trusts law

Series editor: Marise Cremona

Business Law   Stephen Judge
Company Law   Janet Dine and Marios Koutsias
Constitutional and Administrative Law   John Alder
Contract Law   Ewan McKendrick
Criminal Law   Jonathan Herring
Employment Law   Deborah J. Lockton
Evidence   Raymond Emson
Family Law   Kate Standley and Paula Davies
Intellectual Property Law   Tina Hart, Simon Clark and Linda Fazzani
Land Law   Mark Davys
Landlord and Tenant Law   Margaret Wilkie, Peter Luxton and Desmond Kilcoyne
Legal Method   Ian McLeod
Legal Theory   Ian McLeod
Medical Law   Jo Samanta and Ash Samanta
Sports Law   Mark James
Torts   Alastair Mullis and Ken Oliphant
Trusts Law   Charlie Webb and Tim Akkouh

If you would like to comment on this book, or on the series generally, please write to lawfeedback@palgrave.com.

palgrave macmillan law masters

trusts law

charlie webb

Senior Lecturer, Department of Law,
London School of Economics and Political Science

tim akkouh

Barrister, Erskine Chambers, London

Third edition

palgrave
macmillan

This edition first published 2013 by PALGRAVE MACMILLAN

Palgrave Macmillan in the UK is an imprint of Macmillan Publishers Limited, registered in England, company number 785998, of Houndmills, Basingstoke, Hampshire RG21 6XS.

Palgrave Macmillan in the US is a division of St Martin's Press LLC, 175 Fifth Avenue, New York, NY 10010.

Palgrave Macmillan is the global academic imprint of the above companies and has companies and representatives throughout the world.

Palgrave® and Macmillan® are registered trademarks in the United States, the United Kingdom, Europe and other countries.

ISBN-13: 978–1–137–29752–5   paperback

This book is printed on paper suitable for recycling and made from fully managed and sustained forest sources. Logging, pulping and manufacturing processes are expected to conform to the environmental regulations of the country of origin.

A catalogue record for this book is available from the British Library.

Contents

Preface

Our aim in this new edition of the book remains to offer an account of the law which is clear, revealing and stimulating. As before, we think the approach we have taken is different – not radically, but noticeably – from those found in the other texts. Different texts have different objectives, but principally they exist to plot a course through a subject, to give the reader a primary resource which brings together the various strands and sources of law and legal analysis, forming from them something approaching a coherent whole (and, where no such coherence emerges, explaining why this is). In so doing, they seek to help students through law courses and exams.

Law exams do not normally require encyclopaedic knowledge. Instead they aim to test your ability to apply and evaluate a set of core rules and principles. And rightly so, for this is the real challenge of the law. Moreover, if you're ever going to become enthused about law, this is what will do it. Furthermore, whatever its historical and political origins, the law, as a set of rules to be applied to disputes today, can be evaluated and justified, if at all, only by reference to the principles it embodies, the policies and interests it seeks to advance and to protect. Or, in more simple terms, you can't really say whether a rule is a good or bad one without some idea of what that rule is for. Accordingly, if you want to know how these rules might or should apply in problem cases, or to comment on the merits of those rules and possible reform proposals – which is what exam questions typically require – giving some thought to the principles which underlie the legal rules is every bit as important as knowing what those rules are.

The fact that exams are not memory tests and tend to demand depth rather than breadth of knowledge and understanding has, or should have, an impact on the make-up of textbooks. If a text is to do its job of guiding you through a subject, it should set you up with the material you need to address the sorts of questions on which law courses and exams focus. So, when it comes to describing what the law is, you'll be much better served by a focused and more intensive examination of a selection of key cases than you will by a more expansive, though more superficial, survey of a broader range of authorities. Moreover, since you will need to do more than simply know what the law is to do well in your exams, a textbook should also move beyond a purely descriptive account of the cases and statutes, and offer some analysis of the principles and policies they reflect and embody. This is what this book sets out to do.

In one sense, this is an introductory text. It is a book geared primarily for first-time trusts students (though it should also offer something to those already familiar with the subject) and which assumes no prior knowledge of trusts law, or indeed law more generally. It then aims to lead you through an area of the law which can easily appear obscure and inaccessible. However, this book is not introductory in so far as this implies a text which only takes you some of the way. So, while there are plenty of thicker, denser texts out there, with longer tables of cases and packed footnotes, by failing to provide the sort of material on which law courses and exams focus, they can often leave students underprepared. By contrast, we believe that, though shorter, this book, supplemented by reading the key cases and articles, contains all you need to make your way through an undergraduate course on the law of trusts and to set you up for your exams.

As in previous editions, each chapter is split into a series of sections of typically a few pages each. One anonymous reviewer got particularly het up at the length of some of these sections. We nonetheless maintain here the 'old-fashioned' approach of having, at times, up to six or seven pages of unbroken text. For those, like the reviewer, who don't feel up to reading so much in one go and who are soothed by the appearance of a new section heading every few lines, do feel free to pause at any time. You can read this book in whatever order and in as many sittings as you like.

We owe a number of debts to those who have assisted in the preparation of this book. Special mention goes to Charlotte Ford, Sarah Worthington, Aimée-Shirin Daruwala, Ewan McGaughey, Michael Blackwell, Jonathan Jervis, Emily Gillett and Nicholas Le Poidevin QC who read and commented on various drafts. Also, many thanks to Rob Gibson and all at Palgrave Macmillan, who have been patient, generous and professional throughout.

Though we stand jointly behind everything in this book, Tim has been primarily responsible for Chapters 11, 15 and 16 and elements of Chapters 3, 5 and 12. Charlie bears primary responsibility for the rest. We aim to state the law as of the start of December 2012.

Charlie Webb
Tim Akkouh

Acknowledgements

The authors and the publisher are grateful to Sweet & Maxwell Ltd for permission to include the discretionary trust and deeds of appointment and retirement found in Chapter 16 . These have been drawn by the authors using precedents contained in James Kessler QC and Leon Sartin (2012) *Drafting Trusts and Will Trusts: A Modern Approach* (11th edn, Sweet & Maxwell).

Table of cases

Table of legislation

Chapter 1

An introduction to equity and trusts

1.1 What are we doing here?

Those embarking on the study of trusts for the first time face an immediate and significant obstacle: what is a trust? Even before you read your first case or text on, for example, criminal law or contract, you have a basic understanding of what that area of law is (or may be) about. This is important because it gives you a foothold in the subject, a familiarity with the sorts of question it addresses. It means that when you do start reading about the law, you already have a sense of what you are looking at and what you are looking for. None of this is true with trusts. Most people never encounter the concept of a trust unless and until they find themselves confronted with it as an inescapable part of a law degree. Moreover, unlike, for instance, tort law, this is not an area where familiar ideas are simply obscured by unfamiliar terms. This means we have no choice but to start from scratch. It also means that trusts law is a subject which can feel alien for a while. As a first-time trusts student, you are being asked to understand, learn and apply an often complex body of rules without any clear idea of what these rules are for. The only way you will overcome this fully is with time; the more you read and the more you think about trusts, the more the subject will make sense and the more you will get a feel for it. It helps, however, to be shown the way. Accordingly, the aim of this chapter and the next is to give you a headstart, to put in place some of the basic concepts and principles on which trusts law is based. All of these will reappear in the later chapters. Nonetheless it is worth taking some time to introduce them now, as not only do they provide overarching themes and ideas linking the many and diverse applications of trusts law, but they should also make it that much easier for you to get to grips with the details of the cases and statutes when we encounter them later.

So, we must begin by addressing our initial question: what is a trust? The difficulty in offering a straightforward answer is that it seems that there is no single concept of a trust. Instead, there is a collection of related concepts which are all, at least on occasion, referred to as trusts. In simple terms, trusts come in different shapes and sizes, and with different features. It is this diversity and malleability that helps to make trusts so versatile and explains why they play such an important role in English law. However, this also contributes to the trust being an idea which is, at first, difficult to grasp.

Given this multiplicity of trusts and trust-related concepts, one option is to frame a definition of trusts, which covers all angles and accommodates all cases where the language of trusts is applied. Though such formulations have their place and neatly encapsulate the breadth of trusts law, they tend not to offer a particularly clear or immediate sense of what a trust is. A more informative introduction to trusts can be achieved by identifying what may be regarded as a paradigm example or core case of a trust. Other examples of trusts can then be regarded, and examined, as variants on this basic form. So, in the following section we shall describe what may be considered the central case of a trust. To understand this, however, we must first say something about the law of property.

1.2   Property and trusts

Unsurprisingly, the everyday notion that some things – our possessions, belongings – are 'ours' is reflected in the law. The law of property describes our legal claims and entitlements to things. ('Things' here extends beyond physical, tangible objects to cover forms of intangible property, such as company shares, bank balances and trademarks – the word 'assets' gives a more accurate impression.) In relation to your clothes, books, CDs, the money in your pocket and countless other things, you have what is called *legal title* ('legal' meaning here 'under the common law [on the meaning of which see Section 1.5] rules of property' and 'title' having the same root as 'entitlement'). Normally when you have legal title to property you are free to use it for your own benefit and to further your own interests. So, as a general rule – and there are of course exceptions – you can put it to whatever use you see fit, determine and control the use others make of it, sell it, lease it, even destroy it. All these choices are for you, and you alone, to make, and when making them you are free to be entirely self-seeking and self-interested.

Sometimes, however, the law subjects the holder of the legal title to certain obligations, known as *fiduciary obligations*, which require him to hold and deal with the property not for his own benefit and in pursuance of his own interests, but rather for the benefit and in pursuance of the interests of some other person. This person is called a *beneficiary* (or occasionally a *cestui que trust*). The property remains in the hands of the holder of the legal title – in such situations called a *trustee* – and he retains the legal power to deal with the property. But when exercising this power he must do so with the sole objective of furthering the beneficiary's interests. As a corollary of these fiduciary obligations the trustee owes to the beneficiary, the beneficiary has the right that the trustee will act solely in his (the beneficiary's) interests when dealing with the property. Moreover, because of both the extent of the rights he has against the trustee and the protection afforded to him against third parties into whose hands the property may pass (see Section 2.4), the beneficiary is regarded as having a proprietary interest in – a title to – the property. This title is not the same one as that held by the trustee – the trustee still has the legal title – rather, the beneficiary has a new and separate title, an *equitable title* ('equitable' meaning 'deriving from the rules of equity'; see further Section 1.5). In these circumstances, the trustee is said to hold the property 'on trust' for the beneficiary.

1.3   The varieties of trusts

It is this combination of (1) separate legal and equitable titles to property and (2) fiduciary obligations owed by the trustee to the beneficiary, which forms what we may regard as the central instance of the trust. We can usefully note now that there may be more than one trustee and/or beneficiary (in other words, legal and/or equitable title can be shared among more than one person), and that, in such cases, the same person may be both a trustee and a beneficiary. The only limit is that the same person cannot be the sole trustee and sole beneficiary, as it is clearly nonsense to say that the trustee cannot, *as trustee*, deal with the property for his own benefit but must instead apply it for the benefit of himself *as beneficiary*. Such a 'trust' is no more than standard legal beneficial ownership.

We may also briefly see how trusts (and related concepts) may differ from this paradigm:

1. The trustee with legal title may hold the property subject to fiduciary obligations as before, but this time there is a class of potential beneficiaries from which he is to

choose who will receive the benefit of the trust property. In such a case, because none of the potential beneficiaries has any fixed or guaranteed entitlement to benefit from the property, the conventional view is that there is no separate equitable title to the property (though see Section 2.5). This is called a *discretionary trust* (see Section 2.1).

2. The trustee with legal title may hold the property subject to fiduciary obligations as before, but rather than being under an obligation to act in the interests of one or more beneficiaries when dealing with the property, the trustee is required to apply the property towards the achievement of a certain object or purpose. As above, because there is nobody with a fixed entitlement to benefit from the property, there is no equitable title to the property. This is called a *purpose trust* (see Chapter 4).

3. The trustee may hold property subject to fiduciary obligations for the benefit of a beneficiary, but the trustee himself has only an equitable title to the property, whether because he himself is a beneficiary of a trust of that property (in which case there will be what is called a *sub-trust*) or because it is a type of property only recognised by equitable property rules (see eg Law of Property Act 1925, s 1(3)). In such cases both the trustee and the beneficiary will have (distinct) equitable titles.

4. The trustee may hold property to which he has legal title and in relation to which there is a beneficiary who has equitable title, but the trustee owes no fiduciary obligations to the beneficiary in relation to his dealings with the property and instead only a duty to hand over the asset to the beneficiary when he demands it (see further Section 10.12).

5. The 'trustee' (or more commonly here *fiduciary*) owes fiduciary obligations to another party (generally in such instances called a *principal*) but has no legal title to any relevant property, either because the obligations do not refer to dealings with property (eg a solicitor giving legal advice to a client) or because the principal holds the legal title to the property to which the obligations relate (eg an agent handling his principal's goods) (see further Section 10.13).

The bulk of this book constitutes an examination of when a trust (of whatever sort) arises and the precise combination of rights and duties, powers and liabilities each sort of trust involves. Hence, we shall start out by looking at the rules of trust formation – what needs to happen for a trust to arise? From there we shall look at the rules on trustees' duties – what exactly does a trustee have to do, and correspondingly what rights does a beneficiary under a trust have? Finally, we shall examine breaches of trust – what happens when the trustee does not do what he was meant to do?

All this lies ahead of us. It is, however, worth noting now that there exists a basic and important divide in the law of trusts. This is the division between trusts which arise because this is what the parties wanted and trusts which arise for some other reason and on some other basis. More fully, some trusts arise precisely because this is what the property owner (ie the holder of legal beneficial title) intended. These trusts are traditionally called *express trusts* (though, as we shall see, there is a good argument that there are intended trusts which have not been classified as express trusts). By contrast, other trusts are recognised by law irrespective of the owner's intentions. These trusts can, roughly, be said to be *imposed* rather than intended, though this is somewhat misleading as such trusts may happen to coincide with the owner's intentions. (A more precise definition would be to identify these as trusts which arise for reasons other than a desire to give effect to an owner's intentions. Of course, so defined, this category is not particularly revealing. It tells us what these trusts are not – intended trusts – but not what they are.) The traditional classification of trusts assigns these to two classes, *resulting* and *constructive* trusts, which is similarly unrevealing. When and why the law imposes trusts on owners who have not consented to this will be examined in detail in later chapters. The key point to note now is simply that some trusts arise because this is what the parties want, whereas other trusts arise even though the parties may not want this.

This distinction is important for a number of reasons. The rules of trust formation of course differ between intended and imposed trusts. This distinction also bears on the duties that the trustee will be under in handling and dealing with the trust property (see in particular Chapter 10). More generally it is the fact that trusts can be used *both* by property owners, as a way of arranging their affairs and using their property for the benefit of those around them, *and* by the courts, to redirect property when they consider that the current allocation of entitlements is unjust, which makes trusts so versatile and so important in English law (see generally Section 1.10).

We may usefully introduce at this stage some basic terminology. In the case of intended trusts, the trust arises precisely because some property owner decides that this is what he wants to do with his property. He may decide to create a trust while he is alive, in which case the trust is described as *inter vivos* ('among the living'), or he may decide to create a trust to take effect on his death, in which case we call this a *testamentary* trust (see further Section 6.7). In the case of *inter vivos* trusts, we call the creator of the trust a *settlor* (similarly, trusts are sometimes referred to as *settlements*). Where the trust is to take effect on death (ie is created by a will), we tend instead to refer to the creator (if male) as a *testator* or (if female) a *testatrix*.

We may also note here that, when deciding to set up a trust, the settlor can choose to take on the role of trustee himself, in which case we have what is called *a self-declaration of trust*. Alternatively, he can appoint someone else, or a number of other people, or a company to act as trustee(s) (see further Section 6.2). The settlor, of course, gets to choose who are to be the beneficiaries of the trust. The settlor himself can be the, or a, beneficiary of the trust, subject to the standard limitation that he cannot be both sole trustee and sole beneficiary.

1.4   Equity and trusts

In describing the typical trust, we saw that one feature is the separation of legal and equitable titles to the relevant property. We also noted at the time that 'legal' and 'equitable' are here the adjectival forms of 'common law' and 'equity' respectively. We have as yet, however, said nothing as to what common law and equity mean in this context. On one view, if our concern is with understanding the law of trusts *as it is*, as opposed to its historical development, no more need be said about this. 'Legal' and 'equitable' are as such no more than convenient labels for the different titles held by the trustee and beneficiary. Others, however, argue that trusts cannot properly be understood without an appreciation of the nature of equity and its relationship with the common law. Because of this lack of consensus, and because it is important that you make up your own minds on this, it is necessary to say a little now about common law and equity, and why some think it matters that we keep in mind the role of equity in the law of trusts. Accordingly, though this is a book about contemporary trusts law and not a historical overview of the development of trusts, we must make a brief excursus into legal history.

1.5   Equity and the common law

It is not unusual for a legal system to separate the administration of different branches of the law. So, for example, many legal systems, including our own, have separate courts for criminal trials and civil trials. Other jurisdictions divide constitutional or public law cases from the rest of the law. What is far more unusual is for a legal system to have more than one set of courts to deal with disputes of the same kind. Even more unusual, and even more baffling, than this is to have separate sets of courts applying different sets of rules in cases of the same kind. Nonetheless, this is exactly what English law did for a number of centuries.

With the demise of the feudal system and its reliance on local courts applying local rules in resolving essentially local disputes, a national and centralised set of courts was established by the King to apply a single, common set of rules to all relevant disputes between his subjects. This *common law* gave us (eventually) much of the law of contract, almost all the law of torts and the basics of the law of property.

(It is worth noting at this stage that the phrase 'common law' carries a number of different meanings. At its broadest, it identifies a system in which there exists no comprehensive statutory legal code, with courts having on occasion to frame and develop rules for themselves. Here the contrast is between common law and civil law jurisdictions. A second sense of 'common law' identifies *all* judge-made law within such systems. Here the contrast is between common law and statute law. Finally we have the sense of 'common law' we are concerned with now, and which contrasts with equity: the judge-made law deriving from one particular sets of courts, namely the King's courts or courts of common law.)

Problems arose because the common law, as initially developed, was deficient both in its procedure and its substance, leading, at times, to instances of arbitrariness and injustice. Claimants who had got a raw deal from the common law courts started to petition the King to ask him to dispense the justice the courts had failed to administer. And the King would do so, at least on occasion. In time, as the number of such petitions grew, the King passed on the job of dispensing justice to his Chancellor, and ultimately, as one pair of hands was not enough to deal with the influx of petitions, a separate court system developed to deal with them. These were the courts of Chancery. Unsurprisingly, as certain complaints from petitioners tended to recur, and because no judge worth his salt sets out to treat like cases differently, the courts of Chancery developed their own set of rules for the administration of justice. This set of rules became known as *equity*. This then meant that 'the law' in fact consisted of two distinct sets of rules, administered by two distinct sets of courts: the rules set down and applied by the common law courts, and the supplementary rules added and applied by the courts of Chancery.

To see how this worked, let us take an example from contract law. Perhaps the principal focus of the law of contract is to identify the circumstances in which promises are legally binding. The common law identified two such circumstances: first, where the promise was embodied in a formal document, known as a deed, and, second, where the promisor asked for (and got) something in return for the promise he made, in which case there is said to be 'consideration' for the promise. The implication of this is that promises made in other circumstances, and so which did not meet these requirements, had no legal effect under the common law rules. However, this seemed to do injustice on occasion. The problem arose where A made a promise to B, and B, believing entirely reasonably that that promise would be kept, proceeded to conduct his affairs on that basis. If A then broke his promise, B could suffer as a result of his reliance on it. However, unless the promise had been made by deed, or unless A had requested B to act in this way, the common law afforded B no protection. To remedy this injustice, the courts of Chancery developed the doctrine of promissory estoppel, which provided redress to (some) promisees who, in the absence of consideration, had relied reasonably and to their detriment on the promise being kept. This then meant that to know when promises had legal effect, you had to look to both the common law and equity. The common law identified two such situations, promises made by deed and promises supported by consideration, while equity provided a third: (certain) promises which have been detrimentally relied upon. This also necessarily meant that looking at either the common law or equity in isolation gave an incomplete answer to the question of when promises are legally binding.

A similar story underlies the development of the law of trusts. The common law of property identified the basic situations in which individuals became beneficially entitled to particular items of property. As we have noted, in those situations, the individual was said to have legal title to the asset. However, at times, the common law rules determining the location of beneficial entitlement to property worked injustice. There were circumstances in which, because of some undertaking he had made, or by reason of the circumstances in which he got his hands on the property, it would have been unfair to allow the legal title holder to keep the property for himself and to use it in whatever way he saw fit, but to which the common law rules offered no solution. In such circumstances, the courts of Chancery stepped in and ruled that the property must be held by the legal title holder not for his own benefit but for the benefit of someone else, thus resulting in the creation of fiduciary obligations. Moreover, that other person was ultimately regarded by equity as having an entitlement to the property itself, thereby giving rise to the notion of equitable title. This then gave us the trust as we know it today. So, just as the law of promissory estoppel can be seen as a supplement to the common law of contract, the law of trusts is a supplement to and refinement of the common law rules on beneficial entitlement to property. The common law set down a list of circumstances in which an individual, through the allocation of legal title, became exclusively entitled to the benefits of a given item of property. Equity then intervened by adding to that list through the imposition of a separate equitable title where the rules on legal title left the right to benefit from the property in the 'wrong' hands.

Two important points follow from this. First, equity's intervention was needed only where the common law was inadequate. If the common law on a particular issue was perfectly fair and just then equity had nothing more to add. Accordingly, the notion of equitable title was needed, and hence was recognised, only where the location of legal title, if left unqualified, was thought to lead to unfairness. It is because of this that in circumstances where there is no trust, and hence where the common law rules on title are perfectly adequate, no equitable title exists at all, the owner having simply a legal beneficial title (see further Section 2.6). Second, as a matter of form, equity intervened not by repealing the relevant common law rules but by supplementing them. So, where it was considered that the rules on legal title left the wrong person to benefit from the property, equity intervened not by stripping that person of his legal title but by granting a separate equitable title to the individual who it was deemed should be entitled to its benefit. As such, the common law remained intact, but many of its unfair consequences were reversed through the additions and qualifications supplied by equity. It is because of this that equity is often said to be a 'gloss' on the common law.

So we can see that through the development of common law and equity we ended up with two sets of rules which, only when combined, gave a full and accurate representation of 'the law'. However, this created problems. As should be clear, the rules of common law and equity necessarily differed. That, of course, was not all bad. The very point of equity was to be different. Many of the injustices perpetrated by the common law were remedied. But nor was it an ideal solution. One problem was that unwitting claimants would be put to the expense and inconvenience of having to bring two separate claims if they did not know from the outset that the common law would leave them high and dry. Even though it was accepted at least by 1616 that equity's rules were indeed to be treated as trumping the common law where the two were in conflict, so that it was clear that the common law alone did not give the full picture of a claimant's legal rights and duties, still the common law judges would deny claims they knew would succeed in equity. In effect (though of course not expressly) they would be saying that, on the application of only half the relevant rules, you lose, but that if you want the rest of the rules applied – those rules which would enable your claim to succeed – you have to go elsewhere, starting again from scratch. This was manifestly unsatisfactory and the problem was finally solved by the Judicature Acts 1873–75, which led to the creation of a single court system applying the full set of rules, encompassing both those deriving from common law and those arising from equity.

1.6   The fusion of common law and equity

So now there is just one court system applying both the rules which were formulated and, prior to 1875, applied only in the common law courts and the rules which were formulated and, pre-1875, applied only in the courts of Chancery. This is undeniably a good thing. But whether it has solved all the problems to which the common law–equity dualism gave rise is an altogether more controversial matter. On one view, the problems ran deeper. This is why.

1.7   The case for substantive 'fusion'

The common law and equity necessarily dealt with many of the same fact situations, and necessarily (because this was the point of equity) they devised different rules to deal with them. This was, and is, fine where the equitable rule purported to trump the common law's view of the situation; in such cases the common law rule was to all intents and purposes no longer 'the law'. Notwithstanding the misleading maxim 'equity follows the law', equitable relief always effectively reverses some common law rule. In other words, wherever equity intervened, it reached a different solution, and applied a different rule, from the common law, which, to that extent, no longer resolved such cases. But there was still plenty of the common law left untouched by equity and which equity never purported to touch. This created the potential for inconsistency. There would sometimes be arbitrary gaps in the common law, that is, situations where the common law refused a claim despite allowing claims in other situations which were materially similar. Equity would then fill in the gap, so that now there would be a claim on such facts where previously there was none. But equity might fill in the gap differently from the common law rules which applied in the other, materially similar situations. In simple terms, the common law and equity would be offering different solutions to the same basic problem. The gap in the law ends up being filled, but arbitrariness and inconsistency remain, only in a different form.

Take the following example (and see generally Birks, 1996a; Burrows, 2002; Worthington, 2006). The common law set down a series of rules defining when a defendant would be liable for infringing the claimant's interests. This body of rules makes up the law of torts. These rules protected, among other things, individuals' interests in their bodily integrity and mental health, in their property and in their reputation. However, there were certain interests which the common law did not protect. These included rights to intellectual property and confidential information. Accordingly, the early rules prohibiting interference with intellectual property rights and breach of confidence derived from equity. So here equity was filling a gap left by the common law of torts. However, in filling this gap, the courts of Chancery developed their own rules for what remedies were available where such a duty was breached, and these rules differed in certain important respects from the equivalent rules set down by the common law. For instance, at common law a breach of duty would generally give rise only to a claim for compensatory damages. In equity, however, in addition to the possibility of claims for compensation, the courts showed a greater willingness to allow claims for the recovery of gains made by the defendant. This meant that common law wrongs (torts) were remedied differently from equitable wrongs. So, for instance, if A profited from publishing material which was defamatory of B, B could only recover in respect of the loss he had suffered; whereas if A had made a profit by disclosing confidential information in breach of a duty to B, then B would have the option of stripping A of this gain.

This difference in response does not, however, appear to be attributable to some distinctive factual feature unique to cases of equitable wrongs. The arguments for allowing the claimant to recover the defendant's gains seem to apply equally strongly to common law wrongs. The different responses of the common law and equity to wrongful conduct appear simply to be referable to the fact that the respective rules were developed by different people at different times, rather than due to a considered application of the relevant principles. As such, though equity filled in a gap left by the common law, it did so in such a way that an (arguably) arbitrary distinction remained.

Another example can be taken from the law of property. Imagine that property to which I have legal beneficial title is stolen from me and the thief then makes a gift of that property to a third party, who is completely unaware of the fact that the property he is receiving is stolen. In this case, though I have lost possession of the property, I retain title to it as I never intended to give my title away. So, though the innocent third party has physical possession of the property, I am the one who is legally and beneficially entitled to it. As such I have a claim against him. However, the law's response, save in exceptional cases, is not to return the property to me but instead to allow me to recover a sum of money from the third party, reflecting the value of the property and any other losses I have suffered as a result of being deprived of it. Compare this with the situation where the stolen property is an asset to which I have *equitable* beneficial title. Here the law allows me to recover the property itself, rather than compelling me to make do with its money value. By contrast, however, I have here no claim for compensatory damages for any other losses I have suffered by being without the asset for a period of time. So here common law and equity have very different rules to deal with what looks like the same problem. In each case, property to which the claimant is beneficially entitled has been stolen, and in each case it ends up in the hands of an innocent donee. The only difference between the two cases is that in the first the claimant's was a legal title and in the second the title was equitable.

Now, it is clear, as we shall see in more detail in the following chapter (in Sections 2.5–2.6), that legal and equitable titles are different concepts and work in different ways, so we should not automatically assume that they should be subject to matching rules. However, it is far from clear whether, even taking into account the differences between them, we can justify the different responses of common law and equity in our example. For instance, equitable title is generally considered to be weaker than legal title, and yet equitable title seems to be better protected in the event that the property ends up in the wrong hands, as the claimant can recover the asset itself. Once again it appears that common law and equity have devised different and inconsistent solutions to the same basic problem.

The probability of this happening was increased by the dual court system. Despite the traditional language of equity supplementing or acting as a gloss on the common law, the reality is that equity was in the business of contradicting the common law – the common law says the legal position is one thing; equity says it is another. As such, we can hardly expect Chancery judges to have been either striving for or achieving consistency with the common law when formulating new rules. The fusing of the administration of common law and equity within a single court system therefore provides the opportunity to identify and weed out these inconsistencies. This requires, when necessary to achieve consistency of treatment, the application of equitable rules to situations to which, prior to 1875, only the common law rules applied and, conversely, the application of common law rules to situations which, prior to 1875, were governed by equity. So, for instance, if we really do believe that deliberate wrongdoers should not be able to profit from their wrongdoing, we have good reason to extend to the common law tort of defamation the rule derived (largely) from equity that the claimant should be able to recover the defendant's gains, rather than simply seek compensation for his own loss.

This process whereby we look to achieve harmonisation between the rules of common law and the rules of equity is often referred to as *fusion* (or substantive fusion to distinguish it from the administrative fusion of common law and equity brought about by the Judicature Acts). The overall aim is to ensure that like cases are treated alike, and that we are not tied to inconsistency, and hence injustice, for no reason other than that this was the position before the Judicature Acts.

1.8   Anti-fusion arguments

This may all sound perfectly reasonable, and indeed it is, but not everyone agrees. Some believe that we should not attempt or allow any such cross-fertilisation of common law and equitable principles. Rather, they believe that although the administration of common law and equity has been fused, the substantive rules are, and should continue to be regarded as, distinct. This sees the common law–equity distinction as being of more than historical significance, and hence as something to be maintained. Why do they think this? One reason is essentially historical. The Judicature Acts were designed only to fuse the administration of the two bodies of law. They were not designed to alter the substantive law, that is, the actual results of cases. Accordingly, it is contended that those who are arguing for the substantive fusion of common law and equity have misunderstood the purpose of the Judicature Acts and that the legislation provides no support for the greater integration of common law and equity on a substantive level. As such, those arguing for such a substantive change have been accused of committing a 'fusion fallacy' (see Meagher, Heydon and Leeming, 2002, 52–54).

This is right, but it does not take us very far. It is true that the Judicature Acts were not intended to affect the substantive law, and so they do not in themselves provide a good reason for a change of result on a given set of facts. But this does not answer the point made by the advocates of substantive fusion, which we set out in the previous section. The argument there was not that the Judicature Acts justified substantive changes in the law. Rather, such changes are justified by *the need to do justice*: justice requires that we treat like cases alike, which in turn requires us to be on the lookout for situations where the law acts inconsistently or arbitrarily. Where we find inconsistency or arbitrariness, we should remove it, and the courts don't need to appeal to the Judicature Acts, or indeed any other statute, to do this. The significance of the Judicature Acts is simply that, now both the common law and the equitable rules are applied by the same courts, judges have the opportunity to examine the full, combined set of rules and are better placed to excise any inconsistencies to which the existence of dual systems gave rise. In short, the fusion fallacy objection is not incorrect; it just misses the point.

There is, however, a second argument in favour of continuing to maintain a distinction between common law and equity, of which it is less easy to dispose. This posits that equity is by its very nature different from the common law, such that you cannot hope to compare, let alone integrate, legal ('legal' here being the adjectival form of 'common law') and equitable rules and principles because this would not be comparing like with like. Quite what this difference is, however, is a lot harder to pin down.

The standard version of this argument paints the common law as a system of general rules, promoting clarity and certainty, but capable of leading to injustice in occasional cases precisely because of this generality. Equity, by contrast, is viewed as a more flexible, more context-sensitive set of principles, designed to mitigate the occasional injustices of the common law's general rules. Equity accordingly gives the common law a much needed injection of fairness. But if it is to be able to do this job, equity must have, and retain, its own distinct rationale and identity. This argument tends to be supported by reference to the notion of 'conscience', equity operating to prevent conduct which is 'against conscience' or 'unconscionable'. Such language is of course vague and imprecise, but this is necessary if it is to be capable of being applied across a range of cases where the common law's rules require equitable supplementation. This need to retain flexibility means that the application of equitable concepts involves the exercise of judicial discretion in a way that the application of the clear but rigid rules of the common law does not. The sum effect of all this is that equity is to be viewed as ideologically distinct, and attempted integration of the substance of the common law and equity is to be avoided.

This account has historical resonance given the origins of equity. However, we may doubt whether this gives us reason to reject the argument for the substantive integration of the common law and equity. First, it is far from clear that this dichotomy between, on the one hand, clear but inflexible general rules and, on the other, more sensitive but also more vague or abstract moral principles is in fact an accurate representation of the law. It may well be true that broadly framed general rules are never going to achieve morally desirable results across the board. The world is simply too complex and the spectrum of possible eventualities too broad. Accordingly any legal system needs the capacity to deviate from these rules where justice demands. This was the role of equity in the period before the Judicature Acts. However, consider what happens when a court exercises this power to deviate from the existing rules to avoid injustice. Rather than this leaving the rule standing as before, untouched by the decision of the court, we rightly tend to regard the court's decision as a supplement or exception to the rule, replacing the old imperfect rule with a new and improved version. This is because, if we are to treat like cases alike, the 'deviation' must apply not just in the case in which it was first recognised, but also in all materially similar future cases. So, applying this equitable power to deviate from the common law does not give rise to a dichotomy between the common law's general, occasionally unjust rules and a series of equitable ad hoc exceptions or deviations from these rules. Rather, it leads to a single, increasingly complex and sophisticated, but also (it is hoped) fairer, body of rules.

So, though an inherent feature of equity was this 'discretion' to depart from the common law rules, once it did make such a departure, this left us with a new (equitable) rule, which was just as binding as the common law rule it replaced or supplemented. As such, though equitable rules may be sourced in the exercise of some judicial discretion, it does not mean that the courts then have a continuing discretion when it comes to their application (on the different types and meanings of discretion, see Section 9.22). That being the case, there is no reason to view the substantive rules of equity as being any different in nature from the substantive rules of the common law, and so we have no reason to think that they cannot and should not be harmonised.

Second, it is plain that this important job of developing or changing the existing legal rules has historically been performed by both the common law and equity. Though plenty of important legal developments were made by the courts of Chancery, the common law rules did not remain unchanged over the centuries. Rather, while the dual system was in existence, English law happened to have two judicial sources of legal change: sometimes the common law would change itself; sometimes it would be changed by equity. Again, therefore, this gives us no reason to think that the common law and equity are somehow different in kind or nature.

Third, even if, contrary to what we have just said, it were true that the law is made up of a combination of clear but inflexible rules and broad, open-ended principles, it would be impossible to maintain that this dichotomy mirrors the common law–equity distinction. Much of equity, as we shall see, is as inflexible as anything the common law has to offer. Conversely, there are aspects of the common law which seem to involve the same application of flexible but vague standards, which are meant to be the hallmark of equity. A good example of this is the duty of care in the law of torts, where the courts have significant leeway to determine whether a defendant should be held to owe the claimant such a duty. It may well be that historically equity has played up its flexibility and discretion, and that the common law has played these down, but we should be able to look beyond the language used by the courts to see the reality of what they are doing. Similarly, it is impossible to argue that equity is any more concerned with morality or fairness than the common law. Again the development of the tort of negligence is a good example of common law courts developing the law by express reference to moral principles (see *Donoghue v Stevenson* [1932] AC 562). Contrast this with the rules the courts of Chancery developed in relation to, for example, the certainty requirements for express trusts or purpose trusts, which seem to have no inherent moral aspect.

Indeed, there are even examples of equity framing rules, which work *injustice* on the facts of individual cases. As we have noted already, one of equity's most important contributions to the law has been the recognition of fiduciary obligations. As we shall see later, these duties are so strict that a defendant may be held to have breached them, and so be subjected to legal liability, even where we consider that he acted with exemplary motives and did no harm whatsoever to those around him (see in particular *Boardman v Phipps* [1967] 2 AC 46: Section 10.6). Here, it is common to find lawyers explaining that these rules may create occasional injustice but that this is necessary in order to further the broader policy of encouraging the highest standards of conduct from fiduciaries. This may (or may not) be a legitimate approach for the law to take. What is clear, though, is that, in light of such rules, we simply cannot argue that equity has any monopoly on or an unwavering commitment to morality, fairness or individualised justice.

All in all, the argument that the common law and equity are engaged in fundamentally different pursuits looks decidedly weak. Of course none of this is intended to suggest that equity has not developed its own distinctive practices, which can be regarded as distinctive features which set it apart from the common law. It clearly has (on which see Smith, 2005). The point, however, is that we must always ask whether any such continuing distinction can be supported on the basis of principle. If we can account for these differences only by recourse to history then we should be ready to develop and modify the common law and equity so that they form a single body of law which is principled, coherent and fair.

Of course the crucial but difficult question is when differences in approach between the common law and equity are to be regarded as principled responses to (perhaps subtly) different sorts of problem, in which case such differences should be maintained, and when, by contrast, they are alternative and inconsistent responses to the same basic problem, and so require harmonisation. For example, as we have noted and as we shall see in the following chapter (in Section 2.9), proprietary interests recognised by the common law typically function differently from those recognised in equity. This is most evident when the property ends up in someone else's hands. Whereas legal proprietary interests, as a general rule, bind everyone, equitable proprietary interests usually bind only those who know (or should have known) of their existence and those who acquired the property free of charge. As such, there is a divergence of approach between the common law and equity with regard to the treatment of third parties who get their hands on the property in which the claimant has an interest.

However, it does not follow that this difference cannot be justified. The law may, and indeed almost certainly does, have good reason to have two (or more) types or tiers of proprietary interest, one stronger and more durable than the other. If so, we should maintain this distinction between the operation of legal and equitable proprietary interests (though it may be that we should find labels more illustrative of their respective content than 'legal' and 'equitable'). However, we must also ask whether the situations in which proprietary interests have been recognised in equity correspond to the situations in which the claimant merits only the weaker variety of proprietary interest. This is more doubtful. Therefore, though we should keep the distinction between legal/strong and equitable/weak proprietary rights, we may need to reconsider which examples of proprietary interests we allocate to each category.

Finally, we may note one further, very bad argument against the substantive integration of common law and equity, which is still occasionally trotted out on the misplaced assumption that it deals a knockout blow to pro-fusionists. This is most famously encapsulated in a quote from Lord Selborne LC:

> It may be asked ... why not abolish at once all distinction between law and equity? I can best answer that by asking another question – Do you wish to abolish trusts? If trusts are to continue, there must be a distinction between what we call a legal and an equitable estate.

The answer to this should be obvious. The fusion argument does not call on us to pick between common law and equity, with the other then condemned to the scrapheap. Rather it simply asks us to ensure that our combined set of common law and equitable rules forms a single, coherent, principled body of law. The only substantive changes it advocates are where the interplay of common law and equity has led to rules which are contradictory or inconsistent. Only then do we need to make changes to the rules we have, and then only in so far as is necessary to ensure consistency and fairness. In the many cases where common law and equity work happily side by side, without contradiction or inconsistency, nothing would change. This would be the case with trusts. Nobody suggests that trusts are inherently contradictory or unprincipled. They are not, by their very nature, unjust. The division between legal and equitable title, on which the trust rests, may at first glance appear to involve such a conflict (the common law saying that the trustee owns the property, equity saying it is owned by the beneficiary). However, the trust in fact works as a special type of property arrangement whereby the usual rights and powers of 'ownership' are split between two people. So, rather than having conflicting claims to the trust property, the trustee and beneficiary in fact have complementary interests: the trustee having custody of and the power to deal with the property, the beneficiary having the right to whatever benefits may flow from such dealings. In short, nobody advocates the abolition of the trust, and substantive fusion certainly would not force this upon us. The issue is simply whether we should allow historical divisions to impede our pursuit of justice. The answer is plain: we should not.

1.9   The maxims of equity

Among the more unusual features of equitable jurisprudence are what have become known as the 'maxims of equity'. These are a series of propositions, which (purport to) illuminate the functions and workings of equity. They are thought to be significant because, as with other statements of legal principle, they both tell us about the law as it is and offer guidance in resolving disputes where the law is uncertain. However, the maxims of equity do not resemble the sort of principles you will find elsewhere in the law. So while in the law of contract you will find references to the principle that agreements must be performed (commonly in its Latin form, *pacta sunt servanda*), and while in tort we have Lord Atkin's famous neighbourhood principle, that we must take reasonable care not to harm those whom it is reasonably foreseeable may be harmed by our actions (see *Donoghue v Stevenson* [1932] AC 562), in equity we are told, amongst other things, that 'equity abhors a vacuum', 'equity regards as done that which ought to be done' and 'equity will not assist a volunteer'. The problem with such statements is not only that their meaning is far from clear, but that, unlike their common law counterparts, they carry no obvious moral weight. So even once you understand what is meant by a 'volunteer' (it is someone who has not given anything in exchange for a promise or transfer of property), it is far from apparent why such a person does not, at least on occasion, merit 'assistance'. Moreover, when you actually look at the cases, you find that there are in fact plenty of occasions when equity *does* assist volunteers. As such, the maxim would be more accurately stated as 'equity sometimes does not assist a volunteer' or 'equity will not assist a volunteer except where it does'. This makes its redundancy plain.

Here, then, we have a proposition which is not only obscure and has no obvious moral basis, but which is also misleading as it applies only intermittently. Many of the other maxims of equity are similarly problematic. For instance, take the maxim 'equity acts *in personam*'. This appears to suggest, and has been used to support the view, that equity provides only personal rights and claims, and does not grant or recognise proprietary rights and claims (for the distinction between personal and proprietary rights, see Sections 2.4 and 14.2). However, as we shall see (Section 2.4), whatever the position may once have been, trusts law has so developed that a beneficiary is plainly treated as having a proprietary right or interest, namely equitable title, in the trust assets. Moreover, equity has created a range of proprietary interests outside the law of trusts. However, one still finds judges and commentators referring to the maxim as though it nonetheless embodies an important truth about the operation of equity.

Of course there are other equitable maxims which pose fewer problems. For instance, 'equity looks to intent, not to form' is both clear and, largely, accurate. However, the basic point still stands. The maxims of equity are unreliable. Though rarely completely meaningless or false, they have a tendency to obscure and mislead, and to stand in the way of analysis of the real principles and policies which shape the law. They are not the keys to unlock equity and the law of trusts, and, though they cannot be ignored entirely, for the simple reason that some judges persist in using and abusing them (for a good example, see *A–G for Hong Kong v Reid* [1994] 1 AC 324, discussed in Section 9.20), they should be treated with suspicion. So, though it is a fetish of many books (and some courses) on equity and trusts to begin with an examination of the maxims, the better approach is to postpone discussion of specific maxims until we encounter them when examining particular concrete questions later in the book. (Though if this has only served to whet your appetite for these obscure half-truths, see Martin, 2009, 29–34 for a fuller rundown.)

1.10   The uses of trusts

Thus far, we have been dealing with the question of what a trust is. However, we have yet to see what trusts are *for*. Throughout the book, through our examination of the cases, you will get to see many of the diverse applications of trusts. However, it may help to provide some context at the outset for the discussion of the rules and principles to follow.

Here it is useful to return to the fundamental division we introduced earlier (Section 1.3) between *intended* and *imposed* trusts. For present purposes, the significance of this division is that it reflects different uses of trusts in practice. When we look at intentionally created trusts, the reason for the law giving effect to such trusts is plain. The property owner wants a trust, and the law generally enables individuals to make whatever dispositions of their property they desire. The interesting question here is why someone would choose to create a trust. By contrast, when we are looking at trusts which arise for other reasons, the important question is why the law would want to impose a trust against, or irrespective of, the owner's wishes.

So, first, why do people choose to create trusts? The (express) trust is a facilitative institution, which means that it is a device supplied by law, which people can then make use of in order to arrange their affairs in whatever manner best suits their purposes. In this way, the trust ranks alongside contract and much of the rest of the law of property. The simple reason for choosing to create a trust, then, is that it suits your purposes, and does so better than the other facilitative institutions the law makes available. What, then, do trusts have to offer that these other devices lack? Trusts are principally a mechanism for benefiting people through the disposition of one's property. That is to say, trusts are a means of transferring to others the benefit of the property we have at our disposal. Of course, you do not need a trust to do this. If you have property – money, a book, some shares – which you would like someone else to enjoy and benefit from, the simplest and most common option is to transfer the property to them outright, or in other words to make a gift of it. The effect of such a transfer is that the recipient takes over from you as 'owner' and holder of the property. A variant on this is to transfer the property to a number of people, who will then become co-owners (though this possibility is more limited in relation to land; see Law of Property Act 1925, s 1(6) and Trustee Act 1925, s 34). It may also be possible to grant a lease, which gives the other a right to use the property for a fixed period of time. However, these cases aside, the common law gives few options.

For most purposes these choices will be enough. However, on occasion, you may want to do something different, to use your property to benefit another in some other way or in some other form. One possibility then is contract. You can, through the law of contract, give others legal rights to use and to benefit from your property. Moreover, because there is still general freedom of contract, you are given pretty much free rein to mould these rights to suit your ends. In this way, contract offers a flexibility, which the common law of property lacks. However, the big weakness of contractual rights is that they, as a general rule, bind only the parties to the contract. As such, they are effective only so long as the initial owner and contracting party retains the property. So, for example, if your concern is where your property goes after your death, contract is of little use. Moreover, contractual rights offer little protection if the owner becomes bankrupt, because then the relevant property will be sold and its proceeds used to pay off the owner's various creditors (see further Sections 2.4, 8.11). If you want to give someone a right to benefit from property which is not so easily defeated then you need to give that person a right or interest *in* the property.

This is where trusts come in. Trusts in essence allow you to divide up ownership, and to confer beneficial rights to property, in different and more complex ways. For instance, trusts allow for the creation of *successive* rights to property. So, if, for example, you want to leave some property to your partner for life, then to your child for his or her life, and thereafter to your grandchildren, you will need to create a trust. Trusts also enable you to create different forms of *concurrent* interests in property. Whereas common law co-ownership gives all co-owners concurrent shares in *all* aspects of the property and the benefits it brings, under a trust you can, for instance, arrange for the income to go to one person and the capital to go to someone else. Trusts are also useful if you want property to be used for someone else's benefit but without giving them control over it. As we have seen, the distinctive feature of the trust is that while the beneficiary is entitled to any benefits the property has to offer, it is (typically) the trustee who has custody of the trust property and the power to determine how it is to be applied. This may be a more attractive option when the person you want to benefit is unable, because of age or mental incapacity, to make these decisions for himself, or where, because of impulsiveness or stupidity, you do not trust him to exercise these powers responsibly. Similarly, the divorcing of control from beneficial entitlement which trusts entail may be desirable if you want to benefit one person while taking advantage of another's investment acumen. Trusts can also be used if you want to make an immediate disposition of your property while at the same time leaving some flexibility to accommodate changing circumstances. As we shall see later (Section 2.1), it is possible to set up a trust but leave it to the trustee to decide exactly who benefits from the trust property and by how much.

These features have seen trusts used, for instance, by those with dynastic ambitions as a way of ensuring that property is kept in the family line. Trusts also form the basis for many occupational pension and other investment schemes. As we shall see in Chapter 5, trusts are one of the principal mechanisms by which property is donated to and held by charitable organisations. The division of control and benefit, as well as the fact that trusts can usually be created without writing (see Chapter 6), has also seen trusts play a significant role in schemes to avoid or minimise tax liability. Over recent years trusts have also been used increasingly in commercial transactions to provide a form of security in the event of a debtor's insolvency (see eg the discussion of *Quistclose* trusts in Section 8.13 and *Re Kayford Ltd* [1975] 1 WLR 279).

Turning to trusts which arise for reasons other than an owner's intentions, in the majority of cases the aim and effect of imposing a trust is to remove property from one person and give it instead to someone else. Such trusts can, therefore, be understood as a means of redistributing property where an unqualified application of the common law rules of title would lead to injustice. One example of this is where property has been acquired through wrongdoing. In such instances, the law may impose a trust over that property to strip the wrongdoer of his ill-gotten gains and divert them to his victim (Sections 9.19–9.20). Another, though controversial, example is provided by cases of defective property transfers (see Sections 8.10, 9.18). If I transfer property to you on the basis of some mistaken belief or as a result of coercion, the common law will usually say that you take title to the property and that I have merely a personal claim to recover its value. At least on occasion, however, a trust will arise to enable me to recover the property on the basis that I never properly intended to give it away in the first place. The third principal situation in which trusts are imposed to reallocate property occurs in the context of home sharing. Here the courts have, through the law of trusts, granted cohabitants interests in their home on the basis of their contributions to its acquisition and (it seems) to the partnership more generally (see Sections 9.10–9.17). Indeed, in recent years it has been argued that the courts should have a general power to impose trusts, and hence to effect a redistribution of property, wherever they consider that this is what justice demands (Sections 9.21–9.22).

Even without going this far, you can see how versatile trusts are and why, as unfamiliar and awkward as they may appear, they play such an important role in English law (see further Moffat, 2009, 5–13, 33–34; Oakley, 2008, 6–13). Trusts provide a mechanism, which offers extensive freedom and flexibility to owners to dispose of their property in a manner which best suits their objectives, while at the same time providing a means for courts to redirect property where they consider it unjust for a defendant to keep it for himself. Trusts can be used to further the aims of family members and commercial parties alike, and trusts law plays a role in resolving problems ranging from relationship breakdown to corporate insolvency. In short, there are very few areas of law and society in which trusts law does not play some role.

Summary

▶ The term 'trust' describes a particular form (or forms) of property holding. In contrast to standard absolute ownership, where the owner (holder of legal beneficial title) is free to use the property howsoever he wishes, where there is a trust, the legal title holder must apply the property exclusively for the benefit of someone else.

▶ In such a case, the person holding the property is called a *trustee*, and the person for whose benefit he holds it is called a *beneficiary*. The person (if any) who set up the trust is usually referred to as a *settlor*.

▶ In the typical trust, the beneficiary not only has rights against the trustee that the property be applied solely for his benefit, but also his own, equitable title to the trust property. It is this combination of (fiduciary) obligations owed by the trustee to the beneficiary and the split between legal title and equitable title to the property, which describes the core case of a trust.

▶ Some trusts arise because this is what the owner wanted to do with his property. These are typically called *express trusts*. Other trusts are imposed by the law, irrespective of the owner's wishes. These are traditionally allocated to the categories of *resulting* and *constructive trusts*.

▶ For a long time English law had two separate court systems, applying two distinct sets of rules. The common law was applied by the King's courts, whereas equity was applied by the courts of Chancery. The origins of the law of trusts lie in this divide.

▶ The administration of common law and equity has been fused since 1875. However, it is strongly arguable that more needs to be done to ensure that the substantive rules of common law and equity form a coherent and principled whole. None of this would jeopardise the law of trusts.

▶ Trusts are an extremely versatile legal device. Settlors may use them both to provide for family members and to secure their commercial interests. The law imposes trusts to ensure a just division of the family home upon relationship breakdown, to strip gains from wrongdoers and to return misapplied property. It is for this reason that trusts play such a central role in English law.

Exercises

1.1 How does holding property on trust differ from owning it outright?

1.2 What is meant by the 'fusion' of law and equity? What reasons have been given for it? What reasons have been given for rejecting it?

1.3 What would English law lose if it did not recognise the trust?

Further reading

For more on equity and its origins, have a look at the following:

Baker, *An Introduction to English Legal History* (4th edn, Butterworths 2002), 97–115

Holdsworth, *A History of English Law*, vol 1 (7th edn, Methuen 1976), 395–476

Maitland, *Equity: A Course of Lectures* (rev edn, Cambridge University Press 1936)

Further reading cont'd

Meagher, Heydon and Leeming, *Meagher, Gummow and Lehane's Equity: Doctrines and Remedies* (4th edn, Butterworths 2002), 3–121

Smith, 'Fusion and Tradition' in Degeling and Edelman (eds), *Equity in Commercial Law* (Thompson 2005)

Worthington, *Equity* (2nd edn, Oxford University Press 2006)

Chapter 2

Basic concepts and principles

2.1 Fixed and discretionary trusts

The paradigm or central case of a trust, which we described in the previous chapter, is an example of what we call a *fixed trust*. What makes this trust fixed is that the trustee has no discretion as to what property the beneficiary is to receive under the trust, so that what he gets is 'fixed' from the outset. A fixed trust may have any number of beneficiaries, so a trust of property for A for life, remainder to B is fixed, as is a trust for A, B, C and D in equal (or specified unequal) shares. In all cases the settlor has said exactly what property is to go to what person. Consequently, when distributing the trust property all the trustee needs to do is follow the instructions given by the settlor.

But trusts need not work in this way. The settlor may pass property to a trustee to distribute amongst a defined group of individual beneficiaries, but leave it to the trustee to decide exactly who is to get what. Such trusts are known as *discretionary trusts*, for the simple reason that the trustee has a discretion as to how the property is to be distributed amongst the class of beneficiaries, or, as we more usually call them in such cases, *objects*. The discretion given to the trustee may be more or less extensive. So, a settlor may give his trustee free rein to decide what property, if any, each beneficiary is to receive. Alternatively, he may stipulate that each of the beneficiaries must receive something, but leave it to the trustee to determine exactly what each gets. What makes it a discretionary trust is that:

1. the trustee is under an obligation to distribute the property among the specified class of beneficiaries; and
2. he has, in at least some form and to some extent, a discretion to decide how the property is to be distributed among them.

2.2 Trusts and powers

All trusts ultimately require the trustee to distribute the property to the beneficiaries. Where fixed and discretionary trusts differ is simply in relation to who gets to make the decision as to how it is to be distributed. So, although the trustee of a discretionary trust can choose who is to receive the trust property, *he must give it out*. As such, when the trust comes to an end, the trust property will have been exhausted.

Trusts, in this respect, are to be distinguished from *powers of appointment*. Where a trustee (or someone else) is given a power of appointment, he is given the choice as to how much, if any, of the property is to be given out to the named objects. In other words, the holder of a power of appointment is under no duty to distribute the property to the objects, and as such it is implicit in any power of appointment that at least some of the property may not end up being distributed amongst the class of objects.

A trustee who holds a power of appointment therefore has discretion in relation to the distribution of the relevant property. However, it is important to note that this is a different sort of discretion from that held by the trustee of a discretionary trust. In the latter case, the discretion relates to *how* the property is to be distributed or, in other words, the proportions of the trust fund which each beneficiary is to receive. With a power of appointment, the discretion relates to whether the property is to be distributed *at all*. So, there are two sorts of discretion that can be given to a trustee:

a. discretion as to whether (and, if so, to what extent) to distribute the property among the class of objects at all; and
b. (if and to the extent that the property is distributed among that class) discretion as to the proportions in which the trust property is distributed.

A given trustee may be given neither, one or both of these discretions. The presence or absence of discretion (a) determines whether the disposition is a trust or a power and (b) determines whether it is fixed or discretionary. This leaves the following four basic possibilities:

1. The trustee must give the property out to the named objects, and has no discretion in relation to how it is to be distributed (ie he has neither discretion (a) nor discretion (b)). This is a fixed trust.
2. The trustee must give the property out to the named objects, but has a discretion as to how it is to be distributed (ie the trustee has discretion (b) but not discretion (a)). This is a discretionary trust.
3. The trustee has a discretion as to whether (and to what extent) to give out the property to the named objects, *and*, if and to the extent that he decides to give it out, as to the proportions in which he distributes it (ie he has both discretions (a) and (b)). This is a discretionary power of appointment.
4. The trustee has a discretion as to whether to give out the property to the named objects, *but*, if he decides to give it out, he must do so in pre-determined proportions (ie he has discretion (a) but not discretion (b)). This is a fixed power of appointment. (This is the least common of the four: as an example, imagine I leave £1,000 to a trustee directing that he may (but need not) give out a sum of £250 to each of my four children.)

All imposed trusts will be of the first variety. However, when it comes to intended trusts, any of these is possible. It is for the settlor to pick which option he wants, and, where his language is ambiguous, it is for the court to determine what he intended and which of these possibilities best mirrors his intentions. To this end, obligatory language such as 'to be distributed' clearly connotes a trust rather than a power, whereas phrases such as 'as my trustees think fit' tell us that the disposition is discretionary rather than fixed.

Distinguishing between these various possibilities is made more complicated by two factors. First, on a practical level, it is possible for a settlor to combine two or more of these options when making a disposition of a given item of property. Recall that it is implicit in a power of appointment that the trustee may end up not allocating some or all of the property to the objects of that power. Therefore, a well-advised settlor will also make provision for what is to happen to the property in the event that some of the property is left over (if the settlor fails to makes such provision, the default position is that the power-holder is beneficially entitled to the property, meaning that, for instance, if and when he dies, it will pass on under his will as with the rest of his property: *Re Weekes' Settlement* [1897] 1 Ch 289). Any provision the settlor makes as to what will happen to any leftover property will take the form of a trust, which may itself be fixed or discretionary. Moreover, the objects of that trust may be the same as or different from the objects of the power. So, I may give £1,000 to my trustee, with a power to distribute this as he sees fit among my children, and in default of appointment he is to hold it on trust for my children and grandchildren in equal shares. This then describes a discretionary power of appointment in favour of my children, with a fixed trust in favour of my children and grandchildren of any property left over. What this means in practice is that my trustee can decide to distribute some or all of the money, in whatever proportions, to my children, but, if and to the extent that he does not do this, he must divide it equally between my children and grandchildren. Often a settlor's precise intentions will be unclear. For example, in *Burrough v Philcox* (1840) 5 My & Cr 72, the settlor disposed of property to his children, directing them to allocate it as they saw fit between his nephews and nieces or their children. The children died without making any allocation and the question was who was now entitled to the property. The court concluded that it was to be held on trust for the nephews and nieces in equal shares. In doing so it interpreted the provision as giving the children a discretionary power of appointment in favour of the nephews and nieces, with a fixed trust for the nephews and nieces in equal shares in default of appointment.

Second, though these various types of disposition are clearly distinct as a matter of principle, these clear distinctions have been clouded by inconsistent and overlapping terminology. For instance, not only have the courts and texts at times employed the term 'trust power', which in itself invites confusion, they have also used that term at different times to mean different things (for a fuller exposition on the terminological difficulties in this area, see Moffat 2009, 209–16). Here, we shall stick to the terms set out earlier, though be prepared for deviations in the cases and articles.

2.3 The nature of a beneficiary's interest under a trust

We have so far explained the paradigm or central case of a trust as built on two separate features:

1. fiduciary duties owed by the trustee, as holder of the legal title to property, to another, the beneficiary
2. who has his own, distinct equitable title to the property.

However, for some time the very notion of equitable title was a matter of considerable controversy. Originally a beneficiary was conceived as having no more than a right (or combination of rights) against his trustee that the latter should carry out the trust according to its terms, and hence as having no right *in the trust property itself*.

To understand this debate and why we regard the beneficiary as having an equitable title to the trust property, we need first to take some time to consider what is meant when it is said that someone has a right *in* property.

2.4 Property and proprietary interests

The law of property is concerned with the allocation and protection of entitlements *to* or *in* things. A proprietary right or interest is an entitlement to or in respect of a particular thing. (We may note that sometimes the word 'property' is used as a synonym for 'thing' and sometimes to denote the sort of entitlement you can have in a thing. This duplicity of terminology bothers some people, but it is commonplace and rarely causes confusion.) The hallmark of all proprietary interests is exclusivity. Proprietary interests are entitlements *exclusively* to determine how something may be used or enjoyed. That is to say, when you have a proprietary interest, it means that, so far as that interest extends, it is for you and not others to determine how and by whom the relevant thing is to be used or enjoyed.

For example, if you happen to own (have legal beneficial title to) this book, it means that you and you alone may choose how it is to be used. You can, for instance, choose to open it and read it, to make notes in it, even destroy it. Another choice you can make is to transfer your interest in the book to someone else – in other words, to make a gift of it – in which case the recipient replaces you as the person entitled to make all these choices. Short of this, you can choose to allow others to make some more limited and temporary use of the book. For instance, you may lend it to a friend to read over the weekend. Absent such permission, however, nobody is entitled to make any such use of it.

This, then, accounts for what may be regarded as the two most important incidents or features of proprietary rights:

1. so long as they endure, they can be enforced against third parties who happen to receive or come into contact with the property; and
2. they give priority should the person currently in possession of the property become insolvent.

Take the following example. I have been browsing the internet, looking to buy a laptop, and I see that you are advertising to sell one second hand. We e-mail each other, fix a price and enter into a contract of sale. That contract gives me a right that you will transfer the laptop to me. The protection this right gives me, however, is limited. Say you, rather than delivering the laptop to me, choose instead to give it away to someone else. In this case, I can of course sue you for compensatory damages for the loss you have caused me by your breach of contract. But I have no way of getting the laptop you agreed to sell to me: you no longer have it, and you cannot give me what you do not have; and I have no claim against the third party who now has it because my contract gives me rights only against you.

Or say that before you deliver the laptop to me you are declared bankrupt. The basis of bankruptcy is the individual's insolvency. When someone (or some company) is insolvent, it means that they do not have sufficient assets at their disposal to meet their various liabilities. In other words, they do not have the resources to pay off all their debts. What then happens is that an individual known as a trustee in bankruptcy is appointed, whose job it is to sell the bankrupt's assets, thus generating a lump sum of money, which is then used to pay the various creditors. However, as the upshot of the debtor's insolvency is that there is not enough money to go around, it will necessarily be impossible to pay everyone's debts in full. The default rule then is that all creditors get the same proportion of their debts paid, so that they take a proportionate share in the money available but also bear a proportionate part of the total loss. If, therefore, you are declared bankrupt before you give me the laptop, my contractual rights cannot stop your trustee in bankruptcy selling the laptop, along with all your other assets. Moreover, though I have my claim for breach of contract, your insolvency means that, at most, only a fraction of my loss will be compensated.

In both scenarios my position is improved if I can establish that, though you never delivered the laptop to me, I nevertheless acquired legal title to, and hence a proprietary interest in, it. (This may seem strange, but not only is it clear that legal title to the laptop can pass to me prior to delivery, in fact this is the default rule in sales of goods contracts where the goods are specific or ascertained: see ss 17 and 18 of the Sale of Goods Act 1979.) First, my proprietary interest opens up the possibility that I may be able to recover the laptop, or at least to obtain compensation, from the third party to whom you gave it and who currently holds it. My contract only gives me rights against you as the other party to the contract. After all, you were the only person who promised to give the laptop to me. However, having a right in the laptop gives me (potentially at least) a claim against anyone who may come into contact with it. This is because my right, my proprietary interest, entitles me and me alone to decide who can possess, use and benefit from it. I can therefore (subject to defences) recover the laptop, or at least compensation, from anyone who comes into possession of it, for the simple reason that I never consented to their having it and this was my decision to make.

Similarly, my proprietary interest gives me protection in the event that you become bankrupt before delivering the laptop to me (see further Sections 8.11, 9.18, 9.20). As we have seen, your trustee in bankruptcy has the job of selling your assets and distributing the proceeds among your various creditors. However, my title to the laptop means that I can claim it before the trustee in bankruptcy can do this. Again, the simple reason for this is that my proprietary interest entitles me to decide how and by whom the laptop is used, and I have not consented to the trustee in bankruptcy taking it and selling it, nor to your other creditors taking any share of its proceeds. In other words, I can demand that *your* debts are not paid out of *my* property. Because I can recover the laptop before anyone else can get their hands on it or the proceeds of its sale, we tend to say that my proprietary interest gives me priority over other creditors. This priority is significant given that, as we noted, in the ordinary course of events, creditors all bear a proportionate share of the loss entailed by a defendant's insolvency. By establishing a proprietary interest in an asset held by the defendant, I can make sure that none of this loss falls on me.

As an aside, we may also note that this example shows that not all rights which pertain to things or are somehow thing-related are proprietary rights. My contractual right that you will transfer the laptop to me, though it clearly relates to a thing – the laptop – is no more than a right that you keep your promise. As such, it cannot be asserted against anyone other than you and cannot be characterised as a right *in* or *an exclusive entitlement to* the laptop.

These twin features of proprietary interests – that they are capable of being asserted against third parties who come into contact with the relevant thing and that they give priority in the event of the insolvency of whoever currently holds the thing – can also be used to test whether a given right is to be understood as proprietary. In other words, if we want to know whether a right is to be classed as proprietary, as a right in a thing, we can ask whether this right can be asserted against third parties who receive the thing and whether it gives the right-holder priority in insolvency. This then allows us to see why a beneficiary is conventionally regarded as having a proprietary interest – an equitable title – in the trust property.

At first, a beneficiary was regarded as having rights only against his trustee (that the trustee act in good faith and in the beneficiary's best interests, that he exercise reasonable care when dealing with the trust property, that he should not make dispositions of that property to anyone but the beneficiary, etc.). This meant that if, for instance, the trustee did misapply trust property by giving it away to a third party in breach of the terms of the trust, the only claim the beneficiary could bring was against the trustee for his breach of duty. As against the third party, the beneficiary had no claim. Accordingly, the position of the beneficiary was analogous to my position in our example, where I have a contractual right that you transfer the laptop to me, but as yet no title to or right in it. However, over time the position changed. Equity extended the protection it accorded to beneficiaries by giving them claims against certain types of third party. First, it allowed beneficiaries to claim against third parties who received trust property knowing, or with reason to know, that the property derived from a breach of trust. These claims by themselves could be explained simply as a response to the recipient's wrongful interference with the performance of the trust, rather than on the basis that the beneficiary had an interest in the trust property. However, the courts then began to allow claims against third parties who were entirely blameless but who gave nothing in return for the trust property they received. The beneficiary's rights were also recognised as binding those who took the property when the trustee died. Moreover, where the trustee was declared bankrupt, the beneficiary's interest bound the trustee's trustee in bankruptcy, so as to give the beneficiary priority over the trustee's other creditors in the event of the latter's insolvency.

The possibility of bringing such claims appears incompatible with the beneficiary having no more than a right against his trustee for proper performance of the trust and clearly suggests that the beneficiary is to be regarded as having a right in the trust property (see Scott, 1917 and *Baker v Archer-Shee* [1927] AC 844; cf Stone, 1917 and *Webb v Webb* [1994] QB 696 for an alternative view). Accordingly, references to the beneficiary having an equitable title to the trust assets are now commonplace (see, for instance, *Westdeutsche Landesbank Girozentrale v Islington London BC* [1996] AC 669, 705 (per Lord Browne-Wilkinson)).

However, although there is now no doubt that, at least in a standard fixed trust, a beneficiary has more than just a personal right to the trustee performing his trust duties, the conventional view that a beneficiary has a proprietary right in trust assets has recently been challenged: see Smith, 2004a; McFarlane and Stevens, 2010. On this view, the beneficiary's rights are *neither* (solely) personal *nor* proprietary. Instead – so the argument goes – the beneficiary's right should be seen as falling into a third class of so-called persistent rights: see McFarlane, 2008, 206–27. The key difference between a proprietary right and a persistent right is that whereas a proprietary right attaches to a *thing*, and so can, in principle, be asserted against anyone who receives or comes into contact with that thing, a persistent right attaches to a *right* and, as such, is, in principle, assertable against all those who receive *that right* (or some right which derives from it). So, the claim is that the beneficiary has a right not in or to *the trust property* but has instead a right to or against *the trustee's right* (typically a legal title) to that property: see McFarlane and Stevens, 2010.

Why should we understand the beneficiary's rights in this way? It certainly doesn't make the law of trusts any simpler. Far from it. Rather, the perceived advantage of this formulation is that it explains certain features of trusts law which appear inconsistent with the view that a beneficiary has a proprietary right in the trust assets. We have seen already that a beneficiary can enforce his rights against third parties to whom the trustee has wrongfully transferred trust property and that he can also recover that property in priority to the trustee's creditors in the event of insolvency. It is these features which have led the courts and most commentators to treat the beneficiary's rights as proprietary. Yet there are other situations where a beneficiary's rights do not appear to act in the way we would expect them to if they were truly proprietary.

Take the following example: T holds a painting on trust for B. A third party, X, then steals or damages the painting. If – as is widely agreed – B has a proprietary interest in the painting, then we might expect B to have a claim against X. After all, X has stolen or damaged property which is beneficially *his*. But this is not what the courts have traditionally said. Rather they have said that it is T, and T alone, who can sue X for his wrongful taking of or damage to the painting: see *MCC Proceeds Inc v Lehman Brothers International (Europe)* [1998] 4 All ER 675; *Leigh and Sillivan Ltd v The Aliakmon Shipping Co Ltd; The Aliakmon* [1986] AC 785; cf Section 9.19. Now, B can certainly demand that T does indeed sue X, and any damages T then recovers from X will be held on trust for B. But (so this argument goes) it is nonetheless significant that T is required to be party to such a claim and that B cannot simply sue in his own right.

If B does not have a proprietary right, however, but has instead merely a *persistent* right – a right against T's right (ie T's legal title to the painting) – then it appears that we can make sense of these rules. On this view, B has a right which is assertable against those, and only those, who acquire T's right to the painting. X does not do this. Though he steals the painting, he does not thereby take over T's *right* or *title* to the painting. This remains vested in T. And as T's right to the painting has not gone anywhere, B – as *his* right attaches to this (ie T's) right – has no claim against anyone but T. So, B's right enables him to demand that T sue X, but does not enable him to sue X directly. Importantly, this view of the beneficiary's rights can also explain why a beneficiary *can* claim against third parties to whom the trustee has wrongfully transferred trust assets and why he *can* recover those assets in priority to other creditors in the event of the trustee's insolvency. When T misapplies trust property, the third party – unlike the thief – receives T's title to that property. And as B's right attaches to that title, he can now enforce his right against the third party who now holds that title. The same goes where T is insolvent: T's trustee in bankruptcy will receive T's title to the trust assets and B can demand that he, the new holder of that title, give the property to B rather than make it available to T's other creditors.

This is all very clever, but before we rush to abandon the proprietary view, we should sound a few words of warning. First, it does not necessarily follow from the view that a beneficiary's rights are proprietary that we should expect him to have claims against the likes of X, who steal or damage the trust property. True, proprietary rights are, by their very nature, presumptively enforceable against all-comers and entail a right that others not interfere with one's enjoyment of or access to the property. But before we can conclude that the beneficiary should have a claim against X we need to think a bit more carefully about what sort of access to the property the beneficiary's proprietary rights give him. Only if X has done something which infringes the beneficiary's rights to that property would we expect the beneficiary to have a claim.

To see what we mean here, let's put trusts to one side for a second. Imagine I own land which I then lease to you for 10 years. Now, nobody doubts that both my legal title to the land and your legal lease are proprietary rights, nor that these proprietary rights co-exist, that is, that we both have proprietary rights in the land *at one and the same time*. However, if, midway through the lease, a stranger, X, trespasses onto the land, ordinarily it will be you and you alone who has a claim. The reason for this is that, for the duration of the lease, it is you and not me who has the right to immediate possession of the land. As such, the right to use and to control others' use of and access to the land is, for this period, yours and not mine, and so it is your rights, but not mine, which are infringed by X. By contrast, if X causes permanent damage to the land, then I will have a claim as well, because X will then have interfered with *my* property rights too: *Mayfair Property Co v Johnston* [1894] 1 Ch 508.

So, we cannot infer from the fact that a given person has no claim in the event of a defendant's wrongful interference with a particular asset that that person has no proprietary right in that asset. That is *one* possibility. The other is that, though he *does* have such a right, it was not affected or infringed by the defendant's actions. There is good reason to think this might be the case with beneficiaries when trust property is stolen. After all, beneficiaries, unless and until they exercise their *Saunders v Vautier* right (Section 2.7), typically have no right to possession of the trust assets. As such, it is not obvious that we should expect them to have a claim against those who have stolen – and hence taken possession – from the trustee. And, if this is correct, the fact that they have no such claim gives us no reason to doubt that their rights are nonetheless proprietary.

Second, even if on the proprietary view, we *should* expect beneficiaries to be able to sue those who steal or damage trust assets, it is possible to understand why the law has yet to recognise this. We saw earlier that, in the early days of trusts, beneficiaries were seen as having no more than personal rights against their trustees. On such a view, the only person the beneficiary could sue would be his trustee. Over time, however, the courts started to move towards the view that beneficiaries have rights in the trust assets, that is, proprietary rights. So, slowly, beneficiaries began to be given claims against third parties who received trust property with notice, against recipients who had not given value, against a trustee's trustee in bankruptcy etc. We might, therefore, see the rule that says that a beneficiary cannot sue those who steal or damage trust property, and that such a claim must instead be brought by his trustee, as a last vestige of the old view that the beneficiary's only rights were against his trustee. Moreover, we can understand why this rule might have stuck around, given that, as we have seen, the beneficiary can not only demand that the trustee sue the third party but also any damages recovered will go to the beneficiary. In other words, even without a direct claim of his own, the beneficiary ends up protected. And, as such, we can see why the law hasn't needed to take the final step of simply letting the beneficiary sue directly.

Moreover, where the approach of requiring the trustee to sue *is* seen to disadvantage the beneficiary, the courts have shown a willingness to allow the beneficiary to sue and so to recover damages in his own name. For example, in *Shell UK Ltd v Total UK Ltd* [2010] EWCA Civ 180; [2010] 3 WLR 1192, the Court of Appeal allowed Shell, a beneficiary of a trust of oil tanks and pipelines damaged in an explosion caused by Total's negligence, to sue Total to recover the profits it had lost as a result. On the view that a beneficiary has only a persistent right – a right against the trustee's title to the trust property – this case must be wrong. The claim should have been brought by Shell's trustee, and it is at the very least doubtful that the trustee would have been able to recover for Shell's lost profits, for the usual rule is that a claimant can recover its own losses and nobody else's. So, although, as legal title holder, the trustee could recover for the damage to the trust property itself, there seems to be no basis upon which it could recover for the consequential losses suffered by another party, namely Shell. The problem for the persistent rights thesis here is not simply that it is inconsistent with the analysis and result in *Shell* but that this result is plainly just. By contrast, the decision is wholly consistent with – indeed it offers yet further support for – the orthodox view that a beneficiary does indeed have a proprietary right in the trust assets.

Third, even if the persistent rights thesis is conceptually possible – that is, it makes sense on its own terms and supports results such as those we see in the cases – it looks normatively arbitrary. In other words, if we ask *why* beneficiaries should be seen to have persistent rights rather than proprietary rights, we find no good answer. The point here is that if we want to know whether the rules of trusts law are *justified* – whether they make sense as a set of reasonable legal responses to certain real-world events – we need to be able to say why it is that beneficiaries acquire the rights they do in the circumstances in which they acquire them. So, in relation to express trusts, we need to be able to say why it is that a settlor's declaration of trust creates certain rights in the beneficiary.

Now this is a question which cannot be addressed fully here, but we may briefly note that we can offer plausible accounts which can support either the (historic) view that beneficiaries have purely personal rights or the (modern, orthodox) view that they should be seen as having proprietary rights in the trust assets. So (and see Section 2.7 for a fuller analysis of these possibilities) we might see trusts and trust rights as stemming from the trustee's *undertaking* or *promise* to hold the relevant assets for the beneficiary's benefit. This sees trust duties as (broadly) akin to contractual obligations – the trustee's duty, and so the beneficiary's right, is that the trustee adheres to the terms he undertook – and, as in the case in contract law, this would suggest that the beneficiary should have purely personal rights to the trustee's performance of these undertakings. Alternatively, we might see a declaration of trust as amounting to a *disposition* or *grant* by the settlor of his beneficial interest in the trust property to his intended beneficiary. This sees express trusts as closer to gifts than to contracts, and accordingly would justify treating the beneficiary as acquiring rights *in that property* (ie proprietary rights). By contrast, there seems to be no plausible way of conceiving declarations of trust, which would explain why we *should* see them as creating persistent rights, rights against the trustee and those who derive their rights from him, but not against other third parties who might come into contact with the trust property in other ways. Of course, it would be another matter if settlors, when declaring trusts, were intending to create persistent rights of this kind. But it is doubtful that any settlor has ever had this intention.

As a final point, we noted earlier that it is usual now for judges to say that a beneficiary has an equitable proprietary right in trust assets. Moreover, these are not regarded by the courts as controversial statements. By contrast, no judge has *ever* said that a beneficiary has instead a persistent right or a right against a right. This is a concept that only the most academically aware judges will have heard of, and even then only in the last two or three years. There seems little doubt that when the courts talk about equitable proprietary rights, they see them as genuine proprietary rights, albeit ones which differ from their common law counterparts. Now, it is not impossible that these judges have all been wrong, that what in fact they have been unwittingly creating, recognising and applying have not been proprietary rights at all but a new third class of right. But this is not particularly likely. At the very least this should put into perspective the claim that the persistent rights view *better* fits our present rules and practices than the proprietary view.

All in all then, the persistent rights thesis is valuable as it forces us to think seriously about the nature of a beneficiary's rights and whether we can support the present rules detailing who he can and cannot sue. But in the end the better view remains the view which has long been regarded as orthodox: beneficiaries, at least in standard fixed trusts (see Section 2.5 for discretionary trusts), have equitable proprietary rights in trust assets.

2.5　The variety of proprietary interests

Proprietary interests come in different forms. The differences between them can pertain to their *content* and their *durability*. The question of content refers to the scope of the interest – what uses of the asset does it exclusively reserve for the holder? Some proprietary interests give more extensive, or simply different, privileges and powers in relation to the asset's use than others. Durability concerns the strength or resilience of the interest – by whom and in what circumstances will it be defeated? Proprietary interests can, as a general rule, be given away to others. But they can also be lost even in the absence of any such willed transfer by the holder. This happens more readily with some proprietary interests than with others.

As we have noted, in the typical trust there exist two types of proprietary interest. The trustee has legal title, whereas the beneficiary has his own distinct equitable title. One reason these proprietary interests can co-exist is that they differ in content. During the lifetime of the trust, it is the trustee, by virtue of his legal title, who, subject to the precise terms of the trust, is exclusively empowered to hold the trust property and to determine how it is to be applied. For instance, it is he who gets to choose how it is to be invested. Similarly, as we have just seen (Section 2.4), if a third party negligently damages or destroys the trust property, it is the trustee who can sue the third party for damages. By contrast, it is the beneficiary, with his equitable title, who, again subject to the trust terms, is exclusively entitled to whatever benefits may be derived from the property. So, though the trustee decides how to invest the trust property, he must make these decisions with a view to maximising the beneficiary's gains, and any gains so made go to the beneficiary rather than to the trustee. Likewise, though it is typically the trustee to whom third parties owe a duty of care in respect of the trust property and who brings legal proceedings when such duties have been breached (cf *Shell UK Ltd v Total UK Ltd* [2010] EWCA Civ 180; [2010] 3 WLR 1192), any damages are recovered on behalf of the trust and so will ultimately be received by the beneficiary.

Very generally then, at least in the context of a trust, we may say that legal and equitable titles reflect different sorts of claim or entitlement to property. Legal title is an entitlement to determine how the property be used and applied, whereas equitable title is an entitlement to the benefits to be derived from the use and application of that property.

Do all trusts involve this split of legal and equitable titles? Where a trustee, T, holds property on trust for A and B in equal shares, there is no difficulty in viewing A and B as equitable co-owners of the trust property. Similarly, where T holds on trust for A for life, remainder to B, both A and B have equitable proprietary interests in the trust property, though this time these interests are of different kinds, A's being a life interest, B's being an interest in remainder. Greater difficulties are posed by discretionary trusts. As we have seen, in a discretionary trust the trustee gets to choose what share, if any, of the trust property each beneficiary will get. Accordingly, there is a difficulty in viewing any individual beneficiary as having any interest in the trust property. Of course, once the trustee exercises his discretion and makes a distribution, the relevant beneficiary will at that point obtain legal beneficial title to the property distributed to him. However, before any such decision has been made, it would seem that each individual beneficiary has no more than a right against the trustee that he be considered when the trustee comes to exercising his discretion: see *Gartside v IRC* [1968] AC 553 and *Sainsbury v IRC* [1970] Ch 712.

Nonetheless, because we know that the property will be distributed in one way or another among the various objects, one might think that we could view the objects *as a group* as holding equitable beneficial title. Lord Reid rejected this idea in *Gartside v IRC*, 605–06, although this seems the best way to explain the fact that (as we shall see shortly: Section 2.7) the objects can group together to demand that the trustee transfer the trust property to them outright. Moreover, there seems little doubt that if a trustee of a discretionary trust misapplies trust property, that property is potentially recoverable from the third parties who now hold it. This again appears incompatible with the view that the objects of a discretionary trust, whether individually or as a group, have no more than personal rights to the trustee's proper performance of his duties. One clear case where no separate equitable title exists in relation to trust property is where property is held on a purpose trust, for here there is by definition no beneficiary in whom such an equitable proprietary interest could be vested.

2.6 Equitable title and beneficial title

We have seen, then, that in the standard trust the beneficiary's equitable interest constitutes an exclusive entitlement to the benefits derived from the trust property. Reflecting this, it is common to see the beneficiary referred to as having a 'beneficial interest' in or 'beneficial title' to the trust property. Because of this it may be tempting to conclude that the terms 'beneficial interest' and 'beneficial title' are synonymous with 'equitable title'. This is not the case however.

A 'beneficial interest' or 'title' describes an exclusive entitlement to the benefits of a given asset. Of course, in the typical trust, it is the beneficiary who has such an entitlement. Where this is so, his equitable title is a beneficial title. By contrast, where there is no trust – that is, where property is held outright – the person exclusively entitled to benefit from the property is the person who holds *legal* title. In such a case we can say that he has the beneficial title to or interest in the property. Consequently, we use the term 'legal beneficial title' to describe outright ownership, in contrast to the situation where property is held on trust, where we say that the trustee has a 'bare legal title'. As we have noted already though (Section 1.5), where there is no trust there is no equitable title to that property (for recent confirmation of this see *Westdeutsche Landesbank Girozentrale v Islington London BC* [1996] AC 669, 706 per Lord Browne-Wilkinson). There is a legal beneficial title and nothing more. Equitable title arises for the first time upon the creation of a trust and is extinguished the moment the trust comes to an end.

Accordingly not all beneficial titles are equitable titles. Less obviously, not all equitable titles are beneficial titles. To understand how this can be, we need to make a brief diversion. Proprietary interests can typically be transferred to other people. So if you own (ie hold legal beneficial title to) property, you can of course make a gift of that property by making an outright transfer of your interest to someone else. The same is true if you have an equitable interest in property under a trust. This equitable interest can be transferred (or assigned) to others (we shall learn more about this later: see Section 6.19). Another option available to the holder of legal beneficial title is of course to declare a trust. This results in the legal title becoming a bare (ie non-beneficial) legal title and the beneficiary obtaining a new, equitable interest in that property. This option is also available to the beneficiary under an existing trust. He can declare a trust of his equitable interest, whereupon his becomes a *bare* equitable title, and a new, separate equitable beneficial title arises in the new (sub-)beneficiary. This then results in what we call a sub-trust: the original trustee, T, holds his legal title on trust for the original beneficiary, B, who in turn holds his equitable interest on trust for C, the sub-beneficiary (see further Section 6.22). In such a case, both B and C have equitable titles to the property, but only C's is a *beneficial* title, because it is he and not B who is ultimately entitled to the benefits derived from the property.

2.7　The rule in *Saunders v Vautier*

There is one other important aspect to a beneficiary's equitable title. Where a beneficiary, who is of full age (now 18) and of sound mind, has an absolute interest in (at least some part of) the trust property, he may call on the trustee to transfer legal title to that property to him, so bringing the trust (at least so far as that property is concerned) to an end (see generally Matthews, 2006). The result is that the beneficiary ends up with legal beneficial title to the property, or what we recognise as straightforward outright ownership. This is known as the rule in *Saunders v Vautier* named after the leading case, in which this principle was applied (*Saunders v Vautier* (1841) 4 Beav 115). There a testator set up a trust of stock for Vautier. The trustee was directed to accumulate the dividends declared on the stock until Vautier was 25, and only then to transfer the stock and dividends to him. Vautier, then aged 21, asked that the property be transferred to him immediately. The court held that he was entitled to demand such a transfer. Though the settlor had directed that Vautier was not to get his hands on the property until he was 25, the beneficiary's interest was absolute in that there was nobody else who had any beneficial claim to the stock. This meant, the court concluded, that Vautier had the option of demanding the property now rather than waiting till he was 25 as the settlor had stipulated.

The same principle also applies to trusts which have more than one beneficiary. So, for instance, if I set up a trust of £1,000 for A and B in equal shares, A, if of full capacity, can call for the immediate transfer of £500 to him, as he has an absolute interest in half the fund. This will not be possible, however, where allowing one beneficiary to exercise his *Saunders v Vautier* right to demand an immediate transfer of his share of the fund would have an adverse impact on the other beneficiaries: see *Stephenson v Barclays Bank Trust Co Ltd* [1975] 1 WLR 882. For instance, if the trust fund is made up of shares in a private company rather than money, A will not be able to claim half the shares if this would lessen the value of the remaining trust property (ie B's shareholding). Similarly, if A and B have equal shares in land, the only way A could demand an immediate transfer of his share would be to have the land sold and half the proceeds paid over to him. This may also be contrary to B's interests, and, if so, would be denied.

Where no one beneficiary has an absolute interest in any part of the trust fund – and so nobody is able to demand an immediate transfer of any part of it – the beneficiaries can nonetheless group together and exercise their collective *Saunders v Vautier* right jointly. So, where land is held for A and B jointly, though neither A nor B can individually call for a transfer of the land or any part of it, they can together demand that the land be transferred into their joint names. The same applies to discretionary trusts. As we have seen (Section 2.1), under a discretionary trust it is for the trustee to decide what part of the trust fund, if any, each beneficiary is to receive. Accordingly, if I declare a discretionary trust of £1,000 for A, B, C and D, none of the beneficiaries can individually demand the transfer of any part of that fund, because none has any fixed interest in it. Until the trustee decides who is to get what, we simply do not know what, if anything, each beneficiary will get. However, we *do* know that the money will end up being divided among one or more of A, B, C and D in some manner. As such, there is nobody outside these four beneficiaries who has any beneficial claim on the trust fund. It follows that A, B, C and D can *in combination* be said to be absolutely beneficially entitled to the trust property and so can demand that the money be transferred to them jointly (see *Re Smith* [1928] Ch 915).

Of course, in many trusts, particularly the sort of wide discretionary trusts which we shall encounter later (see *McPhail v Doulton* [1971] AC 424; Section 3.12), it will not be feasible to obtain the consent of all those beneficially entitled under the trust. Nonetheless, the principle stands. If all those actually or potentially beneficially entitled to the trust property who are of full age and sound mind do so decide, they can demand that the property be transferred to them outright.

Why does the law allow this? After all, the significance of the rule is that it enables beneficiaries to get their hands on the trust property notwithstanding certain limitations the settlor has placed (or attempted to place) on their right to claim it. This is seen from *Saunders v Vautier* itself. The settlor, though intending that Vautier alone would benefit from the stock, also intended that the stock would be transferred to him only upon his reaching the age of 25. Accordingly the rule effectively allows the beneficiary's intentions to trump those of the settlor. This seems odd, given that the very reason we recognise a trust – and hence why the beneficiary has any rights at all in the trust property – is that this is what the settlor intended. In other words, the beneficiary cannot make out an entitlement to the trust property without reliance on the settlor's intentions, and yet we then allow him to claim the property, on the basis of his entitlement to it, even though this in fact conflicts with what the settlor intended.

One reason for allowing this may be that the law has a preference for property to be owned outright rather than for property held on trust, so that, though the law is prepared to admit and recognise trusts, it encourages attempts to bring them to an end. This is based on the view that trusts act as a fetter on the free use of property. So long as a trust is in existence, the trust property is 'tied up' in that it can be used and applied by the trustee only for the purposes of the trust. By contrast, where property is held outright, the owner is, as a general rule, free to do whatever he likes with it, which includes disposing of it to others. This latter position is viewed as economically preferable as it facilitates the free transfer of property, which is desirable as it enables property to end up in the hands of those who value it the most. So, we may be able to support the rule in *Saunders v Vautier* on the basis that, by enabling an absolutely entitled beneficiary to bring the trust to an end, it facilitates the free transfer of property and this justifies a limited deviation from the settlor's intentions. (We shall see later that the same policy underlies another important rule of trusts law, the rule against perpetuities: Section 4.9.)

The rule in *Saunders v Vautier* may also, or alternatively, be regarded as one particular manifestation of a tension that exists throughout trusts law where the wishes of the beneficiaries deviate from those of the settlor. So, for instance, it is clear that though express trusts arise because this is what the settlor intended, nonetheless the settlor himself has no right to enforce the trust. Instead enforcement is left to the beneficiaries, who, of course, may choose not to sue, or may be unable (eg through lack of resources) to do this. Similarly, it is clear that beneficiaries can authorise the trustees to commit what would otherwise be breaches of trust, so deviating from the terms set down by the settlor (see further Section 13.8). More generally, the trustee's fiduciary duty is to act in the beneficiaries' best interests, not in the settlor's best interests or in what the settlor may consider the beneficiaries' best interests to be. All these instances involve a prioritisation of the beneficiaries' intentions and wishes over those of the settlor, and the rule in *Saunders v Vautier* accordingly fits alongside them.

However, in other respects, in other areas, the settlor's intentions appear to be given primacy. This is of course the case when it comes to determining whether a trust has arisen in the first place and what interest the beneficiaries take under it. Another example is provided by the rules on exclusion clauses. A settlor can provide for the trustee to have the protection of an exclusion clause, absolving him from liability in the event of his committing certain breaches of trust (Section 13.10). This clearly works to the detriment of the beneficiaries, as it deprives them of the right they would otherwise have to recover compensation from the trustee for the losses caused by his breach, yet it is permitted because these are the terms chosen by the settlor and it is his choice to make. Similarly, though they can consent to breaches of trust which the trustee proposes to commit or has already committed, the beneficiaries are not free otherwise to demand that the trustee commit breaches of trust on their behalf. Indeed, the beneficiaries, save by using their *Saunders v Vautier* right to bring the trust to a premature end, are not entitled, while the trust remains in existence, to direct the trustee as to how he is to exercise his powers. For instance, they cannot demand that the trustee invest the property in a particular way, unless this is also what the settlor provided. (For an application of the basic principle see *Re Brockbank* [1948] Ch 206, though the specific point in issue has now been reversed by s 19 of the Trusts of Land and Appointment of Trustees Act 1996: Section 11.2.) It should be noted, however, that much the same result can be achieved by the beneficiaries exercising their *Saunders v Vautier* right to bring the trust to an end and then immediately resettling the property on new trusts, which differ from the original trusts only by imposing an obligation on the trustee to act in the desired way.

More generally, this tension reflects two alternative conceptions of the express trust (see further Section 4.5 and Penner, 2002). On one view, a trust is much like a gift from the settlor to the beneficiary, with the trustee being the medium through which the gift takes effect. And, as with a straightforward outright gift, once the donor has made the transfer, he has no further say over what the recipient does with the property. So, if we treat the creation of a trust as akin to making a gift of the property, it is unsurprising that we should allow the beneficiary to decide how exactly he wants to use and enjoy the equitable beneficial title the settlor has 'given' to him. On another view, however, an express trust resembles a contract between the settlor and his trustee for the benefit of a third party, the beneficiary (see Langbein, 1995). On this view, we should expect the settlor and trustee to fix whatever terms they desire, and the beneficiary only receives whatever they decide he should receive. This approach appears, for instance, to be evident in the law's treatment of trustee exclusion and remuneration clauses.

The question of how we should conceive of express trusts, whether they more closely mirror gifts or contracts, or are in truth analogous to neither, may appear academic. However, though for the most part trusts law can be explained and applied without reference to *why* we give effect to express trusts, ultimately, here as elsewhere, the law is shaped by the principles and policies which underlie it, and, in problem areas, different conceptions of what trusts law is there to do will lead to different results. The above examples demonstrate this. Moreover, greater attention to this question may assist us in resolving some perennial controversies in the law of trusts. We have seen one example of this already (Section 2.4), when we discussed the nature of a beneficiary's rights under a trust. As we saw then, one way of determining how we might best conceive of a beneficiary's rights is to ask why it is that the act of declaring a trust should create rights in a beneficiary. The *kind of rights* a beneficiary acquires should be dependent on our *reasons* for recognising him as acquiring rights (of whatever kind) in the first place. Another example of this can be seen in relation to a rule known as the beneficiary principle. As we shall see in Chapter 4, the law, as a general rule, prohibits purpose trusts, insisting that trusts must instead have people as beneficiaries. However, there is considerable doubt as to whether the conventional explanations for this rule provide adequate justification for it. On the contractarian basis, the rule looks particularly odd: why should the settlor and trustee not be free to arrange for the trustee to hold and apply the trust property in the pursuit of some abstract purpose rather than for the benefit of specified individuals? However, if we view trusts as an offshoot of the law of gifts then the impossibility of creating purpose trusts appears more straightforward, for just as property cannot be given to or received by a purpose, so you cannot make a trust in favour of a purpose.

For now we must make do by saying that, as the law stands, there does not appear to be one single model or conception of express trusts. Different ideas appear to motivate and to shape different aspects of trusts law, and although this does not necessarily mean that the law is contradictory or unprincipled, more analysis is required as to whether, and if so how, these ideas can be accommodated within a single set of rules which is both consistent and fair.

2.8 Trusts and funds

As we have mentioned in passing already, it is common for the trustee to have the power to invest the trust property. Indeed this is often the very point of setting up a trust. Investment of trust property involves the trustee transferring that property to a third party, who in return provides the trustee with some other asset. That newly acquired asset then becomes trust property. So, where, for instance, trust money is invested in shares, the trustee pays trust money to the company or an existing shareholder in return for a transfer of shares. The end result of the transaction is that the company or shareholder receives the money outright – and hence free of the trust – and the shares become trust property in its place. In effect, the beneficiary's equitable title is transferred from the money to the shares.

This reveals another important feature of a beneficiary's equitable title to trust property: his title to specific trust assets can be extinguished by his trustee exercising a power to invest or otherwise disposing of the trust property. This process, whereby the trustee disposes of trust property free of the beneficiary's interest, is known as *overreaching* (see further Section 9.4). Because of this feature of trusts (or at least of express trusts; trustees of resulting and constructive trusts will not usually have powers of investment) and equitable title, it is sometimes suggested that we should view beneficiaries as having a proprietary interest in a fund of shifting assets rather than in each of the specific assets which, at any given point in time, make up that fund (see eg Penner, 2006). This probably goes too far. A beneficiary can claim specific trust assets both from his trustee, in exercise of his *Saunders v Vautier* right, and against third parties (subject to the bona fide purchase rule: Section 2.9) to whom such assets have been wrongfully transferred. This appears inconsistent with the beneficiary having no rights in the constituent elements of the trust fund. Nonetheless, the trustee's capacity to bring about changes in the identity of the property which falls within the trust is an important feature of the typical express trust and a significant qualification to the beneficiary's rights in individual trust assets.

2.9 The bona fide purchase rule

We noted earlier (in Section 2.5) that different types of proprietary interest can vary in two respects: their content and their durability. Until now we have been focusing principally on the content of equitable title, identifying exactly what sort of entitlement a beneficiary has to the property which falls within the trust. However, equitable title also differs from legal title in relation to its durability.

As mentioned previously (Section 2.4), the defining feature of proprietary interests is that they give exclusive entitlements to the use and/or enjoyment of particular things. It is by virtue of this exclusivity that proprietary interests typically bind third party recipients of the relevant property. So, in the most straightforward case, where some third party gets his hands on your property without your consent, you can demand its return simply because it is you and you alone who is entitled to decide how and by whom that thing is to be used. However, few, if any, proprietary interests are binding on all people in all circumstances. Sometimes proprietary interests will be lost even where the holder has not consented to their extinguishment or their transfer to another person. Different types of proprietary interest are more prone to being lost without their holder's consent than others.

Take the following example. We enter into a contract whereby I agree to sell you some computers for your business on credit. So, though I let you have immediate possession of the computers, you do not have to pay me until some specified future date. However, to safeguard my position in the event that you prove unable to pay me when the time comes, the contract also provides that, pending payment, I retain ownership of (ie hold legal beneficial title to) the computers. (This is known as a reservation of title or *Romalpa* clause.) In other words, though you are free to use the computers from the outset, until payment they remain mine. However, let us assume that, before you have paid, you purport to sell those computers to a third party, who is completely unaware that I in fact hold legal title to them. In such circumstances I have not consented to the third party receiving and using the computers, and so you may expect that I can enforce my proprietary interest against him and either recover the computers from him or sue him for using them without my permission. However, section 25 of the Sale of Goods Act 1979 provides that the third party is not only immune from any claim by me, but in fact obtains legal beneficial title to the computers.

As such, section 25 provides one instance where a proprietary interest may be lost even though the holder of that interest has not consented to its transfer. Why does the law do this? In our example, I am prejudiced by the law holding that title has passed to the third party. Of course, I have a claim against you, most likely both in tort and for breach of contract, for your wrongful sale of my property, but this may not help if you are insolvent or cannot be located. However, if title remained in me and I could enforce it against the third party, he would be prejudiced, as he has paid you, expecting to receive title to the computers. Again, he will be able to sue you for breach of contract or to recover the money he paid in a claim for unjust enrichment, but these rights will once more be no good if you have fled the scene or do not have the money to pay. Therefore, the law is faced with a dilemma. There are two equally blameless and equally deserving parties, and yet only one of them can be given title to the property. The law can either protect my pre-existing property rights, or it can protect his expectation of acquiring such rights – it cannot do both. In this instance, the balance is tipped in the third party's favour by the widely held view that the reliability and security of commercial transactions require that people should be able to acquire property without having to concern themselves unduly with the vendor's right to sell.

However, subject to these and similar specific provisions, legal proprietary interests (ie those recognised by the common law) will bind all those who come into contact with the property without the interest holder's consent, and so will be lost only where the interest holder consciously chooses to transfer his interest. In other words, the common law takes as its starting point that proprietary interests will bind all those who come into contact with the property in all circumstances, and then creates a series of limited exceptions to this.

Equity, however, adopts a different stance. As a general rule, equitable proprietary interests will bind only those who either:

1. knew or should have learned that the claimant has an interest in the relevant property (in short, those with *notice* of the claimant's interest); or
2. gave nothing in return for receiving that property (donees).

By contrast, equitable proprietary interests do *not* bind those who both pay, or otherwise give value, for (a legal interest in) the property and who do not know and cannot be expected to know that the claimant has an interest in that property: see *Pilcher v Rawlins* (1872) 7 Ch App 259. We call these people *bona fide purchasers for value without notice*, and we can call the rule that such parties are not bound by equitable interests the 'bona fide purchase rule'.

The bona fide purchase rule may be broken down into three elements:

1. The defendant must have given value in return for an interest in the property. This will be the case where he has given money or other property in exchange for the trust assets. However, it also extends to other actions or performances which have an objective value. So, if you give me trust property in return for my cleaning your windows or singing you a song, I am a purchaser for value. All that matters is that something of value is given; it does not matter how great its value is, or whether its value corresponds to the value of the property received.
2. The rule extends to all defendants who acquire a *legal* (ie common law) interest in the property. This of course covers those to whom the trustee has passed legal title, but it also embraces other types of legal proprietary interest, for instance those who have been granted a legal mortgage over the trust property (for more detail on mortgages, see Sections 8.13 and 14.2).
3. The defendant must not have notice of the claimant's equitable interest in the property. Notice covers both those who know of the claimant's interest (*actual notice*) and those who would have discovered the claimant's interest had they made such inquiries as would have been reasonable in the circumstances (*constructive notice*). A defendant will also be regarded as having notice if his agent, acting on his behalf in the acquisition of the property, has actual or constructive notice of the claimant's interest (*imputed notice*). (The reference in the rule that the defendant must act '*bona fide*' (in good faith) does not appear to add anything to the requirement that he must not have notice of the claimant's interest: cf *Armstrong DLW GmbH v Winnington Networks Ltd* [2012] EWHC 10 (Ch); [2012] 3 WLR 835, [121].)

So, say my trustee holds shares on trust for me and, in breach of trust, sells them to you. If you knew nothing and had no reason to know of the trust and my rights under it, you will receive legal beneficial title to those shares. However, if you did know or should have known that the shares were trust property (in which case you are not 'without notice'), or if you had been given the shares free of charge (in which case you are not a 'purchaser for value'), you would take the shares (and the legal title transferred by the trustee) subject to my equitable interest in them. Importantly, where you can bring yourself within the rule, not only do you take the property free of my interest, but so does anyone to whom you then transfer the property, *irrespective of whether they themselves are bona fide purchasers for value without notice*. In substance, then, the acquisition of the property by a bona fide purchaser for value without notice has the effect of destroying or extinguishing my equitable interest in that property. (There is an exception to this rule where the property or its traceable proceeds are returned to the original trustee, in which case the beneficiary can assert an equitable title to that property against him notwithstanding that it has passed through the hands of a bona fide purchaser: *Wilkes v Spooner* [1911] 2 KB 473 and see generally *Independent Trustee Services Ltd v GP Noble Trustees Ltd* [2012] EWCA Civ 195; [2012] 3 WLR 596.)

Some have suggested that because a beneficiary's interest cannot bind a bona fide purchaser for value without notice, it cannot be said to be proprietary. This is misconceived. There is no reason to demand that proprietary interests must bind all people in all circumstances (though, as proprietary interests are by definition rights in things, they must be capable of binding at least some third parties some of the time). Indeed, as we have noted, even legal proprietary interests, which presumptively bind everyone, can on occasion be defeated without the holder's consent, yet we do not (and should not) doubt that these are genuine proprietary interests. More fundamentally, the fact that one's rights are occasionally trumped by others' rights or are sacrificed for the public interest does not mean that those rights are illusory. For instance, just because you are permitted to manhandle me without my consent in certain cases of necessity and self-defence, it does not follow that I have no right to bodily integrity or autonomy.

The better view then is that the bona fide purchase rule does not compel the conclusion that beneficiaries do not have a proprietary interest – an equitable title – in the trust property. Rather, it means simply that such proprietary interests are by their nature more vulnerable than other proprietary interests recognised in the law.

Finally, we may ask why equity adopts in this respect an approach different from that of the common law, rendering equitable proprietary interests noticeably weaker than their common law counterparts. (Though it is worth noting that the common law applies the bona fide purchase rule to the transfer and receipt of money: *Miller v Race* (1758) 1 Burr 452.) One argument sometimes given is that equitable interests under trusts are typically 'hidden', in that it is the trustee who will usually have physical custody of the property. As such, trusts are apt to mislead third parties. The trustee, by virtue of his possession of the property, will appear to the outside world to be beneficially entitled to it, whereas in fact the beneficial interest lies elsewhere. The bona fide purchase rule therefore protects third party recipients of trust property from the risks created by the fact that the beneficial entitlement of trust property is divorced from its physical possession. This analysis also gains support from section 25 of the Sale of Goods Act 1979, which we came across earlier. Here the common law, exceptionally, applies the bona fide purchase rule to transfers of property by a person in possession of goods which he has agreed to buy but to whom title has yet to be passed. Again, this is a situation where the beneficial interest is hidden, in that the person in possession of the property, and so who appears to all the world to be beneficially entitled to it, is not in fact so entitled.

However, one may doubt whether this in fact justifies applying a different rule in such situations. Certainly it is true that, where proprietary interests are hidden, there is a greater chance that third parties who acquire the property will be unaware of them and so will be unfairly prejudiced if they then find themselves bound by them. But if we really do feel that we should not enforce proprietary interests against those who could not reasonably have discovered them then we should apply the bona fide rule *in all cases*, regardless of the nature of the proprietary interest involved and regardless of the context. In other words, though equitable proprietary interests are more likely to go undiscovered than legal proprietary interests, that should mean simply that the bona fide purchase rule is harder to satisfy in the latter case, not that the rule should not apply at all. As such, a strong argument can be made that this is one of those areas in which, through their separate development, the common law and equity have come up with different and conflicting answers to the same basic problem (see further Section 1.6). Accordingly, though no such reform is on the cards, treating like cases alike may require us to abandon this systematic difference in the treatment of proprietary interests between common law and equity.

Summary

▶ Trusts can be either *fixed* or *discretionary*. In a fixed trust, the settlor sets down exactly who is to get what property. In a discretionary trust, the settlor leaves it, at least to an extent, to the trustee to decide how the property is to be distributed.

▶ Trusts are to be contrasted with *powers of appointment*. Trusts, whether fixed or discretionary, involve an obligation on the trustee to distribute the property amongst the named objects. A power of appointment leaves the 'trustee' free to choose whether the property is to be given out amongst the identified class.

▶ Beneficiaries, at least in standard fixed trusts, have an interest – an equitable title – in the trust property. This, like other proprietary interests, allows the beneficiary to bring claims against (some) third parties who hold or have handled the trust property, and gives the beneficiary priority in the event of the insolvency of the trustee or third party who currently holds the property.

▶ A beneficiary's equitable title to the trust property differs from other forms of proprietary interest. First, it may be overreached by the trustee making an effective disposition of the trust property to a third party, who then takes that property free of the beneficiary's interest. Second, it will be defeated if the property is received by a bona fide purchaser for value without notice. This will be the case where a third party gives something of value in return for receiving a legal interest in the property, and, at this time, he neither knows nor has reason to suspect that the property derives from a breach of trust.

▶ Another aspect of the beneficiary's rights under the trust is that, if he is of full age and sound mind and is absolutely entitled to the trust property (ie there is nobody else with a beneficial claim to it), he may call on the trustee to transfer it to him outright, even if this is inconsistent with the settlor's wishes. This is known as the rule in *Saunders v Vautier*.

▶ Equitable title and beneficial title are not synonymous. Beneficial title is held by whomsoever is currently entitled to the benefit of the property. Where there is no trust, this is the holder of legal title. Equitable title arises only when a trust is created, and endures only so long as the trust lasts.

Exercises

2.1 Does a beneficiary always, or indeed ever, have a proprietary right in the trust property? Why does it matter?

2.2 Is it possible to justify the claims that a beneficiary can bring against third party recipients of trust property without viewing him as having any interest in that property?

2.3 How do the notions of equitable and beneficial title differ?

2.4 Why should we allow an absolutely entitled beneficiary to demand that the trust property be handed over to him even where this is inconsistent with the settlor's wishes?

2.5 Why should a beneficiary's rights in the trust property be defeated by a bona fide purchaser for value without notice? Why should a legal title holder's rights in his property not be defeated in the same circumstances?

Further reading

Birks, 'In rem or in personam? *Webb v Webb*' (1994) 8 Tru LI 99

Harris, 'Trust, power, or duty' (1971) 87 LQR 31

Langbein, 'The contractarian basis of the law of trusts' (1995) 105 Yale LJ 625

Matthews, 'The comparative importance of the rule in *Saunders v Vautier*' (2006) 122 LQR 274

McFarlane, *The Structure of Property Law* (Hart Publishing 2008), 206–27

McFarlane and Stevens, 'The nature of equitable property' (2010) 4 Journal of Equity 1

Penner, 'Duty and liability in respect of funds' in Lowry and Mistelis (eds), *Commercial Law: Perspectives and Practice* (Butterworths, 2006)

Penner, 'Exemptions' in Birks and Pretto (eds), *Breach of Trust* (Hart Publishing 2002)

Scott, 'The nature of the rights of the cestuique trust' (1917) 27 Colum L Rev 269

Smith, 'Unravelling proprietary restitution' (2004) 40 CBLJ 317

Stone, 'The nature of the rights of the cestuique trust' (1917) 27 Colum L Rev 467

Waters, 'The nature of the trust beneficiary's interest' (1967) 45 Can BR 219

3.1 The three certainties

Every express trust has to meet certain basic requirements for validity. As we are concerned here with express trusts, it makes obvious sense that the first requirement is that there is an *intention* on the part of the settlor to create a trust. Additionally, the *subject matter*, that is, the property which is to be held on trust, and the people or purposes (together known as the *objects* of the trust) for whose benefit the trustees are to hold that property, must be sufficiently clear. Together these requirements are known as the three certainties (see also *Knight v Knight* (1840) 3 Beav 148, 173 (Lord Langdale)).

Two different functions are served by these requirements. The first requirement, certainty of intention, looks to whether a reason exists for recognising a trust. Express trusts arise in response, and to give effect, to the intention to create a trust, so without such an intention there is clearly no basis for finding an express trust. The latter two requirements, certainty of subject matter and objects, have a different function. They are concerned with ensuring that the trustees, and if necessary the court, have sufficient information to give effect to the trust intended by the settlor. This is a more textured issue than that of intention, as the courts face a choice as to how much information they should require before holding a trust to be effective. The key question here is to what extent the courts should be prepared to accommodate and to work around a lack of certainty in the trust the settlor has declared, in order to avoid defeating his intentions entirely.

3.2 Intention

In very many cases, it will be obvious that a settlor intended to create a trust. Where the settlor has had legal advice and a trust deed has been drawn up, detailing the duties and powers of the trustees and the manner in which the beneficiaries are to benefit, the case will usually be clear. The use of the technical legal language of trusts law creates, at the very least, a strong presumption that the settlor intended to create a trust.

However, it is entirely possible to create a trust without mentioning the word 'trust', and indeed without having any notion of the trust as a legal concept. What matters is the *substance* of what you intend and not the language you use to express that intention. If what you intend is the set of legal relations which lawyers term a trust, you have created a trust, and it does not matter in the least that you had never previously heard of trusts, trustees, beneficiaries and the like. As Megarry J put it in *Re Kayford Ltd* [1975] 1 WLR 279, 'it is well settled that a trust can be created without using the words "trust" or "confidence" or the like: the question is whether in substance a sufficient intention to create a trust has been manifested.' (To similar effect, see *Re Schebsman* [1944] Ch 83, 104 (du Parcq LJ).)

More difficult questions arise where it is clear that the 'settlor' intended to benefit another party, but it is unclear whether he intended this benefit to be conferred by means of a trust. The starting point is that the law provides a variety of ways in which we may benefit people through a disposition of our property. A trust is one such way but it is not the only one. The most obvious alternative is an outright transfer of property to the intended 'beneficiary' (what we tend to refer to as *gifts*). Indeed, this is the much more common method by which we benefit each other.

As such, if I have, say, some shares which I want to put to your benefit, I have a choice as to how to do this. One option is simply to transfer the shares to you outright. Another is to create a trust of those shares in your favour. The courts generally allow us to choose whichever of these methods best serves our purposes. The problem case is where it seems clear that the property owner intended to make an outright gift but, for one reason or another, the gift is ineffective. If the gift cannot take effect as intended because the rules of property law for the passing of title to the asset are not satisfied, can the 'beneficiary' claim that the failed transfer nonetheless takes effect as a trust in his favour? In other words, can we treat a failed attempt to make a gift as amounting to a successful declaration of trust? Generally the answer is no. The court will hold that a trust arises only if that is what the settlor specifically intended (see further Sections 6.3–6.5).

This can be seen from *Jones v Lock* (1865) 1 Ch App 25. Here, a father had been away on a business trip. On his return, he was chastised by his family for failing to bring a gift for his baby son. In response, he produced a cheque for £900 and, placing the cheque in the baby's hand, said 'look you here, I give this to baby; it is for himself and I am going to put it away for him, and will give him a great deal more along with it'. When his wife expressed concern that the baby might tear the cheque, the father responded that 'it is his [ie the baby's] own, and he may do what he likes with it'. The cheque was then locked in the father's safe. Sadly, the father died six days later. The court then had to determine whether the cheque had been validly given to, or placed in trust for, the baby. It seems clear that the father intended to make an outright transfer of the cheque to his son, but merely handing a cheque to someone is not enough to transfer title to it. Rather, the father would have had to endorse the cheque (ie sign it on the back and write that it had been transferred to his son). The question then was whether the father's words should be read as manifesting an intention to create a trust of the cheque for his son, as a successful declaration of trust did not require the cheque also to be endorsed. The Court of Appeal held that they should not. Although it was clear that the father intended the benefit of the cheque to pass to his son, and that a trust would have been an effective means of doing this, his intention was to make an outright transfer, and the court refused to perfect an imperfect gift by treating a failed outright transfer as a successful declaration of trust.

However, there are cases which seem to display a more indulgent attitude on the part of the courts. The best example of this is *Paul v Constance* [1977] 1 WLR 527 (see too *Rowe v Prance* [1999] 2 FLR 787). Having separated from his wife, Mr Constance moved in with Ms Paul. When he then received £950 in damages after suffering an injury at work, Mr Constance decided with Ms Paul, that he would pay the money into a new bank account. Because they were unmarried, the account was opened in the name of Mr Constance alone. However, Mr Constance repeatedly assured Ms Paul that 'the money is as much yours as mine'. The couple later paid their joint bingo winnings into the account and made a withdrawal of £150, which they split between them. When Mr Constance died intestate, Ms Paul claimed that she was entitled to some of the money in the account on the basis that Mr Constance's words and actions had amounted to a declaration of trust in her favour.

Though Mr Constance never used the word 'trust', as we have seen, this is not decisive. As Scarman LJ held:

> ...we are dealing with simple people, unaware of the subtleties of equity, but understanding very well indeed their own domestic situation. It is right that one should consider the various things that were said and done by the plaintiff and Mr Constance during their time together against their own background and in their own circumstances.

Scarman LJ concluded that, when these factors were taken into account, Mr Constance's words and conduct demonstrated an intention that the bank account money should be held on trust for himself and Ms Paul:

> When one bears in mind the unsophisticated character of Mr Constance and his relationship with the plaintiff during the last few years of his life, counsel for the plaintiff submits that the words that he did use on more than one occasion namely 'This money is as much yours as mine', convey clearly a present declaration that the existing fund was as much the plaintiff's as his own. The judge accepted that conclusion. I think he was well justified in doing so and, indeed, I think he was right to do so. There are, as counsel for the plaintiff reminded us, other features in the history of the relationship between the plaintiff and Mr Constance which support the interpretation of those words as an express declaration of trust. I have already described the interview with the bank manager when the account was opened. I have mentioned also the putting of the 'bingo' winnings into the account, and the one withdrawal for the benefit of both of them.

Scarman LJ did, however, admit that this was a borderline case. Moreover, the case raised difficult questions, which, as things turned out, did not need to be answered. In particular, it was far from clear when this trust arose, as there was no single event relied on by the court as amounting to a declaration of trust.

3.3 Subjective and objective intentions

When it comes to determining whether the intention to create a trust is present, the question arises whether we are looking to what the settlor actually intended (a *subjective* approach) or to what the reasonable person would conclude the settlor intended from what he said and did (an *objective* approach). In contract law it is usual to determine intention from an objective standpoint, and the courts have said that the same approach is to be used when asking whether the settlor intended to create a trust (see eg *Twinsectra Ltd v Yardley* [2002] UKHL 12; [2002] 2 AC 164, [71] (Lord Millett)). This means that it does not matter whether the settlor in his own mind wanted a trust; all that matters is that the reasonable person would have inferred that this was his intention from his words and conduct. This is questionable on two grounds however.

First, as a matter of principle, there is generally no good reason for disregarding or overriding the settlor's true (subjective) intentions in this way. The objective approach is needed in contract law to protect the other contracting party who, when opting into the contract, will tend to rely on what he reasonably believes his counterpart's intention to be. This is shown by the fact that the objective approach will not be used where a contracting party in fact knows what the other's true intention is (*Hartog v Colin and Shields* [1939] 3 All ER 566). When it comes to the creation of express trusts, there is nobody in an equivalent position to the other party to a contract who needs the protection afforded by an objective approach. The same considerations therefore do not apply. So, short of facts which would justify an estoppel claim, a subjective intention to create a trust should be required.

Second, there is an area of trusts law, which shows that, where the subjective and objective approaches give different answers to the question of whether a trust was intended, the courts will take a subjective line. This is where it is argued that a trust purportedly created by the settlor is a sham. A settlor may set up a trust that gives the impression of being a trust for, say, his children, whereas in reality he intends for the property to remain at his disposal. Why, you may ask, would a settlor do such a thing? Well, a dishonest settlor might wish to assert to various people – such as the police, HM Revenue and Customs, creditors or ex-spouses – that he is penniless while, in reality, remaining in control of substantial assets. This way he can avoid having those assets seized when legal proceedings are pursued against him. This type of trust is known as a sham because it is designed to mislead the outside world as to the settlor's true intentions (see eg *Midland Bank plc v Wyatt* [1995] 1 FLR 697). In such cases, if the creditors can show that the settlor and not the named beneficiaries is the true object of the trust, they may be able to have recourse to the trust property to satisfy their claims. But they can prove that the real trust is for the settlor and not for the named beneficiaries only if a subjective approach to intention is used.

3.4   Precatory words

We have seen already that a trust can be created without using the word 'trust' and what matters instead is the substance of a settlor's intentions. On occasion a donor may transfer property to someone, expressing the wish or hope that the recipient will use the property for the benefit of some other named individual. For instance, a testator may leave property to another, 'fully trusting' or 'in the firm expectation' that he will use that property in a particular manner. When these and similar expressions are found in dispositions made by will, they are referred to as *precatory* words. Do expressions such as these manifest an intention to create a trust or do they impose at most a moral obligation on the recipient to comply with the donor's wishes?

For example, in *Mussoorie Bank Ltd v Raynor* (1882) 7 App Cas 321, the testator left property to his wife, 'feeling confident that she will act justly to our children in dividing the same when no longer required by her'. The problem with such a provision is that it is really quite unclear as to what is intended by the settlor. Here there appeared to be three different possibilities. The first is that the settlor intended to leave the relevant property on trust for his three children, with his wife acting as trustee. Under this interpretation, the wife would have no beneficial interest in the property whatsoever. The second is that the property was to go to the wife on trust, for her for life, with the remainder to the testator's children. Here, the wife could use the income produced by the trust property for herself during her lifetime, leaving the capital intact for her children after her death. The final possibility is that the testator left the property to his wife absolutely, imposing only a moral obligation on his wife to provide for the children after her death. The differences between these different constructions (and in particular between the first two and the last) are crucial, as in the last example the wife would be quite entitled as a matter of law to deal with and dispose of the property as she likes and need not leave a penny for her children.

The approach adopted by the courts is now firmly fixed in favour of treating expressions such as these as imposing no legal obligation in respect of the recipient's use of the relevant property and as creating no trust (see *Lambe v Eames* (1871) LR 6 Ch App 597). The best explanation for this approach is that the obligations of trusteeship are onerous and so should not be imposed where the language used is ambiguous or permissive, particularly when the disposition is contained in a document as formal as a will. Such an approach is well demonstrated in *Re Adams and the Kensington Vestry* (1884) 27 Ch D 394, where the testator gave his personal estate to 'the absolute use of my wife, Harriet Smith, ... in full confidence that she will do what is right as to the disposal thereof between my children, either in her lifetime or by will after her decease'. Summarising the shift in approach as to how the courts interpret such expressions, Cotton LJ stated:

> I have no hesitation in saying myself, that I think some of the older authorities went a great deal too far in holding that some particular words appearing in a will were sufficient to create a trust. Undoubtedly confidence, if the rest of the context shews that a trust is intended, may make a trust, but what we have to look at is the whole of the will ... and if the confidence is that she will do what is right as regards the disposal of the property, I cannot say that that is, on the true construction of the will, a trust imposed on her.

(Other examples of precatory words, where no intention to create a trust was found, include 'it is my desire that ...' (*Re Diggles* (1888) 39 Ch D 394) and 'I wish ...' (*Re Hamilton* [1895] 2 Ch 370).)

So the message is clear: if you want your will to create a trust so that there is absolutely no possibility of the person to whom you leave your property not disposing of it in accordance with your wishes, use imperative language, or, even better, use the words 'settlor', 'trust', 'trustee' and 'beneficiaries'.

Cotton LJ also noted that construing the whole of a document is critically important. This is shown by *Comiskey v Bowring-Hanbury* [1905] AC 84. Here, a testator gave his estate to his wife by will, 'in full confidence' that she would devise it on her death to such of the testator's nieces as his wife saw fit. Had this been the extent of the clause, these words would no doubt have been interpreted as imposing only a moral obligation on the wife. But the will went on to state: 'I hereby direct that all my estate and property acquired [by my wife] under this my will shall at her death be equally divided among the surviving said nieces.' These obligatory words were held by a majority of the House of Lords to supersede the prior permissive language and create a trust on the wife's death in favour of the nieces in such proportions as were determined by the wife's will, or, if no such proportions were specified, equally.

3.5   Segregation of trust property

The final issue regarding intention concerns how the trustee treats the trust property. As we saw in the previous chapter, the trustee is subject to fiduciary obligations in respect of his handling of the trust property, the key aspect of which is that he must use it to further the beneficiaries' interests and not his own. Because of this he will clearly have to deal with the trust property differently from the way in which he would deal with his own assets. Therefore, trustees are commonly required to keep the trust property separate from their own assets, and hence a duty to segregate the trust property is a pretty good indication that a trust is indeed what the parties intended. As Channell J put it in *Henry v Hammond* [1913] 2 KB 515, 521:

> It is clear that if the terms upon which the person receives the money are that he is bound to keep it separate, either in a bank or elsewhere, and to hand that money so kept as a separate fund to the person entitled to it, then he is a trustee of that money and must hand it over to the person who is his cestui que trust. If on the other hand he is not bound to keep the money

separate, but is entitled to mix it with his own money and deal with it as he pleases, and when called upon to hand over an equivalent sum of money, then, in my opinion, he is not a trustee of the money, but merely a debtor.

The point here is that, as trustees must deal with trust property differently from the way they use their own property, we should expect that trustees will be prohibited from mixing the trust property with property of their own. However, there is no necessary objection to a trustee holding, and hence mixing, the property of a number of distinct beneficiaries together in a common fund. This led Watkins LJ in *R v Clowes* [1994] 2 All ER 316 to state:

> As to segregation of funds, the effect of the authorities seems to be that a requirement to keep moneys separate is normally an indicator that they are impressed with a trust, and that the absence of such a requirement, *if there are no other indicators of a trust*, normally negatives it. The fact that a transaction contemplates the mingling of funds is, therefore, not necessarily fatal to a trust.

Whether the mingling of funds is inconsistent with the parties having intended to create a trust will depend on whose funds the 'trust' property is to be mixed with. If it is to be mixed with the property of the trustee, then this does appear to suggest that the parties cannot have intended to create a trust. If, by contrast, the property is to be mixed with the property of other beneficiaries, then the arrangement is not necessarily inconsistent with the parties intending that the property be held on trust. The reason for this is that, though the property of each individual beneficiary is not segregated from the property of other beneficiaries, all the beneficiaries' property *is* segregated from the trustee's own property, and it is this latter requirement which is essential to the idea of a trust.

As a final point, there do appear to be exceptional cases where a trust has been found even though the trust property was mixed with the trustee's own property. For example, in *Re Kayford Ltd* [1975] 1 WLR 279, the settlor company was held to have created a trust despite the fact that the money it was to hold on trust was paid into an account which already contained a small sum of its own money. The idea here seems to be that, though there is no reason to think that the settlor was thereby giving up its claim to the money already lying in that account, its intentions were that the money in that account was to be treated differently from its own money located in other accounts. As such, the settlor's intention was that it would not make further deposits of its own money into the 'trust' account nor would it make withdrawals from that account for its own use and enjoyment.

3.6   Subject matter and objects: the need for certainty

As express trusts are intentionally created, it is clear why there should be a requirement that the settlor must intend to create a trust. But trusts come in different shapes and sizes and so, if the settlor's intentions are to be given effect, we need to know what sort of trust he intended. The requirements of certainty of subject matter and of objects flesh out the terms of the trust and ensure that the trustees and the court are in a position to see that the settlor's intentions are upheld.

First, though, it should be stressed that the requirements of certainty of objects and subject matter are distinct from that of certainty of intention. It has been remarked (see eg *Mussoorie Bank Ltd v Raynor* (1882) 7 App Cas 321, 331 (Sir Arthur Hobhouse)) that uncertainty in the definition of the subject matter and/or objects may reflect a lack of any genuine intention to create a trust. In other words, the imprecision may be a sign either that the purported settlor did not intend his directions to have legal effect, or that he had not fully made up his mind. This is true. However, even where such an intention is clear, it must still be asked whether the subject matter and objects are sufficiently certain. If not, no trust will arise despite the settlor's proven intentions.

The reason for this is that the trustees and the court cannot effectively do their jobs unless they know what is required of them. The point of the certainty of objects and subject matter requirements is to ensure that the trustees and the court have the information they need to be able to perform their respective roles in the running of the trust. The trustees have the job of administering the trust, the central aspect of which is distribution of the trust property. Accordingly they need to know what property they are holding on trust and for whom they are holding it, or, in other words, who gets what. It is the role of the court to supervise the conduct of the trustees, in particular checking that they are properly distributing the trust property, that is, giving the right things to the right people. To do this also requires knowledge of the subject matter and objects of the trust. The same information is also required for the court to give directions on the proper administration of the trust when called on to do so by the trustees; indeed the court may even have to take over the running of the trust should the trustees be unwilling or unable to do so. The key question then is how much information do the trustees and the court need in order to do these jobs. What is sufficient certainty?

3.7 Forms of uncertainty

Certainty of intention is at root a simple factual enquiry: either the settlor had the requisite intention or he did not. The certainty of subject matter and objects requirements are a little more complex. One reason for this is that uncertainty comes in different forms. Uncertainty of objects or subject matter occurs where information which the trustees and the court need to ensure the proper distribution of the trust property is missing. We can distinguish different kinds of uncertainty depending on what sort of information we lack.

Our starting point must be the definitions of the subject matter and objects given by the settlor. What we are looking for are clear criteria by which we can identify what is to be the trust property and who falls within the class of objects. There will accordingly be uncertainty where the definition of the objects or subject matter provided by the settlor is, at least in part, imprecise or ambiguous. In such cases the problem is that we cannot be sure what he wants the trust property to be and/or who he intends as its objects. This type of uncertainty is most commonly referred to as *conceptual* uncertainty (though occasionally you will see it called *semantic* or *linguistic* uncertainty). Examples of this would be where the settlor declares a trust of 'some' of his shares or in favour of his 'friends'. In each case it is not clear what exactly the settlor intends. The first example is simple; we just have no idea how many of the shares are to be held on trust. The second case may need a little more explanation. Though (it is hoped) all of us can point to certain individuals who are, without doubt, our friends, things become a lot less clear at the borders. The line between friends and those who are simply acquaintances, colleagues or the like is blurry. To the extent that any of us actually draw such a line in our own minds (which is itself doubtful), different people will draw that line in different places. What to one person is a friend will be merely an acquaintance to someone else.

As such, and unless the settlor has offered further guidance as to who his friends are, we simply cannot be sure who precisely falls within the class of objects.

Clear definitions are only the beginning though. If we are to give effect to the settlor's intentions and see that the right property goes to the right people, these definitions need to be applied in practice. So, even if the settlor has given perfectly clear definitions of the objects and subject matter, there may still be uncertainty if we do not have the factual information at hand to determine what people or property match the definitions the settlor has given. Problems in applying the settlor's definitions to the facts can themselves take a variety of forms. First, giving the right things to the right people (and avoiding giving the wrong things to the wrong people) requires that we have the facts available to determine whether given things are part of the trust property and whether given people are within the defined class of beneficiaries. The subject matter and/or objects will be uncertain if, at least on occasion, ignorance of certain key facts leaves us unable to say whether a given thing or person falls either within the settlor's definition or outside it. For instance, if the settlor declares a trust in favour of all those who have studied law at a certain university, the trustees and the court will need to know whether any individual who comes their way, claiming to be a beneficiary, is or is not within the defined class. This will most likely depend on whether the university has kept full records of all those who studied law there. If such records were never kept, or if they have been lost or destroyed, then it is likely that we will be unsure as to whether some people are beneficiaries or not. This brand of uncertainty is known as *evidential* (or, sometimes, *factual*) uncertainty.

Evidential uncertainty is essentially reactive; it requires that, when confronted with a particular item of property or individual, we can answer 'yes' or 'no' to the question whether it/he/she falls within the definitions of the trust property and objects provided by the settlor. Sometimes, though, it will not be enough simply to be able to identify individual items of trust property and objects when called on to do so. It may also be necessary to know *from the outset* how many things or people match the settlor's definitions. The issue here is *enumerability*. For (an admittedly improbable) example, if the settlor declares a trust for all people over 6 ft tall, we would be able to know whether any given individual fell within the class of objects (we would just need a tape measure), but we would not know the total number of people who qualify. This type of information will, for instance, be relevant where the trust requires equal division of the trust property among the objects, as we then need to know the total number of objects before we can calculate how much any individual beneficiary is entitled to (see further Section 3.13).

A final issue concerns what may be called *ascertainability*. Even where we know of property or people who match the definition of objects or subject matter, we still may not know where to find them. This sort of information is needed if the trust property is to reach the beneficiaries.

You may at this point be wondering why we need go to all this effort to distinguish different forms of uncertainty if in the end they all create common problem: that we do not know what we need to know. The short answer to this is that the courts have themselves drawn these distinctions and have responded differently to different forms of uncertainty. Moreover, some certainty elements (eg enumerability) have greater relevance in relation to certain types of trusts than others. This makes it necessary to identify not just whether the subject matter and objects are uncertain, but also in what way they are uncertain.

3.8 Degrees of uncertainty

The ideal situation is for there to be complete certainty in relation both to the subject matter and to the objects of the trust. At the other extreme, there will, on occasion, be cases where the definition of the subject matter or objects is so imprecise, or the difficulties in applying these definitions in practice so great, that there is no way the trust can be saved (eg the trust of 'some' of the settlor's shares as mentioned earlier – see Section 3.7). However, between these two situations there is a vast middle ground. This is because imprecision and practical difficulty are matters of degree; a definition can be more or less precise, practical difficulties greater or lesser. And, importantly, although complete uncertainty cannot be overcome, a lesser degree of uncertainty may well be remediable.

Take the following example. S declares a discretionary trust of £100 in favour of his friends. Neither the subject matter nor the objects are defined with complete certainty. We are not told which £100 of S's total wealth is to be the trust property. Is it to come out of his bank account? The cash in his wallet? From the sale of other assets of his? Neither is it clear who falls within the class of beneficiaries, because, as we have seen earlier (Section 3.7), 'friend' is a term which is conceptually uncertain, in that it may be impossible to say with certainty, even where the facts are clear, whether a given individual is a friend or merely an acquaintance. However, the uncertainty here goes only so far. It is possible to supplement or to modify the information provided by the settlor so as to ensure that the trust does not fail. So, though we do not know where the £100 is to come from, we *could*, for instance, just take it from his bank account; and though we do not know for sure whom S's concept of friendship encompasses, we *could* formulate some workable definition or criteria of 'friendship' and apply that to S. That way we would, at least in broad terms, be giving effect to S's intentions. The alternative – the failure of the trust – would of course entail S's intentions being entirely defeated.

So should we be prepared to 'remedy' uncertainty in this way? The desire to give effect to settlors' intentions, where at all possible, supports the courts lending a helping hand in such cases. However, this is not the only relevant consideration. We must also ask whether it is legitimate for a court to act in this manner. How is the court to choose where the £100 is to come from, or who is to count as a friend? The settlor's intentions are no guide as the uncertainty stems from us being unclear as to what it is that the settlor wants, and so any choice the court makes runs the risk of appearing arbitrary. Courts are naturally reluctant to engage in arbitrary decision-making, especially where the decision affects the allocation of property rights – that is, who gets what. This leaves us with different factors pulling in different directions. What the courts must do is to decide to which they should give priority, or else to find some compromise between them.

3.9 Subject matter

As trusts involve the imposition of obligations in respect of the holding of property, we need to know to which property the trust relates. Moreover, if there is more than one beneficiary we need to know their respective entitlements in relation to the property; in other words, what part of the total trust fund each beneficiary gets.

Any asset which can be transferred outright (ie bought and sold, given as a gift) can form the subject matter of a trust. This therefore includes not just physical things like land, paintings and horses, but also intangible assets such as debts, shares and intellectual property. Problems arise where the settlor has not made clear what he wants the trust property to be. For instance, in *Palmer v Simmonds* (1854) 2 Drew 221 the settlor sought to create a trust of 'the bulk' of his residuary estate. A trust of the residue under one's will is certain (it is simply what is left of the testator's estate once all the property which has been specifically bequested is removed), but the reference to 'the bulk' meant that the court could not be sure what part of the residue was to be held on trust. Though this terminology is not often used in relation to the subject matter of the trust, the problem here is one of conceptual uncertainty; the settlor has not adequately defined what the trust property is to be.

Palmer v Simmonds may seem a clear case but it can usefully be contrasted with *Re Golay's Will Trusts* [1965] 1 WLR 969. There the trust required 'a reasonable income' to be provided to the beneficiary. Ungoed-Thomas J held that this was sufficiently certain:

> ...the yardstick indicated by the testator is not what he or some other specified person subjectively considers a reasonable income but what he identifies objectively as 'reasonable income'. The court is constantly involved in making such objective assessments of what is reasonable and it is not to be deterred from doing so because subjective influences can never be wholly excluded. In my view the testator intended by 'reasonable income' the yardstick which the court could and would apply in quantifying the amount so that the direction in the will is not in my view defeated by uncertainty.

The distinction being drawn here is between what people (subjectively) *think* is a reasonable income and what truly (objectively) *is* reasonable, and it is the latter, objective figure which the settlor intended to fix the subject matter of the trust. The difficulty, however, is that even if we accept that there is a single, correct answer to the question 'What is an objectively reasonable income?,' if – as seems inevitable – different people, and indeed different trustees and judges, would *in fact* answer that question differently, then this is as clear a case of conceptual uncertainty as you could hope to find. That is not to say that the court in *Golay* was wrong to uphold the trust; rather that it would be better to have admitted that, though 'a reasonable income' was uncertain in this way, the trustees and the court could remedy this by applying their own notions of what was reasonable in the circumstances.

In *Palmer v Simmonds* the source of the trust property was clear – it was to come from the settlor's residuary estate. What was uncertain was how much of this property was to be held for the beneficiary. A slightly different problem arises where the settlor has made clear both where the trust property is to come from and how much of it is to be held on trust, but has failed to identify which of the specific assets from that source are to be the trust property. For instance, the settlor declares a trust of one of his houses or half of his collection of paintings, without identifying which house or which specific paintings. Traditionally the courts have held that such trusts must fail; the settlor must make clear which individual assets (which house, which paintings) from the source are to be held for the beneficiary.

The orthodox position can be seen in *Re London Wine Co (Shippers) Ltd* [1986] PCC 121. This concerned a company in the business of supplying fine wines. When it went into receivership the question arose whether any of the company's stock of wines could be claimed by customers who had ordered and paid for wine but had not yet received delivery. One argument put forward by the customers was that the company held bottles of the relevant wines on trust for them. However, the company had not earmarked any particular bottles of wines for particular customers, and this meant that there was no certainty of subject matter. The principal stumbling block to the customers' claim was that the company had not in fact promised to provide the wine from its current stocks, which meant that there was not even a stipulated source from which the trust property was to come. However, even if the company had said that the wine was to come from current stocks – such that we knew not just how much wine (of the relevant type and vintage) the customer was to receive but also where it was to come from – the subject matter would still have been uncertain and the trust would still have failed. Oliver J stated:

> ... to create a trust it must be possible to ascertain with certainty not only what the interest of the beneficiary is to be but to what property it is to attach. I cannot see how, for instance, a farmer who declares himself to be a trustee of two sheep (without identifying them) can be said to have created a perfect and complete trust ... And it would seem to me to be immaterial that at the time he has a flock of sheep out of which he could satisfy the interest.

So, for there to have been certainty of subject matter it would have been necessary for the company to have gone one step further and to have identified the specific bottles of wine from its stock which were to go to each customer.

3.10 Intangible and fungible property

The rule requiring the settlor to identify the specific trust assets makes good sense where the individual assets from the source are not all identical. This is clearly the case in the examples given above of the trust of one of the settlor's houses and of half of his paintings. No two houses are the same, and this will also be true of the individual paintings in a collection of artwork. Arguably this is also the case with the wine in *Re London Wine Co*, as it is unlikely that all bottles of the same type and vintage will be exactly the same. It therefore makes a difference which house, which paintings, which bottles of wine are to be the trust property. And if the settlor has failed to identify the specific items to be held on trust, the court has no basis upon which to select which of these are to fall within the trust. Any such choice would necessarily be arbitrary. This is accordingly just the sort of situation we want to avoid and which the certainty requirements are designed to deal with.

However, where all the individual assets from the designated source are identical (such assets are generally described as *fungible*), this particular problem does not arise. Even if the settlor has not said which specific items are to be held on trust, the court or the trustees could themselves pick out the relevant number from the source. It would not matter which they selected for the simple reason that all the individual assets are the same. For example, if the settlor declared a trust of £100 from his bank account, provided he has at least that amount in the account, there is no impediment to the court ordering that £100 be withdrawn and treated as the trust property. A trust of half of a quantity of oil could be dealt with similarly.

Despite this, Oliver J in *Re London Wine Co* had taken the view that the same rules apply even where the subject matter is part of 'a homogeneous mass so that specific identity is of as little importance as it is, for instance, in the case of money'. However, when the matter was later considered by the Court of Appeal in *Hunter v Moss* [1994] 1 WLR 452, the court took a different view, holding that whether identification of specific assets was required did indeed depend on what sort of property was involved.

In *Hunter v Moss* the settlor, Moss, owned 950 shares in Moss Electrical Co Ltd (MEL). The court found that he declared a trust of 50 of those shares for Hunter. However, at no point had Moss identified which particular shares were to go to Hunter. The court nonetheless held that the subject matter was sufficiently certain and the trust was upheld. Dillon LJ stated:

> Just as a person can give, by will, a specified number of his shares of a certain class in a certain company, so equally, in my judgment, he can declare himself trustee of 50 of his ordinary shares in MEL, or whatever the company may be, and that is effective to give a beneficial proprietary interest to the beneficiary under the trust.

Hunter v Moss has had a mixed reception. The analogy Dillon LJ draws between declarations of trust and bequests under a will has been heavily criticised (see in particular Hayton, 1994). Moreover, Dillon LJ's rejection of *Re London Wine Co* on the ground that it concerned the passing of property in chattels and not declarations of trust quite simply ignores what Oliver J said in that case. Nonetheless, the decision was followed in *Re Harvard Securities Ltd* [1997] 2 BCLC 369 and has recently been affirmed and elaborated upon in *Re Lehman Brothers International (Europe)* [2010] EWHC 2914 (Ch); [2011] EWCA Civ 1544; [2012] 2 BCLC 151.

There Briggs J, at first instance, considered that the best interpretation of the trust in *Hunter* was not that Hunter became the beneficiary of a trust of 50 of Moss' 950 shares, but that he acquired a 50/950 share of that total shareholding. As such, there were not 50 (as yet unidentified) shares, which belonged in equity to Hunter, with the rest belonging to Moss. Rather the whole fund of 950 shares was co-owned in equity by Hunter and Moss in the proportions 50:900. One argument in favour of this approach is that it reflects the way shares work. Any shareholding is no more than that: a share, a proportionate interest in the company. The 'number' of shares to your name is simply a way of conveying what proportion (ie what total 'share') of the company you own relative to others (see further Goode, 2003). So, when you own 50 shares, there are not 50 separate items you own which are in principle capable of being isolated one by one. Rather you have a single shareholding in that company, its proportion determined by reference to the total 'number' of shares issued. The same is true of debts. A debt of £100 is not really 100 debts of £1 each. If you have a 50% equitable interest in such a debt, there is no question of requiring your 'half' to be identified for there are no separate 'parts' which are capable of segregation.

The clear implication of this understanding of *Hunter* is that it has no application to tangible property, where segregation *is* possible. This was also the view of Neuberger J in *Re Harvard Securities* [1997] 2 BCLC 369. Identification of specific trust assets is therefore still required where the trust is of tangible property, even where the trust property is to come from a collection of identical assets. This is clear from the Privy Council decision in *Re Goldcorp Exchange Ltd* [1995] 1 AC 74, which, on very similar facts, endorsed *Re London Wine Co*.

We may still ask though why it should be that homogeneous tangible assets must be specifically identified before a trust can arise. For though, unlike with intangibles like shares, segregation and specific identification is *possible*, more needs to be said to justify the conclusion that it is *necessary*. After all, as we have noted, the fungibility of such items means that it usually will not matter which specific items are to go to the beneficiary and which not. The usual worry is that we need to know what specific property belongs to the beneficiary if some is lost or stolen: so if I declare a trust for you of an unspecified 50 of the 950 gold bars in my safe, who bears the loss if 500 of those bars are stolen? Yet it is doubtful that we cannot find solutions to these problems (note in particular the tracing rules discussed in Sections 14.8–14.16) or that the mere possibility of such difficulties arising gives us sufficient reason to treat all such trusts as ineffective. (For an excellent discussion of the issues arising from these cases see Worthington, 1999.)

It seems clear – though the position is muddied a little by the *Lehman Brothers* decision (see Section 3.11) – that the rule set down in *Hunter v Moss*, and any possible extension of that approach to cases of homogeneous tangibles, can apply only where the settlor identifies the *source* of the relevant property among his existing stock of assets. In other words, it was vital that Moss declared a trust of 50 of *his 950 shares in MEL*. If he had not identified some collection or 'bulk' of assets to which he had title and from which the trust property was to be taken, no trust would have arisen (see too *MacJordan Construction Ltd v Brookmount Erostin Ltd* [1992] BCLC 350 and *Re Goldcorp Exchange Ltd* [1995] 1 AC 74). Moreover, the Court of Appeal made clear that the collection of assets from which the trust property is to come must be homogeneous. As Dillon LJ held, 'it would not be good enough for a settlor to say, "I declare that I hold fifty of my shares on trust for B", without indicating the company he had in mind of the various companies in which he held shares.'

3.11 'Floating' trusts

Uncertainty of subject matter has also been said to be the reason the courts have refused to allow 'floating' or 'suspended' trusts, whereby S transfers money to T on terms that T may use as much of it as he likes during his lifetime but must on his death leave what is left of it on trust for B. For instance, in *Sprange v Barnard* (1789) 2 Bro CC 585 the testatrix left £300 of annuities to her husband 'for his sole use; and at his death, the remaining part of what is left, that he does not want for his own wants and use to be divided between' the named beneficiaries. The court held that no trust arose and that the husband instead took the property beneficially. Now it is clear that, at the outset, we do not know what property will ultimately be received by the beneficiaries as we do not know how much the trustee will spend in his lifetime. To that extent we may say that the subject matter is uncertain. However, we may question whether this is sufficient reason to invalidate the trust. After all, the beneficiaries have no claim to any of the property until the trustee dies, and at that time we will, or should, be able to determine what is left and so what the beneficiaries are to receive. An analogy may be drawn with trusts of income from specified property, where, though it is impossible to say in advance how much income will be generated and hence what the beneficiary will receive, we will nonetheless be able to work this out when the time comes to pay him.

It may be that the true objection to floating trusts is not uncertainty of subject matter but the perception that it is incompatible with the existence of a trust that the trustee should be free, if only for a period, to use and dispose of the property howsoever he wishes. By virtue of their fiduciary obligations, trustees are generally prohibited from deriving any benefit from the trust property. However, trustees may take a benefit if the settlor so provides, and there seems to be no good reason to prevent settlors from creating floating trusts if this is what they want. For this reason there does not seem to be any sufficiently strong argument for holding that such trusts must fail. Indeed in *Ottaway v Norman* [1972] Ch 698, Brightman J suggested that such a trust may be upheld; though because the case concerned secret trusts (see Section 6.7), some doubt whether his statement is of general application (see further Section 6.14). In any case, the same result can be achieved by the alternative and uncontroversial means of giving the initial recipient only a life interest in the property, though with a power to dispose of the property in that time, with the ultimate beneficiary being entitled to the remainder. A provision similar in its wording to that in *Sprange v Barnard* was given effect in just this way in *Re Last* [1958] P 137.

Re Lehman Brothers International (Europe) [2010] EWHC 2914 (Ch); [2011] EWCA Civ 1544; [2012] 2 BCLC 151 sheds some light here too. There the claimants entered into contracts with Lehmans, under which Lehmans were to acquire securities on their behalf. However, the contract granted Lehmans the freedom to deal with (buy, sell) those securities in the ordinary course of its business, leaving the claimants with a right against Lehmans that it provide them with equivalent securities if and when they later demand them. One issue here was whether there was sufficient certainty of subject matter for there to be a trust of securities in the claimants' favour. Though each claimant was entitled to a specific quantity of securities of a particular kind, no specific securities had been segregated for any given claimant. As we have seen, following *Hunter v Moss* [1994] 1 WLR 452, this posed no problem.

However, the further difficulty here was that Lehmans had no obligation to provide the claimants with securities from their existing holding. Lehman was free to dispose of the securities it held and all the claimants could demand was that Lehmans provide them with equivalent securities in the future. But at any point in time Lehmans may not hold sufficient – or indeed any – securities of that description. This is in contrast to *Hunter* where Moss' shareholding in MEL remained constant throughout. Briggs J however concluded that this wasn't fatal to the trust, holding that '[a] trust does not fail for want of certainty merely because its subject matter is at present uncertain, if the terms of the trust are sufficient to identify its subject matter in the future' [225]. This seems to suggest that it is indeed possible to create a sort of 'floating' trust, which hovers over a range of assets of a given description, but which fastens onto a specific set of such assets only at some defined point in the future. (On this point, compare the Court of Appeal's judgment, which responds to the potential uncertainty in the subject matter once the trust is up and running by saying that it is enough that the subject matter is clear at the outset: [75].)

Finally, the settlor's failure to identify which assets are to go to a particular beneficiary will not be fatal to the validity of the trust if he has left this to the trustees to decide. For example, if in *Re Golay's Will Trusts* (discussed in Section 3.9) the settlor had said that the beneficiary was to receive what the trustees *considered to be* a reasonable income, the case would have been clear cut. It also seems that the settlor may leave such decisions to the beneficiary. For example, in *Boyce v Boyce* (1849) 16 Sim 476, the testator left his houses on trust, directing that his eldest daughter, Maria, should have the one she chose with the others to go to another daughter, Charlotte. In the event, Maria died before her father and the trust failed, as it was then uncertain which houses were to go to Charlotte. However, the assumption is that, had Maria lived and so been able to make the choice, the trust would have been upheld. Similarly, in *Re Barlow's Will Trusts* [1979] 1 WLR 278, the testatrix left a collection of pictures to be held on trust, with a direction to her trustees to allow any of her friends or family to purchase them. The trust was upheld despite the fact that it was not clear which individual would end up getting which paintings. It was enough that it was clear which paintings were to be held on trust, and it was then up to the beneficiaries to determine who got what.

3.12   Objects

The amount of information needed as to the objects of the trust has, rightly, been held to depend on the nature of the trust created, and hence on the nature of the obligations owed by the trustee. Therefore, we shall look at fixed and discretionary trusts in turn.

3.13   Fixed trusts

Fixed trusts can be framed in either of two ways. Each beneficiary's entitlement may be defined so as to be independent of and distinct from those of the other beneficiaries (if any). Alternatively, the beneficial interests may be defined referentially, so that any individual's entitlement cannot be ascertained or quantified without identifying and quantifying the others'. An example of the former would be '£100 to each of my friends'; an example of the latter '£100 to be divided equally between my friends'. This difference is often underplayed, but it is an important one when it comes to certainty of objects. In the former case, once a beneficiary has established himself to be within the class – here that he is one of the settlor's friends – he can claim his £100. It does not matter whether there is any uncertainty as to who or where the others in the class are. His claim in no way depends on that. In this way his claim is freestanding, not dependent on the success or failure of the others' claims. This is not true in the latter situation, where trust interests are defined referentially. If, in the example given, an individual comes forward and establishes himself to be one of the settlor's friends, we know that he should be entitled to *something*, but we do not know what until we know how many other friends the settlor has. In other words, it is not enough for a beneficiary to make out his own claim to a share of the property because the quantum of his share depends on the trustees being able to make out the claims of the other beneficiaries too.

Because of this difference, the two types of fixed trust have different tests for certainty of objects. In the case of trusts conferring independent, freestanding interests, all that is necessary for the claimant to establish an entitlement to his part of the trust property is that he satisfies the trustees (or the court, as the case may be) that he falls within the class set down by the settlor. It does not matter that the trustees cannot be certain of the identities of the other potential beneficiaries, whether because of ambiguities in the definition of the class or a lack of information. So, if I direct my trustee to give £100 to each of my friends, the trust will succeed notwithstanding the fact that 'friend' is an ambiguous, and hence (at least partly) conceptually uncertain, term. Neither will it fail if there are also substantial factual difficulties in showing who my friends are. Anyone who can prove himself to be a friend of mine can show up and claim his £100. Indeed another way of putting this point is that where I say '£100 to each of my friends' this is equivalent to my saying '£100 to friend A; £100 to friend B; £100 to friend C [and so on]'. Such provisions, therefore, effectively provide for a series of discrete dispositions and, as such, the fact that there is difficulty identifying some of my friends and so in giving effect to some of these dispositions is no reason to invalidate those we can give effect to (see *Re Barlow's Will Trusts* [1979] 1 WLR 278). The trust will fail only if the trustees have absolutely no idea of what the words used by the settlor meant, such that they could not find even one person who they could be certain fell within the class of beneficiaries. Accordingly, this test is sometimes called the 'one person' test.

In the second case, by contrast, where the beneficiaries' interests are referentially defined, a much stricter test of certainty is required. Because an individual beneficiary's interest cannot be quantified until the total number of people in the class has been worked out, the trustees must be able to compile a complete list of all the members of the class defined by the settlor in order for the trust to be valid. This requirement is commonly referred to as *list certainty*. The trust will accordingly fail either if there is ambiguity in the definition of the class (so that we do not know even in theory who falls within it) or if there is insufficient evidence, that is factual information, from which we can make out all those who do in practice fall within the definition. In short, fixed trusts of this kind need both conceptual and evidential certainty.

There is some indication that this test may be relaxed where we know the maximum number of people in the class, but do not know if there are in fact fewer than this (see eg *Re Gulbenkian's Settlements* [1970] AC 508, 524). For example, in relation to a trust of £1,000 to be divided equally between the settlor's children, it may not be too difficult to determine how many children the settlor had – say five. There may, however, be greater difficulty in establishing the continued existence of all of them. The trustees may have lost track of one or more, and hence it may be unclear if they are still alive. In such a case it would make sense to allow each child who has been located to claim £200 (one fifth of the fund) on the basis that he or she is clearly entitled to this much at the very least. The shares of the missing beneficiaries could be paid into court pending the discovery of the necessary information, or the court could make an order that those sums be divided among the established beneficiaries on the basis that the others cannot and will not be found.

One point of clarification. The 'one person' test, which we have seen applies to fixed trusts of the '£100 each' variety, is commonly treated in the textbooks as applying only to 'gifts subject to a condition precedent' or 'individual gifts'. The former description is particularly inappropriate. It is true that, in the example given above of a trust of £100 for each of the settlor's friends, each potential beneficiary must first satisfy the trustees that he does fall within the class (ie that he is a friend of the settlor) before he can claim his £100. As such his entitlement might be said to be subject to a condition precedent, namely that he can first establish himself to be a friend and hence within the class of beneficiaries. But this is hardly a defining feature of this sort of case. *All* trusts, whether fixed or discretionary, work in this way. A would-be beneficiary's ability to establish an interest under a trust, whatever the nature of the trust, will always be dependent on his being able to make out that he is indeed a member of the stipulated class, and this is so whether the class is framed in terms of a common characteristic, such as friends or relatives of the settlor, or whether the beneficiaries are identified by name. The second description is closer to the mark but nonetheless misleading. For, although it highlights the fact that in such cases each individual beneficiary's interest is independent and freestanding, the reference to 'gifts' obscures the fact that we are here talking about a test which applies not only to outright transfers but also to (some) fixed trusts (see eg *Re Tuck's Settlement Trusts* [1978] Ch 49; this is also implicit in *Re Barlow's Will Trusts* [1979] 1 WLR 278 where no distinction was drawn between the certainty of objects rules applying to gifts and to trusts).

3.14 Discretionary trusts and powers of appointment

The courts at first held that the objects of a discretionary trust were sufficiently certain only if it were possible to draw up a complete list of all those within the class of beneficiaries: ie the list certainty test we encountered in Section 3.13 in relation to referentially defined fixed trusts (see eg *IRC v Broadway Cottages Trust* [1955] Ch 20). One reason for this was that the courts took the view that the only way they could enforce the trust if called on would be to divide the trust property equally among all the beneficiaries, which of course requires knowledge of who all these beneficiaries are. The idea was that the courts were not entitled to prefer one beneficiary to another, which anything other than equal division entails, unless the settlor had given them a basis upon which to do so. A second factor supporting the list certainty test concerns how discretionary trusts function. As we saw in the previous chapter, discretionary trusts involve the conferral of a dispositive discretion on the trustees. The trustees thus choose who gets what, but in order to make a meaningful choice, they need to be in a position to weigh up the merits of the various members of the class. And though, as Lord Wilberforce was to remark in *McPhail v Doulton* [1971] AC 424, 449, a complete list of names in itself tells you little, it does at least enable the trustees to make the further enquiries needed to acquire the information they *do* need to exercise their discretion.

This was not to last however. In the middle of the last century, mainly for tax mitigation purposes, there developed a trend for discretionary trusts and powers with broadly defined classes of objects, and this culminated in a relaxation of the certainty test. In *Re Gulbenkian's Settlements* [1970] AC 508, the House of Lords endorsed recent Court of Appeal authority that, in relation to powers of appointment (see Section 2.2), the objects were sufficiently certain if it could be said of any given individual that he was or was not a member of the class, thereby rejecting the need for list certainty. And though Lord Upjohn, whose was the leading judgment, appeared clearly to reaffirm the list certainty test for discretionary trusts, *Gulbenkian* was used as a stepping-stone by a majority of the House of Lords in *McPhail v Doulton* [1971] AC 424, to the adoption of the same test for discretionary trusts too.

McPhail concerned a discretionary trust in favour of employees of the settlor's company and their relatives and dependants. It was accepted that the trust would fail for uncertainty of objects if the complete list test was applied, and so the validity of the trust depended on the House of Lords relaxing this test. Lord Wilberforce, giving the majority judgment, emphasised the similarity between discretionary trusts and powers (indeed the *McPhail* trust had been interpreted as a power at first instance and in the Court of Appeal), and hence the undesirability of their having different certainty tests. Importantly, he rejected the view that judicial execution of discretionary trusts could only take the form of equal division amongst the whole class, the view which demanded list certainty. Lord Wilberforce, having remarked that equal division was probably the last thing the settlor wanted in such cases, stated:

> ... the court, if called upon to execute the trust power, will do so in the manner best calculated to give effect to the settlor's or testator's intentions. It may do so by appointing new trustees, or by authorising or directing representative persons of the classes of beneficiaries to prepare a scheme of distribution, or even, should the proper basis of distribution appear by itself directing the trustees so to distribute.

(It should, however, be noted that there may be cases, particularly concerning smaller family trusts, where the settlor *does* (or can be taken to) intend equal division in the event that the trustees fail or are otherwise unable to exercise their discretion: cf *Burrough v Philcox* (1840) 5 My & Cr 72. In such cases, it would follow that we should still require list certainty as equal division is impossible without it.)

So, following *Gulbenkian* and *McPhail*, a single test of certainty of objects applies to both discretionary trusts and powers: can it be said with certainty that any given individual is or is not a member of the class of beneficiaries? What, then, does this test (sometimes called the '*any given postulant*' or '*is or is not*' test) require? On the face of it, there seems to be no complication; we must be able to say of any individual who happens to come our way whether he falls within the class or outside it. The test will accordingly not be satisfied if there are people of whom we are not sure whether they are beneficiaries. We must always be able to answer 'yes he is' or 'no he isn't'; there can be no 'don't knows'. On this basis two sorts of information would be required: we would need a precise definition of the class of objects and sufficient factual information to ensure that we could always tell whether an individual matched that definition. In short we would need conceptual and evidential certainty (see Section 3.7). If either the definition of the class is unclear or there are insufficient facts to establish whether certain individuals meet that definition, there will be some people in respect of whom we are unsure whether they are beneficiaries.

Unfortunately the picture is not so simple. The House of Lords in *McPhail*, having adopted the 'is or is not' test, referred the case back to the High Court to apply the test to the trust at hand, and from there the case went back up to the Court of Appeal as *Re Baden's Deed Trusts (No. 2)* [1973] Ch 9. Of the three judges, only one, Stamp LJ, took the approach set out in the preceding paragraph. Though he did not use the language of conceptual and evidential certainty, it is clear that he regarded it as necessary that there be both a clear definition of the class and sufficient factual information to be able to say who is and who is not a member. A class of 'don't knows' is not allowed. Despite this, Stamp LJ was able to declare the trust valid on the basis that the court could always determine who was a dependant and 'relative' could legitimately be restricted to next of kin.

Sachs and Megaw LJJ interpreted the test differently. Sachs LJ held that the test set down in *McPhail* required only conceptual certainty: 'The court is never defeated by evidential uncertainty.' Rather, where the evidence leaves us unsure as to whether a person meets the definition, that person is to be treated as not falling within the class:

> Once the class of persons to be benefited is conceptually certain it then becomes a question of fact to be determined on evidence whether any postulant has on inquiry been proved to be within it: if it is not so proved, then he is not in it.

Thus all those who, because of factual uncertainty, are 'don't knows' are to be treated as 'nos'. This is clearly a more relaxed view of the 'is or is not' test than that taken by Stamp LJ and allowed Sachs LJ to say the *McPhail* trust was valid even if the term 'relatives' was to be understood as 'descendants from a common ancestor'.

Megaw LJ offered yet another approach. Unlike Stamp LJ, Megaw LJ was willing to tolerate a class of 'don't knows' – people in respect of whom we are unsure whether they meet the settlor's definition. Indeed, he considered that, were it otherwise and we had to be able to answer 'yes' or 'no' to everyone, we would be back with the list certainty test, which had been clearly rejected in *McPhail*. However, neither did Megaw LJ endorse Sachs LJ's view that evidential certainty was an irrelevance. Rather, he took a position somewhere between the two:

> To my mind, the test is satisfied if, as regards at least a substantial number of objects, it can be said with certainty that they fall within the trust; even though, as regards a substantial number of other persons, if they ever for some fanciful reason fell to be considered, the answer would have to be, not 'they are outside the trust', but 'it is not proven whether they are in or out'.

Thus it seems that Megaw LJ was happy to accept *some* evidential uncertainty (though, arguably, not *conceptual* uncertainty) but only so much. There comes a point at which the evidential uncertainty is so widespread that the trust must fail, though what constitutes a substantial number is not elaborated upon and presumably varies from case to case. On this basis, Megaw LJ too was able to uphold the trust, and with 'relatives' bearing the same wide meaning adopted by Sachs LJ.

So where does this leave us? We have three judges all interpreting the same test differently, and with no clear majority and minority. There does seem to be agreement as to the need for conceptual certainty (though this is not wholly clear in the case of Megaw LJ): if there is any imprecision in the definition of the class of objects then the trust will fail. It is also clear that if there is both conceptual certainty and complete evidential certainty, the test will be satisfied. The difficulty only comes in cases where there is conceptual certainty but at least some evidential uncertainty, as each of the three judges has something different to say on the significance of evidential uncertainty. It has been suggested earlier that Stamp LJ's approach is most consistent with the test set down in *Gulbenkian* and *McPhail*; by contrast, Megaw LJ's interpretation in particular appears irreconcilable with the way the test was formulated in these cases. Ultimately, however, which one you find preferable will depend on how far you feel the court should go to uphold a trust. Those who feel that the courts should not be permitted to qualify or modify the settlor's intentions will incline to Stamp LJ's views. Those who think that trusts should be upheld even when the settlor's intentions can be given effect only imperfectly will prefer Sachs LJ's more indulgent approach.

A few remarks are, however, worth making in relation to some of the arguments employed by the judges in *Baden (No. 2)*. First, both Sachs and Megaw LJJ considered that the 'or is not' part of the 'is or is not' test could be dispensed with, so that it was enough that it can be said of any given person that he *is* a member of the class without the need to prove that certain people *are not* members. This then appears to have encouraged both judges to be accepting of at least some evidential uncertainty. But removing the 'or is not' changes nothing; the meaning of the test stays the same whether (or not) we keep the 'or is not' in the formulation. If we are unsure whether someone falls outside the class then we must necessarily be unsure as to whether that person falls within it. Not being able to prove that someone is not a member entails that we are also unable to prove that this person is a member. In this respect the reasoning of both judges must be seen as flawed. Second, Megaw LJ considered that the approach of Stamp LJ, requiring both complete conceptual certainty and complete evidential certainty, amounted to a return to the complete list test. This is wrong. The 'is or is not' test is essentially reactive; it demands that, *as and when confronted with individuals*, we can say whether or not they are beneficiaries. As we have seen (Section 3.7), this does not require, and is not the same as, being able to draw up a list of all these people *in advance*. Third, both Sachs and (it appears) Megaw LJJ were prepared to tolerate (some) evidential uncertainty but not conceptual uncertainty. Given that the presence of *either* type of uncertainty leads to us being unable to say whether some people are beneficiaries or not, you may wonder on what basis we can demand one type of certainty but disregard the other. Sachs LJ dismisses the problems of evidential uncertainty by resort to a burden of proof argument – if, on the facts, a person cannot be proved to be inside the class, he falls outside it. But we *could* do a similar thing in cases of conceptual uncertainty: if the definition is (in part) imprecise, then if any individual cannot be proved to come within that definition, because of such imprecision, he is to be treated as falling outside it.

What if the court had held that 'relatives' was uncertain? Could the trust have been upheld in favour of the other two groups, 'employees' and 'dependants'? The point was not addressed in *Baden (No. 2)*, but *Re Wright's Will Trusts* (1999) 13 TLI 48 says the answer is no. Conceptual uncertainty in any aspect of the class definition will cause the trust to fail. The court has no power to sever the ambiguous part of the definition from the certain part.

One final point. We started off this section on certainty by stating that the point of the certainty of objects requirement is to ensure that the trustees and the court have the information they need to administer the trust. It can be argued that the 'is or is not' test, however interpreted, is inadequate in this respect. We have mentioned already that the *McPhail* test is reactive in nature, requiring only that we are able to identify beneficiaries and non-beneficiaries when they fall for consideration. But the trustees will need to do more than pick out beneficiaries as and when they appear. A proper exercise of the trustees' dispositive discretion will require them first to weigh up the merits of the competing claims of the various beneficiaries. This requires some knowledge both of the size of the class and what sort of people comprise it. As mentioned earlier, one factor in favour of the list certainty test is that it provides the trustees with the raw materials they need to be able to conduct this sort of survey. The *McPhail* test can be satisfied without the trustees having any real idea of the size of the class of beneficiaries, let alone who these people actually are.

3.15 Administrative unworkability

At the end of Lord Wilberforce's judgment in *McPhail v Doulton* (Section 3.14 above) the following passage appears:

> There may be a third case [besides cases of conceptual and evidential uncertainty] where the meaning of the words used is clear but the definition of beneficiaries is so hopelessly wide as not to form 'anything like a class' so that the trust is administratively unworkable or ... one that cannot be executed ... I hesitate to give examples for they may prejudice future cases, but perhaps 'all the residents of Greater London' will serve. I do not think that a discretionary trust for 'relatives' even of a living person falls within this category.

Ever since, lawyers have been trying to work out what exactly this means. It is clear that Lord Wilberforce is saying that there is an additional requirement that discretionary trusts must satisfy if they are to be valid. Even where the 'is or is not' test is passed, the trust will fail if it is 'administratively unworkable'. But when and why will a trust fail on this basis? Lord Wilberforce's words suggest that he is concerned with a problem in the definition of the class, which prevents the trustees and/or the court from administering the trust. Now the obvious problem that may arise in connection with the definition of the class is that it is imprecise – that is conceptual uncertainty – but Lord Wilberforce makes clear that this is not what he is talking about. So, if the definition of the class is clear, how may it nonetheless be problematic?

One suggestion is that the settlor must make clear not just who falls within the class of objects but also the basis on which the trustees and/or the court are to choose between them when it comes to distributing the trust fund. Without such information, how are they to know who should get what? The problem with this argument is that the cases accept (albeit for the most part implicitly) that there is no requirement that the settlor lay down the proper basis for distribution. Rather, he may leave it to the trustees to formulate their own criteria for selection. This is evident from any number of trusts which the courts have upheld despite the lack of any clear basis for distribution in the definition of the objects or the other terms of the trust, the trust in *McPhail* itself being an example of this (see generally McKay, 1974). Moreover, as a matter of principle, there does not seem to be any reason a settlor should not be free to leave such matters to the trustees should he so desire.

Another view is that administrative unworkability concerns the size of the class. If the class is too wide, that is, there are too many people in it, then the trust will fail. This gets superficial support from Lord Wilberforce's example of a trust for all the residents of Greater London, though it should also be said that when you look at the context it is pretty clear that this is not what he was getting at. Moreover, it is difficult to see why a large class of beneficiaries should in itself render a trust impossible to administer. It is true that the trustees are under a duty to survey the class of beneficiaries in order to determine to whom they should distribute the trust property, and so the wider the class the more difficult and expensive it may be to conduct an in-depth survey. But we can simply say that, in such cases, the survey need not be so extensive. This is surely better than saying that the trust fails. Nevertheless this seems to be the way the administrative unworkability test was understood in the one case in which it has been used to invalidate a trust, *R v District Auditor No. 3 Audit District of West Yorkshire Metropolitan CC, ex parte West Yorkshire Metropolitan CC* [1986] RVR 24. There, the County Council sought to create a discretionary trust whereby the trust fund of £400,000 was to be applied for a list of purposes, 'for the benefit of any or all or some of the inhabitants of the county of West Yorkshire'. Lloyd LJ, giving the judgment of the Divisional Court, held, 'A trust with as many as 2 1/2 million potential beneficiaries is, in my judgment, quite simply unworkable. The class is far too large.' Quite why size alone should render a trust unworkable was not made clear. Lloyd LJ was, however, clearly impressed by the similarity between this trust and the residents of Greater London example given in *McPhail*:

> It seems to me that the present trust comes within the third case to which Lord Wilberforce refers. I hope I am not guilty of being prejudiced by the example which he gave. But it could hardly be more apt, or fit the facts of the present case more precisely.

The *District Auditor* case is problematic. Aside from the failure to identify any rationale for the administrative unworkability requirement, the trust should have in any case failed for a far simpler reason. As we shall see later, English law has a rule prohibiting the creation of trusts for non-charitable purposes and, as Lloyd LJ recognised, this is what the County Council had sought to do here. Because of this, the case could and should have been decided without any reference to administrative unworkability. Nonetheless, Lloyd LJ's view that trusts which are simply too large will fail for administrative unworkability has now been endorsed in *Re Harding* [2007] EWHC 3 (Ch); [2008] Ch 235.

3.16 Capriciousness

The administrative unworkability requirement does not apply to powers. Because of this, despite the adoption of the 'is or is not' test in *McPhail*, the validity requirements of discretionary trusts and powers are not completely aligned. This was made clear in *Re Manisty's Settlement* [1974] Ch 17 and *Re Hay's Settlement Trusts* [1982] 1 WLR 202.

In *Manisty*, Templeman J stated, 'The mere width of a power cannot make it impossible for trustees to perform their duty nor prevent the court from determining whether the trustees are in breach.' However, he went on to say that a power (and, it must be assumed, a discretionary trust) will fail if it is 'capricious'. This will be the case where the terms 'negative any sensible intention on the part of the settlor' such that the objects constitute 'an accidental conglomeration of persons who have no discernible link with the settlor or any institution'. Templeman J gave as an example a power to benefit 'residents of Greater London'. This is of course the same example that Lord Wilberforce had used in *McPhail* to explain administrative unworkability. Inevitably, this led some to question whether administrative unworkability and capriciousness really were distinct concepts. That they are distinct is clear from *Manisty* itself though, and this was confirmed by the *District Auditor* case, where the trust failed for administrative unworkability but was held not to be capricious. The capriciousness requirement, like administrative unworkability, is rooted in the need for the trustees and the court to be able to administer the trust. However, the specific problem here is not to do with the breadth of the class definition or the number of people who fall within it, but rather with who these people are and why the settlor picked them. The idea appears to be that the settlor should have a good reason for choosing the objects he has chosen, for if the class appears to be arbitrarily defined (in the sense that the only factor which links them is one which in itself provides no basis for choosing who should be benefited) then the trustees will not be able to pick among them on any sensible basis when it comes to distribution. But this doesn't follow: the fact that the objects are an arbitrary collection of individuals does not mean that the trustees will be compelled to act arbitrarily when they have to decide whom to pay. However the class is defined and whoever is within it, the trustees should be able to formulate sensible and coherent criteria for the exercise of their distributive discretion (again see McKay, 1974).

3.17 Resolving uncertainty

Where a class as defined by the settlor is, or runs the risk of being held to be, conceptually uncertain, the settlor may attempt to rescue the trust from uncertainty and invalidity by stipulating that uncertainties are to be resolved conclusively by a named third party or by the trustees themselves. It was originally held (see *Re Coxen* [1948] Ch 747) that such stipulations, although capable of resolving evidential uncertainty, could not cure conceptual certainty, on the basis that this would effectively oust the jurisdiction of the court on this matter and was thus contrary to public policy. Additionally, some questioned how conceptual uncertainty could be resolved by a third party if it couldn't be resolved by the court. However, the position may have moved on since then.

In *Re Tuck's Settlement Trusts* [1978] Ch 49, the settlor, a baronet, created a trust in favour of future baronets, provided that they be married to a wife who is 'of Jewish blood' and who 'continues to worship according to the Jewish faith'. The settlor further provided that, where this was in doubt, 'the decision of the Chief Rabbi in London of either the Portuguese or Anglo German Community ... shall be conclusive'. The question was whether the trust was void for uncertainty because of inherent ambiguity in the references to Jewish blood and the Jewish faith. Lord Denning MR held that the Chief Rabbi provision was effective to resolve any conceptual uncertainty in these terms. However, as the other two members of the Court of Appeal were able to uphold the trust on other grounds, this was only a minority opinion. Just to make matters even more confusing, there is a third possible approach, which gathers support from some of the cases (see *Dundee General Hospitals Board of Management v Walker* [1952] 1 All ER 896; *Re Leek* [1969] Ch 563, 579 and the judgment of Eveleigh LJ in *Re Tuck*; cf *Re Wright's Will Trusts* (1999) 13 TLI 48). This says that there are in fact two different ways in which a third party may be called in aid of potential uncertainty in the definition of a class. The third party could be called upon to resolve uncertainty in the definition of the class (eg '£100 to my friends, and, where there is any uncertainty, matters are to be resolved conclusively by X'), or, alternatively, the third party's opinion may itself form part of the definition of the class provided by the settlor (eg '£100 to those who in the opinion of X are my friends'). In the former case, the class ('friends') is conceptually uncertain and the third party cannot save it. But, in the latter case, conceptual uncertainty is avoided because a conceptually uncertain class ('friends') is replaced by a conceptually certain class ('friends as defined by X'). In *Re Tuck*, Eveleigh LJ held that the reference to the decision of the Chief Rabbi was of the latter type and so he was able to say that the trust was valid.

A number of points follow from this. First, there is a question as to whether *any* third party's say-so can be used as the reference point through which conceptual certainty is obtained, or whether the third party must have some expertise or knowledge of the class set down by the settlor. For instance, in *Re Tuck's Settlement Trusts*, a potentially conceptually uncertain definition (being of the Jewish faith) was resolved by referring the matter to a Chief Rabbi, someone with obvious expertise. Whether such prior expertise or knowledge is necessary is unclear. It may be that the best approach is simply to ask whether, considering the uncertainty otherwise present in the definition, we think it feasible for the stipulated third party to be able to resolve these difficulties.

Second, you can question whether all conceptually uncertain terms are curable in this way. A word or concept may be uncertain, at least in part, because different people have different ideas about what it means, with the consequence that we do not know which of these meanings of the word was intended by the settlor. This type of uncertainty can be resolved by reference to a third party's opinion because the settlor is thereby saying which of the different meanings of the term he intends. However, conceptual uncertainty may extend beyond this issue of multiplicity of meanings. It may be that there are some concepts which are so ambiguous that, even if you were to limit the inquiry to one person's conception of the term, there would still be some uncertainty. Think of terms such as tall, attractive, intelligent. It is likely that most individuals do not have such concrete conceptions of these terms that they can readily say of *all* people whether they meet that definition. If so, reference in the trust document to a third party's interpretation of the term will not rescue it from uncertainty.

Third, one can argue that this distinction, between cases in which the third party is called on to resolve conceptual uncertainty in a definition and cases in which the third party's opinion forms part of that definition so as to preclude this uncertainty, is overly fine. It is unlikely that most settlors would appreciate any difference between the two, on both occasions intending the third party to tidy up loose ends. Moreover, often it will be difficult to tell from the language used by the settlor whether this is a case of the former type or the latter. As such, it may be questioned whether the validity of the trust should turn on this distinction.

Finally, the courts will, at least on occasion, rescue a definition from conceptual uncertainty by interpreting it in such a way as to make its meaning clear. As Lord Upjohn stated in *Re Gulbenkian's Settlements*:

> It is...the duty of the court by the exercise of its judicial knowledge and experience in the relevant matter, innate common sense and desire to make sense of the settlor's or parties' expressed intentions, however obscure and ambiguous the language that may have been used,

to give a reasonable meaning to that language if it can do so without doing complete violence to it. The fact that the court has to see whether the clause is 'certain' for a particular purpose does not disentitle the court from doing otherwise than, in the first place, try to make sense of it.

In *Gulbenkian* the objects of the power included all those with whom a named individual had at some time been 'residing'. It was argued that this was uncertain; as Lord Reid said, 'It is often difficult in a particular case to determine whether a temporary sojourn amounts to "residence"'. However, their Lordships held that such difficulties could be overcome and that, if necessary, the court could determine whether a given individual matched the description. A similar exercise is evident in *Re Baden's Trusts (No. 2)*, where the court held that 'dependants' was sufficiently certain. It is important to note that the problem in such cases is one of *conceptual* certainty – the problem comes from imprecision in the definition itself: How long does one have to stay to have resided somewhere? How dependent is a dependant? This is sometimes underplayed by the courts (see, for instance, Sachs LJ in *Baden (No. 2)* [1973] Ch 9, 21). The question then is: why don't/can't the courts do this in other cases (friends, etc.)?

3.18   Consequences of uncertainty

What happens if a trust fails due to one or more of the three certainties not being satisfied? If there is no certainty of intention then whoever has legal title to the relevant property keeps it beneficially. So if S transfers property to T and it cannot be proved that S intended T to hold that property on trust, there is an outright transfer to T, who is then free to use the property as he likes. If there is uncertainty of subject matter or objects then, if the settlor sought to create the trust by declaring himself trustee, no trust arises and the settlor remains absolutely entitled to the property. If, by contrast, he sought to create the trust by transferring the property to another person, T, for him to hold on trust, then T will hold that property on resulting trust (see Section 8.7) for the settlor, unless the settlor can be regarded as having intended that, in such circumstances, the beneficial interest should go to someone else, say the trustee or another of the beneficiaries (cf *Hancock v Watson* [1902] 1 AC 14).

Summary

▷ To create a valid express trust, a number of requirements have to be met. The settlor must have intended to create a trust; the trust property must be sufficiently certain; and the beneficiaries must be adequately identified. Together these are known as the three certainties: *intention, subject matter* and *objects*.

▷ Intending to create a trust is not the same as intending to make an outright gift of property, and a trust will be recognised only if this is what the settlor intended. Failed gifts will not be reinterpreted as successful trusts.

▷ An intention to create a trust involves an intention to impose legal obligations on another – the trustee – in relation to his handling of and dealing with the property. Accordingly, no trust will be created if the settlor intended merely to impose a moral obligation on the 'trustee' to use the property for another's benefit.

▷ The courts have said that in establishing whether the necessary intention is present they adopt an objective approach, asking whether a reasonable person would have understood this to be the settlor's intentions, as opposed to asking whether this is what the settlor *actually* (or subjectively) intended.

Summary cont'd

▶ The certainty of subject matter and objects requirements are concerned with ensuring that both the trustee and the courts have sufficient information to administer the trust.

▶ A trust's subject matter and objects may be uncertain in a variety of ways and to differing degrees. The principal forms of uncertainty arise where the words used by the settlor are inexact (*conceptual uncertainty*) and where we do not have enough factual information to apply the settlor's definitions (*evidential uncertainty*).

▶ The law has to decide how much information is sufficient to give sensible effect to the settlor's intentions. The more it requires, the more straightforward the court's job in administering and policing the trust, and the more likely it is that the trust will accurately reflect the settlor's intentions. However, this also makes it more likely that clearly intended trusts will fail to satisfy the law's certainty requirements, thus defeating the settlor's intentions entirely.

▶ In respect of certainty of subject matter, the general rule is that the precise identity and location of the trust property, and what parts of it are to go to which beneficiaries, must be clearly stated. There is, however, an exception with homogeneous intangible property, where it is sufficient to identify the source of the trust property and the proportion of that 'bulk' which is to be held on trust.

▶ The certainty of objects requirement varies depending on the nature of the trust being created. This is because some types of trust require more information to function than others.

▶ Where a settlor creates a fixed trust of the form '£X to each of my friends/relatives/employees etc.', the trust will succeed so long as any one person can be found who falls within the defined class of beneficiaries, even if in all other respects, and for all other people, the definition is unclear.

▶ Where a settlor creates a fixed trust of the form '£X to be divided equally between my friends/relatives/employees etc.', the trust will succeed only if it is possible to draw up a complete list of all those who fall within the defined class of beneficiaries.

▶ Where a settlor creates a discretionary trust, the trust will succeed only if it can be said of any given person that he *is or is not* a member of the class of beneficiaries. Quite what this test requires is, however, uncertain. The suggestion is that the class must be conceptually certain, and so the trust will fail if the definition of the beneficiaries is in any way ambiguous, but that evidential certainty may not be necessary, or at least that a degree of evidential uncertainty will be tolerated.

▶ A discretionary trust will fail, even if its objects are sufficiently certain, if it is held to be either *administratively unworkable* or *capricious*. The content of and relationship between these two tests are unclear. The suggestion, however, is that administrative unworkability is concerned with the size of the class of beneficiaries – is it too big? – whereas capriciousness is concerned with the settlor's reasons for choosing these people as his beneficiaries – did he have a good enough reason for picking them (rather than anyone else)?

▶ It may be possible to cure uncertainty of subject matter or objects by stipulating for a third party to fix any such problems. Such provisions are effective in resolving evidential uncertainty. However, there is considerable doubt as to whether conceptual uncertainty can be cured in this way.

▶ If the settlor seeks to make a self-declaration of trust then any uncertainty will result in him continuing to hold the property absolutely. If he seeks to create a trust by transferring property to another to hold on trust then uncertainty of objects or subject matter will lead to the trustee holding the property on trust for the settlor.

Exercises

3.1 Is the modern relaxation in the requirements of certainty of subject matter and objects, as evidenced by cases such as McPhail v Doulton and Hunter v Moss, a good thing?

3.2 Is there any point in distinguishing different types of uncertainty (eg conceptual and evidential)?

3.3 In relation to certainty of subject matter, can we justify applying different rules to, on the one hand, fungible tangible property (like oil or gold bars) and, on the other, to fungible intangible property (like shares)?

3.4 Ed, a retired singer who lives in New Cross, resolves to divest himself of his wealth while he is alive, and transfers the great bulk of his assets to his only brother, Colman, to hold on trust. The trust contains these provisions:

(a) £500 million to be divided between my children and immediate family;

(b) £50 million to be divided as my trustee sees fit between my many business partners, past and present, in gratitude for their valuable help and support;

(c) £10 to everyone paying local taxes in Greater London;

(d) £5 million to be used to build and maintain a recording studio for the use of students of Goldsmith's College;

(e) each of my good friends is entitled to a guitar from my collection;

(f) the remainder is to be distributed equally between my children.

Ed has been married twice, and has three children from the first marriage. With his second wife he adopted two children. Ed is estranged from one of the children from his first marriage, Tetris, of whom nothing has been heard since he emigrated to Ecuador 10 years ago.
    Advise Colman.

3.5 Should the tests of administrative unworkability and capriciousness also apply to fixed trusts?

3.6 Should a settlor be able to stipulate for a named third party to resolve any conceptual uncertainty which may otherwise exist in his definitions of the subject matter or beneficiaries of the trust?

Further reading

Goode, 'Are intangible assets fungible?' [2003] LMCLQ 379

Hayton, 'Certainty of subject-matter of trusts' (1994) 110 LQR 335

McKay, '*Re Baden* and the third class of uncertainty' (1974) 38 Conv 269

Parkinson, 'Reconceptualising the express trust' [2002] CLJ 657, 663–76

Worthington, 'Sorting out ownership interests in a bulk: gifts, sales and trusts' [1999] JBL 1

Chapter 4

Purpose trusts

4.1 The beneficiary principle

The trusts we have encountered so far have all been trusts for people. However, a settlor may wish to create a trust with a different aim. Instead of seeking to benefit certain specified individuals, he may want to see his property used to further a particular cause or objective. So, a settlor may want to set up a trust to promote the study of law, or to ensure that his pets are looked after. We call such trusts *purpose trusts*.

The basic rule of English trusts law, however, is that trusts must have beneficiaries – people for whose benefit the trust property is held and applied – and hence that it is not possible to create purpose trusts. This rule, known as the *beneficiary principle*, was not always part of English law but, though it has its critics, it is now firmly established. As Lord Evershed MR stated in *Re Endacott* [1960] Ch 232, 246: 'No principle perhaps has greater sanction or authority behind it than the general proposition that a trust by English law, not being a charitable trust, in order to be effective, must have ascertained or ascertainable beneficiaries.' Applying this principle to the facts of *Endacott*, the Court of Appeal held that the testator's attempt to create a trust 'for the purposes of providing some useful memorial to myself' failed. As the reference to charitable trusts in Lord Evershed's statement indicates, however, there are in fact exceptions to the beneficiary principle, and hence to the rule that purpose trusts are invalid. It is also clear that the prohibition applies only to purpose trusts and not to *powers* for purposes (see eg *Re Douglas* (1887) 35 Ch D 472). We will examine these exceptions, as well as further examples where the rule has been applied, in due course. Before then it is worth spending a little time considering why, as a general rule, we do not allow purpose trusts.

The key point to note is that the rule against purpose trusts means that even where we are sure that the settlor intended such a trust, and there is no uncertainty in relation to the property to be held on trust or the purposes for which it is to be applied, the trust will fail. It is true that, because purpose trusts which promote worthy causes will often be valid as charitable trusts, many of the trusts which fall foul of the beneficiary principle will be for rather eccentric or esoteric purposes, but why should we not allow settlors to create such trusts if they so wish? After all, express trusts are facilitative devices; they enable owners to see that their property is used in accordance with their intentions. Here, though, we seem to be saying that no matter how much a settlor may want to ensure that his property is used to further a particular purpose, the law (or at least the law of trusts) will not enable him to. This requires some justification.

4.2 The basis of the rule

The most frequently cited accounts of the basis of the rule come from *Morice v Bishop of Durham* (1804) 9 Ves 399, affirmed (1805) 10 Ves 522. Sir William Grant expressed its rationale as follows:

> There can be no trust, over the exercise of which this Court will not assume a control; for an uncontrollable power of disposition would be ownership, and not a trust. If there be a clear

trust, but for uncertain objects, the property, that is the subject of the trust, is undisposed of, and the benefit of such trust must result to those, to whom the law gives ownership in default of disposition by the former owner. But this doctrine does not hold good with regard to trusts for charity. Every other trust must have a definite object. There must be somebody, in whose favour the Court can decree performance.

To similar effect is Roxburgh J in *Re Astor* [1952] Ch 534, 541–42:

> ...if the purposes [of the trust] are not charitable, great difficulties arise both in theory and in practice. In theory, because having regard to the historical origins of equity it is difficult to visualize the growth of equitable obligations which nobody can enforce, and in practice, because it is not possible to contemplate with equanimity the creation of large funds devoted to non-charitable purposes which no court and no department of state can control, or in the case of maladministration reform.

The argument here is that for a trust to be valid it must be capable of being supervised by the courts, in order to ensure that the trustees' duties are enforced and the settlor's intentions respected. For the court to be able to supervise the running of trusts, there needs to be someone who will take the trustees to court if he thinks that they may be failing to administer the trust properly. If there is no beneficiary – and purpose trusts necessarily have none – there is nobody in the position to do this. This explanation also accounts for the validity of trusts for charitable purposes, as these are enforced by the Attorney-General and the Charity Commission.

This explanation of the beneficiary principle has, however, come under attack in recent years. In essence, the argument rests on two propositions, both of which must be true if we are to be able to justify the prohibition of non-charitable purpose trusts on this basis:

1. a trust which cannot be enforced must fail; *and*
2. only beneficiaries can enforce trusts.

For the most part, critics of the beneficiary principle have accepted the first of these and focused their attention on the second.

4.3   Who can enforce trusts?

It is clear that beneficiaries are the ideal people to enforce trusts. As the trust exists for their benefit, it is they who will lose out if the trustees do not do their job properly. Accordingly, they have an obvious incentive both to supervise the trustees' running of the trust and to take them to court if they consider that they have been breaching their obligations. However, it does not follow from this that beneficiaries are the *only* people capable of enforcing trusts. If, despite the lack of beneficiaries, we can find someone to enforce purpose trusts, this reason for prohibiting them falls away.

So who could fill the role of enforcer of the trustees' duties? One option would be to allow the settlor standing to enforce purpose trusts. The obvious advantage to this is that because it is the settlor himself who created the trust, he will be keen to see the trust carried out properly and so has an incentive to keep an eye on the trustees and go to court if necessary. In spite of this, however, it is a long- and well-established rule of trusts law that settlors have no standing to enforce trusts (though they may do so if they are also beneficiaries). Once the trust is up and running, the settlor has no further input and drops out of the picture. The reasons for this, however, are not entirely clear. One argument is that the settlor may no longer be around to enforce the trust. This will obviously be true of the great number of trusts created by will. But this does not explain why a settlor should not be able to enforce the trust he created when he is still alive and well. Perhaps the rule can be best explained as an example of a particular view of the nature of trusts. On this view trusts are a form of disposition, the settlor transferring – giving up – his beneficial interest in the trust property to the beneficiary. As such, trusts are, in this respect, analogous to gifts. In both cases the settlor/owner makes a transfer of some or all of his interest in the relevant property (see further Sections 2.7, 4.5). And, just as once you make a gift of property you have no right to control what the recipient does with it, so the same is true once you create a trust. The settlor has given away his interest in the property and has no further right to dictate or interfere with its use.

A second possibility would be to allow the settlor to appoint an independent enforcer of the trust. This would involve enabling the settlor to choose someone who, despite not being a beneficiary, would have the job of supervising the trustees and taking them to court where necessary. This argument has been made at length by Hayton (2001) and has been adopted in the trusts legislation of a number of 'offshore' jurisdictions. The principal counter-argument is that, as the enforcer is independent, and hence has no personal interest in the performance of the trust, how can we be sure that he will do the job? (See eg Parkinson, 2002, 680.) Even worse, there is the danger that he and the trustee may collude to divide the property between themselves. To prevent this we would need a second enforcer to supervise the actions of the first, and so on *ad infinitum*. It can readily be admitted that, for these reasons, independent enforcement is not as good as enforcement by beneficiaries. The question is whether we should consider it good enough. Ultimately it comes down to whether we are concerned to see that enforcement is not merely possible but likely. In this regard it should be noted that, for a variety of reasons (lack of resources, ignorance, apathy, etc.), even the presence of beneficiaries does not guarantee that a trust will be enforced.

A final possibility would be to ask if there are any people who, though not beneficiaries, are similarly interested in seeing the trust performed and so would be similarly motivated to enforce it. In relation to purpose trusts, these would be people who would like to see the particular purpose carried out. Though not all purpose trusts would be likely to have people sufficiently interested to take the time and make the effort to enforce the trust, many would, and enforcement by such interested parties would avoid the problems created by independent enforcers. As we shall see (Section 4.8), this argument has received some support in the cases, though its status remains hotly contested. The counter-argument here would be that we should not be giving rights of enforcement to any old person who would like to see the trustees' obligations performed. An analogy can be drawn with contract law, where third parties have traditionally had no rights to sue even where the performance would benefit them and, even following the Contracts (Rights of Third Parties) Act 1999, have such rights only where the parties to the contract have so agreed.

4.4   Must trusts be enforceable?

The upshot of all this is that it is at least arguable that we can find people to enforce trusts even in the absence of beneficiaries. As we have already noted, however, we only need to find an enforcer if we conclude that enforceability is essential for a trust's validity. This too can be questioned (see too Gardner, 2011, 231–36). If we ask why we should be concerned with enforcement, the answer is that without the possibility of enforcement there is a (greater) risk that trustees will not perform their obligations. If we then ask why we should be concerned about unpreventable and unremediable breaches of trust, then, aside perhaps from some general public interest in trustees not abusing their position, our reason must be that this would defeat the intentions of the settlor who created the trust. Accordingly, to minimise the risk that trusts are not performed, and hence that settlors' intentions are thwarted, we say that unenforceable trusts are ineffective, with the beneficial interest in the property reverting to the settlor or his estate (see further Section 8.7).

However, although this approach greatly reduces the chance of the trustees misappropriating the trust property, it *guarantees* that the trust property will not be used in the way the settlor intended, namely to further his chosen purposes. In other words, the effect of the current prohibition of purpose trusts is that, even where the trustees are keen to give effect to the trust and where there is no doubt as to their honesty and competence, the law stops them from performing the trust and applying the property in furtherance of the intended purpose. The alternative approach would be to hold that unenforceable trusts are nonetheless valid. This would mean that trustees who were honest and competent would be free to give effect to the trust as intended by the settlor. Of course, there would be some trustees who would act dishonestly or incompetently, with the result that the settlor's intentions would then be defeated, but, in contrast to the current outright prohibition, there would at least be a *chance* of success. Moreover, seeing that it is for the settlor, in the first instance, to choose whom he wants to be his trustees, there is every chance that the people chosen *would* strive to give effect to the settlor's intentions, even without a beneficiary or other enforcer breathing down their necks. In short, if our concern is with giving effect to the settlor's intentions, there is a strong argument that the present prohibition of purpose trusts does more harm than the alternative of allowing them even where they cannot be enforced. At the very least, if the settlor is willing to take the risk that the trust will not be carried out, there does not seem to be any strong reason for the law to stand in his way.

4.5 Beneficiaries and the nature of trusts

In the light of the arguments rehearsed earlier, both the propositions on which the *Morice v Bishop of Durham* rationale for the beneficiary principle rests appear weak. Perhaps because of this, those who support the principle have looked elsewhere for a justification. Most often the proposition they put forward is that it is somehow of the essence of a trust that it must have beneficiaries, such that a 'trust' without beneficiaries would not be a true trust at all. One such argument is that duties cannot exist without rights. Duties must be owed to someone and that person will in turn have a right to the performance of that duty. As all trusts involve duties on the part of the trustee, they are possible only if we can identify someone to whom these duties are owed (see Matthews, 1996). On this view, a trust needs more than a mere enforcer; it needs someone with a right to its performance, someone to whose benefit the trustee's duties are directed – or, in other words, a beneficiary. Without this, the trustees' duties, and hence the trust, are illusory. A second example of this sort of argument is that property must always have a beneficial owner. This is not a problem where there is no trust or where there is a trust with beneficiaries, but it is when we come to purpose trusts. Accordingly, the impossibility of the beneficial interest in property 'disappearing' or being 'in suspense' means that purpose trusts are necessarily impossible (see eg *Twinsectra Ltd v Yardley* [2002] UKHL 12; [2002] 2 AC 164, [90] (Lord Millett)).

Neither of these arguments is convincing. In response to the suggestion that duties must always be owed to someone, we can question whether this is really true. Certainly, many duties are owed to specific people or groups and so *do* correspond to rights held by other people/groups. For example, if you and I enter into a contract, each one of us comes under a duty to perform, a duty which corresponds to the other's right to performance. Similarly, if I breach my contract with you I owe you a duty to compensate you for your loss. This duty corresponds to your right that I pay you compensation. But it's not uncommon to see duties described without any reference to rights or right holders. This tends to be the case with criminal law duties, which tell us simply not to kill, steal, assault, cause criminal damage and the like. Perhaps we might say that these duties are owed to the members of society whose interests would be threatened by that conduct. But is it nonsensical simply to say 'don't kill/steal', without stipulating or even considering to whom, if anyone, the duty is owed? Even if these duties *are* owed to those who would be threatened by such conduct, can we really say the same about things like parking laws or environmental regulations? An even clearer example is provided by charitable purpose trusts. There is no doubt that these do not have beneficiaries and yet nobody claims that the duties owed by their trustees are meaningless or empty. Nor does it seem right to say that these duties are owed to the Attorney-General or the Charity Commission. Of course it is true that they can *enforce* these trusts and these duties, but if that is all we are concerned with, we are back where we started, with the *Morice* proposition that there must always be someone who can enforce the trust obligations.

Similarly, it is far from clear why there must always be someone or some group who holds the beneficial interest in the property. There are plenty of resources in the world which are owned by nobody (see Gray, 1991) and it would be mysterious if the law could not accommodate the possibility of property capable of ownership not being beneficially held by anyone, at least for a period of time. Indeed, as the law stands, there seem to be a number of situations in which the beneficial interest in an asset is temporarily in abeyance: see for example *Commissioner of Stamp Duties (Queensland) v Livingston* [1965] AC 694 and, again, charitable trusts.

Perhaps the best argument against purpose trusts builds on a particular understanding of the nature of trusts. As we saw earlier (Section 4.3), one view of express trusts is that they operate as dispositions by a property owner of his beneficial interest in that property. Trusts, in this view, are like gifts, the settlor/owner transferring (some part of) his interest to the beneficiary/donee. We saw then that this provided a useful explanation of the rule that settlors cannot enforce trusts – once they have disposed of their interest in the property, it is no longer for them to determine how it is to be used. More importantly, however, this understanding of the nature of express trusts supports the beneficiary principle and the prohibition – or rather impossibility – of purpose trusts. Just as you cannot make a gift (ie outright transfer) of property to a purpose, so, on this view of trusts, you cannot create a trust for – that is dispose of your beneficial interest to – a purpose. In both cases, there needs to be someone on the receiving end. A trust needs a beneficiary in the same way and for the same reason that a gift needs a recipient.

This understanding of trusts as beneficial transfers has a fair amount going for it. It explains why self-declarations of trusts are possible and, as we have seen, where a separate trustee is appointed, it explains why enforcement is a matter for the beneficiary and not the settlor. It also goes some way to explaining why trusts will not fail for want of a trustee, and indeed why the law allows trustees to come and go, allowing old trustees to be replaced and new ones appointed. On this view of the nature of trusts, the identity of the trustee is unimportant. Rather we simply need someone – anyone – to do the job of overseeing and implementing the beneficial transfer initiated by the settlor.

Nonetheless, this argument – like all arguments that purpose trusts are somehow conceptually impossible – faces a major obstacle: the law *does* recognise a series of exceptions to the beneficiary principle, most notably charitable trusts. This leaves the proposition that a trust cannot be a trust without beneficiaries looking decidedly unreal. Moreover, even if it were the case that English law recognised *no* examples of valid purpose trusts, it would not follow that we *should* accept only trusts with beneficiaries. In other words, we need to be able to justify the conceptual structures we are using. If our concept of a trust does not allow for purpose trusts, we still have to ask whether this concept of a trust is worth keeping or whether we would be better off with a new one, one which allowed settlors to create trusts for purposes.

4.6 The impact of the rule

The question of whether and on what basis the beneficiary principle is justified is therefore in some doubt. Nonetheless, the existence of the rule is clear. Good examples of its application include *Re Astor's Settlement Trusts* [1952] Ch 534, where the settlor sought to create a trust for a series of purposes including the 'maintenance ... of good understanding ... between nations' and 'the preservation of the independence and integrity of newspapers'. Roxburgh J held that the trust failed both because of the lack of beneficiaries and because the stated purposes were defined with insufficient certainty (see further Section 4.9). To similar effect is *Re Shaw* [1957] 1 WLR 729. There the testator, George Bernard Shaw, had attempted to leave funds on trust to investigate the possibility of introducing a new 40-letter alphabet. Having determined that the purposes of the trust were not charitable, and that the provision could not be read as setting down a power (which would have been valid, see Section 4.1) rather than a trust, Harman J held the trust to be void.

4.7 Purpose trusts and 'persons' trusts

Of course, the beneficiary principle applies to invalidate a purported trust only where the trust does indeed lack beneficiaries. The problems posed by the principle are therefore avoided if the trust, on examination, is not in fact a purpose trust at all but rather a straightforward trust with beneficiaries, which we may call a 'persons' trust. The distinction between the two is not always clear. After all, the vast majority of purpose trusts will benefit *somebody*, either because there are people interested in the purpose being furthered or because the trust property will ultimately end up in someone's hands. At root, the question turns on whether the trustee is under an obligation to benefit some person or group, with the manner of such benefit secondary – in which case it is a persons trust – or whether his obligation is to apply the fund for the stipulated purpose, irrespective of what benefit, if any, any individuals happen to derive from this – in which case the trust is a purpose trust. In the latter case, though there may well be people who would benefit from the trust's purpose being carried out, they have no right to the trust property or to require that it be applied for their benefit in some other way. The focus of the trust and the trustee's duties is the purpose, not that individual's personal benefit. As a corollary of this, people who would derive benefits under purpose trusts have no *Saunders v Vautier* right to call for the legal title to the property to be transferred to them, thus bringing the trust to an end (see Section 2.7). By contrast, this right seems always to exist in some form, at least potentially, for persons trusts.

Whether a given trust is a persons trust or a purpose trust is therefore a matter of interpreting the trust deed and the words used by the settlor in order to find his true intentions. However, it seems clear that at times the courts have adopted rather strained interpretations of trusts in order to avoid treating them as purpose trusts, whether out of a desire not to defeat the settlor's intentions entirely or simply because this makes disposing of the trust property more straightforward. The best example of this is *Re Bowes* [1896] 1 Ch 507. There the testator left £5,000 to his trustees, to be used 'planting trees for shelter on the Wemmergill estate'. In spite of the apparently clear words used by the testator, and encouraged by the fact that this was far more money than was needed for the purpose of planting trees, North J felt able to treat this as a trust for the benefit of the owners of the estate. This meant that the owners, as beneficiaries and exercising their *Saunders v Vautier* right, were free to use the money as they saw fit.

Re Andrew's Trusts [1905] 2 Ch 48 provides a further example of this approach. Money was collected 'for and towards the education' of the children of a deceased clergyman, and was to be used 'solely' for that purpose. The children's education having been provided for, the question arose as to what was to be done with the money left over. Kekewich J held that, if necessary, he would construe 'education' broadly so as to cover more general provision for the children's needs, but that in any case the reference to education should be understood as identifying merely the motive for the gift. As such the children were beneficially entitled to the remaining funds.

This 'principle of interpretation' was explained by Buckley LJ in *Re Osoba* [1979] 1 WLR 247, 257:

> If a testator has given the whole of a fund, whether of capital or income, to a beneficiary, whether directly or through the medium of a trustee, he is regarded, in the absence of any contra indication, as having manifested an intention to benefit that person to the full extent of the subject matter, notwithstanding that he may have expressly stated that the gift is made for a particular purpose, which may prove to be impossible of performance or which may not exhaust the subject matter. This is because the testator has given the whole fund; he has not given so much of the fund as will suffice or be required to achieve the purpose, nor so much of the fund as a trustee or anyone else should determine, but the whole fund. This must be reconciled with the testator's having specified the purpose for which the gift is made. This reconciliation is achieved by treating the reference to the purpose as merely a statement of the testator's motive in making the gift. Any other interpretation of the gift would frustrate the testator's expressed intention that the whole subject matter be applied for the benefit of the beneficiary. These considerations have, I think, added force where the subject matter is the testator's residue, so that any failure of the gift would result in intestacy.

This seems to leave two alternatives. When faced with an apparent purpose trust, we can say either that the property must only be used for the stipulated purpose, in which case the trust is likely to fall foul of the beneficiary principle, or, alternatively, that the settlor's reference to the purpose has no legal significance and so can be ignored, in which case the trust will be valid though often at the cost of distorting the settlor's intentions. Slightly confusingly, however, there seems to be a third possibility. This is to say that, though the trust is indeed a persons trust, and so is not threatened by the beneficiary principle, the reference to the purpose is nonetheless not to be ignored. Instead the *amount* of the trust fund which the beneficiary is to receive is determined by reference to what is or would be needed to further the relevant purpose.

A possible example of this is provided by *Re Sanderson's Trust* (1857) 3 K & J 497. There the testator created a trust 'to apply the whole or any part of the rents, issues and profits of his real and personal estate and effects for and towards' the 'maintenance, attendance and comfort' of his brother. When the brother died, the question arose as to what was to happen to the money which remained. The court took the view that there were two possibilities. The first was that the trust should be understood as a straightforward trust of all the money for the brother, thus disregarding the reference to the purpose, as in *Re Bowes*. This would mean that the remaining money would form part of the brother's estate. The alternative was that this was a trust for the brother only of such sums as were needed to meet the costs of his 'maintenance, attendance and comfort'. The consequence of this would be that the money left over, absent a beneficiary, would go back to the testator's estate under a resulting trust (see Section 8.7). Given the words used by the testator, the court concluded that this second approach was the correct one on the facts. This appears to suggest that, rather than being a purpose trust, this was a trust for the brother whereby the amount he was to receive was calculated by reference to the costs of his maintenance. In other words, the reference to the purpose identified the *subject matter* of the trust, the property which would go to the brother *as beneficiary*. This view is backed up by the court's statement that if the brother had paid for his upkeep from his own resources, he would have been entitled to have been reimbursed out of the trust fund, such money being received by him absolutely, and which would presumably then be at his free disposal. For what may be another example of this see *Re the Trusts of the Abbott Fund* [1900] 2 Ch 326.

Following on from this, a trust in the form '£100,000 to T to be used for the education of B' (though of course the principles extend beyond education trusts) can be understood in *three* ways:

1. It could be understood as a purpose trust, whereby T is under an obligation to use the money to further the purpose of B's education (for instance through buying books, paying tuition fees). B would have no right to claim any of the money for himself. This will fail by virtue of the beneficiary principle, unless it falls within one of the exceptions (see Section 4.8).
2. Alternatively, it could be understood straightforwardly as a (persons) trust for B, with the reference to education being treated merely as the settlor's motive, which T and B are both free to ignore. B could exercise his *Saunders v Vautier* right to call for the entire sum to be transferred to him, whereupon he would be free to use it as he sees fit.
3. Finally, it could be understood as a (persons) trust for B, with B entitled only to whatever portion of the total sum is required to fund his education. So, by exercising his *Saunders v Vautier* right, B could have transferred to him not the full £100,000 but only the amount it has taken or will take to educate him. However, B would then be free to use that money as he sees fit.

Of course, to decide which interpretation to adopt in a given case, we should be trying to work out which is most in line with the settlor's intentions.

4.8 Exceptions to the rule

The cases we have examined in Section 4.7 avoid falling foul of the beneficiary principle only by interpreting what at first glance appear to be purpose trusts as trusts for individuals. As such they are not strictly exceptions to the beneficiary principle: the trusts were construed such that the principle was satisfied. There is, however, a series of true exceptions to the beneficiary principle, where the courts have upheld purpose trusts *as purpose trusts*. The most significant exception has been mentioned already, namely trusts for charitable purposes. We will examine such trusts in detail in the following chapter. For now, we will address the other exceptions to the rule that trusts must have beneficiaries.

First, there are what have become known as the 'anomalous' purpose trusts. These are purpose trusts which, despite being non-charitable, are upheld for, it seems, no better reason than that the courts have done so in the past. There is no principle or policy justifying or explaining why trusts for these particular purposes work, whereas trusts for other purposes do not. They are simply the results of the accidents of legal history. It seems that there are now only three types of cases falling within this exception:

1. trusts to look after and provide for certain animals. So, in *Re Dean* (1889) 41 Ch D 552, a trust for the maintenance of the testator's horses and hounds and the upkeep of their stables and kennels was upheld (trusts to provide for animal welfare more generally are likely to be effective as charitable trusts: see Section 5.15);
2. trusts for the construction and/or maintenance of graves and funeral monuments – see eg. *Re Hooper* [1932] 1 Ch 38;
3. trusts for the saying of private masses – see *Bourne v Keane* [1919] AC 815.

(A further apparent exception for trusts to promote fox-hunting – see *Re Thompson* [1934] Ch 342 – can now safely be ignored following the ban on fox-hunting.)

The courts, however, have stressed that these anomalous classes of valid purpose trusts are not to be extended, even by analogy. Hence, the court in *Re Endacott* [1960] Ch 232 refused to extend the graves and funeral monuments cases to the testator's attempt to create a trust to erect a memorial to himself. These anomalous trusts are 'enforced' by those who would take the trust property, or what is left of it, in the event of the trust either failing or not exhausting the fund. Given the interests of those who will take in default, this will usually be effective to prevent the trustee misappropriating the property, but provides little guarantee of the intended purpose being carried out. As such, the anomalous purpose trusts take effect much as purpose powers: the trustee will be prevented from using the property outside the stipulated purpose but will usually not be compelled to use it to give effect to that purpose.

A second and controversial – though if correct far more significant – exception comes out of *Re Denley's Trust Deed* [1969] 1 Ch 373. Here, the settlor company transferred land to trustees to be 'maintained and used as and for the purpose of a recreation or sports ground primarily for the benefit of the employees of the company and secondarily for the benefit of such other person or persons (if any) as the trustees may allow to use the same'. In response to the argument that this was a non-charitable purpose trust and must therefore fail by reason of the beneficiary principle, Goff J had this to say:

> I think that there may be a purpose or object trust, the carrying out of which would benefit an individual or individuals, where that benefit is so indirect or intangible or which is otherwise

so framed as not to give those persons any locus standi to apply to the court to enforce the trust, in which case the beneficiary principle would, as it seems to me, apply to invalidate the trust, quite apart from any question of uncertainty or perpetuity. Such cases can be considered if and when they arise. The present is not, in my judgment, of that character, and it will be seen that ... the trust deed expressly states that ... the employees of the company shall be entitled to the use and enjoyment of the land. Apart from this possible exception, in my judgment the beneficiary principle ... is confined to purpose or object trusts which are abstract or impersonal .... Where, then, the trust, though expressed as a purpose, is directly or indirectly for the benefit of an individual or individuals, it seems to me that it is in general outside the mischief of the beneficiary principle.

Accordingly, Goff J held the trust to be valid. The clear suggestion from *Denley* is that a purpose trust will be upheld provided there is an ascertained or ascertainable class of people who would benefit, directly or indirectly, from the property being applied for the stipulated purpose, provided the benefit to such people is not *too* indirect or intangible. On Goff J's view, the beneficiary principle is concerned only with ensuring that trusts are enforceable, and, where there are people interested in the furtherance of the purpose, these people can enforce the trust. As such, not only do we have no reason to invalidate such trusts but we can also give effect to them *without treating them as persons trusts*.

If this is correct, the decision is hugely significant. It would mean that the majority of non-charitable purpose trusts would now be valid. The only hurdles *Denley* sets down are the following:

1. the carrying out of the purpose must benefit an individual or individuals in a way which is not too remote or indirect. Presumably, trusts of the kind found in *Endacott*, *Shaw* and, probably, *Astor* would still fail on this basis;
2. it must be possible to ascertain the individuals who would be so benefited. In relation to this second inquiry, Goff J applied the list certainty test from *IRC v Broadway Cottages Trust* [1955] Ch 20, though given developments since then there is a strong argument that we should be content with a more relaxed test.

On this understanding of the case, the trustee's obligation is to apply the property in pursuance of the stated purpose. And though there are, and need be, ascertainable people who can enforce the trust, these people are not to be regarded as beneficiaries, at least in the orthodox sense of the word. Accordingly, though Goff J did not go into this, we must presume that they would only be able to demand that the property be applied for the purpose, and that they have no *Saunders v Vautier* right such as would allow them to group together and call for the property to be transferred to them absolutely.

However, not all agree that this is the correct interpretation of *Denley*. The decision has been considered in later cases, and the tendency has been to deny its significance and instead to interpret it in line with orthodox trusts law. So, in *Re Lipinski's Will Trusts* [1976] Ch 235, Oliver J, while endorsing the dictum of Goff J quoted earlier as according 'both with authority and with common sense', seemed then to treat *Denley* as a *Re Bowes* type case (Section 4.7), where the purpose is disregarded and the trust upheld as a trust for individuals. Similarly, in *Re Grant's Will Trusts* [1980] 1 WLR 360, Vinelott J held that *Denley* 'falls altogether outside' the category of purpose trusts. Instead, he had the following to say about the decision:

I can see no distinction in principle between a trust to permit a class defined by reference to employment to use and enjoy land in accordance with rules to be made at the discretion of trustees on the one hand, and, on the other hand, a trust to distribute income at the discretion of trustees amongst a class, defined by reference to, for example, relationship to the settlor. In both cases the benefit to be taken by any member of the class is at the discretion of the trustees, but any member of the class can apply to the court to compel the trustees to administer the trust in accordance with its terms.

This sees the trust in *Denley* as no different from a discretionary trust for individuals, and hence, once again, denies its significance with regard to purpose trusts. However, as a number of commentators have noted, the analogy drawn by Vinelott J is false, because there is an important difference between a discretion as to *who* benefits from the property (as in a standard discretionary trust) and a discretion as to *how* the property is to be enjoyed by those entitled to use it.

Where does this leave us? It is hard to view either of these cases as having offered an accurate interpretation of the reasoning of Goff J, which, though at times ambiguous, seems clearly to suggest that the *Denley* trust should be given effect as intended and so as a purpose trust. Moreover, neither overrules or qualifies the authority of *Denley*. But they do reveal a judicial tendency to downplay the significance of the case. This will be welcomed by those who support the beneficiary principle and the prohibition of non-charitable purpose trusts, and regretted by those who do not. This takes us back then to the justification of the beneficiary principle. Is there really anything more to the rule than that trusts must be enforceable? If enforceability is all we are concerned with then it is hard to see why we should have any objection to understanding *Denley* as providing a way of validating certain purpose trusts. If, by contrast, there is something more behind the prohibition of purpose trusts then we need a clearer statement of what this is.

4.9   Other requirements of purpose trusts

Where one of the exceptions to the beneficiary principle applies, and so a given purpose trust does not fail simply because it lacks beneficiaries, there are three further hurdles it must overcome to be valid.

First, the purposes must be defined with sufficient certainty for the court to be able to enforce the trust. This is the equivalent to the certainty of objects requirement we looked at in the previous chapter in the context of persons trusts. *Morice v Bishop of Durham* (1804) 9 Ves 399 provides a good example of this, as does *Re Astor's Settlement Trusts* [1952] Ch 534, where the court held that, even without the prohibition of purpose trusts, the intended trust to maintain understanding between nations and to preserve the independence and integrity of newspapers would fail because it gave insufficient guidance to the trustees and to the court as to how the trust property was to be applied.

Second, it seems that a clearly defined purpose trust will nonetheless fail if the purpose is regarded as capricious or unlawful. The standard example of this is *Brown v Burdett* (1882) 21 Ch D 667, which rather bizarrely concerned a trust to block up the rooms of a house for 20 years.

Finally, non-charitable purpose trusts, and indeed non-charitable persons trusts, will fail if they do not satisfy the rule against perpetuities. This is a rule which, with respect to trusts law, says broadly that trusts must have a time limit, the aim being to ensure that sooner or later property ends up vested absolutely in some individual or group whereupon it may be dealt with without encumbrances. The traditional perpetuity period was framed in terms of a 'life in being' plus 21 years. That is, beneficial interests under trusts have to vest in the intended beneficiaries at the latest 21 years following the death of some stipulated individual alive at the date the trust was created. This remains the relevant period for non-charitable purpose trusts. Elsewhere the rule has been overtaken by statute: first the Perpetuities and Accumulations Act 1964 gave a choice of some fixed period of up to 80 years; now section 5(1) of the Perpetuities and Accumulations Act 2009, applicable to instruments made on or after 6 April 2010, provides that 'the relevant perpetuity period is 125 years (and no other period)'.

4.10 Unincorporated associations

It was at one time thought that a further exception to the beneficiary principle was to be found in the context of unincorporated associations. In fact, these days the orthodox position is that such cases have nothing to do with purpose trusts, though, following *Re Denley*, it may be that purpose trusts may have a role to play here after all. First, though, we must ask what an unincorporated association is and what legal issues arise from them.

It is typical now for accounts of unincorporated associations to begin with a definition offered, in the context of section 526 of the Income and Corporation Taxes Act 1970, by Lawton LJ in *Conservative and Unionist Central Office v Burrell* [1982] 1 WLR 522, 525:

> I infer that by 'unincorporated association' in this context Parliament meant two or more persons bound together for one or more common purposes, not being business purposes, by mutual undertakings, each having mutual duties and obligations, in an organisation which has rules which identify in whom control of it and its funds rests and upon what terms and which can be joined or left at will.

Though this definition was given in the context of interpreting a particular statutory provision, it is conventionally assumed to be of general application. However, it may not be the most helpful starting point. For a start, it is not clear whether all the listed features really need be present in all cases. Most agree that it is not essential that the association can be joined or left at will. We may also add that there is no obvious reason associations with business purposes need be excluded from the rules we are about to look at (cf Partnership Act 1890). Indeed, as a matter of principle, the rules which determine how unincorporated associations acquire and hold property should apply wherever (subject to the point on incorporation below) two or more people join together and pool property for a certain common purpose. Such purposes are multifarious: the group may form to promote a cause, perhaps political, or its members may simply band together to form a club for their own private enjoyment, such as a sports club. In all cases, it is likely both that the group will have a set of rules, or at least informal conventions and understandings, concerning how the group is to function, and that it will require property to help achieve its ends. The three key issues arising from unincorporated associations, on which the following sections will focus, are:

1. how they acquire such property;
2. how it is held once acquired; and
3. what happens to it if the association comes to an end.

The view that purpose trusts had a role to play in answering these questions followed from two observations about the way unincorporated associations work in practice. First, members of such groups generally understand that they are not free to treat the group property as if it were their own. So, for instance, members of a tennis club understand that they are not free to walk off with the club's racquets and other equipment without permission. Second, where you transfer property to an unincorporated association, for example you make a donation to support a local sports club, you expect that that money will be used only for the purposes of the club, and hence that the members will not be free to use that money to treat themselves, for instance, to a holiday or a night out. If we said that the association's property was held on trust for the purposes of the group then we could account for both of these features. Members would not be free to treat the property as their own because it would be held on trust and so would not (beneficially) be theirs, while donors could be sure that their donations would be used only for the group's purposes as that would be the effect of the purpose trust on which such property would be received and held. As such, a purpose trust analysis would seem to fit perfectly with the intentions and expectations of those involved with unincorporated associations.

There was only one problem: the beneficiary principle. Because of the rule that trusts must have beneficiaries, rendering (non-charitable) purpose trusts invalid, this simple solution became regarded as a legal impossibility. The courts then needed to find a way of answering these questions with the legal tools at their disposal. We shall start with the question of how unincorporated associations hold property, for, as we shall see, this also provides answers to the remaining questions of how transfers to unincorporated associations are made and what happens to the property if the association comes to an end.

4.11 How unincorporated associations hold property

This question is problematic because these associations are unincorporated. In other words, they involve groups of people who have not formed a company by incorporating under the Companies Acts. A company is regarded in law as a person. This means that it can owe and be owed obligations and, importantly, own property, distinct from the obligations owed by and to, and the property held by, any of the individuals, or any aggregate of them, involved with the company. This greatly facilitates the analysis of how companies deal with property. This solution is not available in respect of unincorporated associations as these have no separate legal personality. As such, there is no separate legal entity to and by whom property can be transferred and held. Rather, property held 'by' the group must strictly be vested in one or more of its members. The important question of course is who.

This will depend principally on the way the association has chosen to order itself. One possibility is that the property is co-owned in law by all the members, ie legal title to the assets is held by them all jointly. A second possibility is that the property is vested in law in one or more of the members, usually a treasurer or treasury committee, on trust for the members as a whole. In practice, the second is far more common. This is partly because it is simply more convenient to have property vested in fewer individuals and in part because of rules limiting the number of people who may hold legal title to certain types of property (see eg section 34 of the Law of Property Act 1925, restricting the maximum number of legal co-owners of land to four). Accordingly, it is this analysis on which we shall focus.

The first important point to note is that, on this basis, there are no problems with respect to the beneficiary principle. Though there is a trust, there are clearly beneficiaries, and indeed a certain class thereof. Second, in the normal case where property is co-owned, whether at law or, as here, in equity, an individual co-owner can sever his share (relying on the *Saunders v Vautier* rule in the case of equitable co-ownership), at least where practicable, and deal with it as his own property, unconstrained by the other co-owners. However, this possibility is likely to thwart the aims of an unincorporated association. For this reason, it is very likely that the members will have some consensual arrangement whereby each commits to the group property being used exclusively for the purposes of the association. Such an arrangement may be expressed in a formal constitution for the association, or it may be largely tacit and implied from the members' actions. Either way, provided the law would recognise the arrangement as binding, so as to restrain individual members from breaking the group's rules and taking the property for themselves, we can treat the arrangement as contractual. (It should, however, be noted that, in many cases, the contract does not bear too close scrutiny in terms of offer, acceptance, consideration and certainty.) Therefore, on this analysis, at any particular point in time, the property will be held on trust for, and hence beneficially owned by, the members as a whole by one or more treasurer–trustees, but with the members' rights to deal with the property being governed by a contract between themselves.

Even at this stage, the analysis is not entirely unproblematic. Almost always, the membership of the group will change over time. Members will leave and new members will come in. This raises two issues. First, it supposes that, when a new member joins, he thereby enters into a contract, on the terms of the association's constitution or rules, with all the other members individually. This is clearly a convenient analysis and desirable, but it does look a little implausible, at least when viewed in light of the rules of contract formation (though the problem may lie with the narrowness of those rules). Second, and more important, there is the question of what effect shifting membership has on the ownership of the group property. It is generally assumed that the property is held on trust for, and so co-owned in equity by, the members of the association for the time being. Hence, when members leave, they lose any interest they have in the property and, when new members arrive, they acquire such an interest. This is potentially problematic because the law has a series of rules setting down the formal steps to be taken for the effective transfer of proprietary interests. Most notably, as we will see in more detail in Chapter 6 (Sections 6.17–6.22), an effective disposition of one's equitable interest under a trust must be made in writing and signed, by virtue of section 53(1)(c) of the Law of Property Act 1925. As, on the analysis we are looking at, the members all have an equitable interest in the group property held on trust by the treasurer, it looks as though, when a member leaves, his equitable interest must pass to the remaining members, and when a new member joins, he acquires such an interest from the existing members. This would seem to fall within section 53(1)(c), and yet in practice members will often come and go from such associations without any formal documentation.

The courts have never looked into this issue. Penner (2012, 276) offers a solution to the apparent problem by saying that the trust under which the group property is held for the members contains a (generally implied) power to add to or take away from the class of beneficiaries. Hence, when a member leaves, the treasurer–trustee can remove that person from the class, and when a new member joins, he can be added. The important point is that, according to Penner, the exercise of such a power by the trustee does not constitute a disposition of an existing equitable interest so as to call section 53(1)(c) into play. This is clever and would seem to solve the problem, if at the expense of imputing an intention to the parties which, though consistent with their aims, probably never crossed their minds.

Thus the now orthodox analysis of how unincorporated associations hold property is that the assets are beneficially owned by the members under a trust of which the association treasurer is trustee, with a contract between all the members governing the application of the property. This is now widely known as the contract holding theory and was recognised by the courts in *Neville Estates Ltd v Madden* [1962] Ch 832 and *Re Recher's Will Trusts* [1972] Ch 526. Its principal benefit is that it allows us to explain why individual members are not free to treat the group's property as their own but must instead use it only for the group's purposes, yet without contravening the beneficiary principle. It is the contract, rather than the existence of a purpose trust, which prevents individual members severing and walking off with their proportionate share of the group assets. However, there is one important consequence, and perhaps weakness, of the contract holding theory.

As we have seen, the group's property is beneficially held by the members of the group. This beneficial interest would normally entitle individual members to walk off with their share of that property. The only thing preventing them from doing this is that they are under a contractual duty to the other members to use the property only for the purposes of the association. However, contracts can be waived or varied by the parties to them. Accordingly, as was accepted in *Re Recher*, it is open to the members as a whole to agree to put an end to the contract or to vary it so as to remove the legal restrictions it imposes on the individual members' freedom to deal with their share of the property. The members would then be free to divide up the property between themselves, with each then able to apply his portion of the property as he wishes, and without regard to the purposes of the association.

4.12 Gifts to unincorporated associations

Once the question of how unincorporated associations hold property is answered, it becomes easier to give answers to the other two questions set out in Section 4.10: namely how the association acquires property and what happens to such property if the group comes to an end. In respect of the first of these – the acquisition of property – the question involves asking how one goes about transferring property to an unincorporated association.

In *Leahy v A-G for New South Wales* [1959] AC 457, the Privy Council considered that there were three possibilities:

1. the donor could transfer the property beneficially to the current members of the association;
2. he could seek to transfer the property beneficially to present and future members of the association; or
3. he could attempt to transfer the property on trust for the purposes of the association.

(In fact the first method seems to be capable of achievement by two different routes. The donor could make an absolute transfer of legal beneficial title to the members or, alternatively, he could transfer *on trust* to one or more of the members for the benefit of the members as a whole. For present purposes there is no need to distinguish between them.)

One problem with the first approach is that it appears to leave the members free to deal with the property as they see fit, so enabling individual members to walk off with their share of the assets. At least in the vast majority of cases, this would conflict with the intentions of the donor, who wants to see the property used only for the association's purposes. Moreover, a further problem is that it does not seem to provide for the fact of shifting membership of the group (ie the property is beneficially owned by the people who were members at the time of the transfer, regardless of whether they remain members and whether new members have joined subsequently). The second and third methods, however, seem even more problematic. The second – a beneficial transfer to present and future members – provides for the group's shifting membership but, unless qualified, would fall foul of the rule against perpetuities (see Section 4.9). The third – a trust for the purposes of the association – makes clear that the members are to apply the property only for the purposes of the association, but at the cost of infringing the beneficiary principle. Hence, such a disposition would be ineffective unless it could be brought within one of the exceptions to the principle.

With the second and third possibilities therefore ruled out, the first method remains: beneficial transfer to those individuals who are members at the time of the disposition. This seemed to leave the law in a very unsatisfactory position. The only method by which property could be transferred to unincorporated associations would inevitably leave the members free to use that property without restriction and so would defeat the transferor's intentions in making such a transfer in the first place.

The development of the contract holding theory enabled the courts to avoid such an undesirable conclusion. Following the lead of Cross J in *Neville Estates Ltd v Madden* [1962] Ch 832, Brightman J put forward an alternative method by which property could be transferred to and received by unincorporated associations in *Re Recher's Will Trusts* [1972] Ch 526, 539:

> In the case of a donation which is not accompanied by any words which purport to impose a trust, it seems to me that the gift takes effect in favour of the existing members of the association as an accretion to the funds which are the subject-matter of the contract which such members have made inter se, and falls to be dealt with in precisely the same way as the funds which the members themselves have subscribed. So, in the case of a legacy. In the absence of words which purport to impose a trust, the legacy is a gift to the members beneficially, not as joint tenants or as tenants in common so as to entitle each member to an immediate distributive share, but as an accretion to the funds which are the subject-matter of the contract which the members have made inter se.

This passage is not wholly free of difficulty. For one thing, it appears to suggest a third form of beneficial co-ownership beyond joint tenancy and tenancy in common. But, as Lewison J recently noted in *Hanchett-Stamford v A-G* [2008] EWHC 330 (Ch); [2009] Ch 173, [47], we don't need to invoke any new form of co-ownership. Rather, the donor transfers the property to (some or all of) the members beneficially (as either joint tenants or tenants in common), so avoiding the beneficiary principle problem, *but* the property is received by the members *as group property*, as an accretion to the association's funds, meaning that its application falls to be governed by the contract between the members setting out how that property can be used. This, subject to the qualification set out above as to unanimous waiving of the contract, removes the risk of members deciding to sever their share of the transferred property and keeping it for themselves. And, at least if we follow Penner's analysis of the trust on which the treasurer holds the group's property, the problem of shifting membership is solved too.

There is one slight loose end. The passage from Brightman J's judgment in *Recher* works on the basis that donations to unincorporated associations take the form of outright transfers (ie not transfers on trust) to, most likely, the group's treasurer. The question then is how such an outright transfer becomes an accretion to the group's funds. After all, in the usual case, someone who receives property outright can use it however they like. So what stops the treasurer doing the same? How are we to ensure that property transferred to the treasurer is not only held by him on trust for the members but also governed by the same contract as regulates the members' dealings with existing 'group' property? Matthews' (1995) answer is that it depends on the contract: does the contract apply on its terms to this sort of property, acquired in these circumstances? If it does, the treasurer, upon receipt of the donation, will be contractually obligated to hold it on what is essentially the same self-imposed trust on which he holds all the association's property. This means, though, that there is nothing the donor can himself do to ensure that the property is received and applied solely for the purposes of the association. It depends instead on the wishes of the members as manifested in their contract. An alternative partial solution to this is achieved by treating donations to unincorporated associations not as outright transfers to the treasurers but as transfers to them *on trust* for the members generally. However, although this ensures that the beneficial interest in the property passes to all the members, it similarly fails to provide any guarantee that their use of the property will be 'caught' and governed by the members' contract.

It is important to note that the *Re Recher* analysis is really a composite of two elements. First, there is a beneficial transfer of property to some or all of the members. It is this, which allows us to avoid falling foul of the beneficiary principle. Second, there is the contract which exists between the members of the group, which sets down their rights and duties in respect of their use of the property. It is this which, at least until that contract is waived or varied, stops individual members walking off with their share of the property and ensures that the property will be used only for the association's purposes. As such, occasional suggestions that the members' rights to the 'group' property are based in contract are misleading. The contract existing between the members does not 'oust' the members' beneficial ownership of the property. Indeed the contract is vital precisely because the members *remain* beneficial owners of the group's property, and thereby entitled, in the absence of any contract, to deal with their share of the funds in whatever way they choose.

One important point to take from this is that the *Re Recher* approach, whereby a donation to an unincorporated association takes effect as an accretion to the group's funds, applies only where both elements listed earlier are present, and, in particular, *only* where the donor transfers property *beneficially* to the members. Where the donor frames his donation simply as a transfer 'to' the unincorporated association, or as a transfer to the association or its treasurer on trust for the members generally, there is no difficulty in concluding that the *Re Recher* approach will apply. However, problems arise if the donor does not appear to have transferred property to the group and its members *beneficially*.

To see this, imagine that I want to leave money to my former student law society, which we shall call 'The Eldon Society'. We can apply the *Re Recher* approach if I transfer money simply 'to The Eldon Society', as the terms of the transfer suggest that the group – and hence the members – is to take the property beneficially. The same would be the case if I left money 'on trust for The Eldon Society' because, though the disposition is now framed as a trust rather than an outright transfer, the terms again suggest that the beneficial interest is to go to the group, ie the members. Problems arise, however, if I transfer money 'to The Eldon Society for the purpose of hosting drinks parties' or 'so that they may be able to fund a mooting competition'. The problem here is that by qualifying my donation by the reference to a particular purpose or objective for which the money is to be applied by the group, it appears that my intention is *not* that members take the property beneficially. Rather, it appears as though I am seeking to impose an obligation on the association to use that money only for the purpose I have identified. And this of course looks a lot like a purpose trust, and so would fail unless it could be brought within one of the exceptions to the beneficiary principle.

The only way this conclusion can be avoided is if we can find a way of disregarding my reference to the money being used to host drinks parties or to fund mooting, thereby allowing us to treat the donation as a beneficial transfer after all. The obvious way to do this is to argue that when I referred to drinks parties and mooting, these were just suggestions as to how the money *might* be used or simply reflected my motives in making the donation, such that I was not seeking to impose any legal restriction on the group's use of the money. This is effectively the same technique as used in *Re Bowes* [1896] 1 Ch 507 (discussed in Section 4.7), whereby an apparent purpose trust was interpreted as a persons trust on the basis that the reference to the money being used to plant trees on the estate was just a suggestion and imposed no legal obligation, the settlor's paramount intention being to benefit the estate owners.

The court faced just this sort of problem in *Re Lipinski's Will Trusts* [1976] Ch 235. There the court had to determine the validity of a bequest to the Hull Judeans (Maccabi) Association, 'to be used solely in the work of constructing the new buildings for the association and/or improvements to the said buildings'. The issue was whether the testator's direction as to how the money was to be used prevented the bequest being treated as a beneficial transfer to the association, which could then take effect as an accretion to its funds, and instead amounted to an attempt to create a purpose trust which would fail. Oliver J approached the matter as follows:

> There would seem to me to be, as a matter of common sense, a clear distinction between the case where a purpose is prescribed which is clearly intended for the benefit of ascertained or ascertainable beneficiaries, particularly where those beneficiaries have the power to make the capital their own, and the case where no beneficiary at all is intended ... or where the beneficiaries are unascertainable ... If a valid gift may be made to an unincorporated body as a simple accretion to the funds which are the subject matter of the contract which the members have made inter se ... I do not really see why such a gift, which specifies a purpose which is within the powers of the association and of which the members of the association are the beneficiaries, should fail.... Where the donee association is itself the beneficiary of the prescribed purpose, there seems to me to be the strongest argument in common sense for saying that the gift should be construed as an absolute one within the second category [ie as an accretion to the association's funds].

What does this mean? The first point to note is that if we *do* interpret the donor as having directed the association to use the property only for certain identified purposes, this will amount to an attempt to create a purpose trust and so, unless it falls within one of the exceptions to the beneficiary principle, will fail. However, and here is the second point, the transfer will *not* fail if we can find a way of disregarding the donor's reference to the property being used only for a particular purpose and treat it instead as an unqualified beneficial transfer to the group. When are we entitled to disregard the condition that the donor appears to have set down? Oliver J says that we can do this where the donor's intention in identifying a particular purpose for which the property is to be applied is to benefit the members of the association. In such cases, the intention to benefit the members is paramount and the precise purpose identified can be ignored. However, we cannot do this where, in identifying that purpose, the donor's intention was either to confer no particular benefit on anyone or to benefit a collection of people who cannot be ascertained. On this basis, Oliver J was able to conclude that, as the construction and improvement of buildings for the association would benefit the members of the association, the testator's primary intention was to benefit those members. Accordingly, and in spite of the testator's apparently plain words, there was no obligation on the association to use the money for building purposes, and so this was not to be understood as an attempted purpose trust. Instead the members took the property beneficially as an accretion to the association's funds, which they could then use in whatever way the contract between them allowed.

4.13 The distribution of property upon the dissolution of unincorporated associations

The final question is what happens to the group's property if the unincorporated association, for one reason or another, comes to an end. Initially it was assumed either that the property would have to revert back to those who provided it in the first place by way of a resulting trust (see Chapter 8), or else that it was 'ownerless' in which case there was no option but for it to vest in the Crown as *bona vacantia*.

This can be seen in *Re West Sussex Constabulary's Widows, Children and Benevolent (1930) Fund Trusts* [1971] Ch 1. A fund was set up so that allowances could be provided to widows and dependants of deceased members of the West Sussex Constabulary. When the members resolved to wind up the fund, the question arose as to what was to happen to the money left over. Goff J considered that this depended on how the money was raised. In fact, money had been raised in a variety of ways. Some had come from the members themselves, some had been generated from raffles, sweepstakes and the like, some from collecting boxes, and some from donations and legacies. Looking at each in turn, Goff J held that the members' entitlements were fixed by the terms of their contract of membership to the scheme. This provided that, in return for their subscriptions, money would be paid to their widows or dependants in the event of their death. But, beyond this, it gave them no rights in and no claim to the fund, and certainly the contract gave them no right to share in the money left over should the fund be brought to an end. Accordingly, Goff J held that money deriving from the subscriptions of members must be treated as ownerless and hence was *bona vacantia*. Moving on to money raised by raffles and sweepstakes, Goff J held that this too was *bona vacantia*, as those who paid it over did so under a contract (to take part in the raffle or sweepstake) and so, like the members, had no rights beyond those conferred by that contract. Money provided through collection boxes also became *bona vacantia*, this time because contributors must be regarded as having paid that money 'out-and-out', such that they could have had no intention of it being returned in the event of the fund's dissolution. By contrast, those who had left money by donations or legacies could be regarded as having intended that that money should be retained by the donees only so long as the fund was operational, and so anything left over should be returned to them by way of a resulting trust.

There are a number of problems with this decision. First, it seems more than a little arbitrary. Are the intentions of those who leave money in collecting boxes really any different from those who leave more sizable legacies? Moreover, it seems slightly unreal to say that those who make contributions to the fund by buying raffle tickets or entering a sweepstake must be treated as contracting for the chance to win the raffle or sweepstake, rather than simply making a donation in a different way. Second, Goff J's approach is conceptually suspect. He decided that the bulk of the money left over was ownerless and so went to the Crown as *bona vacantia*. However, clearly the money was not ownerless before the fund was wound up, so how did it suddenly become ownerless when the members decided to bring the fund to an end? There are also problems with Goff J's conclusion that money deriving from donations and legacies was to be held on resulting trust for its contributors. It is clear that where A transfers money to B on trust, and that trust then fails, B holds that money on resulting trust for A. This seems to be the sort of resulting trust Goff J had in mind here: those who contributed by way of donation or legacy transferred that money on trust and that trust failed when the fund ended. But the only sort of trust which would be affected by the dissolution of the fund would be a trust for the purposes of the fund. And, as we have seen, the problem with this is that purpose trusts are not permitted. As such, the resulting trust conclusion makes sense only if we say that the money was until then held on a purpose trust, and we cannot say that without contravening the beneficiary principle.

The contract holding theory once again points the way forward. As we saw in Section 4.11, while an unincorporated association is up and running, the property is beneficially owned by the members, albeit that their use of their property is restricted by the terms of their mutual contractual arrangement. If the members resolve to bring the association to an end, all this means is that they decide that they no longer want to pursue, and to apply that property in furtherance of, the purposes the association existed to pursue. The effect of such a resolution is the abandonment of the contract that existed between them, thus removing the restrictions placed by that contract on their use of the property. The members' beneficial interests in that property are unaffected. The only change is that the members, as beneficial owners, are now free to deal with and to use the property as they wish. Thus the default position upon the dissolution of an unincorporated association is that the members at the time of dissolution are each entitled to an equal share in the association's property precisely because they are equally beneficially entitled to that property. This was confirmed in *Re Bucks Constabulary Widows' and Orphans' Fund Friendly Society (No. 2)* [1979] 1 WLR 936.

As we saw, Goff J in *Re West Sussex* rejected the possibility of the members claiming any share of the property on the basis that the contract gave them no such right. But now we can see that the proper answer to this is that they do not need to rely on any contract to claim the property. They can claim it simply because it is (beneficially) theirs. Goff J had also held that distribution of property among the members was possible only where the group existed for the benefit of the members. Walton J in *Re Bucks* dismissed this as irrelevant:

> I can see no reason for thinking that this analysis is any different whether the purpose for which the members of the association associate are a social club, a sporting club, to establish a widows' and orphans' fund, to obtain a separate parliament for Cornwall, or to further the advance of alchemy.

Of course, just as the members are free to set the rules of their association and hence the terms of the contract that bind them, they are also free to agree to some other basis of distribution of the group's property upon dissolution. And even where there is no express term to that effect, the courts have been ready to imply a term that the property is to be distributed on some other basis if they consider that this is what the members intended. This happened in *Re Sick and Funeral Society of St John's Sunday School* [1973] 1 Ch 51, where the association had two classes of member, with half members paying only half the subscription and receiving only half the benefits of full members. In light of this, Megarry J concluded that upon its dissolution each full member should receive a share of the property twice as large as those of half members.

It is important to stress that it is only those who are members at the time of dissolution who can claim any share of the property. As Walton J held in *Re Bucks*, unless there is exceptionally some rule to the contrary, past members have no rights in the group's assets. This of course means it is important to know exactly when the association was dissolved. Often this will be clear enough, such as where the dissolution is brought about by a vote of the members or a court order. It has also been held, however, that an association may end 'where the substratum upon which the society or fund was founded has gone' (*Re William Denby & Sons Ltd Sick and Benevolent Fund* [1971] 1 WLR 973, 979 (Brightman J)), and in such cases the exact date the group ended may be far from certain (see eg *Re St Andrew's Allotment Association* [1969] 1 WLR 229).

Walton J in *Re Bucks* considered that there was one exception to the rule that the group's property is to be distributed among the members upon its dissolution. This is where, by death or resignation, the society is reduced to one member. In such a case, Walton J held that the remaining member could not claim to 'be' the association and so, on that basis, entitled to the property, as one cannot associate with oneself. Instead the property must be regarded as ownerless, and so goes to the Crown as *bona vacantia*. This was always a dubious conclusion, and has now been rejected in *Hanchett-Stamford v A-G* [2008] EWHC 330 (Ch); [2009] Ch 173. Although it is clear that an unincorporated association requires more than one member, and so the association must cease when the membership falls to one, there is no reason this should have any effect on that remaining member's beneficial interest in the relevant property. Ordinarily, where one member of a group dies, his beneficial interest is extinguished, but those of the others remain. If we end up with only two members, A and B, then it is clear that they will share the beneficial interest in the group's property. If B then dies, there is no reason to say that A as well as B must lose his interest, leaving the property ownerless. The better view, now endorsed by *Hanchett-Stamford*, is that the death of B necessarily brings an end to the contract, which previously bound the members (as it is impossible to have a one-person contract) but leaves A, the survivor, with the sole beneficial interest in the property.

Re Bucks, with the gloss added by *Hanchett-Stamford*, clears up the uncertainty and problems created by *Re West Sussex*. However, it has been suggested (see Gardner, 1992) that some uncertainty has been reintroduced into this area by *Davis v Richards & Wallington Industries Ltd* [1990] 1 WLR 1511, in which Scott J applied *Re West Sussex* in determining what was to happen to surplus property left in a pension fund. Scott J held that money contributed by the employer went back to them on a resulting trust, whereas money contributed by employees became *bona vacantia* on the basis that it was impossible to impute to them an intention that the money be returned in such circumstances. The contract holding theory and *Re Bucks* were not discussed.

This may not be problematic however. The beneficial interests of the employees under the trust were set down by the terms of the scheme, calculated by reference to a variety of factors, including the length of time an employee had worked for the company. The effect of this was that the beneficial interests of the various employees were not set in stone but would change over time. It also meant that at any given point there might be more in the trust fund than was needed to meet the beneficial entitlements of the employees. This is indeed what happened: after all the employees received the payments they were entitled to under the trust, there was money left over. Where, as here, the declared beneficial interests fail to exhaust the trust fund, there is at least a presumption that what is left is held on resulting trust for its contributors. So, although we may certainly doubt whether Scott J was correct to hold that this presumption was displaced in respect of the employees' contributions, he was right to conclude that the answer to this case lay in the law of resulting trusts. The *Re Bucks* approach, founded as it is on the members' beneficial interests in the fund, was simply inapplicable, as there were no declared beneficial interests in respect of the surplus.

4.14　Political parties

In two cases it has been held that the contract holding theory of unincorporated associations does not apply to the property holdings of political parties. On both occasions the obstacle has been with finding a contract between the various members of the party which governs their use of such property. In *Re Grant's Will Trusts* [1980] 1 WLR 360, which concerned a bequest to the Chertsey and Walton Constituency Labour Party, the problem was that the rules binding the members of the constituency party could be altered by non-members, namely the National Labour Party. This meant that, unlike in the standard case of an unincorporated association, the members could not unanimously agree to waive the rules and divide the property among themselves. This led Vinelott J to conclude that the *Recher* analysis, whereby donations take effect as accretions to the group's funds and subject to the contract which exists between the members, could not be applied there. Similarly in *Conservative and Unionist Central Office v Burrell* [1982] 1 WLR 522, the Court of Appeal concluded that the *Recher* analysis could not account for donations to the Conservative Party as it was not possible to identify any contract which connected the various limbs, and so the various members, of the party. Brightman LJ realised that this left us without an explanation as to how donations to the party take effect. His suggestion was that we should understand donors to the party as giving a mandate to the party treasurer, which entitles him then to use the property (only) for party purposes. This mandate involves a personal agency relationship, whereby the donor gives the treasurer a permission to use the property in a certain way and the treasurer undertakes a duty so to use it. Because of this, and as Brightman LJ noted, this analysis cannot apply to testamentary dispositions, as no agency relationship can exist where the donor is deceased. Quite how we then account for testamentary dispositions is uncertain.

　　It can be argued that the courts have been too quick to give up on the contract holding theory in these cases. Legal title to property held 'by' political parties will inevitably be vested in some person or group of people. These people will either hold the property beneficially or, far more likely, they will hold it on trust. If they hold it on trust then that trust must have beneficiaries. These beneficiaries are highly unlikely to be free to deal with that property as their own, and that must be because there are rules or conventions which govern their use of it and which require that such property be applied, broadly, for the purposes of the party. Now, it may be that these rules do not easily fit within the orthodox principles of contract law and contract formation, and it may be that the rules are fixed or can be altered by people other than those who hold the beneficial interest in the relevant property. But this should not matter. The essence of the contract holding theory is that the property is held by a collection of people beneficially, but that they cannot do what they like with it because of the existence of a set of rules which is legally binding on them. This must also be the case with political parties. Who sets those rules and whether we should view them as representing a contract (rather than some other form of legally binding arrangement) is, for present purposes, unimportant. And if this is true, it must also be possible for donors to transfer property to political parties such that they take effect as accretions to the party's funds, with the beneficial interest passing to those beneficially entitled to the party's existing assets and falling to be dealt with in accordance with the rules that govern the use of all such property. In short, the *Re Recher* approach can be applied.

4.15 The reintroduction of purpose trusts

As we saw at the beginning of our analysis of unincorporated associations, the obvious way to explain how such groups hold property would be to say that they hold it on trust for the purposes of the group. However, the beneficiary principle stops us from doing this. It was for this reason that the courts were forced to develop the contract holding theory. However, in so far as purpose trusts *are* recognised in the law, they can of course be used to explain how unincorporated associations hold and receive property. So, if the purposes of the association are exclusively charitable, there is nothing to stop us regarding the association's treasurer as holding the property on trust for such purposes. More importantly, *if* we accept that *Re Denley's Trust Deed* [1969] 1 Ch 373 constitutes a further exception to the rule against purpose trusts (on which see Section 4.8), we can use purpose trusts to explain how property is held by perhaps the majority of unincorporated associations. As we saw earlier, *Denley* suggests that purpose trusts will be upheld provided there is an ascertainable class of people who would benefit directly or indirectly from the property being applied for that purpose. Therefore, if the purposes for which an unincorporated association exists and for which it applies its property do benefit an ascertainable class of individuals, *Denley* allows us to say that the association's treasurer holds the property on trust for such purposes; a trust which can then be enforced by those who would benefit from it (presumably whether or not they are members). On this basis, it is only where the unincorporated association has a purpose which is abstract or which would benefit an uncertain class (or nobody at all) that we have to fall back on the contract holding theory. In all other cases, the contract holding theory and a *Denley*-type purpose trust would provide alternative, and mutually exclusive, answers to how the association's property is held.

This has two important implications. First, if we say that the property is held on a purpose trust, there is no possibility of the members dividing the property up amongst themselves as they can under the contract holding theory. This is because, on this approach, they are not beneficially entitled to the property and so have no claim to or interest in it. Second, if the association comes to an end, the property would not go to the members as beneficial owners, as again they have no beneficial interest in the property. Instead the dissolution of the group would mean that the purpose trust on which the property was held would have failed, and so, in principle, whatever property is left should go back to whoever contributed to it on a resulting trust.

Summary

▶ A settlor may wish to set up a trust with a view not to benefiting a particular person or class of persons, but instead to furthering a particular cause or purpose. Such trusts are called *purpose trusts*.

▶ As a general rule, however, the law prohibits the creation of purpose trusts, requiring that trusts must instead be 'for' people. This is known as the *beneficiary principle*.

▶ The traditional rationale for the rule is that beneficiaries are needed to enforce the trust. Without them, there is nobody to supervise the trustee and to ensure that he does his job properly. Whether beneficiaries are needed to enforce trusts and whether enforceability should be essential for a trust's validity are, however, unclear. In response to this, it has been argued that there is more to the purpose trust prohibition than the question of enforceability, and that it is in some sense of the essence or nature of trusts that they must have beneficiaries. On this view, a purpose trust should be viewed as a conceptual impossibility.

▶ Nonetheless, it is clear that the law recognises a number of exceptions to the general rule. The clearest and most significant is trusts for charitable purposes.

▶ Another set of exceptions is provided by the 'anomalous' purpose trusts: trusts to provide for particular animals; trusts for the erection and maintenance of graves and funeral monuments; and trusts for the saying of private masses. The courts have, however, made clear that these categories of purpose trusts are not to be extended, even by analogy.

▶ A final exception may come out of *Re Denley's Trust Deed*, which appears to suggest that purpose trusts will be upheld so long as there is an ascertainable class of individuals who will benefit, directly or indirectly, from the purpose being pursued. These people can then act as enforcers of the trust.

▶ The beneficiary principle is satisfied if an apparent purpose trust turns out to be, on closer examination, a persons trust. In this respect, the courts have occasionally been willing to override or downplay statements by the settlor to the effect that the property must be used to achieve a particular purpose, on the basis that his paramount intention was to benefit those individuals who would benefit from that purpose being pursued.

▶ Unincorporated associations are groups of people who join up, and often pool resources, to pursue a particular (typically non-business) purpose, but without incorporating as a company. The key legal questions concerning such groups are how they acquire and hold property, and what happens to that property when the group dissolves.

▶ For some time it was thought that this was another exception to the no purpose trusts rule. However, the modern view is that the members of the group hold all the relevant property beneficially, but that a contract exists between the members, which restricts them in their use of that property, requiring that they use it only for the group's purposes. This is known as the *contract holding theory*.

▶ Property donated to such groups is therefore given beneficially to the members, but, when received, is 'caught' by the contract that exists between them, which then stops individual members walking off with their share of the property, at least while that contract remains in existence.

▶ When an unincorporated association comes to an end, the result is that the contract which previously bound them is waived or rescinded. This then leaves the individual members free to take their share of the 'group's' property. Accordingly, upon dissolution, and unless some contrary intention can be found, the property is divided equally between the members at that date.

Exercises

4.1 Why must trusts be enforceable?

4.2 Do we have good reason to prohibit non-charitable purpose trusts?

4.3 What does *Re Denley's Trust Deed* decide?

4.4 Annabel leaves £100,000 and her country house to the tennis club of which she was a member. The gift is expressed to be 'for the purpose of providing the club with proper facilities'. The majority of the members would like to turn Annabel's country house into a golf club and propose spending the £100,000 on developing the golf course. Other members, however, claim to be beneficially entitled to a share of Annabel's gift and propose to take it with them when they resign from the club. Some of these individuals joined the club after Annabel's death.

Discuss the validity of Annabel's bequest and advise regarding the members' plans for the use of the gift.

4.5 Have we sorted out all the problems which existed in accounting for how unincorporated associations acquire and hold property?

4.6 Alvin, Beverley, Cassandra and Dooley are enthusiastic nudists. They consider that the current law prohibiting public nudity is cruel and oppressive, so they decide to form a group to campaign for a change in the law. Accordingly, calling themselves The Association of Frustrated Nudists, they rent a flat which is to be the group's headquarters and order posters and pamphlets to be printed. The lease to the flat is put in Alvin's name. A bank account, in Cassandra's name, is also set up, into which the members make regular payments. The money in that account is then used to pay the rent for the flat and to fund all other group activities. Every weekend the members walk up and down Oxford Street with collecting boxes, seeking contributions from members of the public. This money too is paid into the bank account. Finally a substantial donation is made by Ernie, another disgruntled naturist, who hands a cheque for £500 to Cassandra, saying 'This is to help you repeal that awful and unfair law!'

The members never adopt a formal constitution, but there is a tacit understanding that the flat and the bank account are to be used only for the purposes of the group. Over time Beverley and Dooley become disenchanted by the group's lack of progress in getting the law changed, and quit the group. Alvin then dies in a freak industrial accident, leaving Cassandra as the only member. £600 remains in the bank account.

Advise Cassandra as to what is to be done with the money in the bank account.

Further reading

Baughen, 'Performing animals and the dissolution of unincorporated associations: the "contract-holding" theory vindicated' [2010] Conv 216

Gardner, 'New angles on unincorporated associations' [1992] Conv 41

Gardner, *An Introduction to the Law of Trusts* (3rd edn, Oxford University Press 2011), 216–37

Hayton, 'Developing the obligation characteristic of the trust' (2001) 117 LQR 96

Hayton, 'Overview' in Birks and Pretto (eds), *Breach of Trust* (Hart Publishing 2002), 379–83

Matthews, 'A problem in the construction of gifts to unincorporated associations' [1995] Conv 302

Matthews, 'From obligation to property, and back again? The future of the non-charitable purpose trust' in Hayton (ed), *Extending the Boundaries of Trusts and Similar Ring-fenced Funds* (Kluwer 2002)

Matthews, 'The new trust: obligations without rights?' in Oakley (ed), *Trends in Contemporary Trust Law* (Oxford University Press 1996)

Parkinson, 'Reconceptualising the express trust' [2002] CLJ 657, 657–63, 676–83

Chapter 5

Charitable trusts

5.1 Trusts for charitable purposes

We saw in the previous chapter that there are a number of exceptions to the beneficiary principle, that is, the rule that says trusts must have a beneficiary and which therefore invalidates purpose trusts. In this chapter we look at the largest and most well-established of these exceptions: trusts for charitable purposes.

The basic requirements for a valid charitable trust are that:

1. The purpose(s) for which the trust property is to be held and applied must be (exclusively) charitable, and
2. The trust must benefit (some section of) the public.

So to find out in what circumstances a purpose trust will be upheld on this basis, we need to know what purposes the law classes as charitable and what it takes for a trust for such purposes to be regarded as benefiting the public.

It is worth noting at the outset that though much of the work of determining whether these requirements have been satisfied has been done by the courts, these days this responsibility is shared with the Charity Commission, which has significant powers to determine how the provisions of the Act are interpreted and applied. As such, a full understanding of the law here requires us to look beyond the cases and statutes to the decisions reached and documents produced by the Charity Commission.

5.2 Charity, trusts and the law

Charitable dispositions can take different forms:

1. A settlor may simply decide that he wants to see his property applied towards a certain charitable purpose and declare a trust to this effect, either with himself as trustee or, far more commonly, with a third party trustee being appointed.
2. Alternatively, a settlor may choose to transfer his property to a pre-existing charitable body or movement, such as Oxfam or the RSPCA. This could work in two ways:
   a. First, the property could be received by (the members of) the relevant body on trust for their (charitable) purposes. This is in substance no different from the situation in 1 above, save that the trustees who receive the settlor's property are already holding other property on trust for the same purposes. In this sense the settlor is simply adding to a pre-established trust fund.
   b. The second possibility is that the property is not transferred to – and so is not received by – the relevant body *on trust*. Rather it is transferred to, and received by, that body *outright*. This is possible only if the charitable body is *incorporated*, that is it has formed itself into a company. The company then applies what is now its property in line with the charitable purposes set out in its articles of association (the rules setting out the duties, powers and organisational arrangement of the company). (If I transfer property to one or more private individuals, rather than a company, outright, this cannot take effect as a charitable disposition.)

The rules determining what sorts of purposes and what sorts of disposition are charitable are the same in all cases. However, only 1 and 2a involve the law of trusts, so these are the most important for our purposes.

The divide between charitable and non-charitable purposes is of fundamental importance. Not only will trusts for charitable purposes succeed whereas trusts for non-charitable purposes will, usually, fail, but in a variety of other respects the law treats charitable purpose trusts differently from standard private persons and purpose trusts. For instance, charitable trusts can exist in perpetuity (see Section 4.9); they do not need to meet the same standards of certainty as private trusts and the impossibility of achieving the intended charitable purpose does not automatically lead to the failure of the trust (see Sections 5.21–5.23). Just as importantly, charitable trusts are given certain fiscal advantages. They are exempt from income tax and from capital gains tax and stamp duty: Income Tax Act 2007, part 10, Taxation of Chargeable Gains Act 1992, section 256, Finance Act 2003, section 68. Further, charities are entitled to an 80% relief on non-domestic rates (and local authorities have a discretion to grant total relief): Local Government and Finance Act 1988, section 43. Those who give to charity also enjoy tax advantages: charities are able to claim additional gift aid on donations made by taxpayers, and gifts made to charities are also exempt from capital gains and inheritance tax. Corporate taxpayers who donate to charity also enjoy fiscal privileges.

It is no surprise that the law would want to encourage charitable gifts and so has good reason to treat charitable trusts more favourably than standard private trusts. It would therefore be understandable for the courts to be concerned to see that the advantages of a trust being classed as charitable are reserved for those trusts and those purposes which really do merit this sort of favourable treatment. Indeed, how else can a court sensibly decide whether a trust should be upheld as charitable other than by reference to the consequences of such a finding?

This view was articulated by Lord Cross in *Dingle v Turner* [1972] AC 601, 624 (and see too *Re Compton* [1945] Ch 123, 136):

> In answering the question whether any given trust is a charitable trust the courts – as I see it – cannot avoid having regard to the fiscal privileges accorded to charities. ... [T]he law of charity is bedevilled that charitable trusts enjoy two quite different sorts of privilege. On the one hand, they enjoy immunity from the rules against perpetuity and uncertainty and though individual potential beneficiaries cannot sue to enforce them the public interest arising under them is protected by the Attorney-General. If this was all there would be no reason for the courts not to look favourably on the claim of any 'purpose' trust to be considered as a charity if it seemed calculated to confer some real benefit on those intended to benefit by it whoever they might be and if it would fail if not held to be a charity. But that is not all. Charities automatically enjoy fiscal privileges which with the increased burden of taxation have become more and more important and in deciding that such and such a trust is a charitable trust the court is endowing it with a substantial annual subsidy at the expense of the taxpayer. ... It is, of course, unfortunate that the recognition of any trust as a valid charitable trust should automatically attract fiscal privileges, for the question whether a trust to further some purpose is so little likely to benefit the public that it ought to be declared invalid and the question whether it is likely to confer such great benefits on the public that it should enjoy fiscal immunity are really two quite different questions. The logical solution would be to separate them and to say ... that only some charities should enjoy fiscal privileges. But, as things are, validity and fiscal immunity march hand in hand.

However, though the other members of the House of Lords agreed with Lord Cross's judgment on the substantive issue before the court (see further Section 5.19), three of the four – Viscount Dilhorne, Lords MacDermott and Hodson – expressly distanced themselves from his comments on the relevance of fiscal implications to determining the validity of charitable dispositions. Instead, for the most part, the courts have tended to proceed simply by analogy from the existing cases, without appeal to the broader policies and goals which support the distinctive treatment accorded to trusts with charitable status. Indeed, much the same can be said of the Charities Act 2011, which appears largely to codify the case law up to this point.

5.3 Defining charitable purposes

The legal definition of charity is not wholly detached from the everyday understanding of the word, yet it is plain that at times they diverge. Sometimes the legal definition of charity extends to purposes which would not be described as charitable in the ordinary sense. Sometimes the law goes the other way, denying charitable status to purposes which most non-lawyers would view as clearly charitable. In all cases, therefore, the only safe approach is to put the everyday sense of 'charity' to one side and to look instead to the law.

The traditional starting point for determining whether a purpose was charitable was the preamble to the Charitable Uses Act 1601 (often referred to as the Statute of Elizabeth). This statute, which has long since been repealed, was not enacted to define charity but to prevent the abuse of charitable trusts. Nevertheless, a rule of law arose pursuant to which the court would assess whether a purpose was charitable by considering whether that purpose was within the 'spirit and intendment' of the preamble. In other words, a purpose would be held to be charitable if, but only if:

1. it was included in the list of charitable purposes set down in the preamble, or
2. it could otherwise be said to be analogous to one of the purposes set down in the preamble (or indeed analogous to a purpose already recognised as charitable by analogy to one of the 'original' preamble purposes).

As such, the class of charitable purposes developed incrementally from the following, rather haphazard and dated list of purposes identified in the preamble:

> ... [R]elief of aged, impotent and poor people, for maintenance of sick and maimed soldiers and mariners, schools of learning, free schools, and scholars in universities, ... for repair of bridges, ports, havens, causeways, churches, sea-banks and highways, ... for education and preferment of orphans, ... for ... relief, stock or maintenance for houses of correction, ... for marriages of poor maids, ... for supportation, aid and help of young tradesmen, handicraftsmen and persons decayed, and ... for relief or redemption of prisoners or captives, and ... for aid or ease of any poor inhabitants concerning payments of [taxes on chattels], setting out of soldiers and other taxes.

In time, following Lord Macnaghten's speech in *Commissioners for Special Purposes of the Income Tax v Pemsel* [1891] AC 531, 583, it became common to reduce this assorted collection of purposes to four basic categories or 'heads':

1. the relief of poverty;
2. the advancement of education;
3. the advancement of religion; and
4. other purposes beneficial to the community, not falling under any of the preceding heads.

5.4 The Charities Act 2011

The *Pemsel* classification has now been overtaken by the statutory definition of charity provided first by the Charities Act 2006, and now by the Charities Act 2011. Section 2(1) provides that a charitable purpose is one which:

1. falls within one of the 13 purposes set out in section 3(1) of the 2011 Act; and
2. is for the public benefit.

This is the crucial two-stage test that the courts must now apply when considering whether a purpose is charitable.

The 13 purposes set out in section 3(1) are as follows:

    (a) the prevention or relief of poverty;
    (b) the advancement of education;
    (c) the advancement of religion;
    (d) the advancement of health or the saving of lives;
    (e) the advancement of citizenship or community development;
    (f) the advancement of the arts, culture, heritage or science;
    (g) the advancement of amateur sport;
    (h) the advancement of human rights, conflict resolution or reconciliation, or the promotion of religious or racial harmony or equality and diversity;
    (i) the advancement of environmental protection or improvement;
    (j) the relief of those in need because of youth, age, ill-health, disability, financial hardship or other disadvantage;
    (k) the advancement of animal welfare;
    (l) the promotion of the efficiency of the armed forces of the Crown, or of the efficiency of the police, fire and rescue services or ambulance services;
    (m) any other purposes within sub-section –

      (i) that are not within paragraphs (a) to (l) but are recognised as charitable purposes by virtue of section 5 (recreational and similar trusts, etc.) or under the old law,
     (ii) that may reasonably be regarded as analogous to, or within the spirit of, any purposes falling within any of the paragraphs (a) to (l) or sub-paragraph (i), or
    (iii) that may reasonably be regarded as analogous to, or within the spirit of, any purposes which have been recognised, under the law relating to charities in England and Wales, as falling within sub-paragraph (ii) or this sub-paragraph.

Section 4 provides some guidance in relation to the public benefit test. It confirms that a purpose must be for the public benefit if it is to be a charitable purpose and provides 'it is not to be presumed that a purpose of a particular description is for the public benefit': section 4(2).

Though now the question of whether a given purpose is charitable must begin with section 3 of the Act, it is clear that to a significant extent the statutory list of charitable purposes sticks closely to the purposes the courts had already held to be charitable. Indeed, section 3(3) of the 2011 Act expressly provides that where terms set out in section 3(1)(a) to (l) already have a particular meaning under charity law, they are to be taken as having the same meaning when they appear in section 3(1). Moreover, section 3(1)(m) preserves the same incremental approach adopted by the courts previously to the development of new charitable purposes by analogy with the existing categories. As such, much of the old case law remains important in determining the scope of charitable trusts.

Nonetheless, it would be wrong to treat the 2011 Act as no more than a codification of the pre-existing law, as section 3(1) confers charitable status on some purposes which were not charitable – or at least not clearly charitable – under the common law. In what follows, the various purposes listed under section 3(1) will be considered by reference to, where appropriate, previous case law.

An important point to make at the outset is that a charitable trust does not need to fall squarely within just one of these 13 categories. For a start, as we shall see, a number of these categories appear to overlap. More importantly, there is no objection to setting up a charitable trust where, for example, the trust property is to be used *both* to relieve poverty *and* to advance education. Indeed, the courts have held that if a settlor simply declares a trust 'for charitable purposes' without giving any direction as to what particular purposes he intends, the trust will be a valid charitable trust. The court and the Charity Commission then have jurisdiction to establish the specific charitable purposes to which the trust should be directed: Charities Act 2011, section 69. Similarly, a trust expressed as being simply 'for' or 'for the benefit of' a particular locality or its inhabitants will be treated as a trust for charitable purposes in that locality: *Goodman v The Mayor and Free Burgesses of the Borough of Saltash in the County of Cornwall* (1882) 7 App Cas 633.

However, a trust will fail if the expressed purposes include both charitable and non-charitable purposes, unless the non-charitable element can be severed from the charitable element of the trust (as was the case in *Salusbury v Denton* (1857) 3 K & J 529). Hence trusts for 'charitable or benevolent' purposes will fail on the basis that not every benevolent purpose is necessarily charitable: *Chichester Diocesan Fund v Simpson* [1944] AC 341; see also *Morice v Bishop of Durham* (1804) 9 Ves 399 ('objects of benevolence and liberality') and *Re Macduff* [1896] 2 Ch 451 ('charitable or philanthropic purposes'). This rule is sometimes expressed by saying that the purposes of a charitable trust must be *exclusively charitable*.

5.5   The prevention or relief of poverty

Poverty is a straightforward enough idea, but it is also clearly a matter of degree. So, although there will be clear examples of poverty, and indeed plenty of cases where it is plain that the trust cannot be said to relieve poverty, at other times there will be no clear answer. As such, we should not be surprised to find that different courts, deciding cases with very similar facts, take differing views on the question of whether the purpose of the trust can be said to be to help prevent or relieve poverty.

If the trust is expressly stated to be for the relief of poverty then there will of course be no problem treating it as falling under this heading. The same will be true if the trust is directed towards the poor or some other synonymous class: for example those 'in needy circumstances' (*Re Scarisbrick* [1951] Ch 622), 'of limited means' (*Re Gardom* [1914] 1 Ch 664), 'for the permanent aid of distressed gentlefolk' (*Re Young* [1951] Ch 344). The difficulty is where the trust purposes identified by the settlor are not explicitly defined by reference to poverty, the poor or some equivalent term. Here the court must determine whether in substance and effect the trust purposes are nonetheless directed towards the prevention or relief of poverty.

In *Re Coulthurst* [1951] Ch 661, 666, Sir Raymond Evershed MR held that 'poverty does not mean destitution; it is a word of wide and somewhat indefinite import; it may not be unfairly paraphrased for present purposes as meaning persons who have to "go short" in the ordinary acceptation of that term, due regard being had to their status in life, and so forth'. Accordingly, what we are looking for when determining whether a trust falls within this class is whether it is in fact directed towards the needs of (some) such individuals.

It is not enough that those who would benefit from the trust include the poor, if the trust would also benefit other people who fall outside the list of valid charitable objects. Accordingly, in *Re Gwyon* [1930] 1 Ch 255, a trust to provide 'knickers' for boys in Farnham and the surrounding district failed because not all boys in the area were poor. Similarly, in *Re Sanders' Will Trusts* [1954] Ch 265, Harman J held that a trust to provide funds for housing for 'the working classes' was not charitable as not all those who were of the working class were poor. By contrast, in *Re Niyazi's Will Trusts* [1978] 1 WLR 910, funds were to be held on trust to contribute towards the cost of a 'working men's hostel'. Megarry VC was able to distinguish *Re Sanders' Will Trusts* on the basis that the word 'hostel' had 'a strong flavour of a building which provides somewhat modest accommodation for those who have some temporary need for it and are willing to accept accommodation of that standard in order to meet the need'. As such, the trust, when properly construed, was aimed at relief of the poor and was therefore charitable.

5.6   The advancement of education

Like poverty, education is a simple enough concept. The clearest examples of educational charitable trusts involve provision for schools and universities or for the support of students at such institutions. But it is clear that education also covers other forms of learning. So, in *Incorporated Council of Law Reporting for England and Wales v A-G* [1972] Ch 73, the Court of Appeal held that the purpose of providing accurate law reports was charitable, as it facilitated the study and ascertainment of the law. In *Re Hopkins' Will Trusts* [1965] Ch 669, Wilberforce J held that a trust established for the purpose of providing funds to find the Bacon–Shakespeare manuscripts (ie manuscripts showing that plays attributed to Shakespeare were actually written by Francis Bacon) was charitable. Wilberforce J held that a search for such manuscripts was not 'manifestly futile' and that, if discovered, such manuscripts would be 'of the highest value to history and to literature'. In the earlier case of *Re Shaw* [1957] 1 WLR 729, a trust for the testator's residual estate to be directed towards researching the advantages of a 40-letter alphabet was held not to be charitable, principally because the purposes as expressed were directed towards research alone and involved no requirement of teaching or education. Wilberforce J, however, doubted the suggestion that trusts for research could not be classed as educational 'unless the researcher were engaged in teaching or education in the conventional meaning'. Rather he preferred the view ([1965] Ch 669, 680) that education should be understood:

> in a wide sense, certainly extending beyond teaching, and that the requirement is that, in order to be charitable, research must either be of educational value to the researcher or must be so directed as to lead to something which will pass into the store of educational material, or so as to improve the sum of communicable knowledge in an area which education may cover.

Subsequently, Slade J in *Re Besterman's Will Trusts* (1980) [unreported but quoted in *McGovern v A-G* [1982] Ch 321, 352–53] adopted a position somewhere between those of *Re Shaw* and *Re Hopkins*, summarising the relevant principles as follows:

> (1) A trust for research will ordinarily qualify as a charitable trust if, but only if
>
>   (a) the subject matter of the proposed research is a useful subject of study;
>   (b) it is contemplated that knowledge acquired as a result will be disseminated to others; and

(c) the trust is for the benefit of the public, or a sufficiently important section of the public.

(2) In the absence of a contrary context, however, the court will be readily inclined to construe a trust for research as importing subsequent dissemination of the results thereof.
(3) Furthermore, if a trust for research is to constitute a valid trust for the advancement of education, it is not necessary either

(a) that a teacher/pupil relationship should be in contemplation, or
(b) that the persons to benefit from the knowledge to be acquired should be persons who are already in the course of receiving 'education' in the conventional case.

As *Re Hopkins' Will Trusts* suggests, education covers not simply the discovery and spread of factual information and has been held to embrace the development of practical skills and the production, preservation or study of artistic works. For instance, in *Royal Choral Society v IRC* [1943] 2 All ER 101, a trust to 'form and maintain a choir in order to promote the practice and performance of choral works' was upheld because it would educate artistic taste. A trust to 'encourage the exercise and maintain the standards of crafts ... and craftsmanship' was upheld in *Comrs of Inland Revenue v White* (1980) 55 TC 651. And in *Re Dupree's Deed Trusts* [1945] Ch 16, a trust for the purpose of providing an annual chess tournament for those under the age of 21 in Portsmouth was upheld as charitable on this basis. Moral or political learning also counts (though cf Section 5.20). Trusts were upheld in *Re South Place Ethical Society* [1980] 1 WLR 1565 for 'the study and dissemination of ethical principles' and in *Re Koeppler's Will Trusts* [1986] Ch 423 for the 'formation of an informed international public opinion'.

The breadth of 'education' in the context of charitable trusts is perhaps best evidenced by *IRC v McMullen* [1981] AC 1, which concerned a trust established by the Football Association with the objects of, inter alia, providing facilities enabling school and university pupils to play football or other games or sports 'and thereby to assist in ensuring that due attention is given to the physical education and occupation and development of their minds'. The House of Lords, reversing the Court of Appeal, held that such purposes were charitable. Lord Hailsham LC, giving the leading judgment, held that ([1981] AC 1, 18):

> the picture of education when applied to the young which emerges [from the cases and statute] is complex and varied ... It is the picture of a balanced and systematic process of instructions, training and practice containing ... spiritual, moral, mental and physical elements ... I reject any idea which would cramp the education of the young within the school or university syllabus, confine it within the school or university campus, limit it to formal instruction, or render it devoid of pleasure in the exercise of skill.

(See too *Re Mariette* [1915] 2 Ch 284. For the validity of trusts promoting sport outside educational establishments see Sections 5.11 and 5.17 below.)

It does not follow, however, that any purpose that provides for the acquisition and spread of information or practical learning will be upheld as charitable on this basis. In particular, the courts will not recognise a trust as truly educational, and hence charitable, unless the relevant information or knowledge has some value or use ('a college for pickpockets is no charity': *Re Shaw* [1957] 1 WLR 729, 737 (Harman J)). Determining a purpose's usefulness is, of course, a value judgment, on which different people may reasonably take different views. Where necessary, the courts will take assistance from expert evidence.

The courts' approach to such questions can be seen by contrasting two cases concerning aesthetic or artistic subjects. The first, *Re Delius* [1957] Ch 299, examined a trust for the advancement of the musical works of the testatrix's late husband. The trust was held to be valid, in part because of the high standard of Delius' work. The second, the Court of Appeal's decision in *Re Pinion* [1965] Ch 85, concerned the validity of a trust established by a testator for the purpose of keeping his studio and its contents intact and displayed to the public. Harman LJ held that it was 'essential to know at least something of the quality of the proposed exhibits in order to judge whether they will be conducive to the education of the public'. In concluding that the exhibits were of too low a quality to justify charitable status, Harman LJ held, in rather blunt terms, that ([1965] Ch 85, 106–07):

> there is a strong body of evidence here [to show] that as a means of education this collection is worthless. The testator's own paintings ... are said by competent experts to be ... 'atrociously bad' ... Apart from pictures there is a haphazard assembly – it does not merit the name collection, for no purpose emerges, no time nor style is illustrated – of furniture and objects of so-called 'art' about which expert opinion is unanimous that nothing beyond the third-rate is to be found. Indeed one of the experts expresses his surprise that so voracious a collector should not by hazard have picked up one meritorious object .... The judge with great hesitation concluded that there was that scintilla of merit which was sufficient to save the rest. I find myself on the other side of the line. I can conceive of no useful object to be served in foisting upon the public this mass of junk.

5.7 The advancement of religion

Section 3(2) of the 2011 Act is now the starting point for analysis of what constitutes, for trusts law purposes, a religion. It states that religion includes '(i) a religion which involves belief in more than one god, and (ii) a religion which does not involve belief in a god'. Of course, religions which involve belief in one god will also count. Accordingly, monotheistic faiths such as Islam and Christianity will fall within the definition, as will faiths that are multi-deity (such as Hinduism) or non-deity (such as some types of Buddhism).

The principal question that remains is when does a belief system – particularly one which does not include belief in a god – constitute a religion. The Charity Commission (2008b) have stated that the following characteristics of religious belief can be identified from the case law:

- ▶ [B]elief in a god (or gods) or goddess (or goddesses), or a supreme being, or divine or transcendental being or entity or spiritual principle, which is the object or focus of the religion;
- ▶ a relationship between the believer and the supreme being or entity by showing worship of, reverence for or veneration of the supreme being or entity;
- ▶ a degree of cogency, cohesion, seriousness and importance;
- ▶ an identifiable positive, beneficial, moral or ethical framework.

As such, the changes made to the definition of religion by the 2006 and 2011 Acts appear not to dispense with the requirement for worship developed previously by the courts. So, in *Re South Place Ethical Society* [1980] 1 WLR 1565 the court held that a trust for 'the study and dissemination of ethical principles and the cultivation of rational religious sentiment' could not be classed as religious (though it succeeded under the education head: see Section 5.6) on the basis that the 'essential attributes of religion are faith and worship'. As Dillon J put it ([1980] 1 WLR 1565, 1571), religion 'is concerned with man's relation with God, and ethics are concerned with man's relation with man'. For similar reasons, freemasonry and the Church of Scientology were held not to meet the law's definition of religion in, respectively, *United Grand Lodge of Ancient Free and Accepted Masons of England v Holborn BC* [1957] 1 WLR 1080 and *R v Registrar General, ex parte Segerdal* [1970] 2 QB 697.

However, once we remove the requirement of a belief in a god, it is not clear what need or place there is for a requirement of worship. Indeed, where the religion is centred on, in the Charity Commission's words, belief in a 'spiritual principle', a need for worship looks unintelligible.

As a final point, section 3(1)(c) speaks of the *advancement* of religion. In *United Grand Lodge of Ancient Free and Accepted Masons v Holborn BC* [1957] 1 WLR 1080, 1090, Donovan J held that this meant that the purpose must be to 'promote [the religion], to spread its message ever wider among mankind; to take some positive steps to sustain and increase religious belief'.

5.8   The advancement of health or the saving of lives

The preamble to the Statute of Elizabeth referred to the 'maintenance of sick and maimed soldiers and mariners'. It soon became clear that the relief of the sick was a charitable purpose, which clearly included trusts for the funding or support of hospitals. In *Re Resch's Will Trusts* [1969] 1 AC 514, the House of Lords had to consider whether a gift to a private but non-profit-making hospital was charitable. They held that it was. In his leading speech, Lord Wilberforce first noted that the trust was not rendered invalid by the fact that the hospital sometimes made a small surplus (which was largely applied for hospital purposes), as it was not carried on with a view to making profit for private individuals. He then considered whether the trust was beneficial to the community (see further Section 5.18), notwithstanding the fact that patients had to pay for the treatment that they received. He held that there was public benefit, as the fee-paying hospital provided a 'particular type of nursing and treatment' that the nearby general hospital did not, and as the general hospital would benefit from its proximity to the fee-paying hospital (by, for example, having its resources freed up).

Section 3(1)(d) of the 2011 Act refers to advancing health or saving lives. The reference to advancing health includes, by virtue of section 3(2)(b), the 'prevention or relief of sickness, disease or human suffering'. This definition seems wide enough to apply to mental as well as physical health. Indeed, the modern approach to the relief of the sick is shown by the decision in *Funnell v Stewart* [1996] 1 WLR 288, where it was held that spiritual healing qualified. The purpose of saving lives will include organisations such as the Royal National Lifeboat Institution and the Royal Society for the Prevention of Accidents (organisations which were previously charitable under the fourth head of the *Pemsel* classification).

5.9   The advancement of citizenship or community development

Citizenship and community development are relatively modern concepts, as is shown by the fact that it would be difficult to argue that they are analogous to any of the purposes set out in the preamble to the Statute of Elizabeth. Accordingly, there is little useful case law, though some trusts upheld under the fourth *Pemsel* head could fit in here: see for example *Re Webber* [1954] 1 WLR 1500 where a trust to support the Boy Scouts movement was held to be charitable. Greater assistance is provided by section 3(2)(c) of the 2011 Act, which states that this head of charity includes 'rural or urban regeneration' and 'the promotion of civic responsibility, volunteering, the voluntary sector or the effectiveness or efficiency of charities'.

The Charity Commission considered the meaning of 'rural or urban regeneration' in its March 1999 review of the register. It noted that this phrase would include some or all of the following activities:

1. providing financial or other assistance to the poor;
2. providing housing to those in need;
3. helping the unemployed to find work;
4. providing education and training, especially for the unemployed;
5. providing financial or technical assistance for new businesses; and
6. providing, maintaining and improving recreational facilities or public amenities.

In *Helena Partnerships Ltd v The Comrs of Her Majesty's Revenue and Customs* [2012] 4 All ER 111; [2012] EWCA Civ 569, the Court of Appeal held that the provision of housing was not itself a charitable purpose, and so for a housing association to be classed as a charity its purposes had to satisfy some other, distinct head of charity (eg the relief of poverty). The question in the case concerned Helena's tax liability for the period between 2001 and 2004. As such, the case was decided under the common law rules, meaning that the court had to determine whether the association's purposes were within the 'spirit and intendment' of the preamble (see Section 5.3). The court did not consider whether the position would be any different under the 2011 Act.

An example of a charity for the promotion of civic responsibility would be Encams, which runs the 'Keep Britain Tidy' campaign. Volunteering and the voluntary sector are probably relatively well-understood concepts (with charities such as Voluntary Service Overseas falling within their scope). An example of an organisation that promotes the 'effectiveness or efficacy of charities' would be the National Council for Voluntary Organisations, which assists and advises upon the way in which other charities are operated.

A further point can also be noted under this heading: the term 'community development' and some of the purposes contained under this head appear, at first blush, to be very widely defined (eg 'urban regeneration', which could apply to a large housing developer). It can, then, be confidently predicted that the second requirement for charitable status – that of public benefit – will be of quite some importance in relation to this head.

5.10 The advancement of arts, culture, heritage or science

Many of these purposes which were previously dealt with under the education head of the *Pemsel* classification will find a more natural home in this category. Only a few further points need be made. First, 'science' is unlikely to be narrowly construed, as can be seen by the recognition of horticulture as a science in *Re Pleasants* (1923) 39 TLR 675. Second, no definition has been provided within the 2011 Act for the terms 'arts', 'heritage' or 'culture'. Presumably the courts and Charity Commission will be required to make judgments like those in *Re Delius* [1957] Ch 299 and *Re Pinion* [1965] Ch 85 (see Section 5.6). Nonetheless, many cases will be clear cut, and bodies such as the National Gallery, the National Trust and the English National Opera will certainly fall within these respective categories.

5.11 The advancement of amateur sport

We have seen already that funding for sport in schools and universities has been treated as charitable under the education head: *IRC v McMullen* [1981] AC 1; Section 5.6. The treatment of adult amateur sport has been less straightforward.

The starting point is the decision in *Re Nottage* [1895] 2 Ch 649, where it was held that a trust to provide a prize for a yacht race failed on the basis that promoting the playing of sports was not a charitable purpose. The Recreational Charities Act 1958 made some difference here by granting charitable status to the provision of certain recreational facilities (see further Section 5.17). However, the general rule that the playing of sports was not per se charitable remained: see *IRC v McMullen* [1981] AC 1, 15, 21.

The Charities Act 2006 and now the Charities Act 2011 mark a clean break here and recognise charitable trusts which advance all sports and games 'which promote health by involving physical or mental skill or exertion': section 3(2)(d). Recognised sports such as football, rugby, cricket and tennis will, of course, fall within this definition. So too, however, will activities which we might not describe as sports in ordinary speech but which satisfy the test of involving mental skill or exertion, such as chess, bridge or even Sudoku.

5.12 The advancement of human rights, conflict resolution or reconciliation, or the promotion of religious or racial harmony or equality and diversity

This represents a newly established head of charity, though it is likely to catch some cases which were previously considered charitable under the advancement of education or religion categories (and see too *Re Harwood* [1936] Ch 285 where a trust for the promotion of peace was held to be charitable). It is important to note that, as we shall see shortly (Section 5.20), the law has traditionally denied charitable status to trusts whose purposes are political. Unless and until this rule is changed, this will significantly curtail the scope of this class of charitable purpose (on this point, see *McGovern v A-G* [1982] Ch 321, where Slade J held conducting and disseminating research into the maintenance and observation of human rights is charitable, but that the trust failed because its purposes extended to the implementation of policies giving greater protection to human rights).

5.13 The advancement of environmental protection or improvement

The courts had previously upheld trusts for the preservation of 'lands and tenements ... of beauty or historic interest and as regards lands for the preservation ... of their natural aspect features and animal and plant life' (*Re Verrall* [1916] 1 Ch 100) as charitable. This new head confirms that the protection of the environment more generally is a charitable purpose.

The Charity Commission published a review of the register of charities in February 2001 that considered the test which it would apply to determine whether purposes of preservation or conservation were charitable. Although the 2011 Act uses slightly different terminology, the guidance provided by that report is likely to be relevant to the interpretation of this head. In particular, the Charity Commission noted that in order for a purpose of preservation or conservation of the environment or of a particular species to be charitable, it must be demonstrated by independent expert evidence that such species or parts of the environment are worthy of preservation or conservation.

5.14 ## The relief of those in need by reason of youth, age, ill-health, disability, financial hardship or other disadvantage

By virtue of section 3(2)(e) of the 2011 Act, this head includes 'relief given by the provision of accommodation or care to the persons mentioned in [s 3(1)(j)]'. There is clearly overlap here with section 3(1)(a), which provides for the prevention or relief of poverty and section 3(1)(d) concerning the advancement of health. Trusts to relieve the aged have long been considered charitable: see for example *Re Robinson* [1951] 1 Ch 198 ('the old people over 65 of Hazel Slade near Hednesford'). The same is true for trusts for the disabled: see for example *Re Lewis* [1955] Ch 104 (blind girls and boys).

To be charitable, the trust must be directed to the *relief* of those in need by reason of one or more of the stated circumstances. In *Joseph Rowntree Memorial Trust Housing Association v A-G* [1983] Ch 159, a housing association sought charitable status for a housing scheme for those above pensionable age. Pursuant to the scheme, the association intended to grant long leases of small, self-contained flats (specially adapted for the needs of the elderly) in return for the payment of a capital premium (which was below the market value of such leases). Peter Gibson J held that the word 'relief' implies that the beneficiaries 'have a need attributable to their condition as aged, impotent or poor persons which requires alleviating, and which those persons could not alleviate, or would find difficulty in alleviating, themselves from their own resources'. Accordingly, had the scheme been aimed at aged millionaires of Mayfair, it would not have been charitable. As it was, the scheme, being aimed at alleviating particular housing difficulties, was charitable.

5.15 ## The advancement of animal welfare

It has long been clear that trusts to provide funds for carrying out the work of caring for animals in need will be charitable. Thus, in *Re Moss* [1949] 1 All ER 495, a trust for 'the welfare of cats and kittens needing care and attention' was upheld. Similarly in *Re Murawski's Will Trusts* [1971] 1 WLR 707, a gift for the 'provision of care and shelter for stray, neglected and unwanted animals of all kinds and the protection of animals from ill-usage, cruelty and suffering' was held to be charitable. A less obvious example of a trust for the advancement of animal welfare arose in *Re Wedgwood* [1915] 1 Ch 113, where the purpose of the improvement of methods of slaughtering animals was upheld as charitable.

As we have mentioned already, trusts which have political purposes have traditionally been denied charitable status (see further Section 5.20). As such, a trust will not be charitable if one of its purposes is to secure a change in the law concerning animal welfare. This was the case in *Hanchett-Stamford v A-G* [2008] EWHC 330 (Ch); [2009] Ch 173, which denied charitable status to the Performing and Captive Animals Defence League, an unincorporated association formed for the purpose of bringing about a ban on performing animals.

The other important decision in this area is *Re Grove-Grady* [1929] 1 Ch 557, in which the Court of Appeal considered a trust for the establishment of a reserve for 'the purpose of providing a refuge or refuges for the preservation of all animals birds or other creatures not human ... and so that all such animals birds or other creatures not human shall there be safe from molestation or destruction by man'. The Court held by a majority that this trust was not charitable, on the basis that animals within the reserve could not be destroyed by man no matter how necessary such destruction was to other animals or the animal itself, and on the basis that this purpose still left animals within the reserve 'liable to be molested and killed by other [non-human] denizens of the area'. It is likely that this case would be decided differently today, in light of modern views about conservation, although perhaps such a trust would be validated under section 3(1)(i) and not section 3(1)(k).

5.16 The promotion of the efficiency of the armed forces of the Crown, or of the efficiency of the police, fire and rescue services or ambulance services

These purposes were already charitable, falling under the fourth head of the *Pemsel* classification. Thus, in *Re Gray* [1925] Ch 362, a gift for the establishment of a fund for an army regiment for the 'promotion of sport (including in that term only shooting, fishing, cricket, football and polo)' was held to be charitable. These sports might reasonably be supposed to encourage physical efficiency, and it was, held Romer J, 'obviously for the benefit of the public that those entrusted with the defence of the realm should be not only mentally but also physically efficient'. The same reasoning was used in the earlier case of *Re Good* [1905] 2 Ch 60, where it was held that a gift for maintaining a library for the officers' mess of a particular regiment was charitable.

5.17 Other purposes

Section 3(1)(m) of the 2011 Act refers to three further categories of charitable purposes. The first category is other purposes which have previously been established as charitable under existing charity law. This preserves the charitable status of purposes held to be charitable under the earlier case law but which cannot be squeezed into any of the 12 previous categories. Aside from any such miscellaneous leftovers, the other purposes covered here are those set out in section 5 of the Act, which addresses purposes previously covered by the Recreational Charities Act 1958.

The Recreational Charities Act 1958 was introduced after the decisions of the House of Lords in *IRC v City of Glasgow Police Athletic Association* [1953] AC 380 and *IRC v Baddeley* [1955] AC 572, which held that trusts for purely recreational purposes were not charitable. Its provisions have now been incorporated into the Charities Act 2011 in section 5, which provides:

(1) It is charitable (and is to be treated as always having been charitable) to provide, or assist in the provision of, facilities for –

    (a) recreation, or
    (b) other leisure-time occupation,

if the facilities are provided in the interests of social welfare.

(2) The requirement that the facilities are provided in the interests of social welfare cannot be satisfied if the basic conditions are not met.

(3) The basic conditions are –

(a) that the facilities are provided with the object of improving the conditions of life for the persons for whom the facilities are primarily intended, and

(b) that –

    (i) those persons have need of the facilities by reason of their youth, age, infirmity or disability, poverty, or social and economic circumstances, or

    (ii) the facilities are to be available to members of the public at large or to male, or to female, members of the public at large.

(4) Sub-section (1) applies in particular to –

(a) the provision of facilities at village halls, community centres and women's institutes, and

(b) the provision and maintenance of grounds and buildings to be used for purposes of recreation or leisure-time occupation,

and extends to the provision of facilities for those purposes by the organising of any activity.
But this is subject to the requirement that the facilities are provided in the interests of social welfare.

(5) Nothing in this section is to be treated as derogating from the public benefit requirement.

The scope of what was section 1 of the 1958 Act – now section 5(1) of the 2011 Act – was considered by the House of Lords in *Guild v IRC* [1992] 2 AC 310. There, a bequest had been made 'to the town council of North Berwick for use in connection with the sports centre in North Berwick or some similar purpose in connection with sport'. The Inland Revenue Commissioners argued that this bequest was not charitable, and therefore that it did not qualify for tax exemptions, on the basis that recreational facilities should be aimed at meeting the needs of those who suffered from a position of relative social disadvantage. The House rejected this submission, approving the dictum of Bridge LJ in *IRC v McMullen* [1979] 1 WLR 130, 143, where he had stated:

> I can see no reason to conclude that only the deprived can have their conditions of life improved. Hyde Park improves the conditions of life for residents in Mayfair and Belgravia as much as for those in Pimlico or the Portobello Road, and the village hall may improve the conditions of life for the squire and his family as well as for the cottagers.

Lord Keith concluded that, for the purposes of what is now section 5(3)(b)(ii) 'it suffices if [facilities] are provided with the object of improving the conditions of life for members of the community generally'.

The second category of charitable purposes falling within section 3(1)(m) are charitable purposes which are analogous to, or within the spirit of, those charitable purposes falling within sections 3(1)(a) to (l). The third contains purposes which are analogous to, or within the spirit of, any charitable purpose that falls within the second category (ie analogous to any purpose which has been held to be charitable by analogy to the purposes set out in sections 3(1)(a) to (l)). This allows for the same incremental development of the classes of charitable purpose as existed in the case law before the 2011 Act: see for example *Re Foveaux* [1895] 2 Ch 501, 504.

The idea of purposes that are analogous to other analogous charitable purposes is not a particularly easy one. It is perhaps best explained by Lord Reid in *Scottish Burial Reform and Cremation Society v Glasgow Corporation* [1968] AC 138, 147:

> ... the courts appear to have proceeded first by seeking some analogy between an object mentioned in the preamble and the object with regard to which they had to reach a decision. And then they appear to have gone further and to have been satisfied if they could find an analogy between an object already held to be charitable and the new object claimed to be charitable.

Thus in that case the provision of affordable crematoria was upheld as charitable by working through the following process: first, the purpose of keeping up churchyards was found to be charitable by analogy with the reference to upkeep of churches found in the preamble; second, the provision of burial grounds was found to be charitable by analogy to the upkeep of churchyards; and, finally, the provision of crematoria was found to be charitable by analogy to the provision of burial grounds. It is this same process of building analogy upon analogy which is preserved by section 3(1)(m)(ii) and (iii) of the 2011 Act.

5.18 The public benefit requirement

In addition to fitting into one of the 13 categories of charitable purpose set out in section 3(1), a valid charitable trust must also be for the public benefit: section 2(1)(b). In *The Independent Schools Council v The Charity Commission for England and Wales* [2011] UKUT 421 (TCC); [2012] Ch 214, the Upper Tribunal identified what it regarded as two distinct senses of public benefit:

> The first aspect is that the nature of the purpose itself must be such as to be a benefit to the community: this is public benefit in the first sense. In that sense, the advancement of education...has the necessary element of benefit to the community...The second aspect is that those who may benefit from the carrying out of the purpose must be sufficiently numerous, and identified in such manner as, to constitute what is described in the authorities as 'a section of the public': this is public benefit in the second sense.

The distinction drawn here exists, but this may not be a helpful way of expressing it. For a start, we may be better off saying that what the Upper Tribunal regards as two different senses of public benefit in fact marks the two different elements of public benefit, namely: (1) that it is *beneficial* and (2) that this benefit *accrues to the public*. So the first sense of public benefit simply asks whether the purposes are indeed beneficial, whereas the second goes on to ask whether those benefits extend to a sufficient section of the public. So, to frame these as different senses of public benefit – intimating that public benefit means different things at different times – is misleading.

Second, this distinction between the questions (1) what is beneficial and (2) whether the benefit is sufficiently public is, in practice, captured in the distinction we have drawn already (and which is captured in s 2(1) of the 2011 Act) between the question (1) whether the purposes of the trust are of a kind the law regards as (potentially) charitable and (2) whether those purposes are publicly beneficial. In other words, the benefit question is typically answered by establishing that the proposed purpose of the trust is charitable – a question now answered by section 3 of the Act. Once we know this, the only question left over tends to be whether this benefit is sufficiently *public*. In other words, there is an important distinction between what the Upper Tribunal calls the 'two senses' of public benefit. But in reality, when we get to what is traditionally regarded as the 'public benefit' stage of the inquiry, it is usually only this 'second sense' – the question of whether the benefit extends to a sufficient section of the public – which is at stake. A charitable trust must indeed be beneficial. But much of this work is done by showing that it falls within one of the purposes listed in section 3(1). Hence, as we have seen already, a trust will only be regarded as advancing education if it provides for *useful, beneficial* instruction (see eg *Re Shaw* [1957] 1 WLR 729, *Re Pinion* [1965] Ch 85, and generally Section 5.6).

So the question we are looking at now is whether the proposed purposes benefit *the public*. Of course, this does not require that the trust must in fact benefit *everyone*. Rather the requirement is that the charitable purpose must benefit a *section* of the public. The difficult question then is how we determine whether those who stand to benefit from the trust constitute a 'section of the public'. As we shall see, the courts have answered this question differently at different times, and such inconsistencies are likely to remain after the Act.

Section 4(2) of the Act provides: 'In determining whether the public benefit requirement is satisfied in relation to any purpose falling within section 3(1), it is not to be presumed that a purpose of a particular description is for the public benefit.' This provision is included because it was commonly thought that there *was* a presumption of public benefit in relation to certain charitable purposes in the case law before the 2006 and 2011 Acts: see eg *National Anti-Vivisection Society v IRC* [1948] AC 31, 42; cf Hackney, 2008; Luxton, 2009. In fact the Upper Tribunal in *The Independent Schools Council v The Charity Commission for England and Wales* [2011] UKUT 421 (TCC), [2012] Ch 214 has recently confirmed that there never was any such presumption, and that it always has been the case that any given charitable trust, whatever its purposes, had to demonstrate that it benefited the public. We should also note at this stage that the Charity Commission assumes an obligation under section 17 of the 2011 Act to publish guidance as to how public benefit should be assessed; see for example Charity Commission 2008a, 2008b.

Though it is now clear that all charitable trusts must be for the public benefit, it shouldn't be assumed that there is a single, common standard of what counts as public benefit which can be applied to all charitable trusts. As we shall see, prior to the 2011 Act, the public benefit test was applied more stringently to some charitable purposes than to others. There is nothing in the Act to suggest that these differences do not remain. As such, though public benefit must be positively demonstrated for all charitable trusts, *how* this is demonstrated will differ among different charitable trusts (for recent confirmation, see the *Independent Schools Council* case [15]). The upshot of this is that, though it is possible to make a few general statements about the public benefit test, it is unsafe to draw inferences from how the test is applied to one head of charity as to how it will or should be applied to another head. Instead, we must approach each of the four traditional *Pemsel* heads of charity in turn and to see how the public benefit requirement has been applied in each.

So what can we say in general about the public benefit test? The Charity Commission (2008a, C3) has formulated the following principles of public benefit:

1. There must be an identifiable benefit or benefits.

    a. It must be clear what the benefits are.
    b. The benefits must be related to the aims.
    c. Benefits must be balanced against any detriment or harm.

2. Benefit must be to the public, or a section of the public.

    a. The beneficiaries must be appropriate to the aims.
    b. Where benefit is to a section of the public, the opportunity to benefit must not be unreasonably restricted by geographical or other restrictions.
    c. People in poverty must not be excluded from the opportunity to benefit.
    d. Any private benefits must be incidental.

To a significant extent these are statements of the obvious; certainly the two main principles tell us nothing which is not already plain from the phrase 'public benefit'. Just a few points require some elaboration or comment.

First, as principle 1C confirms, before we can conclude that a particular charitable trust is publicly beneficial we must offset any harms or dangers it creates against the benefits it confers. In simple terms, a trust will not be for the public benefit if it will do more harm than good. The leading example of this is the House of Lords decision in *National Anti-Vivisection Society v IRC* [1948] AC 31. There, a society that had the object of suppressing vivisection was denied a tax exemption on the basis that its work was not charitable. The House of Lords, in rejecting the society's appeal, held that the society could not overcome the finding of fact that:

> any assumed public benefit in the direction of the advancement of morals and education was far outweighed by the detriment to medical science and research and consequently to the public health which would result if the society succeeded in achieving its object [of suppressing vivisection], and that, on balance, the object of the society, so far from being for the public benefit, was gravely injurious thereto.

Second, in assessing the benefits flowing from a particular charitable trust, principle 1B states that the benefits must 'be related to' the charity's aims. What does this mean? The idea here appears to be that we are concerned only with the benefits that come from the specific purposes of the trust being pursued, and not with any benefits that come from incidental activities carried out on behalf of the trust. The Charity Commission gives the example of a charity concerned with the preservation of a particular historical building which provides a skating rink in the courtyard to attract visitors and enhance their appreciation of the neighbouring building. Although the enhanced appreciation of the building and its surroundings will count towards the public benefit assessment, the health benefits people may derive from the physical exercise of skating will not count because this does not have sufficient connection with the building preservation aims of the charity.

It does not follow, however, that it is only directly intended benefits that are relevant. A charity's actions in pursuing its charitable purposes may cause beneficial side effects, which though indirect are nonetheless sufficiently closely connected to the trust's primary purposes to be relevant to the public benefit equation. For example, in *Re Resch's Will Trusts* [1969] 1 AC 514, a trust to fund a private but non-profit-making hospital was held to be for the public benefit not simply because of the health gains of those who would be treated there but also because it would relieve the pressure on a nearby public hospital. Similarly, in *Neville Estates Ltd v Madden* [1962] Ch 832, a trust to establish and maintain a synagogue was upheld as charitable, Cross J taking the view that 'some benefit accrues to the public from the attendance at places of worship of persons who live in this world and mix with their fellow citizens'.

Third, charities cannot be run for profit. As such, the trust in *Re Resch's Will Trusts* would have failed, notwithstanding the benefits that it created, if it had been a profit-making hospital, rather than one that charged simply to cover its costs. An earlier version of principle 2B had gone further, stating that 'the opportunity to benefit must not be unreasonably restricted by ability to pay any fees charged'. This was withdrawn, however, following *The Independent Schools Council v The Charity Commission for England*

and Wales [2011] UKUT 421 (TCC), [2012] Ch 214. The case concerned the charitable status of independent, fee-paying schools. Although the Upper Tribunal endorsed the Charity Commission's guidance that, for a trust's purposes to be charitable, the poor must not be excluded from the trust, it concluded that this was compatible with the charity charging fees which would, in practice, exclude some members of the public from accessing its benefits. Whether in fact the fees charged have the effect of excluding the poor depends on the context. Sometimes it will be possible for a charity to charge a fee which excludes many from its benefits, if it nonetheless provides a service at a rate which allows the charity to meet its costs and which is not available at a lower price elsewhere. It follows that 'poor' here will be interpreted more flexibly and more widely that it is in trusts which are specifically for the relief of poverty. The Upper Tribunal nonetheless concluded that those who could afford fees of £12,000 a year could not be said to be poor, and so a school whose purposes were framed so as to make access dependent on an ability to pay such fees could not be said to satisfy the public benefit requirement.

Though they cannot be run for profit, charitable trusts may bring 'private' benefits to particular individuals so long as these are purely incidental to the trust's purposes (eg though a trust to provide professional benefits to lawyers would not itself be charitable, the incidental professional benefit lawyers derive from the publication of law reports does not stop a trust for the publication of law reports from being for the public benefit: *Incorporated Council of Law Reporting for England and Wales v A-G* [1972] Ch 73) or to the trustees doing their job (eg paying them a salary or even funding an annual dinner: *Re Coxen* [1948] Ch 747).

Fourth, as noted at the outset, benefit need not accrue to every member of the public. One reason for this is simple practicality. Even a charity which is, in principle, open to all is likely, in practice, to be able to benefit only a smaller section of the public. For example, funding a public hospital or providing free school books will, at best, benefit only those who need hospital treatment or require such books, and, in practice, will be enjoyed only by the minority who in fact obtain treatment at this hospital or to whom these books are distributed. As the Charity Commission puts it (2008a, F2), '[a] charity is for the public benefit if the benefits it offers are made widely available, even though in practice only a few people from time to time are able to benefit'.

Where the benefit of the trust is not in principle available to all, principle 2B states that the restrictions on the opportunity to benefit must be reasonable. The difficult question is how to determine which restrictions are reasonable and which are not. The Charity Commission states (2008a, F3):

> To be a charity, where the beneficiaries are a 'section of the public', any restrictions on who can benefit must be 'reasonable'. That means the restrictions are legitimate, proportionate, rational and justifiable given the nature of the organisation's charitable aims. It is not charitable to restrict who can benefit by reference to criteria that are unrelated to the charitable aims to be carried out.

A restriction on who can have opportunity to benefit may be reasonable:

▶ where the class of people who can benefit is sufficiently wide or open in nature (given the charitable aims to be carried out and the resources available to the charity) to constitute a sufficient section of the public; or
▶ because the class of people whom the aims are intended to benefit have a particular charitable need which justifies restricting the benefits to them.

In particular, the Charity Commission notes that it is generally reasonable for a charity's aims to be intended to benefit people living in a particular geographical area, such as a village, town, city, county or country. By contrast, restricting benefit to people living in a particular street, or a few named houses, is likely to be too small an area to be considered a section of the public.

However, if there are additional bars to access to the benefits of the trust on top of the geographical restriction, then the trust is likely to have a harder time satisfying the public benefit requirement. For instance, in *Williams' Trustees v IRC* [1947] AC 447, a trust directed at promoting the interests of Welsh people in London, through lectures on Welsh language, art and history, a library for Welsh literature and providing a meeting place for Welsh people in London was held not to be a valid charitable trust primarily because these purposes did not fall within the spirit and intendment of the preamble to the Statute of Elizabeth. However, Lord Simonds was also disposed to hold that, even had the purposes been charitable, the trust did not benefit a sufficient section of the public.

The same point emerges from *IRC v Baddeley* [1955] AC 572, a case concerning a trust of land, including playing fields, to be used to promote the religious and social well-being of present or likely members of the Methodist Church. Again, the trust was held to fall outside the recognised categories of charitable purposes (though see now s 5 of the Charities Act 2011; Section 5.17). However, Viscount Simonds again held that the trust would also have failed the public benefit test. To him, the important distinction was between trusts which provide a 'form of relief extended to the whole community yet by its very nature advantageous only to the few and a form of relief accorded to a selected few out of a larger number equally willing and able to take advantage of it' ([1955] AC 572, 592). Only the former would satisfy the public benefit requirement. The latter would not. He illustrated this with the following example:

> ... a bridge which is available for all the public may undoubtedly be a charity and it is indifferent how many people use it. But confine its use to a selected number of persons, however numerous and important, it is then clearly not a charity. It is not of general public utility: for it does not serve the public purpose which its nature qualifies it to serve.

This requirement that the benefits deriving from a charitable trust not be unreasonably limited to a selected few from a larger group who would otherwise be able to benefit from it is sometimes – though not particularly helpfully – explained by saying that a charitable trust cannot be for a 'class within a class' (*IRC v Baddeley* [1955] AC 572, 591).

A final point stressed by the Upper Tribunal in the *Independent Schools Council* case was that, when determining whether a purported charitable trust is for the public benefit, we must look to the purposes for which it was established rather than how it is and has been operated. In other words, the trust's purposes are one thing, whether it in fact sticks to or achieves these purposes in its operations is another. So a trust is for the public benefit if the purposes for which is was set up are publicly beneficial. That the trust does not in practice benefit the public means not that the trust is not charitable but that its trustees are failing to abide by the terms of that trust. How do we establish what a trust's purposes are if not from what it in fact does? Things are simplest where the charity has a constitution setting out its purposes. Where there is no constitution, the court has to look for other evidence indicating what the trust was set up to do. Whether this question can in practice be answered without at least some inquiry into what the trust does *in fact* do is doubtful.

5.19   Public benefit and personal nexus

It may look from all of this that the public benefit test is essentially straightforward. If the benefit is, in principle, available to everyone, then the trust will be for the public benefit, even if in practice it is only enjoyed by the few. If the benefit is restricted to a certain sub-section of the public, then the trust will be publicly beneficial only if it still enables a sufficient number of people to benefit and if the restriction to these people is reasonable in light of the nature of the trust's purposes. Unfortunately, things are not quite so simple.

As we noted at the start of the previous section, the public benefit test has been applied differently to different types of charitable purpose. To this extent, the apparent uniformity of the general principles set out by the Charity Commission and described earlier is misleading. In particular, the last rule we looked at – the rule that the opportunity to benefit from a charitable trust must not be unreasonably restricted to a particular sub-section of the public – has been interpreted and applied differently as between the four *Pemsel* categories of charitable purpose.

As a starting point, we can say that the rule that the opportunity to benefit from charitable trusts should not be unreasonably restricted should preclude settlors from creating trusts which would benefit only those to whom they have some personal connection or 'nexus', such as family members, friends or colleagues. In all such cases we would expect the courts to hold that these people do not constitute a sufficient section of the public and that it is unreasonable to exclude those who do not fall within these groups and yet whose need is just as great and who are equally deserving of the opportunity to benefit. Yet this is not always what the courts have said.

This is clearest in relation to trusts directed towards the relief of poverty. In *Re Scarisbrick* [1951] Ch 622 the Court of Appeal confirmed the validity of charitable trusts for poor relatives. A few years later, the House of Lords in *Dingle v Turner* [1972] AC 601 held a trust to relieve poverty among the settlor's employees was also a valid charitable trust. (See also *Spiller v Maude* (1881) 32 Ch D 158n, where a trust set up by a company of actors in York to fund funeral expenses, medical bills and to provide for orphans of its members was held to be charitable.) In the poverty cases, therefore, there is no rule that the benefit of the trust cannot be reserved for those with some sort of personal nexus to the settlor. As Evershed MR put it in *Re Scarisbrick* [1951] Ch 622, 639, this can be explained either 'on the basis that the relief of poverty is of so altruistic a character that the public element may necessarily be inferred thereby; or they may be accepted as a hallowed, if illogical, exception' to the general rule. The only requirement is that the trust must, properly interpreted, be for the purpose of relieving poverty, albeit within the narrow class of people defined by the settlor, rather than a trust for the benefit of the class of people identified by the settlor, who also happen to be poor: see for example *Dingle v Turner*. In other words, the trust must be a *purpose* rather than a *persons* trust (Section 4.7), though, of course, in the latter case the trust may nonetheless take effect as a valid, though necessarily non-charitable, private persons trust provided the usual rules of certainty are met.

Is any of this likely to change following the 2011 Act? As we have seen, section 4(2) of the Act stresses that there is no presumption that purposes falling under the various established heads of charity do in fact benefit the public. This might be taken to suggest that the courts and the Charity Commission might begin to apply this requirement a bit more strictly than they have done previously (notwithstanding the conclusion in *The Independent Schools Council* case that there had in fact never been any such presumption). However, the Charity Commission in its guidance on trusts for the relief of poverty (2008c, E3) observed that 'what is a sufficient section of the public for one charitable aim is not necessarily a sufficient section for a different charitable aim', before noting:

> [Although] beneficiaries cannot usually be defined by reference to a personal connection ... , an exception has existed in charity law that has allowed charities for the relief of poverty to have a more narrowly restricted beneficiary class, including one that defines the beneficiaries by reference to a personal connection. The reason for this is that relieving poverty has been considered by the courts to be of such a public character that a more narrowly defined class of beneficiary can still be a sufficient section of the public.

As such, it seems that the old rules and cases such as *Re Scarisbrick* and *Dingle v Turner* remain good law. The Commission did, however, stress that this generous treatment of trusts under the poverty head would not be extended, and that settlors were not free to set whatever arbitrary limits they liked to access to the relevant benefits.

Turning to trusts for the advancement of education, we find that the courts have been a lot stricter in barring trusts where the benefit is open only to those with some personal connection to the settlor (or indeed to some other individual). The leading case here is *Oppenheim v Tobacco Securities Trust Co Ltd* [1951] AC 297. This concerned the status of a trust fund to be applied 'in providing for ... the education of children of employees or former employees of the British–American Tobacco Co Ltd or any of its subsidiary or allied companies in such manner as the acting trustees shall in their absolute discretion think fit'. The number of employees whose children could benefit from this trust exceeded 110,000. A majority of the House of Lords held that because the qualification for benefit was based upon the personal connection of employees with their employer, the class was not a section of the public and the trust was therefore void. Lord Simonds reasoned as follows ([1951] AC 297, 305–06):

> It is a clearly established principle of the law of charity that a trust is not charitable unless it is directed to the public benefit. This is sometimes stated in the proposition that it must benefit the community or a section of the community. Negatively it is said that a trust is not charitable if it confers only private benefits ... . If I may begin at the bottom of the scale, a trust established by a father for the education of his son is not a charity. The public element, as I will call it, is not supplied by the fact that from that son's education all may benefit. At the other end of the scale the establishment of a college or university is beyond doubt a charity ... . The difficulty arises where the trust is not for the benefit of any institution either then existing or by the terms of the trust to be brought into existence, but for the benefit of a class of persons at large. Then the question is whether that class of persons can be regarded as such a 'section of the community' as to satisfy the test of public benefit. These words 'section of the community' have no special sanctity, but they conveniently indicate first, that the possible ... beneficiaries must not be numerically negligible, and secondly, that the quality which distinguishes them from other members of the community, so that they form by themselves a section of it, must be a quality which does not depend on their relationship to a particular individual. ... A group of persons may be numerous but, if the nexus between them is their personal relationship to

a single propositus or to several propositi, they are neither the community nor a section of the community for charitable purposes.

Similarly, in *Re Compton* [1945] Ch 123, an attempted charitable trust for the education of children from three families failed on the basis that this did not confer a public benefit. There the Court of Appeal expressly declined to extend the poor relatives cases by analogy into the head of educational charitable trusts.

As against this, however, the courts have upheld trusts for the education of children of members of a particular profession: for example *Hall v The Urban Sanitary Authority of the Borough of Derby* (1885) 16 QBD 163 (concerning an orphanage for the children of deceased railway workers). Moreover, the validity of these cases was accepted in *Oppenheim*. But this then leaves us with a distinction between, on the one hand, trusts to educate children of employees of a particular company and, on the other, trusts to educate children of members of a particular profession. Following *Oppenheim*, only the latter can be said to be for the public benefit. This creates some odd results however. As their Lordships noted in *Oppenheim*, this means that whereas a trust for the education of children of employees of a major tobacco producer will fail, a trust for the education of children of workers in the tobacco industry generally will be a valid charitable trust. Yet *both* place restrictions on who can benefit from the trust and, depending on the size of the company and the sums of money involved, trusts of the former kind may end up benefiting *more* people than the latter. As such, how can we say that only the latter benefit a sufficient section of the public?

For these reasons, Lord MacDermott dissented from the majority in *Oppenheim*, taking the view that the 'personal nexus' test was 'baffling and elusive', 'arbitrary and artificial'. The arbitrariness and artificiality of this approach are magnified when we see that the courts have allowed trusts which are framed as for the benefit of the public generally (or some sufficient section of the public) but that contain a direction that preference be given to, say, children of a particular company: see *Re Koettgen's Will Trusts* [1954] Ch 252 (where preference was to be given to families of employees of a particular company in respect of up to 75% of the income of the trust); cf *IRC v Educational Grants Association Ltd* [1967] Ch 993. In such cases, however, the trustees will have to be careful that they do not simply treat the trust as a trust for the benefit of the class to be preferred. If they do, they leave themselves open to the criticism that they have failed to comply with the trust instrument or, if the court finds that the settlor really intended that the trust be only for the group to be preferred, that the trust is a sham.

The public benefit requirement, and the rule that trusts which reserve benefits for those who have some personal connection to the settlor, has been applied most stringently to trusts to advance religion and to those falling within the fourth, miscellaneous head of the *Pemsel* classification. For example, in *Gilmour v Coats* [1949] AC 426, the House of Lords considered the validity of a trust for the Carmelite Priory, a community of strictly cloistered nuns who devoted their lives to prayer, contemplation, penance and self-sanctification. The Priory, backed by evidence from an eminent Cardinal, argued that its activities were for the public benefit because of the value of its prayers and because the public would benefit from observing the way in which the Priory's nuns lived their lives. Both arguments were rejected, the first because it was 'manifestly not susceptible of proof'; the second because edification by example was 'too vague and intangible' where the nuns did not mix with the outside world. Just as importantly, there was no suggestion that the present and possible future members of the Priory could constitute a sufficient section of the public.

A different result was reached in *Neville Estates Ltd v Madden* [1962] Ch 832, where a trust for the Catford Synagogue was in issue. Cross J was able to distinguish *Gilmour* on the basis that the members of the synagogue spent their lives in the world, whereas the members of the Carmelite Priory did not. He continued to find that 'the court is ... entitled to assume that some benefit accrues to the public from the attendance at places of worship of persons who live in this world and mix with their fellow citizens'. The public benefit test was also held to be satisfied in *Re Hetherington* [1990] Ch 1, where a trust for the saying of masses for the settlor and her late husband was upheld because the masses would be said in public and therefore be for the benefit of those members of the public who attended. Again, however, in both cases the public benefit test was met only by invoking the (possible) gains that the public at large might derive from these trusts. The clear assumption was that the benefit of those who might attend the synagogue in *Neville Estates* or the masses in *Re Hetherington* could not be said to amount to a *public* benefit.

5.20   Trusts for political purposes

Even if a trust falls within one of the established heads of charity, the courts have held that it cannot be charitable if its purposes are (also) political. 'Political' trusts mean those which promote a particular political party or ideology or which exist to push for a particular change in the law or governmental policy either in the UK or overseas. So, for example, in *McGovern v A-G* [1982] Ch 321, the court struck down a trust set up by Amnesty International whose purposes included attempting to secure the release of prisoners of conscience and procuring the abolition of torture and inhuman and degrading punishment. In *Southwood v A-G* [2000] WTLR 1199, a trust for the 'advancement of the education of the public in the subject of militarism and disarmament' was held not to be charitable as its principal purpose was to challenge the policies of Western governments. And in *Hanchett-Stamford v A-G* [2008] EWHC 330 (Ch), [2009] Ch 173, charitable status was denied to the Performing and Captive Animals Defence League, an unincorporated association formed for the purpose of bringing about a ban on performing animals. The political nature of the purpose was also a second reason the trust failed in *National Anti-Vivisection Society v IRC* [1948] AC 31 (Section 5.18). For examples of failed charitable trusts for political parties, see *Bonar Law Memorial Trust v IRC* (1933) 49 TLR 220, *Re Ogden* [1933] Ch 678 and *Re Hopkinson* [1949] 1 All ER 346.

The courts have offered a variety of (purported) justifications for this stance. The first is that, as charitable trusts can be upheld only if they are for the public benefit, the courts would then have to determine whether the relevant political cause or aim was indeed publically beneficial. And this, so the argument goes, is a question which the courts are not qualified to answer: see *Bowman v Secular Society Ltd* [1917] AC 406, 442 (Lord Parker); *McGovern v A-G* [1982] Ch 321, 336–37 (Slade J).

Second, it has been argued that, aside from the question of expertise, courts cannot determine whether political purpose trusts are for the public benefit without overstepping their remit, because it is the role of Parliament and not of the courts to determine whether and how the law should be changed: *McGovern v A-G* [1982] Ch

321, 337. As Chadwick LJ stated in *Southwood v A-G* [2000] WTLR 1199, the court is 'in no position to determine that promotion of the one view rather than the other is for the public benefit. Not only does the court have no material on which to make that choice; to attempt to do so would be to usurp the role of government'.

A third argument is that, so far as the purpose of the trust is to bring about some change in the law, the court cannot resolve the question whether this change would be beneficial, not (simply) because it does not have the expertise or mandate to make this decision, but because it is incompatible with the court's duty to apply the law as it is. As Lord Simonds said in *National Anti-Vivisection Society v IRC* [1948] AC 31, 62 'each court in deciding on the validity of a gift must decide on the principle that the law is right as it stands'.

None of these arguments is wholly convincing. Courts are often in the business of determining whether particular rules of law are sound or unsound, effective or ineffective, so any suggestion that they *never* have the expertise to determine whether a proposed change in the law would be (publicly) beneficial is nonsense. Indeed, the court undertook just such an evaluation of the merits of the proposed change in the *Anti-Vivisection* case (see Section 5.18). Similarly, it cannot be right to say that they are necessarily overstepping their role to pass judgment on the merits of a change in the law. In a common law system, many changes in the law are authored by the courts and, even where the courts are not authorised to change the law itself, they may nonetheless have to consider its substantive merits, for instance to determine its compatibility with human rights legislation. And, given all this, there is no reason to think that courts cannot pass judgment on the merits of a proposed change to the law while acknowledging their duty, so far as it extends, to apply that law in relevant cases. In any case, none of these three arguments bites where the political purpose is directed to *foreign* governments and laws. Here the most we can say is that recognising such trusts could disrupt relations between the relevant state and the UK: see *McGovern v A-G* [1982] Ch 321, 338–39.

So, although it seems reasonable to conclude that *sometimes* the court will not be able to determine that a trust is for the public benefit for one or other of the reasons offered earlier, it is doubtful whether the present absolute prohibition of all trusts which have political purposes is defensible. It is important to stress that the rule preventing political trusts only applies where one of the trust's purposes is political in the sense described earlier. What the rule does not prevent is charities using political means to further their other *non*-political purposes: see generally Charity Commission, 2008d. Accordingly, a charity such as Oxfam, which is directed towards, inter alia, the relief of poverty, will not lose this status because it sometimes lobbies the Government with a view to securing additional funding for alleviating third world debt.

5.21   The cy-près doctrine

One of the most significant differences between the law of charitable trusts and the law of private (ie non-charitable) trusts is the application of the cy-près doctrine to the former but not the latter. Literally construed, cy-près means something like 'as close as possible'. In short, the cy-près doctrine applies where it is impossible or impractical to implement the precise terms that are contained in a charitable trust, and, where it applies, it works to allow the court to direct that property held under such a charitable trust be held for a purpose that is similar to – though necessarily different from – that stipulated by the settlor.

It might become impossible or impractical to implement a charitable gift or trust for a number of reasons. For instance, a gift could be made to a charitable body that never existed, or which was dissolved before the gift took effect. Or a testator may attempt to create a charitable testamentary trust for a purpose which, although possible at the time that his will was drafted, has since become impossible (for instance, a will trust to preserve a certain species of animal which, by the time of the settlor's death, has become extinct). Another example might be a trust to achieve a charitable purpose which has, by the time it takes effect, already been achieved (say, for instance, a testamentary trust for the advancement of research into the possibility of providing an initial map of the human genome). These three examples are cases of *initial* failure, that is, failure of the intended trust purpose at the outset. Yet another scenario is that the impossibility or impracticality does not occur before the trust comes into existence but at a subsequent stage (say, eg, the purpose of a trust becomes impossible or is accomplished after the trust has been in existence for some time). These are cases of *subsequent* failure.

The distinction between initial and subsequent failure is important. In cases of initial failure, the cy-près doctrine applies only where the trust deed demonstrates that the settlor had a *general* or *paramount charitable intention*: see Section 5.22. There is no such requirement in cases of subsequent failure, where the courts will automatically apply the cy-près doctrine.

Before we delve into the rules governing the application of the cy-près doctrine, it is important to stress that we do not need to concern ourselves with cy-près if, on closer inspection, the trust's purposes have not in fact failed. To see how there might be confusion on this point, take the following example. I want to leave some money for the purpose of supporting down-at-heel former trusts academics, so I make provision in my will for £1,000 to be paid to the Foundation for Impoverished Trusts Scholars. However, let's say that the Foundation has been dissolved by the time of my death, and hence by the time the disposition is to take effect. Of course, it is now impossible to give the money to the non-existent Foundation. But there is nothing impossible about my money still being used to support impoverished former trusts academics; this *purpose* remains entirely possible. So, although I cannot give the money to the Foundation to carry out this purpose, there is nothing to stop some other person or group from holding and applying my money for the very same purpose. Another way of putting this point is that the only impossibility here is with (the members of) the Foundation acting as trustee(s) for my intended charitable purpose trust. And this is no reason for the trust as a whole to fail. As we shall see (Section 12.2), it is a basic rule of trusts law that trusts will not fail for want of a trustee. Rather, all we need do is find and appoint a substitute trustee.

Of course, this is only possible where my intention is to create a charitable purpose trust, for only then is it the purpose which is essential to the success of the trust rather than the identity of the body whose job it is to apply the funds for that purpose. In other words, this solution is available only in relation to dispositions of type 2a as set out in Section 5.2. By contrast, where I intend to make my charitable disposition by way of an outright transfer to an incorporated charitable body (type 2b), there is no way of giving effect to my intended transfer by appointing a replacement trustee for the simple reason that I am not intending to create a trust *at all*. In cases of this latter type, if the body is no longer in existence, my disposition straightforwardly fails: I have tried to transfer property to a company which does not exist. (For judicial recognition of this distinction, see *Re Finger's Will Trusts* [1972] Ch 288).

So if a settlor attempts a charitable disposition to a now defunct charitable body (or indeed a body which was never in existence), the questions we need to ask are as follows (see too *Re Vernon's Will Trusts* [1972] Ch 300n):

1. Did the donor intend to transfer the property to the chosen charitable body *on trust* (for charitable purposes) or *outright*?

   (If the body is *unincorporated* – ie the members haven't formed themselves into a company – then the transfer must necessarily be on trust, because an outright transfer to an unincorporated body can take effect only as a beneficial transfer to its members (see Section 4.12), and a beneficial transfer to a group of private individuals can never be a charitable disposition. If the body is *incorporated*, then both sorts of transfer are possible, so we must work out which of the two the settlor intended.)

2. If the donor (settlor) intended a transfer *on trust*, then are those purposes still capable of being achieved, notwithstanding that the body is no longer in existence?

   a If not, then the trust fails, unless the doctrine of cy-près can be invoked.
   b. If so, then the trust will succeed and simply requires the appointment of a new trustee, *unless* in turn, the settlor intended that the trust should take effect only if the chosen body were available to act as trustee (in which case, as the body no longer exists, the trust will fail).

3. If the donor intended an *outright* transfer, then the trust fails, unless the doctrine of cy-près can be invoked (cf *Re Faraker* [1912] 2 Ch 488 discussed later).

A good example of the application of these principles is found in *Re Finger's Will Trusts* [1972] Ch 286. There, the testatrix gave shares of the residue of her will to 11 named charities, two of which had ceased to exist before her death. One of these – the 'National Radium Commission' (in fact there never was a *National* Radium Commission, but the court assumed she meant the 'Radium Commission') – had been an unincorporated body, whereas the other – the 'National Council for Maternity and Child Welfare' – had been incorporated. Goff J held that the disposition to the Radium Commission – as an unincorporated body – must be read as a transfer to the members on trust for the Commission's (charitable) purposes. Those purposes remained possible and there was no indication that the testatrix only intended that the trust take effect if the Commission itself remained in existence. As such, the trust did not fail and Goff J directed that a scheme be drawn up for how the trust could now be given effect.

By contrast, the National Council for Maternity and Child Welfare was an incorporated body, and, in the absence of any suggestion that the testatrix intended to transfer the property to the Council *on trust*, it followed that the Council was meant to receive it outright. As there was no purpose trust which could be 'saved' by finding a new trustee but simply an attempted outright transfer to a body which no longer existed, the gift failed. The question then was whether the doctrine of cy-près could be deployed to see that the property was nonetheless given to a distinct charitable body fulfilling the same or similar purposes to the now defunct Council. Here, Goff J held that the testatrix had a general charitable intention – a finding made easier by the fact that the testatrix had attempted to give almost her whole estate to charity – and so the cy-près doctrine applied. The end result was that both shares of the residue ended up devoted to the charitable purposes the testatrix envisaged, but the latter only by reason of the cy-près doctrine and only because the court was able to find that she had a general charitable intention.

There is one other way a charitable trust may be 'rescued' without recourse to the cy-près doctrine. This occurs where a charitable disposition is made to a charitable body, which no longer has any independent existence but whose operation has been taken over by a new body. In such circumstances, the court may hold that the gift which is expressed to be to the defunct body should be construed and so take effect as a gift to the new body. For example, in *Re Faraker* [1912] 2 Ch 488, the Court of Appeal had to determine the effect of a disposition to 'Mrs Bailey's Charity, Rotherhithe'. There was no 'Mrs Bailey's Charity', though there was a 'Hannah Bayly's Charity' founded for poor widows in Rotherhithe. This charity had since been consolidated with 13 other charitable bodies into a single charitable fund for the benefit of the poor in Rotherhithe. The court held that the testatrix must have intended 'Hannah Bayly's Charity' and, though this no longer subsisted as an independent charitable body, it continued to 'exist' in the new form of the consolidated charity, notwithstanding its broader objects.

5.22 Initial failure

So it is only where a charitable disposition cannot take effect as intended that any question of cy-près arises. And, as we have noted already, in cases of initial failure, the doctrine of cy-près will apply only where the donor has a general or paramount charitable intention. The question now is what is meant by a general charitable intention and how do we tell whether the donor had one.

The distinction the courts appear to have in mind is as between, on the one hand, a donor whose primary intention is to give to charity, with the precise form or content of that gift secondary and, on the other, a donor whose intention is to make a specific charitable disposition and does not extend to any broader wish to give to charity. As Buckley J put it in *Re Lysaght* [1966] Ch 191, 292:

> A general charitable intention ... may be said to be a paramount intention on the part of a donor to effect some charitable purpose which the courts can find a method of putting into operation, notwithstanding that it is impracticable to give effect to some direction by the donor which is not an essential part of his true intention – not, that is to say, part of his paramount intention. In contrast, a particular charitable intention exists where the donor means his charitable disposition to take effect if, but only if, it can be carried into effect in a particular specified way.

This is all well and good in theory; the difficulty comes in applying this test in practice. The cases suggest that, on similar evidence, some judges have been more ready to find a general charitable intent than others.

So, for example, a general charitable intention was found in *Biscoe v Jackson* (1887) 35 Ch D 460, where the testator set aside £10,000 of his estate for charitable purposes, £4,000 of which was to be used 'in the establishment of a soup kitchen for the parish of Shoreditch, and of a cottage hospital adjoining thereto'. In the event, land could not be acquired for this purpose and so the carrying out of this particular purpose became impossible. The Court of Appeal held that the testator had a general charitable intention, because the clause as a whole exhibited 'an intention on the part of the testator to give £10,000 to the sick and poor of the parish of Shoreditch, pointing out how he desires that to be applied'. Or to put it another way, his paramount intention was to provide for the sick and poor, with the reference to the soup kitchen and hospital being in effect precatory (cf Sections 3.4, 4.6). The Court of Appeal indicated, however, that had the clause stated that the trustees 'must build the particular building', the contrary conclusion would have been reached.

Similarly, the court found a general charitable intent in *Re Lysaght* [1966] Ch 191. There, the testatrix left funds to the Royal College of Surgeons (RCS) to set up medical studentships. However, she specified that these should only be available to the British-born sons of qualified British-born medical men, and then only if they weren't Jewish or Roman Catholic. The RCS would not accept the gift on these terms and so the gift could not take effect as intended. The question was whether the cy-près doctrine could apply so as to enable the RCS to take the money and fund the studentships without these restrictions. Buckley J held that the testatrix had a paramount charitable intent and that the specific restrictions on the availability of the studentships were not an essential part of her intention.

In contrast, no such general charitable intention was found in *Re Rymer* [1895] 1 Ch 19. There, the testator bequeathed a legacy of £5,000 'to the rector for the time being of St Thomas' Seminary for the education of priests in the diocese of Westminster'. Between the date on which the testator executed his will and the date of his death, the seminary had ceased to exist. So, once again the question was whether the testator had a general charitable intent, so enabling the funds to be applied cy-près. The Court of Appeal held that he did not. Lindley LJ held that the Court must 'consider whether the mode of attaining the object is only machinery, or whether the mode is not the substance of the gift. Here it appears to me the gift to the seminary is the substance of the whole thing'.

The same conclusion was reached in *Re Spence* [1979] Ch 483, where the testatrix left half of her residuary estate to 'the Old Folks home at Hillworth Lodge Keighley for the benefit of the patients', an institution which had closed down the year before the testatrix's death. Sir Robert Mcgarry VC held that the specificity of the words used by the testatrix when setting out the gift were inconsistent with her having a broader, more general charitable intention. He stated ([1979] Ch 483, 493):

> If a particular institution or purpose is specified, then it is that institution or purpose, and no other, that is to be the object of the benefaction. It is difficult to envisage a testator as being suffused with a general glow of broad charity when he is labouring, and labouring successfully, to identify some particular specified institution or purpose as the object of his bounty. The specific displaces the general. It is otherwise where the testator has been unable to specify any particular charitable institution or practicable purpose [ie where the named institution never existed or the named purpose was always impossible], and so, although his intention of charity can be seen, he has failed to provide any way of giving effect to it. There, the absence of the specific leaves the general undisturbed.

This approach sounds entirely sensible. The problem is that it is difficult to square with *Biscoe v Jackson* and *Re Lysaght* (and indeed *Re Finger's Will Trusts* which we discussed in the previous section), which likewise contained very specific provisions but where the court nonetheless felt able to identify a general charitable intent. The basic difficulty is, as these cases show, in the majority of cases the donor will simply have directed that his funds should go to a particular charity or be held for a particular charitable purpose. There will be little or no indication as to whether he had a broader, general charitable intention, an intention which does not stand or fall with the success of the specific disposition he has detailed. Indeed, the more fundamental problem is that most charitable donors will not have given any thought at all to this question. They simply decide to fund a particular charitable purpose and never consider what they would want to happen should funding that specific purpose prove impossible. As such, the problem here is not simply one of proof – of identifying what the donor's intentions were – it is that in the majority of cases there will be *no* relevant intention one way or another. It seems then that, though the courts tend to approach this question by asking what the donor *did* intend, in reality the most they can ask is what they think he *would have* intended. And this then opens the door to courts determining the operation of the cy-près doctrine not by reference to the donor's actual or possible intentions but rather by their own views of the merits of the case and where this property may best end up.

This is not to say that we cannot offer any more concrete guidance as to when a general charitable intention will be found. First, as Megarry vc notes in the quote from *Re Spence*, the courts are far more likely to find a general charitable intent where the charitable body named by the donor never in fact existed. Here it is far harder to argue that he intended only to make a gift to that particular body because, necessarily, there never was any such body and so the only way to make sense of his intention is to treat it as a broader charitable intent (see too *Re Davis* [1902] 1 Ch 876; *Re Harwood* [1936] Ch 285).

Second, the courts have been more inclined to find a general charitable intention where the donor makes a series of gifts to charities all sharing common or similar charitable purposes. If one of the charitable bodies named is no longer in existence then the courts have held that the presence of the other gifts to similar bodies clearly intimates that the donor's overriding intention was to see all these funds applied to that particular purpose: see for example *Re Satterthwaite's Will Trusts* [1966] 1 WLR 277; *Re Knox* [1937] Ch 109.

Finally, it should also be stressed that the courts will not apply the cy-près doctrine to save a trust that is not charitable in the first place by substituting a charitable purpose for a non-charitable purpose: see *Re Jenkins' Will Trusts* [1966] Ch 249.

5.23 Subsequent failure

If a gift to charity or a charitable trust initially takes effect – that is, if there is no initial failure – then the courts have held that the relevant property is from that point on 'committed' to charity, such that the charitable disposition cannot fail even if the specific charitable purpose subsequently becomes impossible or if the charitable body to which the gift is directed ceases to operate. As such, there is no possibility of a resulting trust arising, thus sending the property back to the donor or his estate, in the event of failure of the intended purpose as would be the case were there to be a subsequent failure of a non-charitable purpose trust (see Section 8.7; *Re the Trusts of the Abbott Fund* [1900] 2 Ch 326). Rather, in the event of the purpose subsequently becoming impossible or impractical, the cy-près doctrine will automatically apply. Importantly, this rule applies even in the absence of any general charitable intention being shown on the part of the settlor: see *Re Slevin* [1891] 2 Ch 236.

5.24 The meaning of impossibility and impracticability

We have seen above that the cy-près doctrine applies only when the specific charitable disposition intended by the donor fails. But what does 'failure' mean in this context? In the 19th century, the cy-près doctrine was invoked only where a charitable trust had become impossible or impracticable to administer. What this meant was that cy-près could not operate where the specific charitable disposition had become simply inefficient or outmoded. This possibility was made all the more likely given that, as we have seen, charitable trusts can exist in perpetuity. As such, a charitable disposition which functioned sensibly and cost-effectively at the time of its creation may, as a result of changed circumstances, function inefficiently or haphazardly years, or indeed centuries, later. However, the narrowness of the cy-près doctrine meant that, so long as these dispositions could be given effect, the court had no power to modify them with the result that funds were tied to charities which were doing far less public good than the donor intended (or would have intended had he contemplated the changed circumstances).

This strict rule, limiting cy-près to cases of impossibility and impracticability, was finally relaxed by section 13 of the Charities Act 1960, which is now to be found in section 62 of the Charities Act 2011. Section 62 of the 2011 Act sets out various circumstances in which property can be applied cy-près. Where one of the various tests set out by section 62(1) is satisfied, the court can alter the purposes of the trust and make any necessary consequential orders. It provides:

(1) Subject to sub-section (3) below, the circumstances in which the original purposes of a charitable gift can be altered to allow the property given or part of it to be applied cy-près are:

    (a) where the original purposes, in whole or in part –
        (i) have been as far as may be fulfilled, or
        (ii) cannot be carried out, or not according to the directions given and to the spirit of the gift,
    (b) where the original purposes provide for use for part only of the property available by virtue of the gift,
    (c) where–

        (i) the property available by virtue of the gift, and
        (ii) other property applicable for similar purposes,

can be more effectively used in conjunction, and to that end can suitably, regard being had to the appropriate considerations, be made applicable to common purposes; or

    (d) where the original purposes were laid down by reference to –

        (i) an area which then was but has since ceased to be a unit for some other purpose, or
        (ii) a class of persons or an area which has for any reason since ceased to be suitable, regard being had to the appropriate considerations, or to be practical in administering the gift, or

    (e) where the original purposes, in whole or in part, have, since they were laid down –

        (i) been adequately provided by other means,
        (ii) ceased, as being useless or harmful to the community or for other reasons, to be in law charitable, or
        (iii) ceased in any other way to provide a suitable and effective method of using the property available by virtue of the gift, regard being had to the appropriate considerations.

(2) In sub-section (1) above 'the appropriate considerations' means –

    (a) (on the one hand) the spirit of the gift concerned, and
    (b) (on the other) the social and economic circumstances prevailing at the time of the proposed alteration of the original purposes.

(3) Sub-section (1) does not affect the conditions which must be satisfied in order that property given for charitable purposes may be applied cy-près except in so far as those conditions require a failure of the original purposes.

The Court of Appeal exercised its powers under these provisions (then s 13 of the Charities Act 1993) in *Versani v Jesani* [1999] Ch 219, which considered a charity for the provision of facilities for worship at a temple for adherents to a particular sect of the

Hindu religion. Unfortunately, the sect split into two factions on the death of its founder: the first recognised the founder's successor; the second refused to do so. As a result, the two factions refused to worship together, with the second group being excluded from the temple. The Court of Appeal held that the requirement of what is now section 62(e)(iii) of the 2011 Act was made out, as the original purpose of the charity had ceased to provide a suitable and effective method of using the charity's property, having regard to the spirit of the gift. It directed a division of the charity's funds between the two rival factions.

Summary

- Charitable trusts have a number of important differences from private (ie non-charitable) trusts. They do not have to satisfy the beneficiary principle, the rules of certainty and perpetuity do not apply as stringently, and the doctrine of cy-près can apply to save them from failure. They also carry a number of fiscal advantages.

- A valid charitable trust must satisfy two basic requirements:

  1. The purpose(s) for which the trust property is to be held and applied must be (exclusively) charitable, and
  2. The trust must benefit (some section of) the public.

- Traditionally, charitable purposes have been defined by reference to the preamble to the Charitable Uses Act 1601 (the Statute of Elizabeth I). The case law categorised the purposes described in that preamble under four heads, namely:

  1. the relief of poverty;
  2. the advancement of education;
  3. the advancement of religion; and
  4. other purposes beneficial to the community.

- This categorisation has now been overtaken by a new statutory definition contained in the Charities Act 2011, section 2(1) of which provides that a trust will be charitable if it falls within one of the 13 purposes set out in section 3(1).

- As was the case before the 2011 Act, new charitable purposes can be developed incrementally and by analogy to existing categories of charitable purpose.

- Trusts which would bring no discernible benefit to the public or which would prove positively harmful cannot be charitable.

- The public benefit requirement also demands that the opportunity to benefit from the trust should not be unreasonably restricted to a certain sub-section of the public. However, how this rule is interpreted and applied differs depending on the nature of the charitable purpose. Though in some cases the courts have stressed that the opportunity to benefit cannot be reserved for a class of people defined by some personal connection or 'nexus' to the settlor, other cases – particular in the field of trusts to relieve poverty – have allowed this.

- Trusts for political purposes cannot be charitable. This prohibits trusts whose purposes include the promotion of a particular political party or ideology and those which are directed towards securing a particular change in the law or governmental policy either in the UK or overseas.

- If a particular charitable trust or disposition becomes impossible or impracticable to administer or if one of the tests set down in section 62 of the Charities Act 2011 applies, the funds may nonetheless be applied for a similar charitable purpose under the doctrine of cy-près. This doctrine applies automatically in cases of *subsequent* failure – that is where the disposition fails only after having first taken effect. In the case of *initial* failure – where the disposition fails at the outset – the cy-près doctrine will apply only where the donor can be found to have had a *general* or *paramount* charitable intention.

Exercises

5.1   'The Charities Act 2011 merely codifies the principles laid down by the case law.' Discuss.

5.2   What are the main differences between private (ie non-charitable) and charitable trusts?

5.3   Why should the law require that an effective charitable trust fit within (or be analogous to) an existing head of charitable purpose? Why not give charitable status to *all* trusts which benefit a sufficient section of the public?

5.4   Why is a trust to support my poor relatives charitable? Why is a trust to educate my uneducated relatives not charitable?

5.5   What reasons have been given by the courts for denying charitable status to political purposes? Are these reasons justifiable?

5.6   What is the doctrine of cy-près? How does it differ from the approach taken in cases such as *Re Faraker* and *Re Finger's Will Trusts*? Is the requirement of a general charitable intention appropriate and/or workable?

Further reading

The Charity Commission website is an invaluable source of further information about charitable trusts: http://www.charity-commission.gov.uk

Charity Commission, *Charities and Public Benefit* (January 2008)

Charity Commission, *Speaking Out: Guidance on Campaigning and Political Activity by Charities* (CC9, October 2008)

Charity Commission, *The Advancement of Religion for the Public Benefit* (December 2008)

Charity Commission, *The Prevention or Relief of Poverty for the Public Benefit* (December 2008)

Hackney, 'Charities and public benefit' (2008) 124 LQR 347

Harris, 'The politics of the chancery' (1981) 34 CLP 113

Luxton, *Parliament v The Charity Commission* (Politeia 2009) (available at http://politeia.co.uk/p109.pdf)

Mitchell and Moody, *Foundations of Charity Law* (Hart Publishing 2000)

Moffat, *Trusts Law: Text and Materials* (5th edn, Cambridge University Press 2009), 913–1080

Warburton, 'Charitable trusts – unique?' [1999] Conv 20

Chapter 6

Formalities

6.1 Requirements of form

When you have an interest in property, you are generally, perhaps invariably, entitled to deal with that interest in certain ways. You can transfer the interest on to another person. Often you can carve out lesser interests from your own, for example where a land owner grants a lease or mortgage of the property. Somewhere between the two there is of course the possibility of creating a trust of it. If you want to dispose of your property in one of these ways, the law commonly requires you not simply to form and express your intention to make such a disposition, but also to take certain additional steps. Sometimes you are required to accompany the intention with some physical act, such as where title to assets is passed by physical delivery. Sometimes a third party is required to do something to complete the transaction, such as where the donee has to be entered on a register as the new owner. Sometimes you are simply required to manifest your intention in a certain way, often in a signed document. Rules of this final type are known as formality requirements. What rules apply to the proposed dealing will depend primarily on the nature of the property involved (shares, land, chattels, etc.) and what interest you are seeking to confer ('ownership', a charge, a lease, etc.; whether the interest is legal or equitable).

The reasons for putting such rules in place vary with the context. In relation to formality provisions at least, they tend to be reserved for dealings the law regards as having particular significance, and hence where it is in everyone's interests for it to be clear about what exactly is going on, and where the relevant parties are likely to be making use of legal advice in any case, so they will not end up stymied by unknown legal rules. All such rules promote clarity in property dealing because they require something more overt and often more permanent than an oral expression of intent, commonly through documentation or physical transfer, meaning that the parties themselves, and ultimately the courts, are more likely to know what has gone on. It is also often argued that, because of this, such rules serve a 'cautionary' function, allowing and encouraging you to think twice about what you are doing (see generally Fuller, 1941).

Whatever the rules and whatever their reasons, it is vital to appreciate what having rules like these means; namely, that a party must do more than simply form and express an intention to make a particular disposition of his property for that disposition to be effective. Without more, the law will not give effect to the intended disposition and the party's wishes will not be fulfilled. Because of this, it is inevitable that where we have such rules there will be situations where, even though we know for sure what the parties intended, we nonetheless refuse to give effect to their intentions simply because they did not satisfy the procedure the law has set down for such transactions. For instance, it may be beyond doubt that a testator wished his property to go to X on his death, but, because he failed to express this intention in the requisite form, the law says that it must go to Y.

Doing this of course sticks in the throat, because we know that we are defeating the testator's intentions in an area of the law where intentions usually count. Nevertheless, this is a necessary consequence of having such requirements. A rule that a certain type of transaction must take a particular form to be effective is a formality rule. A rule that such a transaction must take a particular form *unless it is otherwise clear that this is what the parties intended* is a rule requiring *no* formality, as it means that we are ultimately concerned only with what the parties intended irrespective of the form in which that intention was expressed.

Because of this, we cannot justify creating exceptions to formality requirements in order to avoid defeating the parties' intentions, as the 'exception' would eat up the rule (though we may be able to defend exceptions with other rationales). In other words, if, despite the presence of a formality rule, we allow informal but clearly intended transactions to be effective because we do not want to defeat the parties' intentions, the formality becomes merely an option rather than a requirement. If we think there are good reasons for imposing a formality requirement, we must be prepared to stomach the apparent injustice done to parties whose intentions are defeated through a failure to satisfy that requirement. We can prevent such injustices only by abandoning the requirement of formality, in which case we lose the benefits of requiring formality. We cannot have it both ways. Nonetheless, as we shall see, it is evident that the courts have on occasion been seduced by the apparent injustices to which such rules can give rise on individual facts. One may well argue that these are prime instances of hard cases making bad law (though see Lord Denning MR's comments on this in *Re Vandervell's Trusts (No. 2)* [1974] Ch 269, 322).

6.2   Modes of transferring the beneficial interest in property

If you own property, one way you can 'deal' with that property is to pass the beneficial interest in it to someone else. The most obvious way of doing this is simply to transfer your entire interest in that asset to the other person. This is what happens when you give a birthday present. It also happens when you hand over money in a shop in exchange for goods. In each case, the recipient or donee gets exactly what you had to begin with. (There is, of course, a difference between the two examples, as in the second case you get something in return for what you gave. We tend not to call these gifts. However, the form of transfer is the same in both cases.)

However, that is not the only way in which the beneficial interest in an asset can be passed. The law provides a facility whereby you can carve off the beneficial part of your interest, retaining what is left. This facility is, of course, the trust. The donee or beneficiary obtains not the interest which you had at the outset but rather a new, equitable beneficial interest in the property. As we have seen, you can create a trust in two ways. You can declare that you will now hold the property, which you previously held outright, on trust for the intended beneficiary. Alternatively, you can transfer your interest to a third party on terms that he then holds it on trust for the beneficiary. In the first case you are the trustee, retaining your interest; in the second the third party becomes trustee and you, having disposed of your interest, drop out of the picture.

This therefore leaves us with three distinct ways of passing the beneficial interest in property:

1. outright transfer of your interest;
2. self-declaration of a trust of that interest, whereby you then hold the property on trust and a new equitable interest arises in the beneficiary;
3. transfer to a third-party trustee on trust for the beneficiary, whereby your interest passes to the trustee and, as before, a new equitable interest arises in the beneficiary.

Although, in a rough sense, all three bring about the same end result, in that the donee receives the right to the benefit of the property (indeed, by virtue of *Saunders v Vautier* (see Section 2.7), they may all enable the donee to get hold of the property), they are distinct modes of transfer. The law leaves you free to choose between them whenever you wish to benefit someone 'through' your property. Which you choose will depend on which best serves your plans. Importantly, however, each method has its own distinct rules, its own steps, which must be followed if the intended transaction is to be effective.

Mode (1) involves the application of those rules which govern how property interests can be passed from one person to another, such that the recipient receives the very same interest that the transferor started off with. So, for instance, transferring legal title to tangible property can be effected by physical delivery of the transfer to the donee, accompanied by an intention thereby to pass title; land transfers require the execution of a deed, and if the land is registered this must be followed by entry of the new proprietor on the register; debts can be transferred by writing accompanied by notice of the assignment to the debtor.

Mode (2), by contrast, involves no such transfer of the donor's interest. Rather, in such cases, the 'donor' retains *his* interest but creates a new interest, an equitable beneficial interest, in the 'donee'. The rules which apply are accordingly different. As we saw in Chapter 3, as a general rule, the law does not require one's intention to create a trust to be manifested in any particular form. In most cases, it is enough that the 'donor' or settlor expresses his intention in *some* way. The two principal exceptions, which we will look at in greater detail below, are trusts of land and trusts which are to take effect on the settlor's death (testamentary trusts).

Mode (3) requires the application of *both* sets of rules just discussed. This is because the settlor is not just creating a trust, as in mode (2), but also transferring *his* interest in the property to a third party, the trustee, calling into play the rules applied in mode (1). Hence, more formal requirements stand in the way of someone who wants a third party to act as trustee for the intended beneficiary, than for someone who is happy to do the job himself. Whereas the latter needs only to declare the trust effectively, the former needs to do both this *and* to ensure that his own interest is transferred to the trustee. This latter requirement – that the trustees have vested in them the property to be held on trust – is known as the rule that the trust be properly constituted. Until the trustee has the settlor's interest transferred to him, the trust is said to be incompletely constituted and so has no effect.

6.3 Imperfect gifts

It can be seen then that, of the modes of beneficial transfer set out in Section 6.2, some require more than others. In particular, mode (2), self-declaration of trust, generally requires much less than modes (1) and (3). The question therefore arises whether a donor, who tries to confer a benefit using modes (1) or (3), but fails because he did not take all the necessary steps, can be treated as having declared himself a trustee for his intended beneficiary under mode (2), because this usually requires nothing more than an expressed intent to create a trust. The argument in favour of doing so would be that, though the donor's chosen method was not effective, we should do what we can to give effect to his more general intention to confer a benefit on the other party. The courts have, however, traditionally rejected this argument, holding that, although individuals are free to pick whichever mode of beneficial transfer they like, once they have made their choice they must stick with it. We saw an example of this in Chapter 3 with *Jones v Lock* (1865) 1 Ch App 25, where the father was unsuccessful in transferring the cheque to his baby son (Section 3.2), and see also *Richards v Delbridge* (1874) LR 18 Eq 11.

The leading case is *Milroy v Lord* (1862) 4 De G F & J 264, in which a shareholder sought to make a transfer of his shares, but used a deed rather than the form required by the company for such transfers. The Court of Appeal held that the attempted transfer failed and that the ineffective outright transfer could not be regarded as an effective declaration of trust. Turner LJ stated the law as follows:

> I take the law of this court to be well settled, that, in order to render a voluntary settlement valid and effectual, the settlor must have done everything which, according to the nature of the property comprised in the settlement, was necessary to be done in order to transfer the property and render the settlement binding upon him. He may, of course, do this by actually transferring the property to the persons for whom he intends to provide, and the provision will then be effectual, and it will be equally effectual if he transfers the property to a trustee for the purposes of the settlement, or declares that he himself holds it on trust for those purposes ... but, in order to render the settlement binding, one or other of these modes must ... be resorted to, for there is no equity in this court to perfect an imperfect gift. The cases, I think, go further to this extent: that if the settlement is intended to be effectuated by one of the modes to which I have referred, the court will not give effect to it by applying another of those modes. If it is intended to take effect by transfer, the court will not hold the intended transfer to operate as a declaration of trust, for then every imperfect instrument would be made effectual by being converted into a perfect trust.

As Turner LJ notes, this refusal to treat an ineffective transfer as an effective declaration of trust is reflected in the maxim 'equity will not perfect an imperfect gift'. If you fail in effecting a gift through your chosen mode, you cannot then ask equity to help you out by treating you as having declared yourself a trustee of that property. Whether this rather unforgiving stance should be supported is far from clear, but this strict approach starts to look all the more questionable when you consider that many would-be donors, unaware of the panoply of options provided by law, will not have in mind any one of these specific modes of gift giving. Rather, many donors will have cruder, generalised intentions to benefit (see further Section 3.2). In such cases, it becomes slightly unreal to maintain that the donor has committed himself to one of these modes, and hence even less justifiable to hold that equity should not intervene to give (some sort of) effect to his intentions.

An unusual and fortuitous avoidance of the harshness of this approach is provided by *T Choithram International SA v Pagarani* [2001] 1 WLR 1. The donor wanted to set up a foundation, to which he would transfer much of his wealth. A trust deed was drawn up to such effect, with the donor himself as one of the trustees, and the donor made an announcement to the effect that he had transferred his wealth to the foundation. However, the donor died before ever executing the documents necessary to transfer legal title to his various assets to the trustees named in the trust deed. The Privy Council was nonetheless able to hold that the trust had been effectively set up.

First, it was held that, given the context, the donor's statement 'I am transferring my wealth to the foundation' was to be understood as meaning 'I am transferring my wealth to the trustees of the foundation on the trusts declared in the trust deed'. Accordingly unlike, for instance, *Jones v Lock*, this was not an attempt to make an outright transfer but was in fact an attempt to create a trust. Second, because the donor himself was one of the trustees, so far as *he* was concerned, no transfer of title to the relevant assets was needed for the trust to be constituted. In other words, he had made an effective self-declaration of trust. Although, as the trust deed provided, it was intended that there would be a number of trustees, the court held that it was enough that title to the relevant assets was vested in one of those trustees (though he would then be under an obligation to have the assets transferred into the names of the other intended trustees as well). Hence, the trust succeeded in *Choithram* only because the donor himself was to be one of the trustees. If it was not for this, the trust would have been ineffective and the donor's intentions thwarted.

6.4 The rule in *Re Rose*

The *Milroy v Lord* approach can also work (apparent) injustice in another way. This is because the failure of the gift may be not be the fault of the donor (or indeed the donee). As was mentioned in passing in Section 6.2 (and see further Section 7.1), sometimes the law requires some third party to act before the transfer of an interest will be effective. This is most commonly the case where there is a register on which the donee must be entered before the property is regarded as having been effectively transferred to him, as is the case in some land and share dealings. In such cases the donor and donee are completely reliant on this third person – a person with whom they will usually have no connection or relationship beyond this transaction – doing his job properly. It is one thing to defeat an intended gift where the parties have only themselves to blame, quite another where they were powerless to do more.

This argument was accepted by the Court of Appeal in *Re Rose* [1952] 1 Ch 499. The donor, Mr Rose, wanted to transfer his shares to the claimants. Accordingly he filled in the relevant share transfer forms, handed these along with the share certificates to the claimants, who then passed them on to the company so that the claimants could be registered as the new shareholders. The company then registered the claimants as shareholders in place of Mr Rose, and the transfer of legal title to the shares was at that point complete. Mr Rose, however, died a few years later and the question arose whether estate duty (a tax on beneficial transfers of property made within a certain period prior to the transferor's death) was due in respect of the transfer. This depended on the exact date at which the claimants became beneficial owners of the shares. The court held that, though legal title passed only when the claimants were registered by the company as the new shareholders, the beneficial interest passed earlier when Mr Rose transferred the completed share transfer forms to the claimants.

Why was this? The court considered that, once he had handed over the forms, Mr Rose was no longer at liberty to cancel the transfer or to retain any dividends subsequently declared on the shares. From this it followed that Mr Rose no longer remained beneficially entitled to the shares. Instead the court decided that he held them on trust for the claimants from the moment he handed over the forms to them and up until the point they were registered as the new shareholders and legal title passed. Hence, though Mr Rose did not intend to create a trust of the shares, intending instead only to transfer them outright to the claimants, the court held that a trust arose pending the completion of that transfer. The court distinguished cases like *Milroy v Lord* and *Jones v Lock* on the basis that there the donors had failed to follow the procedure required for a legally effective transfer of the relevant property. Here, by contrast, the donor had adopted the correct procedure – indeed the gift was ultimately effective – the issue was simply at what date the beneficial interest passed. So the question was not whether equity should intervene to correct a flawed transfer, but simply whether equity should come in to accelerate a transfer which was as yet incomplete but in no way defective.

The factor stressed in the judgments of both Evershed MR and Jenkins LJ was that the donor here, unlike in *Milroy v Lord*, had done everything in his power to make the transfer effective. Accordingly, *Re Rose* has long been regarded as authority for the proposition that, where you seek to make an outright transfer of property, once you have taken all the steps you are required to take to make such a transfer effective and even though there are further steps *others* must take before the transfer will be completed, you will hold the property on trust for your intended transferee. Importantly, the principle applies and the trust arises irrespective of whether the transfer is later completed. Where it is subsequently completed, as it was in *Re Rose*, the trust comes to an end at the moment title passes.

Another example of this principle is *Mascall v Mascall* (1984) 50 P & CR 119, where a father, seeking to transfer land to his son, had executed and handed over to him a deed of transfer and the land certificate. Before the son passed these on to the Land Registry so that he could be registered as the new proprietor, as is needed for the transfer to be complete, the parties fell out and the father changed his mind about the transfer. However, as the father had done everything in his power to make the transfer effective, the court concluded that he held the land on trust for his son.

For a long time the rule in *Re Rose*, though not uncontroversial, was at least clear. However, the position is no longer so certain following the Court of Appeal's apparent extension of the rule in *Pennington v Waine* [2002] EWCA Civ 227; [2002] 1 WLR 2075. There the donor, Ada, wanted to transfer 400 shares to her nephew, Harold. She therefore contacted Pennington, who represented the company's auditors, and instructed him to prepare a share transfer form. She completed this and returned it to Pennington, who placed it on the auditors' files but never passed it on to the company. This meant that Harold was not registered as the new shareholder and so did not acquire legal title to the shares. When Ada died the question arose as to whether Harold had any claim to them. The problem was that here, unlike in *Re Rose*, Ada had not done everything she could have done to effect the gift, as she had not handed over the completed transfer form to either Harold or the company. Nonetheless, the Court concluded that Ada's actions were sufficient to give rise to a trust of the shares in favour of Harold.

Arden and Clarke LJJ both gave judgments, the third judge, Schiemann LJ, agreeing with them both. Arden LJ, echoing the approach of the court in *Re Rose*, asked whether Ada would have been free to go back on the intended transfer. On the facts – particularly that Ada had transferred the form to Pennington with a view to his securing Harold's registration as shareholder, that she had told Harold about the gift and that no action on his part was necessary, and that Harold had agreed to be a director of the company, for which a shareholding was needed – Arden LJ concluded that it would have been unconscionable for Ada to change her mind. Accordingly, Ada held the shares on trust for Harold.

Clarke LJ took a different approach. He began by noting that, whereas legal title to the shares could pass only with registration, an equitable title could be conferred without this. The question then is what steps need to be taken to effect an equitable assignment of the shares. *Re Rose* showed that completion of share transfer forms followed by their delivery to the donee or the company was sufficient for the donee to acquire an equitable interest in shares, and Clarke LJ asked whether this second step of delivery was essential. His view was that there was no reason in principle or in authority for regarding this as a necessary step. Accordingly, Clarke LJ held that, provided the donor intended the transfer to have immediate effect, simply completing the appropriate share transfer form was all it took to confer on the donee an equitable interest in those shares.

The decision in *Pennington v Waine* is problematic. For a start, regardless of whether one considers the principle set down in *Re Rose* as a positive step, it at least left the law in a tolerably certain state. The idea that a trust would arise when, but only when, the donor had done everything in his power to make the transfer effective, could be applied more or less straightforwardly whatever the property being transferred. By contrast, Pennington leaves the law in some doubt. We know what suffices in respect of shares, but what of other forms of property which have different transfer procedures? For instance, what steps are sufficient (following Arden LJ) to make it unconscionable for a donor to deny a transfer of land or (following Clarke LJ) to effect an equitable assignment of that land? Certainly the approaches taken by the Court provide no assistance.

First, Clarke LJ's preference for the language of 'equitable assignment' should not obscure the fact that what he is talking about is the creation of a trust. So, when he says that the key question is what steps are necessary for an equitable assignment of the shares, what he is really asking is what is needed for the creation of a trust of those shares. Now, *if* Ada had sought to create a trust of the shares, it is uncontroversial that no share transfer form would need to be delivered to the beneficiary or to the company; indeed no share transfer form would need even to be completed. But the key point is that Ada was not attempting to create a trust; she intended to make an outright transfer. So, the question Clarke LJ needed, but failed, to answer is why we should treat a failed outright transfer as a successful creation of a trust, the very thing *Milroy v Lord* says we should not do.

Arden LJ's analysis is no better. Her requirement of unconscionability is entirely question begging, as it gives us no basis for determining *when* and *why* it becomes unconscionable for a donor to change his mind about a transfer of property, and hence when and why a trust arises. A comparison with the equitable doctrine of proprietary estoppel is illustrative. In estoppel cases, an owner of property is likewise held to a representation or promise that he will give or has given that property (or some interest in it) to the claimant where it would be unconscionable for him to change his mind. However, the courts have made clear that this will be unconscionable only where the claimant has detrimentally relied on the owner's promise or representation (see eg *Gillett v Holt* [2001] Ch 210, Section 6.7). In *Pennington*, the nearest thing we have to detrimental reliance is Harold agreeing to act as a director, though losing this directorship could scarcely be said to leave Harold in a worse position than he was in at the outset. Certainly Arden LJ made no reference to detrimental reliance, which strongly suggests that she did not view it as necessary (though see *Curtis v Pulbrook* [2011] EWHC 167 (Ch); [2011] 1 BCLC 638, where the trust in *Pennington* is explained on this basis). However, without such a requirement, not only is there an inconsistency between *Pennington* and the law on estoppel, but it also leaves it unclear why the Court should consider that it would have been unconscionable for Ada to have changed her mind. Indeed the same criticism can be made of the Court of Appeal's conclusion in *Re Rose* that Mr Rose would not have been permitted to change his mind about the transfer, notwithstanding that title had yet to pass and the absence of detrimental reliance. Very simply, if nobody would be harmed, why should we not be free to change our minds?

Most recently, the Court of Appeal decision in *Zeital v Kaye* [2010] EWCA Civ 159; [2010] 2 BCLC 1 shows a preference for the original *Re Rose* formulation. Here too the question concerned beneficial title to shares. The deceased was the beneficiary of a trust of two shares, which he had intended in his lifetime to pass to his partner, Stefka. He handed over to Stefka two share transfer forms (one with Stefka's name and address filled in, the other not), but failed also to provide the share certificates. Though the court mentioned *Pennington* without disapproval, it proceeded on the basis that Stefka could establish a beneficial interest in those shares only if the deceased had done all in his power to affect such a transfer. As the deceased had equitable rather than legal title to shares, any such transfer would have to satisfy section 53(1)(c) of the Law of Property Act 1925, which requires documentation signed by the donor. The deceased had not done this, so necessarily he had not done all that he could have done to make such a transfer. The claim therefore failed.

The general issue underlying all of these cases is that, whatever the ambit of the rule in *Re Rose*, but especially if we follow *Pennington v Waine*, we need to be able to explain why equity is entitled to override or circumvent the legal rules as to the transfer of proprietary interests. Although *Re Rose* looks fair because it is an example of equity helping people give effect to their intentions, we must ask why it is that the gift was otherwise ineffective. Why do we need equity's help here? The reason, of course, is that the law has imposed rules as to what is required before proprietary interests can be effectively created and transferred, and these rules have not been followed. As we saw previously (Section 6.1), such rules may further any number of ends, though principally a desire for certainty and clarity in property dealings. In any case, there will invariably be some policy reason for requiring such dealings to go ahead in a certain way. When equity gives (rough) effect to a transaction despite the requisite steps not having been taken, it is effectively overriding these rules and the policies underlying them.

Whether this is a good thing or not depends on your view of how we ought to balance, on the one hand, the policies such as certainty and clarity underlying these formality rules and, on the other, the desire not to defeat people's clear intentions. But, as before, we cannot have it both ways. Having rules which restrict the way property interests are transferred will necessarily mean that on occasion we have to defeat clearly intended transactions. If equity helps the parties out simply on the basis that otherwise their intentions would be defeated, it overrides these rules and disregards the policies which underlie them. If the courts are to be able to justify such intervention, they need to say why we can afford, and why they are entitled, to ignore the clear policy choices that the legal, often statutory, rules on the passing of property embody.

6.5   The rule in *Strong v Bird*

There are three further exceptions to the general rule that equity will not perfect imperfect gifts which are worth flagging up here.

First, there is what is known as the rule in *Strong v Bird* (1874) LR 18 Eq 315. *Strong v Bird* itself concerned the enforcement of debts. A was owed money by B; however, though A had never formally released the debt, A had manifested a clear intention that she would not demand payment. When A died, B was appointed executor of her will. The court held that this, when combined with A's continuing intention to release the debt, had the effect that the debt could not now be enforced by those who would otherwise have inherited it from A.

This rule was subsequently extended to imperfect gifts: *Re Stewart* [1908] 2 Ch 251. Say A intends to make a gift of certain property to B, but fails to fulfil the requirements set down for an effective outright transfer of that property. This leaves us with an imperfect gift. Let us further assume that A has not even taken the steps necessary for the rule in *Re Rose* to apply. Nonetheless, provided A at no point changed his mind about the transfer, the gift will be perfected, and B will take the property absolutely, if A dies and B is appointed as executor of A's will. When you die, all your property becomes vested in your executor, who has the job of paying off your debts and then distributing the remaining property under the terms of your will. Accordingly, as executor, B will receive title to the property A intended to give to him, and the rule in *Strong v Bird* says that he is free to keep it for himself rather than to dispose of it under the terms of A's will. The rule also applies where A dies intestate – in which case no executor will be identified by A – but B becomes administrator of the estate, again the result of which is that the property becomes vested in the administrator: *Re James* [1935] Ch 449; cf *Re Gonin* [1964] Ch 288.

It is important to stress that the rule operates to perfect imperfect gifts and so applies only where A had intended to make an immediate transfer of the property to B. It is not enough that A did intend at some point to make such a transfer, but had yet to take any steps to achieving this: *Re Freeland* [1952] Ch 110.

6.6 *Donationes mortis causa*

Second, there are *donationes mortis causa* or 'deathbed gifts'. These occur where A, contemplating that he may die shortly, hands over property, or something representing that property (eg car keys represent the relevant car, title to land is represented by its title deeds), to B, on the condition that B is to keep the property only if A does indeed die: see *Cain v Moon* [1896] 2 QB 283; *Sen v Headley* [1991] Ch 425. In such circumstances, if A does die as contemplated, B obtains title to the property notwithstanding that the usual formalities for the transfer of such property may not have been satisfied. By contrast, if A does not die – indeed at any point before his death – A can revoke the gift and the property remains at his free disposal. By saying that the gift must be made in contemplation of death, it seems clear that the gift must be made in the context of a particular risk to A's life, typically a life-threatening illness, though there is no reason this should not also cover dangerous journeys or going to war.

Donationes mortis causa tend to be seen to straddle the categories of inter vivos and testamentary dispositions. Like testamentary transfers, the gift becomes irrevocable only upon A's death. On this basis, it is common to see them held up as exceptions to the formality provisions of the Wills Act 1837 (on which see Section 6.9). However, in contrast to ordinary testamentary dispositions, it appears that A must intend to make an *immediate* gift, albeit one which remains defeasible until A dies: see eg *Solicitor to the Treasury v Lewis* [1900] 2 Ch 812; *Re Ward* [1946] 2 All ER 206. As such, it may be that the 'dehors the will' theory, which does such a poor job of explaining secret trusts (see Section 6.13), can be applied here to explain why these dispositions fall outside the reach of the Wills Act.

6.7 Proprietary estoppel

The final exception to the general rule that equity will not perfect imperfect gifts comes from the doctrine of proprietary estoppel. Though the courts have been reluctant to nail down either the precise circumstances in which the doctrine will apply or the basis of the rights it creates, the basic idea is as follows:

1. If A represents or promises to B that B has or will be given some interest in A's property, and
2. B relies on the expectation of having or acquiring such an interest, such that
3. he would suffer a detriment (ie would be left worse off) if A was to deny B such an interest, then B can make a claim on the basis of proprietary estoppel (see eg *Thorner v Major* [2009] UKHL 18; [2009] 1 WLR 776, [29] (Lord Walker); cf *Gillett v Holt* [2001] Ch 210; *Wilmott v Barber* (1880) 15 Ch D 96).

The court then has a discretion as to how this should be remedied. So, although it is common, perhaps usual, for the court to hold that B should receive the very interest he was promised (eg *Pascoe v Turner* [1979] 1 WLR 431), this is not the only possibility. It may instead decide that B should be given some lesser interest in the property or indeed some other award, with the courts, particularly in recent years, stressing that the remedy must be proportionate to B's detrimental reliance (see eg *Jennings v Rice* [2002] EWCA Civ 159; [2003] 1 P & CR 8; Gardner, 2006).

As such, it is clear that proprietary estoppel is far more than a mechanism for perfecting imperfect gifts. Not only does it apply even where no gift has been intended (for instance where A simply *promises* he will give B an interest in his property), the effect of estoppel claims is not necessarily to give B the interest he was promised (or its equitable equivalent). As such it seems that the point of proprietary estoppel is not (simply) to give effect to A's intentions, but rather to make good or pre-empt the harm suffered by those who have detrimentally relied on representations and promises relating to the acquisition of property. (For a fuller analysis of proprietary estoppel see Gardner and MacKenzie, 2012, ch 8.)

6.8　Trusts of land

Creating a trust usually requires nothing more than the formation and expression of an intent to create a trust (though of course it must also meet the requirements of a valid trust, such as the three certainties – see Section 3.1). This means that a trust can usually be declared orally. No additional steps or conduct are required of the settlor for the trust to be fully effective, save to ensure that, where he is not himself to be one of the trustees, the trust is fully constituted by the transfer of his title to the property to the trustees. There are, however, exceptions to this. The first concerns trusts of land.

The relevant statutory provision is section 53(1)(b) of the Law of Property Act 1925:

> A declaration of trust respecting any land or any interest therein must be manifested and proved by some writing signed by some person who is able to declare such trust or by his will.

Also relevant is section 53(2), which states: 'This section does not affect the creation or operation of resulting, implied or constructive trusts.' Why treat land differently from other forms of property? Traditionally land has been the most (socially, economically, politically) important type of property, and hence it matters that much more who has a claim to it. It is accordingly a context in which the policy of certainty and clarity in property dealings exerts a strong pull. Dealings in land also tend to be slow and commonly involve lawyers, so requiring formality is less likely to get in the way or to catch the participants to such transactions unaware. The same connection between land and formality can be seen elsewhere; hence, contracts can usually be made entirely orally, but contracts to dispose of interests in land must be made in writing (see section 2 of the Law of Property (Miscellaneous Provisions) Act 1989).

So what does this provision mean (see too Youdan, 1984)? For a start, it is clear that it does not require that declarations of trusts of land are *made* in writing. The formality requirement is satisfied by any signed document which evidences the existence and terms of the trust. As such, it is enough for the trust to be evidenced by some document drawn up after, even long after, the settlor expressed his intention to create the trust (see eg *Gardner v Rowe* (1828) 5 Russ 258 – a case concerning the forerunner of section 53(1) (b), section 7 of the Statute of Frauds 1677).

What if no signed document exists? Here there is disagreement as to the nature and meaning of the rule set down in section 53(1)(b). One view is that it sets down a rule of validity: unless and until there is a signed document which provides evidence of the trust, *there is no trust*. The alternative view is that it sets out a rule of evidence: it is not that writing is needed to *create* a trust of land, rather signed documentation is needed if a party is going to be able to *prove* the existence of the trust to a court. The wording of section 53(1)(b) could reasonably be understood either way. (It is sometimes assumed that the existence of the word 'evidenced' in the provision shows that the rule set down is a rule of evidence rather than one of validity. But this is obviously wrong. A provision which said 'No trust is valid unless evidenced in writing' would clearly set out a rule of validity.) What distinguishes the two views is the status of 'trusts' which are (as yet) not backed up by any signed documentation. On the former view, there is simply no trust at all; the settlor's attempted declaration of trust has no legal effect whatsoever. On the latter view, we would have to say that there *is* a trust; it is simply that the beneficiary cannot enforce it in court as the court will not recognise its existence without writing.

The cases provide no clear answer. *Gardner v Rowe* tells us that when the document post-dates the settlor's declaration of trust, the trust is seen to have been validly declared when the settlor made his original oral declaration. But this is compatible with the interpretation of section 53(1)(b) as setting out a rule of validity; it would simply mean that, once such a document is in existence, the trust takes effect retrospectively. On the face of it, the courts seem to think that the rule is one of validity (see eg *Gissing v Gissing* [1971] AC 886, 905; *Hodgson v Marks* [1971] Ch 892; *Lloyds Bank plc v Rosset* [1991] 1 AC 107, 129; and, for a particularly recent example, *Hanchett-Stamford v A-G* [2008] EWHC 330 (Ch); [2009] Ch 173, [25]), though often these statements are weakened by the (mistaken) suggestion that the declaration of trust need be *made*, rather than merely *evidenced*, in writing. Moreover, the rule of validity interpretation avoids a number of difficulties created by understanding the provision as establishing a rule of evidence. (For instance, are we to say that the trustee of an oral trust of land is indeed under a duty – albeit an unenforceable one – to administer the intended trust? What if the matter does go to court? The court would presumably hold that, in the absence of admissible evidence, there is no trust of the land. Should we still say that there *is* such a trust, but that it simply is and remains incapable of proof?) As such, it may be that the better view is to follow the courts' lead and to treat the rule as one of validity and to see a declaration of trust of land which is not (yet) backed up by signed documentation as wholly ineffective.

The application of section 53(1)(b) is uncomplicated where the settlor seeks to declare himself trustee of the land. Here the effect of the provision is that the trust is unenforceable and neither the settlor nor his successors can be compelled to abide by the declared trust, leaving them free to keep and use the property for themselves. Things become a little more difficult, however, where, rather than declaring himself trustee, the settlor, A, transfers land to B to hold on trust, whether for A himself or for some third party, C. Section 53(1)(b) suggests that, in the absence of writing, the trust cannot be enforced. However, the transfer of title from A to B would remain fully effective, so the apparent result is that B is, in practice, free to take the land for himself. This is problematic however; not because this would defeat A's intentions (as we have seen, this is an inevitable consequence of any formality rule), but because it would leave B free to treat the property as his own, despite the fact that he undertook to hold the property on trust and that A transferred it to him only on that basis. Of course, we may still feel that the policy of the statute is so important that we must put up with this. But this is not the approach the courts have taken.

The courts have always been reluctant to allow someone to keep for himself property which he clearly understood and agreed was not to be his. The frequently cited maxim in this context is 'equity will not allow a statute to be used as an instrument of fraud'. In other words, you cannot keep property in breach of your promise by falling back on the lack of statutory formality. This is fair enough. However, saying that B cannot keep the property for himself does not tell us for whom he should hold it. One option is to make B hold the property on the agreed terms, that is, for the intended beneficiary, A or C as the case may be. In this case we would be giving effect to the trust A intended and, it seems, simply disregarding the statute. However, there is another option, namely to make B hold it on trust for the settlor, A, on the basis that A's intended trust failed for not satisfying the formality rules, but, as B should not be allowed to keep the property for himself, the equitable interest should revert back to A. This is – or looks like – a resulting trust (we shall examine resulting trusts in Chapter 8). This option would, of course, not give effect to the settlor's intentions, but has the advantage of not trampling all over the statute and its underlying policy.

It is not entirely clear which of these two approaches represents the law. This is because the leading authorities – *Rochefoucauld v Boustead* [1897] 1 Ch 196, *Bannister v Bannister* [1948] 2 All ER 133 – are two-party cases, where A transfers to B to hold on trust for A. (Or at least they tend to be treated as two-party cases. *Rochefoucauld* is in fact a little more complex. There, A owned land which was mortgaged to X. X was to sell the land as mortgagee and A orally agreed with B that B would acquire it for A. As such, B received the land not from A but from X. However, there was no arrangement *as between X and B* that B would hold on trust for A, so it is in any case clear that *Rochefoucauld* does not answer the question we are addressing now.) In two-party cases, whichever of the two approaches we take leads to the same result: that B holds on trust for A. As such, the results in these cases are inconclusive. *Rochefoucauld* suggests that the courts are giving effect to the trust as intended, as there the Court of Appeal described the trust as an express, and hence intended, trust (see further Swadling, 2010). And though *Bannister* classed the trust as constructive (see Section 9.7), the likely explanation for this is the courts' desire to appear not to be overriding the will of Parliament, rather than that they were doing anything other than giving effect to the trust as intended by A. This would mean that where A transfers land to B to be held on trust for C, B would hold on trust for

C notwithstanding the failure to satisfy the statutory formality requirement. This conclusion is further backed up by the approach taken in relation to secret trusts, where the courts have clearly given effect to the trust as intended by the settlor, though the aptness of the analogy rather depends on why we think the courts uphold secret trusts (see Sections 6.11–6.14; see also the different views put forward in Feltham, 1987, and Youdan, 1988).

The end result is that the statutory writing requirement for trusts of land only really bites where the settlor attempts an oral self-declaration of trust. Where he instead seeks to create the trust by transferring the land to a trustee to hold on trust, the effect of the principle found in *Rochefoucauld* is that the trust will take full effect even in the absence of writing.

6.9 Secret trusts

It will come as no surprise that the law allows you to direct where your property is to go on your death, and that, to do this successfully, you must manifest your intentions in a particular way. Requiring formality here is understandable. What happens to our property when we die is one of the more important decisions we make in our lives, so a rule that encourages us to think carefully about this is clearly beneficial. Moreover, necessarily we shall not be around when such dispositions take effect, so it makes sense for the law to put a premium on certainty. Accordingly, the other principal exception to the general rule that declarations of trust require no formality is in respect of testamentary trusts, that is trusts intended to take effect upon the settlor's death. Section 9 of the Wills Act 1837 provides:

> No will shall be valid unless –
>
> (a) it is in writing, and signed by the testator, or by some other person in his presence and by his direction; and
> (b) it appears that the testator intended by his signature to give effect to the will; and
> (c) the signature is made or acknowledged by the testator in the presence of two or more witnesses present at the same time; and
> (d) each witness either –
>   (i) attests and signs the will; or
>   (ii) acknowledges his signature,
>   in the presence of the testator (but not necessarily in the presence of any other witness), but no form of attestation shall be necessary.

Before we look at how the courts have dealt with testamentary trusts, it is worth making a few more general points about wills and the destination of our property on death. First, most wills comprise a series of specific bequests or legacies of specific assets to specific individuals, followed by a residue clause which stipulates who is to receive all those assets not disposed of in those specific provisions. So I might say, 'My house goes to A, my car to B, and everything else to C'. C in this case is my residuary legatee. If any of my specific bequests fail, for instance because of uncertainty or because the legatee dies before me, then that property falls into the residue. Because of such clauses, most wills are exhaustive of the testator's property. However, if the testator does not include a residue clause, or if the residue clause fails, then it is likely that at least some of the testator's property will not be provided for in his will. In such a case, these assets pass under the rules of intestacy, a series of default rules, which say who receives the deceased's property where and to the extent that no will has been made. These rules of course also apply if there is no will at all.

Second, we tend to think of a will as being a single document. This need not be the case though. There may be a principal document which has been signed and witnessed in accordance with the statutory provisions, which makes reference to some other pre-existing document. The terms embodied in the other document are then incorporated into the will by virtue of the reference to them in the principal document, even though the other document has not itself been signed and witnessed. This is known as incorporation by reference. This is worth knowing about, because although the courts have created exceptions to the rule that testamentary trusts must satisfy the Wills Act, there is no need to have recourse to these exceptions if the formalities have in fact been met. This becomes particularly important when we come to look at half secret trusts (see Section 6.10).

The formality requirements of section 9 are pretty straightforward. Note that trusts that take effect on death cannot arise from self-declarations of trust, as the dead cannot act as trustees. An intended testamentary trust will only satisfy section 9 if the will states both who the trustee is and the terms of that trust, which of course includes the identity of the beneficiaries. The clear implication of the Wills Act is that, if the testator intends a trust but does not satisfy these rules, the trust will fail. However, as with section 53(1)(b) of the Law of Property Act 1925, the courts have carved out an exception to the formality rule, giving effect to certain orally declared testamentary trusts. This exception is secret trusts.

These work in a very similar way to the *Rochefoucauld v Boustead* type trusts which we looked at in Section 6.8 in relation to section 53(1)(b). The testator, A, provides for property to pass to B on his death by making a bequest to this effect in his will. However, independently, A tells B that the property is not to be B's beneficially but that he is instead to hold it for some third party, C. This intention is not however manifest in A's will, which will either fail to reveal that B is to hold it on trust at all or will not disclose the terms of that trust. Therefore, you have a situation where a trust is clearly intended but where the requisite formalities have not been complied with. Again, as with *Rochefoucauld v Boustead*, most seem happy to say that it would be wrong for B to keep the property for himself in clear breach of his undertaking. Moreover, rather than concluding that B must hold the property on resulting trust, which would mean that the property would pass to the residuary legatee under the will or otherwise to A's intestate successor (A, of course, being dead), the courts have given effect to such trusts, so that the intended beneficiaries do indeed benefit.

6.10   Fully and half secret trusts

All secret trusts have certain things in common. First, they are trusts which take effect only on the testator's death and, second, they do so in spite of the fact that they do not comply with the provisions of the Wills Act. However, it is conventional to subdivide secret trusts into two classes, fully secret trusts and half secret trusts. This distinction is particularly important because, as we shall see, different rules apply depending on whether the trust is fully secret or half secret.

The distinction is based on whether the testator's intention that the legatee, B, should hold the property on trust is evident on the face of the will. If there is no evidence of this intention from the will itself then the trust is fully secret. If, however, the intention to create a trust is clear from the will, and it is just the terms of this trust which are unspecified, the trust is half secret. So, say I want to create a secret trust of my shares for my illegitimate love child. If the trust were fully secret, it would seem from looking solely at my will that B, my intended trustee, was to receive my shares absolutely. The bequest would resemble any other beneficial bequest, with no indication that I intended B to hold the shares on trust (eg 'my shares are to go to B'). By contrast, if the trust were half secret, examination of the will would reveal not only that the shares were to go to B but also that B would receive them *as trustee*. What would not be revealed are the details of that trust. Hence, a typical half secret trust would take the form 'my shares to B to hold on trust on such terms as I have communicated to him'. Usually it will be plain on which side of the divide a particular trust falls. However, there will occasionally be difficult cases.

For example, say that my will states 'my shares to B, in full confidence that he will deal with them in the manner I shall communicate to him'. Let us assume that from extrinsic evidence it is abundantly clear that I wanted B to hold those shares on trust for C. Accordingly, my intention to create a trust is not in doubt. However, can this intention be gleaned from the document itself? This will determine whether it is a fully secret or half secret trust. This matters because, as we shall soon see, if it is held to be a half secret trust, it would certainly fail (see Section 6.17 and *Re Keen* [1937] 1 Ch 236). Although it may seem clear that this is indeed a half secret trust, it can be argued that it is in fact fully secret, and hence effective. If you remember back to Chapter 3 and the cases on certainty of intention, we looked at the question of precatory words: words attached to a testamentary gift expressing the testator's wishes or motives, but imposing no legal obligation on the recipient (Section 3.4). A good argument can be made that, though it is clear that A did indeed intend a trust, that intention is not to be derived from the terms of the will itself, as the words 'in full confidence' are not in themselves sufficient to establish that intention. If this is true, the trust is fully secret and the would-be beneficiary can make his claim on the basis of the more relaxed rules applying to this type of secret trust.

It is also worth noting that a fully secret trust may be created even where there is no will. Say again that I want my shares to be held on trust for my child C. However, this time I do not make a will but instead simply ask B, the person who would receive my shares under the rules on intestacy, to hold them on trust for C. The basic issue is the same as in the case where I state in my will that the shares are to go to B. The standard rules on testamentary disposition say that the property goes to B beneficially; however, B had agreed privately with me that he will instead hold them on trust for C. Though I have not complied with the Wills Act, the court will give effect to my intended trust as a secret trust. Clearly half secret trusts are not possible where there is no will, as without a will there can be no valid testamentary document saying that B is to receive property on an unspecified trust.

6.11 The basis for upholding secret trusts

Secret trusts have long been upheld by the courts. There is, however, some doubt as to why we enforce secret trusts despite their failure to comply with section 9 of the Wills Act 1837. There are two principal suggestions:

1. they arise to prevent fraud on the part of the trustee; and

2. they arise and operate outside (or 'dehors') the will so as not to invoke the formality rules.

6.12 Fraud

We have already noted the similarity between secret trusts and the *Rochefoucauld v Boustead* trusts where the courts enforce trusts of land despite a failure to meet the requirements of section 53(1)(b) of the Law of Property Act 1925 (see Section 6.8). Accordingly, the traditional purported justification for enforcing secret trusts is the same as is used to support the enforcement of oral trusts of land, namely the principle that equity will not permit a statute to be used as an instrument of fraud (see *McCormick v Grogan* (1869) 4 App Cas 82 and *Re Gardner* [1920] 2 Ch 523). In other words, it would be fraudulent for B, the secret trustee, to say that he is not bound by the trust on which he agreed to hold the property on the basis that it did not comply with the statute, which would then enable him to keep the property for himself. To prevent this, we give effect to the trust despite the absence of formality. However, there are a number of difficulties with this argument.

First, it has been argued that the fraud argument works as a justification for secret trusts only where B is seeking to deny the trust, and hence is acting or seeking to act fraudulently. On this view, it cannot explain the enforcement of secret trusts where B is happy to give effect to the trust, as there is then no danger of fraud. The answer to this is that the courts' concern is with the *potential* of fraud. Because it *would be* fraudulent for the trustee to seek to keep the property for himself or, we may add, to pass it on to someone other than the beneficiary named by the testator, the courts require that the property is held on secret trust. In other words, because we think that B should not be free to choose to keep the property for himself or to divert it to whomever he wishes, we recognise an obligation on him to give effect to the trust as A intended. This means that B must hold the property on trust for C *whether he wants to or not*. The fact that B may well have been willing to give effect to this trust in any case is irrelevant, just as it is irrelevant to the recognition of contractual obligation that the promisor may have been willing to keep his promise with or without the imposition of the obligation.

A second objection poses greater problems. This is that although the fraud argument can explain why B should not be allowed to keep the property for himself, it does not explain why we should require him to hold it on trust *for* C. The point here is that giving effect to the intended trust is not the only way to prevent fraud. An alternative approach would be to require B to hold the property on (resulting) trust for A's estate. The thinking behind this is that B was not intended to receive the property beneficially (which explains why there is a trust) but that the intended trust for C fails because of the lack of formality (which explains why the property goes back to the testator's estate rather than to C). The advantage of this approach is that it would involve less of a contravention of the Wills Act, and hence Parliament's intentions and the policy underlying the Act, because we would not be giving positive effect to a disposition which did not satisfy the statutory formalities (see Section 6.8 for the same argument in respect of exceptions to s 53(1)(b)). So fraud would be prevented, while the policy of the statute would largely be upheld in that testators would know that their property would go to their intended beneficiaries only if they satisfied section 9.

There is no obvious justification for the courts' choice of giving effect to secret trusts ahead of the alternative of sending the property back to the testator's estate. But neither is it surprising that this is the choice they have made. Sending the property back to the testator's estate defeats his intentions, and moreover, as he is dead, this does not afford him a second bite of the cherry to find another way of disposing of his property as he wishes. And though, as we have noted on numerous occasions, taking formality requirements seriously requires us to accept that clear intentions will on occasion be defeated, it is understandable that courts have been particularly reluctant to do this given the significance and necessary finality of testamentary dispositions.

Nonetheless, this suggests that the fraud argument is only partially successful. Although it can explain the need for the courts to intervene to prevent B taking the property for himself, it cannot explain the particular form of intervention the courts have adopted whereby B is required to hold on trust for C, rather than for A's estate. However, the weakness of the fraud argument is compounded when we consider the distinction between fully and half secret trusts, for it appears that even this partial success is limited to fully secret trusts and that fraud completely fails to account for the enforcement of half secret trust.

With fully secret trusts, if we were simply to let the Wills Act govern the situation, then, as the will says that the relevant property goes to B, B would take that property beneficially. So there needs to be some sort of judicial qualification of or derogation from the provisions of the Wills Act if we are to prevent B keeping the property and hence perpetrating a fraud. However, if we left the Wills Act to run its course in relation to half secret trusts, the end result would be that B would hold the property on trust for A's estate. This is because, in half secret trusts, the will makes it clear that B is to hold the property on trust but does not reveal who the beneficiary is. That being so, applying the Wills Act, the trust declared in the will fails due to uncertainty of objects, and so, as in all such cases (Section 3.18), the trustee must instead hold the property on a resulting trust for the settlor or, in this case, his estate. Accordingly, the courts do not need to create *any* exception to the formality rule to prevent fraud as a straightforward application of the Wills Act itself precludes any possibility of this.

Some have attempted to rescue the fraud argument, offering a version of it which can both explain why we give effect to the intended trust for C rather than send the property back to A's estate on a resulting trust and justify the enforcement of half secret trusts. The argument that has been deployed is that the fraud we are trying to prevent lies not simply in B keeping the property for himself or passing it to someone else of his choice, but rather in B not giving effect to the agreement he had with A to hold the property on trust for C (see Hodge, 1980). So on this view the essence of fraud is in defeating the testator's intentions and in depriving the beneficiaries of the property that was intended to come their way (for which reason it is sometimes said that the relevant fraud is a fraud 'on the beneficiaries'). So understood, fraud will be prevented only by requiring B to hold on trust for C, and it explains why we enforce both fully and half secret trusts.

Unfortunately, however, this version of the fraud argument simply does not work. The problem we have with secret trusts is in justifying why we are giving effect to (what appear to be) testamentary trusts which do not comply with the Wills Act. Now, it is clear that were B to deprive C of property which is rightfully his, we could indeed say that he would be both defrauding C and defeating A's intentions. But we cannot say that the property is rightfully C's until we have concluded that the trust is a valid one, and this is the very question we are seeking to determine. As such, the 'fraud on the beneficiaries' argument simply begs the question. More fundamentally, the problem here is that it is not B who defeats A's intentions and deprives C of the property A meant him to have. Rather, it is the *statute* which does this, by virtue of its requirement that, unless the prescribed formalities are met, the trust will fail. This is clearest in half secret trusts. If we applied the Wills Act without exception, the trust would fail for uncertainty of objects and so B would hold on resulting trust for A's estate. A's intentions are defeated and C cannot claim the property, but this is nothing to do with B or any fraud on his part. Indeed, the statute gives B no choice in the matter, so it can hardly be said to be fraudulent or wrongful for him not to give effect to the intended trust.

In truth, this version of the fraud arguments amounts to no more than the assertion that it would be unjust to defeat A's intentions and deprive C of the property meant for him. But the Wills Act says that A's intentions will be given effect, and C will become entitled to property on A's death, only where the requisite formalities are satisfied. To say that we should give effect to A's intentions regardless of the lack of formality is simply to ignore the Wills Act and the policy choice it embodies.

6.13 The 'dehors the will' theory

The end result is that the fraud argument is inadequate as a justification for the law on secret trusts. It can explain the need for the courts to intervene in cases of fully secret trusts, but it cannot explain the particular form of intervention adopted by the courts whereby we give effect to the intended trust, nor can it explain why the courts intervene *at all* in cases of half secret trusts. Because of these deficiencies of the fraud argument, lawyers have looked elsewhere for an explanation for secret trusts. The principal alternative that has been proposed is that secret trusts are not testamentary dispositions at all but instead operate outside or 'dehors' the will.

When the courts first started to make reference to secret trusts arising 'dehors the will', such claims appeared to be no more than assertions. Holding that the trust arose outside the will was simply the courts' way of saying that the Wills Act was not (or should not be) an obstacle to their recognition. It didn't explain *why* or *how* these trusts fell outside the scope of the statute. As such the courts could hardly be said to have been putting forward a rival *theory* of secret trusts. Since then, however, commentators have sought to fill this gap by setting out a principled basis upon which we might say that secret trusts do indeed fall outside the provisions of the Wills Act.

The argument that they have come up with is that secret trusts are not trusts intended to take effect on the testator's death but are instead trusts declared during the testator's lifetime. As inter vivos rather than testamentary dispositions, the Wills Act simply does not apply to them. Instead they are governed by the usual principles of trust formation and hence require neither writing nor attestation. The only thing stopping such trusts taking effect immediately upon communication of the trust to B (and so what makes such trusts *look like* testamentary dispositions) is that the trust is not properly constituted, as A has not yet transferred the property to B. However, when A dies and the property passes to B either under the terms of A's will or by virtue of the rules on intestacy, the trust becomes fully constituted and hence effective. The proponents of this argument do not claim that it can account for all the rules on secret trusts (it would not, for instance, explain the different communication rules for fully and half secret trusts; see Section 6.17), but it would provide an explanation for why we do uphold secret trusts in spite of their informality.

However, though the view that secret trusts arise and operate 'dehors the will' has a fair amount of support in the cases (see *Blackwell v Blackwell* [1929] AC 318; *Re Young* [1951] Ch 344), it must be rejected. The principal flaw in the argument set out in the previous paragraph is that it misrepresents the intentions of settlors who seek to create secret trusts. When A tells B that he will receive property on A's death, which A wants him to hold on trust for C, A is not intending to create an immediate trust (whether we identify this intention subjectively or objectively; see Section 3.3). He instead intends the trust to arise and take effect only upon his death. As such, this is clearly an attempted testamentary disposition, rather than an inter vivos declaration of trust, and so falls within the ambit of the Wills Act (see more generally Critchley, 1999).

6.14 A pragmatic concession?

This leaves the search for a convincing account for the basis of secret trusts looking rather desperate. Fraud can explain the need for some exception to or qualification of the Wills Act to prevent secret trustees from keeping the property for themselves. But it cannot explain the positive enforcement of secret trusts nor judicial intervention when, as is the case with half secret trusts, there is no chance of the trustee walking off with the property. It seems likely that, having decided that, in the case of fully secret trusts, it was necessary to look beyond the terms of the will to see whether B was not meant to take the property beneficially, the courts considered it a small step then to give it to whomever was meant to get it. In other words, once we have decided that we can overlook the statute for one purpose (determining whether B was intended to keep the property), we may as well overlook it for another purpose (determining who will take the property instead). And, once we have decided we can enforce fully secret trusts, it seems only a further small step to enforce half secret trusts, given the (factual) similarity between them. As Lord Sumner said in *Blackwell v Blackwell* [1929] AC 318, 335, 'Why should equity, over a mere matter of words, give effect to them in one case and frustrate them in another?' (cf Hackney, 1987, 103–04). But although this may work as an account of how the law has ended up where it has and hence why we *do* enforce secret trusts, it provides an unsatisfying explanation of why (and indeed whether) we *should* enforce such trusts.

Why does it matter how we explain secret trusts? For the usual reason that the basis of legal rules determines their ambit. It is only by identifying why we should recognise secret trusts that we can identify the circumstances in which secret trusts should arise. Most broadly, if we cannot find a satisfactory justification for secret trusts then it follows that, despite the wealth of cases upholding such trusts, we should no longer give effect to them. More narrowly, our view of how secret trusts may best be explained provides us with answers to a number of more discrete questions concerning their workings.

For example, section 15 of the Wills Act 1837 says that those who attest a will are not allowed to be beneficiaries of legacies under the will. The question then is whether this provision applies to beneficiaries of secret trusts. In *Re Young* [1951] Ch 344 it was held that a witness to the will was able to be the beneficiary of a half secret trust. This was on the basis of the 'dehors the will' theory: if secret trusts take effect outside the will, then the beneficiary of the secret trust is not a beneficiary under the will. Conversely, it should follow from this that section 15 *would* invalidate a legacy to the trustee of a secret trust. If we instead adopted the fraud explanation of secret trusts there is a good argument that the position would be reversed, so that the beneficiary of the secret trust could not be a witness but the trustee could.

Another question that has arisen is whether secret trusts of land need to be evidenced in writing to satisfy section 53(1)(b) of the Law of Property Act 1925. The authorities here are split. In *Re Baillie* (1886) 2 TLR 660 it was held that the normal formality requirement applied to a half secret trust of land, whereas in *Ottaway v Norman* [1972] Ch 698 a fully secret trust of land was upheld without writing, albeit without discussion of this point. As a matter of principle, adopting the fraud explanation of secret trusts gives us reason not to require such trusts to be evidenced in writing for, if the potential of fraud can justify an exception to the formality requirements of the Wills Act, it should likewise justify a departure from any other relevant formalities. Those who favour the 'dehors the will' theory of secret trusts have, by contrast, suggested that, as this would be a straightforward inter vivos trust of land, it requires evidence in writing like any other express trust of land. (However, it would seem that even on this view we could uphold such trusts despite a lack of writing by applying the principle from *Rochefoucauld v Boustead* [1897] 1 Ch 196 (Section 6.9).)

6.15 The basic requirements of secret trusts

It is common to divide the basic requirements for the effective creation of both fully and half secret trusts into three (see eg *Ottaway v Norman* [1972] Ch 698, 711; *Blackwell v Blackwell* [1929] AC 318, 334):

1. A's intention that B hold the property on trust for C;
2. A's communication to B that he intends B to be a trustee of the trust;
3. B's acceptance of or acquiescence to this proposal.

In fact, we may add that the trust must also satisfy the certainty of subject matter and objects requirements, and must not fall foul of either the beneficiary principle or the rule against perpetuities. However, subject to one or two minor points (see Section 6.16), there is no suggestion that these rules apply any differently to secret trusts so there is no need to re-examine them here. Instead we shall focus on the three elements set out above.

6.16 Intention

The first of the three basic requirements of secret trusts is simply the certainty of intention requirement which applies to all intended trusts. The only issue that is raised in relation to secret trusts is as to the standard of proof. Normally it is sufficient to prove simply on the balance of probabilities that the settlor or testator intended to create a trust. However, the suggestion has been made that a higher standard of proof is needed to support an intention to create a secret trust (see *Ottaway v Norman* [1972] Ch 698). In *Re Snowden* [1979] Ch 528, Sir Robert Megarry vc held that the normal balance of probabilities test applies except where the secret trust can only be established by showing that the secret trustee has acted fraudulently. This qualification is unnecessary however. Fraud here occurs where the trustee seeks to defeat the settlor's intentions by keeping the property for himself or passing it on to someone else of his choosing (see further Section 6.12). So, even here, the trust depends on the settlor having intended to create a trust. Moreover, where this intention is established, it makes no difference whether the trustee acts fraudulently or whether he is happy to go along with the settlor's wishes (Section 6.12). As such, there is no reason for requiring a higher standard of proof of intention in the former case, and it would be better to adopt the conventional balance of probabilities test across the board.

In relation to the certainty of subject matter and objects requirements, these also apply in much the same way as with orthodox inter vivos express trusts. With respect to certainty of subject matter, the only point worth noting concerns so-called floating trusts, whereby the settlor leaves property to a trustee on terms that he may use and dispose of that property howsoever he likes during his lifetime but that he must leave whatever is left of it on his death to the beneficiary. As we saw earlier (Section 3.11), such trusts have traditionally failed on the grounds of uncertainty of subject matter.

However, a different view was suggested in *Ottaway v Norman* [1972] Ch 698. There it was argued that the testator left his bungalow, its contents and a sum of money by will to his housekeeper, on a secret trust that required that she would in turn leave the bungalow, contents and what was left of the money upon *her* death on trust for one of the testator's sons and his wife. Brightman J upheld the trust in respect of the bungalow and its contents. The trust of the money failed, however, because, in the absence of an obligation on the housekeeper to keep that money separate from her own, it would be impossible to determine how much of that money she had left. Nonetheless, Brightman J was prepared to assume that, had the money been kept separate or had the housekeeper been required to leave *all* her remaining money to the named beneficiaries, then the trust would have been valid. Whether *Ottaway* signifies that the certainty of subject matter requirement applies with less rigour to secret trusts, or whether it simply suggests that the courts may be taking a more accommodating stance in relation to floating trusts in general, is, however, unclear.

Moving to certainty of objects, again the normal rules apply for the most part. One issue that has arisen in the context of half secret trusts is whether the trustee may also be permitted to be a beneficiary of the trust. The problem here is that the will itself will state that B is to receive the property on trust, which suggests that he is to have no beneficial interest in the property. As such, any claim by B that the testator intended him to have a beneficial share of the property seems to contradict the terms of the will (and hence no such problem can arise with fully secret trusts). For this reason the Court of Appeal in *Re Rees* [1950] Ch 204 held that the trustees of a half secret trust were not entitled to adduce evidence to show that the testator intended them to have a beneficial interest. However, some doubt was cast on this strict approach in *Re Tyler* [1967] 1 WLR 1269. Moreover, given that *all* secret trusts involve some sort of departure from the terms of the will, it would seem strange for us to deny the possibility of a half secret trustee also being a beneficiary simply because it is inconsistent with the will. The sounder approach would be to allow the trustee of a half secret trust to show that the testator intended him to have an interest under the trust, while remaining wary of uncorroborated evidence to this effect.

One final point concerning objects. Normally if I seek to create a trust for someone who, unknown to me, has died, the trust fails, with the result that the trustee holds the property on resulting trust for me rather than for the deceased beneficiary's estate. (The position is, of course, different if the beneficiary dies only after the trust has been created, in which case his beneficial interest in the trust property passes under his will or intestacy along with all his other proprietary interests.) There is, however, authority that the position is different in relation to secret trusts. In *Re Gardner* [1923] 2 Ch 230, the testatrix sought to create a half secret trust for three beneficiaries. However, following communication to the trustee but prior to the testatrix's death, one of the beneficiaries died. Romer J held that this did not cause this part of the trust to fail and so that share of the trust property could be claimed by the deceased beneficiary's personal representative. There seems no good reason for this departure from the normal rule of trust formation, neither the fraud nor the 'dehors the will' theory of secret trusts providing any support. Accordingly, the near universal conclusion is that the case was wrongly decided.

6.17 Communication and acceptance

In general it is not necessary for the creation of an express trust that the trustee should first be made aware of the settlor's intentions, let alone that the validity of the trust depends on the trustee's acceptance of them (though Lord Browne-Wilkinson's statement that trusts will arise only once the trustee's conscience is affected may suggest otherwise: see *Westdeutsche Landesbank Girozentrale v Islington London BC* [1996] AC 669, 705 (Section 8.6)). The intended trustee is free to decline the role, but if he does, the result will be the appointment of a new trustee rather than the failure of the trust. A secret trust will arise, however, only where there has been effective and timely communication to and acceptance by the trustee of the terms of the trust. This follows from the view that secret trusts are upheld to prevent fraud, as no fraud can be committed unless the trustee did indeed agree to hold the property on trust. As such, adoption of the 'dehors the will' theory of secret trusts should lead us to reject these requirements.

It is here that we find the principal differences between the rules on fully secret and half secret trusts. In relation to fully secret trusts, the rule is simple: the terms of the trust must be communicated to and accepted by the secret trustee at some point prior to the testator's death. Things are not quite so straightforward with half secret trusts. The basic rule here is that they must be communicated to and accepted by the trustee prior to or at the same time as the execution of the will. Moreover, there is here a second rule, which says that, in addition to timely communication to and acceptance by the half secret trustee, the terms of the will must be consistent with prior communication to the trustee. In other words, a half secret trust which says 'my house to B to hold on such trusts as I shall communicate to him' will not succeed, regardless of when communication actually took place, because it suggests that communication will (or may) lie in the future. So, a half secret trust will fail if *either* the testator does not communicate the terms of the trust till after the will is executed *or* the terms of the will suggest that communication of those terms will or may occur in the future.

The leading authority for both of these rules is *Re Keen* [1937] Ch 236. The testator here left £10,000 to his executors, 'to be held upon trust and disposed of by them among such person, persons or charities as may be notified by me to them or either of them during my lifetime'. The Court of Appeal held that the terms of the trust had been communicated to one of the trustees prior to the execution of the will, but that the trust failed nonetheless. Lord Wright MR held that not only must the trust intended by the testator be consistent with the express terms of the will but, moreover, '[t]he trusts referred to but undefined in the will must be described in the will as established prior to or at least contemporaneously with its execution'. In short, the will must state that there has been prior communication and there must have in fact been prior (or coterminous) communication. Even on the view (which Lord Wright MR did not accept) that the words 'may be notified' were consistent with the possibility of prior communication, they also clearly implied the possibility of future communication, and so, despite the testator's clear intentions and though there had in fact been prior communication, the trust failed.

This difference between the rules on communication for fully and half secret trusts has received widespread criticism. It is true that the Wills Act does not allow testators to make future unattested dispositions, and so the approach in *Re Keen* ensures greater compatibility with the statute. However, as noted already, *all* secret trusts involve some departure from the terms of the will. As such, it appears arbitrary to require consistency with the will and the Wills Act on this particular issue. Nonetheless, those who doubt whether there is any sound basis for the enforcement of half secret trusts may at least take some comfort from the fact that the rules here are more strict and require at least some adherence to the statutory formalities. What is clear is that, following their (relatively) modern endorsement in *Re Bateman's Will Trusts* [1970] 1 WLR 1463, these stricter rules for the creation of half secret trusts represent the current state of the law.

Having determined when communication and acceptance must take place, we now turn to what counts as effective communication and acceptance. The clearest case is where the testator tells the trustee exactly what he wants the trustee to do with the property and the trustee says that he will do it. It is clear, though, that the courts do not require anything so explicit. First, as regards communication, it has been held that it is sufficient if the testator hands the trustee a sealed envelope containing details of the secret trusts, but which is to be opened only after the testator's death: see *Re Boyes* (1884) 26 Ch D 531 and *Re Keen* [1937] Ch 236. However, *Re Boyes* also held that it is not enough for the testator to tell his intended trustee that he wants him to deal with the property on terms set out in a written document, when that document is never handed over to the trustee but is instead discovered only after the testator's death. Second, it is clear that acceptance can take the form of tacit acquiescence. In other words, if a testator tells you that he wants you to hold the property you will receive under his will on trust for a specified beneficiary, you will be held to that trust unless you positively refuse.

Where the testator wants two people (B1 and B2) to hold the property on trust for his intended beneficiary, whether there needs to be communication to and acceptance by both of them depends on the nature of the bequest and the timing of the communication. In *Re Stead* [1900] 1 Ch 237, Farwell J held that if the will leaves the property to B1 and B2 as joint tenants and, prior to the execution of the will, B1 has agreed to hold the property on secret trust, the trust is binding on *both* of them, notwithstanding that B2 may have known nothing about it. However, if they take as joint tenants but the communication to B1 has occurred only after execution of the will, or if B1 and B2 are to receive the property as tenants in common rather than joint tenants, then B2 cannot be bound by the trust unless he too is told of and accepts the trust. (For the nature of and distinction between joint tenancies and tenancies in common, see Gardner and MacKenzie, 2012, 326–33.)

It should, however, be noted that Perrins (1972) has criticised Farwell J's reading of the cases which led him to this conclusion. He suggests instead that the authorities support the view that B2 should be bound where the testator makes or leaves unrevoked a bequest to B1 and B2 in reliance on B1's promise to hold the property on trust, irrespective of whether they take as joint tenants or tenants in common. Whichever view we adopt, where, because of a lack of communication and acceptance, B2 is not bound by the secret trust then, if the trust is fully secret, he receives his share beneficially and, if half secret, he holds it on resulting trust for the testator's estate.

Another problem arises where there is effective communication and acceptance of a secret trust but then the testator seeks to add to or otherwise change the property that B will receive under the will, without securing B's agreement to hold the new property on trust. In *Re Colin Cooper* [1939] 1 Ch 811, it was held that the secret trust only extends to the property B has agreed to hold on trust. If the testator wants B to hold further property on trust, he must communicate and secure acceptance of this addition to the trust property. If he does not then the secret trust of the additional or new property fails, and so can be kept by B where the trust is fully secret or is held by B on trust for A's estate where the trust is half secret.

Seeing that the valid creation of a secret trust requires the trustee's acceptance, can the trustee subsequently revoke his acceptance, thus defeating the trust? In *Re Maddock* [1902] 2 Ch 220, Cozens-Hardy LJ remarked that he thought a secret trust would fail if the trustee died or disclaimed the trust prior to the testator's death. Dicta in *Blackwell v Blackwell* [1929] AC 318, by contrast, suggest that the court would not let the trustee's disclaimer defeat the trust. Seeing that the trust does not and indeed cannot arise until the testator's death, and that the trustee's agreement is an essential component of such trusts, the former view seems preferable, except perhaps where the trustee disclaims so soon before the testator's death that he has no opportunity to make other arrangements.

6.18 Failure of secret trusts

What happens when a testator who intends to set up a secret trust fails to satisfy the various requirements discussed earlier? The answer depends on whether the trust is half secret or fully secret and why the trust fails. Where a half secret trust fails, because B is identified as a trustee in the will, he cannot keep the property for himself but instead holds it on trust for A's estate, and hence for A's residuary legatees (if any) under his will or otherwise his intestate successors. Where the trust is fully secret, if the trust fails because of a lack of communication or acceptance of the terms of the trust, it will usually result in B taking the property beneficially. If, however, B has agreed to hold on secret trust but the trust fails because the terms of the trust were not properly communicated to him, or because of uncertainty of objects or infringement of the beneficiary principle, then B will hold the property on resulting trust for A's estate: see *Re Boyes* (1884) 26 Ch D 531.

6.19 Dispositions of equitable interests

In the previous sections we have been examining what formalities and other steps are necessary for the creation of a valid trust. If all these requirements are satisfied then, at least if the trust is fixed rather than discretionary (see Section 2.1), the beneficiaries will acquire an equitable interest in the trust property. As we have seen (Section 2.4), such equitable interests are proprietary interests, and can be dealt with (transferred outright, mortgaged, held on trust etc.) like other proprietary interests. The question then is what steps have to be taken to deal effectively with one's equitable interest. The key provision is section 53(1)(c) of the Law of Property Act 1925:

> A disposition of an equitable interest or trust subsisting at the time of the disposition, must be in writing signed by the person disposing of the same, or his agent thereunto lawfully authorised in writing or by will.

As with section 53(1)(b) (see Section 6.8), the provision is qualified by section 53(2), which states that the formality requirement does not apply to the creation and operation of resulting, implied and constructive trusts.

What is the effect of section 53(1)(c)? It clearly imposes a formality requirement in relation to 'dispositions' of equitable interests, so the key issue is what is meant by 'disposition'. The clearest example is an outright transfer or assignment of your equitable interest to another person; in other words, mode (1) of the three forms of beneficial transfer which we set out earlier (Section 6.2), whereby B receives from A the very interest that A held at the outset. What we need to know is what, if any, other dealings with equitable interests count as dispositions and so require writing to be effective.

One point can be cleared up quickly. Ordinary declarations of trust plainly do not fall within section 53(1)(c). When you create a trust, there is no disposition of an equitable interest for the simple reason that, as we saw in Chapter 2 (Section 2.6), where property is held outright, that is not on trust, there is no existing equitable interest in the property but only a legal beneficial title. The equitable interest springs up for the first time upon creation of the trust. Thus there is no subsisting equitable interest which passes from the settlor to the beneficiary when a trust is created. The following sections examine a variety of other dealings one may make with an equitable interest to see which have been held to fall within section 53(1)(c).

We may also usefully ask what the purpose of the sub-section is. The standard justifications for requiring writing and signature are twofold. First, it reduces the risk of beneficiaries being defrauded by people fabricating dispositions of the equitable interests. Holders of equitable interests will not usually be expected to have possession of the trust property, so without a formality requirement it would be that much easier for a dishonest defendant to claim that he has an equitable interest in the property. Second, the formality rule is said to assist trustees in identifying who their beneficiaries are and hence in knowing to whom they should distribute the trust property. So, if someone approaches the trustees claiming to be the new beneficiary of the trust, and so entitled to payments under it, the trustees can require him to show them the signed document by which he acquired the equitable interest.

Neither explanation is entirely satisfying however. As for the first, the same argument would justify imposing a writing requirement wherever equitable interests are created and not simply transferred. That is, if we want to make it difficult for people dishonestly to claim that they have equitable interests in property then we should also require writing for declarations of trust. Without writing, a dishonest defendant will more easily be able to persuade third parties that a trust has been declared in his favour. Yet, as we have seen, declarations of trust can usually be made orally.

The second justification is also problematic. If the purpose of the formality really was to protect the trustees, this could have been done better by requiring that the signed document be passed on to the trustee for the disposition to be effective. A parallel can be drawn with assignments of debts, where it is clearly important for the debtor to know whom he is required to pay. Here the formality rule is that an assignment of the debt must be made in writing *and* notification must be given to the debtor: section 136 of the Law of Property Act 1925. Without a requirement that notification must be given to the trustee, there is the danger that, even after A transfers his equitable interest to B, the trustee will continue to pay A, because he is unaware of the transfer.

As such there is no entirely satisfying account of why we require this particular formality, given that the law imposes either no such requirement or a different one in areas which seem to raise similar difficulties. This poses problems, as we would expect the courts, at least in part, to determine the scope of section 53(1)(c) by reference to its purpose. In other words, when resolving the question whether a particular type of dealing with an equitable interest falls within the sub-section, we would expect the court to consider whether requiring formality here would be consistent with the policy behind the formality rule. Without a clear understanding of the policy, however, this is made more difficult. It may be for that reason that the courts have, with few exceptions, resolved cases on the scope of the section without much analysis of its purpose.

6.20 Direction to the trustee to hold on trust for another

In a typical assignment or transfer of an equitable interest, the initial beneficiary, A, deals directly with his intended transferee, B. However, an alternative way to pass an equitable interest under a trust to another is for A to contact his trustees and to instruct them to hold the trust property for B instead. The end result is much the same as with a direct assignment: B becomes beneficiary of the trust in place of A. Does this amount to a disposition of A's equitable interest? The courts have said that it does. Though the transaction is effected by a different means, with A giving instruction to his trustees rather than dealing directly with B, there seems to be no difference in substance. At the outset the beneficiary of the trust was A and it was A who had an equitable interest in the trust property. The result of A's direction to the trustees is that B becomes beneficiary of the trust, and hence it is B who now holds the equitable interest. As the equitable interest has passed from A to B, it follows that there has been a disposition of the equitable interest. As such, writing and signature are required for the transaction to be effective.

The relevant authority here is *Grey v IRC* [1960] AC 1. Here, a shareholder, Hunter, transferred 18,000 shares to two trustees to be held on trust for himself. These trustees were already the trustees of six trusts in favour of Hunter's grandchildren. Hunter then orally directed the trustees to divide the shares into six separate blocks of 3,000 shares and to allocate one block to each of the existing trusts for the grandchildren. A few days later, the trustees and Hunter executed deeds in which the trustees declared that the shares were held for the six grandchildren's trusts. The case concerned whether ad valorem stamp duty – a tax payable on documents which transfer beneficial interests – was payable on these deeds. Accordingly what the court had to decide was whether the deeds did indeed have the effect of transferring Hunter's beneficial interest in the shares, or whether his interest passed at an earlier stage as a result of the oral direction he gave to his trustees, in which case the deed would not have effected a beneficial transfer and no such tax would have been due. The answer to this question turned on the applicability of section 53(1)(c).

Prior to Hunter's direction to the trustees, the trustees held the shares on trust for him. Accordingly, Hunter had an equitable interest in those shares. Being an equitable interest, it could, by virtue of section 53(1)(c), only be transferred in writing. Importantly for present purposes, the House of Lords held unanimously that Hunter's direction to his trustees that the shares be held on the grandchildren's trusts fell within the meaning of 'disposition' for the purposes of the statute. The direction to the trustees being oral, it therefore followed that it was not effective to 'transfer' the shares to the grandchildren's trusts. This happened only at the later date when the deeds were executed, thus satisfying the formality set down by section 53(1)(c). Accordingly, the deeds effected a beneficial transfer of the shares and the claimed tax was indeed due.

One point to take from *Grey* is that there is a disposition of A's equitable interest where he tells his trustee henceforth to hold on trust for B (or for B and C), even if the terms of the trust on which T held the property for A are different from the terms of the trust on which T holds it for B. Though the difference in the trust terms will mean that the obligations T owes to B (and C) will be different from those he owed to A, the equitable proprietary interest in the trust assets held by the new beneficiary (or beneficiaries) is the same as that previously held by A.

What if, instead of instructing his trustee, T1, to hold on trust for a new beneficiary, B, A tells him to transfer the property to a new trustee, T2, to be held on trust for B? Here not only is there a change in beneficiary but also a change in trustee. The answer must be that this involves two separate dispositions: a disposition of A's equitable interest to B, which under section 53(1)(c) requires writing to be effective; and a disposition of T1's (usually) legal title to the property to T2, the requirements for which will depend on the nature of that property (see Section 7.1).

It has been argued (see Green, 1984) that *Grey* is in fact a case of this sort, on the basis that because the trusts for the grandchildren to which the shares were transferred were pre-existing, the transaction involved not just a disposition of equitable title but also a change in 'legal proprietorship'. The idea is that, whereas at the outset the trustees held on a bare trust for Hunter, at the end they held the shares in their 'separate capacities' as trustees of the grandchildren's trusts. This is a strange argument. It is clear that the terms of the trust for the grandchildren were different from the terms of the trust for Hunter, but this has no impact on the location or the quality of the legal title to the shares which was vested in the same people throughout. Nonetheless, though *Grey* should not be viewed as a case of this type, it seems plain enough that instructing your trustee to transfer the trust property to a new trustee on trust for a new beneficiary involves a disposition of your equitable interest, and will therefore be effective only if the requirements of section 53(1)(c) are met.

6.21   Direction to the trustee to transfer the property to another outright

In *Grey*, what Hunter sought to achieve through the directions he gave to his trustees was that the property, which was initially held on trust for him, would end up being held on trust for his grandchildren. Notwithstanding that the terms of the latter trust differed from the terms of the original, it is clear enough that this is analogous to an assignment of his equitable interest and hence a disposition for the purposes of section 53(1)(c).

What if, however, a beneficiary, A, instructs his trustee instead to transfer the trust property *outright* to another person, B? The key difference here is that the intended result is that, rather than B becoming beneficiary of a trust of that property, the trust is brought to an end, with B receiving the property absolutely. Accordingly, in this case, although A had an equitable interest in the property at the outset, B in the end does not, because there is no longer any trust and, at the risk of labouring a point made many times already, where there is no trust there is no equitable interest in the property. For this reason, this type of dealing looks different, and indeed has a different effect, from a straightforward assignment of A's equitable interest to B. As we have noted, this sort of direct assignment is the paradigm instance of a disposition under section 53(1)(c). The question then is whether, in spite of these differences, a direction to your trustee to bring an end to the trust by transferring the property to B outright nonetheless counts as a disposition and so requires a signed document to be effective. The answer the House of Lords gave in *Vandervell v IRC* [1967] 2 AC 291 is that it does not.

Vandervell wanted to provide funds to the Royal College of Surgeons (RCS) to enable it to set up a chair in pharmacology. Of course, one way of doing this would be simply to pay the RCS the necessary money. However, Vandervell chose to adopt a different route in an attempt to minimise the tax due on the transaction. The plan was for shares in one of Vandervell's companies, which a bank held on trust for Vandervell, to be transferred to the RCS, with the money needed to fund the chair coming from dividends declared on those shares. As Vandervell wanted to make further use of the shares and because the RCS had no need for them once the dividends were declared, it was also arranged that an option to buy back the shares be granted to Vandervell Trustees Ltd (VT), a trustee company set up by Vandervell and which, amongst other things, held property on trust for Vandervell's children. The transaction went ahead as planned: Vandervell directed the bank to transfer the shares to the RCS, dividends were declared, and the shares were then bought back by VT with money coming from the children's trust.

Vandervell v IRC arose out of the Inland Revenue's claim that Vandervell was liable for tax on the dividends declared on the shares while they were held by the RCS. Its argument was that, notwithstanding the transfer to the RCS, Vandervell retained an interest in those shares and so was liable for tax on that basis. The Inland Revenue had two arguments as to why Vandervell should be regarded as retaining such an interest following the transfer. Its first argument was that Vandervell's direction to the bank to make an outright transfer to the RCS of the shares it held on trust for him was an attempted disposition of Vandervell's equitable interest in those shares. As this had not been made in writing it was ineffective and Vandervell retained his equitable interest. Its second argument was that the option to buy back the shares from the RCS, which had been granted to VT, was received by VT not beneficially but on trust, as VT's sole purpose was to be a trustee company. (And, just to make clear, options are a form of property which can, as such, be the subject matter of a trust.) However, Vandervell had never declared the trusts on which VT was to hold the option, so in the absence of any effectively declared trust VT held the option on resulting trust for Vandervell as settlor. The House of Lords rejected the first argument but accepted the second, with the result that Vandervell was indeed liable for tax on the dividends.

It is the court's rejection of the first argument that is relevant here. The House of Lords unanimously held that the direction to the bank, which was trustee of the shares, to transfer them outright to the RCS was not a disposition of Vandervell's equitable interest and so did not need to satisfy the formality requirement of section 53(1)(c) to be effective. Lord Upjohn considered that the situation was analogous to an outright transfer by a shareholder with legal beneficial title to the shares, and held that, as the transfer of legal title to the shares by the bank to the RCS itself required documentation, there was no reason to require an additional document to transfer the beneficial interest. Lord Wilberforce, by contrast, thought the result could be explained as an application of the *Re Rose* principle (Section 6.4), as Vandervell had done everything in his power to transfer the shares to the RCS.

Both lines of argument can be criticised. The analogy Lord Upjohn draws seems misplaced given that here legal title and the beneficial interest were not vested in the same person. Moreover, his point that a second document would be superfluous ignores both the fact that the second document would (unlike the first document) make clear that it was not simply a bare legal title being passed and that other forms of property can be transferred without documentation (see Section 7.1), so that in other cases there will not already be some other document in existence. Lord Wilberforce's application of *Re Rose* is misplaced given that the central question was whether Vandervell needed to satisfy section 53(1)(c). The rule in *Re Rose* applies once we know what steps the transferor needed to take to make the transfer effective. But the rule does not tell us what the necessary steps are, and this was the question which faced the court in *Vandervell*. We can only say that Vandervell did everything in his power to effect the transfer once we have concluded that the sub-section is not applicable, but then we need some prior reason, which *Re Rose* necessarily cannot provide, for holding writing to be unnecessary.

Nonetheless, most seem to be happy with the result. It is clearly convenient and, if we consider the standard account of the policy of section 53(1)(c)'s writing requirement – namely to assist the trustee in determining who are the beneficiaries of the trust (Section 6.19) – it simply does not apply where the trustee is himself a party to the transaction and where, indeed, that transaction has the effect of bringing the trust to an end. Furthermore, there is no suggestion that the sub-section applies in the analogous situation where a beneficiary, in exercise of his *Saunders v Vautier* right (Section 2.7), instructs his trustee to bring the trust to an end by transferring the property absolutely to him (rather than to a third party as in *Vandervell*).

In summary, following *Vandervell* it seems that, just as declarations of trust, whereby equitable interests are created for the first time, do not fall within section 53(1)(c), neither do transactions which bring trusts to an end and hence extinguish the equitable interest that existed previously.

An unusual application of the rule that section 53(1)(c) does not apply to the creation or extinguishment of equitable interests is to be found in another part of the *Vandervell* litigation, the Court of Appeal decision in *Re Vandervell's Trusts (No. 2)* [1974] Ch 269. The claim here concerned the period after the option was exercised, when the shares were bought back by VT with money from the children's trusts. VT wrote to the Inland Revenue saying that the shares were now held on trust for the children. Despite this, the Inland Revenue claimed that Vandervell still had an interest in the shares, so almost four years after the exercise of the option, Vandervell finally executed a deed by which he transferred all rights he might still have had in the option or the shares to VT to hold on the children's trusts. The question that faced the court in *Re Vandervell's Trusts (No. 2)* was whether Vandervell did indeed, as the Revenue had claimed, retain an interest in the shares in the period between VT's purchase of the shares and Vandervell's execution of the final deed.

On what basis might Vandervell have retained such an interest? The argument goes as follows. As held in *Vandervell v IRC*, Vandervell had an equitable interest in the option to buy back the shares granted to VT. VT's exercise of the option effectively replaced one form of property, the option, with another, the shares. As such, just as the option was held on a resulting trust for Vandervell, so would the shares which took its place once the option was exercised. If, as was clear, Vandervell wanted the shares to be held on trust for his children rather than for himself, then this would amount to a disposition of his equitable interest falling within section 53(1)(c). As Vandervell had not done this in writing, he retained an equitable interest in the shares until he executed the deed years later.

The Court of Appeal unanimously rejected this argument, holding instead that VT held the shares throughout this period on trust for Vandervell's children. There were two important steps in the Court's reasoning. First, it held that when VT acquired the shares from RCS a (new) trust was declared, seemingly by VT rather than Vandervell himself, of those shares in favour of the children. (This conclusion has received widespread criticism – see eg Battersby, 1979, Green, 1984 – but we need not consider it here.) Second, it held that this did not need to be in writing. This is the key point in relation to the scope of section 53(1)(c). However, the basis for the Court's conclusion here is not entirely clear.

One argument, which is found in the judgments of both Lord Denning MR and Lawton LJ, was that the option and the shares were distinct items of property. Accordingly, it did not follow from the fact that Vandervell held an equitable interest in the option that he would also have such an interest in the shares. That would only be the case if, as had been the case with the option, no effective trust had been declared of the shares. But, as the court held that there had been a declaration of trust in respect of the shares, no equitable interest in them was ever held by Vandervell. In other words, when VT exercised the option, the option was necessarily 'used up' or extinguished. And as the option no longer existed, neither could Vandervell's equitable interest in it. The shares were new property in which Vandervell had no subsisting equitable interest, and so the declaration of trust in favour of the children did not involve a disposition of any such interest. Accordingly section 53(1)(c) did not apply.

However, a second, broader argument denying the applicability of section 53(1)(c) is suggested by Lord Denning MR and Stephenson LJ. It is best highlighted in the following extract from the judgment of Lord Denning MR ([1974] Ch 269, 320):

> A resulting trust for the settlor is born and dies without any writing at all. It comes into existence whenever there is a gap in the beneficial ownership. It ceases to exist whenever that gap is filled by someone becoming beneficially entitled. As soon as the gap is filled by the creation or declaration of a valid trust, the resulting trust comes to an end. In this case, before the option was exercised, there was a gap in the beneficial ownership. So there was a resulting trust for Mr Vandervell. But, as soon as the option was exercised and the shares registered in the trustees' name, there was created a valid trust of the shares in favour of the children's settlement. Not being a trust of land, it could be created without any writing.

As we shall see in the next chapter, when A transfers to T on trust but no trust is effectively declared, T holds the property on what is called a resulting trust for A. The resulting trust effectively fills in the gap left by A's failure to identify the beneficiaries of the intended trust. However, the resulting trust, and A's equitable interest under it, endures only so long as there is such a gap. The argument here is that if A later effectively declares trusts of the property, his resulting trust interest is extinguished and a new express trust interest arises in the new beneficiary, B. So though this looks superficially like the situation in *Grey v IRC* [1960] AC 1 (Section 6.20), in that at the outset T holds on trust for A and A then directs T instead to hold the property for B; on this view the situation is in fact different because the equitable interest (under the newly declared express trust) received by B is distinct from the equitable interest (under the resulting trust) previously held by A. As such, there is no disposition of A's equitable interest to B, and so the writing requirement of section 53(1)(c) does not apply. Accordingly, on this approach the fact that the trusts were declared at the time the option was exercised was coincidental. There would similarly have been no need for writing had Vandervell (or it seems VT) declared the trust for the grandchildren either before or after the exercise of the option.

6.22 Declarations of trusts of equitable interests

As we have seen, an equitable interest under a trust is a proprietary interest, with which you can deal in pretty much all the ways you can deal with other types of proprietary interest. So, one thing you can do is to give it away to a third party. However, that is not the only option. As a proprietary interest, it can also form the subject matter of a trust. The question then is whether a declaration of a trust of an equitable interest is a disposition for the purposes of section 53(1)(c).

In the usual case, where a settlor has legal beneficial title to property, the effect of a declaration of trust is that the settlor retains his legal title, but the beneficial interest passes to the beneficiary who acquires a new equitable title to or interest in the property. Similarly, where the beneficiary of a trust, B1, declares a trust of his equitable interest, he retains his equitable interest and a separate, new equitable interest arises in the new beneficiary, B2. The end result is the creation of what is known as a *sub-trust*. The trustee of the original trust has legal title to the property which he continues to hold on trust for B1, who in turn holds *his* equitable interest in the property on trust for B2. B1 becomes the sub-trustee and B2 the sub-beneficiary.

As an aside, sub-trusts also show that equitable interests are not always beneficial interests. We have seen already that equitable and beneficial interests are not synonymous (Section 2.6). The clearest example of this is when you hold property absolutely, that is not on trust. In such cases you have a beneficial interest in the property, but you do not have an equitable interest in it. There is no equitable interest as there is no trust. As sub-trusts show, the converse is also true; it is possible to have an equitable interest which is not a beneficial interest. The sub-trustee has an equitable interest in the trust property, but this is not a beneficial interest as he holds his interest on trust for the sub-beneficiary, whose distinct equitable interest is a beneficial interest.

Given that a declaration of trust of your equitable interest does not deprive you of that interest but simply creates a second equitable interest held by the sub-beneficiary, one may expect that this does not involve any disposition of a subsisting equitable interest and hence does not require writing and signature to be effective (unless of course it is a sub-trust of land or a testamentary sub-trust, in which case section 53(1)(b) of the Law of Property Act or section 9 of the Wills Act would apply).

This does indeed appear to be the law; though, at least until recently, this was not as clear as it could have been. The cause of this uncertainty was that a collection of nineteenth-century cases – *Onslow v Wallis* (1849) 1 Mac & G 506, *Grainge v Wilberforce* (1889) 5 TLR 436 and *Re Lashmar* [1891] 1 Ch 258 – were thought to stand as authority for the proposition that sometimes an attempted creation of a sub-trust takes effect instead as a disposition of the initial beneficiary's equitable interest, and so will fall within section 53(1)(c). This was thought to be the case where the sub-trust you try to create is a bare trust. A bare trust is one where your only duty as trustee is to hold it to the beneficiary's order, to do with it as he directs. Where you as beneficiary under an existing trust try to create a bare sub-trust, the argument is that you end up with nothing to do and so become superfluous. The original trustee retains physical custody of the property and has legal title vested in him, whereas it is the new (sub-)beneficiary, B2, who now has the beneficial interest in the property. Accordingly, for you to be interposed between them appears unnecessary. For this reason, the suggestion was that in such circumstances you simply drop out of the picture. Once you and your equitable interest disappear, we are left with not a sub-trust but a simple two-party trust, whereby the trustee who formerly held on trust for you now holds on trust for B2. This means that B2 has effectively replaced you as beneficiary of the trust and so, regardless of the form of the transaction, it looks very much as though the equitable interest which you once had has passed to B2. And if this is true, this appears no different from an assignment of your equitable interest to B2 and so falls squarely within section 53(1)(c).

This view has, however, recently been doubted by the Court of Appeal in *Nelson v Greening & Sykes (Builders) Ltd* [2007] EWCA Civ 1358; [2008] 1 EGLR 59. Lawrence Collins LJ held that though the creation of a bare sub-trust might *in practice* make it more convenient for the trustee to deal directly with the sub-beneficiary – with the sub-trustee having no role to play – this was not the same as saying *as a matter of law* that the sub-trustee's equitable interest was lost or effectively transferred to the sub-beneficiary.

As such, the law now seems clear. Declarations of sub-trust are not dispositions of the beneficiary's equitable interest, and so do not need to satisfy section 53(1)(c). Of course, if a beneficiary, B1, seeks to create a trust of his equitable interest not by self-declaration of trust (mode (2) identified earlier (Section 6.2)) but by transferring his interest to another, C, to hold on trust for B2 (mode (3)), then, even though the declaration of trust need not be in writing, writing will be needed for B1 to transfer his equitable interest to the new (sub-)trustee, C.

6.23 Disclaimers and surrenders

It seems that where a beneficiary surrenders his interest, this does amount to a disposition and so would require writing to be effective under section 53(1)(c): see *Newlon Housing Trust v Al-Sulaimen* [1999] 1 AC 313. A surrender or release is where a beneficiary says that he no longer wants to be a beneficiary of the trust. Accordingly, the equitable interest he held must then either pass to another beneficiary or revert to the settlor under a resulting trust (though here Lord Denning MR's view of the operation of resulting trusts would seem to come into play: see *Re Vandervell's Trusts (No. 2)* [1974] Ch 269 (Section 6.21)). By contrast, it has been held that a disclaimer of one's interest under a trust, whereby the would-be beneficiary rejects any interest under the trust from the outset, does not require writing to be effective: *Re Paradise Motor Co Ltd* [1968] 1 WLR 1125.

6.24 Specifically enforceable contracts to dispose of equitable interests

There is one final situation to be dealt with. Although people often give away their proprietary interests for free – gifts in the truest sense – commonly they ask for something in return. In other words, there will be a contract. A promises to give X to

B, and B promises to do something in return for A (eg paying over a sum of money). In such cases there are (usually) two distinct stages to the transaction. There is the stage of contract formation, whereupon A incurs the obligation to transfer the proprietary interest to B. Then there is the second stage where A actually transfers the proprietary interest to B, thus fulfilling his contractual obligation. In the usual course of events, B will, of course, not acquire the promised interest from A until the second stage is completed. So far, so clear.

If A, in breach of his contractual duty, refuses to transfer the interest, B has a claim for breach of contract. Now, for the most part, the law limits B to the recovery of compensatory damages from A for any losses the breach has caused him. Exceptionally, however, the court will order specific performance, compelling A to do what he promised under the contract – in this case transferring X to B.

Specific performance, having been developed by the courts of Chancery, is an equitable remedy. And where the contract, as in our example, was a contract to transfer a proprietary interest, this made a crucial difference. This is because, in those cases where equity would compel the transfer, resulting in B becoming the 'owner' of that interest, B would be treated, *from the moment of contract formation*, as 'owner' in equity. The thinking was as follows: *because* (1) A is under an obligation to transfer the property and *because* (2) equity would make him do this, then (3) equity would treat the beneficial interest as *already* having passed to B, and hence say that, from the moment the obligation arose, A held the property on trust for B. Thus, although A's own interest is not itself transferred to B until the second stage is complete, a trust of the property arises after stage one. This, similar to the trust in *Re Rose* [1952] Ch 499 (Section 6.4), is a constructive trust, as no such trust was ever intentionally created, even though, in a general sense, it arises to give effect to the intended transaction.

We shall come back to this sort of constructive trust in Chapter 9 (Section 9.5), but it matters here. As we have seen, equitable interests can be transferred from person to person, but section 53(1)(c) says that writing must be used. Without signed documentation the attempted disposition has no effect. However if A, the beneficiary of a trust, enters into a contract to transfer his equitable interest to B *and* that contractual obligation is specifically enforceable, then applying the rule we have just looked at means that, from the moment of contract formation, A holds his equitable interest on trust for B. This constructive trust then means that B acquires a separate equitable interest in the trust property. Moreover, the effect of this constructive trust is that A is no longer beneficially entitled to the property, and instead it is B who has the beneficial interest. The significance of this is that B receives an equitable beneficial interest in the trust property even before the contract is performed, and indeed even if the contract is never performed.

This avoids the writing requirement of section 53(1)(c) in possibly two ways. First, B acquires his equitable beneficial interest from A not by virtue of a transfer of A's equitable interest, but through the creation or imposition of a trust of that interest. In other words, we have a sub-trust. As we have seen, it now seems to be accepted that this involves no disposition of A's equitable interest (Section 6.22). Second, and in any event, this is a *constructive* trust and, as such, is governed by section 53(2) rather than section 53(1)(c), thus avoiding the need for writing. Therefore, there is an effective transfer of the beneficial interest despite the lack of form. This reasoning was considered in *Oughtred v IRC* [1960] AC 206, though without the House of Lords offering any firm conclusion. It has, however, more recently been accepted in *Neville v Wilson* [1997] Ch 144, where the

Court of Appeal favoured the view that writing was not required by virtue of section 53(2).

Finally, it must be stressed that the argument here applies only to contracts which are specifically enforceable. It is the availability of this remedy which gives rise to the constructive trust. You therefore need to know when specific performance is available, which, for present purposes, is essentially where damages would not be an adequate remedy because equivalent substitute property cannot be acquired elsewhere. This is the case with contracts to transfer (or create) interests in land and shares in private (though not public) companies.

Summary

- Sometimes, if you want to make a transfer or other disposition of your property, all you need to do is make clear that this is what you want and the transfer then takes effect. However, often, more is needed. For instance, you may need to express your intention in a particular form, such as in writing, or the transferee may first need to be registered as the new proprietor. In such cases, the transfer will take effect only if and when these other steps have been taken. We can call these additional steps formality requirements.

- Different formality requirements apply to different sorts of dispositions (eg gifts, trusts, etc.) and to different types of property (eg land, shares, etc.).

- If you want to pass the benefit of property to someone else, there are three basic ways of doing it:
  1. you can make an outright transfer (or gift);
  2. you can declare yourself trustee of that property; or
  3. you can transfer the property to some third party to hold on trust for your intended beneficiary.

- The law allows you to choose whichever of these modes of beneficial transfer you like. However, as a general rule, it will not help you if you fail in your chosen mode. Equity will not perfect an imperfect gift.

- A number of exceptions exist to this rule, however. The most significant is the rule in *Re Rose*. This, in its original form, said that if you intend to transfer property outright then, so long as you do all that *you* need to do to make this transfer effective, you will hold the property on trust for your intended donee, notwithstanding that the outright gift is (as yet) ineffective because someone else has failed to do what he needed for the transfer to go through. This rule has been controversially extended so that such a trust will now arise wherever it would be unconscionable for the donor to change his mind about the gift.

- Trusts can usually be created without formality. There are two principal exceptions: trusts of land and testamentary trusts.

- Section 53(1)(b) of the Law of Property Act 1925 requires trusts of land to be evidenced in writing. However, an exception has been recognised, whereby an oral trust of land will take effect in cases where, in pursuance of an oral agreement, a settlor transfers land to his intended trustee to hold on trust for him (or, possibly, some third party). In such cases, the courts will give effect to the trust, despite the lack of writing, in order to prevent the trustee keeping the property for himself.

- You can create trusts to take effect on your death. These must satisfy the requirements of section 9 of the Wills Act 1837, which state that the trust be in writing, signed and witnessed.

- An exception has, however, been recognised to allow trusts which do not satisfy these requirements, where the testator has told the intended trustee that he wants him to hold the property on trust and the trustee has agreed to do this. These are known as *secret trusts*.

Summary cont'd

▶ Secret trusts can be either fully or half secret. In a *fully secret* trust, the will makes no mention at all of the intended trust – instead the will appears to show an outright gift to the intended trustee. In a *half secret* trust, the will makes plain that the property is to be held on trust, but does not reveal the terms of that trust. The courts have developed different rules for fully and half secret trusts. The principal difference lies in relation to the time by which the trust must be communicated to and accepted by the trustee. In a fully secret trust, this can take place at any time up to the testator's death. In a half secret trust, however, the trust must be effectively communicated and accepted by the trustee before or at the time the will is executed.

▶ A beneficiary of a trust will typically have an equitable title to the trust property. This interest, like other proprietary interests, can be transferred to others. Section 53(1)(c) says, however, that 'dispositions' of such equitable interests must be made in writing and signed to be effective.

▶ An outright transfer of a beneficiary's equitable interest clearly counts as a disposition. So too where the beneficiary directs his trustee now to hold the property on trust for someone else. However, there is no such disposition where the beneficiary tells his trustee to transfer the trust property outright to someone else, thus bringing the trust to an end. Neither is there a disposition where the beneficiary declares himself a trustee of his equitable interest in favour of another.

Exercises

6.1 Why do we impose formality requirements in relation to the transfer and creation of proprietary interests? When, if ever, is it defensible to deny effect to a clearly intended transaction or disposition unless it is expressed in the required form?

6.2 Why should we not perfect imperfect gifts?

6.3 Is there a good reason for upholding secret trusts?

6.4 Duncan has led a full and exciting life but, fearing the end is nigh, decides to make a will. By his will, Duncan leaves his house to Joanne, £1,000 jointly to Mike and Tim, and his collection of paintings to Joe, 'in the expectation that he will distribute them in accordance with the directions I shall give him.'

Shortly after executing the will, Duncan speaks to Tim and asks him to hold the money he will receive under the will on trust for Duncan's illicit lover, Eimear. Tim agrees. Tim goes home and tells Mike, who tells Tim he wants nothing to do with 'the sordid little scheme'. Weeks later, and having had no further communication with Mike and Tim, Duncan adds a codicil, increasing the legacy to Mike and Tim to £2,000.

Duncan then sees Joe and gives him a sealed letter, which he tells Joe is not to be opened until after Duncan's death. Joe looks baffled, so Duncan remarks, 'It's about my paintings'. Joe nods and puts the letter in his pocket.

Just before his death, Duncan decides that he wants the house to go to his secret love child, Akshay. He calls Joanne to give her the relevant instructions but she is not in. He leaves a message on her answer machine, telling her that she is to hold the house on trust for Akshay. Duncan dies that night. Joanne does not get the message until the following morning.

Advise.

6.5 What policy underlies the requirement, set down by section 53(1)(c) of the Law of Property Act 1925, that dispositions of equitable interests must be made in writing? Have the courts kept this policy in mind when determining the scope of the sub-section?

Further reading

Battersby, 'Formalities for the disposition of equitable interests under a trust' (1979) 43 Conv 17

Critchley, 'Instruments of fraud, testamentary dispositions, and the doctrine of secret trusts' (1999) 115 LQR 631

Feltham, 'Informal trusts and third parties' [1987] Conv 246

Green, '*Grey, Oughtred* & *Vandervell* – a contextual reappraisal' (1984) 47 MLR 385

Hodge, 'Secret trusts: the fraud theory revisited' [1980] Conv 341

Matthews, 'The words which are not there: a partial history of the constructive trust' in Mitchell (ed), *Constructive and Resulting Trusts*(Hart Publishing 2010)

Nolan, '*Vandervell v IRC*: a case of overreaching' [2002] CLJ 169

Perrins, 'Can you keep half a secret?' (1972) 88 LQR 225

Perrins, 'Secret trusts: the key to the dehors' [1985] Conv 248

Swadling, 'The nature of the trust in *Rochefoucauld v Boustead*' in Mitchell (ed), *Constructive and Resulting Trusts* (Hart Publishing 2010)

Youdan, 'Formalities for trusts of land, and the doctrine in *Rochefoucauld v Boustead*' [1984] CLJ 306

Youdan, 'Informal trusts and third parties: a response' [1988] Conv 267

Chapter 7

Constitution and promises to create trusts

7.1 The constitution of trusts

We saw in the previous chapter that there are two ways a settlor may set up a trust. He may either declare himself trustee or he may appoint someone else to act as trustee for his chosen beneficiary. The former route requires only that the settlor effectively declare, that is express, his intention to create a trust and, as we also saw in the previous chapter, this can usually be done orally and so without any formality. If, however, the settlor does not want to declare himself trustee but wants instead someone else to perform that role, then there is more that he has to do to get the trust up and running. In addition to effectively declaring the trust, the settlor must also ensure that the trust property is vested in his chosen trustee. In other words, the settlor has to transfer his interest in the trust property to the person who is to act as trustee. This second step is known as the *constitution* of the trust, and until the trust is constituted by transfer of the relevant property to the trustees no trust can arise, notwithstanding the clear intention of the settlor.

Now, the rules that the settlor need comply with in order for his interest in the property to pass to the trustee vary depending on the nature of that property and the settlor's interest in it (see further Section 6.1). The law has different rules for the transfer of different sorts of proprietary interests. Legal title to tangible personal property – cars, paintings, bank notes etc. – is typically passed by physical delivery of the relevant thing (when accompanied by an intention to pass title), though it can also be done by the execution of a deed of gift. The transfer of legal title to land requires a deed (Law of Property Act 1925, s 52(1)) and, if the land is registered, also registration of the transferee as the new proprietor in the land register (Land Registration Act 2002, ss 29, 30). Legal title to shares used to be passed by the execution of a share transfer form followed by the transferee being entered as the new owner in the company's records, though now this can also be done electronically (Stock Transfer Act 1963, s 1; Companies Act 2006, ss 770–72). Debts and other choses in actions are transferred in law by writing followed by notice to the debtor (Law of Property Act 1925, s 136), whereas copyrights require signed writing (Copyright, Designs and Patents Act 1988, s 90(3)). We saw in Chapter 3, when discussing *Jones v Lock* (1865) 1 Ch App 25, that the payee of a cheque can transfer his right to payment by endorsing the cheque, that is signing the back of the cheque and writing the name of the new payee. And, as we saw in the previous chapter, where the settlor's interest in the property is equitable then its transfer must be made in writing and signed by the transferor by virtue of section 53(1)(c) of the Law of Property Act 1925.

If the settlor fails to take the necessary steps to pass his interest in the property to the trustee then no trust will arise. The property will remain with the settlor and he remains free to deal with it as he pleases. The only exceptions to this are those we examined in the previous chapter where equity, exceptionally, is willing to perfect what would otherwise be an imperfect gift (Sections 6.4–6.7).

7.2   Trusts of future property

An express trust cannot, therefore, arise unless and until the trustee gets his hands on the intended trust property. One necessary consequence of this is that a settlor cannot create a trust of future property, that is property in which he as yet has no legal (here meaning 'as recognised in law' and so including both common law and equity) interest. However, the courts have been prepared to treat an attempt to create an immediate trust of future property as a *promise* to create a trust of such property as and when it is received: *Re Ellenborough* [1903] 1 Ch 697; *Williams v Cmrs of Inland Revenue* [1965] NZLR 395. The rights of the parties then depend on the law's treatment of such promises.

7.3   Promises to create trusts

One may expect the law to respond to promises to create trusts, or covenants to settle as they are traditionally known, in the same way as it responds to promises generally. In other words, we simply look to contract law, which tells us which promises are legally binding and who can claim what when such promises are broken. However, the law on promises to create trusts seems to deviate in a number of important respects from orthodox contract law. Nonetheless, in principle these promises are to be treated no differently from other sorts of promises, so we shall begin by looking at the basic principles of contract law and how these would apply to promises to create trusts.

First, not all promises are legally binding. It is only in certain circumstances that making a promise gives rise to legal rights and obligations. In English law there are two principal situations in which a promise has some legal effect. The first is where the promise is made in a deed. This is a formal document (see section 1 of the Law of Property (Miscellaneous Provisions) Act 1989), which binds the promisor simply by virtue of the fact that he expressed his promise in that form. A promise made by deed is also known as a *covenant*. The second is where *consideration* has been given for the promise. This is one of the most contested legal concepts, but in essence consideration exists where the promisor has asked for something in return for his promise ('I promise to do X if you do/promise to do Y'). In such circumstances, the promisee is said to have given value for the promise.

It should also be noted that in one important respect equity extended the notion of consideration. It was once common for trusts to be set up on the occasion of a marriage to provide for the couple and their family. Sometimes the property would come from other relatives, sometimes from the couple themselves. In the latter case, often the couple would not only create a trust of property they owned already but would also promise to transfer into the trust other assets which they might receive during their lifetimes. The marriage was regarded as consideration for these promises; moreover such 'marriage consideration' embraced not just the couple themselves but also their children and grandchildren, so that they were all treated as though they had given value in return for the promise.

Importantly, the legal effect of promises made by deed differs from that of promises supported by consideration. Where a promise made by deed but not supported by consideration is broken, the other party (or parties) to the deed can only recover damages for the loss caused by its breach. By contrast, where consideration has been given, there is the possibility that the court will order specific performance, which compels the promisor actually to keep his promise rather than simply to compensate the promisee for the loss caused by not keeping it. As specific performance is an equitable remedy, this gives rise to the maxim 'equity will not assist a volunteer', a volunteer being someone who has not given consideration. (It is worth noting that the scope of this maxim is limited to imperfect gifts and incompletely constituted trusts. It certainly does not mean that equity gives rights or claims only to those who have given consideration. So, if a trust has been validly created, it can be enforced by the beneficiary even if no consideration was given for this: see *Paul v Paul* (1882) 20 Ch D 742. For more on the unreliability of this maxim, see Section 1.9)

One further point should also be noted at this stage. The position stated in the preceding paragraph has now been modified by the Contracts (Rights of Third Parties) Act 1999. The effect of the Act is that where A and B enter into a contract which purports to confer a benefit on C, C will be able to enforce the contract despite neither having himself provided consideration nor (if the promise is made by deed) being named as a party to the deed, unless in turn it appears that A and B did not intend C to be able to enforce it. (Some have doubted whether the 1999 Act applies to promises made by deed. However, there is no good reason for it not to and s 7(3) clearly suggests that it does.) For convenience we shall first examine the law as it developed prior to the Act coming into force, then consider what the impact of the legislation may be.

So, ignoring for the moment the 1999 Act, where S promises to create a trust for B, one would expect the result to be as follows:

1. If the promise was neither made by deed nor supported by consideration, no claim will lie if S fails to keep his promise.
2. If the promise was made by deed but no consideration was provided, the covenantee could recover damages for any loss caused to him by S's breach, but will not be able to compel the promisor to set up the trust.
3. If consideration was given for the promise, the promisee (or, where applicable, those within the marriage consideration) could likewise recover damages for breach, but may alternatively be entitled to specific performance of the contract, thus compelling S to set up the trust as promised.

The cases, however, do not back this up. Although they endorse propositions 1 and 3, they do not support proposition 2. So, it is clear that where the promise is not made by deed and is not supported by consideration, there is no claim, and S can neither be compelled to constitute the trust nor to pay damages for not doing so. Equally, the courts have confirmed that where consideration has been given for the promise then, at least if damages would not be an adequate remedy, they will compel S to declare the trust or transfer the property to the trustees as the case may be. Indeed, where the courts would compel S to set up the trust, he is treated as holding the property on such trusts from the moment he receives it: see for example *Pullan v Koe* [1913] 1 Ch 9. (This is an application of the general rule we encountered in Section 6.24 and which we shall examine in greater detail in Section 9.5, that where you are under a specifically enforceable obligation to transfer identified property to another then, pending that transfer, you hold that property on trust for the transferee.)

The difficulty comes in those cases where S has promised by deed to create a trust but no consideration has been given for the promise. As we noted, in principle the covenantee – whether this is T, the intended trustee, or B, the intended beneficiary – should be able to recover damages for breach of the covenant. However, this is not what the courts have held. Instead they have held that, though B may recover damages if *he* is a party to the covenant (*Cannon v Hartley* [1949] 1 Ch 213), where the covenant is made only with T, neither B nor T is entitled to damages in the event of S's breach.

The leading case is *Re Pryce* [1917] 1 Ch 234, where the court had to determine whether the trustees of a marriage settlement should take steps to recover property, which should have been transferred to them under the terms of that settlement. Despite being parties to the deed, Eve J held that the trustees should not bring any claim against the current holders of the property. He based his conclusion on the fact that the beneficiaries of the trust, as they were not within the marriage consideration, could not seek specific performance of the covenant, and that where specific performance is unavailable a claim for damages must also be denied. Moreover, Eve J held the trustees should not be allowed to claim as this would indirectly give the beneficiaries what they could not directly claim for themselves.

The flaws in Eve J's reasoning are plain. His statement that damages could not be claimed where specific performance is not available is clearly wrong (see too Elliott, 1960). The general rule in contract remedies is that specific performance will not be ordered if damages would be an adequate remedy. In other words, where specific performance is unavailable this is precisely because damages *are* available and adequately remedy the breach. As such, it makes no sense at all to say that damages awards are themselves dependent on the availability of specific performance. Moreover, it is not a valid reason for denying one party's rightful claim that this would benefit someone else who had no claim of their own. Nobody suggests that, if I contract with you to deliver me some flowers, you can escape your obligation to deliver them or to pay damages if you fail to simply by showing that I was only going to give the flowers to someone else. The fact that *that person*, my intended recipient, had no right that you deliver the flowers is neither here nor there. Similarly, the trustees should have been able to enforce their rights under the covenant notwithstanding that it was the beneficiaries who would ultimately receive any property the trustees recovered. Nonetheless, *Re Pryce* was followed in *Re Kay's Settlement* [1939] 1 Ch 329 and *Re Cook's Settlement Trusts* [1965] 1 Ch 902.

What if, contrary to *Re Pryce*, T were to bring a claim for breach of the covenant? It has been suggested that, as T is only to receive the property as trustee, he – as opposed to the beneficiaries – suffers no loss as a result of S failing to hand over the property. As such, some have claimed that, were T to bring a claim for breach of the covenant, he would recover at most nominal damages. This too seems to be a mistake however. It appears that T *is* entitled to recover substantial damages – measured by reference to the value of the property S covenanted to transfer – notwithstanding that he was only ever intended to receive that property on trust: *Re Cavendish-Browne's Settlement Trusts* [1916] WN 341; Elliott, 1960; Goddard, 1988; cf Friend, 1982.

How might the Contracts (Rights of Third Parties) Act 1999 change any of this? Section 1(1) of the Act provides that:

> ... a person who is not a party to a contract ... may in his own right enforce a term of the contract if –
>
> (a) the contract expressly provides that he may, or
> (b) subject to subsection (2), the term purports to confer a benefit on him.

Section 1(2) then provides that section 1(1)(b) 'does not apply if on a proper construction of the contract it appears that the parties did not intend the term to be enforceable by the third party.'

It is plain that promises to create trusts, whether supported by consideration or made in a deed, fall within section 1(1)(b) and so, unless it appears that this is not what S intended, B will have a right to enforce his promise. This will make no difference where B has a claim in any case because he has himself provided consideration or, as in *Cannon v Hartley*, is a party to the deed. Where, however, traditionally B has had no claim, the Act may make a big difference. Consider cases such as *Re Pryce*, where S covenants with T to set up a trust for B. As we have seen, the cases say that neither T nor B has any claim should S fail to keep his promise. However, by virtue of the Act there is now a good argument that both B *and* T can claim. Unless a contrary intention on the part of S could be proved, B would gain a right to enforce the contract under section 1(1)(b). Moreover, as B himself has a claim, the *Re Pryce* argument for denying T's claim must also fall away.

7.4   Trusts of covenants

Prior to the Contracts (Rights of Third Parties) Act 1999 there was one other way a promise to create a trust could be enforced by the would-be beneficiary despite his not having provided consideration nor being named as a party to the deed.

If A and B contract for the sale of A's car to B for £5,000, both A and B acquire rights to each other's performance: A has a right that B pay him £5,000, and B has a right that A transfer the car to him. These rights or claims are a form of property, sometimes referred to as a chose in action. As items of property, A and B can (usually) transfer those rights to someone else. So, A may assign his right that B pay £5,000 to C. This would then mean that it is C who holds the right to £5,000 and so who can demand that payment from B. And just as A may make an outright transfer of his right to C, so he may also declare a trust of it. So if A declares a trust of his right to the £5,000 in favour of C, A will retain his legal right to claim the money from B, but C will then be able to compel A to enforce the claim and C can then demand that the money B pays to A is in turn paid over to him.

Similarly, if S covenants with T that S will create a trust for B, T will acquire a right that S perform the covenant. As we have seen, not being a party to the deed, B will have no right of his own to enforce the covenant. However, if T holds *his* right on trust for B then B will in effect be able to enforce the covenant through T and thereby secure the benefit intended for him: *Fletcher v Fletcher* (1844) 4 Hare 67. This avoids the problems posed by *Re Pryce* (Section 7.3), where T was not able to enforce his rights under the covenant on the basis that this would confer a benefit on B to which B had no right of his own, because here, by virtue of the trust of the covenant, B *does* have a right to that benefit.

It has been suggested that this option is not available where the covenant is to create a trust of *future* property – that is property which is not yet owned by S – on the basis that there can be no present trust of future property: see for example *Re Cook's Settlement Trusts* [1965] 1 Ch 902 and Lee, 1969. However, this thinking is muddled. Although, as we have seen, it is true that one cannot create a trust of future property (Section 7.2), a covenant to create a trust of future property creates an immediate right to enforce that covenant, and *that right*, being present rather than future property, *can* be the subject matter of a trust: see too *Davenport v Bishop* (1843) 2 Y & CCC 451 and *Lloyd's v Harper* (1880) 16 Ch D 290; Meagher and Lehane, 1976. Accordingly, the better view is that if S covenants to transfer asset X to T to hold on trust for B, the right to enforce that covenant can itself be held on trust for B, regardless of whether S currently owns X, and that this puts B in a position to enforce S's covenant.

The only question then is when will T hold his rights under the covenant on trust for B. The position will be clear if the deed contains an express declaration of trust of the rights it creates. So, S may covenant with T to transfer any property he receives under his father's will to T to hold on trust for B, with the covenant going on to state that the rights arising under the covenant are *also* to be held by T on trust for B. If so, there will be a clear intention to create a trust of those rights. As such, if S then receives property under his father's will but refuses to transfer it to T, B, by virtue of the trust of the covenant rights, can require T to sue S and, at least if we view the damages recovered as representing the property S should have transferred to T, there is no problem then saying that T holds that money on trust for B.

But what if the deed says nothing about the rights under the covenant being held on trust for B? One might imagine that, in the absence of any declaration of trust, the obvious conclusion would be that there would be no trust of those rights. However, some have argued (see eg Hornby , 1962; Mitchell, 2010, 71) that T *always* holds his rights under the covenant on trust, even where the deed itself is silent on this issue. Why? The argument is as follows: as T is expressly identified in the deed as a trustee, this means that he must also hold his right to enforce the covenant on trust. The only alternative would be that T holds the right to enforce the covenant not on trust but for his own benefit. This, however, is thought to be implausible as this would mean that it would be up to T to decide whether or not to enforce the covenant. So, on this view, the trustee will always hold his right to enforce the covenant on trust and the only remaining question is who the beneficiary of this trust is.

One might then think the most likely beneficiary is B, as he is the person who is intended to benefit from performance of the covenant. Once again, however, we find another view being proposed: that, in the absence of a clear intention that the rights under the covenant are to be held on trust for B, they must instead be held on trust for S (see Mitchell, 2010, 71–72). The idea here is that, unless S has made clear who the beneficiary of the trust of the covenant is to be, we have a trust which fails for uncertainty of objects. And, as we saw back in Chapter 3 and will examine in more detail in Chapter 8, where a trust fails for uncertainty of objects, the trust property will be held on a resulting trust for the settlor. As such, in the absence of a clearly identified beneficiary *of the rights under the covenant*, T will hold those rights on trust for S. This would, in turn, allow us to endorse the result, though not the reasoning, in *Re Pryce*. Unless S makes clear that the right to enforce the covenant is held by T on trust for B, it must be held on trust for S. And, in such a case, T should not be able to enforce those rights *against* S for the very reason that T holds those rights on trust *for* S. Any such claim would clearly go against S's wishes and hence would conflict with T's duty to act in S's best interests.

However, although this argument neatly accounts for *Re Pryce* there are reasons to be sceptical. The argument has two steps, both of which may be challenged. First, it says that, where S covenants with T to transfer property on trust to T, T necessarily also holds his right to enforce that covenant on trust. But why? It is true if T held this right absolutely then nobody could compel him to sue, but it would not follow that, if he did sue and succeed, he could keep any damages recovered for himself. It would not be difficult to see any damages as representing (or as a substitute of) the property S has promised to transfer on trust to T, and so they would be 'caught' by the covenant and T would be obligated to hold them on trust for B.

The second step of the argument says that, unless S clearly provides that the right to enforce the covenant is to be held on trust for B, it must be held on trust for S. This too seems odd. In the absence of any stipulation one way or another, it would seem a reasonable inference to say that B is the intended beneficiary of the right to enforce the covenant. After all, if we are prepared to infer that T must be a *trustee* of the right to enforce the covenant from the fact that he is to be a trustee of the property to be transferred under the covenant, then why should we not also infer that B is the *beneficiary* of the right to enforce the covenant from the fact that he is to be the beneficiary of the property transferred under it? It is arbitrary to say that we can infer the existence of a trust but not the identity of the beneficiary of that trust. And if we ask who is the most likely beneficiary, the answer is clearly B.

Certainly this is more plausible than inferring that the right is to be held on trust for S, as this effectively deprives the covenant of any legal effect (see too Feltham, 1982). For, if S is the beneficiary, T cannot enforce the covenant against S's wishes, which then effectively leaves S at liberty to break the covenant. By contrast, the conclusion that T holds his rights under the covenant on trust for *B* not only makes the covenant genuinely binding, but it also makes it enforceable by the very person whom the parties were intending to benefit through these arrangements. As such, if we are to endorse the view that T will hold his rights under the covenant on trust, then, in the absence of clear evidence to the contrary, we should presume that the beneficiary of those rights is B and not S.

This all leaves the law looking rather uncertain and very complicated. It seems pretty clear that where S promises by deed that he will transfer property to T to hold on trust for B, B will be able to enforce that promise either where he is himself a party to the deed or where the deed declares that T holds his right to enforce the covenant on trust for B. However, it remains unclear why no claim will lie, whether by T or by B, outside those situations. The one piece of good news is that many of these controversies are likely to be rendered obsolete by virtue of the Contracts (Rights of Third Parties) Act 1999, which will, absent a contrary intention, give rights to B, as a third party beneficiary of the covenant, regardless of whether he is a party to the deed or whether any trust of the right to enforce the covenant has been set up.

7.5 'Fortuitous vesting' of trust property

Needless to say, the problems concerning the enforceability of promises to create trusts only arise if the promisor fails to keep his promise. If the promise is kept, and the promisor transfers the property to the trustees, the trust will be fully constituted. The beneficiaries will then be able to enforce it like any other trust, notwithstanding that, prior to the trust's constitution, they had no right to enforce the promise: *Paul v Paul* (1882) 20 Ch D 742.

Moreover, it seems that, where S has covenanted to transfer property to T to hold on trust for B, the trust will take effect once title to the property is received by T, irrespective of *how* T came to receive the property. So, in *Re Ralli's Will Trusts* [1964] Ch 288, S by deed set up a trust (trust 1) and covenanted to transfer to her trustees certain other property, including S's interest under a separate trust (trust 2) created on the death of S's father. S, however, never assigned her interest under trust 2 to the trustees of her trust (trust 1). When S died, T was the sole trustee of both trusts. Therefore, despite the lack of any assignment, legal title to the property which S had covenanted to assign to T happened to be held by T. Buckley J held that this sufficed to constitute the trust, such that the beneficiaries of the trust S had covenanted to create could claim S's interest under trust 2. The thinking here has much in common with the rule in *Strong v Bird* (Section 6.5), which holds that an imperfect gift (ie transfer of title) will be perfected if the transferor dies and the intended transferee is appointed his executor. As executor, the transferee will receive the title the transferor had intended to pass to him, and so the gift ends up being completed, albeit more by luck than by judgment. The same thing is going on here: S covenants to transfer property to T and T ends up receiving that property, albeit fortuitously. All that matters is that the property is received by T and, once it is, the trust is properly constituted.

Although the result in *Ralli* seems reasonable enough, its authority can be questioned. First, it is not quite right to say that T ended up being vested with the very interest which S covenanted to transfer to the trustees of trust 1. S had covenanted to transfer to T her *equitable* interest under trust 2. What T ended up receiving was the *legal* title to that trust property. As such, it is not clear that the trust was *ever* properly constituted. Second, the decision in *Ralli* appears to conflict with, and was decided without reference to, the earlier decision *Re Brooks' Settlement Trusts* [1939] Ch 993, where, in similar circumstances, no trust was found in spite of the fact that the intended trust property had coincidentally vested in T.

In *Re Brooks'*, S was one of the objects of a trust set up by his mother. He subsequently covenanted to transfer to trustees all interests he had and would receive under that original trust. As in *Ralli*, both trusts had the same trustees. His mother later exercised a power of appointment under the original trust in favour of S, and the question was whether the trustees were to pay that money to S or were instead to hold it on the trusts S had declared in the covenant. Farwell J held that the money was to be paid to S, as no trust of that money had been effectively created. Farwell J focussed on the fact that S had no interest in that money at the time he executed the covenant and that he only acquired such an interest years later when the power of appointment was exercised in his favour. This is uncontroversial. The important question for our purposes, however, was, *now that the power had been exercised and S did have such an interest*, whether a trust of that money was properly constituted on the basis that the money was *now* held by the trustees with whom he had covenanted. Unfortunately, this point simply is not addressed in Farwell J's judgment. As such, given that the question of fortuitous vesting simply was not answered, even considered, we may doubt whether *Re Brooks'* should be treated as an authority opposed to the view in *Ralli* that constitution requires only that the trustee get hold of the trust property, and that it makes no difference *how* he ends up with it.

Summary

▶ A trust cannot arise until title to the intended trust property is vested in the intended trustee. This is the requirement that the trust be properly *constituted*.

▶ Accordingly, a trust will not arise simply as a result of a settlor promising to set up a trust. In such a case, the beneficiary's rights, if any, depend on his ability to enforce such a promise. Promises are usually enforceable only where consideration is provided or where they are made in a deed, and they are usually enforceable only by those who have given consideration or those who are a party to the deed (though this has been extended by the Contracts (Rights of Third Parties) Act 1999). However, as the law stands, there will be no claim to enforce a promise to set up a trust if the promise is made in a deed to which the intended trustee, but not the intended beneficiary, is a party.

▶ An intended beneficiary may also enforce a promise to create a trust if, despite not having himself provided consideration or being a party to the deed, the person who did provide consideration or who was a party to the deed holds his right to enforce that promise on trust for the beneficiary.

▶ Though the authorities are not wholly clear, it appears that where T *does* receive the property S had covenanted to transfer to him, the trust will be properly constituted, irrespective of how or why the property ended up coming into T's hands.

Exercises

7.1 Can we justify the current rules on the enforceability of promises to create trusts?

7.2 In what circumstances will a covenantee hold his rights under a covenant to settle on trust? Who is likely to be the beneficiary of such a trust?

7.3 Can we reconcile the decisions in *Re Ralli's Will Trusts* and *Re Brooks' Settlement Trusts*? If not, which should we prefer?

Further reading

Elliott, 'The power of trustees to enforce covenants in favour of volunteers' (1960) 76 LQR 100
Friend, 'Trusts of voluntary covenants – an alternative approach' [1982] Conv 280
Goddard, 'Equity, volunteers and ducks' [1988] Conv 19
Hornby, 'Covenants in favour of volunteers' (1962) 78 LQR 228
Meagher and Lehane, 'Trusts of voluntary covenants' (1976) 92 LQR 427

Chapter 8

Resulting trusts

8.1 The nature of resulting trusts

The trusts which we call resulting trusts share a common pattern: A transfers property to B, and B ends up holding that property on trust for A. The effect of these trusts is, therefore, to send the beneficial interest in the property back to the transferor. This is indeed how resulting trusts get their name. Resulting means 'jumping back': the beneficial interest 'jumps back' to the person who had it at the outset. (Though, strictly speaking, in the bulk of these cases the beneficial interest doesn't go anywhere. It remains with the transferor throughout.)

So this tells us something about how resulting trusts work. The important questions, however, are when and why trusts like these arise. As we shall see, the when question is easier to answer than the why. One thing, however, which we might think we can take for granted is that these trusts arise for some reason other than the transferor's intention to create such a trust. After all, we already have a category of trusts which covers those trusts which are intentionally created, namely express trusts, which have been our focus till now. As we shall see, things may not be quite so straightforward. However, for now we may simply note that a settlor may choose to create trust in his own favour, by transferring property to a trustee to hold on trust for him. Trusts like these share the same pattern as resulting trusts: the property moves from A to B and B holds that property on trust for A. Yet we don't call this a resulting trust; it's a straightforward express trust, which just so happens to send the beneficial interest back where it started. As such, not every trust which is 'resulting' in pattern is a resulting trust.

8.2 The traditional instances of resulting trusts

Resulting trusts have traditionally been understood to arise in two types of cases. These are summarised in the following passage from the leading judicial statement on resulting trusts, the judgment of Lord Browne-Wilkinson in *Westdeutsche Landesbank Girozentrale v Islington London BC* [1996] AC 669, 708:

> Under existing law a resulting trust arises in two sets of circumstances: (A) where A makes a voluntary payment to B or pays (wholly or in part) for the purchase of property which is vested either in B alone or in the joint names of A and B, there is a presumption that A did not intend to make a gift to B: the money or property is held on trust for A (if he is the sole provider of the money) or in the case of a joint purchase by A and B in shares proportionate to their contributions. It is important to stress that this is only a presumption, which presumption is easily rebutted either by the counter-presumption of advancement or by direct evidence of A's intention to make an outright transfer ... (B) Where A transfers property to B on express trusts, but the trusts declared do not exhaust the whole beneficial interest.

The common practice has been to label type (A) resulting trusts as *presumed* resulting trusts and type (B) as *automatic* resulting trusts (though, as we shall see, Lord Browne-Wilkinson rejected these terms). We shall examine each in turn.

8.3 Presumed resulting trusts

The first situation where resulting trusts have traditionally arisen is where there has been a gratuitous transfer of property. This covers two types of property transfer. First, where A transfers property to B, with B giving nothing in return (eg I give you my car). Second, where A pays some or all of the purchase price for property which is put into B's name (eg I buy a car for you). In both cases, equity, unless it can find a contrary intention, says that B holds that property on trust for A. If A was the sole owner of the property transferred or provided all of the purchase money, he will be the sole beneficiary of the trust (see *Dyer v Dyer* (1788) 2 Cox Eq Cas 92); if the property was initially co-owned or he provided only some of the purchase money, his beneficial interest under the trust will be proportionate to his contribution (see *The Venture* [1908] P 218). So, if A pays £5,000, B £3,000 and C £2,000 for a car for B, then B holds it on trust for A, himself and C with the beneficial interest split between them in the proportions 5:3:2. (In the following sections, unless otherwise indicated, the term 'gratuitous transfers' is intended to embrace both types of cases.)

As mentioned already, things work out this way only if there is no contrary intention on the part of the transferor. Indeed, were it otherwise it would be impossible to make a gift. Equity simply says that if a gift is to take effect, there must be evidence that this is what the donor intended. This is why this type of resulting trust has often been called presumed: there is a presumption that, where A gratuitously transfers property to B, B will hold on trust for A, but this presumption can be rebutted. Quite what sort of evidence and what sort of intention will rebut the presumption of resulting trust is controversial, and we shall look at this in some detail later. Two things are clear though.

First, if the evidence shows that A positively intended to make a gift of the property to B, there will be no resulting trust and B will take the property absolutely. So, if the court knows no more than that A transferred property to B and got nothing in return for it, it will conclude that B holds that property on trust for A. But if there is other information available which sheds light on what A intended when transferring the property to B, the court will weigh up this evidence to come to a conclusion as to what A's intentions were. If, on consideration of all the evidence, the most likely interpretation is that A did intend a gift, there will be no trust.

A good example of this is provided by *Fowkes v Pascoe* (1875) LR 10 Ch App 343. There a wealthy woman, Mrs Baker, bought two sums of stock. One of these she had put in the joint names of herself and Pascoe, a young man who lived with her and whom she treated as a grandson. The other she had put in the joint names of herself and another woman who was her companion. When Mrs Baker died, the question was whether Pascoe held the first sum of stock on resulting trust for her estate, or whether he held it beneficially. The court held that, though the presumption of resulting trust applied, it was on the facts clearly rebutted. Given the circumstances and the relationship between the parties, there was simply no plausible explanation for the purchase except that Mrs Baker intended to make a gift of the stock to Pascoe. As James LJ put it:

> [T]he evidence in favour of gift and against trust is absolutely conclusive. ... The lady had £500 to invest; she had already large sums of stock standing in her own name, besides other considerable property. Is it possible to reconcile with mental sanity the theory that she put £250 into the names of herself and her companion, and £250 into the names of herself and [Pascoe], as trustees upon trust for herself? What trust – what object is there conceivable in doing this?

Second, in some cases equity has traditionally applied a different presumption, the presumption of advancement. As we shall see shortly, Parliament has recently passed legislation which will abolish the presumption of advancement (Section 8.4). However, as this legislation is not yet in force and, moreover, as even then it will only operate prospectively (meaning that for some years to come the courts will have to decide cases concerning property acquired prior to the legislation taking effect and so to which the presumption of advancement will continue to apply), it remains important to see how this presumption operates.

Where this presumption of advancement applies, it effectively reverses the presumption of resulting trust, in that equity presumes that a gratuitous transfer from A to B takes effect as a gift to B rather than as a trust for A. Whether this presumption applies depends on the relationship that exists between A and B. It certainly applies to transfers made by husbands to their wives and by fathers (and others standing in loco parentis, such that they are in a position analogous to a father) to their children. It is less clear whether the presumption of advancement applies to transfers from mothers to children, and, as the law stands, it does not apply to transfers by wives to their husbands. Like the presumption of resulting trust, this too can be rebutted by contrary evidence.

In principle the presumption of resulting trust applies in the same way regardless of the nature of the property being transferred. However, the application of resulting trusts to transfers of land is unclear by virtue of section 60(3) of the Law of Property Act 1925. This provides:

> In a voluntary conveyance a resulting trust for the grantor shall not be implied merely by reason that the property is not expressed to be conveyed for the use or benefit of the grantee.

The suggestion is that this abolishes resulting trusts which would otherwise arise where A conveys his land to B gratuitously, though it would have no impact on resulting trusts arising where A pays for land which is put in B's name. For a long time the courts refrained from offering any firm conclusions on the effect of the sub-section (see eg *Hodgson v Marks* [1971] Ch 892 and *Tinsley v Milligan* [1994] 1 AC 340, 371) and doubts were voiced over whether this was in fact the correct interpretation of the provision. In *Lohia v Lohia* [2001] WTLR 101, Nicholas Strauss QC held that section 60(3) does indeed mean that it is no longer the case that a gratuitous conveyance of A's land to B raises a presumption of resulting trust. On appeal, the Court of Appeal ([2001] EWCA Civ 1691, [2001] All ER (D) 375) expressed some sympathy for this view but held in the end that no firm conclusion on this point was necessary for the disposition of the case. This did not stop the Court of Appeal subsequently in *Ali v Khan* [2002] EWCA Civ 974; [2002] All ER (D) 170 stating that the High Court in *Lohia* had established that the presumption of resulting trust had indeed been abolished in relation to conveyances of land by section 60(3). Of course, even on this view, this does not stop A bringing evidence that a trust was in fact intended, though if A succeeds in proving this then this should be viewed as an express trust rather than a resulting trust.

Moreover, as we shall see in more detail in the following chapter, the presumption of resulting trust now appears to have been abandoned in cases where A and B (or indeed A alone) contribute to the purchase price of land, which is to be their home and which is then registered in their joint names (perhaps with the added condition that the parties also undertake joint responsibility for the mortgage: see *Jones v Kernott* [2011] UKSC 53; [2012] 1 AC 776, [25]; the presumption of resulting trust remains where land is bought in joint names for other purposes). So, if A and B buy a house together, contributing 75% and 25% of the purchase price respectively, and legal title to the house is conveyed to them as joint tenants, then the courts will no longer presume that their *equitable* interests will be proportionate to their contributions. Instead, the presumption will be that they are also joint tenants in equity, and the onus is on the party seeking a greater share than this to show that this is in fact what the parties (can be taken to have) intended.

8.4   The role and significance of presumptions

Later on we shall look in greater detail at how these presumptions work in practice. However, before then it is worth spending a little time thinking about the role presumptions play in the law.

Much of what courts do is determining questions of fact. Was an offer accepted? Was an injury caused by the defendant? Did the defendant intend to harm the victim? Sometimes all the relevant facts are apparent and undisputed, but more often courts are involved in a form of educated guesswork. The defendant may say that when he fired the gun he only wanted to scare the victim, not kill him, but the court (or in this case the jury) must look at all the evidence and come to its own conclusion as to what really happened. The facts that the gun was pointed at the victim's head and that the defendant pulled the trigger may lead to an inference of an additional fact, that the defendant intended to kill. In other words, it is common for certain material facts to be proved 'indirectly', by proving other facts from which one can then infer the presence of the material fact. The courts do this all the time. Sometimes the courts develop a practice of drawing an inference of a certain material fact from the presence of one or more other facts or circumstances. So, if facts A and B are proved, the court will infer or presume that fact C also occurred. Accordingly, if the claimant needs to prove fact C to succeed in his claim, he will satisfy the burden of proof by proving facts A and B. This is a presumption: where facts A and B are present, there is a presumption that fact C also occurred.

A presumption, then, is really a standardised legal inference. The law is effectively saying, 'Because, where facts A and B are present, fact C is usually also present, we will assume, all things being equal, that where facts A and B are proved to have occurred, fact C also occurred'. However, it may be possible for the defendant to establish that, despite A and B having occurred, fact C did not happen. It is, for example, possible to point a gun at someone's head (fact A) and pull the trigger (fact B) without intending to kill that person (fact C), for instance if you did not believe that the gun was loaded. In such a case the defendant will be saying, 'I know that usually when facts A and B are present, so is fact C, but this is one of those unusual cases where fact C did not coincide with facts A and B'. If the defendant succeeds in persuading the court of this, he will have rebutted the presumption.

It is important to appreciate two things here. First, the application of presumptions is really just a standardised application of the sorts of judgment that the courts must make every day when confronted with insufficient or contradictory evidence. Indeed, we make these sorts of inferences all the time in our everyday lives. So, if we want to know whether someone likes us we look for signals, such as smiles, lingering glances, gratuitous physical contact. We do this because we know that, usually, these signals – these facts – are indicative of another fact: that that person likes us. Of course, we know too that these signals may be misleading, and that the person doesn't in fact like us despite the evidence suggesting that he or she does. As such, there is nothing particularly mysterious in the courts doing the same sort of thing.

Second, and more importantly, where a presumption applies and is not rebutted, the court proceeds on the basis that it has been proved that the presumed fact occurred. This can be seen by taking an example from contract law, where the courts use a presumption known as the presumption of undue influence. Very broadly, undue influence occurs when a defendant takes unfair advantage of a position of power or influence over you. If you can establish that you entered into a contract with the defendant as a result of him exercising undue influence over you, you can have that contract set aside. The cases on undue influence show that you can go about proving this in two ways.

One route is to adduce evidence of what exactly the defendant did to make you 'agree' to the contract (ie what he said and did to coerce you). Where undue influence has been proved in this way, the case has traditionally been said to be one of 'actual' undue influence. However, you can make out your case in an alternative way: by proving that the relationship between you and the defendant was one which created the possibility of abuse (usually called a relationship of 'trust and confidence') and that the contract was one which was not obviously beneficial to you (one that 'calls for explanation'). Establishing these two facts raises a presumption of undue influence. In other words, faced with those two facts, the courts will read between the lines and presume or infer a third fact: that the defendant abused his position in the relationship to procure the claimant's entry into the contract. The claimant will then succeed in having the contract set aside, unless the defendant can rebut this presumption by bringing evidence that this is not in fact what happened. These cases have been traditionally labelled as 'presumed' undue influence. However, as Lord Nicholls did a good job of explaining in *Royal Bank of Scotland plc v Etridge (No. 2)* [2001] UKHL 44; [2002] AC 773, despite the different labels, these are just two ways of proving the same thing: that the defendant took unfair advantage of you. (And as an aside, as *Etridge* shows, it is misleading to say that presumptions reverse the burden of proof. A claimant who wants to establish the existence of undue influence by relying on the presumption of undue influence – and likewise a claimant who wants to establish a trust by reference to the presumption of resulting trust – still bears the burden of establishing the facts which raise that presumption.) So at the end of the day, if you can raise the presumption of undue influence and the defendant cannot rebut it, the court concludes – and you have *proved* – that undue influence occurred in just the same way as it would have done had you brought evidence of what exactly the defendant said and did to force or manipulate you into entering the contract.

This, then, is what is happening in the field of 'presumed' resulting trusts. The courts are drawing a presumption or inference of fact (as to the transferor's intentions) from the presence of other facts (namely, a gratuitous transfer between parties in a certain relationship to one another). It also tells you that it is not so much the resulting trust that is presumed; rather a particular fact is presumed, which then leads to the conclusion that a resulting trust has arisen. The crucial question of course is what fact it is that the courts are presuming here, so as to justify a finding of a trust of the property transferred. We shall look at that question in due course. Before we get there though, it should be said that although the application of presumptions or inferences to determine questions of fact is unremarkable, the justifiability of particular presumptions depends on their accuracy. Do they fit the facts? Is it really true to say that, where A and B have occurred, the most likely conclusion is that fact C is also present?

A strong argument can be made that the presumptions we are applying here are, in many cases, simply unreal, in that they do not represent the most likely interpretation of events and so involve implausible factual inferences. So, for instance, it is common to criticise the divergent treatment of transfers between spouses and between parents and their children: see, for instance, the statements of Lord Reid, Lord Hodson and Lord Diplock in *Pettitt v Pettitt* [1970] AC 777. As we have seen, the presumption of advancement applies to transfers by fathers to their children and by husbands to their wives, but not where a mother transfers property to her children or a wife to her husband. The problem here is not (just) sexual inequality, but that it simply is not true to say that the intentions of fathers and mothers typically differ when it comes to transferring property to their children, or that husbands and wives typically intend different things when transferring property to one another. As such there is no good reason to apply different presumptions here. More fundamentally, one may think that, whatever the relationship between the parties, the most probable explanation of a gratuitous transfer is that A intended a gift to B. If so, then we should never apply a presumption of resulting trust and the presumption of advancement should instead apply across the board.

In light of this, Parliament's recent decision to abolish the presumption of advancement should be seen as something of a mixed blessing (see also Glister, 2010). The relevant provision is section 199 of the Equality Act 2010, subsection 1 of which states bluntly: 'The presumption of advancement (by which, for example, a husband is presumed to be making a gift to his wife if he transfers property to her or purchases property in her name) is abolished.' The good news here is that this will put an end to the arbitrarily divergent treatment of husbands and fathers on the one hand and wives and mothers on the other. As soon as section 199 comes into force, transfers from husband to wife will be treated in the same way as transfers from wife to husband, as likewise will transfers from fathers and mothers to their children. As against this, it extends the ambit of the presumption of resulting trust, a presumption which, however understood, is unlikely to mirror the actual intentions of the vast majority of those who make gratuitous transfers of property. So, although the equality between the sexes, which section 199 will achieve is obviously to be welcomed, ideally we should want our presumptions to fit the facts. It might be thought, therefore, that the better option would have been for the presumption of resulting trust, and not the presumption of advancement, to have been sacrificed.

In any case, the content and the justifiability of the presumptions only really matter to the extent that they are determinative of cases in which they may apply. If the presumption is never relied upon to decide cases then we do not need to worry too much about whether it is an appropriate presumption to apply. So, to what extent do the presumptions of resulting trust and advancement affect the outcome of litigation? Although it is perhaps natural to think of presumptions as a starting point, which the parties can then try to rebut or confirm by adducing further evidence, it is better to regard them as evidential longstops (see eg Lord Upjohn in *Vandervell v Inland Revenue Cmrs* [1967] 2 AC 291, 313), which will be determinative of the case at hand only if there is no other information for the court to go on. Almost invariably, there will be further evidence beyond the mere facts of the transfer and the parties' relationship, which shines a light on the intentions of the transferor, and on which the outcome of the case will then turn.

The presumptions are best viewed, then, simply as a tool to assist in determining what really occurred, what the parties actually intended. Accordingly, they have a use, but only in so far as they do in fact assist in this task. It seems that for the most part this is indeed how the courts have approached the presumptions of resulting trust and advancement. *Fowkes v Pascoe* (1875) LR 10 Ch App 343, which we looked at earlier (Section 8.3), illustrates this. However, on occasion the courts appear to have clung a little too tightly to the presumptions, using them as the basis for decisions even where they fly in the face of reality. For example, in *Re Vinogradoff* [1935] WN 68, a woman transferred a substantial sum of stock into the joint names of herself and her four-year-old granddaughter. Clearly the woman cannot have intended that the child act as a trustee of the property for her, and so the only plausible reading of the facts is that the woman intended this as a gift. Nonetheless the court held that the presumption of resulting trust had not been rebutted, and so the child held the property on trust for the grandmother.

Cases like *Re Vinogradoff* are, however, anomalies, the modern tendency being to downplay the role of the presumptions. Recent cases have nevertheless confirmed that there is still one context in which the presumptions may play a vital role: illegality.

8.5 Resulting trusts and illegality

As we have seen, the presumptions will rarely determine the outcome of cases, for there will be other evidence available on which the court can base its decision. However, occasionally the parties will be precluded from adducing evidence of what they actually intended, in which case the presumptions may end up playing a decisive role. This possibility arises where A transfers property to B as part of an illegal scheme.

The problem arises in the following circumstances. Sometimes A may want it to appear that he does not own a particular asset. For instance, A does not want his creditors to be able to demand that the asset be sold to meet their claims, or he wants to appear less wealthy so that he can avoid a tax liability or make benefit claims. Therefore he transfers the property to B. However, he does not intend B to keep the property for himself. Though he wants it to appear to the outside world that B owns the property, it is understood between A and B that A remains beneficially entitled to the asset, therefore allowing A to recover the property when the coast is clear and the illegal scheme is complete or no longer necessary.

What, then, if B refuses to reconvey the property to A, claiming instead to hold it outright? Though A was clearly intended to retain an interest in the property, A has the problem of proving that intention without at the same time admitting his unlawful purpose. In other words, the court is unlikely to be persuaded that A did intend B to hold the property on trust for him without an explanation as to why A wanted to set up such a trust. Understandably, however, the courts are reluctant to lend their assistance to litigants whose claims or defences are founded on their own unlawful activity. What then is the court to do? It is here that the presumptions provide a convenient solution, as they allow the court to determine entitlement to the property without reference to the actual intentions, and hence to the unlawful purposes, of the parties.

This can best be seen through examination of the leading case on resulting trusts and illegality, *Tinsley v Milligan* [1994] 1 AC 340. Miss Tinsley and Miss Milligan bought a house in which to live together as a couple and on the understanding that they would be beneficial co-owners. Legal title to the house was, however, put in Tinsley's name alone. This was done to enable Milligan, with Tinsley's knowledge and consent, to make fraudulent claims for social security benefits. The money then obtained was used for their joint benefit. Later, the couple fell out and Tinsley tried to evict Milligan. Milligan counterclaimed for an order that the house be sold and the proceeds split between them. The court therefore had to determine who was entitled to the property.

By a bare majority, the House of Lords held that Milligan succeeded in establishing an equitable joint interest and so was entitled to an order for sale. For the majority, the key question was whether Milligan could establish an interest in the house without relying on the illegal purpose. If she could, she could enforce that interest, even though the illegality in which the parties were involved was revealed through other evidence or the admissions of the other party. This is where the presumption of resulting trust becomes all important. All Milligan needed to show was a gratuitous transfer from A to B, which was clearly demonstrated by her provision of some of the purchase money to acquire the house. This gave rise to a presumption of resulting trust in her favour. This would give her an interest in the property unless Tinsley was able to rebut it by evidence of what the parties actually intended. However this did not help Tinsley, because not only did the parties indeed intend Milligan to have an interest, but in any case evidence of the parties' actual intentions would have revealed the fraud and so would not have been admissible. In Lord Browne-Wilkinson's words ([1994] 1 AC 340, 371):

> Where the presumption of resulting trust applies, the plaintiff does not have to rely on the illegality. If he proves that the property is vested in the defendant alone but that the plaintiff provided part of the purchase money, or voluntarily transferred the property to the defendant, the plaintiff establishes his claim under a resulting trust unless either the contrary presumption of advancement displaces the presumption of resulting trust or the defendant leads evidence to rebut the presumption of resulting trust. Therefore, in cases where the presumption of advancement does not apply, a plaintiff can establish his equitable interest in the property without relying in any way on the underlying illegal transaction. ... Miss Milligan was not forced to rely on the illegality to prove her equitable interest. Only in reply and the course of Miss Milligan's cross-examination did such illegality emerge: it was Miss Tinsley who had to rely on that illegality.

Here then the presumptions prove decisive and, as Lord Browne-Wilkinson says, everything then turns on which presumption applies. If A transfers property to B in furtherance of some illegal scheme, the presumption of resulting trust will apply and so A will be able to reclaim the property, so long as A is not B's father or husband. If, however, A is B's husband or father (or otherwise stands in loco parentis to B) then the presumption of advancement will apply, and A can only succeed by rebutting this presumption. As this can be rebutted only by evidence revealing the unlawful scheme, A will therefore lose out.

An important exception to the *Tinsley v Milligan* approach exists, however, which means that the presumptions will not always be decisive in cases of transfers for unlawful purposes. This is known as the doctrine of locus poenitentiae and applies where the parties never actually carry out their illegal plan. It is now established that where A transfers property to B in order to effect some unlawful scheme, but the parties withdraw from it before their illegal purpose has been wholly or partly carried into effect, A is not precluded from bringing evidence of his actual (dishonest) intentions in making the transfer in a claim to recover the property. This is the case regardless of whether the parties withdraw from the plan because they have had a change of heart or simply because it turned out that they did not need to put it into action.

This can be seen from *Tribe v Tribe* [1996] Ch 107. There, a father, the majority shareholder of a clothing company, transferred his shares to his son because he feared that he might be forced to sell them to meet liabilities he owed to his landlords. If the landlords then tried to enforce their rights against the father, he could claim that he did not have the resources to meet them as he no longer owned the shares. However, as it turned out, he and the landlords settled their dispute and so he did not need to deceive them by falsely claiming that he was no longer entitled to the shares. When the son refused to reconvey the shares to his father, the father sought an order that the son must give them up.

The Court of Appeal held that because the transfer was from father to son, the presumption of advancement applied. However, the father was able to rebut this by showing that he did not intend to make a gift to his son, even though this required him to bring evidence of his unlawful purpose. This was because the illegal scheme, namely the deception of the landlords, had never been carried into effect. Moreover, it did not matter that the plan was not carried out solely because it never proved necessary rather than because the parties had thought better of it.

Millett LJ summed up the relevant principles as follows ([1996] Ch 107, 134):

> (1) Title to property passes both at law and in equity even if the transfer is made for an illegal purpose. ... (2) The transferor's action will fail if it would be illegal for him to retain any interest in the property. (3) Subject to (2) the transferor can recover the property if he can do so without relying on the illegal purpose. This will normally be the case where the property was transferred without consideration in circumstances where the transferor can rely on an express declaration of trust or a resulting trust in his favour. (4) It will almost invariably be so where the illegal purpose has not been carried out. It may be otherwise where the illegal purpose has been carried out and the transferee can rely on the transferor's conduct as inconsistent with his retention of a beneficial interest. (5) The transferor can lead evidence of the illegal purpose whenever it is necessary for him to do so provided he has withdrawn from the transaction before the illegal purpose has been wholly or partly carried into effect. It will be necessary for him to do so ... if he brings proceedings in equity and needs to rebut the presumption of advancement.

The second part of proposition (4) merits attention as it appears to add a further qualification to the *Tinsley v Milligan* approach. What Millett LJ is saying here is that it may not always be enough for a transferor, A, to rely on the presumption of resulting trust as the transferee, B, may be able to rebut that presumption. There is nothing unusual in this as a matter of general principle, but its application to cases of illegality causes difficulties. The example Millett LJ gives of a situation in which B would be able to rebut the presumption is where A transfers property to B to conceal it from his creditors and then A settles with his creditors on the footing that A has no interest in it. Here, Millett LJ believed that B could give evidence of A's dealings with his creditors to rebut the presumption and show a gift was intended.

Why did Millett LJ think this? If A did indeed intend a gift to B, so that he was not in fact attempting to defraud his creditors, there is of course no problem in B rebutting the presumption. However, if A did not intend a gift and was instead seeking to mislead his creditors, then how can B rebut the presumption of resulting trust? After all, A did indeed intend to retain the beneficial interest in the property, so A's actual intention *confirms* rather than rebuts the presumption (cf *Tinker v Tinker* [1970] P 136). Millett LJ's argument must be that A's dealings with his creditors, *when viewed in isolation*, suggest that A did intend a gift (as A's settlement with his creditors was reached on the basis that the property was no longer A's). So B need only bring evidence of these dealings and need not make any reference to the plan to defraud them in order to rebut the presumption of resulting trust. This would shift the burden of proof back onto A to show that he did not in fact intend a gift, but he cannot do this without himself bringing evidence of his unlawful purpose.

The problem with this is that it is hard to see why the same argument does not also apply to *Tinsley v Milligan*. There Milligan received social security benefits by representing that she had no interest in the house. Surely then, on Millett LJ's view, Tinsley could have rebutted the presumption of resulting trust by bringing evidence of the benefit claims by Milligan, because these, again when looked at in isolation, suggest that Milligan retained no interest in the house and had instead intended her contribution to the purchase price as a gift to Tinsley. If so, Milligan would have lost the case as she would have had to lead evidence of her unlawful purpose to show that no gift was intended. As such it seems impossible to reconcile this part of Millett LJ's judgment (Nourse LJ giving the other full judgment said nothing on this) with the decision in *Tinsley v Milligan*.

Cases such as *Tribe* aside, one important consequence of the *Tinsley v Milligan* approach is that, as we are using presumptions to determine the outcome of cases, it really matters that our presumptions are defensible (see too *Lowson v Coombes* [1999] Ch 373, 385). In this regard we should note that the different treatment of transfers made by fathers and mothers and of transfers made between husbands and wives will lead to different results in cases which seem materially indistinguishable. So if, for example, a man transfers property to his wife or child to defraud his creditors, the presumption of advancement will apply and so the man will not be able to reclaim the property. If, by contrast, a woman transfers property to her husband or child to defraud her creditors, she will be able to recover the property by virtue of the presumption of resulting trust. Yet there is no good reason for treating the two cases differently. Thankfully, the anomalies created by *Tinsley* will be removed once section 199 of the Equality Act 2010 comes into force. However, as noted previously, this provision will operate only prospectively. Property acquired before the section takes effect will fall to be dealt with through the traditional presumptions, and so they will be employed to resolve disputes for a while yet.

Indeed, more generally we can question whether it is appropriate to use such presumptions, even if rid of their present inconsistencies, to resolve these cases. If we are not going to allow the parties to bring specific evidence of their actual intentions, it seems arbitrary still to make use of the presumptions. After all, the only reason the presumptions exist is to act as a guide to what the parties did intend. If, despite the illegality, we wish to give effect to what the parties intended then all evidence as to their actual intentions should be admissible. If we are not concerned with giving effect to the parties' intentions then the presumptions are irrelevant and should be ignored. The *Tinsley v Milligan* approach, as Millett LJ noted in *Tribe v Tribe* [1996] Ch 107, 134, 'does not conform with any discernible moral principle. It is procedural in nature and depends on the adventitious location of the burden of proof in any given case.'

How else could we deal with the problem of transfers for unlawful purposes? One alternative would be to give the courts greater discretion, so that they could determine the rights of the parties to the property either on the basis of a value judgment as to the desirability of the claim (ie would more harm be done by allowing the claimant to recover the property or by leaving it with the defendant?) or by reference to the policy which renders their plan unlawful (ie would the policy supporting the outlawing of such conduct be better served by allowing the property to be recovered or by leaving it with the defendant?).

The former approach, looking to the moral pros and cons of allowing recovery, had been favoured by the Court of Appeal in *Tinsley v Milligan* but was rejected unanimously in the House of Lords. The problem with such approaches is that the flexibility they provide comes at the cost of certainty. By contrast, as *Tinsley* bears out, approaches prioritising certainty lead, on occasion, to arbitrariness and injustice. This seems to be one of those areas where there is no ideal solution. Section 199 of the Equality Act (if and) when it comes into force, will at least ensure that the worst instances of arbitrariness entailed by the *Tinsley* approach are avoided. However, the rejection of the presumption of resulting trust, in cases where land is bought in joint names (see Sections 8.3 and 9.14), would seem to open up the possibility of further anomalies if we continue to resort to the presumptions to resolve the illegality cases.

With this in mind, the Law Commission (2010) proposed that courts be given a structured discretion when dealing with trusts which have been set up to conceal the true beneficial owner of the property for some criminal purpose (whether or not that purpose has then been acted on). As such this would cover cases such as *Tinsley* and *Tribe*. Under these proposals, courts should first determine the parties' interests in light of their actual intentions – a clear break from the *Tinsley* approach whereby such evidence would not be admitted – before going on to consider whether the illegal purpose justifies preventing one or other of the parties from enforcing his interest. The Law Commission's recommendation was that courts should do this only in exceptional circumstances. If the court concludes that the circumstances are indeed exceptional then it must go on to consider whether one or other of the beneficiaries should be prevented from enforcing the trust. In making this determination the Law Commission provided a (non-exhaustive) list of factors the court should weigh up: the conduct and intention of the parties; the value of the equitable interest at stake; the impact of allowing the claim on the criminal purpose; whether refusing the claim would have a deterrent effect on other potential wrongdoers; and the possibility that the person from whom the equitable interest was being concealed may have a claim against the beneficiary's assets. Where the court does conclude that the beneficiary should be prevented from enforcing his interest, the court would then determine who is to receive that interest instead.

However, the Government has now decided not to implement the Law Commission's recommendations, as it was not satisfied that the draft bill would improve upon the present law sufficiently to make legislation worthwhile, especially given that there are relatively few cases where the existing law leads to the wrong result.

8.6   The content of the presumption

It is clear that the effect of the presumption of resulting trust is that, unless rebutted, B, the recipient of a gratuitous transfer, will hold it on trust for A, the transferor. It is also clear that when the presumption is rebutted, whether by contrary evidence or by the presumption of advancement, B takes the property absolutely. As we noted earlier, however, there is some uncertainty as to what exactly the courts are presuming when applying the presumption of resulting trust. We shall now examine this question more closely.

Why does the content of the presumption matter? Besides the intellectual satisfaction provided by knowing exactly what we are doing and why we are doing it, it is crucial in practice as it affects the outcome of cases. As we have seen, the presumption of resulting trust will be rebutted by contrary evidence. But to know what counts as evidence inconsistent with the presumption we must know what we are presuming in the first place. Accordingly, different views of the content of the presumption will lead to different views as to when resulting trusts arise. We have seen (Section 8.4) that when applying the presumption of resulting trust, the courts are drawing a presumption or inference of fact. Moreover, it is clear that the fact relates to A's (and possibly B's) state of mind when transferring the property to B. But what exactly are we presuming A's state of mind to have been?

There are two schools of thought. On one view, where A gratuitously transfers property to B, the presumption is that A intended B to hold that property on trust for him: see Swadling, 1996. On this basis, unless the presumption is rebutted, a resulting trust arises to give effect to A's intentions. The alternative view is that in such circumstances it is presumed that A did not intend B to take the property beneficially: see Birks, 1992; 2004, 185–98; Chambers, 1997. Here the trust exists to prevent B obtaining a benefit A did not intend him to have or, in the standard terminology, to ensure that B is not unjustly enriched. That is, though B acquires legal title to the property, the resulting trust allows A to recover it, thus depriving B of the benefit of the property and redirecting it to A.

In the majority of cases, both views lead to the same outcome. For instance, if the facts show that A intended to make a gift to B then the presumption will clearly be rebutted on either view: A's intent to transfer the property to B absolutely is clearly inconsistent both with A intending that B hold the property on trust for him and with A not intending to benefit B. Similarly, if the evidence shows that A did indeed intend B to hold the property on trust for him, then the presumption will be confirmed and such a trust will arise whichever view we take. However, occasionally the two views of the presumption do depart so as to lead us to different outcomes. Imagine that A transfers property to B while labouring under some mistake, for instance A may pay B money he wrongly believes he owes to B. Can A claim that the money is held on resulting trust for him? As B gives nothing in return for the money, the presumption of resulting trust is clearly raised. The question is whether the presumption is rebutted.

On the first view, what we are presuming is that A intended to create a trust in his favour and this presumption will be rebutted if this can be shown to be not true. The fact that, when A handed the money over to B, he was intending to discharge a debt that he (wrongly) believed he owed to B is clearly inconsistent with A having positively intended that B should take the property as trustee for A. Therefore, on this view of the presumption, it would be rebutted and there would be no resulting trust.

By contrast, on the second view, whereby we are presuming that A did not intend to benefit B, the presumption would not be rebutted and B would hold the money on resulting trust for A. This requires a little explanation. As we have just noted, when A handed over the money, he was intending to transfer it to B outright in order to discharge a perceived liability. So A did indeed have a beneficial transfer 'in mind'. However, A was mistaken; he didn't in fact owe any money to B. This allows A to say that, though he handed over the money intending it to be received beneficially by B, this intention was conditional upon the money in fact being owed to B. In other words A can claim 'I only intended to pay you money I owed. I never had any intention of paying you money I did not owe. Because, as things turned out, I didn't owe you this money, I didn't intend you nonetheless to have the benefit of it.' As such, *in these circumstances*, A did not intend to benefit B (see further Webb, 2010). And so, if we understand the presumption to be a presumption that A did not intend B to receive the property beneficially, the facts confirm rather than rebut the presumption and a resulting trust would arise. The same divergence in outcome between the two views is also evident when A transfers property to B under duress or on the basis of some condition, which then fails, as well as where the property is taken from A and given to B without A's knowledge.

So this is when and why it matters how we view the presumption in cases of presumed resulting trusts. The question then is which view is correct as a matter of law. Here there has been considerable uncertainty. As a matter of history, it is pretty clear that, when first developed some centuries ago, the presumption applied to gratuitous transfers was that A intended B to hold the property on trust for him. However, it does not follow that this is the view that the courts have stuck to ever since. Various formulations of the presumptions can be found in the cases which support one view or the other. However, one can question how much weight they should carry given the judges who offered them were most likely unaware that there were two competing interpretations of the presumptions and hence of the significance of 'choosing' one over the other. When we focus on cases of mistaken, coerced or otherwise 'defective' transfers, where the different views of the presumptions lead to different outcomes, we again find no consensus. Most of these cases give no support for resulting trusts arising in such circumstances, though this can be explained at least in part by the fact that this was never argued. Moreover, there do seem to be a handful of cases in which resulting trusts have been found, which can be explained only on the basis that the presumption is of a lack of intent to benefit rather than of a positive intent to create a trust; see eg *Ryall v Ryall* (1739) 1 Atk 59, and more generally Chambers, 1997, 20–27; 2010; cf Swadling, 2000, 251–57.

The upshot of this is that although the advocates of both views can derive some support from some of the cases, neither camp can claim to have all the cases on their side. However, the argument from authority has been significantly cleared up following the House of Lords' decision in *Westdeutsche Landesbank Girozentrale v Islington London BC* [1996] AC 669. There the claimant bank paid significant sums of money to the defendant local authority under a contract which turned out to be void as it was beyond the powers of the local authority. When this was discovered, the bank argued, inter alia, that there was a resulting trust of the money it had paid to the authority under the void contract. The bank's argument on this point was not fully developed, but in essence would have gone as follows. First, as the 'contract' had no legal effect, nothing had been given in return for the money and hence the presumption of resulting trust was raised. Second, on the view that what is being presumed is a lack of intent to benefit the transferee, the presumption had not been rebutted, as the bank did not intend the authority to have the benefit of the money in the circumstances. (As with our previous example, it intended the authority to have the money only on the condition that this was money it owed by virtue of a valid contractual obligation.) The local authority's argument, by contrast, was that the relevant presumption was of an intent to create a trust in the transferor's favour, and hence it was rebutted as the bank clearly never did set out to create a trust.

The court was therefore faced with a clear choice between the two views of the presumption. The House of Lords unanimously came down on the side of the first view we described earlier: the presumption in cases of presumed resulting trusts is that A intended that B should hold the property on trust for him. The bank had not intended to create a trust, accordingly the presumption was rebutted and its resulting trust argument failed. In support of this conclusion, Lord Browne-Wilkinson, giving the leading judgment, preferred the analysis of the cases put forward by Swadling (1996) to that offered by Birks (1992). Moreover, both he and Lord Goff also considered that the first view of the presumption was supported by legal principle. We shall consider the argument of principle later in the chapter.

For now, the key point is that *Westdeutsche* largely settles the question of what the law is as to the fact presumed where the presumption of resulting trust applies, and hence also as to the sort of evidence which is capable of rebutting this presumption. The fact presumed is that A intended that B hold the property on trust for A himself, and this can be rebutted by any evidence inconsistent with such an intention. This will be the case not simply where A has the positive intention of making a gift to B but also where the evidence shows that A transferred the property to B by mistake, as a result of coercion or on a condition that failed, and indeed where A never intended that the property should end up in B's hands at all.

Two qualifications must be made, however, which mean that the question cannot be regarded as fully settled, even simply as a matter of authority. First, in *Westdeutsche*, Lord Browne-Wilkinson held that it was not simply A's intention that was important in the creation of resulting trusts but also B's. According to him, resulting trusts ([1996] AC 669, 708):

> ... are traditionally regarded as examples of trusts giving effect to the common intention of the parties. A resulting trust is not imposed by law against the intentions of the trustee (as is a constructive trust) but gives effect to his presumed intention.

This suggests that the presumption of resulting trust is not just that A intended for B to hold the property on trust for him, but that *both* A *and* B intended B to hold the property on trust for A. It then follows from this that the presumption will be rebutted if *either* A *or* B can be shown to have had an intention inconsistent with this. In particular it would mean that there could be no resulting trust unless B knew that he was to hold the property on trust for A. Moreover, it seems that B must know, and indeed intend, this at the time of the transfer, and so a resulting trust (as opposed to a constructive trust: Section 9.18) cannot arise if B finds out about it only subsequently. Lord Browne-Wilkinson's view that B's intentions are also relevant followed from his more general view that for any trust to arise (whether express, constructive or resulting), the trustee's 'conscience must be affected'. In his words ([1996] AC 669, 705):

> Since the equitable jurisdiction to enforce trusts depends upon the conscience of the holder of the legal interest being affected, he cannot be a trustee of the property if and so long as he is ignorant of the facts alleged to affect his conscience, ie until he is aware that he is intended to hold the property for the benefit of others in the case of an express or implied trust, or, in the case of a constructive trust, of the factors which are alleged to affect his conscience.

It seems that Lord Browne-Wilkinson's reason for taking this position was that it would not be legitimate to impose the full range of fiduciary duties, such as normally accompany the role of an express trustee, on someone who had no reason to know that he was a trustee. As we shall see, however, the better view is that not every trustee owes all these duties (Section 10.12), and so, although 'unknowing' trustees should not be exposed to such duties and liabilities, this should not prevent a trust, in the sense of a separation of legal and equitable title, arising on such facts (see now *Independent Trustee Services Ltd v GP Noble Trustees Ltd* [2012] EWCA Civ 195; [2012] 3 WLR 596, [80]). Moreover, the cases do not back up Lord Browne-Wilkinson's view that the trustee's conscience must be affected before a trust can arise; indeed a number of cases suggest the opposite (see Swadling, 2000, 257–61). Accordingly, the better view, both in principle and as a matter of authority, is that trusts can arise even without the trustee's knowledge. There is therefore no good reason to regard B's intentions as relevant to the application of the presumption of resulting trust.

Second, the view of the presumption of resulting trust put forward in *Westdeutsche* appears to be challenged by a statement made by Lord Millett in the Privy Council decision in *Air Jamaica Ltd v Charlton* [1999] 1 WLR 1399, 1412. He said:

> Like a constructive trust, a resulting trust arises by operation of law, though unlike a constructive trust it gives effect to intention. But it arises whether or not the transferor intended to retain a beneficial interest – he almost always does not – since it responds to the absence of any intention on his part to pass a beneficial interest to the recipient.

This seems clearly to differ from the position taken in *Westdeutsche*. As we have seen, in *Westdeutsche*, the House of Lords endorsed the view that resulting trusts arise to give effect to A's (and supposedly B's) intention that B should hold the property on trust for A. As such a resulting trust can arise only where A *does* intend to retain a beneficial interest in the property, for an intention to create a trust in one's own favour *is* an intention to retain the beneficial interest in that property. Here, by contrast, Lord Millett is saying that a resulting trust can arise even where A does *not* intend to retain a beneficial interest in the property transferred, and hence even where A intends no trust. Hence Lord Millett's dictum appears to reopen the debate as to the content of the presumption of resulting trust, which *Westdeutsche* looked largely to have settled.

There is an additional complication here. It appears at first glance that Lord Millett is in fact endorsing the view of the presumption taken by Birks (1992), and subsequently endorsed by Chambers (1997), but rejected in *Westdeutsche*. As we have seen, their view was that the presumption is that A lacks an intention to benefit B, so that there would, for example, be a resulting trust where A transferred property to B by mistake, under coercion or on a condition which failed. However, Lord Millett's extra-judicial writing reveals that he in fact has a different understanding of resulting trusts from Birks and Chambers. Thus Millett (1998a, 201–2) agrees with the House of Lords in *Westdeutsche*, in opposition to Birks and Chambers, that no resulting trust arises in the case of mistaken, coerced or conditional transfers. So, although Millett frames the presumption of resulting trust in the same way as Birks and Chambers – and differently from Swadling and the court in *Westdeutsche* – as a presumption that A did not intend to benefit B, he in fact means something different by this.

Millett's view is that, where A transfers property by mistake, this rebuts rather than – as Birks and Chambers argue – confirms the presumption of resulting trust. The reason for this is that, at the time A makes the transfer, he is indeed intending to benefit B (see also Swadling, 2008). It may be that he later regrets it, or he may say 'had I known the truth, I wouldn't have made the transfer', but this cannot change the fact that at the time A did intend a beneficial transfer. Accordingly, in such a case, Millett would say that A *did* intend to benefit B, and so the presumption is rebutted and no resulting trust arises.

As such, Millett has no problem accounting for the result in *Westdeutsche*. There, the bank paid over the money intending that the local authority receive it beneficially, because it (wrongly) believed the contract was valid and the money was owing. In fact, the only situation in which Millett's view leads to an outcome different from the approach endorsed by the House of Lords in *Westdeutsche* is where A had no knowledge of or otherwise gave no consent at all to the property being transferred to B (say B snatches A's property from him). In such circumstances, A cannot be said *in any sense or at any time* to have intended to benefit B, and so, on Millett's view, the presumption is confirmed and a resulting trust arises. By contrast, on the *Westdeutsche* approach, as A was clearly not intending to create a trust, the presumption of resulting trust would be rebutted.

On this point of disagreement between Millett on the one hand and Birks and Chambers on the other, Birks and Chambers' view should be preferred. As we saw at the beginning of this section, although – as Millett rightly identifies – claimants who transfer property by mistake *do* have an intention to benefit their transferees, the mistake is significant precisely because it shows that the claimant's intention to make the transfer was conditional on certain facts being true (in *Westdeutsche*, the condition was the validity of the contract). This means the claimant can genuinely say that, *in the circumstances*, he did not intend to benefit the defendant. So, the bank in *Westdeutsche* clearly *never* intended that the authority should have the money even if the contract turned out to be void. So, if we do take the view that the presumption of resulting trust is a presumption that A did not intend to benefit B, then we should conclude, like Birks and Chambers, that this presumption is *not* rebutted in cases of mistaken or otherwise conditional transfers and a resulting trust ought arise (see further Webb, 2010).

Regardless of whether Lord Millett is right or wrong on this point, his dictum in *Air Jamaica* in no way qualifies the authority of *Westdeutsche*. Nonetheless it is important as it shows that *Westdeutsche* has not settled the debate on resulting trusts and so is unlikely to be the last word on the subject. That being so, the argument of principle – when and why *should* resulting trusts arise? – becomes that much more important. We shall look into this shortly. First, though, we need to look at the second category of resulting trusts: automatic resulting trusts.

8.7   Automatic resulting trusts

The second situation in which it is accepted that resulting trusts arise is where A transfers property to B to hold on express trust, but, for one reason or another, the trusts declared do not exhaust the entire beneficial interest in the property. In such a case, to the extent that the declared (express) trusts fail to exhaust the beneficial interest, this is held on trust for A.

We have come across this idea a number of times already. So, for example, if A transfers property to B to be held on trust, but the trust fails (in whole or in part) for uncertainty of objects, then B will, to the extent that the trust fails, hold the property on resulting trust for A. Hence, if I give £1,000 to you on trust, telling you that £300 is to go to X, £300 to Y, and £300 to Z, but saying nothing about the remaining £100, then a resulting trust of that final £100 arises so that you hold that money on trust for X, Y, Z and myself in the proportions 3:3:3:1. If I give my house to you on trust, to hold for X for life, but without allocating the remainder interest, then you hold the house on trust for X for life and the remainder on resulting trust for me.

Another example of automatic resulting trusts is provided by failed purpose trusts. As we saw in Chapter 4, English law generally invalidates non-charitable purpose trusts. As a result, if A transfers property to B to be held on a purpose trust which does not fall within any of the exceptions to the beneficiary principle, the intended trust will fail and B will instead hold the property on resulting trust for A. To the extent that we recognise exceptions to the rule prohibiting non-charitable purpose trusts, there is also the possibility that a purpose trust which is initially valid will later fail because the purpose has been achieved or is no longer capable of being pursued. In such a case, whatever property remains in the trustee's hands will then be held on resulting trust for the settlor. *Re the Trusts of the Abbott Fund* [1900] 2 Ch 326 appears to be an example of this. There, money was collected for the maintenance and support of two deaf and dumb women. When these women died, the question arose as to what was to be done with the money left over. Appearing to regard this as a valid purpose trust (or possibly a *Re Sanderson* type persons trust: see Section 4.7), Stirling J ruled that the remaining money was held on resulting trust for its contributors.

A more complex but also very important example of this sort of resulting trust is provided by *Vandervell v IRC* [1967] 2 AC 291. We have encountered this case already in the context of formalities (Section 6.21), where we saw that Vandervell arranged for shares to be transferred to the Royal College of Surgeons (RCS), so that the dividends then declared on those shares could be used to fund a chair of pharmacology. As Vandervell considered that it might be advantageous to regain control of the shares after the chair had been established, he also arranged for an option to repurchase the shares to be granted to a trustee company he had set up, Vandervell Trustees (VT). This option would then be exercised once the dividends had been declared and RCS had obtained the necessary money. The plan appears to have been that the shares would be held on trust by VT for Vandervell's children. However, this was not made plain at the time the option was granted, so although it was clear that VT had legal title to the option (an option being a form of property), it was uncertain who was to be beneficially entitled to it. The House of Lords, by a bare majority, held that VT was not intended to hold the option beneficially; instead it held it on trust. The problem, however, was that the beneficiaries of this trust had never been identified. As such, the only conclusion was that, in the absence of any certain objects, the option was held on resulting trust for Vandervell.

8.8 Automatic resulting trusts and intention

In *Vandervell v IRC* it was clear that Vandervell did not intend VT to hold the option on trust for him. The very reason Vandervell and his legal advisors chose to fund the chair by declaring dividends on shares transferred to the RCS, rather than by a simple direct payment, was to minimise the tax payable by Vandervell on the transaction. For this to work though, Vandervell needed to divest himself of any interest he had in the shares. Therefore, the last thing he wanted was a beneficial interest in the option. Moreover, this was acknowledged by the House of Lords. As such, it seems clear that the sort of resulting trust recognised in *Vandervell* does not arise because (the court believes) A intends that B hold the transferred property on trust for him.

Why, then, did the trust arise? Lord Wilberforce explained the result as follows ([1967] 2 AC 291, 329):

> The Court of Appeal, starting from the fact that the trustee company took the option as a volunteer, thought that this was a case where the presumption of resulting trust arose and was not displaced. For my part, I prefer a slightly different and simpler approach. The transaction has been investigated on the evidence of the settlor and his agent and the facts have been found. There is no need, or room, as I see it, to invoke a presumption. The conclusion, on the facts found, is simply that the option was vested in the trustee company as a trustee on trusts, not defined at the time, possibly to be defined later. But the equitable, or beneficial interest, cannot remain in the air: the consequence in law must be that it remains in the settlor.

To similar effect was Lord Upjohn who, having referred to the (presumed) resulting trusts which arise where there has been a gratuitous transfer of property, continued ([1967] 2 AC 291, 313):

> But the doctrine of resulting trust plays another very important part in our law and, in my opinion, is decisive of this case. If A intends to give away all his beneficial interest in a piece of property and thinks he has done so but, by some mistake or accident or failure to comply with the requirements of the law, he has failed to do so, either wholly or in part, there will by operation of law, be a resulting trust for him of the beneficial interest of which he had failed effectually to dispose. If the beneficial interest was in A and he fails to give it away effectively to another or others or on charitable trusts it must remain in him.

Two things seem clear from these extracts. One is that both Lord Wilberforce and Lord Upjohn considered that the kind of resulting trust which arises where an express trust fails is distinct, and operates differently, from the kind of resulting trust which arises by presumption upon a gratuitous transfer of property. Second, resulting trusts which arise from the failure of an express trust do so *automatically*. They are the necessary consequence of the express trust failing, the suggestion being that, if A has failed effectively to dispose of the beneficial interest, it must remain his.

It is this which led Megarry J in *Re Vandervell's Trusts (No. 2)* [1974] Ch 269, 294 to coin the terminology of presumed and automatic resulting trusts, and to offer the following account of their bases:

> Where A effectually transfers to B (or creates in his favour) any interest in any property, whether legal or equitable, a resulting trust for A may arise in two distinct classes of case ...
> (a) The first class of case is where the transfer to B is not made on any trust. If, of course, it appears from the transfer that B is intended to hold on certain trusts, that will be decisive, and the case is not within this category; and similarly if it appears that B is intended to take beneficially. But in other cases there is a rebuttable presumption that B holds on resulting trust for A. The question is not one of the automatic consequences of a dispositive failure by A, but one of presumption: the property has been carried to B, and from the absence of consideration and any presumption of advancement B is presumed not only to hold the entire estate on trust, but also to hold the beneficial interest for A absolutely. The presumption thus establishes both that B is to take on trust and also what that trust is. Such resulting trusts may be called 'presumed resulting trusts'.
> (b) The second class of case is where the transfer to B is made on trusts which leave some or all of the beneficial interest undisposed of. Here B automatically holds on resulting trust to the extent that the beneficial interest has not been carried to him or others. The resulting trust here does not depend on any intentions or presumptions, but is the automatic consequence of A's failure to dispose of what is vested in him. Since ex hypothesi the transfer is on trust, the resulting trust does not establish the trust but merely carries back to A the beneficial interest that has not been fully disposed of. Such resulting trusts may be called 'automatic resulting trusts'.

For many years, this was regarded as representing resulting trusts orthodoxy. However, its standing was challenged by Lord Browne-Wilkinson in *Westdeutsche Landesbank Girozentrale v Islington London BC* [1996] AC 669. Following on from his description of when resulting trusts arise (quoted earlier, Section 8.2), he said:

> Both types of resulting trust are traditionally regarded as examples of trusts giving effect to the common intention of the parties. A resulting trust is not imposed by law against the intentions of the trustee (as is a constructive trust) but gives effect to his presumed intention. Megarry J in *In re Vandervell's Trusts (No. 2)* suggests that a resulting trust of type (B) does not depend on intention but operates automatically. I am not convinced that this is right. If the settlor has expressly, or by necessary implication, abandoned any beneficial interest in the trust property, there is in my view no resulting trust: the undisposed-of equitable interest vests in the Crown as bona vacantia.

On this basis, all resulting trusts – whether arising from gratuitous transfers or from failed express trusts – arise for the same reason: because this is what (we presume) the parties intended. As such, the language of 'automatic' resulting trusts is inapposite and we should instead regard cases of failed express trusts as a second situation in which the presumption of resulting trust applies. In short, there are not different types of resulting trust, but a single type of resulting trust arising in a variety of circumstances.

There are a number of problems with Lord Browne-Wilkinson's approach. The criticisms we have already made in relation to presumed resulting trusts apply here too (Section 8.6). Hence, there is no good reason and no basis in authority for viewing B's intention as relevant to the creation of resulting trusts. Moreover, there does not seem to be a need for B's conscience to be 'affected' for such a trust to come into existence. There is, however, a further reason to be sceptical about Lord Browne-Wilkinson's account, for in relation to 'automatic' resulting trusts, the suggestion that they arise to give effect to A's intentions is contradicted by the cases.

It is likely that in the majority of cases where 'automatic' resulting trusts arise, this will be what A intended or would have intended had he put his mind to it. Where A transfers property to B to hold on trust for C, but that trust fails, more often than not A will want to be able to recover the property. But for Lord Browne-Wilkinson's analysis to be correct, this must always be true. And the big obstacle here is, of course, *Vandervell*. As we have seen, there the resulting trust arose even though it was clear that Vandervell (and for that matter VT) did not intend that he retain any beneficial interest in the property. As such, it is hard to see how it can be described as a case where the trust gave effect to the common intention of the parties. Lord Browne-Wilkinson's reason for saying that 'automatic' resulting trusts, and presumably the resulting trust in *Vandervell*, give effect to A's (and B's) intention is that, if A really does not intend to retain the beneficial interest, he can abandon it. His argument would appear to be that unless an intention to abandon it can be found, A must intend to retain his beneficial interest.

This is questionable. First, it is far from clear that a beneficial interest can effectively be abandoned in the way Lord Browne-Wilkinson suggests (see Hudson, 1984). Second, even if abandonment is possible, it simply does not follow that, in the absence of a positive intent to abandon, A must (positively) intend to retain a beneficial interest in the property. As in *Vandervell*, it is possible to form neither the intention to abandon the property nor the intention to retain an interest in it. A may have simply given no thought *at all* to the question of who should be beneficially entitled to the property; or, to similar effect, he may have chosen that it should pass to C, but this has proved legally ineffective and he has given no further thought to who should have it if the trust for C fails.

8.9   The basis of automatic resulting trusts

It is clear, then, that *Vandervell* cannot be squared with Lord Browne-Wilkinson's account of when and why resulting trusts arise. And as nobody is suggesting that *Vandervell* was, at least on this point, wrongly decided, it cannot stand as an explanation of 'automatic' resulting trusts. However, the account put forward by Lords Upjohn and Wilberforce and Megarry J has come under attack from another angle.

Their explanation was that automatic resulting trusts arise on the basis that A necessarily retains what he has failed effectively to dispose of. This view, sometimes referred to as the 'proprietary arithmetic' argument (see Hackney, 1987, 153–54), has been challenged on the basis that it does not accurately represent how resulting trusts work. As we have seen, and as confirmed in *Westdeutsche* itself, where A holds legal beneficial title to property, there is – and so A has – no *equitable* title to it. Instead an equitable title arises for the first time upon the creation of a trust. Accordingly, it is inaccurate to speak of A 'retaining' his equitable title when a resulting trust arises, as he held none at the outset. As such, the only right A had before the transfer – his legal title – has gone, and the right he *now* has – an equitable title – is a new right. On this view, what we need is an explanation of how and why this new right comes into existence.

This is true, so far as it goes, but it seems to miss the point of the proprietary arithmetic argument. What those who put forward this argument clearly have in mind is that, though, *as a matter of form*, A's rights under the resulting trust are different from those he held before the trust arose, *as a matter of substance*, he does retain something (see too Penner, 2010). And what he retains is the beneficial interest in the property, the right to whatever benefits that property generates. Before the transfer, this was wrapped up in his legal (beneficial) title; following the transfer, though the management and control powers entailed by legal title have passed to B, the beneficial interest remains in A, now as a distinct *equitable* title. Moreover, this seems to fit what is going on in the automatic resulting trust cases. A transfers property to B intending that B receive it *as trustee* and hence that he not receive the property beneficially but should instead hold it for someone else or for some purpose. If for some reason that intended trust fails, we seem to have no effective disposition of the beneficial interest, and so it does not seem unreasonable to say that whatever A has failed to dispose of he retains. To reject the retention argument, one really needs also to reject the idea of beneficial interests, for if you do think that A does have a beneficial interest in the property before the transfer, then we do seem to have something which A *does* retain in automatic resulting trust cases.

The favoured alternative explanation for the operation of automatic resulting trusts is that they arise to prevent or reverse B's unjust enrichment (Birks, 1992; Chambers, 1997). A did not intend B to benefit from the property transferred to him and so, though legal title passed to B, a new equitable title arises in A to ensure that B is not unjustly enriched at A's expense. As we saw earlier, this is the argument that was put forward and rejected as an explanation of the basis of resulting trusts in *Westdeutsche*. However, although it may not work in relation to presumed resulting trusts, it has a lot more going for it as an account of why automatic resulting trusts arise. Importantly, unlike Lord Browne-Wilkinson's approach, it can account for the decision in *Vandervell v IRC*. Although Vandervell may not have wanted the beneficial interest himself, at least on the findings of the majority of the House of Lords, neither did he intend VT to benefit from the option. Therefore, to ensure that VT did not derive an unintended benefit from Vandervell, the resulting trust arose to prevent or reverse VT's unjust enrichment. It is for this reason that some who have argued that presumed resulting trusts are not founded on unjust enrichment have nonetheless been prepared to concede that this may best explain the incidence of automatic resulting trusts: see eg Swadling, 2004, 38 (though see now Swadling, 2008).

It should also be noted that Lord Millett's account of resulting trusts examined earlier (Section 8.6), which sits somewhere between the proprietary arithmetic view and the unjust enrichment analysis of Birks and Chambers, similarly works as an explanation of automatic resulting trusts. As we saw, Millett differs from Birks and Chambers in that he would not find a resulting trust in cases of mistaken transfers, because he believes that the existence of the mistake does not change the fact that A *did* intend B to receive the property beneficially. In relation to automatic resulting trusts, however, as A transferred the property to B *on trust*, it is clear that A never intended B to benefit from the property, and so a resulting trust arises.

Although supporters of the unjust enrichment view of automatic resulting trusts have given short shrift to the proprietary arithmetic argument, the two theories are strikingly similar. After all, on both views, the basis of resulting trusts lies in the fact that A did not consent to B receiving the property beneficially. Moreover, it appears that the unjust enrichment argument is incomplete unless supplemented by something like the proprietary arithmetic view. For instance, the unjust enrichment theory says that a resulting trust arises where A transfers property to B but does not intend B to benefit. But, if so, why is there no resulting trust where A transfers property to B to hold on trust for C (see Gardner, 2011, 302)? We know that if the trust is effectively declared there is no resulting trust for A and no unjust enrichment supporter argues otherwise. Yet this too is a case where A transfers property to B but has no intention to benefit *B*. What this tells us is that the unjust enrichment argument is incomplete when framed simply in terms of A's lack of an intent to benefit B. There is something missing, something which tells us why there is a resulting trust in cases of mistake (etc.) but not where the property is transferred to B to hold on trust for C.

It is here that the unjust enrichment proponents can learn something from the proprietary arithmetic view, for what the proprietary arithmetic argument stresses is the fact that where property is beneficially owned by A, then it is for A (and A alone) to determine how that property should be disposed of (see further Webb, 2009a). Moreover, in the absence of A having effectively disposed of his interest, A should be able to recover the property precisely because this is what having an interest in property entails: it is yours until you give it away (see Gardner, 2011, 295–302, who terms this 'proprietary inertia'). This then explains why A has no claim when he successfully transfers property to B to hold on trust for C, for in such a case, though A does not intend to benefit *B*, he *has* effectively disposed of his interest in the property by passing the beneficial interest to C. In this way, the proprietary arithmetic and unjust enrichment arguments may best be regarded as mutually supporting. Unjust enrichment adds to the proprietary arithmetic approach by telling us that it is when A gives no or only defective (ie mistaken, coerced or conditional) consent to B's receipt of the property, that we can say that A does or should retain an interest in that property. Proprietary arithmetic adds to the unjust enrichment approach by telling us why A's consent to B benefiting from the property is legally significant: it is because A began as owner of the property and so it was for him, and him alone, to determine who should receive and benefit from that property.

8.10 Resulting trusts and unjust enrichment

As a matter of authority, *Westdeutsche* has done much to clear up the law on resulting trusts. A presumed resulting trust will arise where A transfers property gratuitously to B, unless either the presumption of advancement applies or there is evidence incompatible with A having intended that B hold the property on trust for him. Thus the presumption of resulting trust will be rebutted not only by a positive intention to make a gift to B, but also by any evidence, which shows that A did not positively intend to create a trust in his own favour when he transferred the property to B. We know too that an automatic resulting trust will arise where A transfers property to B to be held on express trust, but the intended trust fails in whole or in part.

Yet, as we have seen, this understanding of the presumption of resulting trust has been questioned, notably by Lord Millett, who appears to endorse a variant on the unjust enrichment argument put forward by Birks and Chambers. Moreover, as we have also seen, the unjust enrichment argument – though rejected by Lord Browne-Wilkinson in *Westdeutsche* – *does* appear to offer a better explanation of the operation of automatic resulting trusts (at least when supplemented by the proprietary arithmetic/inertia view). So the unjust enrichment argument has neither received wholesale approval – far from it – nor has it been shown to be wholly mistaken. As such, it is worth taking some time to consider what place unjust enrichment could usefully have in our law of trusts. *Should* resulting trusts be used to reverse unjust enrichment?

We should start by making clear what unjust enrichment means. Though the terminology is sometimes used differently, we have used the language of unjust enrichment to describe the situation where the defendant, B, receives a benefit from the claimant, A, which A did not intend him to receive (see further Webb, 2009b). This will be the case where, for instance, B takes A's property from him without his consent, or where A transfers property to B as a result of a mistake or coercion, or under a condition that fails (eg A gives B a present on the basis that B will pass his exams and B then fails). In such a situation B is said to be unjustly enriched at A's expense, and A can require B to give up that benefit to him. (Claims for the recovery of benefits received by another are called *restitutionary* claims.) The standard remedy in cases of unjust enrichment is for B to pay A a sum of money equal to the value of the benefit B received from him. In other words, A has only a *personal* claim to the value of B's enrichment rather than a proprietary claim such as may enable A to recover the specific asset B received from him. As we shall see, this is particularly important where B is insolvent (for more on the difference between personal and proprietary claims, see Section 14.2).

The argument first made by Birks (1992), then developed by Chambers (1997), was that in those cases where the law presently recognises resulting trusts – ie cases of gratuitous transfers and failed express trusts – it does so because A did not intend B to benefit from the property. The resulting trust therefore arises in order to prevent or reverse B's unjust enrichment at A's expense. However, as we have just noted, it is clear that there are many instances of unjust enrichment in English law where *no* trust is recognised, the claimant instead having merely a personal claim to recover the value of the property transferred. What Birks and Chambers argued was that, if it is true to say that the traditional examples of resulting trusts are cases where trusts have been used to reverse unjust enrichment then, because justice requires that like cases be treated alike, a trust should arise in *all* cases of unjust enrichment. (In fact, neither Birks nor Chambers goes quite so far, and both accept that trusts should be denied to some unjust enrichment claimants, for reasons which need not concern us here: see Birks, 1992, 347–59 and 2004, 194–98; Chambers, 1997, 144–70.) In other words, the existing instances of resulting trusts could be used as a stepping stone from which we proceed to justify the recognition of (resulting) trusts in all sorts of new situations. If resulting trusts were found in all cases of unjust enrichment, this would mean that unjust enrichment claimants would not be limited to personal claims to recover the value of B's enrichment but could instead, by virtue of their equitable beneficial interest under the trust, bring a proprietary claim and recover the asset itself. This would bring a number of advantages, notably in cases of insolvency.

This is what was attempted in *Westdeutsche*. There was minimal authority supporting resulting trusts arising in respect of property transferred under a void contract, but it was argued that the court should recognise a resulting trust by analogy with the existing categories, the common feature being that in all these cases B was unjustly enriched at A's expense. As we have seen, the House of Lords unanimously rejected this argument, denying that the existing categories of resulting trust were to be explained on the basis of unjust enrichment and preferring the view that they arise to give effect to A's (and B's) intention to create a trust. As such, the possibility of using the resulting trust case law as a stepping stone to the increased use of trusts in unjust enrichment cases was pre-empted.

Now, as we have suggested, even as a matter of authority, this seems questionable, given that, in light of *Vandervell*, unjust enrichment (at least when supplemented by the proprietary arithmetic/inertia idea) *does* appear to be the best explanation of automatic resulting trusts. This would then mean that supporters of Birks and Chambers could simply modify their argument, accepting that presumed resulting trusts have nothing to do with unjust enrichment, and focus their attention on automatic resulting trusts (although Chambers continues to fight the corner of unjust enrichment in relation to presumed resulting trusts: Chambers, 2010). For they can still make the same basic argument of analogy: 'If we respond to unjust enrichment in cases of automatic resulting trusts by recognising a trust in favour of the claimant, then, as like cases must be treated alike, should we not also recognise trusts in other cases of unjust enrichment?'

In any case, even if it were true that resulting trusts as traditionally understood and applied by the courts arise *only* where this is what A intended, we should still ask whether the law of trusts should be developed so that trusts *also* arise in cases of unjust enrichment. In short, it is one thing to ask what the law is, quite another to ask what it should be. And if there are strong arguments in principle for recognising trusts in cases of unjust enrichment, then, notwithstanding that this is not what the law presently provides, this is what the courts should do.

So, what factors should we be considering when weighing up the pros and cons of imposing trusts in cases of unjust enrichment? As we have noted already, the most significant consequence of finding trusts in cases of unjust enrichment would be that unjust enrichment claimants would have proprietary rather than merely personal claims. This is important primarily because of the advantages that proprietary claims bring when the defendant is insolvent.

8.11   Unjust enrichment, insolvency and proprietary claims

We introduced the idea of insolvency in Chapter 2. To recap, insolvency describes the situation when an individual's debts exceed the value of his assets. When an insolvent defendant is declared bankrupt (or a company goes into insolvent liquidation), a trustee in bankruptcy (or liquidator) is appointed, whose job it is to sell the defendant's assets to generate a lump sum of money, which is then used to pay off the defendant's various creditors (ie those who have claims against him). However, by definition, the defendant's insolvency means that there is not enough money to go around and so it is impossible to pay off all his creditors in full. The key question in cases of insolvency is how this shortfall should be borne amongst the various creditors; who should get what little money there is, and who should lose out.

The basic rule is that all the creditors bear this shortfall rateably (proportionately), so that if, for example, the defendant has debts totalling £20,000 but his assets are worth only £10,000 – and hence he has only half the money needed to pay off his debts – each creditor will get half the money he is owed. This is known as *pari passu* distribution and ensures that everyone gets what may be considered their fair share of the money available.

However, the position is different for those creditors who have proprietary claims. If you can assert some form of proprietary interest in an asset held by the defendant then, so far as your interest extends, you will usually be able to retrieve that asset or its money value before any other creditors can get their hands on it. In effect, before the trustee in bankruptcy can sell the asset and use the proceeds to pay off the defendant's general creditors, you can step in and say 'that's mine'. This has two important consequences. First, it will mean that you will avoid the pitfalls of pari passu distribution. You can simply walk off with your asset (or its value) and leave those creditors without proprietary claims – known as *unsecured* creditors – to fight over what is left. Because of this, it is often said that proprietary claims give you *priority* in the event of the defendant's insolvency. Second, wherever a proprietary claim is recognised, this necessarily means that that asset (and its proceeds) will not be available to meet the claims of unsecured creditors. So the more proprietary claims there are, the fewer assets will be left to meet the claims of unsecured creditors. In short, in insolvency, every proprietary claim results in unsecured creditors receiving less.

It is because of this that judges and academics start getting twitchy at the thought of allowing unjust enrichment claimants to bring proprietary claims. Unsecured creditors tend to get a raw deal anyway; they will be left in an even worse position if unjust enrichment claimants are added to the list of people who can claim in priority to them. Hence, the basic argument against giving unjust enrichment claimants proprietary claims, and so against recognising trusts as arising in cases of unjust enrichment, is that this would be unfair to other creditors. Assets which would otherwise be used to satisfy the claims of creditors generally would be diverted into the hands of a solitary unjust enrichment claimant, and, so it is claimed, this inequality of treatment is both undeserved and unjustified.

That granting unjust enrichment claimants proprietary claims would lead to an inequality of treatment with other creditors is plain. It can, however, be questioned whether this inequality of treatment is indeed undeserved and hence unjust. Take the following set of facts. You mistakenly transfer to me property worth £1,000. Shortly thereafter I am declared bankrupt, with debts of £4,000 (£2,000 owed to X, £1,000 to Y, as well as the £1,000 I owe you because of the unjust enrichment) as compared to assets to the value of only £2,000, which includes the £1,000 you paid me. If you are given only a personal claim, the effect of pari passu distribution is that X will get £1,000, Y gets £500 and you get £500 (ie you each get half of what you are owed). If, however, you are allowed a proprietary claim, you will be able to take back the assets you transferred (worth £1,000), leaving only £1,000 to be distributed between X and Y. X would then get £666.67 and Y £333.33. This clearly leaves X and Y with less than if you merely had a personal claim.

However, consider what would have been the result had you never made the mistaken transfer, and hence if I had never been unjustly enriched. I would not have the £1,000 you paid to me, and would instead be holding only the other £1,000. This then is the only money that would have been available from which the claims of X and Y could be satisfied. X would, therefore, get £666.67 and Y £333.33. In this situation then, giving you a proprietary claim leaves X and Y *no worse off* than they would have been had you never made the mistaken transfer, and hence they are in no worse a position now than they were prior to that transfer. So what injustice is done to X and Y by allowing you a proprietary claim? Indeed, if you were denied a proprietary claim, it would effectively mean that X and Y would profit from your mistaken transfer, as they would recover more in the event of my insolvency than they would have done had you not made that payment. As such, just as we say that *I* would be unjustly enriched were I allowed to benefit from your mistaken transfer, so we should regard *X and Y* as unjustly enriched if they were allowed to benefit from this (see eg Sherwin, 1989).

Accordingly, a strong argument can be made that there is no necessary unfairness to other creditors in granting proprietary claims to unjust enrichment claimants. Indeed we can go further: the argument in the preceding paragraphs suggests that proprietary claims should, in principle, be available in such cases so as to prevent the unjust enrichment of the defendant's other creditors.

Are there any other reasons to be cautious about recognising trusts in cases of unjust enrichment? Aside from the insolvency argument which we have just examined, Lord Browne-Wilkinson gave two further reasons for rejecting this argument in *Westdeutsche*.

First, if we say that a trust arises where, for example, A mistakenly transfers property to B, this means that if B subsequently transfers the property to C, A may be able to bring a claim against C. This, Lord Browne-Wilkinson considered, would not only be unfair to C, but would also introduce an unreasonable level of risk into commercial dealings. However, in response to this we should note that as A would have only an equitable interest in the property, he would have a claim against C only if C was not a bona fide purchaser for value without notice (Section 2.9). And if C is not a bona fide purchaser for value without notice, it is unclear why we should consider it unfair if A can claim against him (see further Section 14.21). Equally there is little reason this should unnerve commercial parties, as they will almost always give value for the property they acquire and so will risk liability only where they knew or should have known of A's rights in the property. This seems perfectly reasonable.

Second, Lord Browne-Wilkinson thought that imposing trusts in cases of unjust enrichment could work injustice to the recipient. This is because he considered that this would entail that B would be subjected to all the strict duties owed by trustees of an express trust. This would indeed be undesirable, but, as we have noted already (Section 8.6), there is no reason to assume that such duties must be present. Certainly, the need to reverse unjust enrichments only demands that A be given a proprietary right, not that B also be subjected to the same obligations in respect of his handling of the property as someone who has chosen to be a trustee.

In summary, therefore, though the House of Lords in *Westdeutsche* strongly rejected the idea that claimants who make mistaken, coerced or conditional transfers of property should be able to claim that that property is held for them on resulting trust, the argument that unjust enrichment claimants should be accorded proprietary claims is unlikely to go away. The argument of principle is strong and, in automatic resulting trusts, we seem already to have an example of trusts which arise to reverse unjust enrichment, which can then be used as a starting point for the expansion of trusts into the law of unjust enrichment.

8.12 The classification of trusts

It seems then that at least some – and on Lord Browne-Wilkinson's view all – resulting trusts arise to give effect to A's intention that B hold the property on trust for him. But this then raises a question as to the proper classification of these trusts. After all, we already have a category of trusts defined by reference to the fact that they arise to give effect to a settlor's intentions, namely express trusts. In so far as resulting trusts arise because this is what A intends, it becomes difficult to justify not regarding them as express trusts. Here it should be recalled that where a presumption is raised which is not then rebutted, the court proceeds on the basis that the presumed fact has indeed occurred. So if the presumption of resulting trust is a presumption that A intended to create a trust in his own favour, then the trust which arises where that presumption is not rebutted arises because this is what we consider A intended. In other words, the presumption of resulting trust is just one way of proving that A intended a trust. But whether the intent is proved this way or by other specific evidence of A's state of mind, the end result is the same (see further Section 8.4). A trust arises, and precisely because A intended this. And because what matters is *what* is proved rather than *how* it is proved, it simply makes no sense not to classify all these intended trusts as express trusts. (By contrast, were the courts to accept that at least some resulting trusts arise to prevent B's unjust enrichment, then we would have, to this extent, good reason to allocate them to a category distinct from express trusts.)

This not only looks bad, it also leads to indefensible discrepancies in the way we treat these trusts. As we saw in Chapter 6, section 53 of the Law of Property Act 1925 imposes certain formality requirements for the effective creation of trusts of land and disposition of equitable interests. However, by virtue of section 53(2), these formalities do not need to be satisfied in relation to implied, resulting and constructive trusts (though it is unclear what, if anything, is comprised in the category of implied trusts). This means that intended trusts proved by presumption are exempted from the writing requirements which apply to intended trusts proved by other means. Regardless of whether we view section 53(1)(b) as setting down a rule of evidence or a rule of validity (on which see Section 6.8), this distinction is arbitrary and cannot be supported.

Our classification of trusts should reflect genuine material differences that exist among the various trusts recognised in the law (Webb, 2009c; cf McBride, 2000). It is plain that our present classification of trusts does not do this. We have seen here that some resulting trusts appear materially indistinguishable from express trusts. The same may also be true of certain constructive trusts (Section 9.1). This is lousy classification. A principled classification of trusts would categorise trusts by reference to their basis, the various reasons which support the recognition of trusts. One such reason is that this is what the settlor intended. Another is that the trust is needed to prevent or reverse unjust enrichment. As we shall see in the following chapter, there are other reasons besides these. Such a classification would be far more informative than the current categorisation of trusts as express, resulting or constructive. However, so long as section 53 remains good law, it seems that we will be compelled to make do with the present classificatory scheme.

8.13 *Quistclose* trusts

There is one final situation to examine in which it has been held that resulting trusts arise. It has been left until now because it is questionable whether such trusts really should be classed as resulting trusts and, if so, how they fit in with the traditional categories of presumed and automatic resulting trusts. These trusts are known as *Quistclose* trusts and they typically arise in the context of loans.

Usually, when A loans money to B, A's legal beneficial title to the money passes to B, and all A has is a contractual right to repayment of an equivalent sum plus interest. Therefore, if B becomes insolvent before the loan has been repaid, A will be a straightforward unsecured creditor with all the disadvantages that this entails. This is true even if A can show that B has yet to spend the money transferred. A no longer has any interest in the money; he has transferred it absolutely to B, and so cannot recover it.

Normally, if A wants to avoid the risk of B's insolvency he must obtain security from B. Security involves the borrower granting to the lender a proprietary interest in one or more of the borrower's assets. The most familiar example of a security interest is the mortgage. A mortgage is a proprietary interest which entitles the lender, should the borrower fail to repay the loan or become insolvent, to have the debt paid out of the proceeds of sale of the relevant property. Only what is left from the proceeds once the lender's debt has been paid is then available for distribution among the borrower's other creditors. In effect a mortgage gives the lender first call on the money inherent in the mortgaged property. In this way, taking security avoids many of the risks of the borrower's insolvency.

Quistclose trusts offer an alternative means of protection. There is now an established line of authority that, where A lends B money on condition that it is used only for a stipulated purpose, the money will be held on trust for A, at least where it becomes impossible for the money to be used in this way. It is sometimes suggested that A must also require B to keep the loan money separate from B's other assets, though this is not backed up by the cases: see *Re EVTR* [1987] BCLC 646 and Glister, 2002, 229–30 for the view that this element may not be necessary. The better view may therefore be that segregation of the loan money is relevant only in so far as it sheds light on the parties' true intentions, and in particular, whether they really intended that B use the money only for the stipulated purpose. In the end, the crucial question is whether the money received by B is to be at his free disposal, such that he is entitled to spend it how he likes or, alternatively, whether his use of that money is restricted, such that he may use it only for the purpose the parties have agreed. If the former, B receives the money beneficially and there is no trust; if the latter, he receives the property as trustee of a *Quistclose* trust.

Quistclose trusts, therefore, both provide an exception to the general rule that a lender has no interest in the money once lent and give A, by virtue of his equitable interest in the money, a proprietary claim according him priority over B's other creditors in the event of B's insolvency. As an introduction, we shall look at the case which started all this (at least so far as the modern law is concerned): *Barclays Bank Ltd v Quistclose Investments Ltd* [1970] AC 567.

Rolls Razor Ltd was a company in serious financial difficulties. It had already exceeded its overdraft with its bank, Barclays, and, when it declared a dividend on its shares, it found that it did not have the resources to pay its shareholders. Accordingly, it approached Quistclose for a loan of the money needed to pay the dividend. Quistclose agreed and loaned the money, stipulating both that a separate bank account be set up into which the money would be paid and that the money must only be used to pay the dividend. The new account was set up at Barclays and the money paid into it. However, before the dividend was paid, Rolls Razor went into liquidation. Quistclose then sought to recover the money in the account. This was opposed by Barclays, who claimed that they had a right of set-off, enabling them to apply that money in reduction of the debt owed to them by Rolls Razor.

The House of Lords held that Quistclose was entitled to the money. Lord Wilberforce, giving the only reasoned speech, explained the result as follows ([1970] AC 567, 580–81):

> The mutual intention of the respondents [Quistclose] and of Rolls Razor Ltd, and the essence of the bargain, was that the sum advanced should not become part of the assets of Rolls Razor Ltd, but should be used exclusively for the payment of a particular class of its creditors, namely, those entitled to the dividend. A necessary consequence from this, by process simply of interpretation, must be that if, for any reason, the dividend could not be paid, the money was to be returned to the respondents: the word 'only' or 'exclusively' can have no other meaning or effect. That arrangements of this character for the payment of a person's creditors by a third person give rise to a relationship of a fiduciary character or trust, in favour, as a primary trust, of the creditors, and secondarily, if the primary trust fails, of the third person, has been recognised in a series of cases over some 150 years … [W]hen the money is advanced, the lender acquires an equitable right to see that it is applied for the primary designated purpose … : when the purpose has been carried out (ie, the debt paid) the lender has his remedy against the borrower in debt: if the primary purpose cannot be carried out, the question arises if a secondary purpose (ie, repayment to the lender) has been agreed, expressly or by implication: if it has, the remedies of equity may be invoked to give effect to it.

Though the result was clear, the exact legal route taken to get there was not. Lord Wilberforce spoke of two trusts, yet although the focus of the secondary trust in favour of the lender was plain, the primary trust was rather more mysterious. There is a suggestion that this is a trust in favour of the shareholders (ie the people who were entitled to payment of the dividend), yet, if this were so, why should we view this primary trust as having failed so as to enable Quistclose to recover the money? After all, Rolls Razor's shareholders could still have been paid. Then there is a suggestion that this may be a purpose trust (the purpose being the paying of the dividend), but then how can this be squared with the beneficiary principle and the general prohibition of non-charitable purpose trusts? Moreover, on either view, there is no trust for the lender until that primary trust fails, but then what is the nature and basis of the lender's 'equitable right' to see that the borrower spends the money as stipulated?

Later cases seemed to muddy the waters even further. For instance, in *Re Northern Developments (Holdings) Ltd* (1978, unreported) and *Carreras Rothmans Ltd v Freeman Mathews Treasure Ltd* [1985] Ch 207, it was suggested that the person or persons who were intended to receive the money from the borrower had a right to enforce the arrangement, which would seem to suggest that the primary trust is indeed a trust in favour of those people. However, in *Re EVTR* [1987] BCLC 646, a *Quistclose* trust was found where money was loaned for the purpose of buying equipment and hence where there was nobody in a position analogous to Rolls Razor's shareholders who could be said to be beneficiaries of, or at least have right to enforce, the primary trust.

Such uncertainty and mystery may not be good news for judges and litigants, but they warm the hearts of academics, who have for many years strived to find a way to explain the working of *Quistclose* trusts consistently with orthodox legal (and equitable) principles. It would be odd indeed if the combined rules of contract and trusts could not find a way of accommodating this sort of arrangement (though Swadling (2004) maintains that it is indeed impossible). Accordingly, a number of writers have put forward rationalisations of the case law, though usually at the cost of disregarding some of the reasoning. For the most part, the search for a principled explanation of *Quistclose* trusts has been treated like the hunt for the Holy Grail, in that there has been an assumption that there can only be one solution, one analysis which works. In fact, there is no good reason to think that the law might not provide a variety of routes to this result. There is often more than one way to skin a legal cat. It seems this view is now becoming more prevalent: see for example Chambers, 2004; Glister, 2004. Be that as it may, as a matter of authority one interpretation has now gained the upper hand following the decision of the House of Lords in *Twinsectra Ltd v Yardley* [2002] UKHL 12; [2002] 2 AC 164.

Yardley was looking to purchase land and needed to borrow money to do this. Twinsectra agreed to loan Yardley £1 million, but only on the condition that the solicitor acting for Yardley offer a personal guarantee to repay the money should Yardley fail to do so. Leach, the solicitor whom Yardley had instructed to act for him refused to provide the guarantee, so Yardley found another firm of solicitors, Sims, who were willing to do this. Twinsectra accordingly paid the money to Sims, who undertook that the money would only be used for the purpose of enabling Yardley's planned property purchase and that they would retain the money until the relevant purchase was to go ahead. Contrary to these terms, Sims paid over the money to Leach, who in turn paid over the money to Yardley before the planned property purchase was to go ahead and, in the event, some of the money was then used by Yardley for other purposes. When Yardley failed to repay the loan, Twinsectra sued, amongst others, Leach on the basis that, when he received the money from Sims, he thereby dishonestly assisted Sims in committing a breach of trust (on which see further Section 14.23). For this claim to succeed it needed to be established that Sims did indeed hold the money on trust. Lord Hoffmann, giving the leading judgment on this point, simply stated that, as solicitors, Sims necessarily held the money on trust, the terms of which were set down in the terms of the undertaking provided to Twinsectra. Lord Millett, however, gave a fuller analysis of the trust, which he took to be an example of a *Quistclose* trust. In so doing, he offered his views of how these trusts operated.

Starting with Lord Wilberforce's two-trust analysis, Lord Millett noted that the difficulty in explaining *Quistclose* trusts has always been in identifying the nature of the primary trust and hence the location of the beneficial interest in the money prior to the failure of the purpose for which the money was loaned. He therefore examined the various possibilities. The borrower could not be beneficially entitled to the money as this would be inconsistent with the lender having any right to recover the money in the event of the borrower's insolvency (though see Chambers, 1997, Ch. 3; cf Ho and Smart, 2001). Lord Millett also rejected the view that the money was held on trust for those ultimately intended to receive the money (such as the shareholders in *Quistclose*), in particular as there was not always an identified person or group of people in that position. As noted, this was the case in *Re EVTR* as well as in *Twinsectra* itself, where the money was to be used simply 'for the acquisition of property'. Finally, he rejected the possibility of the money being held on a purpose trust, with the beneficial interest accordingly being in suspense, as he considered that this was conceptually impossible (cf Section 4.5); where no provision had been made for the beneficial interest, it would revert automatically to the transferor on a resulting trust.

This left just one possibility which was compatible with both principle and the outcome of the cases: that the beneficial interest was from the outset vested in the lender. This indeed was the analysis which Millett had put forward in a journal article 17 years earlier (Millett, 1985). Under this approach, the borrower holds the money on trust for the lender *throughout*, although the borrower has a power (or, depending on the terms of the agreement with the lender, a duty: cf Smith, 2004b) to apply that money for the stipulated purpose. As beneficiary of the trust the lender can restrain the borrower from using the money for any other purpose (so explaining the 'equitable right' of enforcement identified by Lord Wilberforce). It also seems that the lender can revoke the power to use the money for that purpose and so reclaim the money, even where the money could still be so used, as was the case in *Quistclose*, where the shareholders could still have been paid. If the borrower *does* use the money for the stipulated purpose, the lender is left with his contractual right to repayment. If, however, the borrower misapplies the money then the lender can follow and claim the money from third-party recipients, provided they are not bona fide purchasers for value without notice.

One important consequence of this approach is that it requires that we reject Lord Wilberforce's two-trust analysis. Instead of there being distinct primary and secondary trusts with distinct beneficiaries, the money is only ever held on trust for the lender. Hence the beneficial interest does not change hands when the purpose fails. At most, the failure of the purpose causes a failure of the power which the borrower previously held to apply the money for the stipulated purpose.

One unusual and possibly improper application of these principles occurred in *Re EVTR* [1987] BCLC 646. The claimant lent money to a company on the condition that it be used solely for the purchase of equipment for its business. The company did then use the money to acquire such equipment but went into receivership shortly thereafter. The suppliers were able to retake the equipment they had provided, and in return gave back the money they had been paid by the company, minus certain deductions. The question then was whether the claimant could recover the money repaid by the suppliers. The Court of Appeal held that he could. A standard *Quistclose* trust arose when the claimant paid the money to the company, given the restriction the claimant had placed on its use. And, although the money was indeed used for the stipulated purpose, this purpose subsequently failed and the money repaid by the suppliers was to be treated as received by the company subject to the same trust as the money initially loaned.

The difficulty with this is that, under the conventional analysis, the money is held on trust only until it is used for the stipulated purpose. When it is so used, the recipient takes free of any trust. Hence when the money was received by the suppliers, they took it absolutely and the claimant's equitable interest was extinguished (this is an example of overreaching: Section 2.8). That being so, it is unclear how that equitable interest was spontaneously resurrected when the suppliers later repaid some of this money.

Nonetheless, the decision seems fair and can be justified on the unjust enrichment argument made earlier (Sections 8.10 and 8.11). The claimant intended that the company should have the benefit of the money only to the extent that it was used in the acquisition of equipment. As this purpose ultimately failed, the claimant could say that he intended neither the company nor its creditors to retain any benefit from that money. That being so, the trust ensured that neither the company nor its creditors were unjustly enriched.

8.14 *Quistclose* trusts as resulting trusts

One question remains: are *Quistclose* trusts resulting trusts? In *Quistclose* itself, Lord Wilberforce made no reference to resulting trusts. Rather, his emphasis on the parties' intentions suggests that he would have classified both the primary and secondary trusts as express trusts (see too *Re The Australian Elizabethan Theatre Trust* (1991) 102 ALR 681). In *Carreras Rothmans Ltd v Freeman Mathews Treasure Ltd* [1985] Ch 207, Peter Gibson J preferred to categorise the trust as constructive.

Nonetheless, it is now commonplace to describe *Quistclose* trusts as examples of resulting trusts. This made some sense when Lord Wilberforce's two-trust analysis held sway. According to Lord Wilberforce, the secondary trust in favour of the lender arose upon the failure of the primary trust. On this view, the secondary trust looks and works a lot like a conventional automatic resulting trust. The lender, A, transfers property to the borrower, B, to be held on an express trust. However, that express trust having failed, B holds the property on resulting trust for A. It is no doubt for this reason that Lord Browne-Wilkinson, when offering his account of resulting trusts in *Westdeutsche Landesbank Girozentrale v Islington London BC* [1996] AC 669, listed *Barclays Bank Ltd v Quistclose Investments Ltd* among his authorities for 'type (B)' (ie automatic) resulting trusts.

However, once we reject, as we now seem to have done, this two-trust analysis, the status of *Quistclose* trusts as resulting trusts becomes more doubtful. Of course, nobody can deny that *Quistclose* trusts are 'resulting' in pattern, in that they send the beneficial interest back to the person who transferred the property to the trustee. But as we have seen, it does not follow from this that the trust should be categorised as a resulting trust (Section 8.1). Nonetheless, Lord Millett continued to refer to *Quistclose* trusts as resulting trusts, despite his rejection of the two-trust approach. Revealingly, however, when he put forward much the same analysis in 1985, the terminology of resulting trusts was absent. Moreover, Lord Hoffmann's analysis of the same trust in *Twinsectra* strongly suggests that he considered it to be express.

The answer to the classificatory question should turn on the reason we recognise the trust (Section 8.12). If we consider that A, when lending the money to B, intended that B should hold that money on trust for him, then we should treat this as an express trust (for a clear example of this see *R v The Common Professional Examination Board, ex parte Mealing-McCleod* (2009) 23 TLI 200). If, by contrast, it appears that, although A did not intend B to obtain the beneficial interest in the money, he never formed the positive intention that the beneficial interest should remain in him, then we have reason to class it as a resulting trust. It seems plausible that cases of both kinds exist and hence that some *Quistclose* trusts should be classed as express and others resulting.

Summary

▶ Resulting trusts arise in (at least) two sets of circumstances: gratuitous transfers of property and failed express trusts.

▶ A gratuitous transfer describes the situation where A transfers property to B, or pays for property to be transferred to B, and A neither receives nor is promised anything in return. In such cases, it is presumed that B will hold the property on trust for A. This is often called a presumed resulting trust.

▶ A failed express trust occurs where A intends to set up a trust with B as his trustee, but, having transferred the property to B, the intended trust fails, for example because its objects are uncertain or because it contravenes the beneficiary principle. B will then hold the property on trust for A. This is often termed an automatic resulting trust.

▶ It is clear that presumed resulting trusts arise by virtue of a presumption. This presumption can be rebutted. So, if it is clear that A positively intended to make a gift to B, then B will take the property absolutely and no trust will arise. Occasionally the law applies a different presumption: that A intended to make a gift to B. This is known as the presumption of advancement. As the law stands, this applies only to transfers from fathers to their children and from husbands to their wives. However, section 199 of the Equality Act 2010 will abolish the presumption of advancement when it comes into force.

▶ The presumptions make a difference to the outcome of cases only where there is no evidence as to what the parties actually intended. One such example is where property is transferred pursuant to some illegal scheme. Often, in such cases, the courts will not allow the parties to adduce evidence of their actual intentions and hence of the illegal purpose they had in mind. Where this is so, this leaves the courts with nothing but the presumptions to fall back on.

▶ Although it is clear that the presumption of resulting trust can be rebutted by evidence of a positive intention to make a gift, it is unclear what other evidence may rebut it. The answer to this depends on what it is we are presuming. There are two views here. The first is that we are presuming that A positively intended to create a trust for himself as beneficiary and with B as his trustee. The second is that A did not intend B to benefit from the property.

▶ Though these two views often lead to the same results, occasionally they diverge. This is most clear in cases of unjust enrichment, for instance where A transfers property to B by mistake. In such a case, A never positively intended to create a trust, but we can say that, in the circumstances, he did not intend B to take benefit of the property. So on the first view, the presumption is rebutted and no trust would arise; whereas on the second view the presumption would be confirmed and B will hold on trust for A.

▶ Though there are cases which offer support to each view, the House of Lords in *Westdeutsche* endorsed the first view: that the presumption is that A intended to create a trust for himself.

▶ The better view of automatic resulting trusts is that they do not depend on A having intended that the beneficial interest in the property should revert to him in the event of the intended trust failing. Instead, the trust arises to prevent B being unjustly enriched.

▶ The unjust enrichment analysis of resulting trusts is controversial, principally because it would give many unjust enrichment claimants proprietary rights, whereas, at present, they have merely personal claims. The principal advantage of this is that it would give them priority over B's other creditors in the event of B's insolvency. Such priority may be justified in order to ensure that those creditors are not unjustly enriched by having access to the property A (for instance) mistakenly transferred to satisfy their claims against B.

▶ If A loans money to B on the condition that that money be used only for a stipulated purpose, B will hold that money on trust for A, at least where and to the extent that that money is not used for that purpose. This trust is known as a *Quistclose* trust. This is sometimes categorised as a resulting trust, though it may be that at least some of these trusts arise because this is what the parties intended, and so should be classed as express trusts.

Exercises

8.1 How do resulting trusts differ from express trusts? How do they differ from constructive trusts (see the following chapter)?

8.2 Why does it matter how we identify the fact being presumed where the presumption of resulting trust applies? Why do we have the presumption of resulting trust?

8.3 What problems may arise from the courts' reliance on the presumptions in cases where property is transferred pursuant to some unlawful scheme? Is there a better way of resolving these cases?

8.4 Why do we allow claimants who have transferred property by mistake to bring a claim against the recipient of that property? How do the principles which justify such claims apply where the recipient is insolvent?

8.5 The *Quistclose* trust has been variously described as express, resulting, constructive and even sui generis. Does the proper classification of such trusts matter?

8.6 Is it true that one effect of *Twinsectra Ltd v Yardley* is that there will be a trust every time a lender imposes a contractual obligation on the borrower only to use the money for a stipulated purpose? Is this desirable?

Further reading

As discussed earlier, there has been, and continues to be, significant debate as to the basis of resulting trusts. The articles and extracts from Birks, Chambers and Swadling give the best introduction to the debate.

Birks, 'Restitution and resulting trusts' in Goldstein (ed), *Equity and Contemporary Legal Developments* (Hebrew University of Jerusalem 1992); reprinted in Birks and Rose, *Restitution and Equity: Volume 1 – Resulting Trusts and Equitable Compensation* (Mansfield Press 2000)

Birks, 'Trusts raised to reverse unjust enrichment: the *Westdeutsche* case' [1996] RLR 3

Chambers, 'Is there a presumption of resulting trust?' in Mitchell (ed), *Resulting and Constructive Trusts* (Hart Publishing 2010)

Chambers, *Resulting Trusts* (Oxford University Press 1997)

Penner, 'Resulting trusts and unjust enrichment: three controversies' in Mitchell (ed), *Resulting and Constructive Trusts* (Hart Publishing 2010), 241–66

Swadling, 'A new role for resulting trusts?' (1996) 16 LS 110; reprinted in Birks and Rose, *Restitution and Equity: Volume 1 – Resulting Trusts and Equitable Compensation* (Mansfield Press 2000)

Swadling, 'Explaining resulting trusts' (2008) 124 LQR 72

Swadling, 'The law of property' in Birks and Rose (eds), *Lessons of the Swaps Litigation* (LLP 2000)

Webb, 'Intention, mistakes and resulting trusts' in Mitchell (ed), *Resulting and Constructive Trusts* (Hart Publishing 2010)

The other area on which there is an (over-)abundance of academic writing is the Quistclose trust:

Chambers, 'Restrictions on the use of money' in Swadling (ed), *The Quistclose Trust* (Hart Publishing 2004)

Glister, 'The nature of *Quistclose* trusts: classification and reconciliation' [2004] CLJ 632

Ho and Smart, 'Reinterpreting the *Quistclose* trust: a critique of Chambers' analysis' (2001) 21 OJLS 267

Millett, 'The *Quistclose* trust: who can enforce it?' (1985) 101 LQR 269

Penner, 'Lord Millett's analysis' in Swadling (ed), *The Quistclose Trust* (Hart Publishing 2004)

Swadling, 'Orthodoxy' in Swadling (ed), *The Quistclose Trust* (Hart Publishing 2004)

Chapter 9

Constructive trusts

9.1 Intention and constructive trusts

We noted in the first chapter (Section 1.3) that there is a basic divide in the law of trusts between trusts which are intended and trusts which are imposed. Express trusts, which we examined through the opening chapters, clearly fall on the side of intended trusts. Resulting trusts, the focus of the previous chapter, seem to straddle this divide, with some intended, others not. Here, with the category of constructive trusts, we are squarely in the territory of imposed trusts.

This is reflected in the standard definition of constructive trusts as trusts which arise 'by operation of law', in contrast to express trusts which arise to give effect to the parties' intentions. This presents an opposition between 'by operation of law' and 'to give effect to the parties' intentions'. Some argue that this is a false opposition, as even intended trusts take effect because of rules of law which make this possible. In other words, *all* trusts, as legal devices, necessarily arise by operation of the law. This is true but not particularly helpful. When we say that constructive trusts arise by operation of law, what we mean is that they arise not because a property owner has set out to create a trust, but because the law, nonetheless, has determined that there should be one. The same distinction can be more precisely stated by contrasting trusts which arise to give effect to a settlor's intention and trusts which arise (ie are imposed) for some other reason.

This distinction may seem straightforward but can easily be misunderstood. The second category comprises trusts which arise for some reason other than that this is what the settlor intended. This does not mean, however, that the parties in such cases *did not* want a trust, so that these trusts necessarily defeat or are inconsistent with the parties' intentions. In many cases, the parties will be perfectly happy to see a trust arise. What defines the trusts in this category is that the law's *reason* for recognising the trust is something other than a desire to give effect to the parties' intentions, and a trust may happen to coincide with the parties' intentions without this being the law's purpose in recognising that trust in the first place.

However, even where our reason for recognising a trust is not to give effect to a settlor's intention to create a trust, intention may nonetheless play a role in the 'creation' of the trust. First, there appear to be some instances of constructive trusts where an intent to create a trust is necessary, but in itself insufficient, for such a trust to arise. Instead, some other material element needs to be present for the trust to come into existence. One possible example of this is secret trusts, which we examined back in chapter 6 (Sections 6.18–6.19 and see also Section 9.8; other examples may be provided by oral trusts of land (Section 9.7) and 'common intention' trusts of the family home (Sections 9.10–9.17)). It is clear that no secret trust can arise unless the testator intends to create such a trust. Equally clearly, however, this intention alone is not enough. Rather we also require that the terms of the trust are communicated to and accepted by the intended trustee. Now, as we have seen, there is no agreement on the question of why we enforce secret trusts. However, on one view, such trusts arise *not* to give effect to the intentions of the testator but rather to prevent the fraud that would be perpetrated if the trustee did not fulfil his undertaking to perform the trust and instead sought to keep the property for himself (Section 6.12). In other words, a mere intention to create a trust is insufficient here precisely because our reason for recognising the trust is something other than a desire to give effect to the testator's intentions. Rather, we require something more – the trustee's acceptance of or assent to this trust – because it is *this* which justifies their enforcement. Now, the point here is not whether this understanding of the basis of secret trusts is correct. Rather it is to show that, *if it is*, these trusts are rightly distinguished from express trusts for, although they do happen to give effect to the settlor's intentions and although an intent to create a trust does need to be present for the trust to arise, the *reason* for imposing the trust is something different.

Second, for some constructive trusts, the 'settlor's' intention to benefit the beneficiary may be the *only* material factor explaining the trust. This is true of the trusts which arise under the rule in *Re Rose* (Section 9.6) and in relation to specifically enforceable obligations to transfer property (Section 9.5). In such cases, if we ask why these trusts arise, often the only answer will be that this gives broad effect to the parties' intentions. And yet these trusts are nonetheless rightly classed as *constructive* trusts, because it is plain that the 'settlors' in such cases never intended to create *a trust*. As we saw in Chapter 6, an intention to create a trust is just one kind of beneficial intent, and so a trust which gives effect to a person's intention to benefit another is not necessarily the same thing as an intended – and hence express – trust.

So constructive trusts are, by definition, imposed trusts, trusts which arise for some reason other than a settlor's intention to create a trust. Yet it seems clear that there are imposed trusts which the courts have not labelled constructive. For instance, some of the *resulting* trusts we examined in the previous chapter – notably so-called automatic resulting trusts – appear to be non-intended trusts. If this is right, there is a good argument that we should bring these within the category of constructive trusts (and, while we're at it, those resulting trusts which *are* intended can be placed into the category of express trusts).

Conversely, an argument can be made that some trusts, which the courts have labelled constructive, *do* arise to give effect to a settlor's intentions. This is the alternative view taken of some of the trusts we mentioned three paragraphs previously, such as secret trusts and oral trusts of land. On this view, though the law may require something more than the settlor's intention to create a trust to be proved before the trust will take effect, this does not change the fact that our *reason* for enforcing these trusts is simply to give effect to this intention. And, *if this is right*, these trusts should not be classed as *constructive* trusts at all. Rather we should treat them as straightforward *express* trusts. (Which side you take in these debates turns on whether you think the 'extra' requirements for such trusts – such as that the secret trustee accept the terms of the trust – are part of the rationale for their enforcement, ie whether they provide a reason for giving effect to such trusts *beyond* simply the wish to give effect to the settlor's intention: see further Sections 9.7–9.8.)

The upshot of all this is that, although our definition of constructive trusts is straightforward enough, it can be difficult to apply and there exist disagreements as to which trusts should be classified as constructive trusts precisely because there remain disagreements as to *why* exactly we recognise some trusts.

9.2 Constructive trusts and constructive trustees

A constructive trust is a sort of trust: the beneficial interest in the property resides not with the holder of legal title but with the beneficiary. And although the duties owed by the trustee of a constructive trust will often differ from those owed by the trustee of an express trust, in all cases the trustee is not free to treat the property as his own but must hold it for, and in the end give it up to, the beneficiary.

However, although constructive trusts are trusts, not all people described as constructive trustees are in fact trustees. As we shall see in Chapter 14, a defendant who dishonestly assists a trustee to commit a breach of trust is liable to the beneficiary for the losses occasioned by the breach or any gains the defendant may have made from it. A similar liability is attached to defendants who have knowingly received trust property in breach of trust. In both cases, the defendant's liability does not depend on him having any trust property in his possession. Indeed in the first case, the defendant will typically have never come into contact with any trust property. Nonetheless, it was, until relatively recently, common to see both sorts of defendants described as constructive trustees (and indeed, on occasion, these forms of liability were listed amongst the categories of constructive *trusts*).

The use of the language of constructive trusts and trustees in these cases has been explained on the basis that it is a shortening of the defendant's 'liability to account as a constructive trustee'. This means that the defendant is to be treated for the purposes of liability, *as if he were* a trustee. In other words, the defendant is *not* a trustee but the same sorts of claim will lie against him as lie against a defaulting trustee. Certainly this is true of defendants liable for dishonest assistance, who may never have received trust property and so never held anything on trust for the claimant. Cases of knowing receipt are more difficult, for, although the defendant will often no longer have any trust property to his name, he will have held trust property at some point previously. As such, it is less of a stretch to describe these defendants as trustees (see Mitchell and Watterson, 2010).

What this means is that 'constructive trustee' is a term of which you should be wary. Sometimes it describes someone who holds property on a constructive trust for the claimant – that is, a genuine trustee. Sometimes, however, it refers to someone who is not, and perhaps has never been, a trustee but who is personally liable to the claimant in the same way as if he were a trustee (see *Dubai Aluminium Co Ltd v Salaam* [2002] UKHL 48; [2003] 2 AC 366, [135]–[143] (Lord Millett), and generally Smith, 1999).

9.3 A unifying theory of constructive trusts

We saw in the previous chapter that there is some debate as to whether resulting trusts form a unitary category; that is, whether all instances of resulting trusts are applications of the same basic idea or principle. Though Megarry J in *Re Vandervell's Trusts (No. 2)* [1974] Ch 269 had suggested that automatic and presumed resulting trusts were materially distinct, there have been attempts to explain all such trusts as resting on a single principle, whether unjust enrichment, as contended by Birks and Chambers, or by the need to give effect to the parties' common intentions, as proposed by Lord Browne-Wilkinson in *Westdeutsche Landesbank Girozentrale v Islington London BC* [1996] AC 669.

Occasionally, similar attempts have been made to locate a single principle or idea which can be said to underlie all instances of constructive trusts. Perhaps the most famous is one set down by the American judge, Cardozo J in *Beatty v Guggenheim Exploration Co* (1919) 225 NY 380, 386:

> The constructive trust is the formula through which the conscience of equity finds expression. When property has been acquired in such circumstances that the holder of the legal title may not in good conscience retain the beneficial interest, equity converts him into a trustee.

(To similar effect see *Gissing v Gissing* [1971] AC 886, 905 (Lord Diplock) and *Paragon Finance plc v DB Thakerar & Co* [1999] 1 All ER 400, 408 (Millett LJ).) However, such statements tell us almost nothing as to when and why constructive trusts arise, and certainly fail to identify some common or defining feature of constructive trusts.

This can be seen in two ways. First, to say that constructive trusts arise where 'the holder of legal title may not in good conscience retain the beneficial interest' is to say no more than that constructive trusts arise where this is what fairness or justice demands. This is almost entirely unrevealing. What we need to know is *when* the courts consider that fairness demands a defendant to hold the property vested in him on trust for someone else. Moreover, when we ask when and why it would be unfair for a defendant to keep property for himself beneficially, we find that there are in fact a number of distinct reasons we might feel that fairness supports the imposition of a trust.

So, for instance, some constructive trusts arise to prevent wrongdoers profiting from their wrongdoing (Section 9.20), others seem to exist to reverse unintended transfers and thus prevent unjust enrichment (Section 9.18), yet others appear to exist to give effect to an undertaking made by the defendant (Section 9.9). In all these cases, we can say that the trust is required by fairness or justice, but this glosses over very real and material differences between those cases and the reasons we have for imposing trusts. As such, broad and unqualified references to fairness are insufficiently discriminating.

Second, such broad statements are incapable of differentiating constructive trusts from express and resulting trusts. *All* trusts arise because the law considers that the legal title holder should not (in fairness) be entitled to keep the property for himself. As such, references to constructive trusts being rooted in conscience or fairness not only fail to tell us anything revealing as to when and why such trusts arise, but also give us no basis for distinguishing this class of trusts from other trusts recognised in the law.

Such statements are also dangerous in that they can give the impression that courts are free to impose trusts wherever they think that this is what justice requires. Although this idea has supporters, it is at the very least a misleading statement of the law on constructive trusts and of the powers of the courts. We shall examine this question in some detail at the end of the chapter.

There has also been the occasional suggestion, although more often in the US than in the UK, that unjust enrichment is the basis of all constructive trusts. We have already encountered the terminology of unjust enrichment in our discussion of resulting trusts (Sections 8.10–8.11), where we used it to refer to situations where A confers a benefit on B without A's proper consent. So understood, it is plain that unjust enrichment cannot account for most of the constructive trusts recognised in law. Instead, it seems that those who seek to explain all constructive trusts on the basis of unjust enrichment are using 'unjust enrichment' in a different sense, to describe any situation where B has something (property, a benefit) which he should not be allowed to retain. Necessarily, wherever we impose a constructive trust it means that we feel the defendant/trustee should not be allowed to keep the relevant property for himself; this is why we say that he must hold it on trust for, and ultimately give it up to, the claimant. And so, on this broader understanding of unjust enrichment, we can say that all situations in which constructive trusts are imposed are situations in which the defendant would be unjustly enriched were he allowed to keep the property for himself.

Such an understanding of unjust enrichment has no useful purpose. *Every* legal liability can be explained as an example of unjust enrichment on this basis, regardless of the source of that liability. For example, if you owe me £100 – whether because of a contractual promise or as compensation for an injury you wrongfully caused me or for any other reason – then we could say that you would be unjustly enriched if you do not pay me, and that therefore my claim prevents your unjust enrichment. But using the terminology of 'unjust enrichment' in this way tells us nothing as to the basis of the defendant's liability. What needs to be explained is *why* the defendant is liable, *why* the defendant is required to hold the property on trust. This broad understanding of unjust enrichment does not do this. Once again, it both obscures the diverse reasons the courts recognise constructive trusts and fails to identify any feature which distinguishes them from other trusts recognised in law.

So, it is plain that there is no single principle or theme which underlies and distinguishes all constructive trusts (see too Elias, 1990; Chambers, 1999). Instead the category of constructive trusts is best regarded as a catch-all class embracing a miscellany of cases not caught by the categories of express and resulting trusts. As such, the only way to approach constructive trusts is to look at the various instances of constructive trusts recognised in English law, asking in each case what facts are needed for the trust to come into existence and what principle explains the law's imposition of a trust on such facts. This is what we shall do in the following sections.

9.4 Recipients of trust property

In the usual case the beneficiary of a trust has equitable title to the trust property (Section 2.5). This is a proprietary interest and, as such, is capable of being asserted against third parties into whose hands the property comes. There are two important limitations however. First, like all equitable proprietary rights, the beneficiary's equitable title will be defeated by a bona fide purchaser of the legal title for value without notice. Second, the trustee will often be empowered to dispose of the trust property, for instance to sell it and reinvest the proceeds. If the trustee disposes of the property in accordance with such a power, the recipient of the property will take free of the beneficiary's interest even if not a bona fide purchaser for value without notice. In such a case the beneficiary's interest is said to be overreached (see Section 2.9).

Subject to these two limits, however, the beneficiary can assert his interest against any third party who receives the trust property. So, if the trustee, T, transfers the property to a third party, C, who is not a bona fide purchaser, the equitable title held by the beneficiary, B, will survive the transfer of the legal title from T to C. As a result, C will now hold the property on trust for B.

The convention is to call this a constructive trust and C a constructive trustee, so as to differentiate it from the case where the trustee and beneficiary intentionally put themselves, or are put by a settlor, in the relationship of trustee and beneficiary. However, an argument can be made that the trust should be classified in the same way as the initial trust under which T was trustee. So if, for example, T held the property for B on an express trust, then we should still regard it as an express trust when that property is transferred to C. The reason for this is that B's equitable interest remains unchanged throughout; the interest in the property he is asserting against C is the same one he had when the property was vested in T. So, although the identity of and (often) the duties owed by the trustee have changed, the interest of the beneficiary has not. Accordingly, one suggestion is that we should say in such a case that C is a constructive trustee of an express trust.

9.5 Specifically enforceable obligations to transfer specific property

Many legal obligations are obligations to transfer property to another. However, only some of those obligations are obligations to transfer *specific* property. Take a damages claim. If I breach a contract with you or commit a tort against you, I will owe you compensatory damages for any loss this has caused you. Hence I will come under an obligation to transfer property – a sum of money – to you. But this is not an obligation to transfer any *specific items* of property; there is no identified lump sum of cash which I must pay to you. It does not matter where I get the money from; I can get it from my bank account, I may sell other assets of mine to raise the funds, I could get a loan from someone, or anywhere else.

The same is true if I order a CD from an online store. So, if I place an order for a copy of 'Bonded by Blood' by Exodus, the store comes under an obligation to transfer to me a CD matching that description, but it is not under an obligation to transfer a specific copy of that CD. The store can send me any one of the many copies of the CD it has in its warehouse, or if it does not have any in stock it can satisfy its obligation to me by acquiring one from wherever it likes. The position is different if I contract to sell you my house. Then my obligation is to transfer for you a specific item of property: my house. No other asset will do. Similarly, if we contract that you will sell me your (solitary) copy of 'Bonded by Blood', your obligation is to transfer that specific asset.

If I am under an obligation to transfer specific property to you but I fail to do this, there are typically two types of remedy the court might award. One is simply to order me to pay you compensation for the loss I caused you by my not transferring the property to you. The end result is that you do not actually receive the property you were meant to get, but instead receive a sum of money reflecting its value and other losses caused to you by not getting it. However, occasionally the court will compel me to fulfil my obligation and so to transfer to you the specific property. So, if I breach my contractual obligation to sell you my house, the court could either order me to pay damages to you for breaching my contract, in which case you would get a sum of money but no house, or compel me to perform that contract, in which case you would get the house. This latter remedy is known as *specific performance*. Perhaps surprisingly, specific performance is awarded only exceptionally in English law, the standard remedy being damages. So, the upshot is that only some legal obligations are to transfer property, of which only some are to transfer specific property, of which only a minority are specifically enforceable.

The crucial point is that where (1) A is under an obligation to transfer *specific* property to B *and* (2) this obligation is one which the court will order to be specifically performed, then (3) A will hold that property on constructive trust for B from the moment that obligation arises: see for example *Shaw v Foster* (1872) LR 5 HL 321, *Lysaght v Edwards* (1876) LR 2 Ch D 499, *Walsh v Lonsdale* (1881) 21 Ch D 9.

This is traditionally explained as an application of the maxim 'equity regards as done that which ought to be done'. As specific performance is an equitable remedy, the availability of specific performance means that equity will ensure that the obligation is fulfilled. And as equity would make A transfer the property to B if the matter was to come to court then, applying the maxim, equity treats the parties as though the transfer *has already occurred*, with the effect that B becomes owner in equity (though not at common law) even before the obligation is performed. So, in our earlier example, simply by entering into a contract to sell my house to you, I become a trustee of the house for you. Accordingly, although *legal* title will remain in me until I convey the land to you, you have from the outset an *equitable* title to the house, which then, like any other equitable interest, can be asserted against third parties subject to the usual limitations.

However, although this may suffice as an explanation of how such trusts arise, it does a poor job of explaining why they do. The effect of the maxim is to convert B's right that A transfer him property into an interest *in* that property. This may make no difference between A and B (though see *Re Wait* [1927] 1 Ch 606, 635–41, (Atkin LJ)), but it makes a big difference when it comes to third parties. Now, by virtue of the trust, B has an interest which can bind third parties and which will give B priority over A's other creditors in the event of A's insolvency. Yet there is no obvious reason B should be thought to merit such advantageous treatment.

Moreover, this trust is a rather unusual one. For instance, it is clear that, pending the legal transfer, A can use the property for his own benefit, though with a duty to B to take reasonable care not to damage the property (see generally *Englewood Properties Ltd v Patel* [2005] EWHC 188 (Ch); [2005] 1 WLR 1961). So I can, of course, keep living in my house and can keep any rent or profit it generates after having contracted to sell it, at least until the point you pay me the purchase price. This is in contrast to the usual rule that trustees are not to benefit from the trust property.

Before we leave this type of constructive trust it is worth stressing once again that the trust will only arise where there is both an obligation to transfer specific, identified assets *and* that obligation is specifically enforceable. This makes it important to know a little about when specific performance is available. Very broadly, the court will order specific performance only where damages are not considered an adequate remedy, and this will be the case where there are no other assets of the same kind readily available. So, obligations to transfer land are specifically enforceable (the reason typically given is that each plot of land, each house or flat, should be considered unique), as are obligations to transfer shares in private companies (as there is no market for such shares, unlike shares in public companies). (For a fuller run-down of the rules, see McKendrick, 2011, 378–81.)

9.6   Imperfect gifts and the rule in *Re Rose*

We saw in Chapter 6 that as a general rule 'equity will not perfect an imperfect gift', which is to say, if I attempt to make an outright transfer of property to you but fail to satisfy the legal requirements needed for a successful transfer, the courts will not treat my failed outright transfer as a successful declaration of trust in your favour. However, as we also saw then (Section 6.4), an exception to this general rule was recognised in *Re Rose* [1952] Ch 499 and more recently extended in *Pennington v Waine* [2002] EWCA Civ 227; [2002] 1 WLR 2075. The rule is now somewhat unclear, but may perhaps best be summarised by saying that where A intends to transfer property outright to B, a trust of that property will arise in B's favour where A has done everything in his power to make the outright transfer effective or where it would otherwise be considered unconscionable for A to resile from the transfer.

We shall not re-examine this rule here except to note that the trust is regarded as a constructive trust because, although it gives broad effect to A's intentions, in that B becomes beneficially entitled to the property, A never specifically intended to declare *a trust* of the property for B. In this way it is similar to the constructive trust which arises in the case of specifically enforceable obligations to transfer specific property (Section 9.5). And, as in those cases, the basic question of principle is how, in the absence of any such intention, we are to justify the imposition of a trust given that it effectively overrides the common law rules on the passing of title to assets.

9.7 Oral trusts of land and the rule in *Rochefoucauld v Boustead*

In Chapter 6 we saw that by virtue of sections 53(1)(b) and 53(2) of the Law of Property Act 1925, express trusts of land are unenforceable unless evidenced in writing. However, we also saw that equity has created an exception to this in cases such as *Rochefoucauld v Boustead* [1897] 1 Ch 196 (Section 6.8). So, where A and B orally agree that A will transfer property to B to hold on trust for A, to prevent the statute being used as an instrument of fraud, B will be required to hold the property on trust for A notwithstanding the lack of writing. There is, however, some doubt as to how these trusts should be classified.

On one view, the possibility of fraud justifies an exception to the statutory rule that evidence of A's intentions will not be admissible if not made in writing. On this basis, once the evidence of A's oral declaration of trust is admitted we have a straightforward express trust. This was the approach taken in *Rochefoucauld v Boustead* itself and by Ungoed-Thomas J in *Hodgson v Marks* [1971] Ch 892 (see too Swadling, 2010). However, on another view these trusts arise not in order to give effect to A's intentions but to prevent B's fraud (although, at least in some cases, this will also give effect to A's intentions). On this basis, the trust would be classed not as an express trust but as a constructive trust. This was the position taken in *Bannister v Bannister* [1948] 2 All ER 133 and more recently endorsed by Millett LJ in *Paragon Finance plc v DB Thakerar & Co* [1999] 1 All ER 400. This approach has the advantage of being easier to square with the statute, as section 53(2) exempts constructive trusts from the statutory formality.

9.8 Secret trusts

The same classificatory uncertainty exists in relation to secret trusts. Secret trusts exist as an exception to the usual formality requirements for testamentary trusts set down in section 9 of the Wills Act 1837 (see Sections 6.9–6.18). Again, one view is that these are express trusts where the prevention of fraud justifies a departure from the rule that evidence of the testator's intentions can be adduced only if expressed in the form set down in the statute. And, once more, the alternative view is that these are constructive trusts which arise not to give effect to the testator's intentions but to prevent fraud by the trustee (see *Re Cleaver* [1981] 1 WLR 939, *Paragon Finance plc v DB Thakerar & Co* [1999] 1 All ER 400). This may be easier to square with the statute as we would not then need to view secret trusts as *dispositions*, and so the formalities applicable to testamentary dispositions would not be relevant.

Both of these approaches assume that secret trusts are justified on the basis of preventing the trustee's fraud (Section 6.12). However, as we saw earlier (Section 6.13), there is a competing view that secret trusts are in fact inter vivos trusts and hence are not subject to the requirements of the Wills Act at all. Taking this line, secret trusts would clearly be classed as express trusts.

9.9   Property acquired subject to an undertaking

It has been argued that secret trusts and the cases of oral trusts of land exemplified by *Rochefoucauld v Boustead* are part of a broader category of constructive trusts which arise where B receives property on the basis of some undertaking he has made in relation to his use of it (see Gardner, 2010; McFarlane, 2004).

Also falling within this category would be many of the constructive trusts that arise in cases of mutual wills. The typical mutual wills arrangement sees two parties, A and B, agree that the first of them to die should leave his or her property to the survivor on the condition that the survivor then leaves his or her property to C. Provided that the parties intend this arrangement to be irrevocable, when A, for example, dies having made his will in accordance with their agreement, a constructive trust arises, which ensures that, on B's death, the property will go, as intended, to C. It is now clear, however, that the same principles apply even where A does not leave any property to B by his will and so where B receives no property from A as part of this arrangement. For instance, in *Re Dale* [1994] Ch 31, A and B agreed that they would each split their property equally between their two children. This is indeed what A did on his death, but B then made a new will leaving more to their son than to their daughter. The court held that the son, as executor of B's will, held B's estate on trust for himself and the daughter in equal shares (cf *Healey v Brown* [2002] WTLR 849).

When does this trust arise? The agreement becomes contractually binding on A and B as soon as it is made. However, no trust kicks in until, at the earliest, A's death. At this point, equity will intervene to ensure that B upholds the arrangement. But it doesn't follow that B is disentitled from using and enjoying the relevant property following A's death. So, whereas B cannot defeat the arrangement by disposing of the relevant assets during his lifetime (subject to the terms of A and B's arrangement which may allow for some such dispositions by B), B need not during his lifetime, hold and employ them exclusively for C's benefit as in a standard trust (see eg *Re Cleaver* [1981] 1 WLR 939). As such, the constructive trust in cases of mutual wills appears to be another example of the sort of 'floating' trust we encountered earlier in our discussions of certainty of subject matter and secret trusts (Sections 3.11, 6.16).

Another line of cases which could fit here are those which apply what is known as the 'Pallant v Morgan equity'. In *Pallant v Morgan* [1953] Ch 43, the claimant and defendant were both interested in acquiring some woodland which was being sold at auction. Agents for the two parties agreed that the claimant would not bid for a particular plot in return for the defendant promising then to sell part of that plot to the claimant. The defendant was then able to acquire that plot for a price lower than he would have done had the claimant bid against him in the auction. When the defendant refused to go ahead with the sale to the claimant, Harman J held that the defendant held the land on trust for himself and the claimant jointly. Subsequently, in *Banner Homes Group plc v Luff Developments Ltd* [2000] Ch 372, Chadwick LJ held that such a trust will arise where:

(a) A and B have an arrangement or understanding that B will take steps to acquire property, in which A will then have some interest; and

(b) in reliance on that arrangement or understanding, A does something (or omits to do something) which confers a benefit on B in relation to his acquisition of the property or which is detrimental to A's ability to acquire the property on equal terms.

Such an advantage to B or detriment to A on the back of their arrangement makes it inequitable for B to act inconsistently with that arrangement by keeping the property for himself (see also *Cobbe v Yeoman's Row Management Ltd* [2008] UKHL 55; [2008] 1 WLR 1752, [30] (Lord Scott)).

Where this line of cases fits within the law of trusts generally is a matter of disagreement. Recently, in *Crossco No 4 Unlimited v Jolan Ltd* [2011] EWCA Civ 1619; [2012] 2 All ER 754, a majority of the Court of Appeal held that it had been settled in *Banner Homes* that these cases were just one application of the sort of common intention constructive trust, which arises more commonly in the context of disputes over beneficial entitlement to family homes (see Sections 9.10–9.17). This is a surprising conclusion not simply because *Banner Homes* does not say this (nor indeed does Lord Scott's judgment in *Cobbe*, which the majority in *Crossco* believe endorses this view), but also because the requirements set out by Chadwick LJ are rather different from those we find in the family home cases (see Section 9.10–9.12).

Nonetheless, the majority in *Crossco* endorsed the observation of Etherton LJ in his minority judgment that these cases might better be explained as arising on the basis that a fiduciary relationship existed between the parties, which was breached when the defendant then sought to keep the relevant property for himself. Whether this provides a better understanding of these cases may be doubted. The view that the relationship between the parties in these cases is fiduciary is unobjectionable; indeed it may be seen to go without saying given the finding of a trust on such facts. But the question of the basis of these trusts is not answered by saying that the parties are fiduciaries for this simply raises the further question of why the relationship between the parties should be classed as fiduciary.

A final line of cases which seems to fit this pattern and in which the language of constructive trusts has been used is exemplified by *Binions v Evans* [1972] Ch 359, *Lyus v Prowsa Developments Ltd* [1982] 1 WLR 1044 and *Ashburn Anstalt v Arnold* [1989] 1 Ch 1. These cases arise from situations where A has a right to occupy X's land, and X then transfers that land to B. If A's right is not of a kind which would bind B automatically, but B agrees nonetheless to give effect to it and allow A to continue occupying the land, a constructive trust will arise to prevent B going back on his undertaking.

The nature of this constructive trust is, however, uncertain and the cases have come in for a fair amount of academic criticism: see, for example Swadling, 1998. Perhaps the best view is that these are not 'true' trusts at all, but are instead examples where the courts have simply imposed an obligation on B to give effect to his undertaking (see McFarlane, 2004, 678–82). As such, all A has is a personal right against B, whereas B remains legal beneficial owner of the relevant property. If so, these provide a further example of the language of constructive trusts being misused (Section 9.2).

9.10　'Common intention' trusts of the family home

One of the most important and difficult applications of constructive trusts has come in the context of establishing interests in the family home. The problem typically arises either where a cohabiting couple split up, whereupon the court is called upon to determine their respective entitlements to the property, or where, on failure to keep up with the mortgage repayments, one cohabitant seeks to establish an equitable interest in the home to defeat the bank's claim for repossession.

It should be noted at the outset that the parties are free to arrange for themselves exactly what their respective interests in the property should be. Though the law requires declarations of trusts of land to be evidenced in writing (section 53(1)(b) of the Law of Property Act 1925; Section 6.8), provided the parties satisfy the necessary formalities, they can divide the beneficial interest in the home however they see fit. If they do so, this will determine the parties' rights, and the principles we are about to examine will have no application: *Goodman v Gallant* [1986] Fam 106.

The problem arises because many cohabitees never give any thought to the question of beneficial entitlement to the home and so fail to make any such provision. The question of the parties' respective entitlements to the home only really matters when things go wrong – when they split up or get into financial difficulties – and although these problems are far from uncommon, parties embarking on a relationship and setting up home together will often, and understandably, fail to give any concrete thought to what their legal rights should then be. Of course, when the property is first bought, it will have to be conveyed to someone, but often legal title is taken by one of the parties simply as a matter of convenience, with no intention that he or she alone is to be beneficially entitled to it. Even where the land is taken in joint names, the parties may not spell out whether the beneficial interest is also to be held jointly. So, although the law provides a relatively simple mechanism whereby the parties can fix for themselves how the property is to be held, in many cases this will fail to provide an answer.

One other point should be noted. Where the parties are married and then divorce, the courts have a broad discretion to fix and to reallocate their property rights, including their interests in the family home: see section 24 of the Matrimonial Causes Act 1973, and see also section 37 of the Matrimonial Property and Proceedings Act 1970. Equivalent provisions now apply to civil partnerships: see sections 65, 66, 72 and schedules 5–7 of the Civil Partnership Act 2004. It should be noted that this discretion applies only on divorce (or dissolution of a civil partnership), so the principles we shall be examining here apply not just to unmarried couples but also where, for instance, a married partner tries to establish an interest so as to defeat a claim by a mortgagee. However, these statutory provisions are exceptional and, outside such cases, the courts have no general discretion to divide property up simply because they think that this would be fair. Instead the courts have turned to the law of trusts for a set of principles which determines how beneficial interests in the family home are to be established.

After Lord Denning's failed attempt to institute a notion of 'family property' and having flirted with the idea that reasonable, but fictitious, intentions could be imputed to cohabitants to resolve the question of beneficial entitlement, the House of Lords in *Pettitt v Pettitt*[1970] AC 777 and *Gissing v Gissing* [1971] AC 886 stressed that beneficial interests in the family home could be determined only by reference to the parties' genuine intentions. This appeared to be the necessary consequence of the courts having disclaimed any general power to reallocate beneficial entitlements to the property against the wishes, or at least without the support, of the parties. Since, by virtue of section 53(1) of the Law of Property Act 1925, orally expressed arrangements for the beneficial ownership of land are usually unenforceable (Section 6.8), a requirement of detrimental reliance was added to justify upholding such trusts in the absence of writing.

The best starting point for an examination – and which for now remains, although perhaps not for much longer, the leading statement – of these principles is the judgment of Lord Bridge in *Lloyds Bank plc v Rosset* [1991] 1 AC 107, 132–33:

> The first and fundamental question which must always be resolved is whether, independently of any inference to be drawn from the conduct of the parties in the course of sharing the house as their home and managing their joint affairs, there has at any time prior to acquisition, or exceptionally at some later date, been any agreement, arrangement or understanding reached between them that the property is to be shared beneficially. The finding of an agreement or arrangement to share in this sense can only, I think, be based on evidence of express discussions between the partners, however imperfectly remembered and however imprecise their terms may have been. Once a finding to this effect is made it will only be necessary for the partner asserting a claim to a beneficial interest against the partner entitled to the legal estate to show that he or she has acted to his or her detriment or significantly altered his or her position in reliance on the agreement in order to give rise to a constructive trust or a proprietary estoppel.

> In sharp contrast with this situation is the very different one where there is no evidence to support a finding of an agreement or arrangement to share, however reasonable it might have been for the parties to reach such an arrangement if they had applied their minds to the question, and where the court must rely entirely on the conduct of the parties both as the basis from which to infer a common intention to share the property beneficially and as the conduct relied on to give rise to a constructive trust. In this situation direct contributions to the purchase price by the partner who is not the legal owner, whether initially or by payment of mortgage instalments, will readily justify the inference necessary to the creation of a constructive trust. But, as I read the authorities, it is at least extremely doubtful whether anything less will do.

Thus, if a claimant who does not hold legal title to the property wants to establish a beneficial interest in it, he needs to prove two things:

1. he and the person or persons who do hold the legal title must have had a common intention that the claimant was to have a beneficial share in the property; and
2. he detrimentally relied on this expectation of a beneficial interest in the home.

So the basic equation is:

common intention + detrimental reliance = beneficial interest

There are in turn two ways the claimant can prove the first requirement of a common intention to share the beneficial interest. First, he can show that he and the legal owner discussed the question of beneficial entitlement to the property and agreed that the claimant was to have an interest in it. Second, such an intention can be inferred from the parties' conduct. In effect what the courts appear to be saying here is there are certain things which they consider no person would do unless it had been agreed that he was to have a beneficial share in the property. Hence, where such conduct is proved, this amounts to proof of the necessary common intention. Lord Bridge's suggestion is that the only conduct which will ground such an inference is a direct contribution by the claimant to the purchase of the property, whether by paying part of the initial lump sum or by making some of the mortgage payments (though see Section 9.12).

If the claimant proves the common intention by bringing evidence that the parties expressly agreed that he was to have a beneficial share of the property, he will need also to bring evidence of some further conduct, which amounts to detrimental reliance on the agreement. If, by contrast, the claimant proves the existence of a common intention by showing that he contributed directly to the purchase of the home, he does not need to bring any further evidence to show detrimental reliance, as his contribution to the price also counts as the necessary detrimental reliance.

This means that a claim for a beneficial share in the property can be framed, and the requirements of common intention and detrimental reliance can be proved, in either of two ways:

(a) express discussion with the legal owner(s), through which it was agreed that the claimant was to have an interest in the property, followed by a separate act of detrimental reliance by the claimant on the expectation so created; or

(b) direct contribution by the claimant to the purchase of the house, which *both* supports an inference that the parties intended that the claimant was to have an interest in the property *and* constitutes the necessary detrimental reliance.

It is helpful to look at these two classes of case separately.

9.11 Common intention proved by express discussion

One may think that in these cases proof of common intention would require evidence of a conversation or series of conversations in which the parties resolved that the claimant was to have a beneficial share. The cases that fall within the category tell a slightly different story however. Take two of the leading cases here: *Eves v Eves* [1975] 1 WLR 1338 and *Grant v Edwards* [1986] Ch 638.

In *Eves v Eves*, Mr Eves bought the home in which he and his girlfriend, Janet, lived. The legal title was put in his name alone, and when she asked him why she had not been made a legal co-owner he told her that it was because she was not yet 21. Janet then did significant work in the home, including extensive decoration and, which particularly caught the court's attention, breaking up a concrete patio with a 14 lb sledgehammer. The Court of Appeal ruled that Mr Eves held the house on constructive trust and that Janet had a one quarter share.

In *Grant v Edwards*, Edwards bought a house into which he and his partner, Grant, moved. Legal title was conveyed into the names of Edwards and his brother. Edwards told Grant that she was not included in the conveyance for fear that it might prejudice her in her divorce proceedings. Detrimental reliance was provided by Grant's significant contributions to the household expenses, and the Court of Appeal concluded that she had a half share in the house under a constructive trust.

The striking thing about both of these cases is that in neither was there anything which we would typically call an agreement. Instead, in each case the claimant asked why her name was not on the title deeds and the defendant gave her an excuse. Lord Bridge in *Rosset* would have us believe that such exchanges reveal that the defendant did indeed intend the claimant to have a beneficial share in the property. However, it seems plain that this was not what Mr Eves and Mr Edwards intended. In each case, when faced with a difficult question by the claimant, the defendant, rather than admitting that he did not want to share the legal title or beneficial interest with her, made up a reason which he hoped she might find more palatable. In short, the defendants were fobbing their partners off; giving (disingenuous) excuses for *not* granting them a share of the property, rather than expressing their intentions that their partners *should* have a share. Indeed, this seems to have been acknowledged by the Court of Appeal in *Grant v*

Edwards. Lord Bridge's subsequent reformulation of them as cases of common intention seems to be little more than fiction (see too Gardner, 1993).

The courts' treatment of the detrimental reliance requirement poses similar problems. Normally the point of requiring detrimental reliance is to show that it would be unfair to the claimant for the defendant to defeat the expectations his words or actions have created. This is done by the claimant showing that he did (or refrained from doing) something which:

1. he would not have done but for the defendant's representation; and
2. would leave him disadvantaged if the defendant did not then give effect to the representation.

Without both these elements, the claimant's only real complaint is that he ended up disappointed because his expectations were not fulfilled. There is no reliance – and so no detrimental reliance – if the claimant would have acted no differently had there been no agreement with the defendant about their beneficial shares.

However, requiring genuine detrimental reliance would be particularly problematic in the context of family home trusts. The reason for this is that most people pay bills, do work around the house, bring up children and the like not because they think that they have or will get an interest in the home which they share with their partner, but because this is what family life involves. If you are going to live happily with your partner then this will inevitably require you to do some work and bear some costs, and all but the most clinical and grasping do this not for any pay-off but because these things simply have to be done and because it is wholly out of keeping with a relationship of love and equality to leave the other party to bear all the burdens.

Because of this, the detrimental reliance requirement poses something of a problem for the courts. If they apply it strictly and look for conduct which the claimant would not have engaged in had he not believed that he had an interest in the home, the requirement will almost never be satisfied. This would then leave most cohabitants who have no share of the legal title to the property without any possibility of claiming an equitable beneficial interest. By contrast, if the courts do want to protect those whose names do not appear on the legal title, they can do this only by pretending there is detrimental reliance where there is none. This may bring fairer results but at the cost of introducing further fictions.

The courts have plainly elected the latter route, watering down the detrimental reliance requirement such that there is no need to show true reliance. The approach of the Court of Appeal in *Grant v Edwards* is illustrative. Nourse LJ held that detrimental reliance requires 'conduct on which the woman could not reasonably have been expected to embark unless she was to have an interest in the house'. In other words, this sets down the usual 'but for' causation test for detrimental reliance: the claimant must have acted in a way which he or she would not have done but for the promise or representation of the defendant. However, when it came to applying the test, Nourse LJ rather generously treated Grant's contributions to household expenses, which enabled Edwards then to use his own money to pay off the mortgage, as satisfying this requirement. This is implausible. Mortgages need to be paid if the occupants are going to be able to continue living there, and there is no reason to think that when Grant made such 'indirect contributions' to the mortgage payments she had anything else in mind than to do what was needed to maintain the home she shared with Edwards.

Browne-Wilkinson vc recognised these difficulties and adopted a slightly different, more relaxed approach:

> In many cases of the present sort, it is impossible to say whether or not the claimant would have done the acts relied on as a detriment even if she thought she had no interest in the house. Setting up house together, having a baby, making payments to general housekeeping expenses (not strictly necessary to enable the mortgage to be paid) may all be referable to the mutual love and affection of the parties and not specifically referable to the claimant's belief that she has an interest in the house. As at presently advised, once it has been shown that there was a common intention that the claimant should have an interest in the house, any act done by her to her detriment relating to the joint lives of the parties is, in my judgment, sufficient detriment to qualify.

Grant satisfied this test. Browne-Wilkinson vc held that indirect contributions to mortgage payments (ie contributions which enable the other party to use his money to pay off the mortgage) provide 'a sufficient link between the detriment suffered by the claimant and the common intention'.

This approach has the advantage of not pretending that reliance exists where it does not, but it leaves the detrimental 'reliance' requirement looking rather uncertain. What does it mean to say that an act 'relates to the parties' joint lives'? This language is apt to embrace conduct such as housekeeping or bringing up children, but it is plain that Browne-Wilkinson vc considered that more than this was needed to satisfy the test. However, indirect contributions aside, quite what more is needed for this requirement to be satisfied remains unclear.

More fundamentally, once we remove the need to show that the claimant would not have so acted but for his belief that he was beneficially entitled to the property, it is unclear quite what function the detrimental 'reliance' requirement serves. As we have seen, the point of requiring detrimental reliance is usually to enable the claimant to say, 'If you do not abide by your representation, I will be worse off than when I started.' It is this that makes it unfair for the defendant to defeat the claimant's expectations. However, where the claimant, although expecting or intending to have an interest in the home, would have acted in exactly the same way even had he not thought he was to have such an interest, then such conduct appears to add nothing to the merits of his claim.

9.12 Common intention inferred from conduct

Establishing a beneficial interest on this basis is rather more straightforward. All the claimant need do is show that he made a direct contribution to the purchase of the property, either through providing some part of the initial lump sum payment, or by paying some of the mortgage instalments or indeed by virtue of a discount of the purchase price to which the claimant was entitled (see eg *Springette v Defoe* (1992) 65 P & CR 1, *Oxley v Hiscock* [2005] Fam 211).

As we have noted, direct contributions are significant because, in addition to providing the necessary act of detrimental reliance, they enable the court to infer that the parties had a common intention that the claimant should have a beneficial interest in the home. In short, by proving that he made a direct contribution to the purchase of the property, the claimant proves that there was a common intention that he should have an interest. There are three important points to note about this.

First, the courts are prepared to infer a common intention and to grant the claimant a beneficial interest even where the claimant's direct contributions are only comparatively trivial. In other words, it does not appear that the defendant can argue that the claimant's direct contributions were insignificant and so are insufficient foundation for an inference that the claimant was intended to have a beneficial share. So, for instance, in *Midland Bank plc v Cooke* [1995] 4 All ER 562, the purchase price of £8,500 was raised by a mortgage loan, the husband's savings and a wedding gift from his parents of £1,100. This gift was treated as having been made to the couple jointly, and so half that money was treated as a direct contribution from the wife. On this basis, the wife's contribution was just under 7% of the purchase price, and even this came from money which she was given by her husband's parents. The Court of Appeal nonetheless held that this was sufficient to prove a common intention that she was to have a beneficial interest.

Second, and by contrast, where the claimant has *not* made any direct contribution to the purchase, the suggestion of Lord Bridge's speech in *Rosset* is that no other form of conduct can support an inference of such a common intention. So, although a comparatively trivial direct contribution will *necessarily* give the claimant a beneficial interest, even the most substantial indirect contributions will give the claimant nothing (unless, of course, the claimant can also prove an express agreement to share the property, in which case he can bring himself within the first class of case).

This cannot be defended. If we are concerned with establishing a *genuine* common intention (on which see further Section 9.15) then there is no sense in saying *either* that direct contributions, no matter how small, are both a necessary and a sufficient basis for an inference of common intention *or* that indirect contributions, no matter how great, can never support such an inference. If we consider that a direct contribution of a few hundred pounds suffices as proof that the parties must have intended the claimant to have a share, surely an indirect contribution (through, for instance, payments of other household expenses) of thousands of pounds must likewise demonstrate such an intention. This is backed up even further by the fact that most cohabitants are unlikely to give much thought to, and indeed to care about, who pays for what, so long as all the necessary expenses are met. So, a couple may agree to split all the bills equally, or they may agree that one will pay off the mortgage while the other will pay the council tax and household bills. What choice they make will almost invariably be for reasons of convenience and practicality, rather than a reflection of their intentions as to the beneficial ownership of the home. As such, if we are concerned with finding genuine common intentions, it is unreal for the law both to place such stress on the *form* of the claimant's contribution and to disregard completely the *size* of those contributions. (A useful contrast can be drawn here with the approach taken in Canada, where both direct and indirect contributions are relevant to establishing an interest in the home: see *Peter v Beblow* [1993] 1 SCR 980.)

Accordingly, it is not surprising to find occasional cases where the courts have held that indirect contributions *do* provide a sufficient basis for an inference of a common intention to share the beneficial interest. So, in *Le Foe v Le Foe* [2001] 2 FLR 970, Nicholas Mostyn QC held that the claimant's significant indirect contributions to mortgage repayments enabled the court to infer that there was a common intention that she should have a beneficial interest in the property. Therefore, we can say that the position of a claimant who cannot show that he and the defendant ever discussed their beneficial shares and who did not directly contribute to the purchase of the home is not entirely hopeless. Moreover, further support for such a relaxation of the *Rosset* stance on indirect contributions can be found in the House of Lords decision in *Stack v Dowden* [2007] UKHL 17; [2007] 2 AC 432. Baroness Hale, giving the leading judgment, suggested that Lord Bridge may 'have set the hurdle rather too high in certain respects' [63], whereas

Lord Walker went even further, stating, '[w]hether or not Lord Bridge's observation was justified in 1990, in my opinion the law has moved on, and your Lordships should move it a little more in the same direction' [26].

However, it remains true that, such dicta and cases like *Le Foe* notwithstanding, direct and indirect contributions remain on a very different footing, with the latter (at most) only exceptionally capable of supporting the necessary inference of a common intention. This in turn gives us cause to question whether the courts really are concerned to find a genuinely shared intention that the claimant should have a beneficial interest in the property (see further Section 9.15).

This is confirmed by the third key point. If the constructive trust of the type set down in *Rosset* is based on the parties' common intention to share beneficial ownership, it should follow that where it is proved that there was *no* common intention then there should be no such trust, irrespective of what contributions the claimant may have made. This point arose in *Midland Bank plc v Cooke*.

We have seen already that there the claimant was able to establish a direct contribution to the purchase of the house through the wedding gift made by her husband's parents. Therefore, on the usual *Rosset* principles, the court could then infer that she and her husband had a common intention that she should have a beneficial share in the property. However, the claimant admitted at trial that she and her husband had never discussed the question of beneficial entitlement, and hence had never formed any such common intention. The question the court had to answer was whether this precluded a finding that a 'common intention' constructive trust arose in the claimant's favour. The Court of Appeal unanimously held that the claimant was able to establish such an interest. In the course of his judgment, Waite LJ had this to say about the viability of the common intention requirement:

> The present case is typical of hundreds, perhaps even thousands, of others. When people, especially young people, agree to share their lives in joint homes they do so on a basis of mutual trust and in the expectation that their relationship will endure. Despite the efforts that have been made by many responsible bodies to counsel prospective cohabitants as to the risks of taking shared interests in property without legal advice, it is unrealistic to expect that advice to be followed on a universal scale. For a couple embarking on a serious relationship, discussion of the terms to apply at parting is almost a contradiction of the shared hopes that have brought them together. There will inevitably be numerous couples, married or unmarried, who have no discussion about ownership and who, perhaps advisedly, make no agreement about it. It would be anomalous, against that background, to create a range of home-buyers who were beyond the pale of equity's assistance in formulating a fair presumed basis for the sharing of beneficial title, simply because they were honest enough to admit that they never gave ownership a thought or reached any agreement about it.

This leaves us in the remarkable position that a common intention is not an essential requirement for a 'common intention' constructive trust (see too *Drake v Whipp* [1996] 1 FLR 826). So long as the claimant has made a direct contribution to the purchase of the home, the court will 'infer' a common intention even in the face of an admission by the parties that no such common intention ever existed.

9.13 Quantification of beneficial shares

The previous sections have set out what the claimant needs to prove to satisfy the court that he is entitled to some sort of beneficial share in the relevant property. But what share? So long as the courts were concerned with finding genuine common intentions, we would expect the answer to be reached by inquiring into the content of the parties' common intention: ie what division of the beneficial ownership did they both intend? However, as we have just seen, the courts are sometimes prepared to find a common intention even where it is admitted that there was never any discussion of or thought given to this issue. As such, often we will not be able to answer this question by asking what it was the parties intended. Moreover, even where the finding of common intention is based on conversations between the parties, there will often be no discussion about the precise shares each is to have (see eg *Eves v Eves* [1975] 1 WLR 1338 and *Grant v Edwards* [1986] Ch 638, discussed earlier, Section 9.11).

In *Midland Bank v Cooke* [1995] 4 All ER 562, the Court of Appeal rejected the argument that, where direct contributions had been made, the claimant's share was to be determined solely by reference of the proportion of his contributions to the total purchase price. Instead, Waite LJ proposed the following approach:

> [T]he duty of the judge is to undertake a survey of the whole course of dealing between the parties relevant to their ownership and occupation of the property and their sharing of its burdens and advantages. That scrutiny will not confine itself to the limited range of acts of direct contribution of the sort that are needed to found a beneficial interest in the first place. It will take into account all conduct which throws light on the question what shares were intended. Only if that search proves inconclusive does the court fall back on the maxim that 'equality is equity'.

In other words, although (in the absence of any express agreement or discussion) the claimant can establish an interest only through direct contributions, where the claimant has established she is entitled to a beneficial share on this basis, all sorts of other factors and other conduct can be taken into account in determining what the extent of his interest should be. So although indirect contributions alone will not (usually) entitle you to a beneficial share of the home, where you can establish an interest through direct contributions, your indirect contributions can then be taken into account in fixing the size of your share. On this basis, although she had made a direct contribution of less than 7% of the purchase price, Mrs Cooke was held to have a beneficial half share in the property.

The Court of Appeal endorsed this approach in *Oxley v Hiscock* [2005] Fam 211 and confirmed that it also applies where the claimant's beneficial share is proved through express discussion but no agreement was reached on the exact division of the beneficial interest. Chadwick LJ offered the following account of how the courts should go about answering the question of the extent of the claimant's interest:

> [I]n a case where there is no evidence of any discussion ... as to the amount of the share which each was to have – and even in a case where the evidence is that there was no discussion on that point – the question still requires an answer. It must now be accepted ... that each is entitled to that share which the court considers fair having regard to the whole course of dealing between them in relation to the property. And, in that context, 'the whole course of dealing between them in relation to the property' includes the arrangements which they make from time to time in order to meet the outgoings (for example, mortgage contributions, council tax and utilities, repairs, insurance and housekeeping) which have to be met if they are to live in the property as their home.

Baroness Hale offered a qualified endorsement of this passage in *Stack v Dowden* [2007] UKHL 17; [2007] 2 AC 432, [61], stressing that the question remains what shares must the parties, in light of their conduct, 'be taken to have intended'. As such, the court is not free 'to abandon that search in favour of the result which the court itself considers fair. For the court to impose its own view of what is fair upon the situation in which the parties find themselves would be to return to the days before *Pettitt v Pettitt*.'

This caused some confusion. After all, if – as was acknowledged in cases like *Cooke* – the parties simply never gave any thought to the question of their respective beneficial entitlements, what else can the court do but consider what shares they ought, in fairness, be given? And what use is done dressing up this question as involving an inquiry into intentions which, in truth, the parties never had? It does indeed seem that we have come full circle (see further Section 9.15). Having rejected the possibility of imputing non-existent and hence fictional intentions and agreements to the parties in *Pettitt v Pettitt* [1970] AC 777 and *Gissing v Gissing* [1971] AC 886, the courts appear now to be back in the business of creating agreements the parties never made and locating intentions which they never possessed (albeit only once evidence of express discussions is found or direct contributions are proved). There is simply no other way to account for the finding of a trust in cases like *Midland Bank v Cooke* where any common intention is denied by the parties.

Most recently, Lord Kerr and Lord Wilson JJSC in *Jones v Kernott* [2011] UKSC 53; [2012] 1 AC 776, argued that the time had come to admit that, in such cases, we were leaving the parties' intentions behind and inquiring directly into what beneficial allocation of the property would be fair. However, Lord Walker and Baroness Hale JJSC, giving the lead judgment, were reluctant to let go of the idea of intention, even in those cases where it was admitted that no such intention actually existed [31]:

> [T]he search is primarily to ascertain the parties' actual shared intentions, whether expressed or to be inferred from their conduct. However, there are at least two exceptions. The first...is where the classic resulting trust presumption applies. Indeed, this would be rare in a domestic context, but might perhaps arise where domestic partners were also business partners....The second, which for reasons which will appear later is...not this case but will arise much more frequently, is where it is clear that the beneficial interests are to be shared, but it is impossible to divine a common intention as to the proportions in which they are to be shared. In those two situations, the court is driven to impute an intention to the parties which they may never have had.

Why cling to the idea of intention even where we know such intentions are non-existent? The idea seems to be this. First, where the parties' (real) intentions *can be* discovered, the court has no power to replace these with some other solution which it considers more fair. Second, even where their intentions cannot be discovered – and indeed even where it is admitted that there are no such genuine intentions to be found – the question is not 'What would be the fair outcome?' but rather 'What would the parties, as fair and reasonable people, have intended had they turned their minds to it? (see *Jones*, [47], [60]; cf [51]). There may not seem to be a lot of difference between these two questions, but – at least in principle – what *the court* considers fair may not always be the same as what *the parties* consider fair. The approach of the majority in *Jones* suggests (though they hardly make it clear) that what we are after is the solution which *the parties* would have agreed to. On this basis, although this will in practice involve consideration of what solution they could *fairly* have agreed to, the focus remains the parties and *their* conceptions of what is (or would have been) fair.

9.14 Joint legal ownership

The *Rosset* principles are frequently used where a claimant whose name does not appear on the legal title wants to establish a beneficial interest in that property. However, a legal co-owner may also seek to rely on these principles to establish an interest greater than their legal co-ownership would indicate. For example, if the property is held by A and B jointly, the inference from the way legal title is held is that A and B each have a 50% beneficial share. However, A may seek to use the *Rosset* rules to claim a beneficial interest greater than 50%. This was the nature of the claim in *Stack v Dowden* [2007] UKHL 17; [2007] 2 AC 432 and now *Jones v Kernott* [2011] UKSC 53; [2012] 1 AC 776. Here it was confirmed that where the legal title to land which is bought and used as the parties' home is put in their joint names (with perhaps the further condition that both parties are also responsible for the mortgage: see *Jones v Kernott*, [25], [51]), the presumption is that the beneficial interest is also to be held jointly. As such, the onus is on the party who is claiming a greater interest to show a common intention that the beneficial shares be divided other than equally.

As such, the basic framework of determining entitlement to shared homes by reference to the parties' common intentions applies to both the single and joint legal ownership cases. Nonetheless, it is also clear that the standard *Rosset* formula cannot simply be extended to cases where legal title is held jointly. As we have seen, when dealing with cases where legal title is held by just one of the parties, the courts have tended to approach the question of beneficial ownership in two distinct stages. The first stage is to ask whether the claimant can establish *any sort* of beneficial interest in the property (as set out in Sections 9.11–9.12); the second, to ask, if so, how this interest should be quantified (Section 9.13). This distinction then becomes important when we consider the factors which are relevant to each. At the first stage, the only facts which, in the absence of an express agreement, will support a finding of a common intention to share the property seem to be direct contributions to the purchase price. However, at the second stage, once a common intention to share has been established – and so once we know that the claimant is entitled to *something* – the court can take into account other factors and other sorts of contributions when calculating what exact share the claimant should have. Or to put it another way, the courts have set a fairly high threshold for claimants to establish that the parties' beneficial interests should be different from their legal interests, but, once they make it over this threshold, they will take a wider range of information into account in determining how those beneficial interests should be fixed.

The difficulty is in transplanting this two-stage process into the joint legal ownership context. For, here, unlike those cases where legal title is held by just one of the parties, our starting point is that both parties *do* have a share of the beneficial interest and, typically, the only question is what share each should have: should it be a 50/50 split, as suggested by the legal title, or something different? This makes it look as though we are jumping straight into the quantification issue – the second stage in the standard sole legal ownership cases.

However, in both *Stack v Dowden* and *Jones v Kernott*, the court was keen to stress that claimants in joint legal ownership cases – like claimants who have no share of the legal title – face a tough hurdle in persuading the court that they should be entitled to a greater share of the beneficial interest. As Baroness Hale stated in *Stack* [69], 'cases in which the joint legal owners are to be taken to have intended that their beneficial interests should be different from their legal interests will be very unusual'. The (strong) presumption then is that joint legal owners will be joint beneficial owners.

So how is a claimant to establish that he is entitled to a greater share? Of course, this will be straightforward enough if the parties expressly agreed this (ie the first method of proving a common intention set out in *Lloyds Bank plc v Rosset* [1991] 1 AC 107). But what if, as will often be the case, there were no discussions to this effect? Recall that in

Rosset, the court held that a common intention could also be inferred from conduct, namely the claimant's direct contributions to the purchase price. But this means of inferring common intention cannot easily be transferred to the joint legal ownership cases. Here, not only will the claimant already have a share of the legal title, but he will typically also be arguing for a greater share of the beneficial interest precisely because his contribution to the purchase price was more than half. This was the case in *Stack*, where the claimant's contribution was around 65%, and in *Jones*, where the contribution of the claimant was over 80% (see also *Fowler v Barron* [2008] EWCA Civ 377; [2008] 2 FLR 831). The problem here is that, if the claimant can establish a common intention that he should have a greater share simply by showing that his contribution to the purchase price was greater, the 'presumption' that joint legal owners are also joint beneficial owners would count for nothing. Instead we would have a presumption that beneficial ownership would be in line with the parties' direct financial contributions, and this presumption was explicitly rejected by the majority of the House of Lords in *Stack* (indeed it was on precisely this point that Lord Neuberger dissented from the majority's approach), a decision since endorsed by the Supreme Court in *Jones*.

So if the claimant's (greater) financial contributions are not in themselves enough to ground an inference of a common intention that he should have a greater share – and assuming there was no express agreement to this effect – what sort of evidence will support such a finding? This is where things get a little messy. It appears that the answer is that the court must take the same sort of 'holistic' view of the parties' actions and dealings that the court takes when addressing the quantification question in cases where legal title is held by just one of the parties (Section 9.13). As such, the court looks not only to the parties' direct contributions to the purchase of the property but also look to their broader financial dealings, arrangements and contributions in a bid to identify their intentions in respect to beneficial ownership of the home (for a fuller, though even then non-exhaustive, list of relevant considerations, see *Stack v Dowden*, [69] (Baroness Hale)).

However, there is a crucial difference between the way the courts are to assess these factors in the joint legal ownership cases and how they assess them when quantifying shares to property to which the claimant has no share of the legal title. In the latter case, the court – having already established a common intention that the claimant is to have *something* – starts, as it were, with a blank slate. The court simply looks through all the evidence to see what sort of share of the beneficial interest is most consistent with the way the parties have arranged their affairs. By contrast, in the joint legal ownership cases we are dealing with now, the courts start with a (strong) presumption that the parties are also to be joint beneficial owners. As such, what they are looking for in the parties' dealings is evidence that is sufficient to *displace* this presumption. So, if the indications from the parties' dealings and contributions are mixed, and so give no clear message that joint beneficial ownership was *not* intended, then the beneficial interests will follow the legal title and be held jointly.

In *Stack v Dowden* itself ([2007] UKHL 17; [2007] 2 AC 432), the court concluded that this was, exceptionally, a case where the presumption of joint beneficial ownership was displaced. Besides the fact that the claimant had made a greater direct contribution than her partner – which, by itself, was not sufficient to rebut this presumption – the court was impressed by the fact that the parties, although in a long-standing relationship, had kept their financial affairs largely separate; they had separate bank accounts and had made their own separate savings and investments. However, Baroness Hale, giving the leading judgment, was at pains to stress that this case was 'very unusual'. Typically, there will be a more general pooling of resources, which, when viewed alongside the decision to put the legal title in joint names, indicates an intention that their beneficial shares in the property should not follow their respective financial contributions.

Jones v Kernott [2011] UKSC 53; [2012] 1 AC 776 turned out to be another of these 'unusual' cases. The parties bought a home together, with the claimant making a greater contribution to its purchase price than the defendant. Nonetheless, the claimant acknowledged that, at that time, there was nothing to displace the law's presumption that the parties were to share the house beneficially. Things changed, however, when the couple split up. The defendant moved out and bought a home of his own. From that point on, he made no contribution to the original property, the mortgage payments and household expenses being met wholly by the claimant. The trial judge concluded that it could be inferred that, when the defendant moved out and directed his resources instead to acquiring and funding his own home, the parties intended that they were no longer to remain beneficial joint tenants of the original property. Instead the claimant was to take sole responsibility for that property and hence the sole benefit of any subsequent increases to its value. This finding was endorsed by a majority in the Supreme Court (the minority thought that, although such an intention was likely absent, it ought to nonetheless be imputed to the parties: see Section 9.15). The result was that the claimant was recognised as having a 90% beneficial interest in the property.

In both *Stack* and *Jones*, therefore, the parties – either from the outset or at some later stage – treated their finances and their property holdings as distinct, which then supported a conclusion that their beneficial shares in the home should be split (broadly) in line with their respective contributions. Elsewhere, however, where there is no such evidence that the parties regarded, and so intended to keep, their financial interests and property holdings as separate, the courts have held that the presumption of joint beneficial ownership is not displaced even where the claimant contributed the entirety of the purchase price (see eg *Fowler v Barron* [2008] EWCA Civ 377; [2008] 2 FLR 831).

9.15 Inferred and imputed intentions

We noted at the outset of our discussion that the common intention constructive trust has its origins in the House of Lords' decisions in *Pettitt v Pettitt* [1970] AC 777 and *Gissing v Gissing* [1971] AC 886. The central message of these two cases was that beneficial interests in the family home were to be determined only by reference to the parties' *genuine* intentions. The courts were *not* free to manufacture intentions which – however reasonable or practical – the parties themselves did not have. Now, as we have seen, the courts have, at the very least, had to bend these rules in a bid to do (what they consider to be) justice. Often the parties simply never thought about the question of beneficial entitlement – or at least not until it is too late – yet the courts have been reluctant to say that this must be fatal to any such claim. *Stack v Dowden* gave the House of Lords the opportunity either to reassert the importance of true intentions or to contribute further to the watering down of the 'common intention' requirement. The messages it sent out were, however, rather mixed.

On the one hand, as we noted earlier (Section 9.13), Baroness Hale doubted the suggestion in *Oxley v Hiscock* [2005] Fam 211 that courts should quantify the parties' beneficial interests by reference to what 'the court considers fair having regard to the whole course of dealing between them in relation to the property'. Her criticism of this formulation was precisely its failure to make clear that the court's job was to identify what the parties must be taken to have intended. Indeed, she acknowledged that for the court instead to determine beneficial interests by invoking its own view of what would be fair would be to ignore the lessons of *Pettitt* and *Gissing*.

On the other hand, however, Baroness Hale on a number of occasions appeared to suggest that the court could indeed manufacture intentions the parties themselves never possessed. This can be seen in the references to what the parties 'must be taken to have intended'(eg [2007] UKHL 17; [2007] 2 AC 432, [61] and [69]). Why not simply ask what they *did* intend? The 'must be taken' implies unreality: although they did not *in fact* intend this, we must (for reasons yet to be explained) act on the basis that they did. A further indication comes from Baroness Hale's statement, at [33], that '[t]he search is to ascertain the parties' shared intentions, actual, inferred or imputed, with respect to the property in the light of their whole course of conduct in relation to it'. The trouble here comes with the language of *imputed* intention. Although inferred intentions are, typically, understood to be intentions that the parties actually had, but which are ascertained by inference from the surrounding circumstances (ie we work out what the parties genuinely intended from their words and actions), we tend to use the terminology of *imputed* intentions to describe intentions which the parties did not in fact have, but which we will nonetheless treat them as having (see too *Stack*, [125] and [126] (Lord Neuberger)). And it is exactly this possibility that the House of Lords had rejected in *Pettitt* and *Gissing*.

As we have seen (Section 9.13), the difficulty here is that there seems little difference in substance between resolving these cases by imputing or manufacturing intentions which the parties never had and by explicitly deciding them by the courts' view of what would be fair. For, how is the court to determine what intentions the parties should be treated as having, if not by reference to what intentions they consider would have been fair and reasonable? And yet, as we have seen, Baroness Hale explicitly rejected the view that courts were to ask what division of the beneficial interest would be fair. This apparent inconsistency was picked up by Lord Neuberger in his dissent and subsequently by Rimer LJ in the Court of Appeal in *Jones v Kernott* [2010] EWCA Civ 578; [2010] 3 All ER 423, who concluded that Baroness Hale could not have intended that courts should be free to ascribe to the parties intentions they never formed.

When *Jones v Kernott* was appealed to the Supreme Court, this provided an opportunity for clarification. The court did not speak with one voice (see Section 9.13), but the following points are now clear. First, where the parties' genuine intentions extend to the precise beneficial shares each is to have in the home then these will be conclusive. In other words, to the extent that the parties do have a genuine common intention on the question of their beneficial entitlements, there is no scope for imputation. Second, and by contrast, to the extent that these genuine intentions fail to determine the parties' beneficial shares, it will sometimes be permissible for the court to impute the relevant intention. As all the members of the court accepted, this process of imputation involves constructing – and hence imposing – an intention which the parties themselves likely never had. Third, when identifying what intention should be imputed to the parties – and hence when determining what beneficial shares each of the parties should receive – the court should bear in mind the whole course of dealing between the parties, and hence should consider more than the parties' respective financial contributions to the purchase of the property.

Is imputation possible – or indeed necessary – in every case where the parties' genuine intentions are absent or unclear? Here the court was less clear, but the suggestion appears to be no. The courts are led to imputation only once they have determined that the parties (genuinely) intended their beneficial shares to be other than reflective of their legal interests in the property. In other words, as we have seen, where the land is in joint names, the presumption is that the parties are joint tenants in equity too; conversely, where legal title is in only one name, the court's starting point is that that legal title holder alone is beneficially entitled to the property. In both cases, a claimant who wants to establish a beneficial interest greater than this has to show that the parties had a common intention that he should have such a share. *This* intention – that the claimant should have an equitable interest greater than their legal interest – must, it seems, be genuine. That is, it must either have been expressed by the parties or (genuinely) inferred from their conduct, but cannot (as the law stands) be imputed: see *Jones*, [64], [84]. So where the parties in a single legal ownership case cannot be said truly to have had a common intention that the claimant will have a beneficial share in the property, the court cannot impute such an intention and the claim will fail (cf the discussion of *Midland Bank v Cooke* in Section 9.12). In a joint legal ownership case, if no genuine common intention as to how the property was to be held beneficially can be found, then, again, no imputation is possible and the presumption of an equitable joint tenancy will go unrebutted.

What this means is that imputation is available only to 'complete' an incomplete *genuine* common intention. So if the parties in a single legal ownership case *do* intend the claimant to have a share but failed to form any intention on what concrete share the claimant should have, the courts are free to fill in this gap by imputing such an intention to them. Similarly, in a joint legal ownership case, if the parties *did* intend to be other than equitable joint tenants but again failed to spell out what their shares should instead be, then here too the courts may impute a relevant intention.

Some may question the sense of this distinction: why should imputation be possible at some times and not others? We can all agree that where the parties' genuine intentions can be identified, there should be no scope for the court to impute different intentions to them. But where these intentions are absent or cannot be identified, surely imputation is reasonable in all cases or in none. As such, allowing imputation only at this second stage but not at the first appears arbitrary.

Indeed this is symptomatic of a broader artificiality in how the courts have approached these cases. In the standard case, where the claimant's name does not appear on the legal title, the courts have approached claims to a beneficial interest in two stages: First, can the claimant establish *any sort* of interest? Second, if so, how should that share of the beneficial interest be quantified? As we have noted already, the cases have drawn a distinction between the sort of evidence that may be used to answer the first question and the evidence which is to be factored in at the second stage. The comments of Lord Bridge in *Rosset* to the effect that, where there has been no express agreement, the only evidence from which a common intention can be inferred is direct contributions to the purchase price were directed to the first of these questions. (Whether he would have said that other evidence could be relied on at the second stage is unclear, as this question did not arise.) Once this stage is passed, however, the courts will look at the parties' broader financial arrangements and contributions to identify their common intentions and so to quantify their beneficial shares.

As we have also seen, any such split in the joint names cases is less neat. The fact that the claimant's name appears on the legal title means that we already presume he is entitled to *some* beneficial share. The only question is how much. As such, the inquiry seems to jump straight to the second stage: quantification. The courts have nonetheless attempted to maintain the two-stage approach by saying that the first stage involves asking whether the parties are to be other than equitable joint tenants. Only if that question is answered affirmatively do we get to the second stage of asking what their shares are to be. But even so, it is clear that the initial question raised in these cases is different from that raised in the single legal ownership cases.

This is clear from both *Stack* and *Jones*, where the courts acknowledged that they were not concerned with, and so did not address, the first question raised in the single legal ownership cases: namely whether the claimant could make out any sort of beneficial interest *at all*. As such, it would be wrong to say that Lord Bridge's requirement of direct contributions has been rejected by these decisions. The same goes for the second element of the *Rosset* formula – detrimental reliance – which likewise receives little mention in *Stack* and *Jones* (on which see *Geary v Rankine* [2012] EWCA Civ 555; [2012] 2 FCR 461, where the court clearly proceeds on the basis that the detrimental reliance requirement remains; cf Gardner, 2008). It may well be that, as and when the Supreme Court next considers the question of how a claimant can establish a beneficial interest in a single legal ownership case, this formula will be revised or the factors from which courts can infer that the parties intended that the claimant should have a share will be extended. Certainly there were hints to that effect in *Stack* (see Section 9.12). But we are not there yet.

Nonetheless, the confirmation in both *Stack* and *Jones* that, when addressing the quantification question, the courts can take into account more than the parties' direct contributions to the purchase of the property, raises a fundamental question as to the logic of the two-stage approach. If (or in so far as) the question at both stages is what the parties did intend, then it makes no sense to say that certain factors, such as indirect contributions to the purchase, are relevant at the second stage but not at the first. If we think that such factors do shed light on what the parties intended in relation to the beneficial ownership of the property, then they should be taken into account not only when quantifying a claimant's beneficial share but also when determining if he has such a share in the first place. Conversely, if we think they tell us nothing as to what the parties' intentions might have been, then they should be disregarded at both stages. The present approach, whereby we say that indirect contributions cannot be evidence that the claimant is intended to have a share, while at the same time saying that they are evidence from which we might infer the parties' intentions as to the scope of such a share, is incoherent.

9.16   Context

It has been suggested that *Stack v Dowden* marks an important shift in the law for a further reason, namely that it suggests that different rules are to be applied in domestic contexts from the rules we apply elsewhere. Before *Stack* most thought that the *Rosset* principles, although typically invoked in domestic disputes, applied in all cases where beneficial ownership of land was at stake (for recent judicial discussion of this see *Crossco No 4 Unlimited v Jolan Ltd* [2011] EWCA Civ 1619; [2012] 2 All ER 754). One thing that emerges from *Stack and Jones, however,* is that where land is registered in joint names, the starting point we take depends on whether the context is domestic/ (quasi-)marital or, alternatively, non-domestic/commercial. So, in domestic cases, the presumption is that the parties are to be joint beneficial owners. However, the Supreme Court in *Jones* made clear that in other cases the presumption of resulting trust will still apply, meaning that the parties are presumed to have beneficial shares proportionate to their respective contributions to the purchase of the property (see [2011] UKSC 53, [2012] 1 AC 776, [25], [51]).

Whether this is a particularly significant divergence is doubtful. As we have seen (Section 8.4), presumptions, whatever their content, tend to be viewed as evidential longstops, and in all these cases what we are really concerned with is determining the parties' intentions. On one view, however, the divergence in the way the law deals with domestic and non-domestic disputes is not limited to the presumptions we deploy as starting points or longstops. Rather, the suggestion is that the cases mean that different *rules* apply to domestic cases than apply where the dispute does not concern domestic property. This was certainly how Lord Neuberger understood the majority judgments in *Stack*, and was one of the reasons for his dissent. As he put it ([2007] UKHL 17; [2007] 2 AC 432, [108]; see also *Laskar v Laskar* [2008] EWCA Civ 347; [2008] 1 WLR 2695):

> ... while the domestic context can give rise to very different factual considerations from the commercial context, I am unconvinced that this justifies a different approach in principle to the issue of the ownership of the beneficial interest in property held in joint names. In the absence of statutory provisions to the contrary, the same principles should apply to assess the apportionment of the beneficial interest as between legal co-owners, whether in a sexual, platonic, familial, amicable or commercial relationship.

Quite whether this was what the majority in *Stack v Dowden* were intending is far from clear however. Although Baroness Hale did stress the importance of context ([69]), this was when discussing what sort of factors might shed light on what the parties intended, or might be taken to have intended, their beneficial shares to be. As such, the clear implication is that *in all cases* the central question is what did the parties intend, but that individuals' intentions are likely to differ depending on the context and the nature of their relationship. So, although we can agree with Lord Neuberger that we should be slow to conclude that different rules and principles should be applied as between, on the one hand, domestic property cases and, on the other, commercial property disputes (cf Section 9.17), the better view is that no such difference was advocated or implemented by the majority judgments in *Stack*.

9.17 Evaluation and reform of the common intention constructive trust

A number of criticisms can be levelled at the courts' current approach to constructive trusts of the family home.

First, as we have noted on a number of occasions, although the *Rosset* principles state that such trusts are dependent on proof of common intention and detrimental reliance, it is plain that the courts have found trusts where one or both of these elements is or are absent. The criticism here is not that the courts were wrong to award the claimants beneficial interests in these cases; rather it concerns how they went about this. The courts have laid down a set of rules, which if applied to the letter, would rarely give claimants the protection which most people feel they merit. Accordingly the courts have had to engage in a sort of deception, distorting or disregarding these rules or the facts of the cases before them, to see that justice is done. As such, we have a situation where the courts are saying one thing and doing another. This façade has now finally been admitted (in part) by the Supreme Court in *Jones v Kernott* [2011] UKSC 53; [2012] 1 AC 776 by conceding that the intentions the courts are identifying are intentions the parties themselves may never have had.

Now you may think that we should not be too unhappy about this so long as justice is indeed being done, but we should really demand more from the law. The courts should be able to develop a set of rules which they are happy to apply straightforwardly without manipulation. If the rules currently in place do not meet this standard, they should be replaced. Unless this is done, it is only going to create problems for those who need the law's guidance and assistance.

Moreover, and now we come to the second ground on which we can criticise the law here, it is clear that even with the many liberties the courts have taken in applying the *Rosset* rules, they are not able to do justice across the board. So, we have seen that the courts in cases like *Midland Bank v Cooke* [1995] 4 All ER 562 have found ways to give a claimant, who never thought about her beneficial entitlement to the home in which she lived and who made only a small contribution to its purchase, a sizeable beneficial interest in it. However, if such a claimant had not made that small direct contribution, it seems likely that she would end up with nothing. So, in *Midland Bank v Cooke* itself, in all probability Mrs Cooke would have had no interest at all were it not for the marriage gift made by her husband's parents. Yet one may legitimately ask why a gift of £550 should make the difference between a half share in a property worth significantly more than this and no share whatsoever. As such, even as modified by the courts, the *Rosset* principles require us to draw arbitrary distinctions and so result in unjust differences in the treatment accorded to different cohabitees.

A further criticism is that not only do these rules lead to injustice, but also that it is women who tend to bear the brunt of this. As such the rules are not only unfair but also result in, and arguably promote, a form of sexual inequality. The reason for this is that the *Rosset* rules prioritise financial contributions (such as payments towards the purchase of the house) over other sorts of contributions one may make to family life, which should be viewed as just as valuable. This is problematic because men still earn, on average, significantly more than women in the workplace and, when one party is to stay at home to look after children, this tends to be the woman. As such, women are less likely than men to be in paid work and are likely to earn less when they do work. Accordingly, men tend to be in a better position than women to satisfy the requirements set down in *Rosset* for establishing a beneficial interest in the home (see Moffat, 2009, 649–54). Moreover, it has even been argued that cases such as *Eves v Eves* [1975] 1 WLR 1338 and *Grant v Edwards* [1986] Ch 638 effectively reinforce gender stereotypes, by giving claims to women only when they engage in what would traditionally be regarded as 'man's work' (see Lawson, 1996). So, 'merely' bringing up children and performing household tasks do not satisfy the detrimental reliance requirement, but breaking up a patio with a 14 lb sledgehammer will (see *Eves v Eves*).

A final – although it must be noted far less significant – complaint concerns the corruption of trust law principles these cases have brought about. This stems from *Gissing v Gissing* [1971] AC 886, where the House of Lords was happy to classify the trust as 'resulting, implied or constructive', it being, in Lord Diplock's words, 'unnecessary for present purposes to distinguish between these three classes of trust'.

A similar lack of concern for conceptual divisions is evident in *Rosset* itself, where the court was happy to refer to 'constructive trust or proprietary estoppel'.

It seems clear that the two classes of common intention constructive trust identified in *Rosset* in fact derive from two separate lines of cases: resulting trust cases, where the claimant bases his claim solely on his contribution to the purchase of the property; and cases of estoppel or constructive trust, where the claimant has detrimentally relied on the defendant's representation that he has or will be given an interest in the property. Arguably the courts would not have got themselves into quite so many difficulties, and would not have had to resort to quite so many fictions, if they had not sought to assimilate these two genuinely different types of claim.

However, although it is easy to point out the failings of the current law, it is not so straightforward to identify what we should put in its place. The principal problem is that there is no consensus as to the basis on which we should be awarding beneficial shares in the family home to those whose names do not appear on the legal title. Once we are clear on why we should recognise such interests, it should be straightforward enough to draw up a set of rules saying when such interests arise, as the latter follows from the former. Conversely, until we make clear the reason(s) for giving interests to those who have no share of the legal title, we will have little chance of coming up with a satisfactory alternative to the *Rosset* approach.

The biggest problem is that, since *Pettit* and *Gissing*, the courts have stressed that establishing such claims depends on proving the existence of a common intention, yet we know that these are intentions which most claimants never had (Gardner, 1993). As we noted at the outset, most people never give any thought to the question of beneficial entitlement to the home they are sharing. As such, a set of rules which offers protection only to those who do happen to have considered and discussed such questions is plainly unsuitable (see the first extract from Waite LJ's judgment in *Midland Bank v Cooke* in Section 9.12, Lord Reid's speech in *Gissing v Gissing*). To this extent, the Supreme Court decision in *Jones v Kernott* is a move in the right direction. In allowing intentions which the parties never had nonetheless to be imputed to the parties, we have now at last acknowledged that it is self-defeating to make claims to beneficial interests in the home dependent on claimants having formed intentions and reached agreements which those whom the rules are designed to protect are unlikely to form or reach. (To this end, compare Wall LJ's plea in *Jones v Kernott* [2010] EWCA Civ 578; [2010] 3 All ER 423, [61]: 'Cohabiting partners must ... contemplate and address the unthinkable, namely that their relationship will break down and that they will fall out over what they do and do not own.')

Yet once we admit that the intentions the courts are identifying need not be genuine, what is gained by continuing to frame these claims in terms of 'common intention'? As soon as we go beyond true intentions, we need to find a new basis for explaining why it is that the parties are *to be taken* to intend what they did not, in truth, intend and hence why it is that claimants are being awarded beneficial shares in the property. There seem to be, very broadly, two alternatives (see further Gardner, 1993; 2008). One is for the law to maintain its existing focus on the parties' contributions but to enlarge the type of contributions which will be taken into account. This would eradicate the present unjustifiable distinction between direct and indirect contributions, and would allow various forms of non-financial contribution (such as bringing up children at home and so allowing the other partner to work and so to earn the money which paid for the property) to be taken into account. At the same time, we would get rid of the pretence that contributions are indicative of genuine intentions to share the property and instead admit that they are relevant to the justness of the legal owner being able to keep the property for himself. In other words, the claimant's contributions should give him an interest in the property because it would be unfair for the defendant to walk off with both the house and the benefit of those contributions, while the claimant is left with nothing.

This idea here is essentially one of unjust enrichment. Both parties put a certain amount into the relationship and the home they share, and their contributions are only ever intended to go towards their joint lives. If the relationship then ends, it would be unfair for one party to walk off with a share of the benefits produced by their joint endeavours, which is disproportionate to his own contribution. This would, of course, involve difficulties of calculation, but there seems no reason the courts could not broadly assess the parties' respective contributions and divide the beneficial interest in line with this.

The other option is to move away entirely from the idea of contributions and deserved or earned shares. Instead, shares in the home would be given to claimants simply by virtue of the nature of the relationship that exists or existed between the claimant and defendant. In other words, the claimant would have an interest simply because of his status as a partner of the legal owner. The idea would be that when we enter into certain types of relationship, we owe the other party a duty to provide for him regardless of what he has or has not done.

A good example of this sort of duty is the duty parents owe to their children. A parent's duty to provide for his or her child is not dependent on the child's actions or the contribution he or she has made to family life. Instead it exists simply by virtue of the nature of the parent–child relationship. Similarly, we could say that where you enter into a sufficiently serious cohabiting relationship, you become subject to a duty to protect the other's interests. This could then extend to providing that other with an interest in the property you shared, even where that relationship has now come to an end. Of course, we have an idea similar to this in the law already, namely marriage. The problem then is that if we wanted to adopt this approach, we would either need to limit it to married couples or we would have to come up with a status of relationships short of marriage but which are sufficiently serious and committed to give rise to such obligations. Whether this is plausible or desirable is unclear.

Finally, it should be noted that the Law Commission (2007) published a report only a few years ago, aimed at a partial reform of this area of law. Although it felt unable to put forward an alternative to the *Rosset* principles, it did recommend giving courts a broad discretion to grant financial relief when an unmarried cohabiting couple separates where they have children and, perhaps, where the couple has lived together for a minimum period to be fixed by Parliament. It appears, however, that the Government is not inclined to take these reforms forward.

9.18   Mistaken transfers

We saw in the previous chapter that ordinarily where A transfers property to B by mistake, A has a personal claim to the value of the property, but usually has no interest in and so no claim to the property itself. However, there is some authority that mistakenly transferred property is held on constructive trust by B for A.

In *Chase Manhattan Bank NA v Israel–British Bank (London) Ltd* [1981] Ch 105, Chase Manhattan had been instructed to pay just over $2 million to Israel–British Bank. However, by mistake it paid this sum twice, and shortly thereafter Israel–British Bank went into insolvent liquidation. Goulding J held that 'a person who pays money to another under a factual mistake retains an equitable property in it and the conscience of that other is subjected to a fiduciary duty to respect his proprietary right', and hence Israel–British Bank held the second payment on trust from the moment it was received.

However, this reasoning was rejected by Lord Browne-Wilkinson when giving the leading judgment in *Westdeutsche Landesbank Girozentrale v Islington BC* [1996] AC 669. Lord Browne-Wilkinson saw two principal flaws in Goulding J's approach. First, it cannot be right to say that the payer 'retains' an equitable interest in the money. As we have seen a number of times already, equitable interests arise only once a trust has been created. Prior to this, there is simply legal beneficial ownership and no equitable interest exists. Accordingly, before it made the payment, Chase Manhattan held legal beneficial title to the money and, having passed this to Israel–British Bank, there was nothing left for it to retain. Second, Lord Browne-Wilkinson considered that the conclusion that a trust arose as soon as the money was received by Israel–British Bank could not be correct. As we saw in the previous chapter (Section 8.6), Lord Browne-Wilkinson's view was that trusts arise only when and where the trustee's conscience is affected, meaning that he is aware of the circumstances which support the imposition of the trust. In the context of mistaken payments, this requires that the payee knew not only of the payment but also that it was made by mistake. Yet, typically, as was the case in *Chase Manhattan* itself, the recipient will not know of the mistake till some time later.

Nonetheless, Lord Browne-Wilkinson stopped short of overruling *Chase Manhattan*. As, in his view, the recipient's conscience *is* affected once he learns of the mistaken payment, a trust could arise at this later point. And, on this basis, *Chase Manhattan* may have been correctly decided, because Israel–British Bank knew of Chase Manhattan's mistake before going into liquidation.

As such, the authority of *Chase Manhattan* is doubtful. It is not, however, without supporters. As we saw in the previous chapter, a sustained argument has been made that trusts should be recognised in cases of unjust enrichment, which would include mistaken transfers. Those putting forward this argument have accordingly defended *Chase Manhattan* and the view that mistakenly transferred property is held on trust, even before the recipient learns of the transferor's mistake (although, consistently with the terms in which this argument is made, they suggest that *Chase Manhattan* is better viewed as a resulting rather than a constructive trust). We examined the arguments for and against recognising trusts in such circumstances in some detail in the previous chapter (Sections 8.10–8.11), and we concluded that the imposition of a trust and the priority in insolvency this would give to unjust enrichment claimants can be justified. We will not repeat these arguments here and will instead offer a few remarks on Lord Browne-Wilkinson's suggestion that, although no trust will arise simply upon receipt of a mistaken payment, a trust will (or may) arise once the recipient learns of the mistake.

Lord Browne-Wilkinson took the view that no trust of a mistaken payment could arise unless and until B learned of A's mistake. Conversely, however, he considered that a trust *will* arise where and when B *does* learn of the mistake. As such, Lord Browne-Wilkinson seems to have taken the view that, so long as B retains the relevant property or its proceeds, knowledge of A's mistake is both a necessary and a sufficient condition for a trust to arise.

Now, as we have seen (Section 8.6), Lord Browne-Wilkinson's position on the role of conscience and knowledge appears to be based on the mistaken view that all trustees necessarily owe the same full range of duties as trustees of express trusts. As such, we have in any case good reason to be sceptical about the conclusions he draws about the circumstances in which trusts will and will not arise. However, we may also note that Lord Browne-Wilkinson's conclusion that a trust will or may arise once B learns of the mistake appears inconsistent with the views he expressed as to the injustice and uncertainty that would be created by imposing trusts in cases of unjust enrichment.

Again as we saw previously (Sections 8.10–8.11), among Lord Browne-Wilkinson's reasons for rejecting the argument of the claimants in *Westdeutsche* was that, if trusts were imposed in cases of unjust enrichment, this would be unfair to the defendant's other creditors and would create an unacceptable risk to commercial parties, as they would not have any means of knowing if the property with which they were dealing was subject to a trust. However, if we say that a trust will nonetheless arise when A learns that B's consent to the transfer was defective, there will still be trusts in many cases of unjust enrichment. The only real difference then between Lord Browne-Wilkinson's position and the argument he was rejecting is that, in his view, the trust will arise not immediately upon receipt but at whatever later date the recipient acquires the relevant knowledge. If anything, this would create more uncertainty rather than less (see also *Maqsood v Mahmood* [2012] EWCA Civ 251, [38]).

More fundamentally, given that the principal consequences of recognising a trust are the priority this gives to A in the event of B's insolvency and the potential of bringing claims against third-party recipients of the relevant property, it is hard to see why the availability of a trust should depend on the state of B's knowledge. For example, if, like Lord Browne-Wilkinson, we consider that it would be unfair to give A priority over B's other creditors where B was unaware of A's mistake, why does this suddenly become fair when B *does* learn of the mistake? B's knowledge is a factor which should be considered irrelevant where the competition is between A and B's creditors, or A and a third-party recipient, C.

9.19 Theft

In *Westdeutsche* Lord Browne-Wilkinson held that where A steals B's property or obtains B's property by fraud, A will hold it on constructive trust for B. This may at first sight appear unnecessary in the case of theft. In the usual case, if someone steals your property, although you no longer have it in your possession, you retain your title to it as you never made any effort to give it away. You can then sue the thief for wrongfully handling your property (this is a tort known as conversion). So even without a trust, you have the beneficial interest in the property and can sue the thief.

However, the imposition of a trust gives you two advantages. First, the standard remedy for conversion is that you will recover the monetary value of the property, rather than the thing itself (see section 3 of the Torts (Interference with Goods) Act 1977). By contrast, if you can claim that the defendant holds the property on trust for you, you can require him to hand the property back to you.

Second, your legal title may be lost if the thief mixes your property with property of his own or some other party. So, if a thief steals money from you and pays it into his existing bank account, the orthodox view is that your legal title to the money is lost and you cannot claim that you now have legal (co-)ownership of the bank account instead. Equitable title, by contrast, is not lost simply by the property being mixed with other property, and the beneficiary can instead establish equitable co-ownership of the resulting mixture. So where your money is paid by the thief into his bank account, although he has legal title to the account, you have an equitable interest in it proportionate to your contribution (see further Section 14.8).

The idea that a thief holds the stolen property on trust for its rightful owner has been criticised. The fact that the thief normally does not acquire the true owner's title to the property has raised doubts as to how he could be considered a trustee. But if the thief has no title, how can he be a trustee? (see *Shalson v Russo* [2003] EWHC 1637 (Civ); [2005] Ch 281, [110] (Rimer J)).To be a trustee you need to have some title to the property yourself. But the fact that the thief doesn't acquire the *true owner's* title does not mean he has no title of his own. In fact, it is well established that the possession of property with the intent to treat the property as your own gives you a title to that property, good against all but those with a stronger title: see eg *Armory v Delamirie* (1722) 1 Str 505. So the thief will typically obtain a title of his own and there is no conceptual objection to his holding that title on trust for the true owner so as to enable him to take advantage of equity's more generous rules of tracing and recovery.

9.20 Property acquired in breach of fiduciary duty

All trustees of express trusts and some, if not all (Section 10.12), trustees of constructive and resulting trusts owe what are called fiduciary duties. Moreover, these duties are also owed by certain 'non-trustees'. We shall examine these in some detail in Chapter 10. In essence, fiduciary duties require a defendant to act in the utmost good faith and in the best interests of the beneficiaries. One corollary of this is that trustees and other fiduciaries must avoid putting themselves in a position where their own personal interests may come into conflict with the duty they owe to promote the interests of their beneficiaries, which in turn gives rise to a rule that fiduciaries must not make unauthorised profits from their position. The concern here is that if trustees were able to use their position to make gains for themselves, it is possible that this would divert them from the single-minded pursuit of their beneficiaries' best interests.

If a trustee or other fiduciary does, in breach of this duty, make an unauthorised (or, as is sometimes said, 'secret') profit, it has been long established that the law will require him to give up this gain to his beneficiary. There are two motivations behind this. One is that wrongdoers should not be allowed to profit from their wrongdoing. Where a defendant has consciously acted unlawfully, we should strip him of any gains so made because it is unjust for those who have acted wrongfully to derive an advantage from this. The other motivation is that, even in the absence of moral wrongdoing, requiring the trustee to give up the gains that he has made makes it plain to other trustees that there is no way that they can get away with profiting from their position. In other words, the stricter the rule, the clearer the message it sends out to trustees, and hence (it is hoped) the more likely it is that trustees will act in accordance with it.

Once we have decided that the trustee's gains have to be given up, we are still left with the question of how this is to be done. Say T, a trustee, receives property in breach of his fiduciary duty. There are two ways in which the law could ensure that he derives no benefit from this. One would be to say that T holds that property on trust for the beneficiary, B, which would then allow B to recover the property from him. The other would be to require T to pay to B a sum of money equal in value to the property he has received. This way T retains the property which he received in breach of duty, but the payment to B ensures that T gets no net benefit from this.

Both approaches ensure that T ends up retaining no benefit from his breach of duty, which is the principal aim of the remedy. However, the choice between the two approaches is an important one. On the second approach, B has merely a personal claim to the value of the property T received; the property itself is owned absolutely by T, with B having no interest in it. By contrast, on the first approach, B has an equitable proprietary interest in that asset. This then carries all the usual advantages of such interests over merely personal claims, notably the possibility of claims against third-party recipients of the property and priority in the event of T's (or any other recipient's) insolvency.

It has been clear all along that where T's unauthorised gain takes the form of property acquired in exchange for trust assets then that property will likewise be held on trust. It also seems clear that that property which, although not acquired in exchange for existing trust assets, *should* have been acquired by T on behalf of the trust (or which T should at least have attempted to acquire for the trust), and so which would have become trust assets if T had not acted wrongfully, will also be held on trust for B: see eg *Keech v Sandford* (1726) Sel Cas Ch 61, *Cook v Deeks* [1916] AC 554.

The one doubtful class of case was where the property received by T in breach of his duty was property which would never in the ordinary course of events have become trust assets (although the line between this class of case and the former is at times nigh on impossible to draw). The best example of this is bribe money. I may pay a trustee bribes so that he will invest the trust property in my company, rather than in someone else's. This is clearly an unauthorised gain by the trustee, but it is also pretty clearly not the sort of gain he would be expected to obtain on behalf of the trust, so this is not a case of him taking for his own benefit property which he should have obtained for the trust. For a long time, the rule was that in such cases, although T would be liable to account for the property he received – that is he would have to give up to B a sum of money equal in value to that property – the property itself was not held on trust for B: see *Lister & Co v Stubbs* (1890) 45 Ch D 1. This approach was, however, rejected by the Privy Council in *A-G for Hong Kong v Reid* [1994] 1 AC 324.

The defendant, Reid, worked in Hong Kong as Deputy Crown Prosecutor and, subsequently, Acting Director of Public Prosecutions. This put him in a fiduciary relationship to the Hong Kong government. During this time he accepted substantial bribes to obstruct the prosecution of certain criminals. This money was, amongst other things, used to buy land, some of which was retained by Reid and his wife, with some conveyed to Reid's solicitor. Reid was eventually caught, and the question was whether the Hong Kong government could establish that this land was held on trust for them. The Privy Council held that the bribe money received by Reid, and hence the land he then acquired with it, was held on constructive trust for the government.

Lord Templeman offered the following explanation ([1994] 1 AC 324, 331):

> The false fiduciary who received the bribe in breach of duty must pay and account for the bribe to the person to whom that duty was owed .... But if the bribe consists of property which increases in value or if a cash bribe is invested advantageously, the false fiduciary will receive a benefit from his breach unless he is accountable not only for the original amount or value of the bribe but also for the increased value of the property representing the bribe. As soon as the bribe was received it should have been paid or transferred instanter to the person who

suffered from the breach of duty. Equity considers as done that which ought to be done. As soon as the bribe was received, whether in cash or in kind, the false fiduciary held the bribe on a constructive trust for the person injured.

Hence, a fiduciary holds all property acquired in breach of fiduciary duty on constructive trust for his beneficiary. It then follows that if that property is invested by the fiduciary, those investments will also be held on trust for the beneficiary, and hence any profits deriving from them will also be recoverable. (In the event of the property being invested badly so that it had fallen in value, Lord Templeman held that there would be a personal claim to make good this shortfall.) Moreover, the beneficiary then has an interest in that property which can be asserted against third-party recipients of the property, subject to the bona fide purchase rule, and which will give him priority in the event of the fiduciary or other recipient's insolvency.

In the passage reproduced earlier, Lord Templeman offers two reasons for recognising a trust rather than a simple personal claim to recover the value of the benefit received by the fiduciary. First, he stresses the importance of ensuring that the defendant derives no benefit from his breach of fiduciary duty. If T has profitably invested the bribe money he has received, simply to make him pay B a sum of money equal in value to the bribe will not strip T of all his gains. Lord Templeman then reasons that the only way to prevent T gaining from the bribe is to require him to hold it on trust for B, which would then allow B to recover not just the initial bribe money but also any other property acquired with it. As such, any profitable investments would have to be given up to B.

Second, Lord Templeman sought to explain the imposition of the trust as a straightforward application of the maxim 'equity regards as done that which ought to be done' (Section 9.5). When T receives property in breach of fiduciary duty, he comes under an obligation to hand over that property to B. Since (or if) the courts would compel T to perform that obligation if the matter was taken to court, equity will act as though the property has already been transferred to B, with the result that B acquires equitable title to the property, and hence, from the moment of receipt, T holds the property on trust for B.

Both lines of argument have come in for heavy criticism. On the first point, although all seem to be agreed that we need to ensure that T retains no benefit from his breach, it has been pointed out that the imposition of a trust is not the only way to achieve this (see eg Crilley, 1994). The alternative would be to require T to pay B a sum of money equal not to the value of the initial bribe but instead to the total gains made by T at the time of trial. So, if I receive a bribe of £1,000 and use that money to buy shares which increase in value to £2,000, my beneficiary should be able to bring a personal claim for £2,000, that being the measure of total gains I have made from my breach. (If I had invested badly, so that the shares were now worth £500, the suggestion is that you could still recover £1,000 as the measure of my initial gain.) Accordingly, we do not need to impose a trust to make sure that T is not left better off as a result of his breach.

Turning to Lord Templeman's second argument, as we have seen (Section 9.5), the maxim 'equity regards as done that which ought to be done' leads to the imposition of a trust only where (1) the defendant is under an obligation to transfer specific property, and (2) that obligation is one which the courts will order to be specifically performed. So, if a fiduciary who receives property in breach of duty comes under an obligation to hand that specific property (and not just its value) to his beneficiary *and* if this is an obligation which the courts will require specifically to be performed, then it would follow from applying the maxim that the fiduciary would hold that property on constructive trust for the beneficiary. The key questions then are:

1. Is T's obligation to hand over the property itself or simply to pay B a sum of money reflecting the value of that property? And, if the former,
2. Is this duty specifically enforceable?

However, Lord Templeman simply assumes the duty is to hand over the specific property received, whereas he does not even address the issue of specific performance (see Goode, 1998). As such, he begs the first question and ignores the second. To justify the imposition of a trust on this basis we need to be able to say why Lord Templeman's understanding of T's obligation is preferable and why this is one of those exceptional situations where specific performance would be ordered in the event of breach. Even then we may point out that to say that 'equity regards as done that which ought to be done' offers little in the way of an explanation for why a personal right should be elevated into a proprietary interest (Section 9.5).

Accordingly, Lord Templeman's reasons for imposing a trust are not particularly convincing and the outcome in *Reid* has been challenged. The principal source of dissatisfaction is the impact of such trusts where T is insolvent. The effect of the trust is that the property T received in breach of his fiduciary duty will be recoverable by B and so will not be made available to meet the claims of T's other creditors. Hence, B avoids the losses involved in T's insolvency, whereas T's other creditors are left with even fewer assets from which their claims may be satisfied. Indeed, this was one of the reasons the Court of Appeal gave in *Lister & Co v Stubbs* for holding that no trust arose and that the claimant had merely a personal claim. Lord Templeman, however, saw nothing wrong in this ([1994] 1 AC 324, 331):

> [I]t is said that if the false fiduciary holds property representing the bribe in trust for the person injured, and if the false fiduciary is or becomes insolvent, the unsecured creditors of the false fiduciary will be deprived of their right to share in the proceeds of that property. But the unsecured creditors cannot be in a better position than their debtor.

However, Lord Templeman does not offer any argument by way of support for this assertion and so we may legitimately ask why T's creditors should be in no better a position than T (compare on this point *Lister & Co v Stubbs* (1890) 45 Ch D 1, 15 (Lindley LJ) and now *Sinclair Investments (UK) Ltd v Versailles Trade Finance Ltd* [2011] EWCA Civ 347; [2012] Ch 453, [83] (Lord Neuberger MR)).

At the start we should recall the point we made when examining the justification for recognising trusts in cases of unjust enrichment (Section 8.11): although imposing a trust always creates an inequality of treatment among creditors, with the beneficiary obtaining more and the other (unsecured) creditors less, it does not follow that this is unfair to those other creditors. So, as we argued in the previous chapter, the same principle which justifies B's liability where A mistakenly transfers property to B also justifies allowing A to recover the property in priority to the claims of B's other creditors. A no more intended B's creditors to receive and benefit from the property than he intended that B benefit, and so just as B's liability prevents his unjust enrichment, the imposition of a trust ensures that B's creditors are not unjustly enriched.

Similarly, when discussing the justifiability of imposing trusts over property acquired in breach of fiduciary duty, it is not enough simply to point out that this would give B more and leave T's creditors with less. Instead we need to inquire into the principles which underlie T's liability in such cases and ask whether these principles also justify giving B priority over T's other creditors. So as a starting point we may recall that the reasons we require trustees to give up unauthorised gains are:

1. to ensure that wrongdoers do not profit from their wrongdoing; and
2. to discourage other fiduciaries from seeking to profit from their positions, which in turn promotes higher standards of trusteeship.

However, where T is insolvent, neither of these principles appears to have any application and so they do not give us any reason for prioritising B's claim over those of other creditors.

This is because where T is declared bankrupt, all his property will go towards paying off his various creditors. The only question then is how this property is to be distributed amongst them. As such, however the relevant property is distributed, T will derive no benefit from it. Moreover, T is unlikely to have any particular preference as to how his assets are distributed amongst his various creditors, so it cannot be said that any particular allocation of this property amongst his creditors is to provide a greater incentive to other fiduciaries not to breach their duties. Consequently, the reasons which justify B's claim to the unauthorised gain as against T have no application where, as is the case in insolvency, the competition is between B and T's creditors. This then suggests that we have no reason to give B anything more than a personal claim to the value of T's gain. Indeed one could go further and argue that there is no justification for giving B *any* claim, whether personal or proprietary, in respect of unauthorised gains where T is insolvent, given that in such circumstances there is no danger of T keeping any benefit for himself and hence the reasons for imposing liability simply do not apply.

Nonetheless, there is one remaining argument which may justify giving B more than merely a personal claim. Imagine the situation where T receives property in breach of his fiduciary duty to B and transfers this property to C (or uses that property to acquire other property for C). This is indeed what happened in *Reid*. If a constructive trust arises over the property received by T, B will be able to recover the property now in C's hands, unless C is a bona fide purchaser for value without notice. However, what if, as has been suggested, we were to say that B has only a personal claim to the value of the gain made by T? It would now appear that B has no claim against C unless C dishonestly assisted T in breaching his fiduciary duty in the first place (see Section 14.22). Short of this, C does not seem to have breached any duty owed to B, nor (on this approach) does he hold any property in which B has an interest.

This would suggest that a dishonest fiduciary like Reid could take substantial bribes, which he could then keep out of reach of his beneficiary simply by transferring them to those around him. Indeed this would seem to be the case even if those to whom T transferred the property knew full well that the property had been obtained dishonestly. Such third parties arrive on the scene too late to be dishonest assistants and there is no wrong or unjust enrichment in them receiving from T property which, although deriving from a breach of duty, he owns outright. Of course, B still has his claim against T for the value of the bribe whether or not T retains the property. But T may be insolvent or may not be locatable, and in any case many people would be uncomfortable with the prospect of, for example, T's wife or children being left free to live off the proceeds of T's breach of duty. Moreover, an incentive is given to trustees to make unauthorised gains if they know that, although any benefits they themselves retain will have to be given up, benefits passed on to others will be left untouched. If we agree that it is undesirable for T to be able to palm off his unauthorised gains to C, who will then take the property free of any liability, it would seem that we need to say that B does have a proprietary interest in the assets T acquired. This is what the imposition of the constructive trust achieves. As such, although the reasoning in *A-G for Hong Kong v Reid* is flawed, the outcome may well be correct.

There is a twist in the tail however. In spite of all the criticisms that have been made of *Reid*, it was at least generally assumed that it did represent English law. Although it was a decision by the Privy Council, and so was not strictly binding on English courts, it represented the considered views of some of our most senior judges and it seemed likely that, one way or another, the courts would follow it. Indeed, it had been applied or approved in a series of first instance decisions: see for example *Tesco Stores Ltd v Pook* [2003] EWHC 823 (Ch), [2004] IRLR 618; *Daraydan Holdings Ltd v Solland International Ltd* [2004] EWHC 622 (Ch), [2005] Ch 119. However, somewhat out of the blue, Lewison J in *Sinclair Investments (UK) Ltd v Versailles Trade Finance Ltd* [2010] EWHC 1614 (Ch); [2011] 1 BCLC 202 held that it is *Lister & Co v Stubbs* and not *Reid*, which is the binding precedent for English lower courts. This verdict was backed up when the case came before the Court of Appeal [2011] EWCA Civ 347; [2012] Ch 453.

As such, unless and until the Supreme Court overrules *Lister* and approves *Reid*, we are back where we were before *Reid*, with constructive trusts arising in respect of some unauthorised fiduciary gains but not others. Which gains? Lord Neuberger MR, giving the judgment of the Court of Appeal, considered that the fundamental distinction was between '(i) a fiduciary enriching himself by depriving a claimant of an asset and (ii) a fiduciary enriching himself by doing a wrong to the claimant' [80]. As a result [88]:

> [A] beneficiary of a fiduciary's duties cannot claim a proprietary interest, but is entitled to an equitable account in respect of any money or asset acquired by a fiduciary in breach of his duties to the beneficiary, unless the asset or money is or has been beneficially the property of the beneficiary or the trustee acquired the asset or money by taking advantage of an opportunity or right which was properly that of the beneficiary.

A trustee or other fiduciary who misappropriates his beneficiary's property will accordingly hold that property and any proceeds traceably derived from it on trust for the beneficiary. So too will he hold on trust any property which, although not the beneficiary's, he acquired by exploiting some right or advantage which 'belonged' to the beneficiary, and hence which he was under a duty to acquire – if at all – on the beneficiary's behalf. But where, as in *Reid*, the property acquired by the fiduciary is property which it was not his duty to seek out for the beneficiary and which the beneficiary would never himself have acquired, the beneficiary is entitled to no more than an equitable account, ie a personal claim to the value of the benefit the fiduciary has obtained.

How far does this personal claim extend? The Court of Appeal in *Lister* had considered that the beneficiary was entitled only to the value of the initial bribe and not to any 'secondary profits' derived from it (eg from profitable investment of that money). As Lord Neuberger MR noted, if this were correct, this would go some way to supporting the Privy Council's view in *Reid* that a proprietary remedy was needed. He concluded, however, that extending any remedy to ensure the fiduciary retained no gain from his breach was better achieved by modifying the rules on equitable compensation than by the imposition of a trust, given the impact of trusts on third parties and in insolvency.

One final point. We have seen that there are two principles which might support the imposition of constructive trusts over property acquired in breach of fiduciary duty.

One is the desire to promote higher standards of conduct among fiduciaries. The second is to ensure that wrongdoers do not profit from their wrongdoing. However, this second principle can apply outside the context of fiduciary relationships. Thus, there are occasional examples of constructive trusts being imposed on those who have wrongfully obtained property even in the absence of a fiduciary relationship between the defendant and the claimant. For instance, property acquired by killing is held on constructive trust. Another example may be the constructive trust imposed over stolen property (Section 9.19). Similarly, there appear to be cases where courts have treated the parties as being in a fiduciary relationship simply so that they can then impose a constructive trust over gains made by the defendant. *Reading v A-G* [1951] AC 507 may be an example of this (see further Section 10.13), although, following the line of argument now endorsed in *Sinclair Investments*, we ought impose not a trust but simply a personal remedy to the full extent of the defendant's gains.

9.21 Remedial constructive trusts

In recent years, there has been increasing discussion as to whether English law should, or perhaps does already, recognise the remedial constructive trust. The desirability of such a step of course depends on what exactly is meant by a remedial constructive trust, and hence on what such a change would mean for the law. Here is where things get a little tricky, because those debating the issue have not always clearly identified what they regard as the essence of a remedial constructive trust. Indeed it is likely that different people have used the term to mean different things at different times.

The language of remedial trusts was first used to distinguish two ways in which trusts are used by the law (see Pound, 1920). On the one hand we have trusts which impose active duties on the trustee to manage and apply the trust assets, often for a series of beneficiaries, such as in the traditional family settlement. On the other hand, we have cases where the trust is in reality nothing more than a liability on the defendant trustee to give up a particular asset in his possession to the claimant. In the first case, it is said that we are treating the trust as a 'substantive institution', whereas in the second case the trust is merely used as a 'remedy'. With a slight corruption of language, this then gives us a distinction between institutional trusts and remedial trusts. On this understanding, many (though not all – eg secret trusts, oral trusts of land) of the constructive trusts currently recognised in English law would be classed as remedial.

However, rather confusingly, it is clear that when lawyers now debate the merits of the remedial constructive trust this is not the distinction they have in mind. In other words, although we continue to contrast institutional and remedial trusts, we are now defining these terms differently. So what is this modern understanding of the remedial constructive trust? The leading modern judicial statement on this comes from Lord Browne-Wilkinson in *Westdeutsche Landesbank Girozentrale v Islington London BC* [1996] AC 669, 714–15:

> Under an institutional constructive trust, the trust arises by operation of law as from the date of the circumstances which give rise to it: the function of the court is merely to declare that such trust has arisen in the past. The consequences that flow from such trust having arisen (including the possibly unfair consequences to third parties who in the interim have received the trust property) are also determined by rules of law, not under a discretion. A remedial constructive trust, as I understand it, is different. It is a judicial remedy giving rise to an enforceable equitable obligation: the extent to which it operates retrospectively to the prejudice of third parties lies in the discretion of the court.

This passage identifies two differences between institutional constructive trusts and the remedial constructive trust. The first and principal difference is that institutional trusts arise as a result of the application of rules of law. The law provides a series of rules, which say that on the occurrence of certain sets of facts, a constructive trust is to arise. Accordingly, when such facts are present, a constructive trust will necessarily be recognised. On this basis, once these rules are in place, the court's task is simply to determine whether the necessary facts are present. If they are, the trust will arise; if not, it will not. Remedial trusts, by contrast, depend for their existence not on the application of rules but upon the exercise of judicial discretion. Rather than being constrained by and within a set of rules, the court has the freedom to decide whether, in the circumstances, a trust should be recognised.

The second difference follows from the first. Because institutional constructive trusts are sourced in the application of legal rules, they will arise automatically once all the necessary facts are in place. The court merely has to confirm their existence. Remedial constructive trusts, however, as their recognition is a matter for the court's discretion, will arise and take effect when the court orders. This will usually be the date of the court's judgment, although the court may direct that the trust should have retrospective effect.

It is clear that at least a majority of the constructive trusts presently recognised in English law are of the institutional variety. For example, the constructive trust imposed over unauthorised profits made by fiduciaries (if we were to follow *A-G for Hong Kong v Reid* [1994] 1 AC 324) and the trust arising out of a specifically enforceable contract to transfer identified assets (Section 9.5) do not depend for their existence on any exercise of judicial discretion. However, there are other instances of constructive trusts which share some of the features of remedial constructive trusts.

The constructive trust of the family home, at least in some instances, appears to involve a discretionary element. Although the courts proclaim to be applying a set of clear rules, it is apparent that they have come to conclusions inconsistent with those rules (see eg *Midland Bank plc v Cooke* [1995] 4 All ER 562; Sections 9.12–9.13, 9.17). The appearance of discretion is particularly evident when it comes to quantifying the equitable interest that the claimant is to have in the home. Moreover, the courts openly adopt a discretionary approach when deciding claims on the basis of proprietary estoppel, an area of the law with close connections to the family home constructive trust (on which see *Oxley v Hiscock* [2005] Fam 211; Hayton, 1990). The courts have traditionally denied that these cases involve the exercise of any such discretion and the trusts arising in these cases are invariably treated as arising prior to and independently of the court's judgment (though see Etherton, 2008 and the statement of Lord Scott in *Thorner v Major* [2009] UKHL 18; [2009] 1 WLR 776, [20]). Moreover, it is clear that courts have no general discretion to award a constructive trust whenever they consider it just in the circumstances, or to deny one where they consider that it would be unjust. However, the courts' recent acceptance that, at least on occasion, the intentions which ground these trusts need not be real intentions but can be 'imputed' to the parties (see *Jones v Kernott* [2011] UKSC 53; [2012] 1 AC 776; Section 9.15), moves us nearer once again to the idea that these trusts rest, in part, on the exercise of a judicial discretion and so resemble, to this extent, remedial constructive trusts.

Over time, judicial responses to the idea of the remedial constructive trust have been mixed. In a number of judgments in the early 1970s, Lord Denning MR sought to introduce what became known as the 'new model' constructive trust, 'a trust imposed by law whenever justice and good conscience require it' (*Hussey v Palmer* [1972] 1 WLR 1286, 1289–90; see also *Cooke v Head* [1972] 1 WLR 518; *Eves v Eves* [1975] 1 WLR 1338). This move was, however, quickly scotched following Denning's departure (see eg *Burns v Burns* [1984] Ch 317). More recently, in *Westdeutsche*, Lord Browne-Wilkinson commented favourably on the possibility of the remedial constructive trust's introduction into English law, but declined to offer any firm views on the issue as it was not necessary to decide the case. However, in *Re Polly Peck International plc* [1998] 3 All ER 812, the Court of Appeal held that, where the defendant is insolvent, the award of a remedial constructive trust would contravene the statutory scheme governing the ordering of claims on insolvency. This would effectively deny any application of the remedial constructive trust in commercial disputes, where the principal value of trusts is the insolvency advantage they provide, but may still leave it with some scope in other contexts. More recently, Lord Millett stated in *Foskett v McKeown* [2001] 1 AC 102, 127 (and see too *Cowcher v Cowcher* [1972] 1 WLR 425, 429–30 (Bagnall J)):

> Property rights are determined by fixed rules and settled principles. They are not discretionary. They do not depend upon ideas of what is 'fair, just and reasonable'. Such concepts, which in reality mask decisions of legal policy, have no place in the law of property.

Consequently, the most that can be said is that, although the courts have yet to state that the remedial constructive trust does have a place in the law, there is some, tentative support for its introduction, though with little analysis of the role it would then play.

What would be gained by the introduction of the remedial constructive trust? The perceived advantage is that it would lead to fairer results. As Lord Browne-Wilkinson suggests in the passage from *Westdeutsche* quoted earlier, as institutional trusts follow inevitably from the occurrence of certain facts, the court has no power to decline or alter the terms of such a trust where such facts are present, even if the imposition of a trust would be unfair to the defendant or to third parties. If, by contrast, the existence of a constructive trust lay at the court's discretion, we would not be compelled to reach unjust results. Instead, the court would be free to come to whatever conclusion it considered fair in the circumstances. If it is indeed true that the remedial constructive trust would lead to greater fairness in the law, this gives us a very strong reason to introduce it.

Those who have argued against the introduction of the remedial constructive trust have tended to concede, at least implicitly, the fairness argument and have focused their criticisms elsewhere. One argument is that, although justice is of course a central aim of the law, it is not its sole concern, and that there are other considerations which rightly limit the law's pursuit of justice. The standard version of this argument says that the law needs to be clear and certain, so that people know where they stand and can plan their affairs accordingly. On this basis, the remedial constructive trust would simply introduce too much uncertainty into the law. Such arguments are common, especially in relation to commercial dealings, where it has long been argued that the introduction of even orthodox equitable principles would lead to too much uncertainty (see eg *Manchester Trust Ltd v Furness, Withy & Co Ltd* [1895] 2 QB 539 (Lindley LJ)). However, although there is some truth in this, to be entirely convincing one would need to show why in the particular context certainty should be seen to trump justice. Without more, the argument is no more than an assertion.

A second argument is that, in the absence of statutory authority, a judicial discretion to vary and indeed redistribute property rights would be undemocratic and beyond the legitimate role of the courts (see eg Birks, 1994; 1998; *Re Polly Peck International plc* [1998] 3 All ER 812 (Nourse LJ)). However, although there is no doubt truth in the assertion that the judiciary's powers are not unlimited, this argument goes too far. Principally, it disregards the fact that much of the law of property, including of course the law of trusts, is judge-made. As such, it becomes impossible to argue that questions of entitlements to property are matters beyond the powers of the courts (see generally Rotherham, 2002). Indeed, it can be said that almost all legal obligations are prone to lead to a redistribution of property, because even where the duty does not require the defendant to transfer property to someone else, the *breach* of that duty will usually generate a liability to pay damages, which requires the defendant to give up assets of his, namely a sum of money, to the claimant. Moreover, if that sum is not paid, the court will order other assets of the defendant's to be seized and sold so as to raise the necessary sum. On this basis, any common law legal system necessarily empowers its courts, in at least some instances, to effect a variation of property rights.

Accordingly, if we are to reject the remedial constructive trust, it must be on the basis that the type of redistribution of property it involves is either undesirable or illegitimate. Whether this is so requires us to look a little more closely at the discretion involved in the remedial constructive trust (also see generally Gardner, 1994).

9.22 Rules and discretion

The distinction we drew earlier was between rule-based decision-making on the one hand and discretion on the other. However, this distinction becomes clouded once one considers some basic features of rule-based systems. The first is that a commitment to a rule-based approach does not entail that the rules can never be altered or modified. And in a common law system, many of these changes are effected by the courts. So one could say that within a rule-based approach, courts will, at least on occasion, have discretion to change or qualify the rules to be applied. Once the new rule is in place, however, it binds the courts and dictates the results of cases just as the old rule did, at least until it too is replaced or modified. So, this is a sort of discretion which is perfectly compatible with a rule-based system. Moreover, it is clear from cases such as *A-G for Hong Kong v Reid* [1994] 1 AC 324 (notwithstanding the Court of Appeal's treatment of *Reid* in *Sinclair Investments (UK) Ltd v Versailles Trade Finance Ltd* [2011] EWCA Civ 347; [2012] Ch 453) that this is a 'discretion' that is already part of English law in general, and the law of constructive trusts in particular. As such, supporters of the remedial constructive trust must have something else in mind when talking of discretion.

There is a second sense of discretion, which also is consistent with a rule-based approach. To understand this, it is worth spending a little time considering what we want legal rules to do. In general terms, such rules should tell us what legal consequences (claims, liabilities, etc.) follow from a given set of circumstances or facts, or, to put it the other way around, what facts must be in place for a certain legal result to ensue. Ideally then, legal rules should be reducible to a proposition of the form 'where facts A, B, C and D are present, legal result X follows'. This is the way many legal rules are framed. For instance, the criminal law says that if you cause another's death (fact A) and, when you do so, you intend to kill or to cause grievous bodily harm (fact B), then you have committed the offence of murder (legal result X).

However, sometimes it is impossible to frame a rule in these terms, usually because the circumstances in which the rule is to be applied and which may affect its application are so many and varied that it is impossible to reduce the rule to this simple form. A good example of this can be found in the law of torts. The tort of negligence says that, in certain circumstances, we owe a duty to take reasonable care to see that others are not harmed by our conduct. Ideally what we need is a rule which tells us in what exact circumstances such a duty of care will be owed. The problem, however, is that duties of care can arise in such a wide range of circumstances and their existence can be affected by such a wide array of (moral, political, economic) factors that it is impossible to reduce the circumstances in which a duty of care is owed to a simple proposition of the form 'where facts A, B, C and D are present, then a duty of care is owed (legal result X)'. It is for this reason that the courts have found it so difficult to lay down any clear guidance as to when a duty of care will be found (see *Caparo Industries plc v Dickman* [1990] 2 AC 605).

It does not follow from this, however, that courts in such situations are driven away from a rule-based approach. This can be seen in two ways. First, if a court has held that a duty of care is owed in a particular set of circumstances, this will bind future courts also to recognise a duty of care in future cases sharing the same basic facts (unless the court decides that the law is to be changed in the manner described earlier). Second, even if there is no previous decision which directly covers the circumstances of the case at hand, the court will look to earlier cases to see what kind of factors influenced their decision to find or to deny a duty of care. This is necessary to ensure that, so far as possible, the law develops in a coherent, consistent and principled manner.

Now, we may say that in this second situation, because there is an absence of direct precedent, the court has a discretion as to which result to reach and so how the law is to develop. However, this is again a discretion which is consistent with a rule-based approach to decision-making. In effect, what each case does is to flesh out, to make clearer, a rule which we can at the outset frame only in very loose terms. With each decision the content of the rule becomes clearer, and it guides and binds in the same way as any other rule of law. Accordingly, if the remedial constructive trust is to be meaningfully contrasted with the current rule-based approach, this cannot be the kind of 'discretion' that those advocating its introduction have in mind. Moreover, although perfectly consistent with a rule-based approach, this sort of discretion is really an admission that we are unable to frame our rules as precisely as we would like. As such, it is a discretion which we should support only where the circumstances in which the rule is to be applied really do prevent us from framing the rule more clearly, as with the duty of care in tort. If it is to be argued that this sort of discretion is needed in relation to constructive trusts, it must first be shown why the circumstances in which it is just to impose a constructive trust are incapable of being formulated with greater precision.

If the remedial constructive trust is meaningfully to be contrasted with the institutional constructive trust, it must be on the basis that it involves a discretion which is inconsistent with rule-based decision-making. How would this work? The essence of rules is that they set down a uniform, common standard. Whenever certain facts are present a particular result follows, and so all those who can prove that such facts occurred are treated in the same way. More simply, rules are premised on the idea that like cases must be treated alike. Now that, of course, does not mean that all rules are just. The content of a given rule may be unjustified and may lead to injustice. However, by choosing to decide cases by reference to rules, the law shows a basic commitment to the importance of consistency and equality, ideals integral to and necessary for the pursuit of justice. If discretionary decision-making is to be distinguished from a rule-based approach, it can only be because it involves an abandonment of this concern for consistency and equality, for treating like cases alike. Instead the court would have the freedom – the discretion – at least within a certain field, to do whatever it liked, irrespective of other decisions made in similar disputes. In effect, each case would be looked at in isolation, the judge being guided (presumably) by his own sense of the merits of the case, but without any duty to concern himself with, or to refer to, other cases, and the standards and principles they reflect.

It will only be in very rare cases that we will have good reason to abandon the goal of treating like cases alike. Moreover, it is implausible to suggest that greater fairness would be achieved by disregarding this central precept of justice. As such, if we really do believe that the present law on constructive trusts works injustice, we would be better served by developing better, fairer rules than by abandoning rules entirely in favour of this sort of discretion.

In fact, when we look to those jurisdictions which have openly embraced the remedial constructive trust, we see that the courts have been at pains to make clear that the law must develop in a principled and consistent manner. As McLachlin J put it in the Supreme Court of Canada case of *Soulos v Korkontzilas* [1997] 2 SCR 217, [35]:

> A judge faced with a claim for a constructive trust will have regard not merely to what might seem 'fair' in a general sense, but to other situations where courts have found a constructive trust. The goal is reasoned, incremental development of the law on a case-by-case basis.

Even clearer is Brennan J in the High Court of Australia in *Muschinski v Dodds* [1985] HCA 78 (paras 7 and 8 of his judgment):

> Equity acts consistently and in accordance with principle ... The fact that the constructive trust remains predominantly remedial does not, however, mean that it represents a medium for the indulgence of idiosyncratic notions of fairness and justice. As an equitable remedy, it is available only when warranted by established equitable principles or by the legitimate processes of legal reasoning, by analogy, induction and deduction, from the starting point of a proper understanding of the conceptual foundation of such principles.

As such, whatever discretion these courts *do* have, this does not extend to the third sort of discretion set out earlier: a discretion that leaves courts free to decide cases howsoever they like and irrespective of how other courts have decided similar cases. This should hardly be surprising. As we have seen, this discretion is marked by its rejection of a basic principle of fairness – that like cases must be treated alike. But then this suggests that the remedial constructive trust is not so different from the good old-fashioned institutional constructive trust after all. In both cases, the court's task is to ascertain, develop and apply *rules* which identify when and where constructive trusts arise, rules which are then binding on courts deciding future cases, unless and until they are in turn revised or overruled.

In summary, therefore, it is difficult to know what to make of the argument that English law should introduce the remedial constructive trust. We can concede that appellate courts should have the power, at least in certain circumstances, to alter the rules on constructive trusts, such that they should be free to recognise constructive trusts in new situations and to deny them on facts where such a trust had previously been recognised. But this is a discretion we already have. Less obviously, it may be that we are unable to formulate the circumstances in which constructive trusts are to arise with precision. In which case, courts, on occasion, would require the discretion to determine how the (imprecise) rule is to be applied on a given set of facts. This will only be necessary, however, if the variety of factors relevant to the finding of a trust and the circumstances in which such a finding may be made are so wide that the formulation of precise, clear rules is impossible. An argument to this effect has yet to be made. In any case, this would not involve a move away from a rule-based approach and so would not require or involve the recognition of a new kind of constructive trust. If, however, as the terms of the debate suggest, the remedial constructive trust really does involve a departure from the conventional institutional constructive trust and its rule-based approach, it can only be through a rejection of rules and the need to treat like cases alike. It is difficult to see how this would lead to anything other than greater arbitrariness and injustice.

Summary

▶ Constructive trusts are typically defined as trusts which arise by operation of law, rather than by virtue of a settlor's intentions. However, there are some constructive trusts which seek to give effect to, at least in some general sense, a settlor's or transferor's intentions. Moreover, there appear to be examples of non-intended trusts which are not traditionally categorised as constructive trusts, such as automatic resulting trusts.

▶ Sometimes the language of constructive trusts is used to describe a situation where a defendant is held liable for participating in a breach of trust, despite the fact that he holds no trust property. These are not true trusts, because a trust requires a trustee who holds trust property. The use of the language of constructive trusts in such cases merely describes the nature and measure of the defendant's liability: he is *liable as though he were* a trustee who had committed a breach of trust.

▶ Attempts have been made to identify a single unifying theme or principle behind all constructive trusts. However, these are either over-inclusive (in that they also cover some or all express and resulting trusts) or unrevealing (as they paper over important distinctions which exist between different constructive trusts). The better view is that there is no such unifying principle. Instead, constructive trusts is a catch-all category, embracing all that is left once express and resulting trusts are removed. Therefore, each example of constructive trusts is best analysed and understood on its own terms.

▶ Where trust property is misapplied, the recipient, unless a bona fide purchaser for value without notice, will hold that property on trust for the beneficiary. This is commonly described as a constructive trust, on the basis that the recipient has himself not agreed to hold that property on trust.

▶ If A is under an obligation (often, but not necessarily, contractual) to transfer a specific asset to B, and that obligation is specifically enforceable (ie the courts would compel A to make that transfer, rather than simply pay damages, in the event of breach), then A will hold that property on constructive trust for B until he makes that transfer.

▶ The trusts which arise under the rule in *Re Rose* are typically classed as constructive. Secret trusts and trusts of land which arise by virtue of the rule in *Rochefoucauld v Boustead* have also been categorised as constructive, although an argument can also be made for treating them as express trusts.

Summary cont'd

▶ There is also a category of constructive trusts, which arises where property is received by the defendant on the back of an undertaking he has made to hold it for another's benefit or use.

▶ Perhaps the most important class of constructive trust is the 'common intention' constructive trust of the family home. The courts have held that a claimant, who has no share of the legal title to a home, will be able to acquire an equitable interest in it if there was a common intention between the claimant and the legal owner that the claimant should have a beneficial share of the home and the claimant detrimentally relied on this. The claimant may prove this in either of two ways:

(a) by showing that he directly contributed to the purchase price of the house or;

(b) by showing that the legal owner represented that the claimant would have such an interest and the claimant then engaged in some separate act of detrimental reliance on this.

▶ The law on common intention constructive trusts of the family home is problematic. The reference to intention is often illusory; indeed the courts have found such trusts even where the parties have admitted that they had no such intention. Moreover, the emphasis placed on direct financial contributions to the purchase of the home works to the systematic disadvantage of women. In short, the rules do not seem to be doing what we want them to do. However, although there is widespread acceptance that they need to be reformed, there is no consensus as to what we put in their place.

▶ There is some authority to suggest that mistaken payments are held on constructive trust by the recipient for the payer. This was, however, doubted by the House of Lords in *Westdeutsche*, which held that such a trust could arise only when the recipient becomes aware of the mistake. However, as we saw in relation to resulting trusts, there is a strong argument that such claimants do merit the increased protection offered by trusts.

▶ A thief holds stolen property on trust for its rightful owner.

▶ Trustees, and other fiduciaries, are prohibited from making unauthorised profits from their position. It was till recently thought that all such profits were held on constructive trust for the beneficiary or principal. It now seems, however, that a trust will arise only where the property received by the fiduciary either (1) is or traceably derives from property to which the beneficiary is already beneficially entitled or (2) ought to have been acquired by the fiduciary for the beneficiary. In all other cases, the beneficiary will have only a personal claim to the value of the fiduciary's gains.

▶ A distinction is sometimes drawn between *institutional* and *remedial constructive trusts*, although the nature and location of this divide are not entirely clear. The suggestion is that remedial constructive trusts are discretionary in a way which institutional trusts are not, and that their introduction to English law would give it greater flexibility and scope to reach just decisions.

▶ To evaluate this claim, we must ask what is meant by discretion. Discretion turns out to have a number of meanings, some of which are not only perfectly consistent with a rule-based approach, but which are also presently to be found in the law. The only sense of discretion which can meaningfully be contrasted with proceeding by rules is a freedom not to treat like cases alike. This would lead to more rather than less injustice, and so should be rejected.

Exercises

9.1   Can we distinguish express trusts and constructive trusts on the basis that, although express trusts arise in order to give effect to a settlor's intention, constructive trusts arise by operation of law?

9.2   What does it mean to say that 'equity regards as done that which ought to be done'? Can this justify the imposition of a constructive trust over property, which a defendant is under a specifically enforceable obligation to transfer to the claimant?

9.3   Why do direct financial contributions to the purchase of a home entitle you to a beneficial interest in that home? Should other sorts of contribution also have this result?

9.4   Given that many cohabitees will not have contemplated, let alone discussed, their respective beneficial entitlements to the home they share, and hence that the question of such beneficial entitlement cannot be resolved by reference to their actual intentions, how else can we deal with these cases?

9.5   Should a defendant who receives property by mistake be required to give that property back to the transferor? Should the proceeds of the sale of such property be made available to satisfy the claims of the defendant's creditors?

9.6   Was *A-G for Hong Kong v Reid* correctly decided?

9.7   Does English law currently recognise any examples of the remedial constructive trust? Should it?

Further reading

There is a wealth of academic writing on constructive trusts. For a start, there are some useful general accounts and overviews of constructive trusts:

Chambers, 'Constructive trusts in Canada' (1999) 37 Alta LR 173
Elias, *Explaining Constructive Trusts* (Oxford University Press 1990)
McFarlane, 'The centrality of constructive and resulting trusts' in Mitchell, *Constructive and Resulting Trusts* (Hart Publishing 2010)
Oakley, *Constructive Trusts* (3rd edn, Sweet and Maxwell 1996)
Smith, 'Constructive trusts and constructive trustees' [1999] Cam LJ 294

Then there are more detailed analyses of individual examples of constructive trusts:

Crilley, 'A case of proprietary overkill?' [1994] RLR 57
Eekelaar, 'A woman's place – a conflict between law and social values' [1987] Conv 93
Etherton, 'Constructive trusts: a new model for equity and unjust enrichment' [2008] Cam LJ 265
Gardner, 'Family property today' (2008) 124 LQR 442
Gardner, 'Reliance-based constructive trusts' in Mitchell (ed), *Constructive and Resulting Trusts* (Hart Publishing 2010)
Gardner, 'Rethinking family property' (1993) 109 LQR 263
Goode, 'Proprietary restitutionary claims' in Cornish, Nolan, O'Sullivan and Virgo (eds), *Restitution: Past, Present and Future* (Hart Publishing 1998), 69–73
Lawson, 'The things we do for love: detrimental reliance in the family home' (1996) 16 LS 218
McFarlane, 'Constructive trusts arising on a receipt of property *sub conditione*' (2004) 120 LQR 667

Further reading cont'd

Millett, 'Remedies: the error in *Lister v Stubbs*' in Birks (ed), *The Frontiers of Liability: Vol. 1* (Oxford University Press 1994)

Moffat, *Trusts Law: Text and Materials* (5th edn, Cambridge University Press 2009), 604–68

Sherwin, 'Constructive trusts in bankruptcy' [1989] U Ill L Rev 297

Smith, 'Constructive fiduciaries?' in Birks (ed), *Privacy and Loyalty* (Oxford University Press 1997), 263–67

Swadling, 'The nature of the trust in *Rochefoucauld v Boustead*' in Mitchell (ed), *Constructive and Resulting Trusts* (Hart Publishing 2010)

Swadling, 'The proprietary effect of a hire of goods' in Palmer and McKendrick (eds), *Interests in Goods* (2nd edn, LLP 1998), 492–513

Swadling, 'The vendor–purchaser constructive trust' in Degeling and Edelman (eds), *Equity in Commercial Law* (Thompson 2005)

Finally there has, in recent years, been a significant amount of writing on the remedial constructive trust.

Birks, 'Proprietary rights as remedies' in Birks (ed), *The Frontiers of Liability: Vol. 2* (Oxford University Press 1994)

Birks, 'Rights, wrongs, and remedies' (2000) 20 OJLS 1

Birks, 'The end of the remedial constructive trust' (1998) 12 Tru LI 202

Evans 'Defending discretionary remedialism' (2001) 23 Sydney LR 463

Gardner, 'The element of discretion' in Birks (ed), *The Frontiers of Liability: Vol. 2* (Oxford University Press 1994)

Rotherham, *Proprietary Remedies in Context* (Hart Publishing 2002), 7–48

Chapter 10

Fiduciary obligations

10.1 The variety of trustees' duties

All trusts involve the imposition of duties on someone with title (usually legal but occasionally equitable) to property which bear on his handling of or dealings with that property. As such, all trustees owe duties detailing what they must and must not do with the trust property. Over the next two chapters, we shall be examining what these duties are.

As a starting point, we should note that the content of these duties will vary from trust to trust and so from trustee to trustee. As we have noted on a number of occasions already, one of the defining features of trusts is their versatility. Trusts are used in and by the law for a variety of purposes; they may arise in a wide variety of circumstances, and they may take a variety of forms. It is, therefore, unsurprising that there is no single and indivisible 'package' of trust duties which is present in all cases, but rather an array of duties to which trustees *may* be subject. Which of these duties do apply to a given trustee will then depend on the facts of the case (see further Section 10.2).

It is commonly supposed, however, that, despite these differences, there are certain duties which are fundamental and intrinsic to trusts, and so common to all trustees. On this view, although the duties owed by different trustees may and do differ around the edges, there are certain core duties which can be found in all cases. Without this core, the trust could not function or would not be what we recognise as a trust. This idea is most clearly expressed in the following passage from the judgment of Millett LJ in *Armitage v Nurse* [1998] Ch 241, 252–53:

> [T]here is an irreducible core of obligations owed by the trustees to the beneficiaries and enforceable by them which is fundamental to the concept of a trust. If the beneficiaries have no rights enforceable against the trustees there are no trusts.... The duty of the trustees to perform the trusts honestly and in good faith for the benefit of the beneficiaries is the minimum necessary to give substance to the trusts.

This duty to act honestly, in good faith for the benefit of the beneficiaries is what we identify as the trustee's fiduciary obligation. The view that fiduciary obligations are constitutive of, and so integral to, trusts, and so will be present in all cases, is widespread (for instance, this assumption appears to underlie the judgments of Lords Goff and Browne-Wilkinson in *Westdeutsche Landesbank Girozentrale v Islington London BC* [1996] AC 669). Indeed, way back in Chapter 1, we identified fiduciary obligations as one of the two features of the typical or central case of a trust.

In fact, although there is little authority on this point, it is extremely doubtful whether all trustees in all circumstances owe fiduciary obligations, or indeed whether there is any one duty which is to be found in all trusts (see further Section 10.12). Nonetheless, there is no doubt something distinctive about a trustee's fiduciary duties. Unlike a trustee's other duties, they do not obviously mirror anything to be found in the common law, in contract and tort. As such, they deserve particular attention. Accordingly, we shall begin our analysis of trustees' duties in this chapter with an examination of fiduciary obligations, before moving on, in the next chapter, to look at the other duties to which a trustee may be subject.

The distinction between a trustee's fiduciary duties and his other, non-fiduciary duties has been given increased emphasis in recent years both by the courts and by academic commentators. Typical of this is the following statement from Millett LJ in *Bristol and West Building Society v Mothew* [1998] Ch 1, 16:

> The expression 'fiduciary duty' is properly confined to those duties which are peculiar to fiduciaries and the breach of which attracts legal consequences differing from those consequent upon breach of other duties. Unless the expression is so limited it is lacking in practical utility. In this sense it is obvious that not every breach of duty by a fiduciary is a breach of fiduciary duty.... It is ... inappropriate to apply the expression to the obligation of a trustee or other fiduciary to use proper skill and care in the discharge of his duties. If it is confined to cases where the fiduciary nature of the duty has special legal consequences, then the fact that the source of the duty is to be found in equity rather than common law does not make it a fiduciary duty.

The argument Millett LJ is making here is that:

1. Not every duty owed by a trustee is properly described as a fiduciary duty; and
2. What distinguishes fiduciary duties from non-fiduciary duties are the remedies available to the beneficiary following a breach of duty. In other words, remedies for breach of fiduciary duty differ from those awarded where the trustee has breached some other duty, and so these two classes of duty must not be confused as we need to know what sort of duty the trustee has breached in order to know what the beneficiary can then recover.

In fact, as we shall see later on (Section 13.5), Millett LJ may overstate the differences between the remedies available in the two classes of case. Indeed, it is far from clear, as a matter of present authority, whether there are in fact *any* differences between claims for breach of fiduciary duty and claims for other breaches of trust. Nonetheless, to the extent that the remedies for breaches of fiduciary duty *may* differ from those which follow a breach of some other duty by a trustee, this gives us a further reason for looking at these two classes of duties separately.

Before we move on to examine the content of the various duties trustees may owe, it is, however, worth taking a brief look at the sources of trustees' duties.

10.2   The sources of trustees' duties

Not all trustees owe the same combination of duties. The key question, then, is how we determine which of the shopping list of possible duties attach to the trustee at hand. In other words, if different trustees owe different duties, how are we to know what duties are owed by a particular trustee?

The answer is to be found by looking at the reason the particular trust arises. As we have seen, some trusts arise by virtue of, and in order to give effect to, a settlor's intentions. In such cases – which cover not just express trusts but also other trusts which can, in some way, be viewed as intended (eg secret trusts (Section 9.8), oral trusts of land enforced under the rule established in *Rochefoucauld v Boustead* (Section 9.7)) – the trustee's duties are defined largely by reference to what the settlor had in mind when creating the trust. The basic rule is that, so long as he abides by the rules of what counts as a valid trust (eg the three certainties, the beneficiary principle, the rule against perpetuities), the settlor can shape the trust, and hence the duties of the trustee, however he likes. So, of course, it is the settlor who chooses whether it is to be a persons or (where possible) a purpose trust, whether it is to be fixed or discretionary, who his beneficiaries will be, and the shape and content of their beneficial entitlements. A settlor can also say how he wants the property dealt with during the lifetime of the trust, for instance whether and how he wants it invested. The trustee is then under a duty to administer the trust in accordance with these intentions.

Other duties, however, although they may be modified by the settlor, appear to derive from the general law of trusts rather than from the conscious choice of the settlor. So even if the settlor says nothing about the trustee owing a duty of care to the beneficiary, it is clear that such a duty will exist. The same goes for the fiduciary duties we shall be examining in this chapter. An argument can be made, though, that such duties nonetheless derive from the settlor's intentions, either on the basis that the law presumes, in the absence of any contrary evidence, that the settlor intends the trustee to be subject to such duties, or by saying that, as these duties are inherent to, even constitutive of, trusts, by choosing to create a trust, the settlor has chosen to impose such duties on the trustee.

However, even on this expanded view of a settlor's intentions, we cannot account for all the duties of an express trustee. The clearest example of this is the duty which follows from the rule in *Saunders v Vautier* (Section 2.7): to transfer the trust property to an absolutely entitled beneficiary of full capacity when called on to do so. As we have seen, this will typically thwart, rather than effectuate, the settlor's intentions. So, however we do explain the basis of this duty – and saying that it derives from the general law of trusts is something of a cop out – it cannot be accounted for by reference to the wishes of the settlor.

Other trusts, by contrast, do not derive from the intentions of a property owner but are instead imposed on him, irrespective of his wishes. In such cases, as a matter of principle, the extent of the trustee's duties should be dependent on our reasons for imposing the trust in the first place (see further Section 10.12). In other words, if we ask why the trust arises, our answer should also guide us in fixing the proper content of the trustee's duties. So if, for example, we considered that a given trust arose to prevent the trustee's unjust enrichment, then the scope of the duties to which he is to be subjected should be determined by asking what set of obligations would be necessary and sufficient to achieve this goal.

In line with this (although it should be noted that the case law is largely silent on this point, and certainly cannot be said yet to support the view taken here), there is a strong argument that a trustee who is innocent of any wrongdoing, and who does not know and cannot be expected to know that he is a trustee, becomes subject to duties in respect of the trust property *only when he learns of the trust*. At that point, he comes under a duty to transfer the property to the beneficiary and, pending such a transfer, should owe him a duty to take reasonable care to safeguard the property. Before he has such information, however, it seems unrealistic and unreasonable to expect him to take reasonable care to look after property which he reasonably considers to be his own, let alone to expect him to hold and apply it in active pursuit of an unknown beneficiary's best interests.

10.3 Trustees de son tort

In the previous chapters we have examined the various ways in which a trust may arise and hence the various ways in which someone may become a trustee. So, you can become a trustee if properly appointed as a trustee to an express trust, or if you receive (or hold) property in such circumstances as support the imposition of a resulting or constructive trust. However, you can also be subjected to the same duties as a trustee if, even though you have not been appointed trustee and have not had trust property vested in you, you nonetheless act *as though you were* a trustee under an existing trust. In such a case you are said to be a *trustee de son tort*. Although the language suggests that liability is here based on wrongdoing (this being the meaning of 'tort'), the principle is really based on the defendant's assumption of the powers, and hence also the responsibilities and duties, of a trustee (see *Dubai Aluminium Co Ltd v Salaam* [2002] UKHL 48; [2003] 2 AC 366, where, for this reason, Lord Millett preferred the language of 'de facto' trustees).

When will someone be held to have assumed the role of trustee? It is clear that a trustee may legitimately employ agents, solicitors and other professionals to undertake certain aspects of trust business. However, such people are not to be treated as trustees de son tort simply because they take on a role in the administration of the trust (see *Barnes v Addy* (1874) LR 9 Ch App 244, *Mara v Browne* [1896] 1 Ch 199). The difficulty is in saying at what point someone crosses the line and is to be regarded as having assumed the role of trustee. Some sort of knowledge that one is concerning oneself with a trust and trust property is necessary, but it is clear that more is needed. Some authorities (eg *Re Barney* [1892] 2 Ch 265) say that the defendant must actually receive trust property to become a trustee de son tort. This, however, appears unnecessary, as someone who receives trust property with knowledge of the trust will become a genuine (and not simply a de facto) trustee in any case (Section 9.4). Conversely, the authorities also show that someone who *does* receive trust property, but who at all times holds it as agent for the trust and the trustees, and acts honestly throughout, will not be made a trustee de son tort: see *Williams-Ashman v Price and Williams* [1942] Ch 219. Moreover, there seems no reason for excluding someone who, though at no point vested with the trust property, nonetheless takes on the role of determining how it is to be applied. Accordingly, a requirement that the defendant must have received the trust property appears unnecessary and to miss the point of the principle here.

The basic difficulty in identifying when someone becomes a trustee de son tort is that there are degrees of control, and so the answer to the question of whether the defendant has assumed control of the trust will often be 'yes, to an extent'. As such, we may have to make do with saying that the greater the extent to which the defendant takes on jobs normally done by a trustee, the greater the chance that he will be held to be a trustee de son tort, with the proviso that the courts are generally reluctant to impose liability on honest, though perhaps negligent, professionals who become involved in trust business. If a defendant is held to be a trustee de son tort then not only will he be subjected to the same duties as the 'real' trustees of the relevant trust, but he will also be subject to the same liabilities if he should breach those duties (on which see Chapter 13).

10.4 The content of fiduciary obligations

A trustee's fiduciary obligations are concerned with ensuring that he exercises his powers under the trust for the right reasons. As we have seen, in the typical trust not only does the trustee have physical control of the trust property, he also has a full range of powers to determine how that property is used and applied. However, in contrast to straightforward legal beneficial ownership, the trustee must exercise these powers not for his own benefit or to further his own ends, but rather for the exclusive benefit of the beneficiary. The trustee's fiduciary duties exist to ensure that he does just this: that, when administering the trust, he does not deviate from the single-minded pursuit of what is best for the beneficiary.

Hence, we typically formulate fiduciary obligations as duties to act in good faith in the best interests of the beneficiary. However, it is also common to see fiduciary obligations split into a series of sub-rules or constituent parts. A neat summary is provided by Millett LJ in *Bristol and West Building Society v Mothew* [1998] Ch 1, 18:

> A fiduciary is someone who has undertaken to act for or on behalf of another in a particular matter in circumstances which give rise to a relationship of trust and confidence. The distinguishing obligation of a fiduciary is the obligation of loyalty. The principal is entitled to the single-minded loyalty of his fiduciary. The core liability has several facets. A fiduciary must act in good faith; he must not make a profit out of his trust; he must not place himself in a position where his duty and his interest may conflict; he may not act for his own benefit or the benefit of a third person without the informed consent of his principal. This is not intended to be an exhaustive list, but it is sufficient to indicate the nature of fiduciary obligations. They are the defining characteristics of the fiduciary.

(It makes little difference whether we regard these various sub-rules, detailing the dos and don'ts for fiduciaries, as simply aspects or offshoots of a single fiduciary obligation or as forming a package of discrete, though of course related, fiduciary obligations. You will see both forms of expression in the cases and articles.)

That the law should require trustees to exercise their powers for the exclusive benefit of their beneficiaries is unsurprising. The very point of trusts is to confer benefits upon the beneficiaries, and it is the trustee's job to use his position to secure these benefits for, and pass them on to, the beneficiaries. Trustees are more likely to be successful in securing such benefits if they keep their beneficiaries' interests in mind at all times. What is unusual and significant about a trustee's fiduciary obligations is how far they extend. As we shall see, the cases hold that a trustee can commit a breach of fiduciary duty even where he *has* acted for the right reasons, having sought throughout to advance the interests of his beneficiary.

10.5   Securing performance

Much of the law is concerned with directing people's conduct, promoting certain forms of behaviour and discouraging others. The law's primary tool for achieving this is to set down rules requiring or prohibiting the relevant conduct and imposing sanctions on those who break those rules. So, for instance, we do not want people to go around harming each other, hence we have rules prohibiting assaults and imposing both criminal and civil liability on those who commit them. Respect for the law and/or a desire to avoid the social and legal repercussions of breaking these rules will then cause many people to act in the way the law prescribes. So if you are tempted to hit someone, the knowledge that this is against the law, and the fact that you can get in a lot of trouble if you do, both act as reasons to decide against it.

However, such rules provide no guarantee that all people will act in the way the law encourages them to. Some people are unaware of what the law requires. Others know what the law is but wrongly consider that they are abiding by it. Others still are happy to take their chances and consciously flout the rules. The first class of people can be dealt with by making sure the law is better publicised. As regards the latter two groups, we can try to ensure that they act in the right way by making it harder for them to get themselves, whether deliberately or unwittingly, into the position to break these rules. For example, although we can never prevent all assaults, we can at least make it harder for people to commit serious assaults by prohibiting the possession of certain dangerous articles. That is to say, we have rules against the possession of certain weapons, not because possessing them is undesirable in itself, but because we do not want such weapons to be used to harm others. If we stop people having such weapons at their disposal, we make it that much harder for such harm to be caused.

Two points may usefully be noted about this sort of practice. First, in such cases we are prohibiting conduct which is *not in itself* harmful or (morally) wrongful, because we think that this prohibition will lead to fewer people engaging in distinct, though related, forms of conduct which *are* harmful or wrongful. Second, where people infringe such prohibitions, they are subjected to legal liability even though they have not done anything which we regard as 'wrong' per se. In other words, their liability is explained not by reference to the inherent wrongfulness of what they did, but rather on the basis that it will discourage or prevent others from acting (genuinely) wrongfully in the future. For instance, the possessor of a dangerous weapon may have entirely innocent motives, and yet his liability may nonetheless be justified because this is what it takes to prevent other people, at other times, using such weapons to cause harm. This sort of approach tends to be described as *prophylactic* – it attempts to reduce the incidence of wrongful conduct, by creating a perimeter of further prohibitions which make it harder for defendants to commit the relevant wrong.

The law can be seen to be doing just this sort of thing when we look at the rules on fiduciary obligations. What we want trustees to do is to use their powers as custodians and managers of the trust property for the exclusive benefit of their beneficiaries. Accordingly, we have a rule that trustees must, when exercising those powers, consider only what would be best for their beneficiaries and, conversely, that they must not use their positions as trustees to promote their own or some other person's interests. This rule, and the liability that attaches to those who infringe it, gives trustees a reason to act exclusively in their beneficiary's best interests. Many will do so. But as with all legal rules, it does not guarantee compliance by all people in all circumstances. Therefore, the law goes further. To minimise the incidences of trustees *not* acting in their beneficiaries' best interests, the law sets down rules which aim to prevent trustees getting themselves into a position where they may end up preferring their own or someone else's interests to those of their beneficiary.

To understand how the law seeks to do this, think about why trustees may commit breaches of trust. It is likely that some trustees disregard their beneficiaries' interests out of simple bloody-mindedness or a positive desire to harm the beneficiary. However, a far more common cause of a trustee's failure to do what is best for his beneficiary is that he is led astray by the possibility of personal gain. Take the following example. A trustee has £1,000 of trust money to invest. One possible way he could invest the money would be in purchasing shares, and one of the many companies in which he could choose to acquire a shareholding is a company in which he has a controlling interest. Investing in that company is, therefore, likely to benefit the trustee. Accordingly, there is a risk that the trustee, when deciding how to invest that money, rather than thinking solely of what would be best for his beneficiary, will be swayed by the fact that one particular form of investment will (also) benefit him. Moreover, the danger is not just that the trustee will consciously choose to prioritise his own interests and his own financial gain over those of his beneficiary. It is equally plausible, and similarly undesirable, that the possibility of personal gain will lead the trustee to convince himself that investing in his own company would be a good move for the trust too.

In order to prevent such situations from arising, trustees are under a duty to avoid putting themselves in a position where their duty to act in their beneficiaries' best interests may come into conflict with their own personal interests or with some other duty they owe to a third party. One corollary or aspect of this is that trustees are prohibited from profiting from their position (unless authorised to do so by the settlor or the beneficiaries; as such, the prohibition extends only to *unauthorised* or *secret* profits), and if they do make any such profits, they must give them up to their beneficiaries.

The thinking is as follows (see too *Bray v Ford* [1896] AC 44, 51–52 (Lord Herschell)). To the extent that the trustee is thinking about his own benefit and his own interests when deciding how to apply the trust property, he is necessarily failing in his duty to consider simply what would be best for his beneficiary. For this reason, by prohibiting trustees from getting themselves into situations in which they may be distracted by considerations other than their beneficiaries' interests, the law hopes to encourage adherence to the basic rule that trustees must act exclusively in the best interests of their beneficiaries. Moreover, by requiring all unauthorised profits that a trustee may make from his position to be given up to his beneficiary, any (or, at least, much of the) temptation that a trustee might otherwise feel to attempt to turn the trust to his own advantage is removed.

So, in our example given earlier, the trustee would be prohibited from investing the trust property (without the beneficiary's consent) in the company in which he holds the controlling interest; and if he did so invest, any gains he may make by virtue of an increase in the value of his own private shareholding would be recoverable by the beneficiary. Because of this, the trustee would gain no more from investing in *his* company than he would from investing in some other company in which he has no stake. Without the distraction of the potential of personal gain, it is that much more likely that the trustee will make his decision as to how to invest the trust money purely on the basis of what he considers will best serve his beneficiary's interests.

10.6 The rule against conflicts of interest

The duty to avoid conflicts of interest involves what may be considered a double extension of the basic rule that trustees must act in their beneficiaries' best interests (and must refrain from preferring the interests of others). First, although conflicts of interest can easily lead to a trustee preferring his own interests to those of the beneficiaries, this is not the inevitable consequence. A trustee may in such situations succeed in wholly disregarding his own interests when deciding how to apply the trust property. As such, a prohibition of actual conflicts of interest goes further than simply prohibiting a trustee from preferring his own interests to the beneficiaries'. Second, the duty the law imposes is not simply to avoid *actual* conflicts of interests, but rather to avoid putting himself in the position where his interest *may possibly conflict* with the duty he owes to his beneficiary.

An early example of the application of this rule, which demonstrates its strictness, can be found in *Keech v Sandford* (1726) Sel Cas Ch 61. There, the trustee held a lease of the profits from a market on trust for a child. When the lease was about to expire, the trustee sought to have it renewed for the beneficiary's benefit. The lessor refused, not wanting the lease to be beneficially held by a minor. Given the apparent impossibility of renewing the lease on behalf of his beneficiary, the trustee took the opportunity to take the lease himself, for his own benefit. The beneficiary claimed that the trustee should assign the lease to him and account for all profits he had made in the meantime. The claim succeeded. Lord King LC held:

> I very well see, if a trustee, on the refusal to renew, might have a lease to himself, few trust estates would be renewed to cestui que use; though I do not say there is fraud in this case, yet he should rather have let it run out, than to have had the lease to himself. This may seem hard, that the trustee is the only person of all mankind who might not have the lease: but it is very proper that the rule should be strictly pursued, and not in the least relaxed; for it is very obvious what would be the consequences of letting trustees have the lease, on refusal to renew to cestuique use.

This is a clear statement of the preventative or prophylactic approach. The trustee was held liable not because the court considered that he had acted in bad faith or that he had failed to act in his beneficiary's best interests, but rather because this would reduce the chances of *other* trustees in other cases acting contrary to *their* beneficiaries' interests. If the trustee in *Keech v Sandford* was able to renew the lease for himself then other trustees would be inclined to do the same thing, even where there was still a chance for the lease to be renewed on behalf of the trust instead. By telling trustees that there is no way that, in such circumstances, they can take the lease for themselves, we increase the likelihood that they will do all they can to ensure that the lease is renewed in favour of the beneficiary. By removing the temptation to use their position to advance their own interests, we make it more likely that they will seek to advance their beneficiary's interests.

A similar approach can be seen in the leading case on fiduciary obligations, *Boardman v Phipps* [1967] 2 AC 46. A trust had a shareholding in a private company, Lester and Harris Ltd. The company was doing badly and so, as things stood, the investment in the trust was providing little benefit to the beneficiaries. The defendants, Boardman, a solicitor used by the trustees in relation to trust business, and Tom Phipps, one of the beneficiaries, through their connection to the trust, attended the company's annual general meeting and got access to its accounts. On the basis of the information so obtained, they suggested that the trustees acquire more shares in the company on behalf of the trust, so as to acquire a controlling interest. The trustees would then be in a position to take charge of the company and, it was hoped, turn its fortunes around. The trustees, however, refused to exercise their powers to increase the trust's shareholding on the basis that this would not be a responsible investment. (Moreover, as a purchase of further shares in the company was not permitted under the terms of the trust, the trustees would have required the court's authorisation to do this.) This did not deter the defendants however. They decided that if the trustees were not willing or able to purchase more shares, they (the defendants) would do so themselves, with their own money. To this end, the defendants entered into negotiations with the company and its other shareholders, at times purporting to be acting on behalf of the trust. Two of the three trustees knew of, and consented to, this (the third was senile and took no role in the running of the trust). The defendants also informed the beneficiaries of what they were planning to do, although importantly the court later found that the defendants had not given them full information as to what their exact plans were and what the defendants themselves would get out of the purchase. After protracted negotiations, the defendants succeeded in buying a significant shareholding, took control of the company, sold off a number of its assets and distributed the profits among the shareholders. The end result was that both the trust – and through it the beneficiaries – and the defendants made a significant sum of money.

One might have thought that the beneficiaries would be happy with all of this. Not only did the defendants act in good faith and out of a desire to advance the beneficiaries' interests throughout, but their hard work and willingness to put their own money on the line also brought gains to the beneficiaries which they could not otherwise have hoped to obtain. Nonetheless, one beneficiary, John Phipps, the brother of the defendant Tom, was dissatisfied and brought a claim against the defendants. The claimant contended that the defendants owed the beneficiaries fiduciary obligations and that, by making a profit from their positions, they had breached those obligations. As such, he claimed that the defendants' shareholding and the money they made from their investment in the company were held on trust for the beneficiaries. By a 3:2 majority, the House of Lords upheld the claim, although it also held that the defendants should be accorded an allowance, to be assessed 'on a liberal scale', for the hard work they put in to acquire the shares and make a profit from them.

The success of the claim depended on the claimant showing two things. First, it had to be demonstrated that the defendants owed him fiduciary obligations. Second, he needed to show that, by acquiring the shares and deriving a profit from them, the defendants breached these fiduciary obligations.

All the members of the court were prepared to accept that the defendants were fiduciaries, although they differed in their views on the nature and form of the fiduciary duties they owed. As we shall see shortly (Section 10.13), trustees are not the only class of persons who owe fiduciary obligations. Another such class is solicitors, who owe fiduciary obligations to their clients. (The generic term for someone who owes fiduciary obligations is a *fiduciary*, and the person to whom he owes these obligations is his *principal*.) Accordingly, Boardman was clearly a fiduciary. However, as he was employed by the trustees, he would owe his duties to them, rather than to the beneficiaries. For John Phipps to be able to sue the defendants directly for breach of fiduciary duty, he would in principle need to show that Boardman had also entered into a (distinct) fiduciary relationship with him (and presumably the other beneficiaries). However, it is unclear whether this is what the court decided.

None of their Lordships grounded Boardman's fiduciary position simply on his role as solicitor to the trustees. Instead they emphasised his and Tom Phipps' attendance at company meetings as representatives or agents of the trust. This implies that Boardman's clear fiduciary role as a solicitor to the trustees was insufficient to ground the claim brought by John Phipps, and that the defendants instead became fiduciaries in the relevant sense by acting as proxies at these meetings. From this we may further infer that, through their attendance and participation at company meetings, the defendants assumed or became subject to the same duties as the trustees, and hence owed fiduciary obligations to the beneficiaries. This then allows us to explain why both defendants were held to owe fiduciary duties and why those duties were owed to, and so their breach could found a claim by, the beneficiaries.

Yet none of their Lordships said this explicitly. Indeed, significant portions of the judgments appear inconsistent with this analysis. For the most part, their Lordships described the defendants as owing fiduciary obligations to the trustees or simply, and unhelpfully, 'to the trust'. Lord Hodson went further and held that Boardman was 'in a fiduciary position vis-à-vis the trustees and through them vis-à-vis the beneficiaries' ([1967] 2 AC 46, 112). However, the unorthodox conclusion that owing fiduciary duties to the trustees entailed or resulted in fiduciary duties being owed to the beneficiaries was not explained. In a similar vein, Lord Guest stated that the trustees' unanimous consent would have been needed to authorise the defendants' actions, which would be unremarkable if the fiduciary duties were owed to the trustees, but not if they were owed to the beneficiaries (see further Section 13.8). In this respect, Lord Cohen's approach is preferable, as he regarded the relevant question as being whether *the beneficiaries* consented to the defendants' actions, and hence, by implication, that the relevant fiduciary duties were owed to the beneficiaries rather than to the trustees.

The better view then is that, besides the fiduciary relationship and obligations that arose by virtue of his acting as solicitor to the trustees, Boardman assumed a separate fiduciary relationship and a set of fiduciary obligations when he acted as a representative of the trustees while attending company meetings. These obligations were owed not (or not only) to the trustees but to the beneficiaries. This then enables us to explain how Tom Phipps, the second defendant, who attended these meetings but who, unlike Boardman, held no pre-existing fiduciary role, became subject to fiduciary obligations (a conclusion which all their Lordships were happy to endorse, but which received little analysis because Tom Phipps had declined to distinguish his position from Boardman's).

Accordingly, the key question was whether the defendants breached these fiduciary obligations. It is on this point that the court was split. Of the majority, Lords Hodson and Guest took as their starting point the rule that a fiduciary must not profit from his position without the informed consent of his principal. It was clear that the defendants had made a gain, and the question of consent was not in issue. Therefore, on this basis, their liability depended simply on establishing a link between these gains and their fiduciary position. This link was provided by the fact that the information the defendants obtained concerning the company's financial affairs and the possibility of a profitable reorganisation, which then enabled them to make their gains, came to them, at least initially, by reason of the meetings they attended on behalf of the trust. Indeed both Lord Hodson and Lord Guest viewed this information as itself a form of trust property. It necessarily followed that any profits deriving from its use also belonged to the trust.

The third member of the majority, Lord Cohen, took a different line. In contrast to Lords Hodson and Guest, he held that profiting from information obtained when acting in a fiduciary capacity will not always be a breach of duty. However, Lord Cohen considered that, because the defendants had acquired not just some of the information on which they based their decision to purchase the shares, but also their opportunity to do so (through being introduced to the company's directors), when acting as representatives of the trust, and, moreover, because Boardman professed to be acting for the trustees for much of the negotiations, the defendants should be liable for the profits they made.

Lord Cohen also explained why he considered that, despite appearances, Boardman's conduct had created the possibility of a conflict of interest. Although the trustees had said that they had no interest in acquiring any further shares on behalf of the trust, and indeed although they had no means to do so, it was not impossible that they might have changed their minds. And if they were contemplating such a purchase it is likely that they would have sought Boardman's advice. If so, Lord Cohen considered that ([1967] 2 AC 46, 103–04):

> Boardman would not have been able to give unprejudiced advice if he had been consulted by the trustees and was at the same time negotiating for the purchase of the shares on behalf of himself and Tom Phipps.

Viscount Dilhorne and Lord Upjohn dissented. Viscount Dilhorne held that, so long as the trustees were opposed to purchasing further shares for the trust, there was no possibility of a conflict of interest arising. Indeed, as things stood, the trustees were only too happy to see the defendants acquire a shareholding and so give the trust, and hence the beneficiaries, an advantage it would otherwise not have obtained. Lord Upjohn took a similar view. In response to the argument that a fiduciary's liability is established simply by showing that he acted in such a way that his personal interests possibly may conflict with his duties, Lord Upjohn held ([1967] 2 AC 46, 124):

> The phrase 'possibly may conflict' requires consideration. In my view it means that the reasonable man looking at the relevant facts and circumstances of the particular case would think that there was a real sensible possibility of conflict; not that you could imagine some situation arising which might, in some conceivable possibility in events not contemplated as real sensible possibilities by any reasonable person, result in a conflict.

On this basis, the defendants' actions never created a potential conflict of interest. In any case, Lord Upjohn took the view that although the defendants were acting in a fiduciary capacity when they first attended company meetings on behalf of the trust, this fiduciary relationship ceased long before the defendants purchased the shares, because, once the trustees had made clear that they were not interested in purchasing additional shares, the defendants were plainly attending company meetings and negotiating for a purchase of shares on their own behalf. Accordingly, when they did eventually purchase the shares, this could not constitute a breach of fiduciary duty for they no longer owed any fiduciary duties.

Much of the reasoning of the majority is problematic. For a start, Lords Hodson and Guest's view that the information the defendants acquired during company meetings was trust property has been widely criticised. Many have been quick to point out that English law has not as yet accepted the proposition that information is or can be a form of property (eg, information has been held not to satisfy the definition of 'property' under section 4 of the Theft Act 1968 and so cannot be stolen: see *Oxford v Moss* (1978) 68 Cr App R 183). However, *if* it is true that a trustee must give up to his beneficiary all profits which derive from or are connected to the trust, and if such a connection is provided by the fact that the profit derives from using information acquired in the course of his trusteeship, then it follows that any information obtained by a trustee in his fiduciary capacity can be exploited only for the benefit of his beneficiary. On this basis, describing such information as trust property may not be inappropriate.

The more pertinent inquiry is not as to the rights and wrongs of attaching the label 'property' to information, but rather as to whether Lords Hodson and Guest were right to hold that there should be a blanket rule that all profits derived from one's fiduciary position (including from information acquired when acting in a fiduciary capacity) must be given up to the principal (unless made with his consent). This strict interpretation of the 'no profits' rule gains support from dicta from the earlier House of Lords decision in *Regal (Hastings) Ltd v Gulliver* [1967] 2 AC 134n (the case was decided in 1942 but only included in the official reports following *Boardman v Phipps*). The best example is the following statement from Lord Russell ([1967] 2 AC 134n, 144–45):

> The rule of equity which insists on those, who by use of a fiduciary position make a profit, being liable to account for that profit, in no way depends on fraud, or absence of bona fides, or upon such questions or considerations as whether the profit would or should otherwise have gone to the plaintiff, or whether the profiteer was under a duty to obtain the source of the profit for the plaintiff, or whether he took a risk or acted as he did for the benefit of the plaintiff, or

whether the plaintiff has in fact been damaged or benefited by his action. The liability arises from the mere fact of a profit having, in the stated circumstances, been made.

The benefit of this approach is its simplicity. Once it is shown that the fiduciary made a gain, his liability is established simply by showing a connection between that gain and his fiduciary role. This avoids possibly complex inquiries into the fiduciary's motives and the impact his actions did have or could have had on his principal. Moreover, it sends a simple message to fiduciaries: there is no way you can profit from your position without your principal's approval, so don't even think about it. However, this approach can also be criticised on the basis that it risks detaching the 'no secret profits' rule from its underlying rationale.

The 'no secret profits' rule is itself best regarded as an application of the wider rule that fiduciaries must avoid potential conflicts of interest. As we have seen, trustees and other fiduciaries are under a duty to avoid getting themselves into a position where their personal interests may come into conflict with their duty to act in their beneficiary's best interests. Trustees are therefore prohibited from making gains because this is one way – indeed the clearest and most common way – in which their interests can be affected by the decisions they make when administering the trust, such that they may be diverted, consciously or subconsciously, from the pursuit of their beneficiary's best interests. So we concern ourselves with gains made by trustees because they raise the potential of conflicts of interest. But on this basis, the prohibition of gains made by trustees should be conditional on there being some risk that the prospect of gain might indeed distract the trustee from doing what is best for his beneficiary. In other words, we have no reason to bar trustees from making gains from their position unless, given the circumstances, they give rise to a possible conflict of interest. As such, it may be that the blanket prohibition suggested by Lords Hodson and Guest goes too far.

In this respect Lord Cohen's judgment has two advantages over those of Lord Hodson and Lord Guest. First, it acknowledges that the 'no secret profits' rule need not extend to all profits made from one's fiduciary position, and that the key question is whether there was a possible conflict of interest. Second, it attempts to identify what potential conflict of interest arose on the facts so as to justify the defendants' liability. However, here too we encounter problems. As we have noted, the potential conflict of interest identified by Lord Cohen concerned the (remote) possibility that the trustees might ask Boardman to advise them on the viability of purchasing more shares for the trust. But this can explain only Boardman's liability, and not that of Tom Phipps. He held no similar advisory role to the trustees and so, for him, no such possible conflict of interest arose. However, as we have noted, Tom Phipps agreed to stand side by side with Boardman, so here as elsewhere the basis of his liability received little independent analysis.

Moreover, the conflict identified by Lord Cohen appears to be a conflict between Boardman's personal interests and the duty he owed to the *trustees*, and as such seems incapable of sufficing to establish a claim for breach of duty brought by the *beneficiaries*. We suggested earlier that the claim brought in *Boardman v Phipps* can be supported only on the basis that Boardman, aside from the fiduciary duties he owed to the trustees by acting as their solicitor, also entered into a distinct fiduciary relationship with the beneficiaries, through his attendance at company meetings. Accordingly, for a beneficiary to make out a claim to the profits made by Boardman, he must be able to establish a breach of the fiduciary duty owed *to him*. However, the duty Lord Cohen describes – to give impartial advice to the trustees on the merits of buying more shares

– is a duty Boardman owed to the trustees as their solicitor, rather than a duty arising from his attendance at company meetings and owed to the beneficiaries. Therefore, even if so remote a conflict of interest can suffice to establish a fiduciary's liability, it cannot justify the result that the defendants were liable to the claimant, a beneficiary.

Because of this, many view *Boardman v Phipps* as a step too far and favour the approach of the minority, in particular Lord Upjohn's statement that liability should depend on there being a 'real sensible' possibility of conflict. Moreover, those who do support the outcome in *Boardman v Phipps* tend to do so on the basis that, although no conflict existed on the facts, liability was nonetheless needed to send out a clear message to trustees that they should not, and indeed cannot, use their position for their personal gain. This implicitly admits that the defendants' conduct was in itself unobjectionable, and that we must look instead to the bigger picture to justify their liability. Nonetheless, an argument can be made that the law should seek to discourage fiduciaries from acting in a similar manner to the defendants in *Boardman v Phipps*.

A typical conflict of interest arises where the trustee's interests and his duty to his beneficiary point in different directions. In such situations, the fear is that the trustee will pursue his own interests and hence fail to do what is best for his beneficiary. But this does not appear to be the case in *Boardman v Phipps*. If their takeover and reorganisation of the company was successful, then it meant profits for both the defendants and the beneficiaries. If it had failed, the value of both the defendants' and the beneficiaries' shareholdings was at risk. As such, the interests of the defendants and the beneficiaries, far from being in competition, went hand in hand. At first glance then, it appears impossible to argue that the prospect of personal gain might divert the defendants from their duty to act in the beneficiaries' best interests. If anything, it would encourage the defendants to strive even harder to ensure that their reorganisation of the company was successful, thus benefiting the beneficiaries.

However, on one view, a danger is created by the trustee's own interests becoming interwoven with those of the beneficiaries. This is because people tend to act more dispassionately, with a little more circumspection, when looking after someone else's interests than when dealing with their own. For instance, it is common for people to take greater risks when investing their own property than if they were making investment decisions on someone else's behalf. Indeed, for this reason the courts formulated the standard of care a trustee owed when investing trust property as 'such care as an ordinary prudent man would take if he were minded to make an investment for the benefit of other people for whom he felt morally bound to provide' (*Re Whiteley* (1886) 33 Ch D 347, 355 (Lindley LJ); Section 11.1). Accordingly, it is possible that a trustee with a personal shareholding in a company in which the trust also has a stake will act differently, take greater risks, when exercising his powers on behalf of the trust, than he would if he had no shares of his own. And although sometimes, as in *Boardman v Phipps*, such risks may pay off, at other times they will not. As such, we may consider that, on the whole, beneficiaries' interests are better served by their trustees acting dispassionately, and so trustees should be prohibited from acquiring stakes of their own in companies in which the trust has a shareholding.

10.7 Relaxing the rule?

Irrespective of how we can best explain the decision in *Boardman v Phipps*, its importance lies in its endorsement of a strict version of the preventative approach described earlier.

It makes clear that a trustee (or other fiduciary) may be held to have breached his fiduciary duties and so be liable to give up his gains even where:

1. he has acted in complete good faith and in an attempt to advance his beneficiary's interests;
2. there was at no point any *actual* conflict between his own interests and those of the beneficiary;
3. the trustee's actions not only caused no loss to the beneficiary but actually benefited him, and;
4. the gains made by the trustee could not otherwise have been made by or for the beneficiary.

This strict approach has not gone unquestioned. Other jurisdictions have adopted a more generous stance towards fiduciaries (see eg *Peso Silver Mines Ltd (NPL) v Cropper* [1966] SCR 673 and the Privy Council decision in *Queensland Mines Ltd v Hudson* (1978) 18 ALR 1; cf *Canadian Aero Service Ltd v O'Malley* [1974] SCR 592), and it has been suggested that English courts should follow suit. Most recently, Arden LJ in *Murad v Al-Saraj* [2005] EWCA Civ 959; [2005] All ER (D) 503 commented at [82] and [83] (see too [121] (Jonathan Parker LJ)):

> It may be that the time has come when the court should revisit the operation of the inflexible rule of equity in harsh circumstances, as where the trustee has acted in perfect good faith and without any deception or concealment, and in the belief that he was acting in the best interests of the beneficiary. I need only say this: it would not be in the least impossible for a court in a future case, to determine as a question of fact whether the beneficiary would not have wanted to exploit the profit himself, or would have wanted the trustee to have acted other than the way the trustee in fact did act. Moreover, it would not be impossible for a modern court to conclude as a matter of policy that, without losing the deterrent effect of the rule, the harshness of it should be tempered in some circumstances. In addition in such cases, the courts can provide a significant measure of protection for the beneficiaries by imposing on the defaulting trustee the affirmative burden of showing that those circumstances prevailed. ... In short, it may be appropriate for a higher court one day to revisit the rule on secret profits and to make it less inflexible in appropriate circumstances, where the unqualified operation of the rule operates particularly harshly and where the result is not compatible with the desire of modern courts to ensure that remedies are proportionate to the justice of the case where this does not conflict with some other overriding policy objective of the rule in question.

Nonetheless, as this passage acknowledges, there has yet to be any such relaxation of the rule and, indeed, the strict approach of *Regal (Hastings) Ltd v Gulliver* and *Boardman v Phipps* has been endorsed on a number of occasions since (see eg *Industrial Development Consultants Ltd v Cooley* [1972] 1 WLR 443 and *Guinness plc v Saunders* [1990] 2 AC 663).

Moreover, even those who believe that the current rules do need to be loosened up would modify them only to the extent of requiring, like Lord Upjohn in his dissent in *Boardman*, a real, sensible possibility of a conflict of interest before liability will attach. As such, there appears to be agreement on all sides that liability should not be confined to those who have acted in bad faith or who have failed to act in their beneficiaries' best interests, and should instead extend to some trustees whose motives are impeccable and whose actions resulted in no harm (nor even the threat of harm) to the beneficiaries.

As we have seen, the thinking behind this is that it will promote greater adherence to the basic rule that trustees must act in good faith and exclusively in their beneficiaries' best interests. A clear message is sent out that trustees must steer clear of any situation in which their own interests may even possibly come into conflict with the duty they owe their beneficiaries. Moreover, given that profits obtained by a trustee from his position can be recovered without having to establish bad faith or even the existence of an actual conflict of interest, the chances of a trustee being able to get away with preferring his own interests are almost zero. To this extent, the rules are likely to lead to more trustees making their decisions for the right reasons, and so to more beneficiaries getting the benefits that the trust was set up to give them.

But there are also costs to this approach. First, as cases like *Boardman* show, the rules may in fact dissuade trustees from entering into arrangements which may actually be in their beneficiary's best interests. Thus the strict approach may, on occasion, be counter-productive. Second, and more importantly, the effect of these rules is to impose, on occasion, liability on honest and dedicated trustees whose actions never threatened, let alone harmed, their beneficiaries' interests. The suggestion is that, although this may be harsh on such trustees, it is necessary to serve the greater good of promoting higher standards from trustees generally. Now, undoubtedly, we are right to be concerned with how trustees do their jobs. Beneficiaries are in a position of considerable vulnerability as it is their trustees who, as custodians and managers of the trust property, are empowered to decide how the property is to be applied. As such, their fortunes are in the trustees' hands. If, therefore, we want to protect beneficiaries and the institution of trusts, we need to take steps to ensure that trustees do their job well. Nonetheless, we may question whether this policy is sufficiently strong to outweigh the injustice of attaching liability to innocent trustees who at no point let their beneficiaries down. In this regard, it should be noted that trusts are principally concerned with *economic* gains and losses, and so, when we talk about the need to protect beneficiaries, we are talking about protecting them from economic losses (losses in the value of the trust fund) and securing for them economic gains. So, despite the hyperbolic language occasionally used by the courts (in *Parker v McKenna* (1874) 10 Ch App 96, 124, James LJ proclaimed that these rules were needed 'for the safety of mankind'), we apply such strict standards to trustees not to save life and limb, but simply to ensure that more beneficiaries suffer fewer economic losses and make more economic gains.

However, if we look elsewhere in the law, we see a very different attitude to the importance of economic loss. So, in the tort of negligence, the courts have been very slow to recognise duties of care to avoid purely economic losses (see eg *Spartan Steel and Alloys Ltd v Martin & Co (Contractors) Ltd* [1973] 1 QB 27; *Murphy v Brentwood District Council* [1991] 1 AC 398). And, of course, even in those exceptional instances where such a duty is recognised, liability arises only where the defendant has both failed to take reasonable care and, thereby, caused loss to the claimant. Therefore, it is, at the very least, incongruous that when we turn to the law of trusts and fiduciaries, we see liability imposed, even where the defendant is blameless and no loss has been suffered, on the basis that this is what it takes to minimise the incidence of economic losses in future cases.

As a final point, however, it should never be forgotten that the prohibition applies only to *unauthorised* or *secret* profits. Trustees are free to profit from their position so long as this is authorised by the settlor when he set up the trust or informed consent is subsequently given by the beneficiaries. As such, no matter how strict – and how apparently unjust – the law's stance on liability for gains, this liability can be avoided by the (typically) simple measure of first securing the beneficiaries' consent.

10.8 Payment

One application of the prohibition of unauthorised profits is that, as a general rule, a trustee is entitled to be paid for the work that he does only where and to the extent that the settlor has provided for this in the terms of the trust. However, the rule now has a number of exceptions.

First, the prohibition does not extend to recovery of expenses the trustee has properly incurred in his administration of the trust. This is now governed by section 31(1) of the Trustee Act 2000, which provides:

> A trustee –
>
> (a) is entitled to be reimbursed from the trust fund, or
> (b) may pay out of the trust funds,
> expenses properly incurred by him when acting on behalf of the trust.

Additionally, section 32 provides for authorised agents, nominees and custodians to have their expenses reimbursed and to be paid reasonable remuneration for their services.

Second, the courts have jurisdiction to order that the trustee be remunerated out of the trust fund for his work. The Court of Appeal confirmed in *Re Duke of Norfolk's Settlement Trusts* [1982] Ch 61 that the courts had power both to authorise payment where none had been provided for by the settlor, and to vary the sum fixed by the settlor where provision for the trustee's remuneration has been made. The jurisdiction allows the court to authorise payment both in respect of work already done and for work the trustee will do in the future.

It is important to note that any money the court orders to be paid to the trustee will pro tanto reduce the amount of money available to the beneficiaries. Accordingly, the courts have stressed that the jurisdiction to order remuneration is to be exercised sparingly: *Re Worthington* [1954] 1 WLR 526. In considering whether to make such an order, one relevant factor is whether the beneficiaries' interests would be advanced by payment out of the trust fund so as to secure the services of a particular trustee. As Fox LJ explained in *Re Duke of Norfolk's Settlement Trusts* [1982] Ch 61, 79:

> If ... the court concludes, having regard to the nature of the trust, the experience and skill of a particular trustee and to the amounts which he seeks to charge when compared with what other trustees might require to be paid for their services and to all the other circumstances of the case, that it would be in the interests of the beneficiaries to increase the remuneration, then the court may properly do so.

However, such considerations are clearly irrelevant if the question is simply whether a trustee should be paid for work which he has already done. In such cases, the courts have asked whether it is fair for the beneficiaries to retain the value of the work done by the trustee without him receiving anything in return (see eg *Foster v Spencer* [1996] 2 All ER 672, where the court spoke of the beneficiaries being 'unjustly enriched' should the trustee not be paid for his work). The fact that, at the time the trust was set up, there were no funds from which remuneration could have been provided and that the work of the trustee turned out to be far more onerous than first envisaged are both factors which militate in favour of ordering the trustee to be paid.

Similarly, as we have noted in relation to *Boardman v Phipps* [1967] 2 AC 46, where a trustee or other fiduciary has committed a breach of fiduciary duty and is liable to give up his gains to his beneficiary, the court may order that he retain a portion of this sum as remuneration for the work he has done in generating such gains. However, as the House of Lords stressed in *Guinness plc v Saunders* [1990] 2 AC 663, it will only be in exceptional cases that such an allowance will be given to a defaulting fiduciary. Certainly, as Lord Goff held, such an award will be made only 'where it cannot have the effect of encouraging trustees in any way to put themselves in a position where their interests conflict with their duties as trustees'.

Finally, a general exception to the 'no payment' rule has been created in respect of trust corporations and professional trustees by section 29 of the Trustee Act 2000:

(1) ... a trustee who –

   (a) is a trust corporation, but
   (b) is not a trustee of a charitable trust,

   is entitled to receive reasonable remuneration out of the trust funds for any services that the trust corporation provides to or on behalf of the trust.

(2) ... a trustee who –

   (a) acts in a professional capacity, but
   (b) is not a trust corporation, a trustee of a charitable trust or a sole trustee,

   is entitled to receive reasonable remuneration out of the trust funds for any services that he provides to or on behalf of the trust if each other trustee has agreed in writing that he may be remunerated for the services.

(3) 'Reasonable remuneration' means, in relation to the provision of services by a trustee, such remuneration as is reasonable in the circumstances for the provision of those services to or on behalf of that trust by that trustee.

(4) A trustee is entitled to remuneration under this section even if the services in question are capable of being provided by a lay trustee.

(5) A trustee is not entitled to remuneration under this section if any provision about his entitlement to remuneration has been made –

   (a) by the trust instrument, or
   (b) by any enactment or any provision of subordinate legislation.

Section 28(5) says that a trustee acts 'in a professional capacity':

... if he acts in the course of a profession or business which consists of or includes the provision of services in connection with –

   (a) the management or administration of trusts generally or a particular kind of trust, or
   (b) any particular aspect of the management or administration of trusts generally or a particular kind of trust,

and the services he provides to or on behalf of the trust fall within that description.

The key points to note are that a trustee can claim payment on this basis only where there is no provision for any such payment in the terms of the trust as set down by the settlor and that, in the case of individuals acting as professional trustees, the right to payment is conditional on the consent of the other trustees.

10.9 Directors' fees

Similar rules have been developed in respect of directors' fees obtained by trustees as a result of the shares they hold on trust. Although company directors are fiduciaries, and so are not entitled to profit from their position without their principal's authorisation, they are typically paid for their work, with such authorisation coming either from the company's articles of association (the document which sets down the basic rules detailing how the company is to function) or from a resolution of the shareholders. Usually directors will be elected by the shareholders, and so where a trustee holds shares on trust, this puts him in a position to vote on who becomes director, and hence who is to receive directors' fees.

One might therefore think that the law would prohibit trustees from using their votes to get themselves elected as directors, for otherwise there would be the danger that trustees will be swayed by the prospect of earning such fees to vote themselves into office, rather than giving dispassionate consideration to the question of who would make the best director. However, such a rule would be counter-productive, as it will often be in the interests of the trust for the trustee to take on an active role in the running of the company (indeed in some cases the trustee will be in breach of his duty of care if he fails to secure such a role for himself: see eg *Re Lucking's Will Trusts* [1968] 1 WLR 866). So the courts have instead held that trustees may exercise the votes which attach to the trust's shareholding to elect themselves directors, but must then hold any fees so obtained on trust for their beneficiaries: see *Re Macadam* [1946] Ch 73. Similarly, a trustee who is elected director by other shareholders, but who could have prevented this through the use of the trust's votes, must also account for any gains so received. However, a trustee who is elected by other shareholders and who could not have influenced this result through the exercise of the votes attached to the trust's shareholding, may retain any director's fees: see *Re Gee* [1948] Ch 284. In this regard, a trustee who also has his own private shareholding in the same company may use his own votes however he pleases, including to procure his own appointment as director, keeping such fees for himself. As before, the prohibition of keeping such gains is subject to the authorisation of the settlor (at the time the trust was created) or the beneficiaries.

10.10 The prohibition of self-dealing

The rule that trustees must avoid putting themselves into a position where their own interests may conflict with the duty they owe to their beneficiaries underlies the prohibition of what is known as self-dealing. This describes the situation where a trustee purchases trust property. The problem with this is that it is the trustee who, as manager of the trust property, is legally empowered to sell it, and so any sale to himself necessarily involves a conflict of interest. As trustee, his duty is to extract the highest possible price from the purchaser, thus securing the best possible deal for his beneficiary. However, his own personal interest will be in obtaining the property cheaply. The inevitability of such a conflict between the trustee's duty to his beneficiary and his personal interests has led the courts to prohibit such transactions, unless the informed consent of the beneficiary is first obtained. In the absence of such consent, any sale of the trust property to a trustee can be set aside by the beneficiary, irrespective of whether the sale price appears objectively fair (*Ex parte James* (1803) 8 Ves 337; *Tito v Waddell (No. 2)* [1977] Ch 106, 225) and even where the price is fixed by some third party or is determined by auction (*Wright v Morgan* [1926] AC 788).

An apparent exception to this rule comes out of the Court of Appeal's decision in *Holder v Holder* [1968] Ch 353. There, the defendant was appointed one of the executors of his father's will. He subsequently sought to renounce his executorship, though only after performing certain tasks in this capacity. The remaining executors put up for sale at auction two farms from the deceased's estate, which the defendant bought. The claimant, one of the beneficiaries, sought to have the sale set aside. Executors owe fiduciary duties, and the defendant's counsel admitted at trial that the defendant's attempt to renounce his executorship was unsuccessful. As such, the facts seemed to fall squarely within the self-dealing prohibition. However, the Court of Appeal held that the defendant was free to bid for the farms and that the sale was valid. The Court considered that the facts fell outside the mischief which the self-dealing prohibition was designed to prevent. The defendant played no part in the decision to sell the farms or in fixing the terms of that sale. Consequently, the defendant's actions raised no conflict of interest and posed no threat to the beneficiaries' interests. Accordingly, the Court considered that there was no reason to invalidate the sale. Sachs LJ in particular took the view that a hard and fast rule, prohibiting all such transactions, was unnecessary and could lead to injustice. Instead, courts should be able to examine the facts to determine whether there are sufficient grounds for setting the sale aside. This has a lot in common with the approach taken by the minority in *Boardman v Phipps* [1967] 2 AC 46, by which a fiduciary's liability should be dependent on there being a real, sensible possibility of a conflict of interest.

The decision in *Holder v Holder* is out of kilter with the other case law in this area. One suggestion is that it is an example of hard cases making bad law. The Court of Appeal clearly considered that the defendant's admission that his attempted renunciation of his executorship had failed was wrongly made. Without this, they would have been able to reach the same result on the more straightforward and orthodox basis that the defendant was not a fiduciary, and so could have avoided making inroads into the self-dealing prohibition. Certainly the courts have not taken up the Court of Appeal's suggestion that the self-dealing rules be relaxed, with the traditional approach being reaffirmed by Vinelott J in *Re Thompson's Settlement* [1986] Ch 99. However, in line with the argument made earlier in relation to fiduciary duties generally, there is a strong argument that the courts have for too long adopted unnecessarily stringent rules in this area and, as such, the more sensitive and sensible approach of *Holder v Holder* has a lot to commend it.

10.11 Fair-dealing

Another set of rules, known as the fair-dealing rules, applies to situations where a trustee seeks to purchase his beneficiary's beneficial interest under the trust. As we have seen, the beneficiary, at least in the standard trust, has his own equitable beneficial interest in the trust property, and this, like other proprietary interests, can be transferred to someone else. One such person is the trustee. Because in such cases the transaction is between trustee and beneficiary, fair-dealing does not pose the same risks as self-dealing, where the trustee is at both 'ends' of the transaction. Reflecting this, the courts have adopted a rather less strict approach.

The standard view is that such transactions can be avoided by the beneficiary unless the trustee can show that he paid the beneficiary a fair price for his beneficial interest and obtained his fully informed consent: see eg *Tito v Waddell (No. 2)* [1977] Ch 106, 225. However, a persuasive argument has more recently been made that the authorities in fact require only that the trustee show that the beneficiary gave fully informed consent for the sale to be unimpeachable (see Conaglen, 2006). The 'fairness' of the price paid is, on this view, at best only evidence of whether the beneficiary did so consent. In other words, if the price looks low then this may support an inference that the beneficiary's consent was defective. However, so long as the trustee can show that the beneficiary was fully informed and that his consent was genuine, the sale cannot be set aside simply because the price appears to be low.

It has also been suggested (see again Conaglen, 2006) that, as with the self-dealing prohibition, the rules on fair-dealing derive from the basic rule that trustees must avoid conflicts of interest. This is questionable. The trustee is not an agent for the beneficiary in respect of dealings with the latter's beneficial interest under the trust. Although trustees have extensive powers to dispose of trust assets, they have no such power to transfer the beneficiary's interest under the trust. Such a decision is for the beneficiary alone. To put it another way, a trustee's fiduciary duties concern how he exercises the powers he holds in relation to the trust property and which derive from his own (usually legal) title to that property. However, although these powers may enable him to *shape* the beneficiary's interest (eg by the investment decisions he makes, by his exercise of powers of appointment), his title to the trust assets give him no power to *dispose of* that interest. As such, it is hard to see how there is any actual or potential conflict of interest in fair-dealing situations. The trustee's interests are certainly involved, but it is not clear what duty he owes in relation to such transactions. (The position may be different for other fiduciaries, such as solicitors, who may be under a duty to advise on the merits of such a transaction.)

A better explanation of the fair-dealing rules may be that they have the same, or at least a similar, function to the rules of undue influence. With some contracts, because of the nature of the transaction and/or the relationship that exists between the parties, the courts are suspicious of whether the contract was freely chosen by the parties, or was instead the product of one party having taken advantage of a position of influence or power over the other (see further Section 8.4). In such situations, the vulnerable party will be able to avoid the contract unless the other can show that his consent was genuine and not forced. This seems to be the case with the fair-dealing rules. The court is concerned with the balance of power and information between trustee and beneficiary, and so requires the trustee to show that he did not take advantage of his (possible) position of power or influence over the beneficiary when purchasing his beneficial interest from him.

10.12 Are all trustees fiduciaries?

As we noted at the start of this chapter, it is commonly assumed that fiduciary obligations are inherent to all trusts and so owed by all trustees (though see *Lonrho plc v Fayed (No. 2)* [1992] 1 WLR 1, 12, (Millett J)). As a matter of principle, however, this is highly questionable. As we have seen, fiduciary obligations are unusually strict, requiring the trustee positively to take steps to advance his beneficiary's interests, and can be breached even where the trustee has acted with impeccable motives throughout and has done nothing to harm or threaten the beneficiary's position.

Of course, a trustee cannot complain about this if he has freely chosen to take on such a role. In such cases, the trustee knows or should know what he is letting himself in for. It may also (just about) be possible to justify subjecting a defendant to such duties, even in the absence of any agreement to act as trustee, where he is guilty of conscious wrongdoing or interference with the claimant's property (for instance in cases such as

Reading v A-G [1951] AC 507 (see further later, Section 10.13); cf recipients of misapplied trust property with actual knowledge that the property derives from a breach of trust).

However, it seems unreasonable, and indeed unrealistic, to expect someone who has not agreed to act as a trustee (or in some other fiduciary capacity), and who is justifiably unaware of the trust, to act and to deal with the property in the best interests of the beneficiary. In such cases, the most we can expect of the trustee is that, when he learns of the trust, he keeps the property intact pending the beneficiary's claim and hands the property over to the beneficiary when called on to do so (see too Hackney, 1987, 167–68; Smith, 1997a). Moreover, in such cases, the imposition of fiduciary obligations appears unnecessary as a matter of principle. If, for example, we treat (some) resulting trusts as arising to reverse an unintended transfer of property (Section 8.10), then all we need the trust to do is to impose on the defendant a duty to hand back the property when asked. The same is true where trust property is received by an innocent third-party donee (Section 9.4), and where a constructive trust is imposed under the rule in *Re Rose* (Sections 6.4, 9.6) or as a result of a specifically enforceable obligation to transfer that property (Section 9.5).

On this view, the only duty that such a trustee shares with the trustee of a conventional express trust is the duty deriving from *Saunders v Vautier* (1841) 4 Beav 115 (Section 2.7) to give up the property to the beneficiary when he calls for it. As such, this duty seems to have a stronger claim to being recognised as the 'irreducible core' of trust obligations (see Section 10.1). However, although it seems the *Saunders v Vautier* right and its correlative duty are at least potentially present in some form in all persons trusts (although, where the number of beneficiaries is vast, their exercise may be practically impossible), there is clearly no such right or duty in relation to genuine purpose trusts, because by definition there is no person to demand such a transfer. Of course, some view this as a reason purpose trusts should be considered a conceptual impossibility (see further Section 4.5). This, however, begs the question, because it presumes that a distinct equitable title, with a concomitant *Saunders v Vautier* right, is indeed a necessary feature of all trusts. It is unclear why this should be viewed as essential, and certainly this is not what the law currently says. Thus, the better view is that there is no single obligation found in all trusts, and that there is instead a collection of different duties, which may be found in different combinations at different times in different trusts.

10.13 Fiduciary obligations outside trusts

We have noted already that fiduciary obligations are not unique to trustees. In fact, there are a number of well-established categories of fiduciary relationship. These include solicitor–client, company director–company, agent–principal, commercial partner–commercial partner, bailee–bailor (a bailee is someone who holds goods on behalf or to the order of the owner (the bailor)), and (at least on occasion) employee–employer. Moreover, the courts have on a number of occasions stated that the class of fiduciary relations is not closed. This means that a defendant can be held to owe fiduciary obligations to the claimant even though their relationship does not fall within one of the pre-established categories of fiduciary relationship. (This distinction between these established categories of fiduciary relationship, whereby fiduciary obligations follow automatically from the fact that the parties are in such a relationship, and those relationships which fall outside these pre-established categories but which may, on the facts, nonetheless be held to give rise to fiduciary obligations is sometimes expressed as the difference between *per se* and *ad hoc* fiduciary relationships.)

Before we examine how the courts go about determining whether a given relationship is fiduciary, it is worth considering why categorising a relationship as fiduciary matters. First, and most obviously, the duties owed by fiduciaries are typically more far-reaching than the duties owed by non-fiduciaries. So, for instance, although we are generally under duties not to go around harming each other, we are not usually required to take positive steps to promote others' interests, let alone to do so in preference to our own. This is what fiduciary obligations involve (see Birks, 2002a). So, very simply, if I can establish that you are my fiduciary, I can require you to do things for me which I could not require of you if you were not. Following on from this, if you are a fiduciary, conduct which would otherwise be perfectly legitimate will constitute a breach of duty and so subject you to legal liability. For instance, if the defendants in *Boardman v Phipps* [1967] 2 AC 46 and *Keech v Sandford* (1726) Sel Cas Ch 61 had not been classed as fiduciaries, there would have been no claim against them, for they committed no tort or breach of contract.

Finally, and importantly, where you are liable for a breach of fiduciary duty, your potential liability (ie the sorts of claim that can be brought against you) is typically greater than if you had committed some other breach of duty (the claims that can be brought following a breach of trust, and applicable also to breaches by other fiduciaries, will be examined in detail in Chapters 13 and 14). So, if you commit a breach of contract or a tort, you will usually be liable only to pay compensatory damages to the claimant for the loss you caused him by your breach. If you breach a fiduciary duty, however, you will be liable for any gains you have made from the breach. Moreover, fiduciaries will, at least on occasion, hold their wrongful gains on trust (see Section 9.20), which then gives the claimant priority in the event of the defendant's insolvency and the potential to bring claims against subsequent recipients of such assets (see generally Chapter 14). It also seems, although this is more questionable, that compensatory awards are assessed on a basis which is more generous to the claimant (Section 13.6).

So, in short, establishing whether a defendant is a fiduciary can be relevant:

1. to determining how he must act vis-à-vis the claimant in the first instance; and
2. to identifying what claims may be brought against him and others should he fail so to act.

This is then reflected in two approaches the courts have taken in determining whether someone is a fiduciary.

The first approach is to look at the factual relationship that exists between the claimant and the defendant and ask whether this shares the key features of, and so is analogous to, the established categories of fiduciary relationship. If so, the defendant should be subjected to the same set of duties, essentially on the basis that like cases should be treated alike. Of course, the important question then is what are the key or defining features of fiduciary relationships. This is a question that has occupied judicial and academic minds for decades, and to which no clear answer has emerged; indeed on one view there is no single paradigm of fiduciary relationships but a variety of templates (see eg Sealy, 1962).

It is clear that fiduciary relationships tend to arise where one party is in a position in which some aspect of his affairs or well-being is peculiarly dependent on the actions or decisions of another. So, a beneficiary is largely dependent on his trustee to see that the trust fund is properly managed. A company's affairs lie largely in the hands of the directors who control it. Those who go to solicitors for legal advice are, of course, reliant upon them in relation to the affairs upon which they seek such advice. Accordingly, a key factor in determining if a relationship is fiduciary is whether there exists this sort of dependence between the parties. (This is not to say that there must be an inequality in the parties' respective positions – they may instead be in a relationship of mutual dependence, as with commercial partners.)

It is sometimes suggested that the potential fiduciary must have agreed to take on such a position of responsibility over the other's affairs: see eg *Hospital Products Ltd v United States Surgical Corp* [1984] HCA 64, (1984) 156 CLR 41, 96–97 (Mason J); *Galambos v Perez* 2009 SCC 48, [2009] 3 SCR 247, [77] (Cromwell J); Edelman, 2010. Certainly, some element of undertaking is present in most, if not all, of the established categories of fiduciary relationship. If, however, this is taken to mean that the defendant must choose or undertake not only the role to which his fiduciary obligations attach but also *those specific obligations*, this seems to go too far and is not borne out by the case law. For instance, the courts in *Keech v Sandford* and *Boardman v Phipps* did not decide those cases by asking what exactly the defendants had undertaken. The majority and minority in *Boardman* differed not on their understandings of the scope or content of the defendants' undertakings, but on what duties should be *imposed* on those who put themselves in such positions. So, even if we were to say that fiduciary positions are always undertaken, this cannot operate as an explanation of the specific incidence or content of fiduciary obligations. And it is this question – when and why should we impose on a defendant fiduciary obligations *on top of* those he has undertaken? – which we are seeking to answer.

What an undertaking requirement does stress, though, is that rarely, if ever, will it be fair to impose such far-reaching obligations on a defendant who has not willingly put himself into the position whereby the claimant is dependent on him. Another suggestion is that fiduciary obligations can exist only where the defendant is legally empowered or authorised (as opposed to being merely factually able) to make decisions which affect the claimant's interests (see eg Weinrib, 1975; *Galambos v Perez,* [83] (Cromwell J)). But, once more, although this element is present in many fiduciary relationships, it does not appear to be essential and is inconsistent with those cases in which fiduciary obligations have been imposed on a defendant as a result of his intermeddling in another's affairs (trustees de son tort provide an example of this, Section 10.3).

The second approach which the courts have employed to determine the existence of fiduciary obligations is not to look for an analogy with the established categories of fiduciary relations, but rather to ask whether the claimant should be able to bring the same array of claims as are available to the victim of a breach of fiduciary duty. For instance, as we have seen, unlike torts and breaches of contract, breaches of fiduciary duty entitle the claimant to recover the defendant's gains as a matter of course. On this basis, courts have occasionally classed defendants as fiduciaries in order to facilitate claims to their gains. A good example of this is *Reading v A-G* [1951] AC 507. Reading was an army sergeant stationed in Egypt. On a number of occasions, he was paid by smugglers to assist their smuggling operation by riding in lorries loaded with illegal spirits while wearing his army uniform. The idea was that the lorries would not be searched if an army officer was visibly riding in them. When Reading was eventually caught, the Crown seized the money he had been paid. After his release from prison, Reading brought a claim seeking its return. The House of Lords held that the Crown was entitled to retain the money. Their Lordships gave a variety of reasons for this. One of these was that Reading was a fiduciary, and hence that he was required to give up his unauthorised profits to his principal, the Crown.

If we start from the established categories of fiduciary relations, the conclusion that Reading owed fiduciary duties to the Crown appears dubious. Certainly there seems to be no obvious analogy with any of them, and it seems implausible to say that the Crown or state were peculiarly dependent on him to secure their interests (a useful contrast can be made here with the defendant in *A-G for Hong Kong v Reid* [1994] 1 AC 324 (Section 9.20), who could meaningfully be said to hold such a position vis-à-vis the state). Instead, holding Reading to be a fiduciary seems simply to be a convenient way of explaining why he could not get his hands on his ill-gotten gains.

The same sort of thing can be seen to be going on in *Chase Manhattan Bank NA v Israel–British Bank (London) Ltd* [1981] Ch 105. As we have seen (Section 9.18), the case arose from a mistaken payment of $2 million by Chase Manhattan to Israel–British Bank, which subsequently went into insolvent liquidation. Chase Manhattan argued that the money was held on trust for it, which would enable it to recover the money in priority to the claims of Israel–British Bank's other creditors. One of the apparent obstacles to this claim was that, as the payment was made by electronic transfer, Israel–British Bank did not hold any property previously held by Chase Manhattan, and so the only way Chase Manhattan could succeed was to rely on the rules of tracing (these rules in essence enable you to claim as yours property which was acquired in exchange for your property; we shall be looking at them in detail in Chapter 14). However, it is commonly supposed that a claimant cannot rely on the equitable rules of tracing unless he can establish that a fiduciary relationship existed between the parties to the misapplication (Section 14.5). Goulding J held that the recipient of a mistaken payment owes a fiduciary duty to the payer in respect of the money, and that there was therefore no obstacle to Chase Manhattan relying on the tracing rules.

Again, if we take the established classes of fiduciary relationships as our template, it is difficult to defend the conclusion that Israel–British Bank became a fiduciary simply by receiving Chase Manhattan's mistaken transfer. The best explanation is that Goulding J considered that Chase Manhattan's claim deserved to succeed and he 'manufactured' this fiduciary relationship so that he could arrive at his desired result.

Such instrumental uses of fiduciary obligations and fiduciary terminology are widely deprecated. Certainly, they create the risk of distorting our understanding of what fiduciary obligations are and what they are about. Moreover, there is a danger that they may lead to injustice. Although controversial, there is a strong argument that the result in *Chase Manhattan* is a fair one. However, by basing this result on the existence of a fiduciary relationship between payer and payee – a relationship found to exist only so as to justify the application of the equitable tracing rules – there is a danger that it might lead litigants and other courts to conclude that the recipient of a mistaken payment owes the payer the full range of strict fiduciary duties described in this chapter. This is clearly undesirable.

It is important to stress that the criticism here is not of the results reached in cases like *Reading v A-G* and *Chase Manhattan* but of how the courts got there. Thus we are not saying that Reading should have been able to walk off with the proceeds of his wrongdoing, or that equity's more generous tracing rules should not be available to the likes of Chase Manhattan. Rather, the point is that we should be able to reach these conclusions without having to conjure up fiduciary relationships from thin air. We would be better off in a case like *Reading* stating explicitly that a wrongdoer's ill-gotten gains may, at least on occasion, be recoverable even in the absence of a fiduciary relationship, and then proceeding to investigate the exact circumstances in which such a claim should be made available. Fortunately this seems to be the direction in which the courts are heading.

Finally, when examining the different classes of fiduciary relationship, it is standard to make reference to the warning issued by Fletcher Moulton LJ in *Re Coomber* [1911] 1 Ch 723, 728–29:

> Fiduciary relations are of many different types: they extend from the relation of myself to an errand boy who is bound to bring back my change up to the most intimate and confidential relations which can possibly exist between one party and another where the one is wholly in the hands of the other because of his infinite trust in him. All these are cases of fiduciary relations, and the Courts have again and again, in cases where there has been a fiduciary relation, interfered and set aside acts which, between persons in a wholly independent position, would have been perfectly valid. Thereupon in some minds there arises the idea that if there is any fiduciary relation whatever any of these types of interference is warranted by it. They conclude that every kind of fiduciary relation justifies every kind of interference. Of course that is absurd. The nature of the fiduciary relation must be such that it justifies the interference.

The suggestion is that we should not assume that all fiduciaries owe the full range of fiduciary duties we have examined in this chapter (though necessarily they will owe some of them). However, this statement was made at a time when the fiduciary label was attached to a wider and looser collection of duties and other legal relations (for instance, in *Re Coomber* itself the claimant argued that the defendant was a fiduciary in order to raise a presumption of undue influence). Given the modern tendency to reserve the fiduciary label for the duty to act in good faith in the best interests of the principal and the sub-rules that support it, it is less clear whether it really is true to say that different fiduciaries owe different fiduciary duties (although equally we should not unquestioningly assume that all fiduciaries must owe the same duties). What *is* true is that the *scope* of those duties – that is the range of transactions or dealings to which they apply – will vary from case to case, as will any exemptions arising from the terms upon which the fiduciary has agreed to take on his role and/or the consent of the principal: see for example *Kelly v Cooper* [1993] AC 205; *Hospital Products Ltd v United States Surgical Corp* [1984] HCA 64; (1984) 156 CLR 41, 97 (Mason J).

Summary

▶ All trusts impose duties on the part of the trustee in relation to his use of the trust property. However, the precise content of these duties will vary from trust to trust, and from trustee to trustee.

▶ The content of these duties will depend upon the reasons the trust arose in the first place. So, in express trusts, the trustee's duties will be determined principally, although not exclusively, by reference to the settlor's intentions. In imposed trusts, the trustee's duties should be determined by reference to the principle which supports the imposition of a trust on him. So if the trust arises to reverse unjust enrichment, the trustee's duties should be determined by asking what duties need to be in place to reverse his unjust enrichment.

Summary cont'd

▶ The duties owed by trustees will also be owed by those who, although not strictly trustees, assume the powers and responsibilities of a trustee by acting in relation to the trust and the trust property *as though they were* trustees. Such people are called *trustees de son tort* or *de facto trustees*.

▶ Perhaps the most important of the duties owed by a typical trustee are his fiduciary duties. Fiduciary duties are duties to act in good faith and in the interests of the beneficiary.

▶ What is noteworthy about these duties is their strictness. They not only prohibit the trustee from pursuing his own or someone else's interests in priority to those of the beneficiary. They also prohibit the trustee from putting himself into a position where his interests may possibly come into conflict with his duty to his beneficiary. This entails a further prohibition on trustees making any unauthorised gains from their position, as the prospect of personal gain might otherwise distract trustees from the single-minded pursuit of their beneficiaries' best interests.

▶ If a trustee or other fiduciary profits from his position, he will be liable to give up those gains even if he acted in good faith and in an attempt to further the beneficiary's best interests throughout, even though no loss was caused to the beneficiary, and even though there is no way that the beneficiary could otherwise have got his hands on that gain.

▶ Trustees have no automatic right to be paid for the work they do. Such payment may, however, be authorised by the settlor or by the courts. Further rights to payment for trust corporations and professional trustees are provided by section 29 of the Trustee Act 2000.

▶ Trustees are prohibited from purchasing trust property. This is known as the *self-dealing* rule. This is because such transactions necessarily involve a clear actual conflict of interest: the trustee's job is to secure as high a price as possible for the beneficiary, whereas his personal interest will be in paying as little as possible.

▶ A trustee is entitled to purchase his beneficiary's equitable interest under the trust only if the beneficiary gives fully informed consent to the sale and, possibly, if the price paid is objectively fair. This is known as the *fair-dealing* rule.

▶ It is commonly supposed that all trustees owe fiduciary duties. As a matter of principle, this must be doubted however. Certainly it is hard to see how it is either plausible or fair to expect those who reasonably do not know that they hold property on trust to apply that property solely in the beneficiary's best interests. On this basis, the trustees of many resulting and constructive trusts should not be regarded as owing fiduciary obligations.

▶ It is clear that fiduciary obligations exist outside trusts and can be owed by people other than trustees. For instance, solicitors, agents, company directors and commercial partners all owe fiduciary duties. In determining whether a given defendant is a fiduciary, one approach is to ask whether the relationship that exists between the claimant and defendant is analogous to one of the established categories of fiduciary relationship. A second approach is to ask whether the remedies available where a fiduciary has breached his duty should also be made available to the claimant. This second approach, however, runs the risk of distorting our understanding of what makes a relationship fiduciary.

Exercises

10.1 When, if ever, is it important to distinguish a trustee's fiduciary duties from the other duties he may owe to his beneficiaries?

10.2 Do all trustees owe fiduciary duties? Should they? Is there such a thing as an 'irreducible core' of trustees' duties which all trustees owe?

10.3 Why do we prohibit trustees from putting themselves into a position in which their personal interests and the duty they owe to act in their beneficiaries' best interests may come into conflict?

10.4 Are the rules concerning the liability of fiduciaries for making secret profits too strict? What would happen if we relaxed these rules?

10.5 What is the relationship between the prohibition of self-dealing, the rule on fair-dealing and the general rule prohibiting possible conflicts of interest?

Further reading

Conaglen, 'A re-appraisal of the fiduciary self-dealing and fair-dealing rules' [2006] Cam LJ 366

Hicks, 'The remedial principle of *Keech v Sandford* reconsidered' [2010] Cam LJ 287

Smith, 'Constructive fiduciaries' in Birks (ed), *Privacy and Loyalty* (Oxford University Press 1997)

There is a vast amount of literature on the nature and basis of fiduciary obligations. Finn's book is widely accepted as being the leading account, and Moffat has a good overview of the various theories.

Birks, 'The content of fiduciary obligation' (2002) 16 Tru LI 34

Conaglen, *Fiduciary Loyalty: Protecting the Due Performance of Non-fiduciary Duties* (Hart Publishing 2010)

Edelman, 'When do fiduciary duties arise?' (2010) 126 LQR 302

Finn, 'The fiduciary principle' in Youdan (ed), *Equity, Fiduciaries and Trusts* (Carswell 1989)

Finn, *Fiduciary Obligations* (Law Book Co 1977)

Moffat, *Trusts Law: Text and Materials* (5th edn, Cambridge University Press 2009), 833–86

Sealy, 'Fiduciary relationships' [1962] Cam LJ 69

Weinrib, 'The fiduciary obligation' (1975) 25 UTLJ 1

Chapter 11

Non-fiduciary obligations

11.1　Introduction

We saw at the start of the last chapter that not all the duties owed by trustees are properly described as fiduciary duties. So, although (most) trustees must indeed act in good faith and in the interests of their beneficiaries, this is not all they must do. Indeed, if a trustee's obligations were limited to his fiduciary duties, the trust would not be a particularly useful institution and settlor's wishes would rarely be effectuated. It is all well and good acting for the right reasons (which is the focus of fiduciary obligations), but if the trust is to achieve its purpose – typically conveying certain benefits to certain people – we must also require a certain level of competence from trustees, and, even more clearly, that they adhere to the terms set down by the settlor (eg as to who to pay and when).

This chapter examines these other duties. We shall look at the obligations imposed on trustees in the performance of their administrative functions of dealing with trust property (eg in investing or insuring it) and in relation to the considerations to which trustees must have regard when exercising dispositive discretions vested in them under discretionary trusts or powers of appointment. We shall end by assessing the types of information which beneficiaries and objects are entitled to have about trust funds in which they are interested.

11.2　The duty of care

Until the Trustee Act 2000 ('the 2000 Act') came into force on 1 February 2001, trustees assumed a duty to act as an ordinary prudent man of business would act in managing his own affairs: see *Speight v Gaunt* (1883) 9 App Cas 1. When it came to deciding how to invest the trust property, the standard was modified such that the trustee had to exercise such care as would the prudent man of business when acting for the benefit of those 'for whom he felt morally bound to provide' (Lindley LJ in *Re Whiteley* (1886) 33 Ch D 347, 355).

The test provided by the case law has now been replaced by the statutory standard set down by section 1 of the 2000 Act, namely that a trustee must exercise:

> ... such care and skill as is reasonable in the circumstances having regard in particular to (a) any special knowledge or experience that he has or holds himself out as having, and (b) if he acts in the course of a business or a profession, to any special knowledge or experience that it is reasonable to expect of a person in the course of that kind of business or profession.

This statutory standard of care is applicable to most significant acts carried out by a trustee in the course of his administration of trust assets (see Schedule 1 to the 2000 Act), although not to a trustee's dispositive decisions (in such cases the common law rules continue to apply). In particular, it applies to a trustee's powers of investment, his powers in relation to the acquisition of land, his power to insure trust property, and his powers to appoint agents, nominees or custodians (to carry out some of a trustee's functions for him, for example, by taking investment decisions or by holding trust property).

The test contained in section 1 of the 2000 Act does not impose a standard of care that will apply to all trustees equally, but one that will depend upon the circumstances of each trust. The reason for this is that there is a wide spectrum of different sorts of trusts and of different types of individuals and companies that become trustees.

At one end of the spectrum is the small family trust administered by a person with absolutely no expertise of either trusts or the administration of trust assets. So, to give an example that we will hereinafter refer to as the 'simple will trust', a testator may appoint a family friend, who happens to be a doctor, as the trustee of a trust of £10,000 for his son for life and, thereafter, for a particular grandchild absolutely. It may well be the case that the trust contains no provision for its trustee to be remunerated: the family friend will rather accept the appointment out of loyalty or duty to the testator, and in the knowledge that administering the trust is unlikely to take up a substantial amount of his time.

At the other end of the spectrum comes a very large trust that is administered by a professional trustee or by a corporation that specialises in the provision of trustee services. Take, for instance, a pension trust for the employees of a large public company which is administered by a trust corporation. Such a trust may contain assets with a value of several billion pounds, and its administration is likely to be extremely complicated (involving the investment of the trust property in such a way as to be able to make pensions payments to the thousands of current and former employees who have paid money into the scheme). The trust corporation will probably have several employees dedicated to the administration of such a trust, assisted by specialist professional advisers (for instance, solicitors, counsel, accountants, actuaries and investment advisers). The trustee will undoubtedly be remunerated for the services that it provides.

The most important point to make about the statutory test provided by section 1 of the 2000 Act is that it sets down a variable duty of care depending upon the relevant circumstances, so the trust corporation administering the pension trust will owe a higher duty of care than that owed by the family friend administering a small and simple will trust.

Four other points need be made about the section 1 test. First, it contains both subjective and objective elements. The objective part of the section 1 test can be seen by the reference in section 1(b) to 'special knowledge or experience that it is reasonable to expect' of a person acting in the course of a particular business or profession. Thus, if a solicitor from a small firm becomes a trustee as part of his practice, he will be judged by reference to what it would be reasonable to expect of such a solicitor acting as a trustee, notwithstanding the fact that the actual solicitor may have absolutely no knowledge of trusts or experience of trust administration.

Overlaid on top of this objective standard is the subjective standard imposed by section 1(a), which requires the court to take into account the knowledge or experience that the trustee actually has, or which he holds himself out as having. This factor may apply where a trustee does not act in the course of his business or profession. Thus, in relation to the purchase of stocks and shares, a higher standard may be expected of a trustee whose profession is that of an investment banker specialising in equities, than of a trustee who is a beekeeper. The section 1(a) subjective standard will also apply where a person acting in the course of his business or profession has, or holds himself out as having, knowledge or experience that is in excess of that reasonably expected of that business or profession. So, a solicitor from a small firm who has 20 years of offshore trusts experience may well owe a higher duty of care than his counterpart in a similar firm who does not have such experience (and of whom it would not be reasonable to expect such experience).

The second additional point to make about the section 1 test is that the factors set out in section 1(a) and (b) are not exhaustive. Rather, they are factors that should 'in particular' be taken into account when determining the appropriate duty of care. Other relevant factors will also go to shape the precise duty owed. Such factors could, in particular cases, include the size of a trust fund, the complexity of the trust, and the level of a trustee's remuneration.

The third point to make is that the section 1 test probably does not radically affect the approach previously adopted by the courts when determining a trustee's duty of care. In fact, the section 1 test bears a remarkable similarity to the test formulated by Brightman J in *Bartlett v Barclays Bank Trust Co Ltd* [1980] Ch 515, 534:

> I am of opinion that a higher duty of care is plainly due from someone like a trust corporation which carries on a specialised business of trust management. A trust corporation holds itself out in its advertising literature as being above ordinary mortals. With a specialist staff of trained trust officers and managers, and with ready access to financial information and professional advice, dealing with and solving trust problems day after day, the trust corporation holds itself out, and rightly, as capable of providing an expertise which it would be unrealistic to expect and unjust to demand from the ordinary prudent man or woman who accepts, probably unpaid and sometimes reluctantly from a sense of family duty, the burdens of a trusteeship.

The final point is that the section 1 duty of care can be expressly disapplied by a provision contained in a trust deed (see para 7 of Schedule 1 to the 2000 Act), although it is not thought that many trusts settled after the 2000 Act came into force actually exclude the duty.

Now that we have assessed the nature of the section 1 duty of care, we can move on to consider the area in which it is most important, that of trustee investment.

11.3 Investment of trust property

In virtually all express trusts, trustees will be required to make investment decisions. This point can be seen from a brief consideration of the two trusts discussed in Section 11.2. In the case of the simple will trust, the trustee will have to take the £10,000 settled on trust and decide how to invest it so that he can provide the testator's son, who is the trust's life tenant, with income from the trust property, while also acting fairly in relation to the testator's grandchild, who will take the property after the death of the life tenant. If the trustee simply places the entirety of the trust property into an interest-bearing bank account, he will be able to provide the life tenant with a modest income during his life. But this investment decision will also mean that the value of the grandchild's interest in remainder will slowly be eroded by inflation. This result, as we will see later on in the chapter, may well be a breach of the trustee's duty to act even-handedly between life tenants and remaindermen. Thus, the trustee will need to adopt a slightly more complex investment strategy.

Things get far more complicated when one considers the pensions trust example. Again, the trust corporation will not simply be able to 'invest' the trust property by placing it into an interest-bearing bank account. Rather, it will need to invest the trust assets in a range of different investments in order to safeguard the trust assets from risk, obtain reasonable returns on those investments, and ensure that it will be able to meet the regular pensions obligations that the trust has assumed to thousands of different current and former employees. As can be imagined, this will involve a very complicated investment strategy indeed.

The two examples set out earlier show why trustees will be required to make investment decisions. But how do trustees go about investing trust funds? There are two questions to examine here: first, what sort of investments are open to the trustees, and, second, how are they to go about choosing between alternative permissible investments.

The starting point is now section 3(1) of the 2000 Act, which sets out trustees' general powers of investment. This section provides: 'Subject to the provisions of this Part, a trustee may make any kind of investment that he could make if he were absolutely entitled to the assets of the trust.' Thus, trustees have a very wide pool of potential investments that they can decide to make. Should the settlor, for any reason, be concerned that this might unduly limit the investment possibilities open to the trustee, the range of potential investments can be expanded yet further by an express provision contained in a trust deed (see section 6(1)(a)). Section 3 applies to all trusts, whether settled before or after the 2000 Act came into force, unless it is inconsistent with or excluded by a trust's express terms: see section 7. Accordingly, the previous Trustee Investment Act 1961 regime, whereby trustees were permitted to invest only in certain types of specified 'safe' investments, no longer has any application.

A word or two should be said about what investments are not permitted by section 3. First, trustees may not acquire freehold or leasehold land outside the United Kingdom (see s 8(1)). Second, there is some doubt as to whether a trustee can properly acquire as investments assets that do not produce income (such as antiques or gold, on which see *Re Wragg* [1919] 2 Ch 58, which suggests that such assets do not qualify as investments). (For the contrary and more modern view, see para 22 of the explanatory notes that accompany the 2000 Act.) Nevertheless, one should not devote too much attention to these exceptions to the wide general investment power: their range is limited, and many modern trust deeds contain express investment powers, which expand the section 3 general powers of investment.

11.4 Investment criteria and advice

As discussed in Section 11.2, when making investments trustees must act with such care and skill as is reasonable in the circumstances. Further guidance as to what trustees are expected to do is contained in sections 4 and 5 of the 2000 Act. Section 4 sets down the standard investment criteria to which trustees must have regard when making investments:

(1) In exercising any power of investment, whether arising under this Part or otherwise, a trustee must have regard to the standard investment criteria.
(2) A trustee must from time to time review the investments of the trust and consider whether, having regard to the standard investment criteria, they should be varied.
(3) The standard investment criteria, in relation to a trust, are –
　(a) the suitability to the trust of investments of the same kind as any particular investment proposed to be made or retained and of that particular investment as an investment of that kind, and
　(b) the need for diversification of investments of the trust, in so far as is appropriate to the circumstances of the trust.

So, trustees must have regard to the suitability of particular investments to the trust that they are administering, and also to the need to diversify investments.

We can deal with the 'suitability' requirement relatively easily. If a trust has an extremely small value or is likely to be in existence only for a very short period of time, it will probably be unsuitable to invest the trust assets otherwise than by placing them in an interest-bearing account. Conversely, if a substantial trust is likely to have a long-term existence, it will be unsuitable simply to invest its assets in short-term investments. It will, of course, also be unsuitable for a trustee to invest any substantial part of the trust fund in an investment that is accompanied by a high degree of risk (although, as we shall see, it may not be a breach of trust for a small part of the trust fund to be invested in high-risk investments as part of a diversified portfolio). Finally, it will usually be unsuitable for a trustee to invest trust funds with an eye on whether those investments are ethical in nature (see Section 11.6).

Under section 4(3)(b), trustees must also take into account the need for diversification of trust investments. At one level, this is a simple concept to grasp: trustees should not put all their eggs in one basket. The consequences of failing to adhere to this rule are equally easy to explain: difficulties with a company or sector in which substantial investments have been made could spell disaster for the entirety of the trust fund. Numerous examples of recent corporate collapses can be given to illustrate the point (eg Enron, Royal Bank of Scotland, Lehman Brothers, WorldCom etc.).

But diversification can also be understood at a more detailed and technical level. Where investments are made in the stock market, the risk of investing in a particular company or sector can be offset by investing in a competing sector. Thus the risk of investing in oil or coal companies might be offset by other investments made in renewables; the risk of investing in emerging economies might be offset by a majority of investments being made in developed economies; and the risk of investing in equities might be offset by other investments in government gilts, corporate bonds or property. This way, even if one investment or class of investments proves unsuccessful, the overall portfolio should not be adversely affected to a great extent. These ideas of diversification and offsetting of risk are often referred to as being principles of 'modern portfolio theory'.

Two other points need to be made about sections 4 and 5. First, it is not enough for trustees simply to exercise such care and skill as is reasonable in the circumstances when making initial trust investments. Investments will also need to be periodically reviewed, and changed if they become unsuitable. Such reviews should, as section 4(2) provides, be carried out with the standard investment criteria in mind.

Second, many trustees will simply not have the experience or expertise necessary to decide properly upon which investments a trust should make. In recognition of this point, section 5(1) imposes an obligation on trustees to 'obtain and consider proper advice about the way in which, having regard to the standard investment criteria, [their investment powers] should be exercised'. Such advice must be obtained from a person who 'is reasonably believed by the trustee to be qualified to give it by his ability in and practical experience of financial and other matters relating to the proposed investment': section 5(4). This obligation does not apply where it is unnecessary or inappropriate for advice to be obtained: see section 5(3). For instance, it might be unnecessary to obtain advice if the value of the trust fund or investment at issue is so small that obtaining advice would cost a disproportionately large amount of money, and it might be inappropriate to obtain advice where a trustee is himself an investment expert.

11.5　Even-handedness

In the simple will trust example given in Section 11.2, we have posited a hypothetical trust for a testator's son for life, and then for a named grandchild absolutely. Such a trust entitles the life tenant to the income earned on trust property for the duration of his life, with the remainderman being entitled to the trust capital on the death of the life tenant.

There is an inherent tension in any trust in which different individuals have a life interest and an interest in remainder. The life tenant will want the trustees to invest the trust fund in a manner that maximises the income that he will receive, and he may not mind if such income is generated at the expense of the trust's capital (and therefore the remainderman). By contrast, the remainderman's interests will be diametrically opposed. It is also clear that a trustee's investment decisions will directly affect the financial interests of the life tenant and remainderman. For instance, a trustee might invest in assets such as gold or antiques, which do not produce any income but which may rapidly appreciate in value. At the other extreme, a trustee may use trust capital to invest in wasting assets, which produce a high income but the capital value of which will depreciate over time to zero (for instance, a short lease or a portfolio of patent rights).

What, then, should a trustee do when balancing the interests of the life tenant and remainderman? In summary, he must act honestly and fairly in striking an equitable balance between them (such obligations being part of a trustee's fiduciary duty), acting with such care and skill as is reasonable (pursuant to section 1 of the 2000 Act), and taking into account relevant considerations whilst ignoring irrelevant considerations (on which see Section 11.9).

Does this mean that trustees should always invest in assets that balance the life tenant and the remainderman's interests equally – such as shares, which might be thought to please both interests as they offer the prospect of both income (through dividends) and capital appreciation (through increases in share price) – or that he should balance any investment in an asset that produces no income with an investment in a wasting asset? Not necessarily. Although both of these propositions might be sensible rules of thumb, the principle of holding a fair balance between life tenant and remainderman is not so mechanical. Instead, the circumstances of a particular trust might sometimes call for the life tenant or remainderman to be given preferential treatment. As Staughton LJ remarked in *Nestlé v National Westminster Bank plc* [1993] 1 WLR 1260, 1279:

> At times it will not be easy to decide what is an equitable balance [between life tenant and remainderman]. ... If the life tenant is living in penury and the remainderman already has ample wealth, common sense suggests that a trustee should be able to take that into account, not necessarily by seeking the highest possible income at the expense of capital, but by inclining in that direction. However, before adopting that course a trustee should, I think, require some verification of the facts.

11.6　Ethical investments

Ethical investment is investment guided not by financial concerns but rather by moral or political considerations. Accordingly, a strategy of ethical investment might exclude investments in the tobacco, armaments and fossil fuel industries. A problem with which the courts have had to grapple is whether a trustee can ever pursue a policy of ethical investment and, if he can, whose conception of ethical investment he must follow.

The general principle is that a trustee must put all ethical or moral considerations to one side when investing or administering a trust fund. Two cases illustrate this principle well. The first is *Buttle v Saunders* [1950] 2 All ER 193. Here, trustees had an oral – and hence non-binding – agreement to sell land to a Mrs Simpson for £6,142. An offer of £6,500 was then made for the same land by one of the trust's beneficiaries who, when his offer was refused, applied to court for an injunction prohibiting the trustees from completing the sale to Mrs Simpson because, he said, their duty was to obtain the best price achievable for the trust. Wynn-Parry J granted the injunction, holding:

> ... the trustees and their solicitors acted on an incorrect principle. The only consideration which was present to their minds was that they had gone so far in the negotiations with Mrs Simpson that they could not properly, from the point of view of commercial morality, resile from those negotiations.

Instead, the trustees should have probed the increased offer and, if they decided that the beneficiary was able to proceed to completion of the transaction within a short period, accepted it. It was only by acting in this way that the trustees would comply with their 'overriding duty to obtain the best price which they can for their beneficiaries'.

The second case is *Cowan v Scargill* [1985] Ch 270. Here, trustees of a pension trust for employees and former employees of the National Coal Board (NCB) held assets valued at approximately £3 billion. Five of the ten trustees were appointed by the NCB and the other five were appointed by the union that represented many of the NCB's employees, the National Union of Mineworkers (NUM). The trustees were assisted in making investment decisions by an advisory panel of experts. In 1982, the experts produced an investment plan, but the NUM trustees refused, in accordance with NUM policy, to accept it unless it was amended to (1) prohibit any increase in overseas investments, (2) withdraw overseas investments already held by the trust at the most opportune time, and (3) prohibit any investment in energies competing with coal. The NCB trustees applied to court for directions. Megarry VC held that the NUM trustees were acting in breach of trust by bringing ethical considerations into account when exercising their investment discretions. He held ([1985] Ch 270, 287–88):

> When the purpose of the trusts is to provide financial benefits for the beneficiaries, as is usually the case, the best interests of the beneficiaries are normally their best financial interests. In the case of a power of investment, as in the present case, the power must be exercised so as to yield the best return for the beneficiaries. ... In considering what investments to make trustees must put on one side their own personal interests and views. Trustees may have strongly held social or political views. They may be firmly opposed to any investment in South Africa or other countries, or they may object to any form of investment in companies concerned with alcohol, tobacco, armaments or many other things. In the conduct of their own affairs, of course, they are free to abstain from making any such investments. Yet under a trust, if investments of this type would be more beneficial to the beneficiaries than other investments, the trustees must not refrain from making the investments by virtue of the views that they hold.

So the very strong prima facie rule is that trustees cannot consider ethical considerations when investing trust property. But this rule is not immutable. There are three principal exceptions to it.

The first takes only a moment's thought to understand: the trust deed may itself expressly consent to a policy of ethical investment. Nevertheless, the draftsman must take care when implementing such a wish on the part of a settlor, for the term 'ethical investment' has no settled legal meaning; the draftsman may be better advised to specify that the trustee's power of investment does not extend to those companies whose principal business is carried out in certain sectors. The settlor must also be careful not to restrict trustees' investment powers to such an extent that he is unable to invest in a properly diversified portfolio. It is important not to underestimate the danger of overly restricting the range of permissible investments. For instance, in *Harries v The Church Cmrs for England* [1992] 1 WLR 1241, expert evidence was adduced to show that a decision not to invest in companies that had interests in South Africa would prevent trustees from investing in 24% of the companies listed on the stock market.

The second exception to the general rule on ethical investment will arise in the rare circumstances where all of a trust's beneficiaries are of full age and consent to an ethical investment policy. This exception was explained by Megarry vc in *Cowan* in the following terms ([1985] Ch 270, 288):

> ... if the only actual or potential beneficiaries of a trust are all adults with very strict views on moral or social matters, condemning all forms of alcohol, tobacco and popular entertainment, as well as armaments, I can well understand that it might not be for the 'benefit' of such beneficiaries to know that they are obtaining rather larger financial returns under the trust by reason of investments in those activities than they would have received if the trustees had invested the trust funds in other investments. ... But I would emphasise that such cases are likely to be very rare.

Trustees should, of course, be careful to ensure that all beneficiaries are of full age and that they all consent to a specific policy of ethical investment.

The third exception applies only to charitable trusts. Here, as Nicholls vc held in *Harries v The Church Cmrs for England* [1992] 1 WLR 1241, the prima facie rule remains the same, but it can be disapplied where investment by the trust in a particular type of company would conflict with the objects that the trust is attempting to achieve. Therefore, a trust for scientific research into potential treatments for cancer would be able to adopt a policy pursuant to which it would not invest in shares in tobacco companies. Furthermore, trustees can decide not to invest in companies if the result of making such an investment would be that potential recipients of the trust's aid might be unwilling to accept it because of the source of the charity's money, or where making such an investment might alienate those who provide financial support to the charity. Such cases are likely to be extremely rare. An example of one might be that a trust for the prevention of cruelty to animals would be justified in not investing in companies that carry out research on animals.

11.7 Majority shareholdings

Trustees often find themselves with a majority shareholding in a company. This typically happens when a settlor who has established a successful company decides for tax or other reasons to settle it into a trust. Now, such a settlor will probably not intend that the trust's trustees sell some of the company's shares in order to diversify the trust's investments, and so his lawyers will probably include a clause within the trust deed that has the effect of extinguishing any duty on the part of the trustees to diversify trust investments.

But holding a majority of shares in a company means that a large proportion, or perhaps all, of a trust's assets are tied up with the fortunes of that company. In other words, all or many of the trust's eggs are held within one basket. The courts have recognised the precarious nature of this situation and have responded by imposing particular duties on trustees who hold majority shareholdings. In short, such trustees should obtain information about the companies in which they have shareholdings over and above the information that would be available to an ordinary shareholder. Furthermore, trustees should, if necessary, intervene in the management of such companies if information that they have received reveals that it is not being managed in a prudent fashion (see *Bartlett v Barclays Bank Trust Co Ltd* [1980] 1 Ch 515).

The *Bartlett* principle requires some explanation of the rights which an owner of a share can exercise. As we have seen, a shareholder is entitled to be paid the dividends declared in relation to the shares that he owns (such dividends usually represent the profits which the company has made over the last financial year). But shareholders also have rights to intervene in the management of a company in which they hold shares. The most important of these 'management' rights is the ability, under section 168 of the Companies Act 2006, to call a meeting of shareholders for the purpose of removing, by a simple majority, that company's directors (and, in due course, appointing replacements for them). So, a trustee with a majority shareholding can, quite simply, sack a company's directors if they do not act in accordance with his wishes. Such a trustee is, then, in a position to be able to demand a great deal of information about such a company from its directors. If this information proves unsatisfactory, a trustee can use the threat of exercising his powers under section 168 to bring about a change to policies adopted by the company's directors. Finally, if all else fails, a trustee can remove that company's incumbent directors and appoint himself and/or his nominee as directors of the company.

So what information should a trustee obtain to ensure that the trust's investments in a particular company are not at risk? There is no hard and fast answer other than 'such information as is reasonably necessary to ensure that the company is being properly administered'. This information may often take the form of monthly management accounts, or the agenda and minutes of directors' meetings. What a trustee should not do is simply rely on information available to the company's shareholders and the public at large, such as audited accounts (which are, in any event, usually produced several months after the end of the relevant accounting period).

These principles were applied in *Bartlett v Barclays Bank Trust Co*. There, the trust held 99.8% of the shares in a property company which had been established by the settlor. The company was administered by a board of directors comprising two surveyors, an accountant and a solicitor (none of whom was appointed by the trust company that acted as trustee). In 1960, the board of directors embarked upon a programme of speculative property development and began, in particular, to acquire residential properties near the Old Bailey at a price that was above market value. The trustee took little notice of the new direction of the company, and obtained only such information as was generally available to shareholders. Had the trustee taken proper steps to investigate the company's trading, it would not only have discovered the hazardous nature of the Old Bailey project, but would also have been able to extricate the company from this project without it having incurred any loss. In the event, the Old Bailey investment was retained and eventually sold at a significant loss. Brightman J had no hesitation in holding the trustee liable for the loss.

11.8 An illustration

Several of the different principles discussed earlier can be drawn together by considering the leading pre-2000 Act case of *Nestlé v National Westminster Bank plc* [1993] 1 WLR 1260. There, the testator, who died in 1922, established a will trust which included as beneficiaries his widow, his two sons and their spouses, and his one grandchild. The interests created under the trust worked as follows: the testator's wife was granted a life interest in the family house together with a tax-free annuity; subject to those interests, the testator's two sons were granted annuities between the ages of 21 and 25, and thereafter life interests in half of the trust fund (each having the power to appoint the income of his share to a surviving spouse for her life); finally, the testator's sons' children, of which there was ultimately only one, the claimant Edith Nestlé, were granted interests in the remainder.

Now, the testator's investments were worth some £53,963 on his death in April 1922. In 1986, when the testator's surviving son died and the claimant became absolutely entitled to the trust fund, its capital amounted to £269,203. The claimant claimed that had the fund been properly invested it would have been worth some £1.8 million. There was clear evidence to the effect that the trust company had completely misunderstood an investment clause contained in the trust, that it had failed to conduct periodic reviews of trust investments until 1959, and that it had fallen 'woefully short of maintaining the real value of the fund, let alone matching the average increase in price of ordinary shares'. Furthermore, the Court of Appeal held that the trust company had not acted 'conscientiously, fairly and carefully', that there was 'not much for the bank to be proud of in its administration of the ... trust', and that 'no testator, in the light of this example, would choose this bank for the effective management of his investment'. Yet the breach of trust claim failed.

There are various ways by which this decision can be explained. Two potential explanations depend upon a close analysis of the facts of the case. First, the trustees had adopted a policy of investing in tax-exempt gilts because the testator's two sons were domiciled abroad. Although this meant that the real value of the fund did not increase as significantly as if other investments had been made, it did mean that there was a substantial prospect that the fund would be exempt from inheritance tax on the death of the sons and their wives. A second reason is that the bank appears to have won the battle of the expert witnesses in a hard-fought trial. A particular point of expert evidence that was accepted by the court was the proposition that, before 1959, equities were regarded as risky investments. Thus, Staughton LJ stated ([1993] 1 WLR 1260, 1276):

> ... the trustees' performance must not be judged with hindsight: after the event even a fool is wise, as a poet said nearly 3,000 years ago. ... [O]ne must bear in mind that investment philosophy was very different in the early years of this trust from what it became later. ... Equities were regarded as risky during the 1920s and 1930s ... It was only in 1959 that [they became more popular].

So the trustees could not be criticised for failing to adopt a more aggressive strategy of equity investment before 1959 because the consensus at this time was that equities were imprudent investments. Conversely, as Hoffmann J noted at first instance, 'modern trustees acting within their investment powers are entitled to be judged by the standards of current portfolio theory, which emphasises the risk of the entire portfolio rather than the risk attaching to each investment taken in isolation'. Thus, it may be that modern trustees do not commit a breach of trust by investing a small part of the trust fund in a high-risk investment which subsequently loses all of its value, if by so investing the trustees were merely acting in accordance with modern portfolio theory.

There are also some more general ways of explaining the result in *Nestlé*. In particular, it might be said that the court was unwilling to penalise a trustee who adopts an overly cautious approach (as in *Nestlé*) as compared to trustees who take an overly risky approach (as the company owned by the trust did in *Bartlett v Barclays Bank Trust Co Ltd* [1980] Ch 515). It might also be said that the court, while acknowledging at various places that professional trustees owe an enhanced duty of care, appeared to apply a relatively low standard. Thus, the court referred to the 'undemanding standard of prudence' that was required. Indeed, the court stated that the trustee's failure to diversify was not a 'course which no prudent trustee would have followed', a test which appears to suggest that *Wednesbury* unreasonableness (a standard taken from the public law case, *Associated Provincial Picture Houses Ltd v Wednesbury Corporation* [1948] 1 KB 223; for disapproval of such public law analogies, see *Pitt v Holt* [2011] EWCA Civ 197; [2012] Ch 132, [77], [235]) will be required before a trustee is liable for improper investment decisions. Accordingly, there is a good argument that the *Nestlé* decision would have been different had the court been applying the test set down by section 1 of the 2000 Act.

11.9 Rules governing the exercise of dispositive discretions

Administrative discretions arise in relation to a trustee's administration of trust assets (for instance, decisions concerning investment, insurance and the appointment of agents). Trustees' dispositive discretions, on the other hand, arise under discretionary trusts or powers of appointment, where the trustees must decide which beneficiaries or objects will receive benefits from the trust (on which see Sections 2.1–2.2). Put another way, when trustees exercise dispositive discretions, they decide who gets what.

Let us take an example of a discretionary trust of various different shares for a fixed period of time, under which the trustees have discretion to appoint income and capital amongst 10 beneficiaries. To keep matters simple, let us assume that there is no power to accumulate income, so that income will have to be distributed as and when it arises. Thus, when dividends are paid on shares held by the trust, the trustees will have to decide within a reasonable time which beneficiary or beneficiaries should receive the benefit of those dividends, and make the appropriate payment(s). The trustees will also have to consider, from time to time, whether to distribute the trust capital (ie the actual assets held by the trust). As this is a discretionary trust, the trustees must distribute the trust property amongst one or more of the 10 beneficiaries by the end of the trust period. Had this been a power of appointment rather than a trust, the trustees would be under no obligation to distribute the property: Section 2.2.

The courts have, as we shall see later, developed doctrines over the years that attempt to regulate the way in which trustees exercise dispositive discretions. These doctrines give trustees guidance as to how they should act when exercising dispositive discretions, and thereby seek to ensure that trustees make an appropriate decision on any given set of facts. In the event that a trustee does not comply with his various dispositive obligations, aggrieved beneficiaries will be able to have that trustee's decisions vitiated and may, in severe circumstances, have the trustee removed from office.

The first obligation assumed by trustees when making dispositive decisions is to obey the terms of the trust, in particular by distributing trust property only to those entities which are beneficiaries of a trust or an object of a power. Thus, the trustee of the discretionary trust referred to earlier can only distribute income and capital to the beneficiaries identified in the trust deed. He cannot pay anyone else. Furthermore, as might be expected, he cannot circumvent his obligation to obey the terms of the trust by distributing property to an actual beneficiary on the basis that that beneficiary will pass that property on to the trustee or some other third party (eg the trustee cannot agree with one of the beneficiaries that he will distribute the entirety of the trust property to her in return for a secret commission of 10% of all such distributions). If the trustee makes such an agreement, he is said to commit a fraud on a power (see, for further discussion of the principle, *Vatcher v Paull* [1915] AC 372, 378).

Trustees exercising dispositive discretions must also consider periodically whether those discretions should be exercised. But trustees cannot simply decide to distribute trust property to the first beneficiary or object of a power that they come across. Rather, trustees must first make a survey of the range of objects or discretionary beneficiaries, so as to be in an informed position to make decisions. This research should also include consideration of the size of the trust fund, the amount available for distribution and, if trustees are exercising a power of appointment, the beneficiaries that will be entitled to the funds subject to the power if it is not exercised. Once this survey has been undertaken, trustees need consider the appropriateness of individual appointments.

The obligation on the part of trustees to survey the range of a class might be thought to be problematical in the case of a power of appointment which relates to a very large class of potential objects (eg a power to appoint income to anyone in the world except the settlor, or current or former trustees of the trust). An obligation to conduct an in-depth survey in relation to all of the objects of such a power would be impossible. Trustees, however, need not worry themselves to 'survey the world from China to Peru' (Harman J in *Re Gestetner Settlement* [1953] Ch 672, 688–89). Rather, they need merely have 'an appreciation of the width of the field, and thus whether a selection is to be made merely from a dozen or, instead, from thousands or millions' (Megarry VC in *Re Hay's Settlement Trust* [1982] 1 WLR 202, 210).

Unsurprisingly, trustees cannot act for whatever reason tickles their fancy. This obligation is often said to be a duty not to act capriciously. As Templeman J explained in *Re Manisty's Settlement* [1974] Ch 17, the court will intervene if the trustee acts for reasons which:

> ... could be said to be irrational, perverse or irrelevant to any sensible expectation of the settlor; for example, if they chose a beneficiary by height or complexion or by the irrelevant fact that he was a resident of Greater London.

A good example of this obligation being breached occurred in *Klug v Klug* [1918] 2 Ch 67. There, a trustee refused to exercise her discretion to approve the making of a distribution to her daughter, a beneficiary of the trust, on the basis that the daughter had married without her consent. When this decision was challenged, the court ordered the trustees to make the distribution, to which the trust's other trustee consented.

The final obligation on the part of trustees when making dispositive decisions is related to the rule set out in *Re Manisty*. It is the obligation only to take account of all factors relevant to any given decision and to ignore all factors that are irrelevant. Importantly, a decision made for the wrong reasons may not only constitute a breach of duty on the part of the trustee but may also be set aside by the court. It is this latter feature which made this aspect of trusts law particularly popular with beneficiaries, and indeed trustees, who wanted to avoid the consequences of an ill-considered disposition or decision.

Over the past 20 or so years, the courts developed what became known as 'the rule in *Hastings-Bass*' (after *Re Hastings-Bass* [1975] Ch 25). The breadth of the rule is clear from the formulation given by Lloyd LJ in *Sieff v Fox* [2005] EWHC 1312 (Ch); [2005] 1 WLR 3811, [119]:

> Where trustees act under a discretion given to them by the terms of the trust, in circumstances in which they are free to decide whether or not to exercise that discretion, but the effect of the exercise is different from that which they intended, the court will interfere with their action if it is clear that they would not have acted as they did had they not failed to take into account considerations which they ought to have taken into account, or taken into account considerations which they ought not to have taken into account.

The rule was particularly popular where a trustee's decision had resulted in greater tax liability than had been planned or envisaged. For example, in *Abacus Trust Co v NSPCC* [2001] WTLR 953, trustees took advice as to the best way to minimise the trust's taxation liabilities, but failed to implement that advice by executing the tax avoidance scheme before instead of after the end of the tax year. In *Green v Cobham* [2000] WTLR 1101, a resettlement by the trustees of some of the trust fund meant that a catastrophic capital gains liability was incurred when one trustee's residential status changed. In both of these cases, the decisions would not have been taken had all relevant factors been taken into account. And in both cases the decisions were set aside and the tax liabilities avoided.

As such, what had started as a rule setting out a further duty trustees must keep to in their management of the trust became a tool of that management, enabling them a second bite of the cherry when their decisions had turned out to be mistaken. This development has now, however, been brought to an abrupt halt by the Court of Appeal in *Pitt v Holt* [2011] EWCA Civ 197; [2012] Ch 132. The decision addressed two conjoined appeals. In the first, the claimant's husband was seriously injured in a road accident. Following the settlement of the husband's claim for damages, the claimant (as her husband's receiver, meaning she was acting in a fiduciary capacity) set up a trust of the money for her husband and other members of the family. When her husband died, a large inheritance tax liability arose in respect of the trust. This liability could easily have been avoided by the inclusion of an additional provision in the trust deed. Accordingly, the claimant sought to have the disposition set aside on the basis of her failure to take this into account. In the second appeal, the trustees of a discretionary trust made a series of appointments from the fund in such as way as they thought would avoid capital gains tax. In fact they had misconstrued the statute and significant capital gains tax liabilities arose. The trustees therefore sought a declaration that the various dispositions were in fact void.

The Court of Appeal held that the starting point must be to consider whether the trustee's purported exercise of a dispositive power in fact fell within the scope of the power given to the trustee. If, on examination, the power does not extend to the sort of disposition the trustee has made, then we in fact have no effective exercise of the power *at all*, so the result is that the disposition is void.

If the disposition falls within the proper scope of the relevant power, the next question is whether the trustee nonetheless exercised that power in such a way as involves a breach of fiduciary duty, which includes (at least for these purposes) the duty to take into account all relevant considerations and not to take into account any irrelevant considerations. An exercise of a power which is within the limits of that power but which involves a breach of fiduciary duty is voidable – not void – at the behest of the beneficiary and subject to the court's discretion and any applicable defences. This is the proper basis and formulation of the rule in *Hastings-Bass* (although, as the Court of Appeal noted, this is a misnomer because *Re Hastings-Bass* itself was not a case of this kind).

If an exercise of a discretionary power is both within the terms of that power and involves no breach of fiduciary duty by the trustee, then the rule in *Hastings-Bass* does not allow it to be set aside simply because the exercise of the power had unforeseen or unintended results. In such circumstances, the only remaining possibility is to seek relief on the basis that the disposition was made by mistake. Here though the Court of Appeal held that the mistake must either go to the legal effect of the transaction or to some existing fact which can be said to be the basis of the transaction, and even then only if the mistake is of sufficient gravity as to make it unjust for the recipient of the property to retain it.

Following this approach, neither of the dispositions to which the appeals were addressed were to be set aside. Although the tax implications of a disposition were (in appropriate circumstances) a consideration which trustees ought to factor into the exercise of such powers, the fiduciaries here had made the relevant dispositions having received legal advice. The Court of Appeal concluded that, where trustees, aware of the need to consider relevant matters, seek advice from apparently competent advisors in relation to the exercise of their dispositive powers, no breach of duty is committed if they then exercise these powers on the basis of that advice (unless the process of seeking or acting on advice was itself open to challenge). To this extent, therefore, the duty to take into account all relevant factors is satisfied by acting on such advice, even if some relevant considerations are not thereby (properly) considered. The dispositions could not, therefore, be challenged under the rule in *Hastings-Bass*. Nor was the mistake they made as to the tax implications of these dispositions of sufficient gravity to have the dispositions set aside.

11.10 Rights to information

The preceding sections of this chapter have explained what obligations are owed by trustees to beneficiaries or objects of a power in carrying out their administrative and dispositive functions. But such rights are meaningful only if beneficiaries or objects have information in relation to the trust, so that they can assess whether the trustees have complied with their duties and, if they have not, take appropriate steps to have the trust fund reconstituted, the relevant decision declared invalid, and/or the misbehaving trustee(s) removed from office.

There are three separate strands to the broad principle that beneficiaries and objects of powers are prima facie entitled to information about a trust. First, trustees are obliged to inform beneficiaries and sometimes objects of a power of the fact that they are beneficiaries or objects. Second, the court will sometimes oblige a settlor or another person involved with a trust to disclose to beneficiaries details of a trust's current trustees. Finally, the courts have a broad discretion to order trustees to disclose information about a trust to beneficiaries and objects.

The obligation on the part of a trustee to inform beneficiaries of their status as such arises upon a beneficiary obtaining the age of majority, namely 18 years (see *Hawkesley v May* [1955] 3 WLR 569). It applies whether or not a beneficiary has a fixed or discretionary interest under the trust. A trustee is not, however, obliged to inform absolutely all objects of a power of their status, for powers of appointment can vary in nature to an enormous degree. At one extreme, there could be a power of appointment exercisable for a long period of time of which there were only a handful of objects. Here, the trustee will assume a duty to inform the objects of their status. But where there is a very wide power of appointment, such as an intermediate power (ie a power to appoint trust property to anybody in the world except certain specified people), the trustee will assume an obligation to inform only those who are the primary objects of the power.

The 'primary objects' test raises the obvious problem of identifying just who those objects are. This is really a question of fact, which will depend on the particular circumstances of a given case. In *Re Manisty's Settlement* [1971] Ch 17, for example, Templeman J held that in the case of a power in favour of the settlor's issue, relatives and employees of a company owned by the trust, the trustees were only under an obligation to inform the settlor's issue of their status as objects. The reason for this rule is that the courts do not want trustees to become overburdened by having to contact, and then deal with, remote objects of a power, who have no more than a theoretical chance of receiving any distribution from the trust. An example of such a remote object might, on the facts of *Re Manisty*, have been a low-level temporary employee of the company owned by the trust.

The second strand of the broad principle that beneficiaries and objects are prima facie entitled to information about a trust, applies where a beneficiary or an object knows of his status under a trust, but does not know the identity or contact details of the trust's current trustee(s). Here again, the courts have a discretion to order a person who is or has been involved with the trust to provide information about the current trustee(s). In the leading case on this point, a settlor was compelled to provide such information to a beneficiary of a discretionary trust (see *Murphy v Murphy* [1999] 1 WLR 283). The court's discretion was exercised in the beneficiary's favour as he was one of the settlor's children, and so could not be described as a remote beneficiary, and as he was not well-off. These factors suggested that the beneficiary had a real prospect of receiving a distribution from the trust fund. Had the beneficiary seeking disclosure been a remote beneficiary who was already financially secure, the court may not have exercised its discretion in his favour.

There is no reason the *Murphy* principle should be limited to beneficiaries of trusts. In appropriate circumstances, a court might well exercise its discretion in favour of a primary object of a power of appointment. Indeed, there is no reason an order might not be made against a person other than the settlor of a trust. For instance, former trustees or former or current trust advisers may well have information about the current trustee of a trust, and it would not normally impose an onerous burden on such individuals to require them to provide the current trustee's contact details. It is unlikely, however, that an order will be made against a third party with no previous connection to the trust, who by chance happens to know the identity and contact details of the trust's current trustee.

The third strand of the principle is that the court has discretion to compel trustees to provide documentary and other information about the trust to those interested under it. The leading case in this area is the Privy Council's decision in *Schmidt v Rosewood Trust Ltd* [2003] UKPC 26; [2003] 2 AC 709, which held that the right to seek an order from the court compelling trustees to provide information could be obtained by beneficiaries of fixed and discretionary trusts and also by objects of a power of appointment. However, the Privy Council stressed, there was no absolute right vested in any particular beneficiary or object to receive information, especially where a beneficiary or object had 'no more than a theoretical possibility of benefit' under the trust.

When exercising its discretion to order disclosure, the court will, of course, be careful to consider the potential adverse consequences that disclosure may have. For example, a court will be careful to limit disclosure of personal information about beneficiaries which may cause embarrassment (because, for instance, it refers to a beneficiary's medical or financial circumstances). It will also be quick to limit disclosure of sensitive commercial information if such disclosure could have a negative effect on the financial position of the trust (because, for instance, it may upset a commercial deal that the trustees are negotiating). The court will also be keen not to impose substantial additional burdens on trustees in having to locate and copy documentation (although the general rule is that beneficiaries seeking information will have to pay for it to be copied).

The Privy Council's reasoning has been criticised, on the basis that it introduces uncertainty into this area of law (as no beneficiary can now say that he is absolutely entitled to see any particular trust document) and on the basis that it may create an antagonistic relationship between trustee and beneficiary (with the latter seeking to obtain, and the former attempting to withhold, disclosure). In practice, however, there will need to be some compelling reason before a principal beneficiary will be prevented from seeing core trust documentation, such as the trust deed or trust accounts showing how the trust fund has been invested and distributed by the trustees.

There is a further specific exception to the type of documents which trustees can be compelled to disclose under the *Schmidt v Rosewood* principle: trustees are not obliged to disclose any document which reveals the reasons that have caused them to make a particular decision (see eg *Re Beloved Wilkes' Charity* (1851) 3 Mac & G 440). This principle was endorsed by the Court of Appeal in *Re Londonderry's Settlement* [1965] Ch 918, where a beneficiary who was unhappy with the amounts which the trustees proposed to distribute to her sought information about the trust. The members of the Court of Appeal gave various explanations for holding that trustees need not disclose the reasons for their decision, noting that any other rule would cause family strife, would lead to fruitless litigation, or would make the role of trustees 'impossible'. This doctrine has undoubtedly been accepted by most subsequent decisions, although it was roundly criticised by Kirby P in the Australian case of *Hartigan Nominees v Rydge* (1992) 29 NSWLR 405, who opined that it would not be unduly burdensome for professional trustees to provide reasoned decisions, which, he argued, would be less likely to cause strife than decisions for which no reasons were given. (For a discussion of the rights of beneficiaries to see letters of wishes, and the recent decision of *Breakspear v Ackland* [2009] Ch 32, see Section 16.3).

Summary

▶ The standard of care expected of trustees when they make administrative decisions is set down by section 1 of the Trustee Act 2000: trustees must exercise such care and skill as is reasonable in the circumstances, a standard that takes into account whether a trustee acts in the course of his business or profession and whether he has or holds himself out as having special knowledge or experience.

▶ Section 3 of the 2000 Act authorises trustees to make virtually any type of investment, as long as the trust deed does not expressly or impliedly restrict this power. When making investments, trustees must have regard to the standard investment criteria, namely the suitability of any particular investment and the need for diversification. Trustees must also take advice on investment decisions, unless it is unnecessary or inappropriate to do so.

Summary cont'd

▶ Trustees must, in particular, act even-handedly between life tenants and remaindermen. They must also almost always ignore ethical considerations when investing. Further, they must take particular care to obtain information when they hold majority shareholdings in companies.

▶ There are a number of different rules that deal with how a trustee should exercise his dispositive discretions. In particular, trustees must obey the terms of the trust by distributing trust property only to beneficiaries or objects of powers of appointment. Furthermore, trustees must survey the range of beneficiaries or objects to whom they could distribute before making a particular dispositive decision. Finally, trustees must not act capriciously and must take into account relevant factors and ignore irrelevant factors when they act.

▶ Beneficiaries and objects of powers have three principal rights to information: first, to be told that they are beneficiaries or objects of a power; second, to seek details about the current trustees of a trust; and, third, to seek information and documentation about a trust from trustees.

Exercises

11.1 'The statutory standard of care set down by the Trustee Act 2000 is far too high and will discourage individuals from agreeing to become trustees.' Discuss.

11.2 You are approached by a trustee of a trust which holds a majority interest in a family company. The company has not traded well for the last few years, and the trustee tells you that he suspects, from looking at the company's last set of accounts, that it is being mismanaged. He tells you that he wants to sell the shares in the company and invest all of the proceeds in a company that sells solar panelling, because both he and the settlor are very keen on renewable energies. What steps should he take?

11.3 You are approached by a beneficiary of a trust who tells you he suspects that the sole trustee is having an affair with another beneficiary, because that other beneficiary has received 90% of all distributions from the trust fund over the past five years, despite being one of 10 discretionary beneficiaries and notwithstanding the fact that the beneficiary is independently wealthy. What duties might the trustee have breached and what information will the beneficiary be able to obtain about the trust? How would your answers differ (if at all) if the person who approached you was an object of a power rather than a discretionary beneficiary?

Further reading

Davies, 'Correcting mistakes: wither the rule in *Re Hastings-Bass*' [2011] Conv 406

Getzler, 'Duty of care' in Birks and Pretto (eds), *Breach of Trust* (Hart 2002)

Lord Nicholls, 'Trustees and their broader community: where duty, morality and ethics converge' (1995) 9 TLI 71

Mitchell, 'Reining in the rule in *Re Hastings-Bass*' (2006) 122 LQR 35

Chapter 12

The administration of trusts

12.1　Introduction

This brief chapter brings together several aspects of how trusts function once they are up and running. We shall start by looking at two issues – changes in the identities of the trustees and variation of trusts – which arise from the fact that express trusts often endure over a significant period of time (for the limits on this, see the discussion of the perpetuity rules in Section 4.9). From there, we shall look at the circumstances in which a trustee may delegate the exercise of his powers, before finally looking at two of the most important of these powers – the powers of maintenance and of advancement.

12.2　The appointment and removal of trustees

The first question to be addressed concerns the role of trustee. In the first instance, the choice of trustees is (in relation to intended trusts) a matter for the settlor. He can decide how many trustees he would like and who they will be. The law imposes few limitations on this freedom. One is that a child cannot act as trustee: section 20 of the Law of Property Act 1925. Another is that, in respect of trusts of land, there may be no more than four trustees: section 34 of the Trustee Act 1925. Of course, those chosen by the settlor to act as trustees are free to refuse. However, this will not lead to the failure of the trust. The principle is that a trust will not fail for want of a trustee and the court will ensure that another, willing trustee is appointed. In the last resort, the trust will be taken on by the Public Trustee, a corporate trustee provided by the state.

Over time, it may be convenient or indeed necessary for existing trustees to leave their posts and for new trustees to take their place. For instance, a trustee may die or become too ill to continue, or he may simply no longer want to have to shoulder such responsibilities. Accordingly, the law allows trustees to retire and new trustees to be added.

The basic rules are set down in section 36 of the Trustee Act 1925:

(1) Where a trustee, either original or substituted, and whether appointed by a court or otherwise, is dead, or remains out of the United Kingdom for more than twelve months, or desires to be discharged from all or any of the trusts or powers reposed in or conferred on him, or refuses or is unfit to act therein, or is incapable of acting therein, or is an infant, then ...

(a) the person or persons nominated for the purpose of appointing trustees by the instrument, if any, creating the trust; or
(b) if there is no such person, or no such person able and willing to act, then the surviving or continuing trustees or trustee for the time being, or the personal representatives of the last surviving or continuing trustee;

may, by writing, appoint one or more other person (whether or not being the persons exercising the power) to be a trustee or trustees in the place of the trustee so deceased, remaining out of the United Kingdom, desiring to be discharged, refusing, or being unfit or incapable, or being an infant, as aforesaid.

(2) Where a trustee has been removed under a power contained in the instrument creating the trust, a new trustee or new trustees may be appointed in the place of the trustee who is removed, as if he were dead ...

...

(7) Every new trustee appointed under this section as well before as after all the trust property becomes by law, or by assurance, or otherwise, vested in him, shall have the same powers, authorities, and discretions, and may in all respects act, as if he had been originally appointed a trustee by the instrument, if any, creating the trust.

The court has jurisdiction to remove trustees, where it is clear that their continuance in office would be detrimental to the execution of the trust (see *Letterstedt v Broers* (1884) LR 9 App Cas 371), and may appoint new trustees where it is expedient to do so *and* it is inexpedient, difficult or impracticable to do so without the court's assistance, in particular where the existing trustee is mentally ill or bankrupt: see section 41 of the Trustee Act 1925 and *Re Tempest* (1866) LR 1 Ch 485. Moreover, where the settlor has not provided for somebody to decide upon the appointment of new trustees, the beneficiaries, if all of full age, sound mind and together absolutely entitled to the trust property, can by writing direct existing trustees to retire or to appoint new trustees: section 19 of the Trusts of Land and Appointment of Trustees Act 1996.

Where there is more than one trustee, the trustees will hold the trust property as joint tenants. The essence of joint tenancy is that none of the individual co-owners is regarded as having his own distinct interest or share in the property, which would then pass to his successors on his death. Instead, the death of one joint tenant simply leaves the title in the surviving owner(s). Therefore, where one trustee dies, he simply falls out of the picture, leaving the trust property vested in the remaining trustee(s). It is only where the last remaining trustee dies that title to the trust property passes to, and the role of trustee is cast onto, the personal representative of the deceased trustee.

12.3 The variation of trusts

It is for the settlor to fix the terms of the trust. However, given that trusts often have a long lifetime, changing and unforeseen circumstances may lead to the original trust terms becoming unsuited to securing the benefits, which the trust was set up to provide to the beneficiaries. In other words, terms which seemed a good idea at the time may become obstacles both to effectuating the settlor's basic intentions and to advancing the interests of the beneficiaries. So, for instance, the settlor may have prohibited investment in a certain type of commodity because the market was, at the time, notoriously unstable and so such investments would pose too great a risk to the trust fund. However, years down the line it may be that the risks of such investments have largely disappeared, such that the prohibition, rather than protecting the beneficiaries, merely shuts off one potential route by which their interests could be served.

The courts are able to vary the terms of trusts in cases of unforeseen emergency (see eg *Re New* [1901] 1 Ch 534) and expediency (section 57 of the Trustee Act 1925). For the most part, this jurisdiction stretches only to extending the trustees' management powers, and so does not authorise variations to the quantum or form of the beneficiaries' interests under the trust: *Chapman v Chapman* [1954] AC 429. One exception, however, is that, where a trust for a family provides that the income from the trust property is to be accumulated rather than distributed to the beneficiaries as and when it accrues, the court may nonetheless authorise the trustees to make immediate payments to child beneficiaries to ensure that they are adequately provided for.

Another possibility is for the beneficiaries to bring about such a variation through exercise of their *Saunders v Vautier* rights (Section 2.7). This right enables them to bring the trust to an end, leaving them free to resettle the property on new trusts on their new, preferred terms. However, this option is available only where all the beneficiaries are of full age and sound mind, and hence capable of exercising such rights. It will not be possible where there are minor beneficiaries, or beneficiaries who are mentally ill or incapable. These gaps are filled by the Variation of Trusts Act 1958. This effectively empowers the court to provide consent on behalf, and for the benefit, of those who cannot exercise their *Saunders v Vautier* rights for themselves (eg children and the mentally ill, plus others who are merely potential beneficiaries under the trust), and thereby to authorise variations of trusts. Consistent with this, the Act cannot be used to authorise variations in the absence of the consent of all beneficiaries who *are* of full age and sound mind, just because it is impractical to obtain their consent or because a minority of them refuse to consent, to the detriment of the interests of the majority.

As noted earlier, the court will authorise a proposed variation only where this is for the benefit of those beneficiaries who are unable to consent to it themselves (cf section 1(1)(d) of the Act). The courts have made clear that benefit is not to be assessed solely in financial terms and extends, in appropriate cases, to physical, emotional or even 'moral' well-being. For instance, in *Re Weston's Settlements* [1969] 1 Ch 223, the court refused to endorse a proposed variation, which would have been financially advantageous to the child beneficiaries but which would have required them to relocate to Jersey. Another example is provided by *Re Remnant's Settlement Trusts* [1970] Ch 360, in which the court accepted a proposal to strike out an original term of the trust, which would have denied an interest to any child who was or married a practising Catholic. One half of the family was brought up Protestant and the other half Catholic, and so the variation deprived the Protestant children of property which would otherwise have come their way. Nonetheless, the court considered that, despite being to their financial disadvantage, the variation was to their benefit as it would promote familial harmony and marital choice (though compare *Re Tinker's Settlement* [1960] 1 WLR 1011).

Many variations authorised by the courts under the 1958 Act will deal with unforeseen eventualities and would have been supported by the settlor had he taken such matters into consideration. However, as cases like *Re Remnant's Settlement Trusts* show, the courts' powers under the Act extend beyond such cases, and they may accept proposals to vary trusts even where this is plainly inconsistent with the settlor's intentions. Rather, the settlor's intentions are relevant only where and to the extent that they shed light on what would be beneficial to the relevant beneficiaries (*Goulding v James* [1997] 2 All ER 239). This is consistent with the rule in *Saunders v Vautier*, which, as we have seen (Section 2.7), provides an example of the courts resolving conflicts between, on the one hand, the beneficiary's interests and wishes, and, on the other, the intentions of the settlor in favour of the beneficiary.

One tension appears to exist between the rule in *Saunders v Vautier* and the provisions of the Variation of Trusts Act 1958. Despite the wide wording of the statute ('the court may ... approve ... any arrangement ... varying or revoking all or any of the trusts'), it has been held that the Act cannot be used to revoke completely the existing trusts and to institute entirely new ones: see eg *Re T's Settlement Trusts* [1964] Ch 158; *Re Holt's Settlement* [1969] 1 Ch 590. (On the question whether a proposed 'variation' really amounts to a revocation, see *Re Ball's Settlement* [1968] 1 WLR 899.) If this is correct then it leaves us in the odd position that, where all the beneficiaries are of full age and sound mind, and so able to exercise their *Saunders v Vautier* rights, their only option is a complete revocation and resettlement; whereas where one or more is not of full capacity, and so the Act must be relied on, only a variation of the existing trusts is possible. In principle, there is no sound reason both options should not be available in both cases.

12.4 Delegation of trustees' powers

A trustee may want to delegate his powers for two main reasons. He may be unable to discharge his duties for a period of time, perhaps owing to temporary illness or absence from the country. Alternatively, he may want to delegate specific powers, say powers of investment, which he does not have the expertise to discharge. There are two principal ways by which trustees can delegate their powers, namely under the Trustee Act 1925 and under the Trustee Act 2000.

Section 25 of the Trustee Act 1925 permits a trustee, acting by power of attorney, to delegate all of his functions to any other person (known as the 'donee') for a period of 12 months or less. Notice of the trustee's appointment of a donee must be given to all other trustees and to any person who has the power to appoint new trustees under the trust. Such notice must be given before or within seven days of the date on which the appointment is made, and must give information as to 'the date on which the power comes into operation and its duration, the donee of the power, the reason why the power is given and, where [only some of the trustee's powers] are delegated, the trusts, powers and discretions delegated': see section 25(4) of the Act. There is no restriction on the powers which can be delegated under section 25, or on the type of people who can be appointed as donee (which can include a co-trustee or a beneficiary), although a trustee who delegates his powers under this section is liable for the acts and omissions of the donee as if they were his own acts or omissions: see section 25(7) of the Act. This last rule means that section 25 is, in practice, an unpopular means of delegating a trustee's powers.

The other important enactment under which trustees can delegate certain more limited functions is the Trustee Act 2000 (although, in relation to trusts of land, see also section 1 of the Trustee Delegation Act 1999). So long as the requirements of Part IV of the 2000 Act are complied with, trustees can delegate any of their delegable functions to an agent. In the case of a private trust, the delegable functions consist of any function except the following (see section 11(2)):

1. any function relating to whether or in what way any assets of the trust should be distributed;
2. any power to decide whether any fees or other payment due to be made out of the trust funds should be made out of income or capital;
3. any power to appoint a person to be a trustee of the trust; or
4. any power conferred by any other enactment or the trust instrument which permits the trustees to delegate any of their functions or to appoint a person to act as a nominee or custodian.

Broadly speaking, then, a trustee's administrative, but not dispositive, functions can be delegated under the powers contained in the 2000 Act. It is noteworthy that these powers of delegation extend to the appointment of nominees or custodians to hold trust property on behalf of trustees. Delegable functions are defined more restrictively in respect of charitable trusts: see section 11(3).

A trustee can delegate functions to another trustee under section 11, although not to a beneficiary (regardless of whether that beneficiary is also a trustee): section 12. The agent to whom functions are delegated must comply with any guidance the Act gives in relation to the exercise of such functions: section 13. Thus, for example, an agent to whom a trustee's general power of investment is delegated must make investments in accordance with the section 4 standard investment criteria.

Trustees must, of course, act in accordance with the section 1 duty of care when appointing agents, by exercising such care and skill as is reasonable in the circumstances. To take an extreme example, a trustee cannot appoint a family friend with no investment experience to exercise his general powers of investment over a large trust fund: section 23. But if a trustee has acted in accordance with his duty of care, he is not liable for losses caused by the agent's subsequent negligence. It is for this reason that appointment of an agent under the 2000 Act is a more attractive course than appointing a donee under the 1925 Act.

Trustees will, of course, have to negotiate specific contractual terms with those that they wish to appoint as agents (for instance, terms as to the duration of the agent's appointment and as to what he will be paid for doing the job). Trustees are, generally speaking, given a relatively wide discretion when negotiating such terms, although they cannot agree, unless reasonably necessary, to terms allowing an agent to appoint a substitute, allowing an agent to act where he has a conflict of interests or allowing an agent to restrict his liability to the trustees or beneficiaries of the trust: section 14.

Special restrictions apply to the delegation of asset management powers. Here, trustees are obliged to produce a policy statement explaining how asset management functions are to be exercised: section 15(2)(a). Any agreement with an agent covering asset management powers must be in writing and must include a term that the agent will comply with the requirements of the trustee's policy statement or any updated version of it: see section 15(1) and (2).

12.5 Powers of maintenance

Trustees often hold property for minor beneficiaries. This gives rise to obvious difficulties. It is clearly not sensible to transfer to a minor property in which he has an absolute interest. In fact, trustees assume no obligation to do so until the minor attains the age of majority, that is, 18 years of age. Likewise, it will not be sensible to transfer income that arises in respect of property over which a minor has a life interest to that minor.

Trustees' duties to deal with income arising in trusts in which a minor has an interest are provided for, subject to any contrary term contained in the trust instrument, by section 31 of the Trustee Act 1925. Section 31(1) covers how a trustee should deal with property held on trust for a minor who has 'any interest whatsoever', whether vested (eg on trust for 'my son' or for 'my son for life') or, provided it satisfies the requirements of section 31(3), contingent (eg on trust for 'my son for life if he attains the age of 27'). If these conditions are satisfied, the trustees may, during the beneficiary's infancy, pay such income as they deem reasonable to his parent or guardian, or otherwise for or towards his maintenance, education or benefit: see section 31(1). In making the decision as to whether such payments should be made, trustees must take into account the age of the infant, his requirements and the circumstances of the case (including whether income from other sources can be applied for the same purposes). (It should be noted that the Law Commission (2011) has recently recommended changing the wording of s 31, replacing the reference that the income so applied must be 'reasonable', with such income 'as the trustees think fit' and removing the list of factors trustees ought consider when making such a decision.) If trustees do not apply income for the maintenance of a minor in one year, they must accumulate it. Nevertheless, trustees can, during an infant's minority, still apply income accumulated during any previous year for his benefit in a subsequent year: see section 31(2).

If a beneficiary is absolutely entitled to the entirety of a trust fund upon marriage (which includes entering into a civil partnership) or reaching the age of 18, or if he is entitled to a vested life interest in that trust fund during his minority, he must be paid all income that has been accumulated under the power of maintenance upon reaching the age of 18 or upon marrying at a younger age. If, on the other hand, the beneficiary does not satisfy these conditions, the accumulations must be added to the other capital held by the trustees. For this reason, trustees are well advised to consider appointing all accumulated income in favour of beneficiaries who are not entitled to accumulated income shortly before they reach their eighteenth birthday, for once this age is reached the power will disappear.

12.6 Powers of advancement

It may often be sensible for a trustee to apply trust capital to a beneficiary sooner rather than later. For example, a beneficiary whose interest is contingent upon him reaching the age of 40 may need funds to start a business or enter a profession before he reaches that age. Alternatively, a beneficiary with an entitlement to an interest in remainder, subject to a life interest in favour of a life tenant who is of the same age, will not derive any personal benefit from his interest if he dies before the life tenant.

In order to cater for such circumstances, section 32 of the Trustee Act 1925 gives trustees a power to pay or apply any capital money subject to a trust for the advancement or benefit of a beneficiary with an absolute or contingent interest. This power applies notwithstanding that the interest of such a beneficiary is 'liable to be defeated by the exercise of a power of appointment or revocation or to be diminished by the increase of the class to which he belongs': see section 32(1).

Section 32 imposes limits on the scope of the power of advancement. First, money paid or applied for the advancement of a beneficiary is not allowed to exceed one half of the value of that beneficiary's presumptive or vested share in the trust property. Therefore, if a beneficiary has a contingent interest in a trust fund currently valued at £100,000, he can only be advanced the sum of £50,000 (and, if such an advancement is made, he cannot be advanced more even if there is a subsequent increase in the value of the trust fund). The Law Commission (2011) has, however, proposed the removal of this limit, extending the trustee's power of advancement to the entirety of that beneficiary's share of the trust fund. Second, any advancement made to a beneficiary must be taken into account when that share falls absolutely and indefeasibly into possession (ie a beneficiary who has already had one half of the trust's capital advanced to him is only entitled to receive the additional one half later on).

The final limit applies where trustees contemplate advancing capital to a remainderman. Such an advance will have a direct effect on the life tenant's interests under the trust, as an advancement of half of the trust's capital is also likely to cut the life tenant's income in half. To cater for the potential unfairness caused by such an advancement, section 32 requires the written consent of a life tenant before any prejudicial advancement can be made.

We have seen that the power of advancement can be used for the advancement or benefit of a beneficiary. These terms have been widely construed, extending to purchasing a commission in the army, furnishing a house, establishing the beneficiary or his spouse in a business, paying debts or estate duty, or even making payments to a charity to which the beneficiary in question felt a 'moral obligation' (see *Re Clore's Settlement Trusts* [1966] 2 All ER 272). A power of advancement can even be used, if there are special personal or tax reasons, to settle the property advanced upon new trusts (see *Pilkington v IRC* [1964] AC 612).

Summary

▶ The law provides significant latitude for existing trustees to leave their office and for new trustees to be appointed. A trustee who refuses to carry out, or who is unfit or incapable of carrying out, his functions can be removed and replaced under section 36 of the Trustee Act 1925. Further powers to remove trustees exist at common law and under section 41 of the Trustee Act 1925.

▶ The court has powers to vary trusts under section 57 of the Trustee Act 1925 and under the Variation of Trusts Act 1958. The former provision permits the court to approve variations in cases of unforeseen emergency and expediency, although this does not extend to variations to beneficial interests. The latter provision allows the court to provide consent on behalf of minor or mentally ill beneficiaries to a proposed variation of an existing trust, including variations in beneficial entitlement, provided those beneficiaries who are of full age and sound mind also consent.

▶ Trustees can delegate their functions under two principal statutory provisions: section 25 of the Trustee Act 1925, and Part IV of the Trustee Act 2000. Under the former provision, a trustee can, by power of attorney, delegate any of his powers to a donee, although he is liable for the acts and omissions of that donee as if they were his own acts or omissions. Under the latter provision, trustees can appoint an agent to exercise any delegable functions, and assume only a general obligation to comply with their duty of care in selecting and appointing such an agent.

▶ Sections 31 and 32 of the Trustee Act 1925 sometimes confer on trustees the power to maintain infant beneficiaries (ie to transfer income produced by the trust property for their benefit, for example to pay for such a beneficiary's school fees) and the power to advance trust capital to those who are not yet entitled to be paid (ie to apply up to half of such a beneficiary's presumptive share to him, so that he can, for instance, start to run a business).

Exercises

12.1   You are approached by an elderly sole trustee of a significant family trust. He is very keen to remain a trustee, notwithstanding his age and the fact that he suffers from mild dementia. He provides you with a copy of the trust deed. It provides:

   (a) that the trustee is to accumulate income until 2015;
   (b) that subject to that accumulation, there should be a discretionary trust of income to the settlor's five children until 2050; and
   (c) subject to that discretionary trust of income, there should be a fixed trust for those of the settlor's children alive in 2050 in equal shares.

   The trustee tells you that he wants to apply the trust's income for the benefit of the discretionary beneficiaries, some of whom are minors, at the moment. He also tells you that he would like to appoint capital to the trust's beneficiaries within the next 10 years, rather than in 2050 (when the youngest of the deceased's settlor's children will be 50). Lastly, he lets slip that he has got the entirety of the trust fund invested in his current account at National Westminster Bank, yielding interest at a rate of 3% per annum. He asks you what steps he should take to properly administer the trust.

12.2   'The rules governing variation of trusts are frequently too inflexible to be of any use to the beneficiaries of trusts.' Discuss.

Further reading

Harris, *Variation of Trusts* (Sweet & Maxwell 1975)

Chapter 13

Breach of trust and trustees' liability

13.1 Breach of trust

A breach of trust is a breach of a trustee's obligations to his beneficiary. The content of these obligations was the focus of Chapters 10 and 11. The question now is what happens when things go wrong, when the trustee fails to perform his duties. Once you know what duties a given trustee owes, establishing a breach of duty is a relatively straightforward process, involving little more than an examination of the facts to see whether the trustee has indeed done what he was meant to. Accordingly, in this chapter we shall be focusing not on identifying when a breach of trust occurs, but rather on how the law responds to breach. Here the key questions are: What claims can the beneficiary bring? What will he recover if his claim succeeds? What defences may be available to the trustee?

As we shall see, where there has been a breach of trust, it is not only the trustee that the beneficiary may be able to sue. Trusts law provides for a number of claims against third parties or, as they are sometimes called, strangers to the trust. For convenience, however, we shall postpone examination of these other claims until Chapter 14. Accordingly, this chapter is concerned solely with claims brought against a trustee for his breach of trust.

13.2 Duties, wrongs and remedies

When looking at the claims a beneficiary can bring against his trustee, it is useful to distinguish two kinds of duties recognised in law. First, there are the duties setting down what conduct is expected of us as we go about our daily business. So, we must take care not to harm others, we must not say things injurious to others' reputations, we must perform any contracts we enter into and so on. These duties are sometimes referred to as *primary* duties, and set down the basic standards which the law expects us to meet. These primary duties are mirrored by primary rights held by those to whom such duties are owed. So, your duty to take reasonable care not to injure me correlates to my right that you take reasonable care not to injure me; your duty to perform your contractual undertakings is mirrored by my right to that performance.

In addition to these, however, there is a second type of legal duty. These are duties which arise upon the commission of wrongs – in other words where other (primary) duties have been breached – and which exist to reverse or to undo (some of) the consequences of that breach of duty. So, if you breach your duty to take reasonable care not to injure me or to perform the contract that exists between us, you will come under a further duty to compensate me for any losses you have caused me by your breach. At other times there will be a duty to give up to me any gains you have made as a result of your breach. These duties are typically termed *secondary* duties. And once again these secondary duties are mirrored by secondary rights. Your duty to compensate me for injuries you have caused me by breaching your duty of care correlates to my right that you so compensate me.

These two types of rights and duties are reflected in two different types of claims that a claimant may be able to make when the defendant breaches a duty owed to him. First, the claimant may seek to enforce his primary rights. In other words, he asks the court to compel the defendant to do what he should have done all along. Second, he may seek to assert his secondary rights, whereby he asks the court to require the defendant either:

1. to make good the losses caused to him (compensation); or
2. to give up to him the gains made by the defendant (disgorgement/restitution), as a result of the breach of duty.

The key point to note is that, with the second type of claim, the primary duty remains unperformed but the claimant ensures either that he does not lose out or that the defendant does not gain because of this.

This distinction is perhaps most clear in relation to claims for breach of contract. If I contract with you for you to build me a swimming pool, and you breach that contract by not building it, then there are two possibilities. One is that I can ask the court to compel you to build it, so that at the end of the day, albeit after some delay and only with the assistance of the court, the contract is performed and I get my swimming pool. The other possibility is that I ask for damages for the losses you caused by not building me the swimming pool. This does not give me the swimming pool I asked for, but it does ensure that I am left no worse off as a result of not getting it.

It should be noted, however, that the law does not always give claimants a choice between these alternative types of claim. Sometimes it is no longer possible for the defendant to perform his primary duty. Say your duty was not to injure me, or to keep certain information confidential. Once such a duty has been breached, it can no longer be performed. Injuries may heal but they cannot be undone; information once passed on cannot be taken back. At other times, although performance of the primary duty is still possible, the law may nonetheless decide that the defendant should not be made to perform it, usually because it would be unfair on him or because it would be a waste of resources. This is the case, for example, with employment contracts, which the courts will not order to be performed because requiring antagonistic parties to continue to work at close quarters would involve too great an interference with the defendant's liberty and too great a risk of further disputes arising. In such cases the claimant will be limited to his (secondary) claim to compensatory damages and, occasionally, a claim for disgorgement of the defendant's gains.

This distinction, between these two types of duty and the two types of claim that may be brought following a breach of duty, is just as applicable to the law of trusts. As we saw in Chapters 10 and 11, the law recognises a series of duties detailing how the trustee should act when administering the trust. So the trustee must, for example, take reasonable care when deciding how to invest the trust property, he must act in good faith and exclusively in the best interests of his beneficiary, he must distribute the trust property only to beneficiaries and only in accordance with the terms of the trust. These are the trustee's primary duties, and a breach of trust occurs when one of these primary duties is not complied with. In such cases, the trustee then comes under secondary duties to make good any losses he has thereby caused to the beneficiaries and to give up any gains he has made through his breach.

Thus, if you are my trustee and you breach one of your trust duties, I may seek, and the court may order, your performance of that duty. Alternatively, I may seek, and the court may order, that you undo the consequences of your not performing that duty, by making good any losses your breach has caused me (compensation) and/or giving up any gains you have made (restitution/disgorgement). So, very generally, we can divide up the claims that a beneficiary may bring against his trustee in the event of a breach of trust as follows:

1. Primary claims for performance of the breached duty.
2. Secondary claims, which can in turn be subdivided into:
    (a) compensation claims for losses caused by the defendant's breach;
    (b) restitution/disgorgement claims in respect of gains made by the defendant through his breach.

However, although this distinction between primary claims and secondary claims is real and important, it is often ignored or obscured. This, as we shall see, is particularly the case in the field of equity and trusts where, as so often, the terminology used is at best unrevealing and at worst misleading. Because of this, there is a danger that we will lose sight of the materially different objectives of different claims and awards following a breach of trust. So, although the terminology of primary and secondary claims has yet to be embraced by the courts and is only just starting to creep into the academic literature in this area, we shall use it here because the distinction it identifies is significant. Moreover, there are signs that the law is now starting to take shape so as to reflect this divide better.

13.3 Primary claims

Equity has long been more willing to enforce primary duties than the common law (see also Chambers, 2002). In keeping with this, it seems that where performance of the trustee's duty is still possible, the court will compel the defaulting trustee to perform. So, a trustee who fails to distribute the trust property in accordance with the terms of the trust will be made to hand it over to the relevant beneficiary (see *Re Locker's Settlement Trusts* [1977] 1 WLR 1323). Similarly, a beneficiary can obtain an injunction to prevent the trustee from distributing the trust property improperly (eg *Fox v Fox* (1870) LR 11 Eq 142). Another example of this can be seen where a trustee makes an unauthorised investment of the trust fund. Here the beneficiary can require the trustee to sell that investment and reinvest the proceeds in an authorised manner (although if the unauthorised investment is profitable, he is likely to choose to adopt that investment).

In all these cases the beneficiary is asking the court to compel the trustee to do what he should have done all along. The result is that the trust ends up being carried out according to its terms. However, on one view, the class of primary claims is significantly wider. This requires us to examine the notion of the trustee's liability to account.

13.4 Liability to account

The phrase 'liability to account' seems to have more than one meaning. At its most basic, it simply means that the trustee is under a duty to provide an account of his dealings with the trust property: how it has been invested, distributed, etc. This is a basic, albeit essentially administrative, primary duty owed by all trustees of express trusts and, probably, some trustees of constructive and resulting trusts. This assists the beneficiaries in keeping tabs on the trustee and to ensure that the trust is being administered in the correct manner. If the trustee has not kept a proper account then the beneficiary may of course take the trustee to court in order to compel him to do this. This is a straightforward primary claim. The trustee has failed to perform his obligation to keep an account and the court is being asked to make him do this.

However, more commonly the language of liability to account is used to describe a different sort of duty, one which extends beyond a duty simply to keep an adequate record of the trustee's dealings with the trust property. Take the following examples. Imagine a trustee commits a breach of duty by failing to take reasonable care when exercising his power of investment or by giving the property away to a non-beneficiary. Of course, the trustee should be and is liable for the losses caused by his breach. But this seems to have nothing to do with the trustee's duty to keep an account of his dealings with the trust property, save that a fully accurate account should say that this is indeed what the trustee (wrongfully) did with the trust property. Nonetheless, courts have typically explained the claims that follow from such breaches in terms of the trustee's liability to account.

This comes about as follows (see generally Millett, 1998b). In the first case, where the trustee caused a loss to the trust through investing the trust property negligently, the beneficiary is said to be entitled to 'surcharge' the account. This means that the beneficiary can compel the trustee to alter the accounts so that they now read as though the trustee had invested the property properly. In other words, rather than showing an investment which lost money, the accounts are changed so that they now show an investment which made the amount of money that would have been earned had the trustee not been negligent. Of course, once this alteration to the accounts has been made, there arises a discrepancy between what the accounts *say* is the value of the trust fund and the amount of money/property the trustee actually *has*, because the accounts say that the investment earned more money than it actually did. The trustee then comes under a liability to make good this discrepancy by making up for this shortfall from his own pocket. The end result is that the trustee is obligated to make good the loss caused by his breach of duty.

The position is similar in the second case, where the trustee's breach lies in giving away trust property to a non-beneficiary. This time the beneficiary can require the account to be 'falsified'. An accurate account would show that the trustee gave away the relevant property. However, as he should not have done this, the beneficiary can require that that entry be erased from the account. This then means that, according to the account, the relevant property is still held by the trustee and, as before, the result is that there is a discrepancy between the contents of the trust fund as identified in the accounts and what the trustee actually has in his possession. And again, the trustee is then liable to ensure that the trust fund mirrors the accounts by paying in the money needed to make up for this discrepancy. Once more, this means that the trustee must compensate the beneficiary for the losses caused by his breach.

On this approach, the claim the beneficiary brings in both these cases is conceptualised as a claim to enforce the trustee's duty to provide an account of his dealings with the trust property and his concomitant duty to ensure that the trust fund corresponds with the state of the accounts. And this then appears to enable us to treat these as *primary* claims, aimed at securing the trustee's performance of his (primary) trust duty to keep a full and accurate account, rather than as secondary claims aimed at compensating the beneficiary for the losses caused by the breach (although it may indirectly have this effect): see Birks, 1996a, 44–48. A similar argument proposes that claims of the second type, where trust property has been misapplied, should be understood as claims for a form of 'substitute' performance. The trustee is under a primary duty to safeguard and apply the trust property as required by the terms of the trust. If the trustee makes an unauthorised disposition of trust property, although it may be too late for him to ensure that *that property* is applied for the benefit of the beneficiaries, the beneficiary can still demand that he perform this duty by paying into the trust fund the monetary *equivalent* of the property he wrongfully disposed of. Again, the end result is that the trustee will have to balance the trust accounts with money of his own: see Elliott, 2002, 589–91; Elliott and Mitchell, 2004, 23–28.

Why does it matter how we explain the beneficiary's claim in such cases? After all, whether we view this as a claim for compensation for losses caused by a breach of duty or as a claim that the trustee perform his duty to provide proper accounts, the end result seems to be the same: the trustee is liable to pay a sum of money to the beneficiary and the beneficiary's loss is made good. However, occasionally these two different ways of understanding the claim will lead us to different results. Take the following example (modified from Penner, 2012, 331–32). I hold a valuable painting, worth say £100,000, on trust for you, keeping it in a secure storage facility. Mistaking the terms of the trust, I give the painting away to a third party who then leaves the country and can no longer be traced. However, a few days later, the storage facility where I was previously holding the painting is burnt down, and all its contents destroyed. In other words, there is no doubt that, had I not wrongfully disposed of the painting, it too would have been destroyed in the fire. What can you claim? Well, there is no doubt at all that I committed a breach of trust. I failed to administer the trust according to its terms. The difficulty is in determining what, if anything, you can recover from me.

It is too late to order specific performance of my obligation to hold the property for you. The painting has gone and cannot be traced. Equally, I have made no gain from the breach. Can you recover for the *loss* of the painting from me? On the view that yours is a straightforward secondary claim for compensation, the question we must ask is what loss has been caused to you by my breach. The problem you face here is that, but for the breach, you would have lost the painting in any case. As such, you cannot say that you are worse off now than you would have been had I properly performed my obligations under the trust. In other words, you would have suffered the same loss, albeit by a different route, in any event. So, having caused you no loss, I owe you no compensation.

The position is different if we regard your claim as a primary claim for proper performance of the trust. I made an unauthorised disposition of trust property by giving away the painting. You can accordingly demand that the trust accounts be falsified to strike off this transaction. Therefore, although the painting has long since gone, the trust accounts still say that it forms part of the trust property. My obligation is then to make sure that there is no discrepancy between the trust accounts and the true state of the trust fund. As I cannot repurchase a replacement on the market (the painting is unique), this must be done by me paying into the trust fund a sum of money equal to value of the property I wrongfully gave away. So, if the claim is framed this way, you can recover £100,000 – the value of the painting – even though you would have suffered the same loss had I not breached the trust. The reason for this is that, on this basis, the gist of your complaint is not that you are worse off, but simply that I have a (primary) duty to administer the trust in accordance with its terms and that this includes a duty to ensure at all times that the trust fund is properly constituted by reference to the trust accounts.

So, does the law allow you to frame your claim as a primary claim and thus recover £100,000 from me? The obvious question is why should it (see also Burrows, 2004, 604–06). It is true that you have suffered a breach of trust, but it is also true that this breach of trust has made no difference to you. You have suffered a loss but it is a loss which you would have suffered in any case. You should be entitled to demand performance from me where this is still possible. But the contention that you are entitled to £100,000 as a form of substitute performance of my (primary) obligations under the trust is plainly unreal. After all, in our example, my duty was not to dispose of the painting in the first place. You are not asking me to undo or to reverse that disposition. Indeed you cannot as it is too late. Therefore giving the beneficiary a sum of money, *however it is measured*, is not a form of compelled performance of *that* obligation.

Moreover, to say that the claim is for a form of 'substitutive' performance is unhelpful. The language of 'substitution' fails to distinguish, on the one hand, claims which give the claimant the performance to which he was entitled but in a different form and, on the other, claims which give the claimant something different from, and which can in no way be equated with, the performance he was due (see further Webb, 2006). So if, for instance, I am under a contractual obligation to give you 1,000 shares in X Plc, and I fail to perform, an order to pay you the sum of money it would take for you to go out and buy 1,000 of those shares from another source can be said to amount to an alternative or substitute form of performance. Albeit by a slightly different route, you end up with the performance you were entitled to all along, as you get the shares I was obligated to give to you. But this cannot be said of our example. You would get something different from, and indeed something more than, the performance you were due.

Given this, the only plausible claim you can bring is a secondary claim, complaining of and seeking to reverse the *consequences* of my breach. But then, of course, we must ask what those consequences are, and this requires an inquiry into causation. Here, you are in just the same position as you would have been had I not breached my duty. Therefore, you cannot demand that my primary duty be performed, because it is now too late, and, although you can demand that any losses I have caused be made good, as events have turned out you have suffered no such loss. In short, you have no basis for recovering anything from me. So, although such claims in such cases may traditionally have taken the *form* of primary claims (the beneficiary asking for the trust to be properly performed), *in substance* they can only be secondary claims (the beneficiary asking to be compensated for loss caused by the trustee's failure to perform). To the extent that in the past the courts have allowed beneficiaries to recover the value of misapplied trust assets, even where it can be shown that they suffered no such loss as a result of the breach, such decisions should be regarded as unprincipled.

13.5 Compensation claims

Fortunately, the courts now appear to have committed themselves to the view that, where trust property is misapplied and cannot be recovered, the beneficiary can succeed only if he can show that the trustee's breach did indeed cause him a loss. The leading case here is *Target Holdings Ltd v Redferns* [1996] AC 421. Target, a finance company, agreed to loan £1.525 million to Crowngate for the purchase of property, in return for a mortgage on that property. As is standard practice, this money was paid to the solicitors acting for Crowngate, a firm called Redferns, on the condition that they would forward it to Crowngate only when the purchase was complete and the mortgage executed. Until that time Redferns were to hold the money on trust for Target. Redferns, however, released £1.49 million to a separate company, Panther, before the purchase was completed. Nonetheless, the sale eventually did go through and a mortgage was executed in Target's favour. When Crowngate subsequently failed to pay off the loan and went into insolvent liquidation, Target was able to recover only £500,000 from the sale of the property. This left Target bearing a significant loss. It therefore sought to recoup this from Redferns by claiming for breach of trust.

That Redferns committed a breach of trust when they paid over the money to Panther was plain. The complicating factor was that, on the facts as they were assumed to be, Target would have suffered exactly the same loss even if Redferns had properly performed their duties and released the money only when the mortgage was executed. That is to say, Target would still have ended up with a mortgage on a property worth only £500,000, and so inadequate to pay off the debt Crowngate owed to it. As such, applying the 'but for' test of causation, it could not be said that Redferns' breach caused any loss to Target. The question was whether this precluded Target from recovering the money misapplied by Redferns.

The Court of Appeal had held that a misapplication of trust property generated an immediate liability on the part of the trustee to reconstitute the trust fund, which did not depend on showing that the loss would not have been suffered but for the breach. On this basis, Target was entitled to recover the full amount paid out by Redferns in breach of trust, subject only to it making allowance for the sum it recovered through sale of the mortgaged property. The House of Lords, however, allowed Redferns' appeal, holding that Target could recover compensation only for losses, which could be shown to have been caused by Redferns' breach. Giving the leading judgment, Lord Browne-Wilkinson stated ([1996] AC 421, 432):

> At common law there are two principles fundamental to an award of damages. First, that the defendant's wrongful act must cause the damage complained of. Second, that the plaintiff is to be put 'in the same position as he would have been in if he had not sustained the wrong for which he is now getting his compensation or reparation'.... Although, as will appear, in many ways equity approaches liability for making good a breach of trust from a different starting point, in my judgment those two principles are applicable as much in equity as at common law. Under both systems liability is fault-based: the defendant is only liable for the consequences of the legal wrong he has done to the plaintiff and to make good the damage caused by the wrong. He is not responsible for damage not caused by the wrong or to pay by way of compensation more than the loss suffered from such wrong. The detailed rules of equity as to causation and the quantification of loss differ, at least ostensibly, from those applicable at common law. But the principles underlying both systems are the same.

In *Target Holdings*, the trustee was under a primary duty not to pay away the trust money until the mortgage was executed. This primary duty, however, once breached, could not then be performed. The money had gone. As such, Target necessarily had no (primary) claim to enforce the duty the trustee had breached. In such circumstances, *Target Holdings* confirms that the only option available to a beneficiary is to bring a (secondary) claim to recover the losses he had suffered as a result of the breach. In this case, however, the success of the claim depends on the beneficiary being able to establish that, but for the breach, such losses would not have been suffered.

Those who argue that the beneficiary should be able to recover a sum of money equal to the value of the misapplied property, irrespective of such a causal link, whether on the basis of 'falsifying' the trust accounts or as a form of 'substitute' performance, have of course criticised the reasoning (although not necessarily the result: see Millett, 1998b) in *Target Holdings*. But, as we have seen, such arguments have little going for them as a matter of principle, and now, following *Target Holdings*, gain little support from (modern) authority.

We say 'little' support because the clear message of *Target Holdings* has been confused by dicta from some of the more recent case law. This confusion appears to derive from the following passages from Lord Browne-Wilkinson's judgment in *Target Holdings* ([1996] AC 421, 434–35):

> The basic right of a beneficiary is to have the trust duly administered in accordance with the provisions of the trust instrument, if any, and the general law. Thus, in relation to a traditional trust where the fund is held in trust for a number of beneficiaries having different, usually successive, equitable interests, (eg A for life with remainder to B), the right of each beneficiary is to have the whole fund vested in the trustees so as to be available to satisfy his equitable interest when, and if, it falls into possession. Accordingly, in the case of a breach of such a trust involving the wrongful paying away of trust assets, the liability of the trustee is to restore to the trust fund ... what ought to have been there. The equitable rules of compensation for breach of trust have largely been developed in relation to such traditional trusts, where the only way in which all the beneficiaries' rights can be protected is to restore to the trust fund what ought to be there. In such a case the basic rule is that a trustee in breach of trust must restore or pay to the trust estate either the assets which have been lost to the estate by reason of the breach or compensation for such loss.... But what if at the time of the action claiming compensation for breach of trust those trusts have come to an end? Take as an example again the trust for A for life with remainder to B. During A's lifetime B's only right is to have the trust duly administered and, in the event of a breach, to have the trust fund restored. After A's death, B becomes absolutely entitled. He of course has the right to have the trust assets retained by the trustees until they have fully accounted for them to him. But if the trustees commit a breach of trust, there is no reason for compensating the breach of trust by way of an order for restitution and compensation to the trust fund as opposed to the beneficiary himself. The beneficiary's right is no longer simply to have the trust duly administered: he is, in equity, the sole owner of the trust estate. Nor, for the same reason, is restitution to the trust fund necessary to protect other beneficiaries. Therefore, although I do not wholly rule out the possibility that even in those circumstances an order to reconstitute the trust fund may be appropriate, in the ordinary case where the beneficiary becomes absolutely entitled to the trust fund the court orders, not restitution of the trust estate, but the payment of compensation directly to the beneficiary. The measure of such compensation is the same, ie the difference between what the beneficiary has in fact received and the amount he would have received but for the breach of trust.

A little later, Lord Browne-Wilkinson continued ([1996] AC 421, 435–36):

> Even if the equitable rules developed in relation to traditional trusts were directly applicable to such a case as this, as I have sought to show a beneficiary becoming absolutely entitled to a trust fund has no automatic right to have the fund reconstituted in all circumstances. Thus, even applying the strict rules so developed in relation to traditional trusts, it seems to me very doubtful whether Target is now entitled to have the trust fund reconstituted. But in my judgment it is in any event wrong to lift wholesale the detailed rules developed in the context of traditional trusts and then seek to apply them to trusts of quite a different kind. In the modern world the trust has become a valuable device in commercial and financial dealings. The fundamental principles of equity apply as much to such trusts as they do to the traditional trusts in relation to which those principles were originally formulated. But in my judgment it is important, if the trust is not to be rendered commercially useless, to distinguish between the basic principles of trust law and those specialist rules developed in relation to traditional trusts which are applicable only to such trusts and the rationale of which has no application to trusts of quite a different kind.... I have no doubt that, until the underlying commercial transaction has been completed, the solicitor can be required to restore to client account moneys wrongly paid away. But to import into such trust an obligation to restore the trust fund once the transaction has been completed would be entirely artificial. The obligation to reconstitute the trust fund applicable in the case of traditional trusts reflects the fact that no one beneficiary is

entitled to the trust property and the need to compensate all beneficiaries for the breach. That rationale has no application to a case such as the present. To impose such an obligation in order to enable the beneficiary solely entitled (ie the client) to recover from the solicitor more than the client has in fact lost flies in the face of common sense and is in direct conflict with the principles of equitable compensation.

A lot has been made of these passages, in particular the second, which is why we have quoted so extensively from them. For instance, some have argued that Lord Browne-Wilkinson is here advocating the development of a separate law of 'commercial trusts', which only broadly mirrors the law of trusts first developed and applicable in the context of family settlements. Whether this is what Lord Browne-Wilkinson intended is highly doubtful. The better view is that, despite the expansive language and tone, he was merely noting that, although the same basic principles of trusts law apply across the board, what they actually require of the parties will depend on the context. To take an analogy, equitable interests under a trust will in all cases bind purchasers of trust property with notice that the property derives from a breach of trust, but what constitutes notice may well vary between commercial and non-commercial transactions, reflecting the sorts of inquiry we expect purchasers to undertake in each case (see further Section 14.20).

Be that as it may, it is clear that Lord Browne-Wilkinson was not suggesting that different rules applied as between commercial and non-commercial trusts when it comes to the type of claim that may be brought or the amount then recovered in cases of breach of trust (cf *Bairstow v Queens Moat Houses plc* [2001] EWCA Civ 712; [2002] BCC 91). As he makes clear at a number of points in these passages, *in all cases*, the beneficiary can recover only for losses which he would not have suffered *but for* the trustee's breach. What Lord Browne-Wilkinson is stressing is simply that the *form* of this compensation will vary depending on the nature of the trust.

In the simplest case, where there is only one, absolutely entitled beneficiary, any loss caused by the trustee's breach will be suffered by that beneficiary alone and any compensation may as well be paid directly to him, rather than be paid by the trustee 'into' the trust fund, such that he (or a replacement trustee) then holds that money, along with any other remaining trust property, on trust for the beneficiary on the same terms as the original trust. Where, by contrast, there are a number of beneficiaries with differing interests under the trust (for instance, in Lord Browne-Wilkinson's example of a trust for A for life, remainder to B), it will usually be impossible or arbitrary to allocate that loss as between the various beneficiaries. Thus, the only possibility is for the compensation to be paid back into the trust, such that it is then held on trust for the beneficiaries on the same basis as the property the trustee earlier misapplied. So, in Lord Browne-Wilkinson's example, the sum received as compensation would be held on trust for A for life and remainder to B, rather than be paid directly to one or both of A and B.

Accordingly, when Lord Browne-Wilkinson speaks of 'restoration' or 'reconstitution' of the trust fund, he is simply referring to a form of compensatory claim, whereby the trustee must pay back into the trust a sum of money corresponding to, and hence no greater than, the loss caused by his breach. He is not using this language, as others have done, to describe a claim to recover the value of the property misapplied, irrespective of what loss (if any) the breach caused.

However, it seems that the courts have not always picked up on this. The first sign of continuing confusion came in *Bristol and West Building Society v Mothew* [1998] Ch 1.

There, Millett LJ stressed the importance of distinguishing fiduciary obligations from the non-fiduciary obligations owed by a trustee, such as the duty to exercise reasonable care and skill, stating that, in relation to the former, the remedies for breach are 'primarily restitutionary or restorative rather than compensatory'. The clear suggestion here is that claims following a breach of fiduciary duty have a different aim and function from those brought after the breach of a non-fiduciary duty. Moreover, as is plain from the opposition of 'restorative' and 'compensatory', it is clear that Millett LJ sees a claim for restoration of the trust fund as something distinct from a claim for compensation. This is in stark contrast to Lord Browne-Wilkinson who used the language of restoration to describe a particular form of compensatory recovery. It would then seem to follow that, in Millett LJ's view, *Target Holdings* and the rule that a beneficiary can recover only in respect of losses which he would not have suffered but for the breach apply only to breaches of *non-fiduciary* duties. Where, by contrast, the trustee has breached a *fiduciary* duty, Millett LJ is suggesting that different considerations apply, which appears to open up the possibility that a beneficiary may be able, in such cases, to recover the value of misapplied trust property even where the breach caused no loss.

A similar position was taken by Evans LJ in *Swindle v Harrison* [1997] 4 All ER 705, who stated that, where a defendant trustee commits a fraudulent breach of duty, a beneficiary was entitled to recover damages to put him in the position he was before the breach (which he misleadingly referred to as the 'restitutionary' measure and the 'stringent test of causation'), rather than the position he would have been in had the breach not occurred. Again, on this basis, the beneficiary may be able to recover for losses which he would have suffered in any event.

Although Evans LJ thought that his view was supported by Lord Browne-Wilkinson's judgment in *Target Holdings*, it is plain that both his position and that taken by Millett LJ in *Bristol and West Building Society v Mothew* are flatly inconsistent with the approach the House of Lords set down in *Target Holdings*. There, Lord Browne-Wilkinson simply stated that, where a breach of trust occurs, the beneficiary can recover only for those losses which he would not have suffered but for the trustee's breach. He gave no indication that his comments were restricted to breaches of non-fiduciary duties or to non-fraudulent breaches, and there is no reason in principle his remarks should be so limited. The better view, supported by Mummery and Hobhouse LJJ in *Swindle v Harrison* [1997] 4 All ER 705 and Tuckey LJ in *Collins v Brebner* [2000] Lloyd's Rep PN 587 (cf *Bairstow v Queens Moat Houses plc* [2001] EWCA Civ 712; [2002] BCC 91 and *Revenue and Customs Cmrs v Holland* [2010] UKSC 51; [2010] 1 WLR 2793, [48]–[49]) is that *Target Holdings* applies to *all* breaches of trust, whatever the nature of the duty breached or the manner of its breach. As such, save where the primary duty is still capable of being performed, the beneficiary is limited to claiming compensation for the losses caused by the breach or disgorgement of any gains thereby made by the trustee. And, where the beneficiary seeks compensation for losses, he will have to show that he would not have suffered those losses had the breach not occurred.

13.6　Limits on the recovery of losses

Target Holdings Ltd v Redferns [1996] AC 421 clearly shows that compensation is recoverable only in respect of losses that the beneficiary would not have suffered but for the trustee's breach. However, only rarely does the law allow a claimant to recover in respect of *all* losses in fact caused by a defendant's breach of duty. For instance, common law claims for compensatory damages in contract and tort tend to be limited by rules of remoteness, restricting recovery to those losses which it was reasonably foreseeable would follow from the defendant's breach. Similarly, it is typical for the law to say that losses which would not have been suffered but for the breach will nonetheless be irrecoverable if there has been a 'break in the chain of causation' or 'novus actus interveniens', such as where the loss was more directly caused by the act of some independent third party. An as yet unresolved question is the extent to which such, or similar, rules apply to limit compensatory claims following a breach of trust.

In *Target Holdings*, Lord Browne-Wilkinson stated that although the beneficiary needed to show that the loss would not have been suffered but for the breach, in claims for equitable compensation 'the common law rules of remoteness of damage and causation do not apply'. The example he gave of this was that a trustee does not avoid liability by showing that the immediate cause of the loss was the dishonesty or failure of a third party, such as would at common law be treated as breaking the chain of causation. He also endorsed dicta of McLachlin J in the Canadian case *Canson Enterprises Ltd v Boughton & Co* (1991) 85 DLR (4th) 129, to the effect that the common law rules on remoteness, limiting recovery to reasonably foreseeable losses, are also inapplicable.

In so doing, as elsewhere in his judgment, Lord Browne-Wilkinson drew no distinction between different types of breach of trust (see also *Caffrey v Darby* (1801) 6 Ves 488). However, in *Bristol and West Building Society v Mothew* [1998] Ch 1, Millett LJ said that the rules determining what losses were recoverable should depend on the nature of the duty breached by the trustee. As we have seen, trustees owe a duty of care and skill to their beneficiaries. This duty of care, although developed in equity, is to all intents and purposes identical to the sort of duty of care recognised in the (common law) tort of negligence. On the basis that we should treat like cases alike, Millett LJ rightly held that there is 'no reason in principle why the common law rules of causation, remoteness of damage and measure of damage should not be applied by analogy' to claims against a trustee for breach of his duty of care. By contrast, breaches of fiduciary duty do not mirror standard common law claims in contract or tort, and, given the strictness of fiduciary duties, it may be justifiable, as Lord Browne-Wilkinson suggests, not to limit recovery to foreseeable losses.

Finally, we may note that a strong argument can be made that the application of remoteness rules and other limits on the recoverability of losses caused by a trustee's breach should depend not on the nature of the duty breached but on the *character* of that breach: see Elliott, 2002. On this basis, innocent or negligent breaches of fiduciary duty would be treated no differently from standard breaches of a trustee's duty of care. This would then bring equitable claims more into line with the common law where, as a general rule, no foreseeability limit is applied where the defendant intended the relevant loss or where it was a direct consequence of an intentional breach of duty: see *Smith New Court Securities Ltd v Citibank NA* [1997] AC 254.

In calculating what losses have been caused to the beneficiary by the trustee's breach of duty, the courts will in general make no deduction in respect of gains the trustee has brought to the beneficiary through other aspects of his administration of the trust. So, if the trustee had for a number of years invested the trust property profitably but then makes a series of negligent bad investments, the trustee cannot argue that the losses so caused should be set off against the gains he made earlier. The beneficiary's complaint is that he is worse off because of the trustee's breach. Any earlier gains the trustee brought him are causally unconnected to the breach and hence beside the point. In other words, the question is how the beneficiary's position has been affected *by the trustee's breach*, rather than how it has been affected by the trustee's running of the trust throughout. A trustee should not escape the consequences of a breach of duty simply because in other respects he has done his job well, even very well.

By contrast, the court *will* offset gains and losses that flow from the same breach of duty. The difficulty then is in identifying the relevant breach of duty. For instance, is a history of making unauthorised investments to be regarded as a single, continuing breach of duty, or as a series of separate breaches each time a new investment decision is made? At least on occasion it seems that the courts are willing to treat what may appear to be separate breaches as aspects of a single composite transaction, so allowing gains and losses to be offset. One example of this is *Bartlett v Barclays Bank Trust Co Ltd* [1980] Ch 515 (see Section 11.7), where the trustee failed in its duty to oversee and influence the actions of a company in which the trust had a majority shareholding. The company's directors invested in two high-risk building developments, one of which caused a huge loss to the company and hence to the trust, whereas the other turned out to be profitable. Brightman J held that the gain from the successful venture should be set off against the loss from the failed investment.

One final terminological point. At common law, it is standard to refer to money paid as compensation for loss caused by a breach of duty as 'damages'. In equity, by contrast, the tradition has been to avoid the term 'damages' and to speak instead of 'equitable compensation'. Although some seem keen to perpetuate this difference in language, it is needless and can wrongly suggest that the common law and equity are here involved in different pursuits. The adoption of a common, consistent terminology when analysing such claims would be a welcome move. In the meantime, you need only note that when equity judges and lawyers speak of equitable compensation, they typically mean the same as common law judges and lawyers do when they speak of (compensatory) damages.

13.7 Disgorgement claims

We have already seen that trustees, as fiduciaries, are under a duty to avoid making unauthorised profits from their running of the trust (Section 10.6). Accordingly, the simple fact of making a gain from one's position as trustee will usually generate a liability to give up that gain to the beneficiary. There may be an exception to this in certain cases of constructive and resulting trusts, where the trustee is (reasonably) unaware that he holds property on trust, in which case the better view may be that he owes no fiduciary duty to the beneficiary (Section 10.12).

Earlier in the chapter we saw that, where a beneficiary seeks compensation for losses resulting from the trustee's breach, he must show that he would not have suffered these losses but for the breach. However, when it comes to recovery of a trustee's gains, things are a little different. The courts have made clear that a trustee who has profited as a result of his breach of trust cannot escape liability to give up those gains by showing that he would have made similar gains even if he had not breached his duty. For example, the defendants in *Boardman v Phipps* [1967] 2 AC 46 (Section 10.6) would have had to give up their gains even if they had persuaded the court that, had they not used their money and expertise to take control of Lester and Harris Ltd, they would have made just as much money by investing their time and energies in some other commercial venture. In other words, the test is not whether the trustee would have made those (or equivalent) gains *but for* his breach of trust (see eg *Gwembe Valley Development Co Ltd v Koshy (No. 3)* [2003] EWCA Civ 1048; [2004] 1 BCLC 131). Rather we have to ask where those gains *did in fact* come from. If those gains *did in fact* derive from a breach of trust then the trustee must give them up, notwithstanding that he *could have* made such gains legitimately.

A recent example of this is provided by *Murad v Al-Saraj* [2005] EWCA Civ 959; [2005] All ER (D) 503. The Murads and Al-Saraj entered into a joint venture for the purchase of a hotel. The purchase price was stated to be £4.1 million with cash contributions of £1 million from the Murads and £500,000 from Al-Saraj. In fact Al-Saraj did not make this payment. Instead his 'contribution' was by way of a set-off of unenforceable debts owed to him by the vendor of the property, including a commission to Al-Saraj for arranging the sale. Al-Saraj thereby breached his fiduciary duties to the Murads, both by his fraudulent misrepresentation as to the real price being paid for the property and by his negotiation and receipt of the secret commission. The Murads accordingly sought to recover from Al-Saraj the gains he had made from the investment in the hotel on the basis that these were profits deriving from his breach of fiduciary duty. The complication was that the trial judge had held that if Al-Saraj had not breached his duties, but had instead revealed to the Murads the true nature of the transaction, they would still have been prepared to invest with him, but would have demanded a greater share of the hotel and its profits. As such, Al-Saraj argued that his liability should be reduced to reflect the fact that he would have made some of these profits in any case. In other words, he contended that he should have to give up only those profits which he would not have made *but for* his breach of duty.

The Court of Appeal, by a majority, rejected this argument. It is not open to a defaulting fiduciary to reduce his liability to disgorge unauthorised gains by showing that he could have made some such gains in an authorised manner. In simple terms, the question is what he did, not what he might otherwise have done. And, on the facts, the court held that Al-Saraj's gains were wholly unauthorised and so were wholly derivable from his breach of duty. (This conclusion has been criticised, but in effect the court took the view that the transaction the Murads consented to was a different transaction from that which they entered into and, as such, no part of Al-Saraj's gains could be said to have been authorised).

Why do we require 'but for' causation for the recovery of losses but not for the recovery of gains? The court in *Murad* considered that this rule stemmed from the difficulty in determining what would have happened had the fiduciary not breached his duty. But courts have to answer hypothetical questions of this sort all the time and it seems absurd to say that they can answer this question for the purposes of establishing a fiduciary's liability for losses but not for gains. As Arden LJ noted ([2005] EWCA Civ 959, [2005] All ER (D) 503, [82]; see Section 10.7), especially given advances in the rules of evidence and civil procedure, there is no reason to consider courts incapable of addressing these questions and, if so, the time may have come to relax the rule that a trustee's liability to give up gains does not require proof that he would not have made those gains but for his breach.

The corollary of the rule that a trustee must give up all gains deriving from a breach of fiduciary duty is, of course, that a defaulting trustee is free to retain gains which are *not* attributable to his breach. For example, we have already come across the rule in *Keech v Sandford* (1726) SelCasCh 61, which says that a trustee who holds a lease on trust must also hold any renewal of that lease on trust for his beneficiary (Section 10.6). However, it has been held that if the new lease includes *more* land than the original lease, then the beneficiaries are entitled to the benefit of the new lease only to the extent of the land covered by the original lease: *Giddings v Giddings* (1827) 3 Russ 241. More generally, the Court of Appeal in *Murad* confirmed that a fiduciary could retain any gains which are to be regarded as the product of his own skill and labour, rather than his breach of duty. Drawing the line, however, between profits deriving from a fiduciary's breach and those which are attributable to his efforts and endeavour is easier said than done.

A useful example here is provided by the High Court of Australia decision in *Warman International Ltd v Dwyer* [1995] HCA 18; (1995) 128 ALR 201 (see also *Docker v Somes* (1834) 2 My & K 655, *Vyse v Foster* (1872) 9 Ch App 309). The defendant, a director of the plaintiff company, took up for his own benefit a business opportunity which had first been presented to, although declined by, the plaintiff. The court held that, although the defendant had breached his fiduciary duty to the plaintiff by taking up this opportunity on his own account, it did not follow that he should be made to give up all the profits the business generates:

> In the case of a business it may well be inappropriate and inequitable to compel the errant fiduciary to account for the whole of the profit of his conduct of the business or his exploitation of the principal's goodwill over an indefinite period of time. In such a case, it may be appropriate to allow the fiduciary a proportion of the profits, depending upon the particular circumstances. That may well be the case when it appears that a significant proportion of an increase in profits has been generated by the skill, efforts, property and resources of the fiduciary, the capital which he has introduced and the risks he has taken, so long as they are not risks to which the principal's property has been exposed. Then it may be said that the relevant proportion of the increased profits is not the product or consequence of the plaintiff's property but the product of the fiduciary's skill, efforts, property and resources.

Accordingly, the court held that the defendant should have to give up only the profits he made during the first two years of the business.

Now, the decision reached in *Warman* seems sensible and practical – to hold the defendant liable to give up all profits he might *ever* derive from the business would be clearly excessive – but we may question whether it makes sense to ask whether (or to what extent) the fiduciary's profits are attributable to his own skills and efforts *rather than* his breach of duty. The reason for this is not that this line is hard to draw but that, in truth, there is no such line. The defendant's fiduciary duty means that, so far as that duty extends, he must employ his skills and efforts for the benefit of his principal. In other words, his breach of duty lies in the very fact that he uses his own skills, labour, knowledge etc. to further his own interests rather than the interests of his principal. So, the question we should be asking is not whether the profits are attributable to the fiduciary's skills and efforts – almost inevitably they will be. Rather we should be inquiring into the scope of his fiduciary duties: how far do they extend? To what extent do they require the defendant to employ his skills and efforts on behalf of the principal? Once we know this, we are in a position to work out what profits derive from his breach. And, if we think that requiring the defendant to give up all those profits would be unjust or unworkable – as would have been the case in *Warman* – then we should say this, rather than pretending that such profits did not derive from the fiduciary's breach in the first place.

Even where it is found that a trustee's gains *do* derive from his breach of fiduciary duty, and so must prima facie be given up to the beneficiary, the court retains a discretion to allow the trustee to retain some of his profit as remuneration for the work he put in to generate that profit. Such an allowance was made in *Boardman v Phipps* (Section 10.6), and it is more likely that this discretion will be exercised where, as in *Boardman*, the trustee acted honestly and in good faith throughout. However, as both *Murad* and *Warman* show, even a fiduciary who has acted dishonestly may, on occasion, be given an allowance for the work he put in making the profits.

Finally, where a trustee or other fiduciary makes an unauthorised profit, there are two ways in which the law might strip those profits from him. First, it might require the trustee to pay the beneficiary a sum of money equal in value to the unauthorised gain. Alternatively, it might say that the specific property (or its traceable proceeds, see generally Chapter 14) received by the trustee is held on trust for the beneficiary and so must be handed over to him. Following the Privy Council decision in *A-G for Hong Kong v Reid* [1994] 1 AC 324, which, as we saw earlier (Section 9.20), held that property acquired in breach of trust or fiduciary duty is held on constructive trust for the beneficiary, it appeared that the law gave the beneficiary a choice between a personal claim to the value of that property and a proprietary claim to the property itself. However, the Court of Appeal in *Sinclair Investments (UK) Ltd v Versailles Trade Finance Ltd* [2011] EWCA Civ 347; [2012] Ch 453 held that *Reid* does not, as yet at least, represent English law. On this basis beneficiaries looking to recover a trustee's unauthorised gains will have only the option of a personal claim to the value of those gains. This, in contrast to the claim recognised in *Reid*, leaves the beneficiary as a simple unsecured creditor and so gives no priority in the event of the trustee's insolvency.

13.8 Defences: consent

A number of defences exist on which a trustee may be able to rely when facing a claim for breach of trust. The first we shall examine is consent.

A trustee will avoid liability in respect of what would otherwise amount to a breach of trust, if he has obtained the free and informed consent of all relevant beneficiaries. We have seen this already in relation to fiduciary duties: although a trustee is not ordinarily permitted to profit from his position, he may do so if authorised to do so by the beneficiaries. The same goes for other trust duties. Such consent may be given before or after the trustee has acted. So the trustee may seek, and the beneficiaries may give, their consent to a planned breach. Alternatively, a breach of trust may be adopted or authorised by the beneficiaries after the event. In either case, the beneficiaries are then precluded from bringing a claim for breach of duty. However, it is important to stress that what is needed is actual consent. As we saw from *Murad v Al-Saraj* [2005] EWCA Civ 959; [2005] All ER (D) 503, it is no defence for a trustee to show that the beneficiary *would have consented* to the trustee's actions, if only he had been asked.

It is sometimes suggested that the basis of the trustee's defence here is that it is unfair for a beneficiary who has consented to the breach then to turn around and sue the trustee. Hence Wilberforce J, in *Re Pauling's Settlement Trusts* [1962] 1 WLR 86, 108, held that, to determine whether a beneficiary's consent provides a defence to a defaulting trustee, the court must ask whether, in the circumstances, it would be 'fair and equitable' to allow him to sue the trustee. This works adequately when the trustee commits the breach in reliance on the beneficiary's earlier authorisation, but does not do a very good job of accounting for the effectiveness of authorisations given *after* the breach has been committed. Perhaps a better explanation may be that the trustee's duties exist for the benefit and protection of the beneficiaries, and so, should the beneficiaries decide that this is not what they want, the law should respect their choice. Where a beneficiary authorises a breach of trust, his wishes effectively trump those of the settlor who imposed the relevant duty on the trustee in the first place. As such, the rule that a beneficiary can authorise what would otherwise be a breach of trust shares parallels with the rule in *Saunders v Vautier* (Section 2.7).

The beneficiary's consent will have the effect of absolving the trustee from liability only if the beneficiary was of full age and sound mind, he was informed of all relevant information and he was not subject to any duress or undue influence. Informed consent requires that the beneficiary knows of all the key facts concerning what the trustee is to do (or has done) and the surrounding circumstances. However, it appears that it is not (or need not be) necessary that he also knows that the trustee's actions amount to a breach of trust: see for example *Holder v Holder* [1968] Ch 353.

Where only one of a number of beneficiaries consents to the breach, the court may order that that beneficiary's interest under the trust be 'impounded'. This means that compensation for the breach will be provided out of his share of the trust fund, rather than being paid by the trustee. This is likely to happen only where the beneficiary instigated the breach or derived some benefit from it: see *Chillingworth v Chambers* [1896] 1 Ch 685; Trustee Act 1925, section 62.

13.9 Defences: section 61 of the Trustee Act 1925

A second defence is provided by section 61 of the Trustee Act 1925:

> If it appears to the court that a trustee, whether appointed by the court or otherwise, is or may be personally liable for any breach of trust ... but has acted honestly and reasonably, and ought fairly to be excused from the breach of trust and for omitting to obtain the directions of the court in the matter in which he committed such breach, then the court may relieve him either wholly or partly from personal liability for the same.

To determine whether section 61 will provide a defence to a trustee who has committed a breach of trust, three questions need to be asked:

1. Did the trustee act honestly?
2. Did he act reasonably?
3. Would it be fair to excuse him in the circumstances?

It should be stressed that the defence will be available only if all three questions are answered affirmatively, and the burden of proof in respect of all three is on the trustee. In particular, it does not follow that just because the trustee did act honestly and reasonably, he should be absolved from liability. After all, the effect of so holding is that any loss caused by the trustee will be borne by the beneficiaries. As such, the court should consider whether the trustee, despite his honesty and reasonableness, should nonetheless bear the loss ahead of the beneficiaries, who of course are likely to be just as, or even more, blameless (though see *Perrins v Bellamy* [1898] 2 Ch 521 (Kekewich J)).

As the section itself suggests, the courts have a broad discretion here, and it is impossible to set down any concrete test for when a trustee will be excused on this basis. A few general remarks can be made however. First, a trustee who has breached his duty of care is unlikely to be able to satisfy the requirements of section 61. Although we should not unquestioningly assume that reasonableness requirements bear the same meaning or identify the same standard in all cases, it seems improbable that a court will view a trustee as having acted reasonably despite having failed to show reasonable care. Instead section 61 will tend to be available only to those who have innocently breached *strict* duties, for example where a trustee has honestly and reasonably misconstrued the trust instrument and ended up paying the wrong person (see eg *Re Allsop* [1914] 1 Ch 1).

Second, the courts are more understanding of the failings of lay trustees than they are when a professional trustee commits a breach of trust. Consequently, it will only be in very rare cases that a professional trustee will be excused under section 61 (see eg *National Trustees Company of Australasia Ltd v General Finance Co of Australasia Ltd* [1905] AC 373; *Re Pauling's Settlement Trusts* [1964] Ch 303). Third, although it does not necessarily follow that a trustee will be excused from liability simply because he acted in reliance on professional advice, a trustee, particularly if inexperienced and inexpert, who has so relied on the advice of a professional when (unwittingly) committing a breach of trust will find it easier to satisfy the requirements of section 61: see *Marsden v Regan* [1954] 1 WLR 423.

13.10 Exclusion clauses

A settlor who wishes to create a trust, but who does not want to act as trustee himself, will usually obtain his intended trustee's consent before declaring the trust and transferring the property to him. (If he does not, and the intended trustee does not want to take on the job, the trust will not fail. Although nobody can be made an express trustee against his will, it is a basic principle of trusts law that a trust will not fail for want of a trustee. Instead a new trustee will be appointed: see generally Section 12.2.) Where the settlor does first approach the trustee, the intended trustee may say that he is willing to act as trustee only on certain conditions. As we have seen, trusteeship is onerous and trustees' duties, in particular fiduciary duties, are strict. This can make acting as trustee an unattractive proposition.

One thing the trustee may ask for, to make taking on such a job more appealing, is that he receives some form of payment for the work he is to do. Although trustees, as fiduciaries, are normally prohibited from profiting from their position, they are entitled to be paid for their work if the settlor agrees (Section 10.8). Another thing a trustee may demand in return for taking on the role of trustee is that he is shielded from some of the duties and liabilities which ordinarily attach to trustees. In other words, he may ask that it be made a term of the trust that he is spared some of the duties to which trustees are normally subject, or that he should not be liable for certain breaches of those duties. So, for example, a trustee will normally be expected to exercise reasonable care and skill in his running of the trust, and will be liable for any losses caused by a failure to exercise such care. However, the trustee may ask either that no such duty of care is imposed on him in the first place (in which case, a failure to take reasonable care does not constitute a breach of trust), or that he is excused from having to compensate the beneficiaries in the event that he does act carelessly (meaning that, although the trustee remains under a duty to take reasonable care, no liability will attach to him if he breaches it). Such provisions are typically referred to as exclusion or exemption clauses.

Of course, faced with such demands, the settlor may choose to go elsewhere and to pick another trustee. However, he may decide that, even with such conditions, he still wants this person to be the trustee. If so, the basic rule is that these conditions become binding terms of the trust. Thus, as we have noted, although the default rule is that trustees are not to be paid for their work, it has been long been accepted that the settlor may stipulate otherwise, in which case the trustee then has a right to such payment as the settlor provided for in the trust instrument. Similarly, the settlor is free, as a general rule, to agree to exclusion clauses proposed by the trustee. In such cases, so far as the exclusion clause extends, the trustee will have a defence to claims for breach of trust.

Both trustee remuneration clauses and exclusion clauses necessarily work to the disadvantage of the beneficiaries. Any payment the trustee receives will come out of the trust property, and so represents money which would otherwise have gone to the beneficiaries. Exclusion clauses deprive beneficiaries of claims they could otherwise bring and compensation they would otherwise receive. Moreover, to the extent that the trustee knows that he will not be liable for his failings, there is less of an incentive to do the job well, and hence such clauses may lead to lower standards of trusteeship. Why, then, do we allow this?

One reason may be a desire to make the office of trustee more palatable. We think trusts are a good thing and that they serve a variety of useful purposes, but if such purposes are to be achieved then we need people who are willing to act as trustees. Given that the job is a tough one, there may be good reason for the law to offer sweeteners to attract people to it. More fundamentally, however, the validity of such clauses reflects the basic principle that it is for the settlor to decide upon the terms of his trust. If he is happy for the trustee to be paid for his work, or for his liability to be limited or excluded, that is a choice he should be free to make and which the law should respect. Of course, the beneficiaries may rather wish he had not included such provisions. But they have no greater cause for complaint than someone who is unhappy that they have not been given a bigger and better birthday present.

Nonetheless, in recent years there has been increasing debate as to the extent to which exclusion clauses should be effective to exempt the trustee from liability for what would otherwise be breaches of trust. The leading authority is the Court of Appeal decision in *Armitage v Nurse* [1998] Ch 241. Here, Millett LJ held that, although it was possible, provided the clause was appropriately framed, to exclude liability for negligent and even grossly negligent breaches of trust, any attempt to exclude liability for dishonest breaches would fail. This was on the basis that the trustee's fiduciary duty to act honestly and in good faith for the benefit of the beneficiaries formed an 'irreducible core' that must be present in all trusts (see further Section 10.1). In other words, a trust is not a trust unless the trustee is required to act in good faith and in the beneficiaries' best interests.

Three points can usefully be made here. First, although, on this approach, the trustee's fiduciary duty cannot be wholly excluded, it may nonetheless be limited by the terms of the trust instrument. The reason for this is that, as we saw in Chapter 10, it is possible to commit a breach of fiduciary duty even though one has acted with complete honesty and with a view to promoting the interests of the beneficiaries. Given that Millett LJ draws the line at attempts to exclude liability for *dishonest* breaches, it is still possible to exclude liability for *honest* breaches of fiduciary duty. This is consistent with the fact that, as we have seen, a settlor may provide for the trustee to be paid for doing his job, although of course he is ordinarily prohibited, by reason of his fiduciary duties, from making any profit from his position.

Second, even if we accept Millett LJ's view of the irreducible core of trusts, we may doubt his conclusion that excluding liability for dishonest breaches of trust leaves the trust stripped of this core content. It is a misconception, albeit a common one, to view the content of (primary) duties as defined simply by reference to the claims which lie following their breach. In other words, it does not follow from the fact that you cannot sue for breach of a duty, that the duty itself must be illusory. There is an important analytical and practical difference between saying, on the one hand, that the trustee need not act honestly and, on the other, that he must act honestly, although he will not be liable for losses caused (or gains made) through failing to do so. In the first case, we send out the message that the trustee is free to act as he likes, and this may very well be viewed as incompatible with the existence of a trust. In the second case, however, we are still saying that the trustee is required to act honestly – that the primary fiduciary duty exists. It is only the secondary duty, to make good losses through a failure to perform the primary fiduciary duty, which is negatived. Unless we believe that trustees are motivated to fulfil their duties only by the prospect of being sued if they fail to do so, there is no reason to assume that these different messages will not be understood, and acted upon, differently. In short, excluding liability for dishonest breaches does not make the duty to act honestly meaningless or devoid of content (see further Penner, 2002).

Third, Millett LJ was of the view that deliberate breaches of trust were not necessarily dishonest. A trustee may commit what he knows to be a breach of trust because he believes that this will nonetheless be in the beneficiary's best interests. For instance, he may make an unauthorised investment on the basis that it will bring a higher return. The courts have a rather ambivalent attitude to such 'judicious' breaches of trust. They are reluctant to give trustees the impression that they can deviate from the terms of the trust whenever they consider it appropriate, but are nonetheless aware that there may be times when the beneficiaries would not be best served by blind adherence to such terms (see eg *Perrins v Bellamy* [1899] 1 Ch 797). In keeping with this, Millett LJ held that in these circumstances the trustee could not be said to have acted dishonestly, preferring the view that dishonesty connoted either knowledge that one is acting contrary to the beneficiaries' best interests or reckless indifference as to whether this is the case (see too *Spread Trustee Co Ltd v Hutcheson* [2011] UKPC 13, [2012] 2 WLR 1360, [60]; Section 14.24). On this basis, liability for deliberate but well-intentioned breaches of trust can be excluded. In *Walker v Stones* [2001] QB 902, the Court of Appeal added the qualification that, at least in the case of professional or 'expert' trustees, dishonesty could be established by showing that no reasonable trustee could have considered that such actions were in the beneficiaries' interests.

The Privy Council in *Spread Trustee Co Ltd v Hutcheson* [2011] UKPC 13, [2012] 2 WLR 1360 has recently confirmed that *Armitage v Nurse* correctly states English law on the validity of trustee exclusion clauses. Nonetheless, many consider that the current rules on exclusion clauses set the bar too low and are unduly favourable to trustees. This question was not too long ago the subject of a Law Commission Report (2006). In an earlier consultation paper, it had recommended that professional trustees should no longer be able to exclude liability for negligent breaches of trust. However, responses to this recommendation were mixed, and in the final report the Law Commission abandoned the idea of legislative reform, proposing instead a 'practice-based approach' whereby paid trustees should take reasonable steps to ensure that settlors are aware of the meaning and effect of exclusion clauses. The merit of this approach is that it recognises that the real objection to exclusion clauses is not their unfairness to beneficiaries but the danger that they are not the product of genuine consent on the part of the settlor. If a settlor's preferred trustee will agree to take on the job only with the protection of an exclusion clause, and if the settlor is happy with this, then it is hard to see on what grounds the beneficiaries can object and why the law should intervene to prevent it.

13.11 Limitation

For most legal claims, there is a time limit within which they must be brought if they are to be successful. Where the relevant time limit has passed, the claim will fail irrespective of the merits. However, section 21(1) of the Limitation Act 1980 provides:

> No period of limitation prescribed by this Act shall apply to a beneficiary under a trust, being an action –
>
> (a) in respect of any fraud or fraudulent breach of trust to which the trustee was a party or privy; or
> (b) to recover from the trustee trust property or the proceeds of trust property in the possession of the trustee, or previously received by him and converted to his use.

So, there is no time limit for claims that the trustee hand over trust property to the beneficiary or where the trustee has committed a fraudulent breach of trust. By contrast, if the trustee commits an innocent or negligent breach of trust (eg by breaching his duty of care or by misconstruing the terms of the trust) and the breach does not leave trust property in his hands, then the claim must be brought within six years: Limitation Act 1980, section 21(3).

In those cases where the Limitation Act imposes no time limit, the beneficiary's claim may nonetheless be barred under the doctrine of 'laches', if there has been an unreasonable delay in bringing the action such that it would be unfair to the trustee to let it proceed.

Defendants who are liable for knowing receipt or dishonest assistance, although occasionally described as constructive trustees, are not trustees in the true sense as they hold no relevant property on trust for the beneficiary (see Section 9.2). Accordingly, such claims do not fall under section 21: see *Paragon Finance plc v DB Thakerar & Co* [1999] 1 All ER 625. Instead, the limitation periods applicable to corresponding common law claims apply by analogy. This again is six years.

13.12 The liability of co-trustees

Where there is more than one trustee of a given trust, the trustees are required to act unanimously. This means that when, for instance, the trustees have to decide how to invest the trust property, although one trustee may in practice take the lead in proposing and assessing potential investments, the decision to commit to a particular investment must be made jointly. As a consequence each of the trustees will be liable in the event that their joint actions amount to a breach of trust. Even where one trustee acts independently of the others and, in so doing, commits a breach of trust – for example if one of the trustees unilaterally misappropriates some part of the trust fund – his co-trustee will also be liable if he can be shown to have breached his duty of care by failing to intervene or prevent this: see for example *Bahin v Hughes* (1886) LR 31 Ch D 390.

Where two (or more) trustees have committed a breach of trust, in so far as both breaches have contributed to the same loss to the beneficiary, the trustees are jointly and severally liable. This means that the beneficiary can sue either trustee for the whole loss. That trustee can then bring an action for contribution from his co-trustee, recouping some of the compensation he has had to pay: Civil Liability (Contribution) Act 1978, section 1. How much the trustee can recover from his co-trustee will depend on the court's view of what proportion of the liability each trustee should bear, although traditionally, in keeping with the rule that trustees are to act jointly, each trustee will be required to make an equal contribution.

Summary

▶ A breach of trust is committed whenever a trustee fails to perform one of his trust duties. The beneficiary can then bring a claim for breach of trust.

▶ Breaches of trust may, broadly, be remedied in two ways. First, the court may order the trustee to perform the very duty he breached, and so to do what he should have done all along. These we may label *primary claims*. Second, the court may order that the trustee undo some of the consequences of his failure to perform his duty, either by compensating the beneficiary for the losses this has caused him, or by giving up any gains the defendant has made from his breach. We can label these *secondary claims*.

▶ Traditionally many claims against trustees have been expressed through the language of the trustee's *liability to account*. It is important to note, however, that this does not and should not have a bearing on the nature of these claims. In particular, if the duty breached is no longer capable of performance, the beneficiary is limited to recovering either the trustee's gains (if any) or the losses he has suffered. In the latter case, the beneficiary must show that he would not have suffered such losses but for the trustee's breach of trust.

▶ It is unclear whether compensation claims for breach of trust are limited in the same way as compensation claims in the common law, which are subject to rules of remoteness, mitigation and the like. The authorities suggest that equity has similar rules, but that they are not as strict as their common law counterparts.

▶ A number of defences exist to claims for breach of trust. One is that no claim will lie if the beneficiary consented, either before or after the event, to the trustee so acting.

▶ A second defence is provided by section 61 of the Trustee Act 1925. This says that a trustee will escape liability for a breach of trust if he acted honestly and reasonably and ought fairly to be excused.

▶ A settlor may agree that a trustee is to have the protection of an exclusion clause. So far as they extend, such clauses have the effect that the trustee is exempted from liability for breaches of trust. It has been held that, so long as it is adequately worded, an exclusion clause can be effective to avoid liability even for grossly negligent breaches of trust. However, liability for dishonest breaches of trust cannot be excluded.

▶ Individual trustees are liable only for their own breaches, although a trustee who sits by while his co-trustee commits a breach of trust may himself be liable for his own failure to prevent this.

Exercises

13.1 What is a trustee's liability or duty to account? Does it help explain the claims that a beneficiary may bring following a breach of trust?

13.2 Is there ever a good reason to require a defaulting trustee to compensate the trust for losses which the trust would have suffered even if no breach had been committed? Do we have good reason for holding a trustee liable to give up gains which he would have obtained even if he had not breached the trust?

13.3 Virginia and Louise are trustees of a trust for Manolis. The only restriction imposed by the settlor on their power of investment is that they are not to invest in companies which manufacture, promote or market alcohol. Virginia is a director of, and shareholder in, Y Ltd. The company is not successful at present, but she is sure that with a bit of investment it will become profitable. She accordingly suggests to Louise that they should invest £5,000 of the trust fund in shares of Y Ltd. Louise does not feel like arguing with Virginia and so agrees. As a result of the trust's investment, Y Ltd is indeed able to turn its business around, resulting in the shares doubling in value, and Virginia is rewarded with a bonus of £1,000.

    Meanwhile, Louise is in the pub one evening and gets chatting to her friend, Hugh. She tells Hugh all about the trust and that she is looking for investment opportunities, so long as they are not alcohol-related. Hugh has just set up a business, Z Ltd, to market a new artichoke-flavoured alcoholic drink he has developed, and is in need of extra funds. He suggests to Louise that she should invest in Z Ltd, although he tells her that the drink is non-alcoholic. Louise thinks this is a top idea, and she and Virginia agree to acquire £2,000 of shares in Z Ltd for the trust. However, it turns out that there is little demand for artichoke-flavoured beverages, and these shares drop dramatically in value, such that the trust's shareholding is now worth only £500.

    Advise.

13.4 Why is a beneficiary's consent a defence to a claim for breach of trust?

13.5 Is there any reason for limiting the freedom of settlors and trustees to agree to whatever exclusion clauses they see fit?

Further reading

Birks, 'Equity in the modern law: an exercise in taxonomy' (1996) 26 Univ WAL Rev 1, 44–48

Burrows, *Remedies for Torts and Breach of Contract* (3rd edn, Oxford University Press 2004), 597–636

Chambers, 'Liability' in Birks and Pretto (eds), *Breach of Trust* (Hart Publishing 2002)

Elliott, 'Remoteness criteria in equity' (2002) 65 MLR 588

Elliott and Mitchell, 'Remedies for dishonest assistance' (2004) 67 MLR 16

Millett, 'Equity's place in the law of commerce' (1998) 114 LQR 214

Payne, 'Consent' in Birks and Pretto (eds), *Breach of Trust* (Hart Publishing 2002)

Penner, 'Exemptions' in Birks and Pretto (eds), *Breach of Trust* (Hart Publishing 2002)

Chapter 14

Proprietary claims and the liability of third parties

14.1 Breach of trust and third parties

Where a trustee has breached his trust obligations, the beneficiary of course has a claim against the trustee for breach of trust. We examined this sort of claim in the previous chapter. However, as we noted then, the law provides a range of other claims against the trustee and, in particular, third parties which may be available to the beneficiary following a breach of trust. These claims can be divided into three basic categories:

1. Proprietary claims against holders of trust assets.
2. Personal claims for knowing receipt against third parties who received misapplied trust property.
3. Personal claims for dishonest assistance against third-party accessories to a breach of trust.

We shall examine each of these in turn in due course. However, first some general points need to be made about the differences in the types of claim a beneficiary may have against a third party.

14.2 Personal and proprietary claims

A key distinction that must be kept in mind when examining the claims that may arise following a breach of trust is between personal and proprietary claims. We have come across this a number of times already, notably when looking at the role of resulting trusts in cases of unjust enrichment (Sections 8.10–8.11) and at constructive trusts of property acquired in breach of fiduciary duty (Section 9.20). You should be familiar with this distinction already. However, we shall recap and say a little more about it now.

A proprietary claim is an assertion of some proprietary interest in an asset held by the defendant. In its most basic form, it amounts to saying 'that thing is mine'. So, a claim that a particular asset in the defendant's hands is held on trust for you is equivalent to pointing to that asset and asserting that it is (beneficially, and in equity) yours. The court gives effect to that claim by recognising your interest and allowing you to call for the defendant to transfer it to you. Anything that can be held on trust, that is anything the law recognises as property, can be the subject matter of a proprietary claim. This therefore includes both tangible (eg cars, houses, notes and coins) and intangible (eg shares, bank accounts and other debts) assets.

An assertion of beneficial ownership, as where you claim that the property is held on trust for you, is not the only type of proprietary claim that may exist however. Other types of proprietary interest are recognised in law, and so other types of proprietary claim can be made. We could perhaps say that all proprietary claims amount, *in some sense*, to saying 'that is mine', but that things can be 'yours' to different extents and in different ways. One clear example is that property can be co-owned (in law or in equity), so rather than saying simply 'that thing is mine', you may instead (if this is what the facts reveal) be able to assert 'that thing is half mine'. Here your claim is essentially of the same kind (beneficial ownership), just less extensive (beneficial co-ownership rather than sole ownership).

A second, slightly more complex example is where the claimant asserts a charge or lien against or in the property. A charge (or lien, the terms are effectively interchangeable) is a right to the money value of the property up to a certain sum. So, if I have a charge against your house to the value of £100,000, I have the right to £100,000 from the proceeds of its sale. This is how a mortgage of land works. It is a proprietary interest as it is capable of binding transferees of the property and because it gives priority in bankruptcy (the charge holder can take the relevant sum from the proceeds of sale before other creditors can get their hands on it). Here, the property is mine in the sense, and to the extent, that the value inherent in it is mine.

Due to their nature, proprietary claims are available only to the extent that there is property in which you, as claimant, can establish an interest. And it is not enough that you can identify property in which you had an interest at some point in the past; you must make out a *subsisting* interest. As a beneficiary under a trust, you have a proprietary interest in the trust assets, and, as a proprietary interest, it is capable of binding third parties who receive or acquire an interest in those assets (Section 9.4). However, as your proprietary interest is an *equitable* one, it will be defeated by anyone who acquires a legal interest in those assets for value and without notice of your interest. Therefore, if you are to make out a claim to misapplied trust property, you must establish that it has not come into the hands of a bona fide purchaser for value without notice in the meantime (see generally Section 2.9).

Another limitation on the availability of proprietary claims is that, even if your interest in the property has never been destroyed, your claim will also be extinguished if the property itself is physically destroyed, for example, if one's bank notes are burned or one's food is consumed. All this makes equitable proprietary interests, and hence equitable proprietary claims, rather fragile. However, as we will see later, this is significantly ameliorated by the rules of tracing, which allow a beneficiary to establish an interest in assets other than those which were originally held on trust for him.

Personal claims are different. Personal claims are assertions of personal rights. As every personal right is mirrored by a corresponding obligation on the part of the other party, personal claims also amount to claims that the defendant perform an obligation he owes to the claimant. So, whereas a proprietary claim amounts to asserting 'that thing is mine', personal claims say 'do this'. In almost all the personal claims we shall be looking at in this chapter, the 'this' that the defendant is under an obligation to do is to pay over a sum of money, measured either by reference to a loss caused by the defendant to the claimant (compensation) or by reference to a gain made by the defendant (restitution or disgorgement). This should not, however, lead you to conclude that personal claims are 'money claims'.

There are two reasons for this. First, the obligation enforced by a personal claim need not be an obligation to pay over a sum of money. Where a contracting party brings a claim for specific performance, this is a personal claim, but the thing the claimant is compelling the defendant to do is to perform his contractual obligations (eg to build a swimming pool) not pay a sum of money. Second, as money – both in the sense of specific notes and coins *and* debts such as bank accounts – is property, one can have a proprietary claim to identified money in the defendant's hands. This is a crucial distinction. Saying that you are under an obligation to pay me (ie you owe me) £100 is significantly different from saying that a specific £100 in your wallet/bank account, etc.

is mine. The former is a personal claim, the latter proprietary. The latter claim will fail if that identified £100 has been destroyed or passed through the hands of a bona fide purchaser for value without notice; the former will not. The latter will give me priority in the event of your bankruptcy (ie I can take out that £100 before your other creditors can claim any of it); the former claim will not (I, like other unsecured creditors, will receive only my proportionate share of the money I am owed, by virtue of the *pari passu* principle (Section 8.11)).

Although the distinction between personal and proprietary claims is fundamental and clear, it is important to note that questions of property law may be relevant to claims of *both* kinds. At the heart of any proprietary claim will be the question of whether the claimant can establish a proprietary interest in the relevant asset. The same question may, however, also be central to the making of certain personal claims. Say, for instance, I want to claim compensation from you on the basis that you wrongfully interfered with or damaged an asset of mine. This is a personal claim – I am demanding that you do something: compensate me for my losses. However, it is clear that my claim will not succeed unless I can show that you did indeed interfere with one of my assets, which in turn requires that I show that the asset you interfered with was, at the time, *mine*. So, although the claim is personal, its success depends (in part) on a question of property law: on establishing that the claimant does or did have a proprietary interest in the relevant asset. One example of this is the personal claim referred to as knowing receipt, which we shall look at in detail later on (Section 14.18–14.21). A key element to such a claim is that the claimant was beneficially entitled to the property when it was received by the defendant. However, unlike a proprietary claim, which requires that the claimant has a *subsisting* proprietary right in the relevant asset, a personal claim along these lines requires only that the claimant had a proprietary right in the asset at some earlier time, namely when the defendant received or interfered with the asset. It does not matter for the personal claim that the claimant does not *now* have any interest in the asset.

14.3 Tracing

So, the question of whether the claimant can establish a proprietary interest in a certain asset is not only central to the success of a proprietary claim, it is also an essential prerequisite to certain types of personal claim. How, then, do you identify property as, in a relevant sense, yours? As we saw in Section 14.2, the original trusts assets, which have been misapplied, will continue to belong (beneficially and in equity) to the beneficiary so long as they have not been destroyed and have not passed through the hands of a bona fide purchaser for value without notice. (It is worth re-emphasising here that the important question is not whether the property is *now* in the hands of a bona fide purchaser, but rather whether it *has been* in the hands of a bona fide purchaser since misapplication. This is because the effect of the bona fide purchase rule is that it extinguishes the claimant's equitable interest (see further Section 2.9). So, once a bona fide purchaser acquires the property, the claimant's interest is destroyed as regards *that* asset, and so the status of subsequent transferees (ie whether they provided value and whether they had notice) is irrelevant.)

However, a trust beneficiary can also, in certain circumstances, establish an interest in assets other than those originally held on trust for him. This is by virtue of the rules of *tracing* (or the combined effect of the rules of tracing and claiming, in deference to those who say we should not confuse the two). The basic principle of tracing is that a beneficiary can claim as his any property acquired in exchange for trust property. For example, if a trustee misapplies trust money by using it to purchase shares for himself, the beneficiary is able to claim those shares as his own.

The position is clearest in cases of *clean* substitutions, that is, where the newly acquired property was acquired in exchange solely for trust property. However, the rules also extend to cases where property is acquired in exchange partly for the beneficiary's property and partly for someone else's. For example, I take money from your trust fund and combine it with my own (or some third party's) money to purchase shares. In such cases, you will acquire a more limited interest in the purchased property (although, as we shall see, the rules by which you can identify the property as yours and what sort of proprietary interest you get in that property vary depending on whether the trustee mixes the trust money/property with his own or an innocent third party's and where the mixing takes place).

Another way of explaining tracing is to say that it is concerned with locating the *value* of the original trust property. So when the trustee uses trust money to buy shares, we can say that the value inherent in the money is now to be found in, or is represented by, the shares. If those shares are then exchanged for a car, that value is then located in the car. On this basis we can contrast tracing with *following* (see *Foskett v McKeown* [2001] 1 AC 102, 127 (Lord Millett)). Whereas tracing is the process of locating the value that was inherent in a particular asset, following is the process of locating the asset itself. So every time a trust asset is misapplied, the beneficiary has two basic options: to follow it into the hands of the recipient; or to trace its value into property acquired in exchange for it.

So, in summary, if you want to show that an asset which a defendant holds (or held) is (or was) a trust asset, there are two ways to go about this. One is to show that the asset is one which the trustee originally held on trust for you and which, following its misapplication, worked its way into the defendant's hands. Second, you may be able to establish an interest in an asset which the trustee did not, at the outset, hold on trust for you, if it was nonetheless acquired by the trustee or a third-party recipient in exchange for, and so is a substitute of, an original trust asset (indeed if that substitute asset is then exchanged for another asset, you can trace into that asset too – the substitute of the substitute).

Following and claiming original trust assets is straightforward enough. However, the identification of an asset as a traceable substitute of a trust asset and the claims which can then be made against such assets are not quite so simple. We shall examine these rules in some detail shortly. First, though, we may ask why it is that the law allows you to claim substitute assets in this way.

14.4 The basis of claims to traceable substitutes

Why do we allow beneficiaries to claim as trust property assets over which no trust was declared and in which they had no prior interest? This is a question to which the courts have until recently paid little attention. However, a sustained argument has been made in the academic literature that these claims are founded on unjust enrichment. The idea is that if I use your trust money to buy myself a car, I would be unjustly enriched if I could keep that car for myself. As such, allowing you to claim equitable beneficial title to the car reverses or prevents my unjust enrichment (see eg Birks, 1995; Burrows, 2001).

There are, however, difficulties with this analysis. For instance, if I go on to exchange the car for shares it is clear that you can then assert title to the shares. However, it seems artificial to say that, as a result of this second exchange, I have been unjustly enriched *again* (for general criticisms of the unjust enrichment approach, see Rotherham, 2002). Moreover, this explanation of the operation of the tracing rules has been rejected by the House of Lords in *Foskett v McKeown* [2001] 1 AC 102. However, their Lordships did not offer much by way of an alternative rationale, simply stating that tracing was a matter of property law not the law of unjust enrichment. As Burrows (2001) shows, this is unsatisfactory. Even if we are all agreed that it is a standard incident of having a proprietary interest in an asset that one becomes entitled to any property acquired in exchange for it, we should still be able to explain *why* this is the case. *Foskett* effectively says 'well, that's just the way property works', which is no explanation whatsoever.

Perhaps a better explanation can be found by inquiring more closely into the notion of beneficial title to property. Such title, whether legal or equitable, amounts to an exclusive entitlement to the benefits derived from the relevant asset. Now, where you are exclusively entitled to property and the benefits derived from it, it does not mean that you have to keep all these benefits for yourself. Of course you can do this if you want, but another option is to pass at least some of these benefits on to others. So, for instance, if I am the beneficiary of a trust of some shares, I could choose to keep all the dividends for myself. Alternatively, however, I could give away that money, or indeed my entire interest under the trust, to someone else. Moreover, I can choose to set the terms of any such transfer. So, I can say that I will pay the dividends over to you only if you give me something – some other property – in return. Because of this, my beneficial interest brings with it the potential of acquiring other property through exchanges. I can swap my beneficial interest in the trust property, or some aspect of it, for property you own.

In other words, one of the benefits of a beneficial interest in property is that, so far as that interest extends, it puts you, and you alone, in a position to use that property to acquire other, 'new' items of property. This is a 'use' of the property reserved for you and of which you alone are entitled to take advantage. On this basis, recognising the beneficiary as having a beneficial interest in assets acquired in exchange for original trust assets makes sense as, by doing this, we ensure that the beneficiary, and the beneficiary alone, benefits from dispositions of these original trust assets. (Of course, in relation to trusts, this aspect of the beneficiary's beneficial interest may be qualified by the terms of the trust, in particular any powers the trustee might have to overreach the beneficiary's interest: see Section 2.8.) In short, as the beneficiary's beneficial interest means that he alone is entitled to any benefits deriving from use of the asset and as one such 'use' is to exchange that asset for other assets, allowing the beneficiary a beneficial interest in such substitute assets can be seen to give effect to (one aspect of) his beneficial interest in the original trust asset.

Why does it matter how we explain claims to traceable substitutes? The reason we concern ourselves with the basis of rules is that this should determine the content and scope of those rules. So, where we are uncertain about what the rules are or what they should be, these uncertainties can be resolved only by asking what these rules are there to do in the first place. Thus, for example, if it is true to say that claims to traceable substitutes are unjust enrichment claims then it would seem to follow that the defence of change of position should apply to them (on which see Section 14.17), as this is a standard defence to claims in unjust enrichment (indeed some have gone further and suggested a radical reformulation of the tracing rules so that they square better with unjust enrichment principles: see eg Evans, 1999). By contrast, if such claims are not based on unjust enrichment, then at the very least it would be far less clear whether this defence should apply. So the question remains far from settled and, given its importance, it is unlikely to go away.

14.5 Prerequisites to tracing

It is clear that the tracing rules we shall be examining apply not just in cases of the misapplication of trust property, but also to other instances of property being misapplied in breach of fiduciary duty. So say, for example, your agent has some of your property in his possession. Normally, that property is legally and beneficially yours, and the agent (unlike a trustee) does not even have a bare legal title to the property. He does, however, owe you fiduciary duties in respect of his dealings with your property (see Section 10.13). If he then wrongfully gives away or sells that property, you can use equity's tracing rules to bring claims in respect of assets acquired in exchange for the original misapplied assets.

However, it has long been thought that such rules cannot be called in aid of a claimant whose property was taken where no trust or fiduciary relationship in respect of that property existed at the outset. Hence, the rule developed that the existence of a relevant fiduciary relationship was a prerequisite to the application of the equitable tracing rules: see *Re Diplock* [1948] Ch 465. (The common law had its own set of tracing rules, which, it was thought, were considerably narrower in that they could not cope with mixed funds, only with clean substitutions.) Accordingly, claimants, desperate to have recourse to the more generous equitable rules, bent over backwards to try to pinpoint some fiduciary relationship on the facts. This, in turn, led courts on occasion to extend the ambit of fiduciary relationships so as to allow claimants, whose claims they considered meritorious, to succeed. A good example of this is Goulding J's conclusion that a fiduciary relationship existed between the two banks in *Chase Manhattan Bank NA v Israel-British Bank (London) Ltd* [1981] Ch 105 (Section 9.17). This, however, came at the cost of a coherent and principled law on fiduciary relationships.

The position is changing, though, as a result of two factors. First, over the last few years an argument has been made that the common law and equitable tracing rules should be the same, as the process of identifying what was acquired in return for your property (ie into which substitute assets it can now be traced) is value neutral and so should have nothing to do with the way the property was held in advance (ie whether it was held by a fiduciary): see Birks, 1995, 295–300; Smith, 1997b, 120–30. Indeed, the argument has gone further and it has been suggested that the common law rules not only *should be* the same, but, on a correct reading of the authorities, *are* the same, and that the courts have been misinterpreting the old case law (see eg Smith, 1995a). This view is gaining support and, although it did not fall for decision there, some members of the House of Lords in *Foskett v McKeown* [2001] 1 AC 102 gave it their backing.

The second factor is Lord Browne-Wilkinson's dictum in *Westdeutsche Landesbank Girozentrale v Islington London BC* [1996] AC 669, 716, that a thief holds stolen property on (constructive) trust for the victim of the theft (Section 9.19). This trust relationship, like any other, then permits the application of the equitable tracing rules should the stolen property subsequently be exchanged for other property. As we have seen, this analysis has been questioned on the basis that a thief generally acquires *no* title to stolen goods and so it is difficult to see how standard trusts principles apply (which require a trustee himself to have an interest in the property). However, Lord Browne-Wilkinson's view conveniently solves the problem of a beneficiary whose property has been misapplied being in a better position than the victim of a theft. If this view takes hold, then this effectively removes the significance of the differing tracing rules in common law and in equity. This is because it is hard to think of many situations where property has been misapplied without *either* a breach of fiduciary duty *or* a theft. And if there are cases left over in which we want the equitable tracing rules to apply, then Lord Browne-Wilkinson's dictum supports the view that a *pre-existing* fiduciary relationship may not be needed.

One final argument that can be made in favour of dropping the need for a fiduciary relationship before a claimant can take advantage of the equitable tracing rules is that we already appear to be doing this as a matter of course in certain cases of resulting trusts. If A and B both contribute to the purchase of property put in B's name, B will hold it on trust in shares proportionate to the parties' contributions (Section 8.3). So, although A started off with legal beneficial title to the money, he ends up with (a share of the) equitable beneficial title to the purchased property. This looks to be an example of tracing, and yet the resulting trust clearly arises irrespective of whether there was any fiduciary relationship between the parties in advance of the purchase. Thus, if we allow claimants to trace into property acquired with their money under the law of resulting trusts even in the absence of a pre-existing fiduciary relationship, we should not require a fiduciary relationship before applying equity's tracing rules in other contexts.

14.6 Proprietary claims

Having set the scene, we can now turn to the detail of the rules on proprietary claims. At the outset, we should note that it has become increasingly popular to stress the distinctiveness of, on the one hand, the rules of *following* and *tracing* – by which assets are identified as representing or deriving from trust assets – and, on the other, the rules of *claiming* – by which the claimant's entitlement to recover such assets is determined (see eg Birks, 1995; Smith, 1997b). As a matter of logic this is no doubt true. However, the cases have made little or no attempt to keep these questions separate. Moreover, when we look at the relevant rules, it is often far from clear which should be classed as identification rules and which as claiming rules: see for example the rules applicable where trust property is mixed or combined with the trustee's own property (Sections 14.8 and 14.11). In any case, following and tracing are legally irrelevant save in so far as they form a necessary step to some form of claim. For these reasons, no effort will be made to keep these questions separate in the sections which follow.

14.7 Following trust property

As we have seen (Sections 2.4 and 9.4), a beneficiary's equitable title to trust property (whether original trust assets, property subsequently acquired by the trustee, or traceable proceeds of misapplied trust assets) can be asserted against, and enables the beneficiary to recover the property from, all holders of that property unless and until the beneficiary's title is either:

1. overreached by the trustee effectively exercising a power to dispose of the property free of the beneficiary's interest; or
2. extinguished by the property being acquired by a bona fide purchaser for value without notice (Section 2.9).

Such cases aside, the only obstacle to a beneficiary's claim to recover trust assets is his ability physically to locate them. Two points are worth noting in this respect.

The first concerns payments into a bank account. Although we tend to speak of money 'in' a bank account, which suggests that one who pays money 'into' an account is simply depositing money with the bank for safekeeping, this is not in fact the legal reality. Rather, a bank account is not a repository of money but a claim against the bank for payment of a sum of money equal to the account's balance or, in short, a debt owed by the bank to the account holder. Accordingly, when the money is paid to the bank, an exchange takes place. The payer transfers his title to the money to the bank and the bank in return gives the account holder (provided the account is not overdrawn) a claim against the bank for repayment of an equivalent sum plus interest: *Foley v Hill* (1848) 2 HL Cas 28. Therefore, as with any exchange, a beneficiary whose trust money is paid into a bank account has two basic options. First, he may be able to follow the money into the hands of the bank and, second, he may be able to trace its value into the debt owed by the bank to the account holder.

Claims based on following the money into the bank's hands will rarely succeed as the bank gives value, in the form of the right it gives to repayment plus interest, and hence it will usually be a bona fide purchaser for value without notice. By contrast, claims to money 'in' the account are in fact claims based on tracing rather than following. The beneficiary is claiming that (at least some part of) the account holder's right to payment from the bank (itself a form of property known as a 'chose in action') is held on trust for him. This would then enable the beneficiary to say that it is he, rather than the named account holder, who can demand payment of the relevant sum from the bank. (We shall examine the rules on tracing into and out of bank accounts in more detail shortly: Sections 14.9–14.11.)

The second point concerns physical mixtures. If, for example, my oil or my sugar is mixed with someone else's, it can be followed into the resulting mixture. However, it will be impossible either to identify which parts of the mixture are mine or to separate out my contribution. What, then, am I able to recover? The law distinguishes two situations. Where my trust property is mixed with the property of another innocent party then I am entitled to a share of the mixture proportionate to my contribution. So, where 2,000 litres of my oil is mixed by my trustee with 1,000 litres of your oil, the resulting mixture of 3,000 litres will be held for us in the proportions 2:1. Subsequent withdrawals or losses from this mixture will then be borne in the same proportions.

By contrast, where my trust property is mixed with the property of the trustee or some other wrongdoer (eg a purchaser with knowledge of the breach of trust) then there is some support for the view that the entire mixture is held on trust for me (see eg *Frith v Cartland* (1865) 2 H & M 417, 420 (Page-Wood vc)), although the likelihood now is that here too the parties would acquire beneficial shares proportionate to their contributions. However, the position is likely to differ where some of the mixture is withdrawn or lost. Here, as with the equivalent tracing rules dealing with mixed substitutions

(Section 14.8), the beneficiary will be able to claim that any losses or withdrawals from the mixture should, where possible, be treated as coming from the defendant's share, leaving his own intact, unless it is to his advantage to claim otherwise. So if my trustee mixes 2,000 litres of my oil with 1,000 litres of his own and 500 litres is subsequently lost, that 500 litres will be treated as coming from the oil he contributed, and hence the remaining mixture of 2,500 litres represents 2,000 litres of my oil and only 500 litres of the trustee's.

Of course, it is no longer possible to follow, and so to claim, given items of property if they cease to exist. So, if a painting held on trust for me is burned or my wine is drunk, there is (save for the empty bottles in the latter case) nothing left for me to claim. Sometimes, though, it is difficult to determine if and when a particular asset is lost. This problem is most apparent where property is used as part of a manufacturing process, such that it is combined with other property to produce some new asset. It is clear that if my property remains both physically identifiable and separable, I can follow and claim it. For example, if I have an equitable interest in tyres which are then fitted to a car, my claim is not thereby defeated and I can recover the tyres.

More problematic is where it is impossible to return the beneficiary's contribution to the finished product. These cases fall somewhere in between following and tracing. There is no exchange as such – we cannot really say that the original asset is transferred in return for another – but the fact that the original asset no longer has any distinct existence means that it raises rather different issues from a straightforward case of following. There is authority that in such cases the beneficiary's property has in essence been 'consumed' and so no claim will lie in respect of the finished product: see *Borden (UK) Ltd v Scottish Timber Products Ltd* [1981] Ch 25. However, this was a case concerning a permitted use of the claimant's property. Where trust property has been wrongfully used as part of a manufacturing process, it seems improbable that the courts would leave the beneficiary with no claim to the resulting product.

The question then is what the beneficiary can recover. Again the position is likely to differ depending on who provided the other property in the manufacturing process. If the other property came from a wrongdoer, then it would seem that the beneficiary could claim the entire product for himself. Where, by contrast, the other property comes from another innocent party, perhaps the best solution is, by analogy with the rules on tracing, to split beneficial ownership between the various contributors by reference to the value of their contributions (though note that the perceived practical difficulties of such an approach dissuaded the Court of Appeal from adopting it in *Borden*). For further analysis of this problem, see Akkouh and Worthington, 2006.

14.8 Claims based on tracing

The preceding section concerned claims to existing trust assets as they change hands and/or are combined with other assets. However, as we have noted, the law also enables a beneficiary to claim as trust assets property not previously held on trust for him, where that property was acquired in exchange for existing trust assets. In such cases, the beneficiary can trace into the substitute asset and will usually be able to treat it, and so recover it, as he would a pre-existing trust asset. Tracing becomes particularly important where claims based on following are no longer available because the original trust property has passed into the hands of a bona fide purchaser for value without notice.

The simplest case is where there has been a 'clean' substitution. This describes the situation where trust property alone was given in exchange for the substitute asset. Here the beneficiary is able to claim that the property acquired in return for the trust property is likewise held on trust for him. So, if £1,000 of my trust money is used to buy a painting, or if my shares are exchanged for a car, I can assert an equitable title to the painting or car.

Greater problems are posed by 'mixed' substitutions. These occur when property from different sources is given in return for the substitute, for example where A's £1,000 and B's £1,000 are used to buy a painting, or where C's shares and D's gold bars are exchanged for a car. Where trust property has been transferred as one part of a mixed substitution, the claims available to the beneficiary vary depending on who provided the other property given in exchange for the substitute.

The more straightforward case is where all contributions come from innocent parties. The position here is that the substitute property will be held on trust for the contributors in proportion to their contributions. Unless it is feasible physically to divide the substitute property into such shares, the likely outcome will be that the substitute is sold and the proceeds then divided between the contributors proportionately. So if a trustee, T, misappropriates £2,000 from A's trust fund and £1,000 from B's trust fund, and then uses that money to buy a painting, T will hold that painting on trust for A and B in the proportion 2:1. This means that if the painting increases in value, A and B will proportionately gain from that increase. If, by contrast, it falls in value, this loss is also borne by A and B in proportion to their contributions (although in this case any resulting loss can be claimed from T as compensation for his breach of trust).

Things become a little more difficult where the other property given in return for the substitute came from a wrongdoer (as before, this covers not just the defaulting trustee but also those who later acquire trust property with knowledge or, possibly, notice of the breach). Take the following example: a trustee, T, takes £3,000 from the trust and £2,000 of his own to buy a painting. Here, as the House of Lords confirmed in *Foskett v McKeown* [2001] 1 AC 102, the beneficiary, B, has a choice. First, he can, as where all contributors to the purchase are innocent, claim a share of the substitute proportionate to his contribution. In our example this would give B a 60% share in the painting. However, there is another option. As an alternative, he can claim a charge over the substitute to the value of his contribution. This would give B a right to have the painting sold and to take £3,000 from the proceeds of sale.

The significance of this choice is made apparent where the property has dropped in value since its purchase. So, say the painting originally bought for £5,000 is now worth only £4,000. If B could claim only a proportionate share in the painting then he would bear a proportionate part of this loss, leaving him with an interest worth only £2,400 (this being 60% of £4,000). However, by allowing B to assert a charge over the painting for the value of his contribution, he can have the painting sold and recover the full £3,000 he contributed to its purchase from the proceeds, notwithstanding the drop in value. This then leaves T to bear all the loss brought about by the painting falling in value. Of course, if the value of the painting falls below £3,000, B's charge will not give him back the full £3,000 he contributed but only so much as the sale of the painting can now raise (though again the shortfall can be recovered by a (personal) claim against the trustee for breach of trust). If, by contrast, the substitute has increased in value, the beneficiary will want to assert his right to a proportionate share, as this will give him a proportionate part of this increase, whereas asserting a charge would limit him to recovery of the value of his initial contribution.

The upshot of all this is that where trust property is combined with property of a wrongdoer to acquire a substitute asset, the beneficiary will choose to claim a proportionate share in the substitute where the substitute has increased in value since its acquisition and will choose to assert a charge against the substitute where it has since fallen in value. Where its value remains the same both types of claim leave the beneficiary in much the same position.

Why does the law give the beneficiary this choice? The courts understandably want to protect beneficiaries as they are innocent victims of the trustee's breach of trust. This being so, it makes sense to hold that, where a loss is to be borne, it should be borne by the trustee (or other wrongdoer) rather than by the beneficiary. This is the effect of allowing the beneficiary to claim a charge. Any loss brought about by the substitute falling in value is borne first by the wrongdoer and only in the last resort by the beneficiary. This also explains why the option of a charge is not open to a beneficiary in cases of mixed substitutions where the other contribution comes from the property of another innocent party. In that case, as both parties are equally blameless, we have no basis for preferring one over the other and so for requiring one to bear more of the loss than the other. Accordingly, we ensure equality of treatment by restricting the parties to a claim to a proportionate share of the substitute.

However, it is arguable the law should go even further in preferring beneficiaries over wrongdoers in cases of mixed substitutions. In *Foskett v McKeown*, Lord Millett suggested that the beneficiary is given the choice between a proportionate beneficial interest and a charge to ensure that the wrongdoing trustee does not profit from his use of the trust property. But the current rules do not ensure this. As we have seen, where the substitute increases in value, the beneficiary can claim a proportionate share in the property, thus giving him a proportionate share of its increased value. But that, of course, means that the trustee or other wrongdoer also takes his proportionate share of this increase. So if the painting in our earlier example is now worth £6,000, B would have a share worth £3,600 and T a share worth £2,400. But, as T contributed only £2,000 of his own money, this means he ends up £400 better off. If we really do want to ensure that T does not profit from his position as trustee then *all* the increase in value should go to B. This would effectively leave T with, *at most*, a charge to recover the value of his contribution (though of course this should not be available to him if the asset has fallen in value).

It should be stressed that the preferential treatment given to beneficiaries when there has been a mixed substitution involving a wrongdoer's property depends on who *contributed* to the exchange, rather than on who currently holds the substitute. So say, in our example, T then gives the painting away to C, a third party who gives no value but knows nothing about T's breach of trust. In such a case, B remains entitled to the same choice between a proportionate share and a charge as he had when the painting was in T's hands, notwithstanding that C is himself innocent.

14.9   Tracing into and out of bank accounts

As we have seen, where trust money is paid into a bank account, the beneficiary has the option of following the money into the hands of the bank or tracing its value into the account holder's right to payment from the bank. If the trust money is the only money that has been paid into the account, this is a straightforward clean substitution. Any withdrawals or transfers from the account must be referable to the deposits of trust money and so can be traced by the beneficiary. However, more commonly trust money will be paid into an account which is already in credit, or into which money from another source is later added. This then involves a question of mixed substitutions: the account holder's claim to payment from the bank derives in part from the deposit of trust money and in part from the deposit of money belonging to someone else, or, more simply, the money 'in' the account is partly the beneficiary's and partly someone else's.

The position is not particularly complicated so long as no money is withdrawn from the account. The account holder holds his rights against the bank on trust for the contributors in shares proportionate to their contributions. So, if £1,000 of trust money is paid into an account which was already £2,000 in credit and into which a further £1,000 of non-trust money is later paid, leaving the balance at £4,000, the beneficiary is entitled to a one-quarter beneficial share in the account as he provided one-quarter of the money deposited in it. Problems arise, however, where money is later withdrawn or transferred from the account, because we then need to be able to say from whose share of the account that money came. In other words, when money is transferred out of the account, how much, if any, should be treated as trust money?

14.10 Bank accounts where all contributors are innocent

As with other mixed substitutions, the courts have developed different rules depending on whether the other contributor to the exchange was an innocent party or a wrongdoer. We shall begin by looking at the case where the other money paid into the account comes from an innocent party. Say that a trustee, T, wrongfully takes £1,000 from B's trust fund and pays it into a newly set-up account. Then a few days later he wrongfully takes £1,000 from C's trust fund and pays that into the same account, raising the balance to £2,000. As we have just noted, at this stage T holds the account on trust for B and C in equal shares, reflecting their equal contributions. However, what then happens if T subsequently withdraws £500 from the account? Given that prior to the withdrawal B and C had equal shares in the account, one might expect that any withdrawals would be attributed to the parties in the same proportions, such that, on these facts, £250 would be treated as coming from B's share and £250 from C's. However, this is not what the courts have held.

Traditionally the courts applied what is known as the 'first in, first out' rule or the rule in *Clayton's Case* (1816) 1 Mer 572. This states that withdrawals from the bank account are to be treated as being made in the same order as the initial deposits. So, the first money paid into the account is regarded as the first money paid out. In our example, therefore, the £500 withdrawal would be regarded as coming entirely from B's share, as B's money was paid into the account first. C's money would be treated as withdrawn only once all of B's money had been taken out. So, if instead T had withdrawn £1,500, this would be regarded as constituting all £1,000 of B's money and £500 of C's, the remaining £500 in the account being C's alone.

What if money from two different sources is paid in at the same time? In that situation, as between those two contributions, relevant withdrawals are shared proportionately. Take the following example: T simultaneously pays into the account £1,000 of B's money and £500 of C's, and then at a later date pays in a further £500 of B's money. At this stage B has a 75% share in the account, and C, a 25% share. If £1,000 is then withdrawn, applying the first in, first out rule means that that £1,000 is to be attributed to the first £1,000 paid into the account. As the first deposit was of a total of £1,500, with B's £1,000 providing two-thirds of this and C's £500 one-third, the withdrawal of £1,000 will be treated as coming from B and C in the same proportions, ie 2:1. In other words, £666.67 would come from B's money and £333.33 from C's. As before, the final deposit of £500 from B's trust fund would be treated as withdrawn only once the entirety of the initial deposit of B and C's money had been fully disposed of.

The advantage of the 'first in, first out' rule is its convenience. Chronologically tallying deposits and withdrawals is a straightforward enough process. However, it can lead to rather bizarre and capricious results. Say £1,000 of B's money is first paid into the account and the following day £1,000 of C's money is deposited, and then years later £1,000 is withdrawn to buy shares which double in value. Applying the 'first in, first out' rule, the £1,000 used to buy the shares is deemed to come from B's money, and so B receives the entire windfall brought about by the increase in the shares' value and C gets none. The disparity is even greater if we imagine that the next £1,000 withdrawn is then frittered away gambling or on a (very) fancy meal, so as to leave no traceable proceeds. In such circumstances, B could trace his money into shares now worth £2,000, whereas C would be left with nothing. It is questionable why such unequal results should follow from the fact that, years before, B's money happened to be paid into the account a day before C's.

Of course, it is not always the first contributor who will benefit from the 'first in, first out' rule. If our example were altered slightly so that the first £1,000 withdrawn was frittered away with the second £1,000 being used to acquire the shares, then it would be C and not B who would gain. The point is that the 'first in, first out' rule leaves the rights of beneficiaries dependent on the fortuitous ordering of deposits and withdrawals, with nothing but convenience and simplicity in its favour. Moreover, the problem is not simply that the rule can lead to inequality and unfairness between the contributors; it is also unreal. Whatever the order in which the money is deposited, once it is deposited there is simply one debt owed by the bank to the account holder. That debt may derive from a series of distinct deposits but it is nonetheless one composite whole, rather than a series of smaller, individual debts referable to the individual deposits. As such, it is entirely artificial to say that the money first withdrawn is, or represents, the money first paid in.

Because of this the 'first in, first out' rule has come in for considerable criticism. Thankfully, it seems now to be on the way out. The Court of Appeal considered the rule in *Barlow Clowes International Ltd v Vaughan* [1992] 4 All ER 22. Noting the criticisms that have been levelled at the rule, the court held that, although this was the default rule to be applied where the money of innocent parties is mixed in a bank account, there are nonetheless cases where the rule should not be applied.

First, the rule will not apply if this is, or can be presumed to be, the intention of the contributors to the account. This will be the case where the contributors intended that the account would be treated as a common fund and, as such, that individual withdrawals were not to be treated as attributable to specific deposits. In *Barlow Clowes v Vaughan* itself, the 'first in, first out' rule was not applied for just this reason. The various contributors to the account had advanced money to a company to be invested as part of a collective fund; in other words, specific investments were not to be earmarked for specific investors. Because of this, the court was able to infer that the contributors could not have intended that withdrawals from the account and investments then purchased with such money be attributed among the contributors by reference to the order in which their contributions were made.

In *Barlow Clowes*, the contributors knew that their money would be paid into an account into which others' money would also be paid. As such, it made sense to ask what their intentions were (or may be presumed to have been) as to how withdrawals should then be allocated. However, in the typical case of a breach of trust, where a trustee misappropriates money from the trust fund and then pays it into his or someone else's bank account, the beneficiary never intended, and most likely will never have considered the possibility of, his money being paid into a mixed account. Consequently, the search for his intention as to whether the 'first in, first out' rule should apply will be either futile or fictitious. Nonetheless, Woolf LJ's judgment in *Barlow Clowes* supports the view that we can ask what the contributors *would have* intended had they known what was to happen to their money. If this is correct, it is hard to imagine a case involving misapplied trust money where the 'first in, first out' rule would apply.

More generally, Woolf LJ expressed the view that the 'first in, first out' rule would not be applied where it would be 'impracticable or result in injustice'. Again, if this statement is taken at face value the rule will rarely, if ever, apply because, although it is usually uncomplicated, it will lead to unfairness in the majority of cases (and where it does not, this will be by happy coincidence, rather than by design). It should be noted that neither Dillon LJ nor Leggatt LJ went so far as Woolf LJ, although Leggatt LJ in particular shared Woolf LJ's distaste for the rule. However, Woolf LJ's position has found support in later cases. In *Russell-Cooke Trust Co v Prentis* [2002] EWHC 2227 (Ch); [2003] 2 All ER 478, Lindsay J noted the readiness of the courts to limit the role of the 'first in, first out' rule, observing 'in terms of its actual application between beneficiaries who have in any sense met a shared misfortune, it might be more accurate to refer to the exception that is, rather than the rule in, *Clayton's Case*.' Subsequently, in *Commerzbank Aktiengesellschaft v IMB Morgan plc* [2004] EWHC 2771 (Ch); [2005] 2 All ER (Comm) 564, Lawrence Collins J endorsed Woolf LJ's broader statements and rejected the 'first in, first out' rule on the basis that 'it would be both impracticable and unjust to apply it'.

If, as in *Barlow Clowes*, the 'first in, first out' rule does not apply, how are withdrawals allocated among the contributors? Consider the following example. On Day 1, a trustee, T, wrongfully takes £1,000 from B's trust fund and pays it into a newly set-up bank account. On Day 2, T misappropriates £1,000 from C's trust fund and pays this into the same account. On Day 3, T withdraws £1,000 from the account and spends all that money on a lavish night out. Finally, on Day 4, T wrongfully takes £2,000 of D's trust money and pays this into the account, leaving the balance at £3,000. Of course, if the 'first in, first out' rule were to apply, it is B's money which would be treated as having been withdrawn and dissipated, leaving C's £1,000 and D's £2,000 intact.

Two alternatives to the 'first in, first out' rule have been proposed. The first is known as the 'rolling charge', 'rolling pari passu' or 'North American' approach (the last of these names stemming from the fact that this is the approach favoured in certain North American jurisdictions: see eg *Re Ontario Securities Commission and Greymac Credit Corp* (1986) 55 OR (2d) 673). This says that, at each stage, the account is treated as a fund in which the contributors have a share proportionate to their contributions. So, on Day 2, following the deposit of C's money, B and C have equal shares in the balance of £2,000. Then the following day, when £1,000 is withdrawn, this money is allocated between B and C in the same proportions, so that the remaining £1,000 in the account is again shared equally between B and C. Finally, when D's money is paid in, the balance is raised to £3,000. Of this D has contributed £2,000, leaving him with a two-thirds (£2,000) share, with B and C with a one-sixth (£500) share each.

The second approach is the simple pari passu, or 'pari passu ex post facto', approach. This simply tots up the total contributions made by the contributors and gives each contributor a share in the final balance of the account proportionate to their share of the total contributions made, *irrespective of when they made their contributions*. So, in our example, in total £4,000 was deposited in the account, one-quarter (£1,000) by B, one-quarter (£1,000) by C and one-half (£2,000) by D. The end balance of £3,000 is then divided among the contributors in proportionate shares. Accordingly, B and C would each get £750, with D getting £1,500.

As noted by Woolf and Leggatt LJJ in *Barlow Clowes*, the rolling charge approach is the fairer and more coherent one. In our example, T withdrew and dissipated money from the account before D's money was deposited. Therefore, there is obvious sense in not attributing any of the money withdrawn to D. The simple pari passu approach, by contrast, imposes on D a proportionate share of the loss caused by T's dissipation of funds from the account, even though none of this money could possibly have derived from D's deposit. However, the rolling charge approach clearly involves more complex calculations than the simple pari passu approach. For this reason the Court of Appeal in *Barlow Clowes* preferred the rougher justice of the simple pari passu approach over the complex, and perhaps costly, precision of the rolling charge method. It should be noted, however, that where, as in our example, there have been only a small number of deposits and withdrawals, and so the complexity and cost of the calculations are not prohibitive, *Barlow Clowes* supports the adoption of the rolling charge approach. This approach has since been endorsed by Rimer J in *Shalson v Russo* [2003] EWHC 1637 (Ch), [2005] Ch 281.

As a final point, it should be noted that the 'first in, first out' rule only ever applies to bank accounts (so it would not apply where, for instance, coins from two or more innocent contributors are placed in the same bag or store), and even then the suggestion is that it applies only to current accounts and not to savings accounts.

14.11 Bank accounts where one contributor is a wrongdoer

The rules of tracing into and out of bank accounts differ where the other contributor to the account is a wrongdoer. As we noted earlier, where a beneficiary and a wrongdoer have competing claims to a traceable substitute asset, the law tends to prefer the beneficiary, ensuring that any losses, so far as possible, fall on the wrongdoer. The same practice is evident where a wrongdoer pays trust money into his bank account.

Take the following example. A trustee, T, misappropriates £1,000 of trust money and pays it into his bank account, into which he had already paid £1,000 of his own. Over time he then adds more money of his own, totalling £3,000, to the account, and also makes a number of withdrawals, totalling £2,000, which do not leave any traceable products (for instance, he spent the money on holidays, meals and paying bills). The resulting balance is therefore £3,000. The question then is what the beneficiary, B, can claim.

If we apply the 'first in, first out' rule, the trust money deposit would be amongst those which would be treated as having been withdrawn and therefore lost. Therefore, T would be absolutely entitled to what remains in the account, and B would be left with no proprietary claim (although he could of course still sue the trustee and obtain compensation for the breach of trust). If we instead applied the simple pari passu approach, then B would have a share in the end balance of £3,000 proportionate to his contribution to the account. This would give him a 20% share (his contribution being £1,000 and the total payments into the account being £5,000), which would then allow him to claim £600. This gives B more than the 'first in, first out' rule would, but still leaves him bearing some of the loss caused by the withdrawals. Neither approach is therefore adequate if we want to give full protection to the beneficiary.

The Court of Appeal faced just this problem in *Re Hallett's Estate* (1880) 13 Ch D 696. The solution adopted by the majority was to apply a presumption that a trustee or wrongdoer who mixes trust money with his own is presumed to spend his own money first. This way it is only once T's own money has been withdrawn from the account that the court will begin to attribute withdrawals to B. Therefore, in our example, all the withdrawals are attributed to T, which then means that all the losses are borne by him, leaving B's money preserved in the account and allowing him to recover it in full.

This approach, therefore, does justice on the facts of our example and on the analogous facts of *Re Hallett*. However, it can easily be seen that the way the Court framed the rule in *Re Hallett* will not always favour the beneficiary and so is capable of leading to injustice. Consider the following variant on our example. Again, T takes £1,000 of B's trust money and pays it into an account already containing £1,000 of his own. Again he makes a series of further deposits of his own money totalling £3,000. This time, however, the first withdrawal T makes, of £1,000, is used to acquire shares, which subsequently double in value. T then makes a series of further withdrawals, these leaving no traceable proceeds, which end up exhausting the funds in the account. Therefore, at the end of the day T has a bank balance of £0 but holds shares worth £2,000. What, if anything, can B claim?

If we apply the 'first in, first out' rule, B again gets nothing, as the first deposit of £1,000 was of T's own money. Applying the simple pari passu approach would give B an interest in the shares proportionate to his contribution to the account, which would end up giving him £400 (one-fifth of £2,000). As such, we have a problem similar to the one we encountered in the previous example and which faced the court in *Re Hallett*, in that neither of the traditional approaches adequately protects B. However, if we apply the solution set down in *Re Hallett*, whereby T is presumed to spend his own money first, B is this time left with nothing. The shares were bought from the first withdrawal from the account, and so should be treated as purchased with T's own money. B's money is then to be treated as falling within the money later withdrawn and lost.

This problem came before the court in *Re Oatway* [1903] 2 Ch 356. Joyce J held that the following approach was to be adopted where a trustee has paid trust money into his bank account ([1903] 2 Ch 356, 360):

> If, then, the trustee pays in further sums, and from time to time draws out money by cheques, but leaves a balance to the credit of the account, it is settled that he is not entitled to have the [first in, first out] rule in *Clayton's Case* applied so as to maintain that the sums which have been drawn out and paid away so as to be incapable of being recovered represented pro tanto the trust money, and that the balance remaining is not trust money, but represents only his own moneys paid into the account.... It is, in my opinion, equally clear that when any of the money drawn out has been invested, and the investment remains in the name or under the control of the trustee, the rest of the balance having been afterwards dissipated by him, he cannot maintain that the investment which remains represents his own money alone, and that what has been spent and can no longer be traced and recovered was the money belonging to the trust.

> In other words, when the private money of the trustee and that which he held in a fiduciary capacity have been mixed in the same banking account, from which various payments have from time to time been made, then, in order to determine to whom any remaining balance or any investment that may have been paid for out of the account ought to be deemed to belong, the trustee must be debited with all the sums that have been withdrawn and applied to his own use so as to be no longer recoverable, and the trust money in like manner be debited with any sums taken out and duly invested in the names of the proper trustees.

In other words, a trustee cannot claim that the money wasted was the beneficiary's, although the money saved or successfully invested was his own. Rather, money profitably invested is to be attributed to the beneficiary and money wasted to the trustee, regardless of the order in which their respective payments into the account were made; or, in other words, the beneficiary can 'cherry-pick' which withdrawals should be treated as 'his' and which the trustee's. Applied to our example, this means that B can say that the £1,000 used to buy the shares corresponds to the £1,000 of trust money deposited into the account and all losses are therefore borne by T. And, on this basis, although it is sometimes doubted whether the *Re Oatway* approach gives the beneficiary anything more than a charge against the property so acquired up to the value of his contribution, it should follow that he can claim a beneficial interest in that property proportionate to his contribution. Where, as in our example, B is the sole contributor to the purchase, this would mean that B alone would benefit from the increase in the shares' value.

There is, perhaps, one loose end concerning the interplay of *Re Hallett* and *Re Oatway*. If, in our last example, having made the first withdrawal of £1,000 to purchase the shares, T went on to withdraw and dissipate a further £3,000, leaving £1,000 in the account, what would B be able to recover? The difference here is that if we were to apply the *Re Hallett* presumption that a trustee spends his own money first, B would be entitled to claim the £1,000, which remains credited to the account. The question then is whether B can nonetheless claim that the money used to buy the shares, now worth £2,000, is to be attributed to the trust money deposited. In other words, does the *Re Oatway* approach apply only where the *Re Hallett* presumption would leave the beneficiary to suffer a loss, or is a beneficiary always free to 'cherry-pick' which withdrawals are to be treated as withdrawals of trust money, so that he can have the best of all worlds? In *Turner v Jacob* [2006] EWHC 1317 (Ch); [2008] WTLR 307, Patten J held that the *Hallett* presumption applies – and so the beneficiary is left with a claim against the money in the account – where the trustee has maintained sufficient funds in the account to repay the beneficiary.

However, there is much to be said for the view that a beneficiary should have the option of cherry-picking in all cases. This received the support of Rimer J in *Shalson v Russo* [2003] EWHC 1637 (Ch); [2005] Ch 281, [144] and appears to be more in keeping with the way the law responds in the analogous situation of *physical* mixtures (Section 14.7; see also *Foskett v McKeown* [2001] 1 AC 102, 132 (Lord Millett)). This would mean that, in our modified example, B would be able to assert that the £1,000 withdrawn to purchase the shares corresponds to the £1,000 of trust money paid into the account, and so here too he could claim equitable ownership of the shares.

Even on this cherry-picking approach, the beneficiary can claim an interest in withdrawals only up to the value of the trust money deposited in the account (plus any interest on such sums). In other words, if, as in our example, £1,000 of trust money was paid into the account, the beneficiary can only trace into £1,000 of withdrawals and purchases. So, if the trustee withdrew £2,000 which he profitably invested in shares, then the most the beneficiary can claim is that £1,000 of that money was trust money, and so at most he has a 50% equitable interest in those shares. Similar thinking underlies another rule limiting the beneficiary's right to trace into withdrawals from a mixed account. This is known as the 'lowest intermediate balance rule'.

Consider the following example. On Day 1, T pays £1,000 of trust money into his bank account, which is already £1,000 in credit. Then, on Day 2, T withdraws £1,500, which he spends paying off his council tax, before finally on Day 3 paying in £2,000 of his own, leaving a balance of £2,500. In such circumstances, even with the benefit of the preferential treatment accorded to beneficiaries by the combined effect of *Re Hallett* and *Re Oatway*, the most that B can claim is £500 (a one-fifth share) of the balance of the account. This is because, although £1,000 of B's money was paid into the account, when the £1,500 was withdrawn on Day 2, at the very least £500 of that must have come from the money B contributed, because T had only £1,000 of his own money in the account at the time. Consequently, B's interest is effectively capped at the lowest balance of the account in the period between the deposit of the trust money and the date of B's claim. Accordingly, if the account was *overdrawn* at any point in this intervening period, B would have no proprietary claim *at all* to the account, no matter how much it is now in credit. This rule was set down in *James Roscoe (Bolton) Ltd v Winder* [1915] 1 Ch 62 and endorsed by the Court of Appeal in *Bishopsgate Investment Management Ltd v Homan* [1995] Ch 211. As a corollary of this, sums later added by the trustee from his own funds, which raise the balance of the account, cannot be claimed by the beneficiary, unless the trustee (genuinely) intended such later sums to constitute repayments of the trust money earlier dissipated. Such an intention will rarely be present.

14.12 Tracing through the payment of a debt

Not every exchange of trust property will produce a substitute into which the value of the trust property can be traced. This will be the case, for example, where money is spent on a holiday, on a visit to a cinema or gallery, or on a meal (at least once that meal is consumed). Traditionally, the use of trust money to pay off a debt has been considered a further example of this. The payment of a debt can be regarded as an exchange, as the creditor gives up or loses his claim against the debtor in return for the payment. However, this exchange leaves no substitute property in the debtor's hands. As such, it would appear that although money used to pay a debt may be followed into the hands of the creditor who received it, there is no property in the hands of the debtor to trace into and so which could be claimed by the beneficiary. It is for this reason that it has long been thought that a beneficiary is unable to trace where trust money is paid into an overdrawn bank account. Where a bank account is overdrawn, this means that the account holder owes the bank money; in other words, there is a debt which the account holder owes to the bank. Therefore, where money is deposited in an account which is overdrawn, this pro tanto discharges the debt owed by the account holder.

14.13 Backwards tracing

In recent years, however, there has been increasing support for the view that the payment of trust money to discharge a debt need not mark the end of the tracing process (see in particular Smith, 1995b; cf Conaglen, 2011). The argument is that we should look at how the debt was acquired in the first place. If the debt was accrued through the purchase of property, the beneficiary should then be able to trace into that property when trust money is later used to pay off that debt. So if, for example, I buy a car on credit, so that I get the car now and have to pay only later, a debt arises as between myself and the vendor. If I then use trust money to pay off this debt, the beneficiary should be able to say that the car is the traceable product of his payment. This is known as *backwards tracing* and the argument is in essence that it should not matter whether an exchange occurs instantaneously – for instance, I pay over the money at the same time I acquire the car – or with a delay, as with purchases on credit. Either way, there is an exchange, and so the beneficiary should be able to trace into the property acquired through that exchange.

This argument received some judicial examination in *Bishopsgate Investment Management Ltd v Homan* [1995] Ch 211. At first instance, Vinelott J had been willing to accept what he considered to be examples of backwards tracing in two circumstances. The first is where property is acquired with money withdrawn from an overdrawn account and one could infer that, when this money was withdrawn, the defendant intended that it should be repaid with trust money. The second is where trust money is paid into an overdrawn account so as to free up the defendant's overdraft limit and enable him to purchase a particular asset. In the Court of Appeal, Dillon LJ endorsed these statements, saying that on such facts it was 'at least arguable' that the beneficiary would have an equitable charge against the relevant asset. By contrast, Leggatt LJ saw backwards tracing as impossible ([1995] Ch 211, 221):

> [T]here can be no equitable remedy against an asset acquired before misappropriation of money takes place, since ex hypothesi it cannot be followed into something which existed and so had been acquired before the money was received and without its aid.

The third judge, Henry LJ, offered no views on this issue, simply agreeing with both judgments.

Bishopsgate v Homan has done little to advance the debate on the status of backwards tracing. Not only was there no agreement among the members of the Court of Appeal on its viability, but the examples posited by Vinelott J and accepted by Dillon LJ are problematic. As Smith (1994) has noted, in the first example, it is not apparent why the trustee's intention to use trust money to repay the overdraft he incurred to acquire the asset should be relevant. After all, tracing is simply an exercise of identifying exchange products, and the parties' intentions seem to play no role in determining whether asset A was acquired in return for, and so is a substitute of, asset B. In simple terms, all that matters is what the trustee *did* exchange and not what he *intended* to exchange.

Meanwhile, the second example does not seem to be an example of backwards tracing at all. Where trust money is used to pay off a debt and that debt was generated through the acquisition of property, the backwards tracing argument is that the beneficiary should be able to trace into that property. In short, the debt the trust money paid off is the same debt as arose through the acquisition of the asset the beneficiary seeks to claim. In Vinelott J's second example, however, trust money is used to discharge one debt, which then allows the trustee to incur *another* debt (the re-extended overdraft), and it is this second debt and the property acquired in return for it that he suggests the beneficiary can trace into. In other words, Vinelott J's suggestion is that money used to pay off one debt can be traced into property the acquisition of which generated a second debt, on the basis that, but for the first debt being discharged (so freeing up the trustee's overdraft facility), this second debt could not have been accrued and the relevant asset could not have been acquired. But even if we can say that the trustee would not have been able to acquire the asset but for his use of the trust money to discharge this first debt, there is no way in which we can say that the trust money was *exchanged for* that asset.

We cannot, therefore, say that there has been any explicit judicial acceptance of the possibility of backwards tracing. However, the argument by analogy with 'standard' instances of tracing through instantaneous exchanges is strong. Indeed, if we were to limit tracing to truly instantaneous, simultaneous exchanges then, given the way most contracts for the sale of goods work (whereby title to the goods passes before payment), claims based on tracing would be very limited indeed (see further Smith, 1997b, 146). Moreover, there appear to be cases where the courts have allowed backwards tracing, though without any explicit acceptance, and perhaps without any awareness, that this is what they were doing: see eg *Agip (Africa) Ltd v Jackson* [1990] Ch 265, *Foskett v McKeown* [2001] 1 AC 102.

14.14 Subrogation

Irrespective of whether it is possible to trace through the payment of a debt, it is clear that the law provides another mechanism on which a beneficiary whose trust money is used to pay off a debt may rely to ground a claim. Where a debt is discharged by the payment of trust money, the beneficiary is allowed to take over the rights of the creditor whose debt has just been paid off. This is known as *subrogation*, and the beneficiary is said to be 'subrogated' to the rights of the creditor.

So, if the trustee, T, owes £100 to a creditor, C, and uses trust money to discharge this debt, the beneficiary, B, acquires C's right to claim £100 from T. Of course, where, as here, the debtor is the defaulting trustee this does not make much difference to B, as he already has a claim against T for £100 as compensation for the loss caused by the breach of trust. However, subrogation gives B a distinct advantage in two instances.

First, where trust money is held and used by an innocent donee to pay off a debt. In such a case, no claim would otherwise lie against the debtor (as he is not a knowing recipient (Section 14.18) and, we may assume, holds no traceable proceeds which can then be the subject of a proprietary claim). Here, then, subrogation enables B to bring a claim against a party where otherwise none would lie. Second, if T, or some subsequent recipient, uses trust money to pay off a debt which is secured by a mortgage or charge (Sections 8.13, 14.2), subrogation allows the beneficiary to take over not just C's (personal) right to recover the debt but also his (proprietary) rights under the mortgage or charge. So, if T uses trust money to pay off the mortgage he took out to buy his home, B obtains the same rights the bank or building society held against T as mortgagee (see eg *Boscawen v Bajwa* [1996] 1 WLR 328). B therefore has a proprietary claim to T's house, bringing all the usual advantages of proprietary interests over personal rights.

14.15 Tracing and the 'swollen assets' theory

Assume you receive £1,000 of my trust money and that you, although innocent, gave no value for the receipt of the money and so are not a bona fide purchaser for value without notice. Of course, so long as I can locate that money or what you have spent it on, I will, subject to defences, be able to recover that money or its traceable proceeds from you. However, say that I am unable to identify the money in your hands (you have money in your possession but I cannot tell if it is the trust money you received), or let's say it can be shown that you spent the trust money paying a bill. In both these cases, on conventional tracing principles, I cannot trace into, and so am unable to claim, any property currently in your hands. Let us further assume, though, that I *can* show that the only money you spent between receiving the trust money and now was used to pay bills or other expenses that you would have had to incur in any event.

In such cases, we can say for sure that, although there may no longer be any trust property in your hands, you remain enriched by having received the trust property. For, by spending the trust money, you thereby avoided spending money of your own which you would otherwise have had to spend. In other words, if you had not spent £1,000 of *my* trust money on paying *your* bills, you would have had to spend £1,000 of your own. As such, I can say that there remains a net increase in the total funds at your disposal, and that this derives from your receipt of trust property. An argument can therefore be made that I should have a charge over your total assets for the repayment of £1,000, being the value of the trust money you received. This does no injustice to you as it simply puts you back in the position you should have been all along, no better but no worse off than you would have been had you never received the trust money.

This view, known as the 'swollen assets theory', is consistent with the (controversial) view that proprietary claims to traceable substitutes are unjust enrichment claims (Section 14.4). In other words, *if* we believe that claimants should be able to claim substitute assets acquired in exchange for trust property because this is necessary to ensure that the defendant is not unjustly enriched, we have good reason to allow me to recover £1,000 from you in our example. This is because, even though I cannot pinpoint any particular asset held by you as a substitute of my trust property, we know that you have been and remain unjustly enriched at my expense. Giving me a charge over your total assets to recover £1,000 therefore ensures that neither you nor your creditors (in the event of insolvency) end up unjustly enriched (ie with more than they would have had but for the receipt of my trust property).

This view was given some judicial support by Lord Templeman in *Space Investments Ltd v Canadian Imperial Bank of Commerce Trust Co (Bahamas) Ltd* [1986] 1 WLR 1072. However, the courts have since retreated from this in favour of the conventional view that tracing only enables a beneficiary to establish a proprietary interest in identified assets acquired in return for trust property: see *Re Goldcorp Exchange Ltd* [1995] 1 AC 74 and *Bishopsgate Investment Management Ltd v Homan* [1995] Ch 211. Accordingly, though strong in principle, the swollen assets theory currently has no place in English law.

14.16 Trust money spent improving, maintaining or repairing property

If trust money is spent on the improvement, maintenance or repair of property then an exchange occurs: the money is exchanged for the labour of whoever is effecting the repairs. Clearly that labour is not an asset which can form the subject matter of a proprietary claim, but can the beneficiary trace into the property on which the work is performed? The case law here is unclear.

In *Foskett v McKeown* [2001] 1 AC 102, 109, Lord Browne-Wilkinson suggested that where a wrongdoer uses trust money to improve, maintain or repair his own property, the beneficiary will have a charge against that property securing repayment of the trust money spent on it. This seems to be the case whether or not the expenditure increases the value of the property. If the work does increase the value of the property, there is a good argument that the beneficiary should have the option of a charge over the property to secure a claim to the value of this increase, in order to ensure that the wrongdoer does not profit from his use of the trust money. Sir Richard Scott VC, in the Court of Appeal in *Foskett v McKeown* [1998] Ch 265, 278, even went so far as to suggest that in such circumstances the beneficiary should be entitled to a beneficial share in the property reflecting the share of the property's total value contributed by the use of the trust money.

Where trust money is used to improve, maintain or repair an innocent party's property, there is authority suggesting that no claim will lie. The leading case here is *Re Diplock* [1948] Ch 465, where a number of charities had wrongly been paid money, some of which had then been used on the improvement and repair of property. The Court of Appeal rejected the beneficiary's claim of a charge over that property. Lord Greene MR's reasons for rejecting the claim are brought out in the following passage ([1948] Ch 465, 547–48):

> The beneficial owner of the trust money seeks to follow and recover that money and claims to use the machinery of a charge on the adapted property in order to enable him to do so. But in the first place the money may not be capable of being followed. In every true sense, the money may have disappeared. A simple example suggests itself. The owner of a house who, as an innocent volunteer, has trust money in his hands given to him by a trustee uses that money in making an alteration to his house so as to fit it better to his own personal needs. The result may add not one penny to the value of the house. Indeed the alteration may well lower its value. ... Can it be said in such cases that the trust money can be traced and extracted from the altered asset? Clearly not, for the money will have disappeared leaving no monetary trace behind. ... But it is not merely a question of locating and identifying the ... money. The result of a declaration of charge is to disentangle trust money and enable it to be withdrawn in the shape of money from the complex in which it has become involved. This can only be done by sale under the charge.... But if what the volunteer has contributed is not money but other property of his own such as land, what then?... Is it equitable to compel the innocent volunteer to take a charge merely for the value of the land when what he has contributed is the land itself?... In our opinion it cannot.

There appear to be two lines of reasoning here, one related to tracing, the other to claiming. The first argument is that the beneficiary cannot trace into the property on which the trust money has been expended because the property may well not have increased in value, and where this is the case the use of the money simply generates no traceable proceeds. The second argument is more difficult, but it appears to be that, even were tracing possible, it would be unfair to the innocent property owner to require him to sell his property to make good the beneficiary's claim.

The first argument takes us only so far. It seems right that there should be no claim where the work, and the money spent on it, results in no increase to the asset's value, but it does not tell us why tracing should not be possible where there *is* such an increase. There is a good argument that, in such cases, the beneficiary should be able to recover a sum of money equal to this increase, perhaps capped by the total sum of trust money so spent. As for the second argument, it does indeed seem unfair for the beneficiary to be able to compel an innocent party to sell his property, especially if, as in *Re Diplock*, this is a significant land holding. Millett LJ in *Boscawen v Bajwa* [1996] 1 WLR 328, however, suggested that this should not have sufficed to deny the claim in *Re Diplock*, and that the court should instead have held that enforcement of such a claim should be delayed until the innocent party has a reasonable opportunity to obtain the money from another source. Nonetheless, in *Foskett v McKeown* [2001] 1 AC 102, 109, Lord Browne-

Wilkinson endorsed the *Re Diplock* view that no proprietary interest should be awarded to a beneficiary whose trust money is used to improve or maintain another innocent person's property if granting such an interest would be unfair.

14.17 Change of position

Another way to account for the result in *Re Diplock* [1948] Ch 465 is to say that, although it was possible to trace the trust money into the improved property, the beneficiaries' proprietary claims were nonetheless rightly denied on the basis that the innocent defendants could be regarded as having a valid defence, known as change of position.

Change of position is a defence developed in relation to unjust enrichment claims (Section 8.10). If, for example, I mistakenly pay you £100, I have a claim that you pay me an equivalent sum of money. Say, however, that before you learn of my mistake, and thinking that that money is rightfully yours, you decide to treat yourself to something nice, say a good meal or some new clothes. If this is an expenditure which you would not have incurred but for your receipt of the mistaken payment (because without it you would not have felt as though you could afford such luxuries), you can claim that it would be unfair to have to pay back that sum to me. This is because you can argue that this would leave you worse off than when you started. You have already forked out money which you would not have done but for your belief that the £100 received was yours; so if you then have to pay the claimant £100, you will be left out of pocket. The change of position defence comes in to defeat the claim to the extent of that expenditure (so if you spent £80 on the meal, then I can recover only £20). Accordingly, change of position works to ensure that unjust enrichment claims do not leave innocent defendants worse off.

It can be argued that this defence could have been applied to defeat the beneficiaries' proprietary claim in *Re Diplock*. The innocent recipients of the trust money used it to fund improvements and repair work on their land, which they would not have undertaken (and so would not have paid for out of their own funds) had the trust money not been received. Although this work may have resulted in an increase in the value of this property, it would nonetheless prejudice the defendants if they were required to sell the land to repay this increase in value. This is because this money could only be generated by selling the property, and the defendants would then be left only with their share in the proceeds of its sale, whereas what they want, and value more, is the land itself.

The application of change of position to proprietary claims to misapplied trust assets is, however, controversial. Millett LJ offered some support for this in *Boscawen v Bajwa* [1996] 1 WLR 328. However he, and the other members of the House of Lords, appeared to pour cold water on this suggestion in *Foskett v McKeown* [2001] 1 AC 102. As we have seen (Section 14.4), the court rejected the idea that claims based on tracing were founded on unjust enrichment, holding instead that such proprietary claims were concerned simply with the vindication of property rights. In discussing the difference between unjust enrichment claims and claims to misapplied trust assets, Lord Millett said ([2001] 1 AC 102, 129):

> ... a claim in unjust enrichment is subject to a change of position defence, which usually operates by reducing or extinguishing the element of enrichment. An action like the present is subject to the bona fide purchaser for value defence, which operates to clear the defendant's title.

The clear implication is that change of position is not a defence to proprietary claims to trust property (see eg Rotherham, 2003). Indeed, if this is not what Lord Millett intended then it is hard to see what the point of these comments was. Nonetheless, extra-judicially Millett (2005, 324–25) has stressed that he did not intend to shut the door to the development of change of position as a defence in such cases. On this basis, its status here is still uncertain.

14.18 Knowing receipt

Proprietary claims are founded simply on the fact that the defendant holds something to which the beneficiary, by reason of his equitable beneficial title, has a stronger claim. This then entitles the beneficiary to demand that the defendant hand over the relevant property. Necessarily though, proprietary claims are available only against those who presently hold trust assets. A recipient of trust property may, however, also be subject to a distinct, personal claim for the way he conducted himself while the trust property was in his possession. This claim we call *knowing receipt*. Importantly, such claims are not dependent on the defendant's continued retention of trust assets. Instead liability is imposed on the basis of the defendant's wrongful conduct when in possession of the trust property. As such, we can say that although the proprietary claim is founded on what the defendant *has*, liability in knowing receipt is based on what he *did*.

We may note at the outset that there is considerable debate as to whether personal claims against recipients of trust property should, or need, be based on their wrongdoing (cf Mitchell and Watterson, 2010). We shall examine this argument in some detail later (Section 14.21). However, it is clear that knowing receipt developed, and exists to this day, as a claim based on wrongdoing. The defendant is liable on the basis of his wrongful handling of or dealing with the beneficiary's trust property. It is for this reason that, as the name suggests, liability depends not just on the defendant having received trust property, but also on his having some knowledge that the property in his hands derives from a breach of trust.

We can now see that knowing receipt is in one way broader and in another way narrower than the proprietary claim. It is broader in that, unlike the proprietary claim, it does not require that the defendant *retain* any trust property in his possession. It is, however, narrower in that liability in knowing receipt requires fault, whereas a proprietary claim does not depend on the defendant having any knowledge of the fact that the property derives from a breach of trust (although this may be relevant if the defendant seeks to establish that he is a bona fide purchaser for value without notice). As such, although a beneficiary may often be able to bring *both* a proprietary claim *and* a claim in knowing receipt against a given defendant, at other times only one of these claims will be available.

14.19 The elements of a knowing receipt claim

We can split a claim in knowing receipt into two constituent elements. First, there is a conduct requirement: did the defendant receive trust property? Second, there is a mental or fault requirement: did the defendant, when receiving or handling the property, have sufficient knowledge of the fact that the property derived from a breach of trust? We shall look at each of these in turn.

The first requirement – that the defendant was at some point in receipt of trust property – involves applying the same rules of following and tracing we examined in relation to proprietary claims. So, the beneficiary needs to show that the defendant received an asset which either:

1. was originally held (and misapplied) by the trustee on trust for the beneficiary; or
2. is a traceable substitute of an asset originally held and misapplied by the trustee.

And, as with a proprietary claim, there will be no claim in knowing receipt if the defendant is a bona fide purchaser for value without notice, or if the asset he received passed through the hands of a bona fide purchaser following the initial breach of trust but prior to its receipt by the defendant, because in such cases the assets the defendant received will, by that time, no longer be *trust* assets.

There appears to be one additional aspect to the requirement that the defendant has received trust property, which does not exist in relation to proprietary claims. This is that the property was received by the defendant 'for his own use and benefit': see *Agip (Africa) Ltd v Jackson* [1990] Ch 265, 292 (Millett J); *El Ajou v Dollar Land Holdings plc* [1994] 2 All ER 685, 700 (Hoffmann LJ); *Twinsectra Ltd v Yardley* [2002] UKHL 12, [2002] 2 AC 164, [105] (Lord Millett). The effect of this is to exclude from liability those, such as agents, who receive property only on behalf of, and so hold it only for the benefit of, someone else. Such cases are sometimes referred to as instances of 'ministerial receipt'.

In *Agip*, Millett J held that, because of this, banks can be liable in knowing receipt only where they receive and apply trust money to reduce or discharge a customer's overdraft, because in all other cases banks pay and receive money as agents of their customers. This is questionable. Where money is paid to a bank by or 'on behalf of' an account holder that money is received beneficially by the bank whether or not the relevant account is in credit or overdrawn (cf Mitchell, 2002, 182–87). The only difference between payments 'into' an overdrawn account and payments 'into' an account which is in credit is that, in the former case, the payment discharges or reduces a debt owed by the account holder, whereas in the latter the payment creates or increases a debt owed by the bank to the account holder. No debt could be discharged or created unless the bank received the money beneficially.

We may also question why those who receive property on behalf of others should be immune from liability in knowing receipt. The key point to note is that the effect of this rule is that such a person will escape liability even if he knew full well that the property derived from a breach of trust but, rather than returning it to the beneficiary, handed it over instead to his principal. In such a case, the defendant's conduct is just as inconsistent with the beneficiary's interest in the property as if he had handled the property for his own benefit. It is difficult to see why no claim should lie against him. The requirement that the defendant receive the property beneficially *would* make sense if knowing receipt claims were based on the defendant's unjust enrichment rather than wrongdoing, because there can be no unjust enrichment if the defendant is not benefited. Indeed this is the view of knowing receipt favoured by Lord Millett, who endorsed the beneficial receipt requirement in *Agip* and *Twinsectra*. However, although, as we shall see, there is a strong argument that receipt claims should be developed along such lines, we are not there yet and the authorities remain tied to the wrongdoing approach. As such, unless and until the courts do adopt Millett's preferred unjust enrichment analysis of knowing receipt claims, we may be better off rejecting his view that liability can attach only to those who receive property for their own benefit.

14.20 The necessary level of knowledge

What does a defendant who has received trust property have to know to be liable in knowing receipt? It is plain that the defendant will be liable if he knew that the property he was holding derived from a breach of trust. The question is if and when liability will be imposed where the defendant does not know about this but could and should have done.

For a number of years, when approaching this question, the courts made use of a framework put forward in *Baden v Société Générale pour Favouriser le Développement du Commerce et de l'Industrie en France* [1993] 1 WLR 509 (the case was decided in 1983). This identified five types or degrees of knowledge that a recipient of trust property may have:

1. Actual knowledge.
2. Wilfully shutting one's eyes to the obvious.
3. Wilfully and recklessly failing to make such inquiries as an honest and reasonable man would make.
4. Knowledge of circumstances which would indicate the facts to an honest and reasonable man.
5. Knowledge of circumstances which would put an honest and reasonable man on inquiry.

One may doubt whether this exhausts all possibilities, and indeed whether it can be viewed (as it has tended to be) as a sliding scale. Nonetheless, it does at least give some indication of the different sorts of factual situations with which a court may be confronted, and hence the choices it has to make when determining where the line is to be drawn. However, no consensus developed as to which of these five 'categories' sufficed for the imposition of liability in knowing receipt. The principal division was between those who thought only categories 1 to 3 would do (eg *Re Montagu's Settlement Trusts* [1987] Ch 264) and those who thought that all 5 were sufficient (eg *Agip (Africa) Ltd v Jackson* [1990] Ch 265).

At other times the courts chose to approach the question by asking whether the defendant needed to have actual knowledge (or notice) of the breach of trust, or whether liability could be founded simply on constructive knowledge (or notice). However, here too there was no agreement, and indeed it seemed that these terms were used differently by different judges (compare again *Re Montagu* and *Agip v Jackson*). Other decisions suggested that the requirements should vary depending on whether the case involved commercial transactions and/or on the type of property involved (see eg *Eagle Trust plc v SBC Securities Ltd* [1993] 1 WLR 484 and *Cowan de Groot Properties Ltd v Eagle Trust plc* [1992] 4 All ER 700).

In short, the authorities are a mess of conflicting decisions. However, an opportunity to clear things up arose in *Bank of Credit and Commercial International (Overseas) Ltd v Akindele* [2001] Ch 437. There, the Court of Appeal noted the inconsistencies in the case law and acknowledged the need for a single standard. Accordingly, it set about the task of framing a knowledge or fault requirement which could then be applied in all future cases, and so rid the law of its earlier inconsistency and ambiguity. The court's conclusion is set down in the following passage from Nourse LJ's judgment ([2001] Ch 437, 455):

> [J]ust as there is now a single test of dishonesty for knowing assistance, so ought there to be a single test of knowledge for knowing receipt. The recipient's state of knowledge must be such as to make it unconscionable for him to retain the benefit of the receipt. A test in that form, though it cannot, any more than any other, avoid difficulties of application, ought to avoid those of definition and allocation to which the previous categorisations have led. Moreover, it should better enable the courts to give commonsense decisions in the commercial context in which claims in knowing receipt are now frequently made.

So now, in all cases of receipt of trust property, the court must first inquire into what the defendant knew of the breach of trust. Then, when this information has been ascertained, it must determine whether, in such circumstances, it would be unconscionable for the defendant to keep the benefits he derived from his receipt and use of the trust property. In other words, what we must ask is: 'Given what he knew (and didn't know) about the connection between the property he held and the breach of trust, would it be unconscionable if he were to retain the benefit that property brought him?'

Of course, the key question then becomes what facts, what sort of knowledge, will support a finding of unconscionability. It is when we try to answer this that the weaknesses of the *Akindele* test start to become apparent. The problem is that the Court of Appeal offers us little or no guidance as to when the defendant's knowledge will justify the conclusion that it would be unconscionable to allow him to keep the benefit derived from receipt of the property. Thus, while *Akindele* tells us what question we should be asking, it offers few clues as to how it should be answered.

Take the following example. A defendant receives trust property, and although he never discovered that it derived from a breach of trust, he had ample opportunity to discover this and failed to do so only through laziness or stupidity. Is he liable for knowing receipt? We *could* say that such incompetent failure to learn that he is holding trust assets establishes unconscionability. But we could just as well say that unconscionability requires something more, some form of conscious wrongdoing. Neither approach would involve a misuse of language; both are defensible as a matter of principle. Which is right? Unfortunately *Akindele* does not tell us and, more importantly, does not seek to tell us.

The trouble arises from the language of unconscionability. As we have seen elsewhere (eg Sections 6.4, 9.3), 'unconscionability' is the equity lawyer's terminology of choice when seeking to describe a defendant's conduct or a given result as unjust, unfair or wrongful. And, as with the language of (un)fairness and (in)justice, any rule we might care to put forward can be framed in terms of unconscionability. So, for example, the rule 'promises supported by consideration are legally binding' can be reformulated as 'it is unconscionable (or unfair) not to perform promises supported by consideration' or 'conscience (or fairness) requires promises supported by consideration to be performed'. Now there is nothing wrong in reformulating the rule in this way, but it should be plain that by doing so we add nothing to the rule's content and clarify nothing as to its application. They are simply different ways of saying the same thing. So, if you wanted to know (as many people do) *why* promises supported by consideration are binding, to be told 'because conscience/fairness requires this' or 'because it would be unconscionable for the promisor not to perform' would tell you nothing. What you are looking for is the *reason* we consider it unfair or unconscionable to break such promises. Similarly, we can (at least roughly) summarise the rules of contract by saying that promises are legally binding where (the law considers that) this is what fairness/justice/good conscience demands. Yet this provides only the vaguest indication of when in practice contracts arise. Moreover, in borderline cases, where there are good arguments on both sides as to whether the promise should be legally binding, references to fairness or conscience provide no assistance whatsoever.

The point is that, although the law *is*, at least broadly, concerned with achieving fairness and preventing injustice and unconscionable conduct, and so the content of the law is, again broadly, determined by what is fair/just/in good conscience, statements to the effect that 'the law requires what is fair or in good conscience' give us, at best, only the most vague of notions as to what the law actually is and what it requires of us. Otherwise all law textbooks could be slimmed down to just a sentence or two saying something along the lines of 'contracts arise when it would be unfair/unconscionable for a promise to be broken', 'a tort is committed when someone unfairly/unconscionably infringes another's interests', 'trusts arise where it would be unfair/unconscionable for a property holder to keep the asset for himself'. The fact that law books and courses choose to say rather more than this serves to demonstrate that simple references to fairness, justice and good conscience leave all the difficult questions as to the law's content and its reasons unanswered.

So, returning to the conditions of liability in knowing receipt, our problem is that 'unconscionability', like 'unfairness', is capable of describing any number of alternative approaches and different levels of fault (indeed, on occasion, instances of strict liability have been explained on the basis of unconscionability: see eg *Kelly v Solari* (1841) 9 M & W 54). What we need to know is what counts as unconscionability *here*. Does it require actual knowledge, or will constructive knowledge suffice? If the latter, what exactly counts as sufficient constructive knowledge so as to make retention of the benefit of the property unconscionable?

In *Akindele* itself, the court concluded that, given that the defendant neither had knowledge of the relevant frauds, nor sufficient reason to question the propriety of the transaction by which he received the misapplied funds, it was not unconscionable for him to retain this benefit. But this finding tells us nothing we didn't know already. Translated into the traditional language, the defendant had *neither* actual *nor* constructive knowledge, so it is hardly surprising that he escaped liability. Given the defendant's lack of knowledge, we get no indication of what sort of knowledge would have been sufficient.

Indeed we can see that we are left in exactly the same position as we were before *Akindele* was decided. Previously, there was no clear answer to the question of if and when a defendant who had only constructive knowledge – that is, who did not know, but could and should have known – that the property derived from a breach of trust could be liable in knowing receipt. *Akindele* takes us no further. It redresses the same old debate in the language of unconscionability, but takes us no nearer to a resolution.

This can be seen from some of the post-*Akindele* decisions. In *Armstrong DLW GmbH v Winnington Networks Ltd* [2012] EWHC 10 (Ch); [2012] 3 WLR 835, [132] the judge, Stephen Morris QC, faced with the uncertainties left by *Akindele*, retreated to the five types of knowledge set out in *Baden* and listed at the start of this section. He concluded that, 'in a commercial context', all five types of knowledge render receipt unconscionable, although with the gloss that knowledge types 4 and 5 suffice 'only, if on the facts actually known to the defendant, a reasonable person would either have appreciated that the transfer was probably in breach of trust or would have made inquiries or sought advice which would have revealed the probability of the breach of trust.' This is in effect a standard of constructive notice (see also *Starglade Properties Ltd v Nash* [2010] EWHC 148 (Ch); [2010] WTLR 1267, [57].)

In *Arthur v A-G of the Turks and Caicos Islands* [2012] UKPC 30, by contrast, the Privy Council appeared to assume that unconscionability required something more than constructive notice: 'Knowledge, in the knowing receipt sense, means not merely notice, but, in accordance with *Akindele*, such knowledge as to make the recipient's conduct unconscionable and to give rise to equitable fraud' [36]. In short, we are back where we were, with one group of cases holding that unconscionability can be established by showing that the defendant had constructive knowledge that the property received derived from a breach of trust and another group of cases requiring something more.

The problems we face in relation to the knowledge requirement can best be understood by considering why we have legal rules and what we want them to do. When deciding cases, courts use rules to determine what legal results follow from the occurrence of certain facts, or, viewed from the opposite end, what facts must be established for a given legal result to follow. Ideally then (although, as we have seen, this is not always possible: Section 9.22), legal rules should be of the form 'when facts A, B and C are present, legal result X follows'. A court then knows, when determining the availability of X, that it must look for facts A, B and C. In relation to knowing receipt, the problem is that although we know some of the facts needed to establish such a claim (beneficial receipt of trust property), we do not yet know what the other fact is (save that we know that it concerns the defendant's state of mind). Accordingly, at the moment the equation stands as:

(A) beneficial receipt of trust property + (B)? = (X) knowing receipt.

What the courts need to do to if we are to have a workable rule which determines the circumstances in which claims in knowing receipt will arise, is to fill this gap. This can be done only by identifying what extra *fact* is needed; in other words, what sort of state of mind or knowledge the defendant must be shown to have. *Akindele* fails because it does not answer this question. Unconscionability does not itself describe a state of mind (no more than unfairness or injustice does), and it provides no assistance in determining what state of mind (and so what fact) is needed to complete the equation. Indeed, it is because of this that we may say that tests based on or employing unconscionability will *always* make for incomplete and so unsuccessful legal rules, as they necessarily fail to indicate what facts need to be present to generate liability.

The only argument that can be made in support of an unconscionability standard, and what the Court of Appeal in *Akindele* appears to have had in mind, is that it gives the courts greater flexibility and so (supposedly) greater freedom to do justice on the facts of the case – in other words, the standard argument for leaving the courts with a discretion rather than formulating a binding rule. Now, as we have seen (Section 9.22), we may question whether such discretion really does lead to fairer results, rather than simply greater uncertainty and an increased risk of arbitrary and so unjust decisions. But we may also ask why the court might consider this an area which requires a more flexible approach.

It is true that there is a difficult balance to be struck here. The stricter the standard (ie the lower the level of knowledge sufficient to generate liability), the greater the risk run by those receiving property, and so the greater the inquiries they have to make to ensure that they will not be subjected to liability. This then is likely to be to the detriment of commercial parties, who want to be able to deal with their assets quickly and without hindrance. However, a strict approach will promote higher standards of conduct amongst those in the business of buying and selling property, compelling them to take greater steps to ensure that the assets with which they are dealing are not the proceeds of a fraud. Moreover, this would give greater protection to the beneficiary and to trusts and trust interests more generally. But although the fact that the competing arguments are more or less evenly weighted means that framing the necessary standard will be both difficult and controversial, it does not follow that it would be better for the courts to give up on this and leave it to individual judges to decide on a case-by-case basis. The argument for 'flexibility' here is effectively to allow different courts at different times to apply different standards for no better reason than a disinclination to bite the bullet and make a tough decision.

A further argument for flexibility is that this enables the courts to take a different approach in commercial cases from that adopted in non-commercial cases. As we have just noted, the principal argument against a stricter standard of knowledge is that it could lead to a slowing down or disruption of commercial dealings. However, such considerations do not apply where the parties are not engaged in commercial dealings or are engaged in a transaction which is not particularly fast moving (such as transfers of land). As such, it can be argued that the level of knowledge sufficient to impose liability on a commercial party should be greater than that sufficient for liability in other cases (for judicial support for this view, see *Eagle Trust plc v SBC Securities Ltd* [1993] 1 WLR 484, 504–6 (Vinelott J); *El Ajou v Dollar Land Holdings plc* [1993] 3 All ER 717, 739 (Millett J)). Of course, we may question whether we should water down the usual conditions of liability simply because commercial parties find them troublesome and inconvenient. However, even if we were to go along with this view, all this would mean is that we should be looking to frame two rules (one for commercial dealings, one for others) rather than one. It certainly does not justify leaving the court carte blanche to make things up as they go along, as *Akindele* does.

Whatever uncertainty there may be as to what knowledge a recipient of trust property needs to have to be liable in knowing receipt, it is at last clear *when* he must have it. Contrary to what the words 'knowing receipt' may appear to suggest, it is enough that the defendant gains the necessary knowledge at any point while the property remains in his possession. In other words, it is not necessary to show that he had this knowledge when he first received the property, so long as he gained it before he parted with those assets and their proceeds.

Thus, as the law stands, the position of a recipient of property which, immediately prior to receipt, can (by the rules of following and tracing) be identified as trust property may be summarised as follows:

1. If he had no knowledge of the fact that the property derived from a breach of trust, and no reason to suspect this, *and* he gave value, then he is a bona fide purchaser for value without notice and immune from any liability, whether proprietary or personal.
2. If he did not know, and could not have been expected to discover, that the property derived from a breach of trust, but *did not* give value for it (ie he is an innocent donee), then so long as that property or its proceeds are in his possession, he is subject to a proprietary claim for the recovery of such property. If, however, he no longer retains such property, he will be under no liability.

3. If he did not know that the property derived from a breach of trust, but could and should have found out that it did then, whether or not he gave value, a proprietary claim will lie so long as he retains that property or its proceeds (as he is a purchaser *with notice*). If he no longer retains any such property, however, he will be personally liable in knowing receipt only if the court concludes that his conduct makes it unconscionable for him to retain the benefit of that property.

4. If he *did* know that the property derived from a breach of trust, or avoided such knowledge only by deliberately turning a blind eye to this, then he is subject both to a proprietary claim, so long as such property remains in his possession, *and*, alternatively, to a claim in knowing receipt.

An important point to take from this is that, as proposition 3 suggests, depending on how the *Akindele* test of unconscionability is applied, there may be a class of recipients who, although not sufficiently 'innocent' to be classed as bona fide purchasers for value without notice (and so who may then be subject to a proprietary claim while the asset is in their hands), are not sufficiently 'guilty' or knowledgeable to be liable as knowing recipients (the same point is made by Sir Robert Megarry vc in *Re Montagu's Settlement Trusts* [1987] Ch 264, 277–78 and by Sir Terence Etherton in *Arthur v A-G of the Turks and Caicos Islands* [2012] UKPC 30, [36]). Consequently, when considering the potential liability of recipients of trust assets, you should always distinguish the question of whether the defendant is a bona fide purchaser from the question whether he may be liable for knowing receipt.

14.21 Justifying personal claims against recipients of trust property

As if this uncertainty as to the level of fault or knowledge needed for liability in knowing receipt was not enough, there is increasing and powerful support for the view that the personal liability of recipients of trust property should not be fault-based *at all*, but should instead be strict. As we noted at the outset, knowing receipt developed as a form of wrongdoing, as something akin to an 'equitable tort', imposing liability for wrongful handling of or dealing with another's trust property. On this basis, it makes sense to require some sort of fault or 'mens rea' element on the part of the recipient before liability will attach to him.

However, over recent years it has been argued that we may be able to justify personal claims against recipients of trust property on an entirely different basis, namely unjust enrichment. The argument here is that, whether or not the defendant acted wrongfully in his acquisition or subsequent handling of the property, he should be liable to give up any benefits he derived from it for the simple reason that these benefits are exclusively reserved for the beneficiary. If this argument holds good (and we shall have a look at this shortly),we can justify imposing liability on defendant recipients of trust property even where they have no knowledge whatsoever of the breach of trust, and hence are entirely faultless. In short, the reason for imposing liability on recipients matters because it will determine the scope of such liability, ie *who* will be liable.

The argument matters for another reason. It is important to know not just who is liable, but what they are liable for. That is, we need to know what the claimant can recover in the event that the defendant's liability is established. Different reasons for attaching liability will justify different types of remedy. So if we adopt the conventional wrongdoing analysis of recipient liability, when liability is made out we can, in principle, justify requiring the defendant to give up gains he has made and/or to make good losses he has caused through his wrongful dealing with the trust property. By contrast, as we shall see, on the unjust enrichment approach, although liability will be strict, it can only justify requiring the defendant to give up any benefits he retains from his receipt and use of the trust property. In other words, his liability should be limited to the extent of his (continued) unjust enrichment.

It is important to stress at the outset that although there are doubts as to what level of fault or knowledge should be required, nobody doubts that someone who wrongfully receives or deals with another's trust property should be liable for his actions. So although at one point the argument was whether strict liability in unjust enrichment should *replace* the current system of fault-based liability for wrongdoing, the better argument is whether an unjust enrichment claim should *supplement* the existing fault-based claim for knowing receipt (see also Nicholls, 1998; Birks, 2002b). If so, this would mean that there would be two alternative types of personal claim that may lie against recipients of trust property:

1. Claims based on wrongful handling of or dealing with trust property. These would be dependent on fault but would then justify both loss- and gain-based claims (moreover, it may be that such claims should then be subsumed within the wrong of dishonest assistance: Section 14.22);
2. Claims based on unjust enrichment. These would not be dependent on fault but would justify liability only to the extent of the defendant's subsisting unjust enrichment.

The argument that there should be a distinct strict liability claim in unjust enrichment can best be understood by using an example. Imagine you receive £1,000 of misapplied trust money, though without any knowledge or suspicion that it derives from a breach of trust. You then use that same money to meet a necessary expenditure, for instance you use it to pay your rent or your gas bill. As you no longer retain the money or any traceable substitute, there is no possibility of the beneficiary bringing a proprietary claim against you (unless we were to accept some version of the 'swollen assets' theory: Section 14.15). Therefore, as the law stands, you will be personally liable only if you had such knowledge as merits a finding of unconscionability under *Akindele*. As you neither knew nor had any reason to know of the breach of trust, such a claim will fail.

However, we can see that, if matters are left like that, you end up better off as a result of your receipt and use of the trust property. If you had not used the trust money to pay the rent or the gas bill, you would have had to find this money from your own funds. Your use of the trust money, although completely innocent, has saved you from spending money of your own, and hence has resulted in you now having more money at your disposal than you would have had had you never received the trust money. In other words, although the trust money is now gone, you remain enriched. Why, then, should you be free to retain this undeserved benefit, while the beneficiary is left (subject to any other claims he may have) to bear the loss? Instead (so the argument goes) the claimant should be able to demand that you give up this unjust enrichment by handing over an equivalent sum of money. You can hardly complain about this as you are only being made to hand over the money you saved when you used the trust money to pay the bill, and so you are simply left in the position you should have been in all along.

This last point is important. The natural instinct is to view strict liability as harsh on defendants, as it suggests that the defendant is being held liable despite not having done anything 'wrong'. This is true, however, only in so far as such liability requires the defendant to bear a loss, and so leaves him worse off than he would have been had things gone to plan. So, say we are on a crowded bus and, as it turns a corner, I stumble into you, causing you an injury. If the law required me, despite being blameless, to compensate you for any injuries you suffered, I would be left to bear a loss. I will have to pay you a sum of money, and so I will be left worse off than if the accident had never happened. Many people would consider this unfair, because (as we are assuming) there really was nothing I could reasonably have done to avoid injuring you and hence I cannot be said to have been at fault in causing your injury. For the most part (and there are a number of important exceptions) the law agrees, and so shifts losses onto people only if they were at fault in causing such losses or if they undertook to bear them (which may then justify the strict liability imposed in the law of contract).

The position is different where the effect of imposing liability is not to shift a loss onto the defendant but simply to remove a gain from him which, if events had gone to plan, he would never have received. So if you go to a shop and the assistant ends up giving you too much change, you are liable to return the excess even if you have not noticed and cannot be blamed for it. Indeed, you are liable to return this even though the assistant himself is to blame. The reason is that you are simply being asked to give back what you should never have received in the first place, meaning that you are only being deprived of a gain rather than being required to bear a loss.

The argument for imposing strict liability in respect of the receipt of trust property is in essence the same as the argument for imposing strict liability on you when you receive too much change in a shop. In both cases, you get something that the person (originally) beneficially entitled to the property (the shopkeeper in the one case, the beneficiary in the other) never intended you to have, and the effect of liability is to require you to give up a sum of money equal to the value of the benefit you received, thus leaving you no better, but no worse, off than you should have been all along.

However, consider the following variation on our example. Again you innocently receive £1,000 of misapplied trust money, and again you spend it paying your rent or a bill. At this stage, as we have seen, despite the expenditure, you remain £1,000 better off through your receipt of the trust money. However, let us assume that you then spend £800 on a holiday which you booked only because you had (and believed you were entitled to) this additional £1,000 in your bank account. In this case, you can argue that if you are required to pay back the full £1,000 you received, you will be left worse off than you would have been had you never received the trust money. This is because you would in that case never have spent £800 on the holiday, preferring to save what money you had to meet other, more necessary expenses. In such a case, it is argued that you should have a defence of *change of position*. We have encountered this already, in our discussion of proprietary claims (Section 14.17). As there, the aim of the defence is to ensure that claims against innocent defendants do not leave them worse off. It does this by reducing the amount the claimant can recover by the sum of any expenditure or other loss the defendant has incurred, which he would not have incurred but for his receipt of the trust property. So here, you would not have spent £800 on the holiday had you not received the trust money, so the claimant is entitled to recover only £200, this being the sum of your remaining enrichment.

In summary then, the argument put forward is that there should be strict liability for recipients of trust property, tempered by the defence of change of position, which ensures that innocent recipients lose nothing but also gain nothing from their receipt and use of the trust property. This would then mirror the position which already exists at common law where (non-trust) property is transferred by mistake, under coercion or on a condition which fails. As we saw with the example where the shopkeeper pays you too much change, liability is strict. Moreover, here the courts have in recent years recognised the change of position defence: see *Lipkin Gorman v Karpnale Ltd* [1991] 2 AC 548. So if, having walked out of the shop, you see that you have more change than you thought you had (although without realising or suspecting why this is) and so decide to buy a magazine or a muffin which otherwise you would not have treated yourself to, you have a defence to the extent of that expenditure. As such, another way of representing this argument is to say that the receipt of misapplied trust assets is, like the receipt of a mistaken or coerced transfer of non-trust property, an unjust enrichment, and that the common law and equity ought to have a common response to cases of unjust enrichment.

The argument that strict liability should attach to recipients of trust property gains only minimal support from the case law. The most we can point to are a few obiter remarks, albeit by leading judges, endorsing this approach. So, for example, in *Twinsectra Ltd v Yardley* [2002] UKHL 12; [2002] 2 AC 164, [105], Lord Millett offered the following view:

> Liability for 'knowing receipt' is receipt-based. It does not depend on fault. The cause of action is restitutionary and is available only where the defendant received or applied the property for his own use and benefit. ... There is no basis for requiring actual knowledge of the breach of trust, let alone dishonesty, as a condition of liability. Constructive notice is sufficient, and may not even be necessary. There is powerful academic support for the proposition that the liability of the recipient is the same as in other cases of restitution, that is to say strict but subject to a change of position defence.

(Cf *Criterion Properties plc v Stratford UK Properties LLC* [2004] UKHL 28, [2004] 1 WLR 1846, [4] (Lord Nicholls))

By contrast, in *Westdeutsche Landesbank Girozentrale v Islington London BC* [1996] AC 669, 707, Lord Browne-Wilkinson, also obiter, supported the traditional view that liability requires fault. More pertinently, if we look at the cases where liability for the receipt of trust property has been directly in issue, they all go one way. As we have seen, the question which has divided the courts in these cases has been as to the level of knowledge required to establish liability in knowing receipt. The clear implication of this is that some knowledge, and hence some fault, is a prerequisite for liability. In other words, the debate over whether a defendant with constructive knowledge could be liable in knowing receipt would be largely irrelevant if there existed an alternative form of personal liability for the receipt of trust property which required no fault whatsoever.

The authorities on knowing receipt therefore do little to advance the unjust enrichment argument. Because of this, its proponents have had instead to rely on the analogous situation where property is misapplied by an executor of a will (the difference between these cases and misapplications of trust property being that, unlike beneficiaries of a trust, the intended legatees under a will have no equitable interest in the property that is to come their way: *Cmr of Stamp Duties (Qld) v Livingston* [1965] AC 694). In such cases, the courts have held that the recipients of the property misapplied by the executor come under a strict personal liability to give up the value of the property they received: see *Re Diplock* [1948] Ch 465 and *Ministry of Health v Simpson* [1951] AC 521. As this is an equitable, rather than a common law, claim, these cases are then used in support of the argument that equity has not set its face against strict personal liability as a response to unjust enrichment.

The reliance on cases such as *Re Diplock* may be thought rather futile. If the argument as to the strict liability of trust recipients is to be resolved on the basis of authority, there is no doubt which side would win. All the direct authorities support a fault requirement, and against these *Re Diplock* carries little or no weight. If, however, we approach this argument on the basis of principle – asking whether we *should* allow a strict liability claim – then it is neither here nor there what, if any, authorities happen to support it.

So how do the arguments of principle weigh up? The basic argument in support of this has been outlined already: receipt of misapplied trust property, like the receipt of mistakenly transferred non-trust property, constitutes an unjust enrichment, and this enrichment should then be given up to the beneficiary. This argument has been doubted on two grounds.

First, some have contended that the introduction of strict liability would lead to adverse practical consequences; in short, that it would lead to unfair or undesirable results. This was the view of the Court of Appeal in *Bank of Credit and Commercial International (Overseas) Ltd v Akindele* [2001] Ch 437. As we have seen, it was there that the Court put forward the test based on unconscionability. In so doing, Nourse LJ also commented briefly on the suggestion that the law should be developed so as to make liability for the receipt of trust property strict ([2001] Ch 437, 456):

> While in general it may be possible to sympathise with a tendency to subsume a further part of our law of restitution under the principles of unjust enrichment, I beg leave to doubt whether strict liability coupled with a change of position defence would be preferable to fault-based liability in many commercial transactions, for example where, as here, the receipt is of a company's funds which have been misapplied by its directors. Without having heard argument it is unwise to be dogmatic, but in such a case it would appear to be commercially unworkable ... that, simply on proof of an internal misapplication of the company's funds, the burden should shift to the recipient to defend the receipt either by a change of position or perhaps in some other way.

In other words, whereas at present the beneficiary is required to show *both* that the defendant received trust property *and* that he had the necessary knowledge, under the strict liability approach all he need do is prove the defendant's receipt of trust property. The onus then shifts onto the defendant to avoid liability by showing that he changed his position.

Why is this problematic? There may be two concerns here. The first is that it will be easier for beneficiaries to establish prima facie claims against recipients of trust property, with the result that such recipients will more often be put to the time and cost of defending such claims. So although, by virtue of the change of position defence, they will avoid liability, this will involve more hassle than the current rules where, without some evidence of the defendant's knowledge, a claim cannot get off the ground.

The second, and more significant, concern is that not only will the defendant bear a greater burden if he is to avoid liability, but he may not be able to discharge this burden simply because of a lack of evidence that he incurred expenditure which he would not have incurred but for his receipt of trust property. So if we go back to our earlier example, if you receive £1,000 of trust money but then book a holiday for £800 which you would not otherwise have booked, *in theory* you should have a defence. However *in practice* that defence will be available only if you can satisfy the court that you would not have booked that holiday but for your receipt of the trust money. And, of course, this may be difficult to prove, as there will often be no evidence to back up your story. As such, the court may not believe you and so you may be held liable, even though in principle no claim should lie. In short, the concern here is that the change of position defence, although sound in theory, may through difficulties in proof fail to do justice in practice.

These concerns are reasonable. Two points may, however, be made in response. First, all seem to agree that claims against recipients of trust property will, even if strict, continue to be subject to the bona fide purchase rule. Indeed this is also a defence to common law unjust enrichment claims. Therefore, aside from change of position, a recipient of property deriving from a breach of trust will also be able to avoid liability by showing that he is a bona fide purchaser for value without notice. Now this too places some burden on the recipient. However, the burden of proving that you gave value and that you had no notice of the breach of trust will be easier to satisfy. Indeed it is just this burden which recipients who still hold trust property already have to bear to defeat proprietary claims. Thus, most parties, and almost all commercial parties (which was Nourse LJ's particular cause for concern), will have a defence without having to prove change of position. The only parties who will be required to fall back on the change of position defence, and so to whom the introduction of strict liability would make a practical difference, are those who gave no value for the property they received, ie innocent donees. These are likely to account for only a small minority of the cases.

Second, even where the recipient does have to rely on change of position, the suggestion from the common law unjust enrichment cases, where the defence has been applied for a number of years now, is that it works pretty well. Conscious of the difficulty of proving what expenditure a defendant would and would not have incurred but for his (unjust) enrichment, the courts have not set the evidential bar too high and have been sympathetic to claims by innocent defendants that they would not have spent so much money had they not received the mistaken payment: see for example *Philip Collins Ltd v Davis* [2000] 3 All ER 808. So if strict liability subject to change of position has not proved unworkable (whether commercially or otherwise) in respect of common law unjust enrichment claims, there seems no reason to think that it should prove unworkable if extended to the receipt of misapplied trust property.

This brings us to the second type of challenge that has been made against the introduction of strict liability. Here the argument is that it is wrong to view the receipt of trust property as an unjust enrichment which is to be equated with – and so treated in the same way as – the receipt of mistakenly transferred non-trust property. In other words, the analogy that proponents of the strict liability approach draw between receipt of trust property and conventional examples of common law unjust enrichment claims is misplaced.

There are a number of strands to or versions of this argument. One points to the differences between legal beneficial title and equitable beneficial title (see eg Smith, 2000, 418–34). Another questions whether receipt of trust property can fit within the framework used by the courts and commentators to analyse and describe unjust enrichment claims. So, for instance, it has been questioned whether the recipient of trust property can really be said to be enriched and whether there is in such cases some 'unjust factor', such as mistake or coercion, which justifies the claimant's demand that any enrichment be given up to him (see eg Smith, 2000, 414–25; Penner, 2012, 401–04).

Again, some of these criticisms are well made. It is probably fair to say that supporters of the unjust enrichment approach have failed to offer a wholly convincing account of *why* we should view receipt of trust property as an unjust enrichment and as parallel to common law unjust enrichment claims. But these gaps can be filled. Claims in respect of misapplied trust property depend in the first instance on the beneficiary's interest in that property, so the starting point must be an examination of equitable beneficial title. Although this sort of interest is different from, and in some respects weaker than, *legal* beneficial title – in particular, it can be defeated by overreaching and by a bona fide purchaser for value without notice (Sections 2.9, 9.4) – so long as it endures, it, like legal beneficial title, gives the beneficiary an exclusive right to the benefits of the property. To this extent, the analogy with common law claims is apt. Where, therefore, trust property is misapplied, any benefit the defendant recipient derives from it is a benefit which, by virtue of his equitable beneficial interest, is reserved for the beneficiary. This then justifies the beneficiary's claim that the defendant give that benefit up to him, irrespective of whether the defendant had any knowledge of the beneficiary's interest in those assets.

The only principled basis on which we can continue to deny beneficiaries a strict liability claim to the benefits recipients derive from trust property would be to reject the now orthodox view that beneficiaries have a beneficial interest *in*, and so are entitled to benefits derived from, the trust property (which seems to be the position taken by Smith, 2004a, and, possibly, Penner, 2010). As we have seen though (Section 2.4), there are good reasons to regard beneficiaries as having a proprietary interest in individual trust assets. As such, we should support the introduction of strict personal liability in respect of receipt of trust property.

14.22 Dishonest assistance

As we have seen (Section 14.18), knowing receipt, as traditionally understood, is a form of personal liability for wrongful dealing with trust property. Accordingly, such claims can be brought only against those who have come into possession of trust assets. By contrast, there exists a second type of personal liability which may attach to third parties which does not depend on their having received any trust property. This is the claim now known as *dishonest assistance*. Again, this is a claim based on wrongdoing, the wrongful conduct this time being helping or procuring the trustee to breach his trust obligations. As such, dishonest assistance is a form of what we call accessory or secondary liability, as liability derives from the defendant's participation in or contribution to a wrong committed by someone else, namely the trustee. The most obvious and illustrative parallel is with the criminal law rules on aiding and abetting. (For more on the nature of liability for dishonest assistance and its connections to the 'primary' liability of the trustee see Elliott and Mitchell, 2004; Ridge, 2012.)

As with knowing receipt, we can divide the requirements for a claim for dishonest assistance into two. First, there is a conduct element: did the defendant assist or procure a breach of trust by the trustee? Second, there is a fault requirement: did the defendant do this dishonestly?

Looking first at the conduct element, there is not a huge amount of case law as to what sort of participation in a breach of trust suffices to attract liability (for more information, see Mitchell, 2002, 171–77). It is clearly enough that the defendant procures, by encouragement or direction, the trustee's breach: see *Eaves v Hickson* (1861) 30 Beav 136. Assistance can be more problematic however. Many cases will be straightforward. So clearly, the forging of documents or the active concealing of evidence of the breach will be enough. At the borderline, though, things may not be as clear-cut.

A good example is provided by *Brinks Ltd v Abu-Saleh (No. 3)* [1996] CLC 133. There, the defendant's husband was involved in laundering the proceeds of a theft of gold bullion, which required him to drive to Switzerland on a number of occasions with cash hidden in his car. On some of these trips he was accompanied by the defendant. One question the court had to decide was whether this could amount to assistance for the purposes of liability. Rimer J held that it did not, and that the defendant had accompanied her husband on these trips 'in the capacity' of his wife, rather than, as the claimant suggested, to provide cover for his money laundering. And although the husband may have enjoyed the defendant's company on the trips, such that we could say that it made his breach a more pleasant experience, this was not 'assistance of a nature sufficient to make her an accessory to the breach of trust'.

It was at one point thought that a defendant, no matter how dishonestly he acted and no matter how great his role in the breach of trust, could be liable for procuring or assisting a breach of trust only if the trustee was also dishonest: see eg *Belmont Finance Corp Ltd v Williams Furniture Ltd* [1979] Ch 250. This, however, made little sense because, although the defendant's liability is derivative of the trustee's own liability for breach of trust, in that it derives from the defendant's role in that breach, nonetheless the defendant is still being held liable for what *he* did. There is, then, no good reason for making the defendant's liability dependent on the trustee's state of mind. Moreover, this leaves a gap where a dishonest third party engineers a breach of trust by an innocent and unwitting trustee. This was accepted by the Privy Council in *Royal Brunei Airlines Sdn Bhd v Tan* [1995] 2 AC 378. So now, provided there is a breach of trust, the trustee's state of mind is irrelevant to the question of the defendant accessory's liability.

Liability for dishonest assistance, unlike knowing receipt, does not depend on the defendant having received any trust property (although there is no reason why, in appropriate circumstances, a knowing recipient cannot also be liable for dishonest assistance). Moreover, there seems to be no reason for there to have been any misapplication of trust property at all. As we have seen, a trust can be breached in a number of ways, only some involving the misapplication of trust assets. So long as the defendant has dishonestly procured or assisted a breach of trust, it should not matter what sort of duty the trustee breached. It should also be stressed that liability in dishonest assistance covers not just those who assisted the initial breach of trust, but also those who subsequently assisted in covering it up, for example by hiding and disposing of any proceeds from the breach: see *Twinsectra Ltd v Yardley* [2002] UKHL 12, [2002] 2 AC 164, [107] (Lord Millett).

14.23   Dishonesty

For a long time the same sort of uncertainty existed in relation to the fault requirement for assistance claims as it did (and probably still does) for knowing receipt claims (see Section 14.20). The courts could not agree on what level or type of knowledge was sufficient for liability to attach to the defendant, with a split between those requiring actual knowledge of the breach of trust and those considering that some form of constructive knowledge or notice would suffice (for this reason, this form of liability was then referred to as 'knowing' assistance). This uncertainty appeared, however, to have been resolved by the Privy Council's decision in *Royal Brunei Airlines Sdn Bhd v Tan* [1995] 2 AC 378. There, Lord Nicholls, giving the judgment of the Board, held that, rather than framing a fault requirement in terms of knowledge or notice, the correct question was to ask simply whether the defendant was dishonest.

Of course, the key question then is what exactly is meant by 'dishonest'. Lord Nicholls gave the following explanation ([1995] 2 AC 378, 389):

> Whatever may be the position in some criminal or other contexts ... in the context of the accessory liability principle acting dishonestly, or with a lack of probity, which is synonymous, means simply not acting as an honest person would in the circumstances. This is an objective standard. At first sight this may seem surprising. Honesty has a connotation of subjectivity, as distinct from the objectivity of negligence. Honesty, indeed, does have a strong subjective element in that it is a description of a type of conduct assessed in the light of what a person actually knew at the time, as distinct from what a reasonable person would have known or appreciated. Further, honesty and its counterpart dishonesty are mostly concerned with advertent conduct, not inadvertent conduct. Carelessness is not dishonesty. Thus for the most part dishonesty is to be equated with conscious impropriety. However, these subjective characteristics of honesty do not mean that individuals are free to set their own standards of honesty in particular circumstances. The standard of what constitutes dishonesty is not subjective. Honesty is not an optional scale, with higher or lower values according to the moral standards of each individual.

Lord Nicholls is making a couple of points here. The first is clear. A defendant cannot establish that he was not dishonest simply by showing that *he* personally did not consider his conduct dishonest. Dishonesty therefore does not depend on the morality of the particular defendant. In this sense honesty is objective; the same standard is applied to everyone, regardless of whether they happen to accept it.

The second is a little less straightforward. The application of this common, objective standard requires consideration of what the defendant actually knew about what he was doing and the surrounding circumstances. In other words, we cannot determine whether an individual acted dishonestly without having some idea of what he was thinking at the time. Consider the following example. I am waiting to collect my luggage after a flight, and a bag comes around on the conveyor belt which looks like, but is not, mine. I pick it up and walk off. Am I dishonest? This depends entirely on what I was thinking at the time. If I positively believed that the bag was mine then, no matter how careless I may have been, I am not dishonest. If, however, I am fully aware that the bag belongs to someone else and thought I would take advantage of its similarity to mine to steal it, I am certainly dishonest. If I merely suspect it is not mine but take it anyway, then this too would most likely be viewed as dishonest.

The key point here is that our conclusion as to whether a defendant is dishonest will be determined by what the defendant was thinking at the relevant time. In fact it is impossible to form a judgment on someone's honesty without this information. It is futile, indeed meaningless, to ask whether I am honest in the above example until you know something of my beliefs and intentions. I am dishonest *because* I know or suspect the bag is not mine. Because of this, as Lord Nicholls notes, dishonesty necessarily involves some sort of 'subjective' inquiry, in that it requires us to look into the defendant's mindset, his intentions and beliefs. None of this, however, means that the standard we are applying is any less objective or common. We are not inquiring into the defendant's mindset to see what he thought (morally, normatively) about his actions: whether they were right or wrong, justified or unjustified. Rather, we are looking at what the defendant knew or believed *the facts* to be. Given this knowledge, we then apply our common, objective standard of honesty. Effectively the question is, 'Is it dishonest to do what the defendant did given what he knew and believed at the time?'

On this basis, the subjective inquiry into the defendant's beliefs is a precursor to the application of the objective standard of honesty. Matters were, however, subsequently confused by the House of Lords decision in *Twinsectra Ltd v Yardley* [2002] UKHL 12, [2002] 2 AC 164. As we have seen already (Section 8.13), this case concerned a *Quistclose* trust of money loaned to Yardley. This money was received by the defendant solicitor, Leach, on the condition that it was only to be made available to Yardley for the purpose of purchasing property. However, Leach paid the money to Yardley without seeking any assurances that the money would be used for the stipulated purpose, and Yardley did indeed use some of this money for other purposes. An action was brought against Leach for dishonest assistance in this breach of trust. Leach knew the terms of the loan but claimed that he believed that he held the money to Yardley's order. On this basis, the judge at first instance, Carnwath J, held that he was not dishonest. The Court of Appeal reversed this, and found him liable. Leach then appealed to the House of Lords. By a 4:1 majority their Lordships upheld the decision of Carnwath J and so Leach escaped liability. In so doing, they gave a detailed examination of the dishonesty test.

The leading judgment on this point came from Lord Hutton. He held that the dishonesty requirement set down in *Royal Brunei Airlines v Tan* had two elements. First, the defendant's conduct must be dishonest when judged by the ordinary standards of reasonable and honest people. Second, the defendant himself must have realised that by the ordinary standards of reasonable and honest people his conduct was dishonest. This Lord Hutton termed the 'combined' test, because it requires us to ask two questions, one 'objective' and the other 'subjective':

1. The *objective* test: would honest and reasonable people view the defendant's conduct as dishonest?
2. The *subjective* test: did the defendant realise that honest and reasonable people would view his conduct as dishonest?

Only if both questions are answered affirmatively will the defendant be found to be dishonest.

Lord Hutton supported this interpretation of the dishonesty requirement on two grounds. First, he considered that this was the test that Lord Nicholls had in mind in *Royal Brunei Airlines v Tan*. Despite Lord Nicholls never having mentioned the need for the defendant to have realised that his conduct was dishonest by the standards of honest and reasonable people, Lord Hutton considered that this was the only way to make sense of Lord Nicholls' reference to dishonesty having a subjective element or aspect.

Second, Lord Hutton considered that this second question was also important as a matter of principle [35]:

> A finding by a judge that a defendant has been dishonest is a grave finding, and it is particularly grave against a professional man, such as a solicitor. Notwithstanding that the issue arises in equity law and not in a criminal context, I think that it would be less than just for the law to permit a finding that a defendant had been 'dishonest' in assisting in a breach of trust where he knew of the facts which created the trust but had not been aware that what he was doing would be regarded by honest men as being dishonest.

Lord Millett dissented on this issue, disagreeing with both of Lord Hutton's reasons for adopting the combined test. He considered that Lord Nicholls had intended an objective standard whereby the defendant's honesty would be determined by reference to the standards of honest and reasonable people, taking into account the defendant's (subjective) knowledge, experience and intelligence, but without the need for the defendant to have appreciated that he was transgressing these standards. Moreover, Lord Millett believed that this approach was sound in principle [127]:

> Consciousness of wrongdoing is an aspect of mens rea and an appropriate condition of criminal liability: it is not an appropriate condition of civil liability. This generally results from negligent or intentional conduct. For the purpose of civil liability, it should not be necessary that the defendant realised that his conduct was dishonest; it should be sufficient that it constituted intentional wrongdoing.

There seems little doubt that Lord Millett's reading of Lord Nicholls' judgment is the correct one. In particular, it is plain, as we have seen earlier, that we can explain his reference to dishonesty having a subjective element without the need for the second 'subjective' test introduced by Lord Hutton. However, in relation to the arguments from principle, neither is particularly persuasive. Lord Hutton's argument that the second 'subjective' limb is required if we are to justify stigmatising the defendant as dishonest, gets things the wrong way around. Our labels ('dishonesty', 'fraud', 'unconscionability', etc.) should be determined by the content of the relevant rules, not vice versa. If the complaint is with labelling the defendant 'dishonest', rather than with the attribution of liability to him, then the label should change to better reflect the rule, not the rule change to fit the label. However, neither are Lord Millett's reasons for rejecting the second limb of the combined test altogether convincing. Although it is true that the civil law is prepared to find fault and liability where the criminal law finds none, it does not follow that in all cases the civil law should apply a watered down notion of fault, or that it should not be concerned with genuine moral wrongdoing. After all, whether we are concerned with criminal or civil law, we need a good reason to justify the imposition of liability. Moral wrongdoing is such a reason; 'wrongdoing' empty of any genuine culpability is not.

There are nonetheless good reasons for rejecting the combined test and its requirement that the defendant realise that he is transgressing the standard of honesty held by honest and reasonable people. First, it makes it that much easier for genuinely dishonest defendants to escape liability. So long as a defendant can persuade the court that he had not considered how honest and reasonable people would view what he did, he will escape liability. Of course, the court will not simply take the defendant's word for it, and the more implausible claims of such 'moral ignorance' are likely to be dismissed. Nonetheless, it does provide a potential escape route for wrongdoers.

Now this is a necessary consequence of all 'subjective' mens rea requirements. There is rarely any direct evidence of the defendant's state of mind, so it is always possible that the defendant will lie about his true state of mind. As such, this sort of escape route will always be available. However, we should be particularly wary of giving defendants this opportunity of avoiding liability, if the requirement makes little or no moral difference to the case against the defendant. It seems to be assumed on both sides in *Twinsectra* that genuine moral fault requires consciousness that you are breaching the standards of honest, reasonable people. But this may not be true. It can be argued that those who are aware that they are transgressing such standards at least show some awareness of the expectations of the law and of other members of society. By contrast, we may think that those who are not even aware of these standards, or who are able to convince themselves that their own actions would be considered acceptable, show an even greater disregard for the law and social mores and pose an even greater danger.

Second, both the majority and minority in *Twinsectra* appear to misunderstand what is meant by 'subjective' fault or mens rea in the law generally and in the criminal law in particular. Normally, when we describe a fault requirement as 'subjective' rather than 'objective', we mean that the defendant must himself have intended or foreseen some relevant consequence of his actions, or have believed that certain facts existed. By contrast, a fault requirement is 'objective' when it is enough that a reasonable person would have – and hence the defendant should have – foreseen some consequence of his actions or been aware of certain surrounding circumstances. So, 'subjective' recklessness requires that the defendant foresaw the relevant risk (eg of injuring the victim, damaging his property), whereas 'objective' recklessness requires only that a reasonable person would have foreseen this (see *R v G* [2003] UKHL 50; [2004] 1 AC 1034).

Therefore, what makes a fault requirement 'subjective' is that it judges the defendant by reference to the *facts* as he believed them to be and the *factual* outcomes he intended to, or thought he may, bring about. We *do not* usually say that 'subjective' fault requirements require the defendant himself to have been aware or to have accepted that his actions were morally or legally wrongful. So, to be guilty of murder the defendant must intend to kill or to cause grievous bodily harm. It is no defence to say that, although you did intend to kill or cause GBH, you did not think that what you did was against the law and/or contrary to societal moral standards (if this seems an implausible claim, imagine a case of euthanasia or the deliberate killing of an escaping burglar). Similarly, in offences that require subjective recklessness, the defendant must have foreseen the relevant risk, but there is no requirement that he should consider the risk an unreasonable one to take, or that he be aware that honest, reasonable people consider this risk unreasonable.

In short, in all these cases, although the fault requirement is subjective in that it asks what the defendant himself factually intended, foresaw and believed, the *standard* we apply is objective. Moreover, we do not require the defendant to have been aware of or to have accepted that standard. The only significant exception to this in the criminal law is the test for dishonesty, established in *R v Ghosh* [1982] QB 1053, where the Court of Appeal set down the same test as Lord Hutton later adopted in *Twinsectra*. But there, as here, the requirement that the defendant must be aware that he is transgressing the standards of reasonable people is anomalous and unnecessary, and was introduced by the Court of Appeal only because the Court wrongly believed that this was necessary to make the test 'subjective'. In fact, the dishonesty test set down by Lord Nicholls *is* subjective in the sense in which that term is conventionally used in the criminal law. Although the standard applied is 'objective' in that it is imposed on the defendant whether or not he likes it, and whether or not he knows of it, it judges him by reference to what *he* knew and intended.

So the better view is that, contrary to Lord Millett, *subjective* fault is an appropriate basis for liability for assistance in a breach of trust, but that, contrary to Lord

Hutton, this does not require the addition of a requirement that the defendant be aware that he is acting in a way which honest and reasonable people would consider dishonest.

Thankfully, Lord Nicholls' approach has more recently been reaffirmed by the Privy Council in *Barlow Clowes International Ltd v Eurotrust International Ltd* [2005] UKPC 37; [2006] 1 WLR 1476. Rather unconvincingly, in giving the judgment of the Board, Lord Hoffmann claimed that there was no difference in approach between Lord Nicholls in *Royal Brunei Airlines v Tan* and Lord Hutton (and the other members of the majority) in *Twinsectra*, instead saying that there was simply 'an element of ambiguity' in Lord Hutton's judgment [15]:

> ... which may have encouraged a belief ... that the *Twinsectra* case had departed from the law as previously understood and invited inquiry not merely into the defendant's mental state about the nature of the transaction in which he was participating but also into his views about generally acceptable standards of honesty.

Lord Hoffmann, however, held that this second step was not necessary and confirmed that the only relevant question was whether the defendant, given what he knew about the transaction he was involved in, was dishonest by the standards of honest and reasonable people. As Lord Hoffmann put it [10], '[a]lthough a dishonest state of mind is a subjective mental state, the standard by which the law determines whether it is dishonest is objective.'

Barlow Clowes v Eurotrust is a decision of the Privy Council and so *Twinsectra* remains the leading case here. However, accepting the line that it simply clarifies, rather than departs from, what was said in *Twinsectra*, the courts have followed the approach set out in *Barlow Clowes*: see for example *Abou-Rahmah v Abacha* [2006] EWCA Civ 1492; [2007] 1 All ER (Comm) 827; *Al Khudairi v Abbey Brokers Ltd* [2010] EWHC 1486 (Ch); [2010] PNLR 32; *Starglade Properties Ltd v Nash* [2010] EWCA Civ 1314. As such, a finding of dishonesty does not depend on establishing that the defendant appreciated that his conduct would be considered dishonest by honest and reasonable people.

Barlow Clowes v Eurotrust also makes another point clear. In *Brinks Ltd v Abu-Saleh (No. 3)* [1996] CLC 133, the defendant did not know that her husband was assisting a breach of trust, instead believing or suspecting that he was involved in tax evasion. Rimer J held that this was insufficient for liability in dishonest assistance, and that it was necessary for the defendant to know of the existence of the trust or at least of the facts giving rise to it. Lord Hoffmann held that this was incorrect, and that it was sufficient that the defendant knew or suspected that he was assisting in a misappropriation of money or other property.

14.24 A return to 'knowing' assistance?

This leaves us with one unresolved issue. If, as we have seen and as Lord Hoffmann stressed in *Barlow Clowes v Eurotrust*, a finding of dishonesty depends on and derives from the defendant's knowledge of the transaction in which he was involved – that is whether he knew or suspected that he was participating in or assisting a breach of trust or other unlawful scheme – then how is a requirement of dishonesty any different from a requirement of knowledge? Indeed, Lord Millett in his dissent in *Twinsectra* considered that there was no difference between dishonesty, so understood, and a test framed in terms of knowledge. A defendant will be dishonest, and hence liable, if he knows that he is participating in a breach of trust, or if he suspects this but chooses to go ahead without asking questions (see also *Barlow Clowes International Ltd v Eurotrust International Ltd* [2005] UKPC 37; [2006] 1 WLR 1476, [10]).

This question matters because 'dishonesty' as a fault requirement brings some of the same problems we encountered earlier in relation to the test of 'unconscionability' in knowing receipt (Section 14.20). As we have noted a couple of times already (Sections 9.21–9.22 and 14.20), ideally we want our legal rules to identify the circumstances, the facts, which need to be established for liability to arise. 'Dishonesty' is not a fact, 'knowledge' is. Therefore, a test framed in terms of dishonesty will always require us to ask 'on what facts is someone to be regarded as dishonest?' But this is what our fault requirement should be doing; it should be telling us what fact, what mental state, is needed for the defendant to be liable. As such, a test of dishonesty fails to tell us what we need to know (unless dishonesty is to be equated with knowledge, in which case why introduce the notion of dishonesty in the first place?).

In *Royal Brunei Airlines v Tan* (Section 14.23), Lord Nicholls preferred a dishonesty requirement to a test framed in terms of knowledge because he considered that this avoided the difficulties that the courts had encountered in framing the correct level of knowledge needed for liability. However, given that a defendant's honesty can only be determined by reference to what he knew and intended, the dishonesty test does not avoid the need to inquire into the defendant's state of mind and to identify what type or degree of knowledge is necessary for liability. We may question, therefore, whether we would be better off forgetting dishonesty and instead stating clearly what sort of knowledge or state of mind the defendant must possess to be liable. This seems to be the direction in which the courts are going, in which case we may soon be talking of 'knowing' assistance once again.

The only advantage a dishonesty test has over one framed in terms of knowledge is that there may be situations in which the defendant had knowledge that he was assisting a breach and yet we nonetheless feel that he did not act wrongfully (or not so wrongfully as to merit liability). This may be the case where the trustee commits a 'judicious' breach of trust, that is, a breach designed to benefit the beneficiary. If we do indeed feel that a defendant who knowingly assisted a breach of trust because he (perhaps misguidedly) believed that this was in the beneficiary's best interests should not be held liable, it is clearly inadequate to frame a test which makes liability dependent purely on the defendant's knowledge of the breach.

A solution would be to frame the fault requirement in terms of intention and/or recklessness rather than knowledge. For instance, we could say that a defendant will be liable if he either intended to act contrary to the beneficiary's interests, or if he was reckless (or indifferent) as to whether his actions would be contrary to the beneficiary's interests. This is preferable to an unqualified and hence imprecise dishonesty requirement, as it identifies what specific fact – what precise state of mind – needs to be proved to generate the defendant's liability.

14.25 Combining claims

We have seen that a number of claims may in principle be open to a beneficiary who has suffered a breach of trust. He can, of course, sue his trustee for breach of trust, recovering either the losses, if any, he has suffered or any gains the trustee has made from his breach. He may make similar claims against third parties who either have knowingly received trust property, or have dishonestly assisted in the trustee's breach or its cover up. Finally, he can recover property in which he can establish some subsisting equitable interest. So, in some cases, a beneficiary may have a number of different claims against a number of different defendants. The question then is to what extent he is required to choose among them.

As a matter of principle, a beneficiary should be able to combine claims so long as:

1. they do not lead to double recovery; and
2. they are not mutually inconsistent.

To the extent that the beneficiary does then need to make a choice between alternative claims, he needs to make that choice only once judgment is given and hence when he knows exactly which claims are successful and what they would enable him to recover: *Tang Man Sit v Capacious Investments Ltd* [1996] AC 514.

Double recovery is where the claimant seeks compensation twice over in respect of the same loss. Clearly, once one defendant has compensated B for the loss caused by his breach, B cannot then claim compensation for that loss from another defendant, because necessarily that loss no longer exists. So if, for example, the beneficiary has claims against both his trustee and a third-party dishonest assistant, both are in principle liable to make good whatever loss the beneficiary has suffered. However, although the beneficiary can choose from whom he shall demand compensation, he cannot obtain full compensation from them both, as this would give him more than his total loss.

Another example of this arises where the trustee makes a gain and the beneficiary suffers a loss by virtue of a breach of trust. Recovery of this gain from the trustee necessarily has the effect, to that extent, of making good the loss suffered by the beneficiary. Therefore, the beneficiary cannot recover both full compensation *and* the full profits made by the trustee: see *Tang Man Sit v Capacious Investments Ltd*; cf Birks, 1996b.

Inconsistent claims are best understood by an example. Say a trustee, T, wrongfully sells shares which he holds on trust to a third party, D, who knows that T is acting in breach of trust. In this case, if D retains the shares and T retains the money he received for them, the beneficiary has two potential proprietary claims. He can follow the shares into D's hands, or he can trace into the money acquired by T. However, he is not allowed to claim both the shares and the money. The idea behind tracing is that the substitute (here the money) may be treated as representing or embodying the 'value' of the original trust property (the shares): see Section 14.3. Clearly, then, the beneficiary cannot say that the value of his original trust property is now to be found in the money while at the same time maintaining that the shares remain his. The language of 'substitution' makes the same point. The substitute takes the place of the original trust asset and so cannot be claimed in addition to it. For the same reason, if D had since given the shares away, so leaving no traceable substitute, the beneficiary could not bring both a proprietary claim for the money against T and a claim in knowing receipt against D. This is because the knowing receipt claim involves treating the shares, when held by D, as trust property, and this is incompatible with the beneficiary's claim that the money received in return for those shares is also trust property.

It is sometimes said that, where a trustee misapplies trust property, a beneficiary cannot combine a personal claim against the trustee for compensation with a claim (whether proprietary or in knowing receipt) dependent on tracing. Take the following example. The trustee, T, wrongfully uses £10,000 of trust money to buy a car, which he then gives away to a third party, D. As D has given no value, he is not a bona fide purchaser for value without notice. The car is now worth only £6,000. The beneficiary, B, has a claim that T compensate him for his loss as well as a proprietary claim against D for the car, as it is the traceable substitute of the trust money. Of course, B cannot claim both the car and the full £10,000 from T as compensation, as the recovery of the car reduces B's loss. But can B recover both the car from D and £4,000 from T? After all, if B recovers the car, he remains £4,000 worse off, so recovering this from T would not amount to double recovery.

It has been suggested, however, that B cannot do this (see Penner, 2012, 368–70). The argument is that, when B traces into substitute assets acquired in exchange for original trust property, he 'adopts' the transfer or sale of the trust property made by T. In other words, although T should not have used the trust money to buy the car, and hence it constitutes a breach of trust, B can choose to treat this as an authorised application of trust money, and so treat the car as purchased on behalf of the trust. This makes T's otherwise wrongful use of the trust money a legitimate one. However, if this is so, B no longer has any claim against T for breach of trust and hence for compensation for any losses caused by T's actions. In other words, B can regard the purchase of the car as wrongful, in which case he can sue T for breach of trust but has no claim to the car, or he can treat it as an authorised purchase, in which case he can recover the car but has no claim for breach of trust. Claiming the car *and* compensation for any remaining loss would therefore involve inconsistent and incompatible claims.

This adoption theory of tracing has more than an air of unreality. Moreover, it is unnecessary, for there seem to be alternative and more plausible ways of understanding why we allow beneficiaries to trace into substitute assets. As we have seen (Section 14.4), one popular view is that claims to traceable substitutes arise as a response to unjust enrichment. The House of Lords' preferred view in *Foskett v McKeown* [2001] 1 AC 112 was that the ability to claim substitute assets was simply one aspect or corollary of a beneficiary's equitable beneficial interest in the trust property. Neither of these views involves the beneficiary authorising or endorsing the trustee's apparent misapplication of trust property, and neither of them compels us to regard claims dependent on tracing as incompatible with claims for breach of trust. Moreover, on the adoption view, we could not explain the operation of tracing where the defendant has no power to dispose of the trust property. This is likely to be the case in most cases of constructive and resulting trusts. Furthermore, it would leave us requiring a different explanation for tracing at common law, where necessarily there is nobody in a position analogous to a trustee with powers to dispose of the claimant's property.

Accordingly, neither principle nor (recent) authority supports this adoption view. As such, we should allow a beneficiary both to claim title to traceable proceeds of misapplied trust assets *and* to claim from his trustee (or a third-party wrongdoer) compensation for any remaining loss caused by the breach.

Summary

▶ Where a breach of trust has been committed, the beneficiary may of course bring a claim against his trustee for that breach. However, the law also recognises three other types of claim. These are:

1. *proprietary claims* against current holders of misapplied trust assets;
2. claims in *knowing receipt* against third parties who at some point received misapplied trust assets; and
3. claims for *dishonest assistance* against those who procured or assisted in the breach.

▶ In understanding these various claims and the differences between them, it is important to keep in mind the distinction between *personal* and *proprietary* claims. A proprietary claim amounts to an assertion by the beneficiary that he has an interest in some asset held by the defendant, and that, as such, the beneficiary should be able to recover it (or some part of it or its value). A personal claim is, by contrast, simply a demand that the defendant do something to or for the beneficiary (eg pay him compensation for losses he has caused).

▶ Proprietary claims, therefore, endure only so long as both the relevant property and the beneficiary's interest in that property remain in existence. Personal claims need not be so limited. By contrast, proprietary claims will give the beneficiary priority in the event of the defendant's insolvency, whereas beneficiaries bringing personal claims against an insolvent defendant will receive, at most, a proportionate share of the money they are owed, and so bear at least some of the shortfall in the defendant's assets.

▶ Where trust property is misapplied, the beneficiary may recover it from whoever currently holds it, unless that property is held by, or has passed through the hands of, a bona fide purchaser for value without notice. A beneficiary can also claim property which has been acquired in exchange for pre-existing trust property. This process is known as *tracing*.

▶ Claims to traceable substitutes – ie property acquired in exchange for trust property – are straightforward where there has been a clean substitution, that is, where only trust property was transferred in exchange for the substitute. In such cases, the beneficiary can demand that the substitute be given up to him.

▶ Mixed substitutions pose greater problems. These occur where the substitute property was acquired in exchange for the beneficiary's trust property and property from some other source. If the other property came from another innocent party, the beneficiary can claim only a share of the substitute proportionate to his contribution to the cost of its acquisition. So, if £100 of trust money and £100 of another innocent party's money are combined to buy a painting, the beneficiary can claim no more than a half share of the painting.

▶ If, however, trust property is combined with the property of a wrongdoer, such as the trustee or a knowing recipient, then the beneficiary has a choice. He can either claim a proportionate share of the substitute reflecting his contribution to the exchange *or* he can claim a charge over the substitute to the value of his contribution. This latter option entitles the beneficiary to have the substitute sold and to recover a sum equal to the value of his contribution from the proceeds of sale. So, if £100 of trust money and £100 of the trustee's own money are combined to buy a painting, the beneficiary could claim either a half share in the painting or a charge over the painting to the value of £100. Claiming a proportionate share will be advantageous if the painting has since increased in value, whereas claiming a charge will be preferable if its value has fallen.

Summary cont'd

▶ Particular difficulties are encountered when trust money is paid into another person's bank account. Again, different rules apply depending on whether the other money in the account derives from another innocent party or from a wrongdoer. Where all contributors to the bank account are innocent, the traditional solution is to apply the 'first in, first out' rule. This says that money is to be treated as withdrawn from the account in the same order in which it was paid in. This rule can, however, lead to arbitrary and unjust results, and in such cases the courts have been willing to take a different approach – namely, to treat all withdrawals as being shared between all contributors to the account in proportion to their contributions to the total deposits into that account. So, on this basis, if half the money paid into the account came from the trust, then half of every withdrawal would be viewed as constituting trust money.

▶ Where the other money paid into the account comes from a wrongdoer, the 'first in, first out' rule does not apply. Instead, it seems that the courts allow the beneficiary to 'cherry-pick' which withdrawals from the account are to be treated as withdrawals of trust money (and, by contrast, which contributions are to be treated as coming from the wrongdoer's own money). The only limit is that the beneficiary cannot claim as his a withdrawal which could not possibly be made up of trust money. The clearest example of this is the *lowest intermediate balance rule*, which says that the beneficiary can claim no more from the account than the lowest sum credited to that account in the period between the trust money being paid into it and the date of the claim. This is because, when the account reached this lowest point, it became impossible to argue that there was any more trust money in the account than this sum.

▶ It is impossible to trace if nothing is acquired in exchange for a transfer of trust property. Traditionally, it has been thought that this is the case where trust money is used to pay off a debt. However, it has been argued that, where the debt arose as a result of buying property on credit, the beneficiary should be able to trace into that property. This is known as *backwards tracing*.

▶ A proprietary claim, whether to the originally misapplied trust property or to a traceable substitute, can succeed only so long as the defendant retains such property. However, there exists a second type of claim which may be brought against recipients of trust property, and which does not require the defendant to retain any such property. This is the claim we call *knowing receipt*.

▶ Such a claim has two elements:

1. the defendant must have received trust property; and
2. when he received it, or at some point while it was in his possession, he knew, or perhaps ought to have known, that that property derived from a breach of trust.

▶ As the preceding formulation shows, it is uncertain what exact level of knowledge is needed to establish a defendant's liability. Actual knowledge is clearly enough. What is uncertain is whether constructive knowledge – where the defendant could and should have discovered the facts – suffices. The latest authority suggests that liability will attach only where the defendant's knowledge is such that it would be 'unconscionable' to allow him to retain the benefit of the property. This, however, takes us no further in determining what level of knowledge is sufficient for the claim to succeed. Moreover, it has been argued that *no* knowledge should be required, and that liability should instead be strict, subject to the defence of change of position.

▶ A beneficiary also has a claim against any third party who dishonestly procured or assisted a breach of trust. The test of dishonesty requires the court to ask whether, given what the defendant knew of his actions and the surrounding circumstances, honest and reasonable people would call his conduct dishonest.

Exercises

14.1 What differences exist between personal and proprietary claims? When will each be advantageous to a claimant?

14.2 Can the rules for the tracing of equitable property rights be reduced to a rational set of principles?

14.3 Leigh is a trustee of a substantial settlement. His friend and sometime business partner, Dan, tells him that if he invests some of the trust fund in Dan's new business venture then the beneficiaries will obtain a great return. Dan also promises Leigh that he will give him a commission in respect of any profits made from the investment. Leigh thinks this all sounds fantastic and immediately writes a cheque, transferring £100,000 from the trust fund to Dan.

In fact Dan had no new business venture in mind and simply wanted to get hold of some money to be used for his own ends. He took the cheque and paid it into his account at Barclloyd's Bank. When he handed over the cheque, Venetia, the cashier, joked, 'You haven't just robbed a bank have you?' Dan smirked and replied, 'This is to be kept between you and me', and slipped Venetia a £50 note. Flustered, Venetia pocketed the £50.

Venetia was too embarrassed to tell her superiors at the bank what had happened. She kept the £50 and used it to buy lottery tickets. One of these earned her a prize of £1,000 which she gave to her brother, Jeremy. Over time, the money is dissipated from the bank account. The evidence reveals only that Dan used £50,000 to pay off the mortgage on his home. It is not known where the rest of the money went. Leigh never received any cut of the money.

Advise the beneficiaries.

14.4 Why do some people argue that personal liability for receipt of trust property should be strict? Does it make sense to allow those who have innocently benefited from another's trust property to retain those benefits?

14.5 Saunders is waiting outside Subway to buy a sandwich, when Morrell and Red approach him. Morrell snatches Saunders' wallet from his hand and throws it to Red. While Morrell restrains Saunders, Red goes through his wallet and takes out a £5 note. She then goes into Subway and asks for a can of coke. Jamie, who is working behind the till, has seen what happened and says to Red, 'You really should give him his money back'. Red glares dismissively back at Jamie, who then accepts the stolen £5 note from Red in payment for the can of coke.

Having drunk the coke, Red throws the wallet to the ground. She and Morrell then run off, leaving Saunders to pick up his wallet, now short of £5.

Still with the change left from the £5, Red and Morrell go to the newsagents. Morrell, who was going to buy some lottery scratch cards in any case, uses some of this money to buy a scratch card. He scratches off the panels and finds that he has won £10,000.

Advise Saunders on any equitable claims he can bring against Morrell, Red and Jamie.

14.6 How do we establish whether a defendant is dishonest in relation to claims for dishonest assistance?

Further reading

Academic writing in this area tends to focus on one of two questions. First, there are discussions of the basis and content of the tracing rules. Smith's book here is the leading work. Second, there are a huge number of articles and essays on (knowing) receipt. The best starting point here is Nicholls' essay, which neatly sets up the basic issues, on which the more difficult pieces by Smith and Birks then build.

Akkouh and Worthington, '*Re Diplock* (1948)' in Mitchell and Mitchell, *Landmark Cases in the Law of Restitution* (Hart Publishing 2006)

Birks, 'Overview: tracing, claiming and defences' in Birks (ed), *Laundering and Tracing* (Oxford University Press 1995)

Birks, 'Receipt' in Birks and Pretto (eds), *Breach of Trust* (Hart Publishing 2002)

Burrows, 'Proprietary restitution: unmasking unjust enrichment' (2001) 117 LQR 412

Conaglen, 'Difficulties with tracing backwards' (2011) 127 LQR 432

Evans, 'Rethinking tracing and the law of restitution' (1999) 115 LQR 469

Hayton, 'Equity's identification rules' in Birks (ed), *Laundering and Tracing* (Oxford University Press 1995)

Martin, 'Recipient liability after *Westdeutsche*' [1998] Conv 13

Mitchell, 'Assistance' in Birks and Pretto (eds), *Breach of Trust* (Hart Publishing 2002)

Mitchell and Watterson, 'Remedies for knowing receipt' in Mitchell (ed), *Constructive and Resulting Trusts* (Hart Publishing 2010)

Nicholls, 'Knowing receipt: the need for a new landmark' in Cornish, Nolan, O'Sullivan and Virgo (eds), *Restitution: Past, Present and Future* (Hart Publishing 1998)

Smith, *The Law of Tracing* (Oxford University Press 1997)

Smith, 'Tracing into the payment of a debt' [1995] Cam LJ 290

Smith, 'Tracing, "swollen assets" and the lowest intermediate balance: *Bishopsgate Investment Management Ltd v Homan*' (1994) 8 Tru Ll 102

Smith, 'Unjust enrichment, property, and the structure of trusts' (2000) 116 LQR 412

Smith, 'W(h)ither knowing receipt' (1998) 114 LQR 394

15.1 Equitable remedies

We saw in Chapter 1 that the rules of equity developed in order to mitigate the hardship that could be caused by a strict application of the common law. Thus, the usual common law remedy was an order that the defendant pay a sum of money to the claimant. Although such an order would and does provide adequate relief in the vast majority of claims that come before the courts – such as a claim in debt arising between two companies, or a claim for personal injury arising out of negligent driving or a professional negligence claim against an architect – there are other cases where relief of a different type is required to do justice.

Say that a group of travellers are about to set up camp on a land belonging to a claimant, or an ex-employee of a claimant has stolen confidential information and intends to use it to set up a rival business, or a claimant brings a claim against an alleged fraudster and there is a real risk that the latter will hide his assets in order to prevent the claimant from enforcing any eventual judgment, or that a claimant believes its patented products are being illegitimately copied and that incriminating evidence will be destroyed by a defendant if he is given notice of the claimant's claim. In each of these situations a monetary judgment will or may be inadequate – whether because the defendant is unwilling or unable to meet the judgment or because the damage that may be caused is incapable of monetary remedy.

It was to respond to these situations that the courts of equity started to grant injunctions, that is, orders requiring a defendant to a claim to do something (a *mandatory* injunction) or to refrain from acting in a certain manner (a *prohibitory* injunction). Thus, in an appropriate case, the travellers might be ordered not to set up camp on a claimant's land, the ex-employee might be ordered to deliver up the secret information to the claimant and not to establish a rival business, or a defendant might be ordered not to deal with his assets prior to judgment (a freezing order), or to permit a claimant's solicitors to access his premises in order to seize and copy relevant documents stored therein (a search order).

But so what? If a defendant is acting in an improper manner, what is to say that he will take note of the court's order? The answer lies in the following text, called a penal notice, found on the front page of every injunction issued by the courts:

> If you, [the defendant's name is inserted here], disobey this Order you may be held to be in contempt of court and may be imprisoned, fined or have your assets seized.

So the court has the power to send those who breach its injunctions to prison for contempt of court. Although in years gone by, the Court could impose indeterminate sentences – essentially saying to a defendant who had breached its orders (a contemnor) that he would stay in prison until he could persuade the Court that he would obey in the future – the statutory maximum is now set by section 14 of the Contempt of Court Act 1981 at two years.

Equity developed further remedies to deal with other situations in which the common law did not provide an effective response. For instance, its courts sometimes ordered those who had entered into a contract to complete their bargain (say that a defendant had agreed to sell 100 shares in a private company to a claimant but subsequently reneged on the deal). This is called the remedy of specific performance. On other occasions, it granted a declaration that a contract or gift had been rescinded (for instance, because a gift from a claimant to a defendant had been vitiated by undue influence). Finally, equity sometimes declared that a formal agreement did not represent the true intentions of the parties (say there had been a word processing error in drawing up a contract and the consideration was said to be £10 million rather than £1 million); in such circumstances, the courts would declare that the true agreement between the parties provided for consideration of £1 million.

The equitable remedies and orders described in the previous paragraph – specific performance, rescission and rectification – are important but are typically covered in some depth in contract texts and courses. Here, therefore, we shall focus on the first of the remedies we encountered in this section: the injunction.

15.2 Types of injunction

We have already mentioned two species of injunction: those ordering a defendant to do something (a mandatory or positive injunction), and those ordering a defendant not to do something (a prohibitory or negative injunction). A second important distinction is between an injunction granted at the conclusion of a trial, at which point the court has determined the parties' respective rights, known as a *final* or *perpetual* injunction, and an injunction granted before trial, known as an *interlocutory* or *interim* injunction. Finally, there are injunctions which are granted after a hearing at which both parties have the opportunity to appear and make representations (an *inter partes* or 'on notice' injunction) and, on the other hand, injunctions granted after a hearing at which only the person applying for the injunction is heard (an *ex parte* or 'without notice' injunction).

15.3 When are injunctions granted?

The next thing is to consider the test that the court applies when deciding whether to grant an injunction. As we shall see, the basic rule is that injunctions will only be made in support of a cause of action to protect against the actual or threatened invasion of the claimant's legal rights. The remainder of this chapter will then consider three topics which have exercised the courts over the past half century: first, when the court should grant an interim injunction (ie an injunction before trial, requiring a party against whom nothing has been proved to do something or refrain from acting in a certain manner); second, in what circumstances is it appropriate for the courts to grant a freezing injunction, requiring a defendant to refrain from dealing with his assets; and third, when it is appropriate to grant a search order, an order requiring a defendant to permit a claimant's solicitors access to his premises in order to seize and copy documents.

When a judge of the High Court grants an injunction, he does so pursuant to section 37 of the Senior Courts Act 1981. That section provides:

> The High Court may by order (whether interlocutory or final) grant an injunction … in all cases in which it appears to the court to be just and convenient to do so.

Equivalent text is contained in section 38 of the County Courts Act 1984, the Act regulating inferior civil courts. At first blush, this section appears to be drafted in almost unlimited terms. Does this mean that anyone can apply for an injunction because they disapprove of the actions of another on moral or other grounds? Can a claimant seek an injunction prohibiting his neighbour from conducting an extra-marital affair, or against a politician requiring him not to implement legal policies an applicant finds unpalatable, or against Prince Harry prohibiting him from returning to Las Vegas?

Common sense suggests that the answer must be no. If the courts were able to grant relief whenever anyone objected to the actions of another on moral grounds, they would be overrun with often petty disputes. The legal reasoning in support of this answer was supplied by the House of Lords in a series of cases decided in the 1970s and 1980s. The first such decision is *The Siskina* (*Siskina (Owners of Cargo lately Laden on Board) v Distos Compania Naviera SA*) [1979] AC 210. That was a case in which a claimant did have a cause of action against a defendant, but it was one which was not actionable in this jurisdiction. The House of Lords therefore held that the English courts had no jurisdiction to grant an injunction in aid of the claimant's position. More importantly, Lord Diplock laid down the following classic statement of principle:

> ... an injunction is not a cause of action. It cannot stand on its own. It is dependent upon there being a pre-existing cause of action against the defendant arising out of an invasion, actual or threatened by him, of a legal or equitable right of the [claimant] for the enforcement of which the defendant is amenable to the jurisdiction of the court. The right to obtain an injunction is merely ancillary and incidental to the pre-existing cause of action.

Thus, in the vast majority of cases in which an injunction is granted, the order is made in response to an actual or threatened invasion of a right held by the claimant. For instance, where a court orders squatters to leave land to which they have no right to possession, it acts to vindicate the claimant's proprietary rights to that land, which gives the claimant a cause of action in trespass. And where a court orders that a neighbour cease playing loud music all night long, the defendant is committing a private nuisance, which again gives the claimant a cause of action against him.

Moreover, the court's powers are flexible enough to allow the court to act where there is a 'threatened' invasion of a legal or equitable right of the claimant. Thus, the court can prohibit a group of travellers from entering onto land before they have even done so, if the claimant has evidence to suggest that this is how the travellers propose to act. Such an order is called a *quia timet* injunction, meaning literally 'because he/she fears'.

But not all injunctions which the courts grant are obviously made in relation to the actual or threatened invasion of a legal or equitable right held by a claimant. Take, for instance, a freezing order (see Section 15.6). The claimant has no cause of action against a defendant if the defendant deals with his assets before judgment; but, as we shall see, a freezing order has the effect of prohibiting the defendant from dealing with his assets in very fundamental respects. The same point can be made in relation to search orders (see Section 15.7): before a claim is started, a claimant has no general legal right to prevent a defendant from destroying his own documents or deleting files from his computer.

Other examples can be given. Take a *Norwich Pharmacal* disclosure order (named after *Norwich Pharmacal v Customs & Excise Cmrs* [1974] AC 133), often made against third parties who have innocently become caught up in a wrong committed by the true defendant, requiring them to name or provide other information about the true defendant. The courts routinely grant such orders, which require third parties to provide specified information and therefore amount to mandatory injunctions, even though the claimant has no cause of action against the third party himself.

Lord Brandon recognised that Lord Diplock's account of the availability of injunctions needed extending in *South Carolina Insurance Co v Assurantie* [1987] AC 24. He considered that injunctions should be granted where either a party had invaded or threatened to invade a legal or equitable right of another party which is amenable to the jurisdiction of the court (in agreement with Lord Diplock in *The Siskina*), *or* where a party had behaved or threatened to behave in an unconscionable manner. (For discussion of the idea of unconscionability and the problems it raises, see Sections 6.4, 14.20.)

Lord Brandon recognised, however, that even this extended statement of principle was incomplete as it did not explain the jurisprudential basis on which a freezing order is granted. Neither does it account for the grant of *Norwich Pharmacal* relief, because this is often made against third parties who have not acted unconscionably (as happened in the *Norwich Pharmacal* case, where the order was made against the Customs & Excise Commissioners, to whom the defendant's identity had been disclosed when certain goods which were alleged to contravene the claimant's patent were imported).

There are two ways around this difficulty. One is simply to say that there are exceptions to the general rule set out by the House of Lords in *The Siskina* and *South Carolina*. But this tells us nothing other than that the rule as stated is incomplete and that it fails to explain why the court has acted as it has. The second is to say that the court can also grant injunctions where it is just and convenient to do so in support of or to render more effective a legal or equitable right held by a claimant. This would explain why freezing, search and *Norwich Pharmacal* orders are made: to render more effective a cause of action vested in a claimant by ensuring that the claimant can enforce his judgment, obtain documents that assist its case, or obtain information about a wrongdoer.

Of course, this still leaves much unclear and appears to leave courts with a fair amount of latitude when it comes to deciding whether to grant an injunction. This impression is compounded by repeated declarations that equitable remedies are discretionary. In reality, however, this equitable discretion is exercised in accordance with more or less settled norms and practices.

The issue we have been addressing in the preceding paragraphs concerns the grant of injunctions other than in situations where the claimant's rights have been or may be infringed by the defendant's conduct. However, it should not be thought that an injunction is available as of right every time the claimant's rights are threatened or even infringed by a defendant. Here too the court has discretion. In particular, the court may refuse to grant an injunction when the wrong complained of is trivial, or where the claimant has acquiesced in the wrong or unreasonably delayed in seeking relief, or where the claimant himself has acted improperly in some relevant manner, or where it would practically speaking be impossible for a defendant to comply with an injunction, or where an injunction would cause unreasonable hardship to a defendant.

15.4 Damages in lieu of an injunction

Where no injunction is granted, the claimant may still be entitled to damages for any infringement of his legal rights. Traditionally the courts of Chancery did not award damages for equitable wrongs. This was changed, however, by the Chancery Amendment Act 1858 (also known as Lord Cairns' Act; the relevant provision is now section 50 of the Senior Courts Act 1981), which allowed for damages to be awarded in lieu of or in addition to an injunction or an order of specific performance.

The significance of the Act is that it enabled courts to order damages in situations to which the common law jurisdiction to award damages did not extend. This was the case where the cause of action was equitable, and so the common law recognised no claim in the first place, but also where, although a common law claim existed, no damages were available. For instance, the common law did not allow awards of damages for future losses. This new jurisdiction to award damages granted by the Act extends only to cases where an injunction or specific performance is in principle available. So it does not extend, for example, to contracts which the court would never order to specifically be performed (although in such cases, damages are available under the common law jurisdiction). However, so long as specific performance or an injunction is potentially available, damages can be awarded under the Act even if, on the facts, specific performance or an injunction would be denied. Indeed these are the cases where the jurisdiction to award damages is most significant.

The courts have often stated a preference for damages awards over forms of specific relief. So, in contract law, the basic rule is that specific performance is available only where damages would be an inadequate remedy. However, when it comes to awarding damages in lieu of an injunction, the courts take effectively the opposite starting point. The following 'good working rule' when determining whether to make an award of damages rather than grant an injunction was set down by A L Smith LJ in *Shelfer v City of London Electric Lighting Co* [1895] 1 Ch 287, 322–23:

1. If the injury to the plaintiff's legal rights is small,
2. And is one which is capable of being estimated in money,
3. And is one which can be adequately compensated by a small monetary payment,
4. And the case is one in which it would be oppressive to the defendant to grant an injunction –
   then damages in substitution for an injunction may be given.

As A L Smith LJ went on to say, it does not follow that the presence of all four of these requirements means that the court *ought* to award damages. For instance, an injunction may still be ordered where the defendant has acted in reckless disregard of the claimant's rights. He also stressed that the interpretation of the four requirements will vary from case to case. So, what constitutes a small injury may differ depending on the parties and the situation in which they find themselves. As a final point, the courts have stressed that this jurisdiction is to be used only in exceptional cases and that it does not enable the courts to legalise wrongful acts or to enable the defendant to 'buy out' the claimant's right that he act or refrain from acting in a particular way (compare here *Miller v Jackson* [1977] QB 966 and *Kennaway v Thompson* [1981] QB 88). Damages awardable under this jurisdiction are assessed on the same basis as common law damages: *Johnson v Agnew* [1980] AC 367.

15.5 Interim injunctions

One feature of modern litigation – and a particular feature of larger litigation – is that there is a considerable delay before cases come to trial. The time lag between the commencement of a claim and its final determination (perhaps on appeal) can range from several months to years. This time lag may seem surprising at first sight. But any claim brought before the court will go through a number of procedural stages: first, the parties explain their positions in documents called pleadings; then the parties disclose relevant documents to each other; then they produce witness statements and (perhaps) reports of expert witnesses. Only then can a trial take place (for which space will need to be found in the court's and counsel's diaries, the witnesses will need to be given notice, and substantial preparation carried out).

This time lag presents the court with a unique difficulty when confronted with a claimant who asks it to grant an injunction against a defendant before trial: it is being asked by the claimant to make an order against a defendant before the claimant has proved its case. Accordingly, if the claimant's case fails, the defendant's freedom to act will have been restricted without good reason. To make matters more difficult, such an injunction can often be of critical importance to a claimant and defendant alike.

Take, for instance, a struggling company whose managing director suddenly quits. A few days later, the company's shareholders learn that the managing director is intending to open a rival business notwithstanding restrictive covenants in his employment contract that seem to prohibit him from doing so for two years, and with the benefit of the claimant's contact list. They go to see their solicitor, who tells them that the former managing director may well be in breach of the restrictive covenants contained in his employment contract (although there is an argument that they might be unenforceable because they are too wide) and that the contact list may also qualify as a confidential information, which the company can prohibit the managing director from using (although this again isn't particularly clear because a lot of the information in the contact list is of a general nature). This is a case where the court will be asked to grant injunctions pre-trial on the basis of causes of action which may, or may not, be established. If the court does not grant the injunction, the claimant may go out of business (although this may happen in any event). And if it does, it will have to prevent the managing director from pursuing a business opportunity which he may, at trial, establish is entirely open to him. Indeed, after the conclusion of the trial the managing director's opportunity to establish his own business may be gone for good.

It was to cater for cases such as this that the House of Lords laid down what have become known as the *American Cyanamid* principles in *American Cyanamid v Ethicon Ltd* [1975] AC 396. The first principle is for the court to consider whether there *may* be substance to the claimant's claim. After all, the court should not make invasive orders against a defendant where the claimant's claim is fanciful or speculative. A good example of a claim that was so weak that it could not justify the grant of an injunction is found in *Morning Star Co-Operative Society Ltd v Express Newspapers Ltd* [1979] FSR 113. There, the claimant, who published the left-wing Morning Star newspaper, complained that the defendant's proposal to publish a newspaper called the Daily Star would lead to the Daily Star being passed off as the claimant's own newspaper. In reality, the two papers were different in just about every respect, with the judge memorably commenting that 'only a moron in a hurry would be misled'. So the claimant's prospects of success were remote and could not found the grant of an interim injunction.

But the courts have not insisted that a claimant must establish a very strong claim, or a claim that is likely to succeed, prior to the grant of an interim injunction. Rather, a claimant must merely demonstrate that his claim raises a 'serious issue' to be tried. Lord Diplock justified this rule in *American Cyanamid* as follows:

> It is no part of the court's function at this stage of the litigation to try to resolve conflicts of evidence on affidavits as to facts on which the claims of either party may ultimately depend nor to decide difficult questions of law which call for detailed argument and mature consideration.

In other words, it is undesirable at the outset of the litigation, when the issues in dispute have not been carefully framed and when the court has not heard oral evidence from witnesses, to conduct a mini-trial as to which side is likely to be found to be correct. So long as a claimant's claim has substance, or there is a 'serious issue' to be tried, the first *American Cyanamid* principle is overcome.

The second principle requires the court to consider whether an award of damages in the claimant's favour would provide him with an adequate remedy. Lord Diplock formulated this principle as follows: 'If damages in the measure recoverable at common law would be an adequate remedy and the defendant would be in a financial position to pay them, no injunction should normally be granted.' In a contractual dispute, an award of damages will usually be an adequate remedy. For example, if a seller of goods or a supplier of services fails to comply with their obligations under a contract, and those goods/services can be obtained elsewhere, then a claimant can adequately be compensated for the defendant's breach of contract by an award of damages (in the amount required to pay for substitute performance together with interest).

Conversely, damages may be inadequate where there is a serious doubt as to whether the defendant will be able to pay them at trial, or the wrong cannot be compensated in money (eg the loss of the right to vote), or the damage is non-pecuniary, or there is no available market for the goods/services which should have been provided, or damages would be difficult to assess (eg where, as in the scenario describe earlier, the failure to grant the injunction may kill off a business). In such circumstances, the second limb of the *American Cyanamid* test will also be satisfied.

The third limb of the test focuses on the effect of the injunction on the defendant. In particular, the court considers whether, if it turns out at trial that the injunction ought not to have been granted because the claimant's case fails, the defendant can adequately be compensated for losses caused by having to comply with the injunction in the meantime. If the defendant can be so compensated, the court will consider whether the claimant would be in a financial position to provide compensation for such losses. If so, the court will require the claimant to promise (or undertake) to make good such losses in the event that an interim injunction is granted but the claimant's claim fails. This is called the claimant's *undertaking in damages*. The court may require the claimant to 'fortify' their undertaking in damages in the event that there is any doubt as to the claimant's solvency, by (for instance) paying money into court or obtaining a bank guarantee.

In the event that a damages award appears fair to the defendant but would be inadequate to the claimant, the court must assess what Lord Diplock called the 'balance of convenience', but which elsewhere has been described as the 'balance of the risk of doing an injustice' (May LJ in *Cayne v Global Natural Resources plc* [1984] 1 All ER 225). This is a wide principle, and Lord Diplock expressly refrained from attempting to list the various matters which may need to be taken into consideration at this stage and the relative weight to be attributed to them.

The final stage of the analysis only arises where the factors which the court decides to weigh under the 'balance of convenience' stage of the test are of even weight. In this situation, the court should, as Lord Diplock held, take such measures as are calculated to preserve the status quo. Where there has been no delay by a claimant in seeking relief, the 'status quo' means the state of affairs which prevailed immediately before the defendant carried out the activities complained of. Hence there is on this basis a stronger case for granting an injunction to prevent a course of conduct which has not yet been commenced than there is to bring an end to an ongoing state of affairs.

Before leaving this topic, we should make two final points. First, the *American Cyanamid* test is the test that is generally applied by the courts. But there are exceptional cases which justify a different tack. For instance, the court will be far more willing to grant an injunction where it seems clear without the examination of detailed evidence that the claimant's claim is very strong. By contrast, the court will be more cautious about granting an interim injunction where it will, in reality, amount to the final disposal of the claimant's claim (because, say, the question will be academic by the time of trial and neither party is interested in the award of damages), or in defamation cases where interim injunctions are not normally granted where the defendant intends to plead justification because of the overriding importance in protecting free speech.

Second, what order is the court likely to make on the hypothetical scenario set out earlier? Let's work through the *American Cyanamid* principles. It seems clear that the claimant's claim raises a serious issue to be tried, even though it will not necessarily succeed at trial. And there is real doubt as to whether damages will be an adequate remedy for the claimant, because its business may be 'killed' by its former managing director's actions. But the claimant is already in dire financial straits, and so it may well have serious difficulties in providing a solid undertaking in damages to satisfy the third limb of the test. It is difficult to anticipate the decision the court would make at the balance of convenience aspect of stage – this would depend on factual points such as the likely effect of the former managing director's competition with the claimant, and the financial, personal and professional effect on the managing director if the injunction were to be granted. In the event that all such factors are evenly balanced, and assuming no delay by the claimant, the court would grant the injunction sought on the basis that it preserved the *status quo* before the defendant's allegedly wrongful actions.

15.6 Freezing orders

A freezing order is a prohibitory injunction which, subject to certain exceptions, orders a defendant not to deal with, dispose of or dissipate his assets prior to trial. The text of the most important paragraphs of the standard form worldwide freezing order used in the Commercial Court are as follows:

5. Until the return date or further order of the court, the Respondent must not-

    (1) remove from England and Wales any of his assets which are in England and Wales up to the value of £ [the maximum value of the claimant's claim, together with interest and an estimated amount of the legal costs the claimant will incur during the litigation]; or
    (2) in any way dispose of, deal with or diminish the value of any of his assets whether they are in or outside England and Wales up to the same value.

6. Paragraph 5 applies to all the Respondent's assets whether or not they are in his own name, whether they are solely or jointly owned and whether the Respondent is interested in them legally, beneficially or otherwise. For the purpose of this order the Respondent's assets include any asset which he has the power, directly or indirectly, to dispose of or deal with as if it were his own. The Respondent is to be regarded as having such power if a third party holds or controls the asset in accordance with his direct or indirect instructions.

It can be seen at once that these are very restrictive provisions, preventing the defendant from dealing with anything that might conceivably be classed as one of his assets (up to the value of the claimant's claim). They are subject to a few small exceptions, described later. This exceptional remedy is of particular use in civil fraud claims and other cases involving allegations of dishonesty against a defendant. After all, a claimant does not want to spend considerable resources and time obtaining a judgment only to find that the defendant has spirited away his assets so that they cannot be enforced against.

But the potent nature of freezing orders means that the courts are careful only to grant them in appropriate cases. Although the grant of freezing relief is always a matter of discretion, most commentators argue that a four-stage test should be applied.

The first question is whether the claimant has a cause of action that is justiciable in England and Wales. If not, so the reasoning runs, there is no cause of action in support of which an invasive injunction should be granted. In practice, the point is not quite so clear-cut. Section 25 of the Civil Jurisdiction and Judgments Act 1982 confers on the court jurisdiction to grant interim relief, including freezing relief, in support of actions commenced in foreign jurisdictions. But in so doing the Court will always tread carefully and accord substantial weight to the views and practice of the court in which the claim is being tried; in other words, it will aim to assist the foreign court rather than interfere with its process.

The second question is whether a claimant has a 'good arguable case'. This is a higher standard than is generally applied in relation to the grant of interim injunctions – the general test is whether there is a 'serious issue' to be tried – because of the particularly serious nature of freezing relief. But, beyond this, it is difficult to say precisely what constitutes a 'good arguable case'. The most authoritative assistance was provided by Kerr LJ in *Ninemia Maritime Corp v Trave* [1983] 1 WLR 1412: a good arguable case is plainly capable of serious argument, although it does not need to be one which the judge believes has a greater than 50% chance of success.

At this point in the analysis, we should mention a point of practice. Freezing injunctions are invariably obtained at a without notice hearing (ie a hearing held in private of which the defendant has no warning and therefore no opportunity to make submissions). The reason is obvious: if you give a person who is liable to dissipate his assets notice of your intention to freeze those assets, he may well move the assets before the order is made. But the making of orders on a without notice basis is equally obviously a strong thing to do: natural justice requires a hearing at which both sides are able to make representatives.

A number of points flow from this difficulty. First, the courts will only make without notice orders where there is remarkable urgency or where an inter partes hearing may undermine the relief being sought (as is the case with freezing orders). Second, where a party seeks a without notice order, he comes under a duty of full and frank disclosure: ie a duty to present all relevant information to the court (especially that which is unhelpful to the party making the application). Third, when a without notice order is made, the court will always require that its order be re-considered at an on notice or inter partes hearing to be held within a short period of time (almost always less than a week) – so he has an opportunity to challenge the order within a short timeframe. This hearing is known as the 'return date'. The court will discharge an injunction at the return date hearing if the person in whose favour the injunction was granted failed to comply with his duty of full and frank disclosure.

This digression was necessary in order to explain that a person applying for a freezing injunction will need to persuade the court that he has a good arguable case while also complying with his duty of full and frank disclosure. So he will need to draw to the court's attention difficulties in his case and the potential defences which the defendant may raise.

The third question posed by the court is often said to be whether there are assets in the jurisdiction against which a freezing order can take effect – for instance bank accounts, real property, shares, chattels etc. But this is a misleading statement of the law: see the decision of the Court of Appeal in *Derby v Weldon (Nos 3 & 4)* [1990] Ch 65. This established that the court has power to grant a worldwide freezing injunction against a defendant who is properly subject to the jurisdiction even if that defendant has no assets in England and Wales. So all that the third question is designed to ensure is that there may be assets – wherever in the world they are situated – against which the freezing order can have effect.

The fourth question is often the most difficult. It is whether there is evidence to show that there is a real risk that the defendant will dissipate his assets if given the opportunity to do so. To put the point another way, the court will not grant freezing injunctions against upstanding members of the community who will comply with any judgment entered against them. Whether there is a real risk of dissipation is a question of fact, which the courts assess by reference to factors such as whether there is evidence to suggest that the defendant has been dishonest, whether the defendant has previously defaulted on judgments entered against him, whether there is evidence to suggest that the defendant has already taken steps to remove or dissipate his assets, and whether the defendant's assets are liquid in nature (such that they could be moved at speed).

We have already mentioned that defendants who fail to comply with injunctions can be sent to prison for contempt of court. In the recent JSC BTA Bank litigation, a number of defendants have been subjected to lengthy prison sentences for failing to comply with various aspects of freezing injunctions. The longest sentence, of 22 months, was handed out to an oligarch who wrongfully concealed and then dealt with assets: see *JSC BTA Bank v Ablyazov* [2012] ECWA Civ 1411.

There are three other factors that ensure the effectiveness of freezing injunctions. The first is that injunctions are not simply effective against the person to whom they are directed. Rather, as the text contained in the penal notice states:

> Any other person who knows of this Order or does anything which helps or permits the Respondent to breach the terms of this Order may also be held to be in contempt of court and may be imprisoned, fined or have their assets seized.

So a third party, such as a bank, who is served with a freezing injunction and who nevertheless permits the respondent to draw on his account in breach of a freezing order will also be in contempt of court. Naturally, institutions such as banks and their directors are keen to avoid this outcome, so they have in place systems to put a stop on all drawings from a respondent's account as soon as they are served with a freezing order. Other third parties such as the Land Registry and company secretaries responsible for maintaining share registers will also be assiduous in preventing a respondent from breaching the terms of a freezing order, lest they open themselves up to a contempt application.

The second factor is that the grant of a freezing order is almost always coupled with the grant of a mandatory injunction requiring the defendant to disclose to the claimant the nature and details of all of his worldwide assets. The courts have gone so far as to say that freezing injunctions cannot normally be effective without such disclosure: see *JSC BTA Bank v Ablyazov* [2012] EWHC 455 (Comm). This is for at least three reasons: when a respondent identifies his assets, the claimant is able to serve the freezing injunction on third parties who are involved in administering the same (thus substantially decreasing the chances of those third parties assisting the defendant in dealing with the assets); a claimant is also sometimes able to keep a watch on the relevant assets to ensure that they are not marketed or can publicise the fact that a particular asset is frozen; and a defendant is less likely to deal with an asset in breach of a freezing injunction when he has already disclosed that he owns that asset.

The third factor is that, where there is a 'measurable risk' that the grant of a freezing injunction does not provide a claimant with effective relief, the court can appoint receivers over the defendant's assets. In this context, a receiver is an individual appointed by the court to hold and safeguard a piece of property pending the conclusion of trial. This happened in *JSC BTA Bank v Ablyazov* [2010] EWCA Civ 1141; [2011] Bus LR D119, where the principal defendant had given highly unsatisfactory disclosure as to his assets, which were held through opaque structures and therefore difficult to secure. His actions left the court unable to 'trust' him to comply with the freezing order such that the further and more invasive relief of a receivership order was necessary.

Before leaving this topic we should describe three small exceptions to the blanket prohibitions on dealing with, disposing or dissipating assets contained in freezing orders. The first, called the ordinary living expenses exception, entitles a defendant to spend a certain defined sum each week on such expenses. The second, called the legal expenses exception, entitles the defendant to spend a reasonable sum on legal advice and representation – so that he can defend himself in the proceedings brought against him. The final exception – called the ordinary course of business or *Angel Bell* proviso (after *The Angel Bell (Iraqi Ministry of Defence v Arcepey Shipping Co SA)* [1981] QB 65) – permits a defendant to continue to carry out routine trading transactions in the ordinary and proper course of business; so a corporate defendant would be able to continue to buy supplies and pay its employees notwithstanding the grant of freezing relief against it.

15.7 Search orders

Freezing injunctions have been described as one of the law's two nuclear weapons: see *Bank Mellat v Nikpour* [1985] FSR 87, 92 (Donaldson LJ). The other such weapon is the search order. The point of a search order is to locate and safeguard evidence the claimant needs to make out a claim against the defendant. For example, in *Anton Piller KG v Manufacturing Processes Ltd* [1976] Ch 55, the claimant, who manufactured computer parts, believed that the defendants, who acted as their selling agents, were selling confidential information acquired about the claimant's products to its competitors. It couldn't prove this, however, without access to documents held by the defendants. The Court of Appeal ordered that the defendants permit the claimant to enter their premises with a view to discovering and inspecting such documents. (Following this decision these orders became known as *Anton Piller* orders.) The courts' jurisdiction to make these orders is now provided by section 7 of the Civil Procedure Act 1997.

(1) The court may make an order under this section for the purpose of securing, in the case of any existing or proposed proceedings in the court –

(a) the preservation of evidence which is or may be relevant, or

(b) the preservation of property which is or may be the subject-matter of the proceeding or as to which any question arises or may arise in the course of the proceedings.

...

(3) Such an order may direct any person to permit any person described in the order, or secure that any person so described is permitted –

(a) to enter premises in England and Wales, and

(b) while on the premises, to take in accordance with the terms of the order any of the following steps.

(4) Those steps are –

(a) to carry out a search for or inspection of anything described in the order, and

(b) to make or obtain a copy, photograph, sample or other record of anything so described.

The order does not in itself entitle the claimant to enter the defendant's property. However, as the order directs that the defendant permit the claimant to enter, any refusal by the defendant to allow the claimant entry to the property is a contempt of court. Moreover, a refusal to grant access to the claimant may support adverse inferences against the defendant if the case comes to trial (ie the court may well think that the defendant has refused to let the claimant in precisely because he has something to hide). The claimant must make an undertaking in damages: Section 15.4. Further conditions attached to the enforcement of the order include: the claimant should be accompanied by his solicitor, the search must take place during office hours so as to enable to defendant to obtain legal advice, the claimant must list the items to be removed for copying.

As the object of search orders is to locate and secure material which it is suspected the defendant might destroy or conceal, these orders are made ex parte (ie without notice: see Section 15.6). The reason for this is to ensure that the defendant is not forewarned, meaning that he is less likely to dispose of the relevant material in advance of the order being executed. What this means, however, is that search orders make a significant inroad into the defendant's ordinary civil liberties. As such, the courts have stressed that not only their execution but also their availability must be tightly controlled. In *Anton Piller* ([1976] Ch 55, 62), Ormrod LJ set out the following 'essential pre-conditions' for the making of a search order:

> First, there must be an extremely strong prima facie case. Secondly, the damage, potential or actual, must be very serious for the applicant. Thirdly, there must be clear evidence that the defendants have in their possession incriminating documents or things, and that there is a real possibility that they may destroy such material before any application inter partes can be made.

Nonetheless, it is plain that this formula is sufficiently open that courts are left with a significant amount of leeway when it comes to deciding whether to make such an order. And indeed, although the Court of Appeal in *Anton Piller* stressed that they were to be made 'only ... in the most exceptional circumstances', the criticism has been made that the courts became far too ready to grant these orders (see eg *Columbia Pictures Industries Inc v Robinson* [1987] Ch 38 (Scott J), *Lock International plc v Beswick* [1989] 1 WLR 1268 (Hoffmann J)).

It has sometimes been thought that search orders may run counter to a defendant's privilege against self-incrimination (see eg *Rank Film Distributors Ltd v Video Information Centre* [1982] AC 380). This privilege means that defendants are entitled to refuse to do things – eg to answer questions – which may incriminate them in respect of criminal proceedings against them. What relevance does this have to search orders? In *Rank Films* it was thought that, although the privilege did not extend to allowing the defendant to refuse entry to the claimant for the purposing of discovering evidence, it did mean that he could not be compelled to answer questions or, more importantly, to disclose any relevant documents. The idea that the privilege extends to the disclosure of documents kept on the defendant's premises has, however, been criticised (see *C plc v P* [2007] EWCA Civ 493; [2008] Ch 1; Zuckerman, 2007). In any event, section 72 of the Senior Courts Act 1981 creates an exception to the privilege against self-incrimination in relation to certain proceedings for infringement of intellectual property rights (for similar exceptions, see eg section 13 of the Fraud Act 2006).

Summary

▶ Whereas the common law would typically order only damages in response to a successful claim, equity developed alternative remedies such as the injunction, specific performance, rescission and rectification.

▶ Injunctions can be either *mandatory* – requiring a defendant to a claim to do something – or *prohibitory* – requiring a defendant to refrain from acting in a certain manner. An injunction may be awarded at the conclusion of a trial which fully determines the parties' respective rights and obligations (a *final* or *perpetual* injunction) or before trial, pending such a determination (an *interlocutory* or *interim* injunction).

▶ Injunctions are granted in two sorts of situation: (1) where a party has invaded or threatened to invade a legal or equitable right of another party and (2) where it is just and convenient to do so in support of or to render more effective a legal or equitable right held by a claimant.

▶ The grant of an injunction is at the discretion of the court. The court also has discretion to award damages in lieu of an injunction, although this is done only exceptionally.

▶ An interim injunction may be granted where the claimant has an arguable case, an award of damages would not provide an adequate alternative remedy and the balance of convenience supports the grant of such an injunction.

▶ Freezing orders are a special form of injunction which prohibits the defendant from dealing with some of his assets. These orders are made when it is feared that, prior to trial, the defendant may dispose of his assets in order to defeat the claimant's claim.

▶ A search order may be made where it is thought that the defendant has on his premises material which would enable the claimant to make out his claim and which it is feared the defendant may otherwise destroy or dispose of.

Chapter 16

A trust in practice

16.1 Introduction

We started this book by suggesting that most people do not encounter the concept of a trust unless and until they find themselves confronted with it as an inescapable part of a law degree. It is equally true to say that many law students finish their law degree without seeing what a trust deed looks like or having much insight into the mechanics of a trust's operation.

We address these gaps in this chapter, by examining some of the documents produced over the life of a hypothetical trust. We start with a potential settlor going to see his solicitor to discuss estate planning; he is advised to establish a trust, and we will examine the trust deed and letter of wishes that are drafted on his behalf; we will then see how our trust's trustees carry out their functions (by, for instance, making distributions and preparing accounts); next we will examine the mechanism by which the trustees retire and are replaced; finally, we examine what happens when a trustee acts improperly and is sued for breach of trust.

The leading work on drafting trust documents is Kessler and Sartin (2012) *Drafting Trusts and Will Trusts: A Modern Approach* (11th edn, Sweet & Maxwell). The discretionary trust and deeds of appointment and retirement found in this chapter have been based on precedents contained in that work.

16.2 The decision to create a trust

Bernard is a successful if sometimes irascible entrepreneur, having made his money through establishing a chain of seaside hotels. He has been retired for a few years and one day goes to see his solicitor about his not inconsiderable estate. He has a wife, Sarah, three children (the eldest of whom is 22) and a number of other relatives, for whom he wishes to provide. He also wishes to benefit a number of his former employees, who provided important contributions to the success of his business. On the other hand, he does not want his children to become (as he says) 'layabouts', in the expectation of receiving millions on or before the death of their 'old man'. (In this, he has something in common with Lord Denning, who remarked in *Re Weston* [1969] 1 Ch 223, 245: 'Many a child has been ruined by being given too much'.)

Bernard's solicitor suggests that he create a discretionary trust. He explains that by so doing, Bernard can defer the date on which decisions are made as to the distribution of his fortune. He also tells Bernard that he can communicate his thoughts regarding distributions to his trustees in a confidential document called a 'letter of wishes'. Bernard thinks that this structure will meet his needs, and so, after taking tax advice from his accountant, gives his solicitor instructions to draft the necessary documents.

A few weeks later, Bernard signs a deed of trust and sends a letter of wishes in the following terms.

Deed of trust

The Bernard Flewty Settlement 2011

THIS SETTLEMENT is made on the 1st day of May 2011 between:

1.   Bernard Flewty of Flewty Towers, Ilsham Road, Torquay, Devon TQ1
        1BF ('the Settlor') of the one part and

2.1   Abigail Tomms of 14 Almond Tree Cottages, Goosenargh, Pudding
        Pie Lane, Berkshire BK2 8H and

2.2   Lord Melton of 62 Acacia Avenue, Brey, Oxfordshire OX7 4HN ('the
        Original Trustees') of the other part.

WHEREAS:

1.1   The Settlor has a wife and three children:

1.2   Sarah Flewty (nee Chesterton)

1.3   Stewart Flewty ('Stewart') who was born on 7 March 1991

1.4   Madeline Flewty ('Madeline') who was born on 17 November 1993
        and

1.5   Gwendolyn Flewty ('Gwendolyn') who was born on 26 January 1995

1.6   This settlement ('the Settlement') shall be known as the Bernard
        Flewty Settlement 2011.

NOW THIS DEED witnesses as follows:

1. Definitions

In this settlement:

1.1   The 'Beneficiaries' means:

1.1.1   The descendants of the Settlor.

1.1.2   The Spouses of the descendants of the Settlor.

1.1.3   The Surviving Spouses of the descendants of the Settlor.

1.1.4   The Surviving Spouse of the Settlor.

1.1.5   Any current or former employee of the Bernard Flewty Group Plc.

1.1.6   Any Person or class of Person added to the class of Beneficiaries
        by the Trustees by deed with the consent in writing of:

1.1.6.1 the Settlor or

1.1.6.1 two Beneficiaries (if the Settlor has died or has no capacity to
        consent).

1.2   'Spouse' includes a civil partner within the meaning of section
        1 of the Civil Partnership Act 2004 and a person is a 'Surviving
        Spouse' whether or not they have remarried or entered into
        another civil partnership.

1.3   'Person' includes a person anywhere in the world and includes a
        trustee.

1.4   'The Trustees' means the Original Trustees or the trustees of
        this Settlement for the time being.

1.5   'The Trust Fund' means:
1.5.1   property transferred to the Trustees to hold on the terms of this Settlement.
1.5.2   all property from time to time representing the above.
1.6   'The Trust Period' means the period of 125 years beginning with the date of this Settlement. That is the perpetuity period applicable to this Settlement under the rule against perpetuities.
1.7   The 'Trust Property' means any property comprised in the Trust Fund.

2. Trust Income

Subject to the Overriding Powers below:
2.1   The Trustees may accumulate the whole or part of the income of the Trust Fund during the Trust Period. That income shall be added to the Trust Fund.
2.2   The Trustees shall pay or apply the remainder of the income to or for the benefit of any Beneficiaries, as the Trustees think fit, during the Trust Period.

3. Overriding Powers

The Trustees shall have the following powers ('Overriding Powers'):
3.1   *Power of appointment*
3.1.1   The Trustees may appoint that they shall hold any Trust Property for the benefit of any Beneficiaries, on such terms as the Trustees think fit.
3.1.2   An appointment may create any provisions and in particular:
3.1.2.1   discretionary trusts;
3.1.2.2   dispositive or administrative powers; exercisable by any Person.
3.1.3   An appointment shall be made by deed and may be revocable or irrevocable.
3.2   *Powers of advancement*
3.2.1   The Trustees may pay or apply any Trust Property for the advancement or benefit of any Beneficiary.
3.3   The Overriding Powers shall be exercisable only:
3.3.1   during the Trust Period; and
3.3.2   at a time when there are at least two Trustees, or the Trustee is a company carrying on a business which consists of or includes the management of trusts.

4. Default Clause

Subject to that, the Trust Fund shall be held on trust for Stewart, Madeline and Gwendolyn in equal shares absolutely.

5. Appointment of Trustees

The power of appointing trustees is exercisable by the Settlor during his life and by will.

6. Further provisions

The standard provisions of the Society of Trust and Estate Practitioners (1st Edition) shall apply.

7. Irrevocability

This Settlement is irrevocable.

In witness whereof, the parties hereto have set their hands and seals or common seal (as the case may be) on the day and year first above written.

Signed as a deed by Bernard Flewty

In the presence of

Signature of witness:

Name of witness (BLOCK CAPITALS):

Address of witness:

Signed as a deed by Lord Melton

In the presence of

Signature of witness:

Name of witness (BLOCK CAPITALS):

Address of witness:

Signed as a deed by Abigail Tomms

In the presence of

Signature of witness:

Name of witness (BLOCK CAPITALS):

Address of witness:

Letter of wishes

**Flewty Towers,
Ilsham Road,
Torquay,
Devon TQ1 1BF**

1st May 2011

Dear Lord Melton and Ms Tomms,

Thank you for agreeing to become trustees of the Bernard Flewty Settlement 2011.

I write to give you some insight into why I put the Settlement in place, and to outline other relevant considerations which I would ask you to consider in your administration of the Settlement (and, in particular, when making discretionary dispositive decisions). I, of course, understand and acknowledge that the contents of this letter are not legally binding, but I nevertheless hope this letter will be helpful.

The Settlement confers wide discretionary powers on you, my trustees. But I consider that my wife, Sarah, and my three children should be viewed as the Settlement's principal beneficiaries. In particular, I consider that my wife should be able to live in the style to which she has become accustomed for the rest of her life, expensive though this is. As for my children, I am particularly concerned that they are not given too much money too young, as I fear that this will have detrimental consequences for their chosen careers. On the other hand, their education should be supported to the fullest extent possible, and suitable provision should be made for their housing needs in due course (though I do not think that this should necessarily extend to purchasing large properties for them outright).

This is not to say that other relatives should not receive distributions, though I would not expect these to be anything like as large as those sums distributed to my wife and children. I would hope that distributions to my other relatives, and in particular my nieces, would assist with their educations and with providing deposits for the acquisition of residences.

I do not wish my former employees to be overlooked. My business success was in good measure attributable to their hard work. I do not expect very substantial distributions to be made to this class of beneficiaries, though I hope the Settlement will at least provide funds to assist in hard times. One employee, Michael Gonzales, calls for particular mention;

though I did not always show it, I became very fond of him during his
many years of service.

I should, finally, refer to the fact that (so I am told by my solicitor)
the Settlement contains a term that allows other people to be added as
beneficiaries. I have inserted this clause principally in case any of my
old friends fall on hard times. If so, they can, so I am told, be added
as beneficiaries with my consent or, if I am gone, the consent of two
other beneficiaries.

I trust that you will give the wishes set out above appropriate
consideration.

Yours sincerely,

Bernard Flewty

16.3 Commentary on the deed of trust and letter of wishes

The introductory parts of our deed of trust are self-explanatory, setting out the date on which the settlement was executed and the parties to the deed. There is then the word 'WHEREAS', which is followed by details of the Settlor's wife and children and the name of the settlement. This section of the deed, known as 'the recitals', is included to assist the reader by explaining the relevant background.

Note that there are two trustees. This is the industry standard where the trustees are individuals for two main reasons. First, there are some relatively minor restrictions on what a sole trustee can do: for instance, he cannot give a valid receipt for sums derived from the sale of land (see section 14 of the Trustee Act 1925 and section 27(2) of the Law of Property Act 1925). Second, as we have seen (Section 13.12), trustees of private trusts must act unanimously, and so having two trustees makes it harder for an errant trustee to misapply trust property.

There are then the words 'Now this deed witnesses as follows:'. This is really just verbiage (though older deeds are worse, saying 'Now this deed made in pursuance of the said desire witnesseth:'). It is no more than a marker to show that the operative provisions of the trust deed follow.

Clause 1 contains definitions used in the trust deed. Some trust deeds define terms as and when they arise, but having the principal definitions at the beginning means that the subsequent drafting can be simpler. Many of the definitions are self-explanatory, but some call for comment:

▶ The Beneficiaries of the trust are defined with some care, in order to ensure that nobody who could reasonably be classed as a relative is excluded. For instance, the drafting ensures that the civil partners of the descendants of the settlor are included, as are spouses of those descendants even where they have remarried. Also included are employees and former employees of Bernard's company. This introduces a relatively wide class of discretionary beneficiaries, but does not cause any difficulties with the certainty of objects requirements because it satisfies the 'is or is not' test (see Section 3.14 and in particular the discussion of *McPhail v Doulton* [1971] AC 424). Further, provision is made to add to the class of Beneficiaries, subject to the consent of Bernard (if he is able to give it) or two other beneficiaries; this increases flexibility and may be useful in the medium or long term (eg to add as a beneficiary one of Bernard's old friends, as he mentions in his letter of wishes, or the long-term (but unmarried) partner of one of Bernard's children).

▶ The Trust Period is set at 125 years, the longest period permissible under English law (see section 5 of the Perpetuities and Accumulations Act 2009; Section 4.9). There is no definition that refers to an accumulation period for the trust, as the rule that income could only be accumulated for 21 years was abolished by section 13 of the 2009 Act.

Clauses 2 to 4 are the really important provisions, containing the trust's dispositive provisions.

Clause 2 deals with income (eg the rent paid on real property owned by the trust, the dividends paid in respect of the trust's shares, the interest paid on the trust's bank deposits etc.). It provides that the trustees can decide to accumulate it (ie add it to the other trust property (usually called the 'capital'), which is dealt with in accordance with Clauses 3 and 4). But if they do not decide to exercise their power to accumulate income, it is held on a discretionary trust in favour of the beneficiaries. In practice, the trustees may decide to use this clause to make monthly payments of, say, £5,000 to Sarah in order to fund her living expenses, or termly payments to or for the benefit of Bernard's children to pay school or university fees.

Clauses 3.1 and 3.2 contain wide powers of appointment and advancement of the trust's capital in favour of the beneficiaries. As we saw in Chapter 2 (Section 2.2), such powers permit but do not oblige the trustees to make appointments in favour of a beneficiary. The simplest way of providing a benefit to a beneficiary is by deciding to advance money to that beneficiary direct. So the trustees may, for example, use the Clause 3.2 power to pay a substantial sum towards the purchase of a house for one of Bernard's children (note that Clause 3.2 does not reproduce the strict requirements of section 32 of the Trustee Act 1925, on which see Section 12.6). We see an example of how the trustees might exercise the power of advancement under Clause 3.2 later on. Another way by which the trustees might decide to benefit a beneficiary/ies is by either varying the terms of the trust (specifically contemplated by Clause 3.1.1) or establishing a sub-trust in his/their favour (see Clause 3.1.2.1). This is often done where a trustee wants to be fair between a settlor's children and their families; in such circumstances, the trustee may establish sub-trusts for each of the settlor's children and their families and divide the trust fund between those sub-trusts equally, thus ensuring that each branch of the family (or the 'stirps', as trust lawyers say) receives the same amount.

Clause 3.3 makes it clear that the Overriding Powers will only operate during the Trust Period (ie for 125 years). At that stage, the default trust contained in Clause 4 kicks in. It also provides that decisions cannot be made under Clause 3 unless there are two individuals acting as trustee (or, alternatively, a professional trust corporation); this introduces a 'four eyes' requirement into decision-making – as noted earlier, the theory being that if two people have to agree, it is more likely that sensible decisions will be made (and less likely that trust assets will be misapplied by a dishonest trustee).

Clause 4 contains the default trust, namely the trust that takes effect if there is any undistributed trust property at the end of the Trust Period. It is no more than a long-stop provision, with it being exceedingly likely that the Trust Fund will be distributed before then. Although individuals have been chosen as the default beneficiaries, it is also common for the default beneficiary to be a charity (often the Red Cross).

Clause 5 is included to give Bernard some continuing power over the trust. As we have seen, trustees must act unanimously. So if Bernard does not like what is going on, he has the power to add an additional trustee who can refuse to consent to decisions (and even make an application to the Court for directions as to how the trust should operate in the future). Of course, it is hoped that there will be no difficulties, and Bernard hopes that his choice of trustees will ensure this; but as trusts are long-term vehicles, Clause 5 may become relevant. (Bernard could have retained a power to remove trustees, although such a power is relatively unusual in the on-shore context.)

Clause 6 deals with administrative provisions, such as the trustee's power of investment, powers of delegation, the trustees' remuneration and the liability of the trustees for breach of trust. It is common practice to incorporate the Society of Trust and Estate Practitioners' (STEP's) standard provisions by reference (although they could also be included in a schedule to the trust deed). Older settlements tend to run to at least 20 pages, and set out detailed administrative provisions verbatim. This is now considered unnecessary for most cases. By simply incorporating administrative provisions by reference, the length of the document is reduced; the layman is told what he is most interested in (ie who gets what); the risk of accidental omission or incorrect inclusion of provisions is eliminated; and the practitioner familiar with the STEP standard provisions will not waste time construing bespoke provisions in every case. The STEP provisions, which were updated in October 2011, are available at http://www.step.org/publications/standard_provisions.aspx.

Clause 7 confirms that the settlement is irrevocable. This is, of course, the default position; for once you have effectively given away your property there is (absent vitiating factors) no way to recover it. But as the tax consequences of a revocable settlement are dire, it is expressly stated.

There are, finally, the execution provisions, which provide (as is the norm) for the trust to be executed as a deed (see further section 1 of the Law of Property (Miscellaneous Provisions) Act 1989). These provisions are self-explanatory, and not repeated in full below.

The letter of wishes is an increasingly common feature of a discretionary trust. In order to explain its function, we need to take a step back and consider the wide discretions that modern trusts often confer on their trustees. Bernard's trust is a good example, with the beneficiaries including not only his spouse and descendants, but also the current or former employees of his company (see also the trust in *McPhail v Doulton* [1971] AC 424).

The drafting advantages of wide discretionary trusts, or wide discretionary trusts coupled with wide powers to add additional beneficiaries, are numerous. First, drafting in a wide manner reduces the prospects of leaving out someone important. Second, having a wide discretionary class means that trustees can react to changed circumstances (eg a lottery win for one side of the family; the illness of the other side's main breadwinner; the drug dependency of a particular beneficiary). Third, the absence of a fixed entitlement provides an incentive for younger beneficiaries to make their own way in life (and not become, as they are sometimes called in the industry, 'trust babes' or (more controversially) 'trustafarians'). Finally, the absence of a fixed entitlement helps to shield assets from claims brought against them by the creditors or the former spouse of a beneficiary.

But there is an obvious drawback to a wide discretionary trust. If the class of discretionary beneficiaries numbers, say, 1000, how is the trustee meant to choose among them? The trustee cannot resolve the problem by simply deciding to distribute the fund equally among the 1000 beneficiaries; indeed, the last thing that Bernard will have intended is for a cleaner who worked for three months at the Bernard Flewty Group to receive the same level of distributions as his wife and children.

What the trustee needs is some guidance as to the reasons underlying the establishment of the trust. Such information will form the background against which he can exercise his dispositive discretions, taking into account more recent developments.

It is not usual for background matters to be recorded in a trust deed. Aside from anything else, they may be of a very private nature. Take, for instance, the settlor who wishes one child to receive greater distributions than another; or the settlor who wishes to provide for a relative of whom most of his family disapprove; or the settlor who wishes to make provision for an illegitimate child. It would be most embarrassing for such matters to be aired on the face of a document, which the beneficiaries will be shown.

The solution that the industry has developed is for the settlor to record the relevant background – the reasons underlying his decision to establish a trust – in a document called a letter of wishes. The letter is usually, as it is in this case, sent to the trustees at around the same time as the trust deed is executed.

The letter of wishes is a confidential document: *Breakspear v Ackland* [2009] Ch 32. Once the trust is up and running, that confidence is held by the trustees, who can maintain it (by refusing to disclose the letter of wishes to beneficiaries, perhaps because they feel it might create family difficulties), judiciously relax it (by, for instance, disclosing the letter of wishes to a handful of principal beneficiaries, in a redacted form), or abandon it completely (by providing it to any beneficiary who asks).

It is, finally, important to stress that a letter of wishes should not purport to give the trustees orders as to what they should or should not do in any given situation. Such a letter of wishes might be viewed by a disgruntled beneficiary as being inconsistent with the settlor's intention to create a discretionary trust, and might therefore lead to a challenge to the validity of the trust at a later date (with consequential uncertainty, legal costs and the risk of significant tax liabilities in the event that the discretionary trust is held to be invalid). As the reader will have seen, these pitfalls have been avoided in Bernard's letter of wishes, which specifically provides that the letter of wishes is not intended to be legally binding.

16.4 Transfer of property to the trustees

So the trust documentation is in place. But a trust cannot exist without assets being placed into it. How does this happen? The answer varies depending on the nature of the property which the settlor wishes to transfer into the trust. The most common types of property are dealt with below (see also Section 7.1):

- **Money.** One of the first things trustees will do is open a trust bank account. In our case, it will probably be opened under the name 'The Bernard Flewty 2011 Settlement'. Once this is done, the settlor may decide to make a bank transfer to the account.
- **Real property.** Real property cannot be dealt with quite so easily. It is transferred (if registered) by the settlor completing a land transfer form in favour of the trustees, and the trustees registering that form at the Land Registry (the TR1 form would usually be used, available at http://www.landregistry.gov.uk/). If unregistered, the settlor will need to formally convey the land to the trustees, who should thereafter apply for its registration.
- **Shares.** Shares are transferred by executing a stock transfer form (see the example found at http://www.macmillan.org.uk/Documents/Donate/stock_transfer_form. pdf), after which the trustees should seek their entry on the shareholders' register maintained by the relevant company.
- **Chattels.** Chattels are usually transferred by deed of assignment, although delivery to the trustees may also suffice.

16.5 The trust up and running: some accounts and an appointment

Let us return to the Bernard Flewty Settlement 2011. Bernard has executed his trust deed and letter of wishes. Over the course of the next month, he transfers the following property to the trustees: £1,500,000 in cash, which the trustees thereafter invest in a number of shares; six seaside apartments, which generate an income when they are let to holidaymakers; and a number of shareholdings, in particular, his remaining shareholding in the Bernard Flewty Group plc.

Thereafter, the trustees make discretionary distributions of income to Sarah, to fund her living expenses, and to Bernard's children, to pay their school and university fees. At the end of 2011, the trustees produce the following accounts:

Accounts

The Bernard Flewty Settlement 2011
Trust accounts for the period 1 May 2011 to 31 December 2011

Balance sheet

	Note	2011
		£
CASH		
Held in First Direct trust account number 12345678		348,592
STOCKS, SHARES, GILTS AND BONDS		
iShares FTSE tracker (137,594 units)		886,282
BP ordinary shares (nominal value $0.25) (20,428 shares)		98,345
Vodafone ordinary shares (nominal value 10p) (45,348 shares)		156,293
UK Government 10-year gilts (234,934 units)		765,483
iShares Sterling Corporate Bond (30,984 units)		412,834
Bernard Flewty Group plc (45,000 shares)		12,000,000 (est.)
REAL PROPERTY		
6 apartments in Seaview Towers, Lighthouse Lane, Bournemouth BM1 3JH		1,800,000 (est.)
ASSETS		16,467,829
ACCOUNTS PAYABLE		
Accountancy fees (KPMG)		16,400
Legal fees (Farrer & Co.)		7,500
Trustee fees		4,200
LIABILITIES		28,100
NET ASSETS		16,439,729
REPRESENTED BY:		
CAPITAL ACCOUNT		16,119,237
INCOME ACCOUNT		464,387
DISTRIBUTIONS PAID	1	(143,895)
		16,439,729

Capital account
For the period 1 May 2011 to 31 December 2011

	Note	2011
COST OF INVESTMENTS		16,023,449
GAIN ON INVESTMENTS		95,788
		16,119,237

Income account
For the period 1 May 2011 to 31 December 2011

	Note	2011
INCOME		
Bank interest		34,228
Dividends from shareholdings		343,282
Dividends from gilts		28,347
Dividends from corporate bonds		19,383
Rental income from Seaview Towers		76,300
		501,600
EXPENSES		
Tax paid to HM Revenue & Customs		25,816
Professional fees		4,500
Bank charges		1,082
Insurance		978
Trustee fees		4,837
		37,213
INCOME ACCOUNT, end of year		464,387

NOTES
Note 1: Distributions paid

	£
Sarah Flewty	98,100
Stewart Flewty (university fees)	11,995
Madeline Flewty (school fees)	16,900
Gwendolyn Flewty (school fees)	16,900
	143,895

We have set out above the three principal parts of a trust's accounts, the balance sheet (which gives a snapshot of the current position of the trust), the capital account (which shows how the trust's capital has grown over the accounting period, in this case from 1 May 2011 to 31 December 2011) and the income account (which shows the income earned by the trust and the expenses paid from the trust over the relevant accounting period). Between them these three statements give fairly detailed information as to the financial state of the trust at the end of the relevant accounting period. They are supplemented by notes; one has been included above, but it is common to see many more referring, for instance, to details of professional fees incurred. The accounts of a private trust do not have to be audited, and those produced above are not. It should, finally, be noted that the accounts set out above show the current value of the trust's investments; but many trust accounts, especially where they refer to assets which have no readily ascertainable market value (eg land, paintings etc.), do not contain the current value of assets but rather the historical or purchase price.

Early in 2012, the trustees decide to make a more substantial capital distribution to Stewart. They make this decision on the basis that Stewart, having obtained a law degree and completed half of his training contract, is looking to buy a property. After having discussions with Stewart, and telephoning Bernard to ascertain his views, the trustees resolve to appoint £120,000 to Stewart in order that he can put down a substantial deposit on the £400,000 flat he plans to buy. The trustees record this distribution in a deed of appointment dated 17 March 2012:

Deed of appointment

THIS DEED of appointment is made on this 17th day of March 2012 by:

(1) Abigail Tomms of 14 Almond Tree Cottages, Goosenargh, Pudding Pie Lane, Berkshire BK2 8H and

(2) Lord Melton of 62 Acacia Avenue, Brey, Oxfordshire OX7 4HN (together called 'the Trustees')

WHEREAS:

(A) This deed is supplemental to a settlement ('the Settlement') made on 1 May 2011 between (1) Bernard Flewty and (2) the Trustees.

(B) Clause 3.2.1 of the Settlement confers on the Trustees the following power ('the Power of Appointment'):

   'The Trustees may pay or apply any Trust Property for the advancement or benefit of any Beneficiary.'

(C) The Trustees are the present trustees of the Settlement.

NOW THIS DEED WITNESSES as follows:

1. In this deed:

   (1) Stewart means Stewart Flewty of 54 Candy Wharf, Bow, London E3 6HN;

   (2) Words defined in the Settlement have the same meaning in this deed.

2. In exercise of the Power of Appointment the Trustees appoint the sum of £120,000 to Stewart.

IN WITNESS whereof etc.

Once this document has been executed, the trustees will go about transferring the £120,000 – probably by bank transfer to Stewart or to his conveyancer.

16.6 Retirement of a trustee

In mid-2012, Lord Melton realises that he is becoming forgetful and decides to retire as trustee. When he discusses his decision with Bernard, Bernard suggests that both Lord Melton and Abigail Tomms retire in favour of a trust company called Eureka Trustees Ltd, which his new financial adviser, a flash city trader, has recommended. Everyone agrees that this seems like a good idea, and the trust's solicitors draw up the following deed of retirement and appointment (which relies upon the provisions relating to the retirement and appointment of trustees contained in section 36(1) of the Trustee Act 1925 (see Section 12.2)):

Deed of appointment and retirement

THIS DEED of appointment and retirement is made on this 1st day of July 2012 between:

(A) Bernard Flewty of Flewty Towers, Ilsham Road, Torquay, Devon TQ1 1BF ('the Settlor') of the first part

(B) Eureka Trustees Ltd, a company carrying on the business of managing trusts, of Eureka Street, Serendipity Lane, London EC3 6ON ('the New Trustee') of the second part and

(C) Lord Melton of 62 Acacia Avenue, Brey, Oxfordshire OX7 4HN and Abigail Tomms of 14 Almond Tree Cottages, Goosenargh, Pudding Pie Lane, Berkshire BK2 8H ('the Retiring Trustees') of the third part

WHEREAS

(A) This deed is supplemental to the deed of settlement ('the Settlement') made on 1 May 2011 between the Settlor and the Retiring Trustees.

(B) Clause 5 of the Settlement confers on the Settlor the power of appointing new trustees.

(C) The Retiring Trustees wish to retire from the Settlement.

NOW THIS DEED WITNESSES as follows

In exercise of the power conferred by section 36(1) of the Trustee Act 1925, the Settlor appoints the New Trustee to be the sole Trustee of the Settlement in place of the Retiring Trustees.

IN WITNESS whereof etc.

16.7 Breach of trust

So Eureka Trustees Ltd take over the reins of the Bernard Flewty Settlement 2011. And at first little changes. The trust's investments remain productive, yielding sufficient income to meet the beneficiaries' needs; and so the beneficiaries and Bernard are happy. But Eureka Trustees Ltd is then taken over, and a number of its senior management change. In particular, a trust administrator called Vernon Dobson is appointed to look after the settlement.

Quite why Mr Dobson was ever given a job with Eureka Trustees Ltd we do not know, for he is a dishonest individual with more than one criminal conviction. Within months, he manages to convert the trust's stocks and shares into cash (over £5m) and transfer the money to a company incorporated in the British Virgin Islands called Lucky Investments Ltd. Lucky Investments is not, in fact, anything other than the alter ego of Mr Dobson, having been incorporated by him to assist in misappropriating the trust's money.

Sarah, Bernard's wife, discovers that a fraud has been perpetrated on the trust over the next few months. She consults solicitors, who advise her to institute proceedings against Eureka, Vernon and Lucky Investments. Counsel is instructed, and he settles the following Particulars of Claim.

Particulars of claim

IN THE HIGH COURT OF JUSTICE
CHANCERY DIVISION
B E T W E E N:

Claim no: 2010CH023457

SARAH FLEWTY

Claimant

and

(1) EUREKA TRUSTEES LIMITED
(2) VERNON DOBSON
(3) LUCKY INVESTMENTS LIMITED

Defendants

PARTICULARS OF CLAIM

Introduction

1. The Claimant is a principal beneficiary of a trust established on 1 May 2011 and known as the Bernard Flewty Settlement 2011 ('the **Trust**').

2. The First Defendant ('**Eureka**') is a company incorporated in England and Wales under company registration number 123754939 on 14 November 1998, carrying on the business of the administration and management of trusts. Eureka was appointed as the sole trustee of the Trust on 1 July 2012.

3. The Second Defendant ('**Mr Dobson**') was an employee of Eureka from 3 January 2013 until his employment was terminated by Eureka on 1 May 2013. During that period, Mr Dobson held the position of 'Senior Trusts Administrator' and took all decisions relating to the administration of the Trust.

4. The Third Defendant ('**Lucky Investments**') is a company incorporated in the British Virgin Islands under company registration number 234846 on 6 January 2013. Lucky Investments was incorporated on the instructions of Mr Dobson, who has at all material times thereafter been its sole director and shareholder.

The Trust

5. By deed of settlement dated 1 May 2011, Bernard Flewty established the Trust. The Trust's principal beneficiaries were named as, and have at all material times thereafter been, the Claimant and Bernard Flewty's three children.

6. The Trust's initial trustees were Lord Melton and Abigail Tomms ('the Original Trustees').

7. By deed of retirement and appointment dated 1 July 2012, the Original Trustees retired in favour of Eureka. Shortly thereafter, the property subject to the Trust was transferred by the Original Trustees to Eureka. That property included:
   a. 137,594 units in the iShares FTSE tracker exchange traded fund;
   b. 20,428 BP ordinary shares;
   c. 45,348 Vodafone ordinary shares;
   d. 234,934 UK Government 10-year gilts;
   e. 30,984 units in the iShares Sterling Corporate Bond exchange traded fund.
   (The investments referred to in (a) to (e), above, are hereinafter referred to as the Publicly Traded Investments.)

The misappropriation

8. On a date or dates currently unknown to the Claimant but thought to be in about January 2013, Eureka entered into contracts for the sale of the Publicly Traded Investments. Pursuant to those contracts, Eureka, as trustee of the Trust, received the sum of £5,182,494 on or around 7 February 2013 in consideration for the Publicly Traded Investments.

9. On or about 9 February 2013, Mr Dobson, acting on behalf of Eureka, procured the transfer of the sum of £5,180,000 to Lucky Investments by way of direct bank transfer ('the **Transfer**'). The Trust received no consideration in return.

Breach of trust by Eureka

10. The Transfer was effected in breach of Eureka's duties as trustee.

PARTICULARS OF BREACH OF TRUST

---

(1) The Trust received no consideration whatsoever in return for the Transfer;

(2) The Transfer was made for the personal benefit of an employee of Eureka; and

(3) Eureka failed to implement any or any adequate system of supervision in relation to Mr Dobson and therefore failed in all the circumstances to use such care, skill and prudence as is required of a professional corporate trustee.

Dishonest assistance by Mr Dobson

11. Mr Dobson, by procuring the making of the Transfer, provided assistance in the breaches of trust of Eureka particularised above.

12. In providing the said assistance, Mr Dobson acted dishonestly.

PARTICULARS OF DISHONESTY

Mr Dobson's knowledge is to be inferred from the following facts and matters:

(1) Mr Dobson procured the making of the Transfer for his own personal gain;

(2) The Trust received no consideration in return for the Transfer; and

(3) Mr Dobson procured the making of the Transfer to Lucky Investments in an attempt to disguise his wrongful misappropriation of trust property.

13. As a result of the matters set out above, Mr Dobson is liable to account as a constructive trustee for the sum of £5,180,000 together with interest thereon, as particularised below.

Knowing receipt of Lucky Investments

14. Lucky Investments received the sum of £5,180,000 on or about 9 February 2013, which sum was transferred to it by Eureka in breach of trust.

15. In receiving the said funds, Lucky Investments acted unconscionably.

PARTICULARS OF UNCONSCIONABILITY

Lucky Investment's knowledge is to be inferred from the following facts and matters:

(1) Lucky Investments knew that it had provided no consideration whatsoever in return for the making of the Transfer;

(2) Lucky Investments knew or ought to have known that it was not a beneficiary of the Trust, such that the Transfer could not lawfully be made to it; and

(3) The knowledge of Mr Dobson, the sole director and shareholder of Lucky Investments, is attributable to Lucky Investments. Accordingly, Lucky Investments is deemed to have known that Mr Dobson was involved

in a dishonest scheme of misappropriating the Trust's property for personal gain.

16. As a result of the matters set out above, Lucky Investments is liable to account as a constructive trustee for the sum of £5,180,000 together with interest thereon, as particularised below.

Loss and damage

17. By reason of the matters set out above, the Trust has suffered loss and damage in that the sum of £5,180,000 has been misappropriated from it.

Equitable proprietary claim

18. Further or alternatively, the sum of £5,180,000 was transferred from the Trust in breach of trust to a party who was not a bona fide third party purchaser of the same. Accordingly, the said sum can be followed and traced in equity. The Claimant, by this claim, seeks the return of the said sum and/or its traceable proceeds and seeks all appropriate orders, accounts and declarations for the return of the same.

Interest

19. The Claimant claims compound interest pursuant to the equitable jurisdiction of the Court and/or interest pursuant to section 35A of the Senior Courts Act 1981, for such period and at such rate as the Court deems fit.

AND the Claimant claims:

1. All necessary orders, accounts and declarations relating to the return of the £5,180,000 misappropriated from the Trust and/or the traceable proceeds of the same;

2. Equitable compensation from Eureka for breach of trust;

3. Equitable compensation from Vernon Dobson for dishonest assistance in breach of trust;

4. Equitable compensation from Lucky Investments for knowing receipt of moneys transferred in breach of trust;

5. Such further or other relief as the Court deems just;

6. Interest; and

7. Costs.

A. COUNSEL

As noted above, this document is usually described as a claimant's 'particulars of claim' (although it is also referred to as a 'statement of case' or a 'pleading'). It is one of the two formal documents by which a claimant commences an action in the English courts (the other document, called a 'claim form', is far shorter and contains formal information such as the names and addresses of the parties, a brief description of the claim, the amount claimed and the amount of the court fee). Particulars of claim are drafted in order to: (1) set out the nature of the complaint that the claimant is making against the defendant(s); (2) explain how that complaint gives rise to a cause of action against each defendant; and (3) explain what relief is sought by reason of the existence of those causes of action. As can be seen, Sarah's particulars of claim start by outlining the identities and roles fulfilled by the claimant and the three defendants. It goes on to summarise the background to the Trust and to explain how money was misappropriated from it.

The next three sections are important because they set out the various causes of action relied upon by Sarah against the three defendants. Eureka is sued for breach of trust because it misapplied trust funds. The breach itself is obvious: Eureka transferred trust moneys away for no consideration, and for the personal gain of an employee. A third particular of breach has been pleaded, out of an abundance of caution: it is said that Eureka failed to act in an appropriate manner because it failed properly to supervise Mr Dobson. Mr Dobson is himself sued for dishonest assistance in breach of trust. It is not necessary to plead many facts to explain how Mr Dobson assisted the breach of trust or acted dishonestly – he was the person who actually carried out the misappropriation for his own gain. Finally, Lucky Investments is sued on the basis that it knowingly received money transferred in breach of trust. It is easy to plead Lucky Investment's receipt of trust funds. Its unconscionability (as to which see Section 14.21) is a little harder to establish; this is done by pleading that Lucky Investments provided no consideration for the transfer, knew or should have known that it could not lawfully benefit under the trust, and should also have Mr Dobson's knowledge attributed to it.

The remainder of the pleading sets out the consequences which flow from these causes of action. First, the claimant wants compensation for the losses the trust has suffered. Second, the claimant wants to bring a claim to recover the misapplied property or its traceable proceeds, in case the misappropriated funds have not passed to bona fide third-party purchasers. Finally, the claimant wants interest, in order that the trust is not disadvantaged by the fact that it has been unable to invest the misappropriated funds.

The final part of the particulars of claim, starting with the words 'AND the Claimant claims', is called the 'prayer'. Its purpose is to summarise the relief claimed. It is customary for the barrister who drafts (or 'settles') the particulars of claim to add his name to the document after the prayer.

Although the facts and particulars of claim have been somewhat simplified, they nevertheless give a flavour of how a breach of trust claim is launched. Happily, all ends well for the trust: Mr Dobson realises the error of his ways, and agrees to repay the misappropriated funds with interest; Eureka agrees to retire; and Bernard, to his considerable relief, executes a deed of appointment and retirement by which his solicitor and accountant replace Eureka.

Bibliography

Akkouh and Worthington (2006) 'Re Diplock [1948]' in Mitchell and Mitchell (eds), *Landmark Cases in the Law of Restitution* (Hart)

Battersby (1979) 'Formalities for the Disposition of Equitable Interests under a Trust' (1979) 43 Conv 17

Birks (1992) 'Restitution and Resulting Trusts' in Goldstein (ed), *Equity and Contemporary Legal Developments* (Jerusalem)

Birks (1994) 'Proprietary Rights as Remedies' in Birks (ed), *The Frontiers of Liability: Volume 2* (OUP)

Birks (1995) 'Overview: Tracing, Claiming and Defences' in Birks (ed), *Laundering and Tracing* (OUP)

Birks (1996a) 'Equity in the Modern Law: An Exercise in Taxonomy' (1996) 26 W Aus LR 1

Birks (1996b) 'Inconsistency Between Compensation and Restitution' (1996) 112 LQR 375

Birks (1998) 'The End of the Remedial Constructive Trust' (1998) 12 Tru LI 202

Birks (2002a) 'The Content of Fiduciary Obligation' (2002) 16 Tru LI 34

Birks (2002b) 'Receipt' in Birks and Pretto (eds), *Breach of Trust* (Hart)

Birks (2004) *Unjust Enrichment* (2nd edn, OUP)

Burrows (2001) 'Proprietary Restitution: Unmasking Unjust Enrichment' (2001) 117 LQR 412

Burrows (2002) 'We Do this at Common Law and that in Equity' (2002) 22 OJLS 1

Burrows (2004) *Remedies for Torts and Breach of Contract* (3rd edn, OUP)

Chambers (1997) *Resulting Trusts* (OUP)

Chambers (1999) 'Constructive Trusts in Canada' (1999) 37 Alta LR 173

Chambers (2002) 'Liability' in Birks and Pretto (eds), *Breach of Trust* (Hart)

Chambers (2004) 'Restrictions on the Use of Money' in Swadling (ed), *The* Quistclose *Trust* (Hart)

Chambers (2010) 'Is There a Presumption of Resulting Trust?' in Mitchell (ed), *Resulting and Constructive Trusts* (Hart)

Charity Commission (2008a) *Charities and Public Benefit*

Charity Commission (2008b) *The Advancement of Religion for the Public Benefit*

Charity Commission (2008c) *The Prevention or Relief of Poverty for the Public Benefit*

Charity Commission (2008d) *Speaking Out: Guidance on Campaigning and Political Activity by Charities* (CC9)

Conaglen (2006) 'A Re-Appraisal of the Fiduciary Self-Dealing and Fair-Dealing Rules' (2006) 65 CLJ 366

Conaglen (2011) 'Difficulties with Tracing Backwards' (2011) 127 LQR 432

Crilley (1994) 'A Case of Proprietary Overkill' (1994) RLR 57

Critchley (1999) 'Instruments of Fraud, Testamentary Dispositions and the Doctrine of Secret Trusts' (1999) 115 LQR 631

Edelman (2010) 'When Do Fiduciary Duties Arise?' (2010) 126 LQR 302

Elias (1990) *Explaining Constructive Trusts* (OUP)

Elliott (1960) 'The Power of Trustees to Enforce Covenants in Favour of Volunteers' (1960) 76 LQR 100

Elliott (2002) 'Remoteness Criteria in Equity' (2002) 65 MLR 588

Elliott and Mitchell (2004) 'Remedies for Dishonest Assistance' (2004) 67 MLR 16

Etherton (2008) 'Constructive Trusts: A New Model for Equity and Unjust Enrichment' (2008) 67 CLJ 265

Evans (1999) 'Rethinking Tracing and the Law of Restitution' (1999) 115 LQR 469

Feltham (1982) 'Intention to Create a Trust of a Promise to Settle Property' (1982) 98 LQR 17

Feltham (1987) 'Informal Trusts and Third Parties' [1987] Conv 246

Friend (1982) 'Trusts of Voluntary Covenants – An Alternative Approach' [1982] Conv 280

Fuller (1941) 'Consideration and Form' (1941) 41 Col LR 799

Gardner (1992) 'New Angles on Unincorporated Associations' [1992] Conv 41

Gardner (1993) 'Rethinking Family Property' (1993) 109 LQR 263

Gardner (1994) 'The Element of Discretion' in Birks (ed), *The Frontiers of Liability: Volume 2* (OUP)

Gardner (2006) 'The Remedial Discretion in Proprietary Estoppel – Again' (2006) 122 LQR 492

Gardner (2008) 'Family Property Today' (2008) 124 LQR 422

Gardner (2010) 'Reliance-Based Constructive Trusts' in Mitchell (ed), *Constructive and Resulting Trusts* (Hart)

Gardner (2011) *An Introduction to the Law of Trusts* (3rd edn, OUP)

Gardner and MacKenzie (2012) *An Introduction to Land Law* (3rd edn, Hart)

Glister (2002) '*Twinsectra v. Yardley*: Trusts, Powers and Contractual Obligations' (2002) 16 Tru LI 223

Glister (2004) 'The Nature of *Quistclose* Trusts: Classification and Reconciliation' (2004) 63 CLJ 632

Glister (2010) 'Section 199 of the Equality Act 2010: How Not to Abolish the Presumption of Advancement' (2010) 73 MLR 807

Goddard (1988) 'Equity, Volunteers and Ducks' [1988] Conv 19

Goode (1998) 'Proprietary Restitutionary Claims' in Cornish, Nolan, O'Sullivan and Virgo (eds), *Restitution: Past, Present and Future – Essays in Honour of Gareth Jones* (Hart)

'Goode (2003) 'Are Intangible Assets Fungible?' [2003] LMCLQ 379

Gray (1991) 'Property in Thin Air' (1991) 50 CLJ 252

Green (1984) '*Grey, Oughtred* and *Vandervell* – A Contextual Reappraisal' (1984) 47 MLR 385

Hackney (1987) *Understanding Equity and Trusts* (Fontana)

Hackney (2008) 'Charity and Public Benefit' (2008) 124 LQR 347

Hayton (1990) 'Equitable Rights of Cohabitees' [1990] Conv 370

Hayton (1994) 'Uncertainty of Subject-Matter of Trusts' (1994) 110 LQR 335

Hayton (2001) 'Developing the Obligation Characteristic of the Trust' (2001) 117 LQR 96

Ho and Smart (2001) 'Reinterpreting the *Quistclose* Trust: A Critique of Chambers' Analysis' (2001) 21 OJLS 267

Hodge (1980) 'Secret Trusts: The Fraud Theory Revisited' [1980] Conv 341

Hornby (1962) 'Covenants in Favour of Volunteers' (1962) 78 LQR 228

Hudson (1984) 'Is Divesting Abandonment Possible at Common Law?' (1984) 100 LQR 110

Kessler and Sartin (2012) *Drafting Trusts and Will Trusts: A Modern Approach* (11th edn, Sweet & Maxwell).

Langbein (1995) 'The Contractarian Basis of the Law of Trusts' (1995) 105 Yale LJ 625

Law Commission (2006) *Trustee Exemption Clauses* (Law Com No 301)

Law Commission (2007) *Cohabitation: The Financial Consequences of Relationship Breakdown* (Law Com No 307)

Law Commission (2010) *The Illegality Defence* (Law Com No 320)

Law Commission (2011) *Intestacy and Family Provision Claims on Death* (Law Com No 331)

Lawson (1996) 'The Things We Do for Love: Detrimental Reliance in the Family Home' (1996) 16 LS 218

Lee (1969) 'The Public Policy of *Re Cook's Settlement Trusts*' (1969) 85 LQR 213

Luxton (2009) *Parliament v The Charity Commission* (Politeia) (available at http://politeia.co.uk/ p109.pdf)

McBride (2000) 'On the Classification of Trusts' in Birks and Rose (eds), *Restitution and Equity: Volume 1 – Resulting Trusts and Equitable Compensation* (LLP)

McFarlane (2004) 'Constructive Trusts Arising on a Receipt of Property *Sub Conditione*' (2004) 120 LQR 667

McFarlane (2008) *The Structure of Property Law* (Hart)

McFarlane and Stevens (2010) 'The Nature of Equitable Property' (2010) 4 J Equity 1

McKay (1974) '*Re Baden* and the Third Class of Uncertainty' (1974) 38 Conv 269

McKendrick (2011) *Contract Law* (9th edn, Palgrave Macmillan)

Martin (2009) *Hanbury and Martin: Modern Equity* (18th edn, Sweet & Maxwell)

Matthews (1995) 'A Problem in the Construction of Gifts to Unincorporated Associations' [1995] Conv 302

Matthews (1996) 'The New Trust: Obligations Without Rights?' in Oakley (ed), *Trends in Contemporary Trust Law* (OUP)

Matthews (2006) 'The Comparative Importance of the Rule in *Saunders v. Vautier*' (2006) 122 LQR 266

Meagher, Heydon and Leeming (2002) *Meagher, Gummow and Lehane's Equity Doctrine and Remedies* (4th edn, Butterworths)

Meagher and Lehane (1976) 'Trusts of Voluntary Covenants' (1976) 92 LQR 427

Millett (1985) 'The *Quistclose* Trust: Who Can Enforce It?' (1985) 101 LQR 269

Millett (1998a) 'Restitution and Constructive Trusts' in Cornish, Nolan, O'Sullivan and Virgo (eds), *Restitution: Past, Present and Future – Essays in Honour of Gareth Jones* (Hart)

Millett (1998b) 'Equity's Place in the Law of Commerce' (1998) 114 LQR 214

Millett (2005) 'Proprietary Restitution' in Degeling and Edelman (eds), *Equity in Commercial Law* (Thompson)

Mitchell (2002) 'Assistance' in Birks and Pretto (eds), *Breach of Trust* (Hart)

Mitchell (2010) *Hayton and Mitchell: Commentary and Cases on the Law of Trusts and Equitable Remedies* (13th edn, Sweet & Maxwell)

Mitchell and Watterson (2010) 'Remedies for Knowing Receipt' in Mitchell (ed), *Constructive and Resulting Trusts* (Hart)

Moffat (2009) *Trusts Law: Text and Materials* (5th edn, CUP)

Nicholls (1998) 'Knowing Receipt: The Need for a New Landmark' in Cornish, Nolan, O'Sullivan and Virgo (eds), *Restitution: Past, Present and Future – Essays in Honour of Gareth Jones* (Hart)

Oakley (2008) *Parker and Mellows: The Modern Law of Trusts* (9th edn, Sweet & Maxwell)

Parkinson (2002) 'Reconceptualising the Express Trust' (2002) 61 CLJ 657

Penner (2002) 'Exemptions' in Birks and Pretto (eds), *Breach of Trust* (Hart)

Penner (2006) 'Duty and Liability in Respect of Funds' in Lowry and Mistelis (eds), *Commercial Law: Perspectives and Practice* (Butterworths)

Penner (2010) 'Resulting Trusts and Unjust Enrichment: Three Controversies' in Mitchell (ed), *Resulting and Constructive Trusts* (Hart)

Penner (2012) *The Law of Trusts* (8th edn, OUP)

Perrins (1972) 'Can You Keep Half a Secret?' (1972) 88 LQR 225

Pound (1920) 'The Progress of the Law, 1918–1919: Equity' (1920) 33 Harv LR 420

Ridge (2012) 'Participatory Liability for Breach of Trust or Fiduciary Duty' in Glister and Ridge (eds), *Fault Lines in Equity* (Hart)

Rotherham (2002) *Proprietary Remedies in Context* (Hart)

Rotherham (2003) 'Tracing Misconceptions in *Foskett v. McKeown*' [2003] RLR 57

Scott (1917) 'The Nature of the Rights of the *Cestui Que Trust*' (1917) 27 Col LR 269

Sealy (1962) 'Fiduciary Relationships' (1962) 20 CLJ 69

Sherwin (1989) 'Constructive Trusts in Bankruptcy' (1989) U Ill L Rev 297

Smith (1994) 'Tracing, "Swollen Assets" and the Lowest Intermediate Balance: *Bishopsgate Investment Management Ltd v. Homan*' (1994) 8 Tru LI 102

Smith (1995a) 'Tracing in *Taylor v. Plumer*: Equity in the Court of King's Bench' [1995] LMCLQ 240

Smith (1995b) 'Tracing into the Payment of a Debt' (1995) 54 CLJ 290

Smith (1997a) 'Constructive Fiduciaries' in Birks (ed), *Privacy and Loyalty* (OUP)

Smith (1997b) *The Law of Tracing* (OUP)

Smith (1999) 'Constructive Trusts and Constructive Trustees' (1999) 58 CLJ 294

Smith (2000) 'Unjust Enrichment, Property, and the Structure of Trusts' (2000) 116 LQR 412

Smith (2004a) 'Unravelling Proprietary Restitution' (2004) 40 Can Bus LJ 317

Smith (2004b) 'Understanding the Power' in Swadling (ed), *The* Quistclose *Trust* (Hart)

Smith (2005) 'Fusion and Tradition' in Degeling and Edelman (eds), *Equity in Commercial Law* (Thompson)

Stone (1917) 'The Nature of the Rights of the *Cestui Que Trust*' (1917) 27 Col LR 467

Swadling (1996) 'A New Role for Resulting Trusts?' (1996) 16 LS 110

Swadling (1998) 'The Proprietary Effect of a Hire of Goods' in Palmer and McKendrick (eds), *Interests in Goods* (2nd edn, LLP)

Swadling (2000) 'The Law of Property' in Birks and Rose (eds), *Lessons of the Swaps Litigation* (LLP)

Swadling (2004) 'Orthodoxy' in Swadling (ed), *The* Quistclose *Trust* (Hart)

Swadling (2008) 'Explaining Resulting Trusts' (2008) 124 LQR 72

Swadling (2010) 'The Nature of the Trust in *Rochefoucauld v. Boustead*' in Mitchell (ed), *Constructive and Resulting Trusts* (Hart)

Webb (2006) 'Performance and Compensation: An Analysis of Contract Damages and Contractual Obligation' (2006) 26 OJLS 41

Webb (2009a) 'Property, Unjust Enrichment, and Defective Transfers' in Chambers, Mitchell and Penner (eds), *Philosophical Foundations of the Law of Unjust Enrichment* (OUP)

Webb (2009b) 'What is Unjust Enrichment?' (2009) 29 OJLS 215

Webb (2009c) 'Treating Like Cases Alike: Principle and Classification in Private Law' in Robertson and Tang (eds), *The Goals of Private Law* (Hart)

Webb (2010) 'Intention, Mistakes and Resulting Trusts' in Mitchell (ed), *Constructive and Resulting Trusts* (Hart)

Weinrib (1975) 'The Fiduciary Obligation' (1975) 25 U Tor LJ 1

Worthington (1999) 'Sorting Out Ownership Interests in a Bulk: Gifts, Sales and Trusts' (1999) J Bus L 1

Worthington (2006) *Equity* (2nd edn, OUP)

Youdan (1984) 'Formalities for Trusts of Land and the Doctrine in *Rochefoucauld v. Boustead*' (1984) 43 CLJ 306

Youdan (1988) 'Informal Trusts and Third Parties: A Response' [1988]Conv 267

Zuckerman (2007) 'The Privilege Against Self-Incrimination May not Confer a Right to Refuse Disclosure of Incriminating Documents which Came into Existence Independently of the Disclosure Order' (2007) 26 CJQ 395

Index

Printed and bound in Great Britain by
TJ International Ltd, Padstow, Cornwall